EYEWITNESS TRAVEL

CALIFORNIA

DK

D0003388

DK | Penguin Random House

Produced by Duncan Baird Publishers, London, England

Managing Art Editor Clare Sullivan
Editors Slaney Begley, Joanne Levêque, Zoë Ross
Editorial Assistant Leo Hollis
Designers Christine Keilty, Susan Knight, Jill Mumford, Alison Verity

Main Contributors Jamie Jensen, Barry Parr,
Ellen Payne, J Kingston Pierce, Rebecca Poole Forée,
Nigel Tisdall, John Wilcock, Stanley Young

Photographers
Max Alexander, Peter Anderson, John Heseltine, Dave King,
Neil Lukas, Andrew McKinney, Neil Setchfield

Picture Research Lindsay Hunt

Illustrators
Arcana Studios, Joanna Cameron, Stephen Conlin,
Dean Entwhistle, Nick Lipscombe, Lee Peters, Robbie Polley,
Kevin Robinson, John Woodcock

Printed and bound in China

First American Edition, 1997
16 17 18 19 10 9 8 7 6 5 4 3 2 1

Published in the United States by
DK Publishing, 345 Hudson Street,
New York, New York 10014

**Reprinted with revisions 1999, 2000, 2001, 2002, 2003, 2004,
2005, 2006, 2007, 2008, 2009, 2010, 2012, 2014, 2016**

Copyright © 1997, 2016 Dorling Kindersley Limited, London

A Penguin Random House Company

Published in the UK by Dorling Kindersley Limited.

A catalog record for this book is available from the Library of Congress.

ISSN 1542-1554
ISBN 978-1-46544-113-3

Floor are referred to throughout in accordance with American usage,
i.e., the "first floor" is at ground level.

MIX
Paper from
responsible sources
FSC FSC™ C018179
www.fsc.org

Front cover main image: Giant sequoia trees in Yosemite National Park, California

◀ Oceanside shoreline, San Diego

Contents

Half Dome in Yosemite National Park

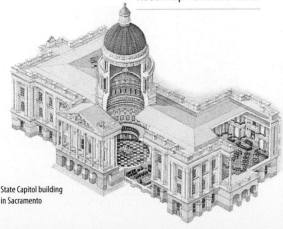

State Capitol building
in Sacramento

HOW TO USE THIS GUIDE

This guide helps you to get the most from your stay in California. *Introducing California* maps the whole state and sets it in its historical and cultural context. Southern and Northern California are divided into ten regional chapters, plus there is a section each for *Los Angeles* and *San Francisco and the Bay Area*, describing key sights with maps, pictures, and illustrations, as well as introductory features on subjects of regional interest. Suggestions on restaurants, accommodations, shopping, and entertainment are in *Travelers' Needs*, while the *Survival Guide* has tips on arriving in the US and getting around the state. LA, San Francisco, and San Diego have their own *Practical Information* sections.

Los Angeles and San Francisco and The Bay Area

The centers of the two major cities have been divided into a number of sightseeing areas. Each area has its own chapter that opens with a list of the sights described. All the sights are numbered and plotted on an *Area Map*. Information on each sight is easy to locate within the chapter as it follows the numerical order on the map.

Sights at a Glance lists the chapter's sights by category: Historic Streets and Buildings, Shops, Modern Architecture, etc.

A locator map shows where you are in relation to other areas of the city center.

2 Street-by-Street Map
This gives a bird's-eye view of the heart of each sightseeing area.

A suggested route for a walk covers the most interesting streets in the area.

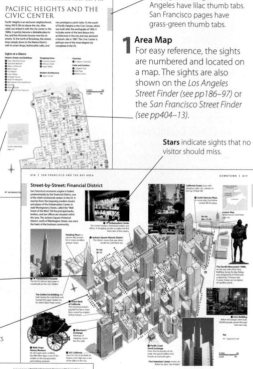

All pages relating to Los Angeles have lilac thumb tabs. San Francisco pages have grass-green thumb tabs.

1 Area Map
For easy reference, the sights are numbered and located on a map. The sights are also shown on the *Los Angeles Street Finder (see pp186–97)* or the *San Francisco Street Finder (see pp404–13)*.

Stars indicate sights that no visitor should miss.

3 Detailed information
All the sights in Los Angeles and in San Francisco and the Bay Area are described individually. Addresses and practical information are provided. The key to the symbols used in the information block is shown on the back flap.

Story boxes explore specific subjects in more detail.

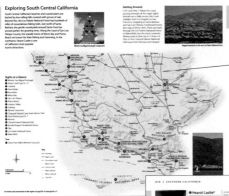

SOUTH CENTRAL CALIFORNIA

South Central California is a land of lonely passes and wooded streams. Broad sandy beaches stretch for miles along the gentle coast with empty, tawny hills as their only backdrop. It is a region of small and friendly towns, scattered farms and vineyards nestled in scenic valleys. Further inland is Los Padres National Forest, where mountain lions roam freely, and eagles and condors soar overhead.

The region's Spanish heritage is highly visible, and no more so than in Santa Barbara. Here the area's most important garrison and the legendary structure that came to be known as "Queen of the Missions" *(see pp226–7)* can be found. The city's red-tile Mission Revival-style architecture *(see p215)* has been imitated throughout the State.

Following the breakup of the wealthy missions during the 1830s, the land was divided into a handful of sprawling ranches, then the 1849 Gold Rush brought an influx of Easterners to California. The newcomers subdivided the large estates and set up small farming communities. They touted the land throughout the world as a "semitropical paradise" where the first season's crops would pay for the cost of the land.

In the early part of the 20th century, the Central Coast was a popular vacation destination, drawing thousands of people each summer to seaside towns such as

Pismo and Avila Beach. Farther north, at San Simeon, millionaire William Randolph Hearst built his own personal playground, the fabulous private museum now known as Hearst Castle™.

Today, South Central California provides a wealth of activities, from wine-tasting tours on horseback in the scenic Santa Ynez Valley to relaxation on empty beaches. The more active can try kayaking on the Kern River near Bakersfield. Offshore, the Channel Islands offer a unique view of the area's ecosystems and an opportunity to see the annual passage of the magnificent gray whales. The ease of the region is dominated by the Los Padres National Forest, an area of breathtaking beauty with miles of hiking trails and drives through mountain scenery. Here, too, are signs of the Chumash Indians who once lived in thriving communities along the coast. Their enigmatic petroglyphs remain as silent reminders of their presence throughout these hills.

1 Introduction

The landscape, history, and character of each region is described here, showing how the area has developed over the centuries and what it offers to the visitor today.

Northern California and Southern California

Apart from San Francisco and the Bay Area and Los Angeles, California has been divided into two regions (Northern and Southern California), each of which has five separate area chapters. The most interesting towns and places to visit are numbered on a *Regional Map* at the beginning of each chapter.

Each area of California can be identified quickly by its own color coding, which is shown on the inside front cover.

2 Regional Map

This shows the main road network and gives an illustrated overview of the whole area. All entries are numbered, and there are also useful tips on getting around the region.

3 Detailed Information

All the main towns and other places to visit are described individually. They are listed in order, following the numbering on the *Regional Map*. Within each entry, information is given on the most important sights. A map reference refers the reader to the road map inside the back cover.

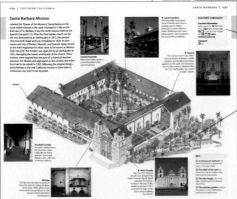

For all the top sights, a visitors' checklist provides the practical information you need to plan your visit.

4 California's top sights

These are given two or more full pages. Historic buildings are dissected to reveal their interiors; museums and galleries have color-coded floor plans to help you locate the most interesting exhibits; national parks and forests have maps showing facilities and trails.

INTRODUCING
CALIFORNIA

DISCOVERING CALIFORNIA

California is huge and varied with distinct geographical regions, from coast and desert to mountain. Covering the state in detail would take several weeks, but if you focus on a particular region, route planning is straightforward, and the following six itineraries can help get your planning started. Some long-distance journeys are inevitable, but travel distances have been kept realistic. First there are two-day tours of San Francisco and San Diego, followed by a ten-day road trip that runs the length of the Pacific Coast, plus two four-day tours, one of the desert and one of the Wine Country. Finally a week-long tour takes you into Gold Country and Yosemite National Park. Pick from and combine tours for a customized itinerary, or simply use them as inspiration.

Eight Days Along the Pacific Coast

- Take in the glamor and relax on the beach in Santa Monica.

- Stroll the Mediterranean-inspired streets of Santa Barbara and visit the mission.

- Tour spectacular Hearst Castle®, then revel in the scenic drive along Big Sur.

- Explore the beautiful Monterey Peninsula and stop by the aquarium.

- Hop on an old cable car in San Francisco, and head to Chinatown for dim sum.

- Wonder at the towering ancient redwoods in Redwood National Park.

Joshua Tree National Park
The famous trees thrive in this desert landscape of pink and grey rocks and boulders.

A Week in Gold Country and the High Sierras

- Stroll the boardwalks of Old Sacramento and admire the California State Capitol.

- Tour the shores of Lake Tahoe and delight in the stunning scenery.

- Pan for gold in a Gold Rush town at Columbia State Historic Park.

- Wander the time-weathered streets of Sonora and Jamestown.

- Hike to the waterfalls in Yosemite National Park, then clamber up to Glacier Point for panoramic views.

- Walk beneath the redwoods in Yosemite's Mariposa Grove and enjoy the wildflowers in Tuolumne Meadows.

- Count the birds at otherworldly, salt-water Mono Lake.

OREGON

Crescent City

Yreka

Redwood National Park

Klamath

Eureka

Redding

Scotia

Avenue of the Giants

Leggett Valley

Sacramento

Mendocino

Sacramento

See Wine Country map above

Bodega Bay

Point Reyes Station

Muir Woods and Beach

Sausalito

San Francisco

Half Moon Bay

Santa Cruz Mountains

Año Nuevo State Reserve

Santa Cruz

Monterey

Carmel-by-the-Sea

Big Sur

Pacific Ocean

Key

— Pacific Coast tour

— Gold Country and the High Sierras tour

— Desert tour

— Wine Country tour

◄ *Yosemite Valley* (1868) by Albert Bierstadt

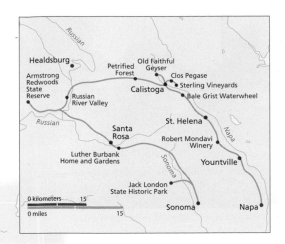

Four Days in Wine Country

- Tour a winery and savor gourmet fare in Napa.

- Get soaked by Old Faithful in Calistoga, then steep in a mineral mud bath.

- Sample the finest vintages at hilltop Sterling Vineyards.

- Marvel at the towering coast-redwood trees in Armstrong Redwoods State Reserve.

- Smell the flowers at Luther Burbank Home and Garden in Santa Rosa.

- Explore downtown Sonoma, discovering where the state of California was born.

Santa Monica
The sweeping beach at Santa Monica, a wealthy suburb on the Pacific shore of Los Angeles.

Four Days in the Desert

- Discover desert wildlife at The Living Desert, Palm Springs.

- Hike past odd Joshua trees and eerie rock formations in Joshua Tree National Park.

- Climb the towering sand dunes at Kelso Dunes.

- Brave the heat at Badwater Basin, Death Valley, North America's lowest point.

- Explore Scotty's Castle and peer into Ubehebe Crater in Death Valley.

Two Days in San Francisco

The City by the Bay has an overwhelming number of must-see sights, including superb museums, Chinatown, Golden Gate Park, and the Golden Gate Bridge.

- **Arriving** San Francisco International Airport is located about 14 miles (22 km) south of the city. Oakland International Airport is closer to downtown San Francisco. Both are linked to the city by the light rail system, BART.

- **Transport** Trams run downtown, and the famous cable cars operate on three tourist routes. BART is handy when heading farther afield. Taxis are ubiquitous, but expensive; Uber and Lyft are popular and less-expensive alternatives.

Day 1
Morning Start with a stroll around the downtown **Financial District** *(pp316–17)*, beginning at the waterfront **Ferry Building** *(p320)*, today housing a farmers' market and boutique stores, and taking in the **Wells Fargo History Museum** *(p318)*, to learn about the early Pony Express stagecoach mail system.

Then head over to **Yerba Buena Gardens** and explore all it has to offer *(pp326–7)*. Take a stroll around the Martin Luther

The Conservatory of Flowers in Golden Gate Park, San Francisco

King Jr. Memorial, grab a coffee, and relax among the locals at the park, or visit one of the many museums nearby, such as the **Museum of Modern Art** *(pp322–3)* or the **Contemporary Jewish Museum** *(p324)*. Now walk up to busy **Union Square** *(p324)*, where huge department stores tempt shoppers and the clanging of passing centenary cable cars adds to the bustle.

Afternoon Hop aboard a cable car to take you to **Chinatown** *(pp330–31)*, teeming with oriental apothecaries, Chinese restaurants, and curio shops. Continue on to the vibrant Italian neighborhood of **North Beach** *(p344–5)*, with its many delicatessens, cafés, and bohemian bookstores; step down for brief strolls. Then head to **Fisherman's Wharf** *(pp338–9)*

to watch the sea lions swimming amid the fishing fleet, to sample fresh crab, and to explore **PIER 39** *(p340)*; children and the young-at-heart might be tempted by the Venetian Carousel. End your day admiring the historic ships, including old clippers and even a World War II submarine, at the **San Francisco Maritime National Historic Park** *(p341)*.

Day 2
Morning Explore **Golden Gate Park** *(pp370–73)*, being sure to include the art collection in the **de Young Museum** *(p371)*; the nature exhibits in the **California Academy of Sciences** *(pp374–5)*, with its fantastic dioramas of dinosaurs, California wildlife, and local marine life; and the botanical exhibitions at **Strybing Arboretum** *(p372)*, with its vast Victorian-era glasshouse.

Afternoon Continue north to the **Legion of Honor** *(pp378–9)*, with artworks from around the globe spanning 4,000 years. Then drive the meandering, tree-lined road through the scenic **Presidio** *(pp380–81)*, a former military base, to reach **Golden Gate Bridge** *(pp384–5)*. Wrap up against the cold and walk out onto the bridge for a spectacular view of San Francisco.

> **To extend your trip...**
> Take a boat ride to the prison island **Alcatraz** *(pp342–3)*, joining a guided tour.

Golden Gate Bridge, an impressive feat of engineering built in 1937

For practical information on traveling around California, see pp602–5

Two Days in San Diego

With an enviable setting on the Pacific, this handsome city teems with sights of interest. Do not miss Balboa Park, San Diego Zoo, or La Jolla.

- **Arriving** San Diego's airport is about 3 miles (5 km) west of downtown.
- **Transport** The San Diego Trolley operates on three separate lines.

The cliffs along the shore surrounding the resort town of La Jolla

Day 1

Morning Plunge straight into San Diego's glory days by exploring the **Gaslamp Quarter** *(pp256– 7)*, a once notorious 19th-century district renowned for its bawdy nightlife. Today the grid of streets is lined with historic red-brick buildings harboring antique shops, boutique hotels, and restaurants. Walk the few blocks north to the **Museum of Contemporary Art** *(p255)*, which features changing exhibits by cutting-edge artists. Explore the adjacent, compact quarter of **Little Italy** *(p255)*, which was settled over a century ago by Italian immigrants. The Italian influence is recalled in the district's wall murals and its many Italian restaurants, perfect for lunch.

Afternoon Walk west to the waterfront Embarcadero to visit the **Maritime Museum** *(p255)*, where you can board several fascinating historic sailing ships. Continue the short distance to the **USS Midway Museum** *(p255)* where up on deck you can check out the refurbished war planes, and below deck you can peek into the crew's sleeping quarters and explore the engine room of this retired World War II-era aircraft carrier. Time permitting, take a taxi to **Point Loma** headland *(p259)* for a bird's-eye view over San Diego Bay at sunset. Interpretive signs help to identify the military ships to-ing and fro-ing below.

Day 2

Morning Immerse yourself in San Diego's early days at **Old Town San Diego State Historical Park** *(p258)*, which preserves the city's original wooden buildings and features actors dressed in period costume. Next, head to **Balboa Park** *(pp260–63)*, with its numerous museums, such as the not-to-be-missed **San Diego Museum of Man**, the **San Diego Museum of Art**, and the **Reuben H. Fleet Science Center**.

Afternoon You will need an entire afternoon to explore **San Diego Zoo** *(pp263)*, with its thousands of animals from around the world – do not miss the polar bears and flamingos. End your day with sunset cocktails and dinner at the grand dame **Hotel del Coronado** *(p259)*, a National Historic Landmark that has attracted presidents since 1888.

> **To extend your trip…**
> Spend a day in the upscale seaside resort of **La Jolla** *(p265)*, allowing time for the Museum of Contemporary Art and Birch Aquarium at Scripps, plus dinner at one of the many cliff-top restaurants.

A flock of wading flamingos at San Diego Zoo

Eight Days Along the Pacific Coast

- **Arriving** Los Angeles' international airport, LAX, is about 14 miles (23 km) south of Santa Monica. From San Diego there is a train service to LA.

- **Transport** You will need a car for this tour.

- **Booking ahead** For Hearst Castle®, book a tour online or call in advance.

Day 1: Santa Monica and Santa Barbara

Start in cliff-top **Santa Monica** (pp80–83), whose peaceful streets are good for strolling, before heading up the Pacific Coast Highway past surfing beaches such as Surfrider County Beach at **Malibu** (pp68–9). Spend the afternoon exploring downtown **Santa Barbara** (pp224–5), including the Presidio and **Santa Barbara Mission** (pp226–7).

> **To extend your trip...**
> Head inland to **Ojai** (p229) to shop for antiques and enjoy a spa treatment at the Ojai Valley Inn & Spa (p532), 40 miles (64 km) east of Santa Barbara.

Day 2: Santa Ynez Valley to San Luis Obispo

Head inland to **Solvang** (p223) to admire its Danish architecture, and spend the morning exploring the wine country around **Santa Ynez** (p222). Continue to **Pismo Beach** (p220), allowing time to stroll the famous sand dunes before arriving in the delightful town of **San Luis Obispo** (p220).

Day 3: Hearst Castle®and the coast to Carmel

Admire Morro Rock at **Morro Bay** (p220) as you drive north to San Simeon for a guided tour of **Hearst Castle**® (pp216–19), the astonishing mountain-top manse of media tycoon William Randolph Hearst (be sure to book ahead). After lunch at San Simeon, revel in the exhilarating drive up the rugged **Big Sur coast** (pp518–19), arriving in **Carmel-by-the-Sea** (p514) by the evening. Carmel has dozens of fine inns and restaurants.

Day 4: The Monterey Peninsula and Carmel Mission

The extraordinarily beautiful **17-Mile Drive** (p515) exploring the Monterey Peninsula deserves a full morning to enjoy at a relaxed pace; be sure to stop at Lone Pine Rock and Spanish Bay. Then visit restored **Carmel Mission** (pp516–17) for an impression of 18th-century mission life. In the afternoon, continue to **Monterey** (pp512–14), focusing your time on exploring the **Monterey Bay Aquarium** (p514) and bay-front **Cannery Row** (p514), made famous by John Steinbeck's novels. Then continue north, curling around Monterey Bay to reach **Santa Cruz** (pp510–11) for sunset.

> **To extend your trip...**
> Travel via **Salinas** (p520), birthplace of writer John Steinbeck, to the well-preserved mission town of **San Juan Bautista** (p509), 33 miles (53 km) northeast of Monterey.

Day 5: Santa Cruz and north via Half Moon Bay

Browse Santa Cruz's downtown cafés, bookstores, and galleries, and the **Santa Cruz Surfing Museum** (p511). Later head into the Santa Cruz Mountains to

Towering redwood trees typical of the forests of California state

ride a steam train at **Roaring Camp Railroads** (p508). In the afternoon, view elephant seals close up at **Año Nuevo State Reserve** (p508), while active travelers might hike in **Big Basin Redwoods State Park** (p508). Continue north via **Half Moon Bay** (p417) and enjoy the thrilling coastal drive to San Francisco.

Day 6: San Francisco

Pick a day from the city itinerary (p12) or follow the **49-Mile Scenic Drive** (pp312–13) for an all encompassing tour of the city.

Day 7: Sausalito and Mendocino

Cross the Golden Gate Bridge to stroll the waterfront in

Sweeping shoreline and perfect surf in Malibu

For practical information on traveling around California, see pp602–5

upscale **Sausalito** *(p418)*, then drive over the Marin Headlands via **Muir Woods and Beach** *(p418)* to **Point Reyes Station** *(p418)*. Follow the shore of Tomales Bay, to arrive in **Bodega Bay** for lunch *(p464)*. Next, marvel at sensational vistas as you follow the winding coast road north to the quaint cliff-top village of **Mendocino** *(p462)*, with its New England-style architecture.

The dramatic desert hills of Death Valley National Park

To extend your trip...
Journey along the wild **Point Reyes National Seashore** *(p418)* to the Point Reyes Lighthouse Visitor Center, 40 miles (64 km) west of Point Reyes Station.

Day 8: Avenue of the Giants and Redwood National Park
After roaming the Mendocino Headlands, travel north via Fort Bragg to the **Leggett Valley** *(p462)*. You will be awestruck by the tallest trees in the world as you pass through the **Avenue of the Giants** *(p451)*. Later in the day, visit the ornate Carson Mansion in **Eureka** *(p450)*, then wind through **Redwood National Park** *(p452–3)* to end your coast tour in Crescent City.

To extend your trip...
If you wish to hike amid the redwoods, extend Day 8 over two days; the most impressive stands are in the **Tall Trees Grove** *(p452* of Redwood National Park.

Four Days in the Desert

- **Arriving** Palm Springs International Airport is located about 2 miles (3 km) east of downtown. Palm Springs is also within easy reach of LA/Ontario airport and LA's LAX.

- **Transport** This tour is most easily done by car.

Day 1: Palm Springs
The desert resort town of **Palm Springs** *(pp278–80)* is a perfect place to ease into the desert. Do not miss the Palm Springs Art Museum, displaying world-class contemporary works; there is also a section devoted to indigenous desert cultures. Then learn about desert ecosystems as you wander the trails of The Living Desert, a zoo and botanical garden displaying plants and creatures from various desert environments.

To extend your trip...
Take the **Palm Springs Aerial Tramway** *(p279)* and spend the day hiking the trails of Mount San Jacinto State Park.

Day 2: Joshua Tree National Park and the Mojave
Head into the High Desert via the **Yucca Valley** *(p277)* and

Oasis palms in Palm Springs

Pioneer Town *(p277)*, built in 1947 as a Western film set. Driving through **Joshua Tree National Park** *(pp282–3)* takes you past eerie Joshua trees and strange rock formations. Exiting at Twentynine Palms, head north into the Mojave National Preserve to admire or climb the **Kelso Dunes** *(p292)*. Continue via the ancient lava flows of **Cinder Cone National Natural Landmark** *(p292)*, and stay overnight at Baker.

To extend your trip...
Head to **Las Vegas** *(p293)*, the 24-hour gambling and entertainment capital of the world, 95 miles (153 km) east of Baker in Nevada.

Day 3 and 4: Death Valley National Park
Enter **Death Valley** *(pp294–7)* at Shoshone and explore the major sites south to north, being sure to include Badwater *(p295)*, the Devil's Golf Course *(p295)*, Artist's Palette *(p297)*, and the Furnace Creek Visitor Center *(p294)*; then Zabriskie Point *(p297)* and Dante's View *(p297)* on the afternoon of Day 3. On Day 4, explore the remains of the Harmony Borax Works *(p294)* before driving north for a guided tour at Scotty's Castle *(p295)*. Nearby, walk the rim of Uhebebe Crater *(p296)*, an ancient volcanic cone, before returning to Furnace Creek or exiting the park.

A Week in Gold Country and the High Sierras

- **Arriving** San Francisco International Airport is located about 88 miles (140 km) southwest of Sacramento, which has its own airport served by domestic flights.
- **Transport** A car offers the most flexibility for exploring.
- **Booking ahead** If you would like to rappel at Moaning Cave, call ahead for reservations.

Day 1: Sacramento
California's capital city, **Sacramento** (pp476–9), was born with the Gold Rush of 1848; strolling the wooden boardwalks of **Old Sacramento** (pp476–7) will bring that past alive. Be sure to visit the fascinating California State Railroad Museum and Delta King Riverboat. In the afternoon take a guided tour of the Neo-Classical **California State Capitol** (p478).

Day 2: Nevada City, Truckee, and Lake Tahoe
Drive through the Sierra foothills to **Nevada City** (p475), where hillside streets are lined with exquisite Victorian buildings. Visit the **Empire Mine State Historic Park** (p474) to tour a restored 19th-century gold mine before continuing through pine forests to **Truckee** (p490), a Wild West town retaining much of its original character. Continue via Hwy 267 to **Lake Tahoe** (p491) and stay on the north shore.

Day 3: Lake Tahoe, Placerville and Sutter Creek
Circle the western shore of the emerald and sapphire lake, stopping to photograph **Emerald Bay State Park** and **Vikingsholm** (p491). Then follow the scenic Lincoln Highway (Route 50) to **Placerville** (p480) and visit the El Dorado County Historical Museum before continuing south to **Sutter Creek** (p480), a pretty Gold Rush town full of antique shops.

Day 4: From Volcano to Angels Camp
Head uphill to the quaint hamlet of **Volcano** (p481) and visit **Indian Grinding Rock State Historic Park** (p481), one of the best-preserved Native American sites in the country. Stop in **San Andreas** (p482) to explore the Calaveras County

Bridalveil Fall, Yosemite National Park

Historical Museum, then overnight in the former gold-mining center of **Angels Camp** (p482).

Day 5: Columbia State Historic Park and Sonora
From Angels Camp, head off the main highway to **Murphys** (p482), one of Gold Country's prettiest and most peaceful towns. Nearby, explore **Moaning Cavern** (p483) on a guided tour before continuing to **Columbia State Historic Park** (pp484–5) for an afternoon panning for gold and otherwise enjoying this perfectly preserved Gold Rush town. End your day in the lovely town of **Sonora** (p483).

Day 6: Jamestown and Yosemite National Park
Pause in **Jamestown** (p485) and check out the old steam trains on display at Railtown 1897 State Historic Park. Then head into the High Sierras and **Yosemite National Park** (pp492–5). Dedicate the after-noon to exploring Yosemite Valley, with its spectacular monoliths and waterfalls.

> **To extend your trip...**
> Take an extra day to hike to either **Vernal Fall** or the top of **Yosemite Falls** (p494).

Columbia, an unusually well-preserved Gold Rush town, now Columbia State Historic Park

For practical information on traveling around California, see pp602–5

Day 7: Yosemite and Mono Lake

Drive to **Glacier Point** (p495) for jaw-dropping vistas of Yosemite Valley and Half Dome. Continue to **Mariposa Grove** (p495) to hike among giant sequoia trees. In summer, ascend to **Tuolumne Meadows** (p495) to marvel at the wildflower display. Exit the park via the Tioga Pass and head to **Mono Lake** (p498), studded with strange alkaline towers.

> **To extend your trip…**
> Visit the largest ghost town in California at **Bodie State Historic Park** (p498), 30 miles (48 km) north of Mono Lake.

Vineyards of the Russian River Valley

Four Days in Wine Country

- **Arriving** San Francisco International Airport is located about 58 miles (93 km) southwest of Napa. Oakland International Airport is a little closer.

- **Transport** Shuttle buses connect the airports to Wine Country, but a car offers the most flexibility for exploring.

- **Booking ahead** Call ahead to book wine tastings at Clos Pegase.

Day 1: Napa Valley towns and wineries

Explore the streets of historic downtown **Napa** (p467 and tiny **Yountville** (p467), known for its Michelin-starred restaurants. Dozens of wineries line Hwy 29, but one not to miss is the mission-style **Robert Mondavi Winery** (p466), which has guided tours. Arriving in **St. Helena**, walk along Main Street, lined with charming shops, galleries, and wine-tasting rooms; then visit the **Bale Grist Waterwheel** (p466), a still-functioning 19th-century mill wheel.

Day 2: Calistoga and Napa Valley wine tours

Outside **Calistoga** (p465) marvel at the **Old Faithful** **Geyser** (p465) as it spouts boiling water. Then head to **Clos Pegase** (p466) winery to admire its superb modern art collection and sample its wine. Nearby, take the aerial tram to reach **Sterling Vineyards** (p466), a Mediterranean-style winery with magnificent views of the valley from its hilltop perch. Fnd the day by steeping in a mineral mud bath in Calistoga.

> **To extend your trip…**
> Thrill to an early-morning **balloon ride** over the Napa Valley (p586), and enjoy a journey on the **Napa Valley Wine Train** (p467).

Day 3: Hiking the Russian River Valley

Lace up your hiking boots and visit the **Petrified Forest** (p465) before heading via Healdsburg to the **Russian River Valley** (p463), a pine-clad vale dotted with wineries. Stands of redwoods tower overhead at **Armstrong Redwoods State Reserve** (p463), perfect for a hike to view the ancient 308-ft (94-m) Colonel Armstrong. Retrace your route through the valley and overnight in **Santa Rosa** (p464).

Day 4: Santa Rosa and the Sonoma Valley

In Santa Rosa, admire the cartoons of artist Charles M. Schultz at the **Snoopy Gallery and Gift Shop** (p465). and tour the rose garden at **Luther Burbank Home and Gardens** (p464) before driving through the **Sonoma Valley** (pp468–9). Head to the charming town of **Sonoma** (p468) for lunch and explore the historic sites around Sonoma Plaza on foot. If you are feeling active, enjoy an invigorating hike in **Jack London State Historic Park** (p465).

Tuscan-styled Castello di Amorosa, just outside Calistoga

Putting California on the Map

California is the third largest state in the US (after Texas and Alaska) and, with over 38 million people, the most populous. Situated on the Pacific Coast, it is 800 miles (1,300 km) long and 250 miles (400 km) wide, covering an area of 158,710 sq miles (411,060 sq km). The state has two major cities: San Francisco and Los Angeles. Most visitors arrive via the airports in one of these cities; the main cities and towns are linked with each other and with other states by an extensive rail (Amtrak) and road system.

For additional map symbols *see back flap*

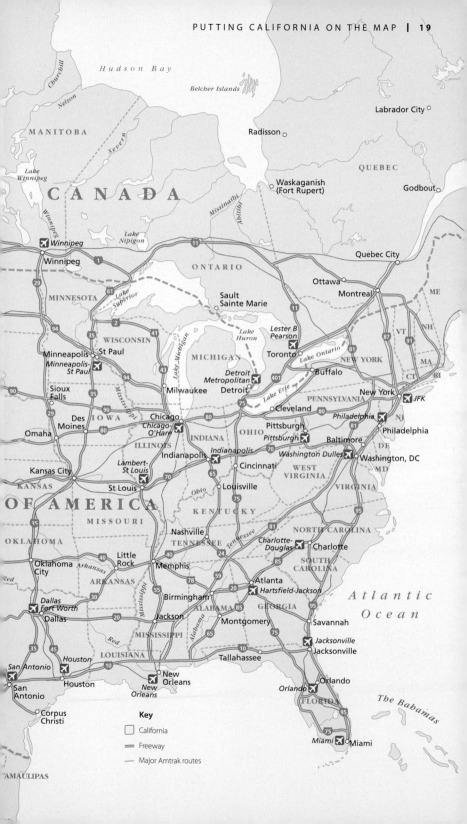

Key
☐ California
— Freeway
— Major Amtrak routes

A PORTRAIT OF CALIFORNIA

Impressive for both its size and its sway over modern culture, California symbolizes the United States' diversity and sense of prosperity. Here can be found towering forests, deserts within half a day's drive of ocean beaches, and two of the world's foremost cities, San Francisco and Los Angeles.

Perceptions of California vary so greatly that some now joke that there are two states. The first is geographic: California is the third-largest state in the Union (after Alaska and Texas), containing its largest county, San Bernardino, which covers 20,155 sq miles (52,200 sq km) – larger than Vermont and New Hampshire combined. This California has 840 miles (1,350 km) of coastline and measures 365 miles (587 km) at its widest point. It claims the second highest peak in the country (Mount Whitney) and its lowest expanse of dry land (Death Valley). More than 1,500 plant species grow here that cannot be found anywhere else on earth. Roughly one in every eight Americans is a Californian, making this the most populous of the 50 states, represented by the largest congressional delegation.

And that other California? It is a realm of romance, formed by flickering celluloid images. Think "California" and pictures are immediately conjured up of bikini-clad beachcombers, middle-class suburban families in ranch houses, and film stars emerging from limousines into hordes of autograph-seekers. These stereotypes are perpetuated by the entertainment media.

Hollywood is only partly to blame for this blurring of fact and fiction. It goes back to Spanish legends of an exotic outpost called California, flung out at the edge of the sea. Most of the world, though, knew nothing of this spot until the Gold Rush of 1849. Tales of the riches to be found encouraged thousands of would-be Croesuses to invade the region. Whether they found their fortunes or not, prospectors spread the same message: California was not as colorful or seductive as they had been told. It was even more so.

Sun-worshipers on Manhattan Beach, Los Angeles

◀ Sunset in Napa Valley

Joshua Tree National Park

Society and Politics

If the US as a whole is a melting pot of people, California is an ethnic microcosm. It receives the highest number of immigrants (more than 250,000 annually), and the racial make-up is the most diverse in the nation. The percentage of whites and African-Americans is lower than the national average, but the Asian residency is more than triple the national level. Hispanics, many from neighboring Mexico, account for more than a quarter of all Californians – three times the US average. Walk through any of the four most-populated cities (Los Angeles, San Diego, San Jose, and San Francisco), and you receive an immediate taste of this ethnic cocktail. It is still more potent during Mexican Cinco de Mayo (May 5) festivities, Chinese New Year bashes, and other multicultural events held around the state.

Racial prejudice has plagued the state since its early days. Abolitionists prevented California's 1849 constitutional convention from barring the entry of blacks into this land, but in the 1870s nativist orators such as Denis Kearney endorsed violence against Chinese immigrants, said to be "stealing" white jobs. With its size and population, California is sometimes viewed as operating as an independent country; government leaders have had to navigate huge challenges concerning everything from water shortages, law enforcement, and overcrowding in schools to balancing the state's enormous budget.

But the most inevitable result of population growth has been an altered balance between rural and urban sectors. More people means that more

Surfer

Golden Gate Bridge, San Francisco

Red Rock Canyon in the Mojave Desert

land is needed for housing. The value of California's agricultural goods still outranks that of all other states, but its farmland has declined steadily since the 1950s. Lumber workers have also had

California oranges

a hard time, because of conservation measures and a continuing shrinkage of the state's forests. The fastest-expanding job markets now are in service industries and high technology, which suggest a more metropolitan than pastoral future.

Visitors usually come to California to see one of two cities: San Francisco or Los Angeles, for very different reasons. In the north and south of the state respectively, these cities define the opposing sides of its character: San Francisco is older and more compact. Although California in general is recognized for its eccentricities and is still the birthplace of new trends, San Francisco is particularly proud of its nonconformity and open-mindedness. It was here that the "Big Four" railroad barons built their millionaire's mansions, but the city has since evolved into a pro-labor hotbed, with a history of activism (the Bay Area was a hub of the

anti-Vietnam War movement). It also has one of the world's largest concentrations of gays and lesbians, with a substantial gay vote.

In contrast to the bustling life of San Francisco, LA is a sprawling city without a real focal point. The car rules, demanding a network of freeways that have hemmed in some of the city's historical buildings and which grind to smoggy standstills during rush hours. The facades of wealth, fame, and glamour leave LA as a dimensionless creation of bright lights and fairly conservative politics.

Wild poppies in Antelope Valley

This is not to say that the north is entirely Democrat (left wing) and the south, Republican (right wing). Hollywood is a chief sponsor of liberal causes, and there are pockets of antigovernment rebels in the northeast. But the conflicting power that the two cities exert on state government in Sacramento and the state's representatives in Washington, DC explains why California may appear a little schizophrenic.

Poster for *LA Story* (1991)

Culture and Leisure

High- and low-brow art enjoy comparable support here. For most people, the state's contributions to culture are the many blockbusters made by Hollywood movie studios or televised sitcoms shot on LA sound stages. This is art in unashamed pursuit of the almighty dollar, complete with tabloid scandals and giant movie billboards, which blot out the Los Angeles sun.

But another creativity reveals itself through the state's history of landscape painting, portraiture, and 20th-century Avant-Garde art. Modern artists John McLaughlin and Elmer Bischoff, and ceramists Peter Voulkos and Robert Arneson have all made international reputations. So have a few pioneers of photographic art, such as Imogen Cunningham and Ansel Adams. British artist David Hockney lived here for many years, capturing the state's sun-soaked image on canvas. California is also home to some of the world's finest art museums, including LACMA, the Oakland Museum, the San Francisco MOMA, and the two J Paul Getty Museums. Victorian architecture in the Bay Area has always been a major tourist attraction, as have the many historic buildings across the state designed by Californians such as Willis Polk and Bernard Maybeck. Visiting designers Frank Lloyd Wright and Daniel Burnham have left their mark here, too. Recent influential architects include residents Frank Gehry and Joe Esherick.

The state has seen many writers over the years, including Nobel prize-winner John Steinbeck and Beat authors Jack Kerouac

Napa Valley Train in Wine Country

El Capitán *(left)* and the Three Brothers at Yosemite National Park

and Allen Ginsberg. The tradition continues with Armistead Maupin *(Tales of the City)*, detective novelist Sue Grafton, and Amy Tan *(The Joy Luck Club)*, among others. Music also plays a major role, whether the work of the cities' orchestras or rock musicians. Outdoor music venues and festivals are common throughout the state, as the temperate climate is conducive to enjoying the sounds of rock, pop, jazz, and classical concerts in the open air. This is where the Beach Boys, Janis Joplin, the Grateful Dead, and Red Hot Chili Peppers launched their careers.

Californians love to eat out, and chefs Wolfgang Puck and Alice Waters have made their names promoting "California cuisine" – a blend of local ingredients and Asian techniques. There is a widespread appreciation for world-class wines and both local and ethnic cuisine – proof that Californians take care of their palates. Yet residents are also body-conscious, aware that they live among the "beautiful people" who come here with dreams of film stardom. So they become slaves to the gym or take up a sport. On any weekend, in various parts of the state, you will see cyclists, surfers, in-line skaters, even whitewater rafters. Californians are eager supporters of professional baseball and football, but they like to be active themselves. Luckily, surrounded by some of the nation's most beautiful countryside and the gentlest climate, they do not have to go far to enjoy a satisfying outdoor experience.

Petco Park, home to the San Diego Padres Major League Baseball team

California's Landscape and Geology

California's dramatic landscape includes the highest and lowest points in the lower 48 states of the US, Mount Whitney in the High Sierras, and Death Valley in the southern deserts. Millions of years ago, subduction of the Pacific Ocean floor beneath the North American Plate created the Coastal Range, the Central Valley, and the granitic rocks of the Sierra Nevada Mountains. Later, the granites were uplifted and tilted westward. The movement of tectonic plates along the San Andreas Fault is still changing the shape of California.

The Coastal Range along the Pacific Coast was created around 25 million years ago, when fragments of the ocean floor and oceanic islands were pushed up by plate movements.

How the West was Made

Over a period of 150 million years, ending about 15 million years ago, the movement of the Pacific Plate and North American Plate formed the western margin of California.

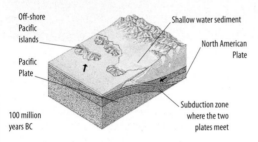

Off-shore Pacific islands

Shallow water sediment

North American Plate

Pacific Plate

Subduction zone where the two plates meet

100 million years BC

1 The North American Plate, moving westward, sweeps up any off-shore islands.

25 million years BC

Coastal Range

2 As the ocean floor moves north, the fragments of off-shore islands are scattered along the coast. They are then pushed up to form the Coastal Range.

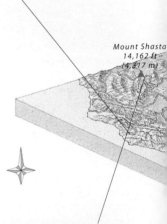

Mount Shasta
14,162 ft
(4,317 m)

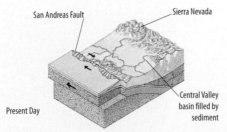

San Andreas Fault

Sierra Nevada

Central Valley basin filled by sediment

Present Day

3 The boundary between the North American Plate and the Pacific Plate is marked by the San Andreas Fault (see pp28–9).

Mount Lassen *(see p457)* and Mount Shasta *(see p456)* are part of the Cascades, a range of extinct and active volcanoes (including Mount St. Helens) created by a subduction zone beneath the northwestern corner of the North American Plate. Both Mount Lassen and Mount Shasta are still considered active. When young, the Sierra Nevada range must have resembled the Cascades.

Lemon trees flourish in central California. The highly fertile surface sediments of the flat Central Valley come from erosion of the surrounding mountains. The sediments have accumulated over the last few hundred thousand years.

Mount Whitney *(see p499)* in the High Sierras is the highest point in the continental United States, rising to 14,494 ft (4,418 m). The process that raised the Sierra Nevada Mountains began more than 50 million years ago, but peaked a few million years ago.

0 kilometers 100
0 miles 100

North Palisade
14,242 ft (4,341 m)

Mount Dana
13,053 ft
(3,979 m)

Mount Whitney
14,494 ft
(4,418 m)

Death Valley

Big Pine Mountain
6,826 ft (2,081 m)

Oil wells sprang up at a frantic pace when oil was discovered in California in the late 19th century. The drilling was so intense that the extraction of oil and gas deflated the land. Part of Los Angeles County subsided 28 ft (8.5 m) before oil companies were required to pump sea water down the wells to replace the extracted fuels.

Death Valley *(see pp294–7)* in the Mojave Desert has extreme height variations. Surrounded by some of the highest mountains on the continent, the valley floor lies 280 ft (85 m) below sea level. Death Valley was formed less than 15 million years ago when the North American Plate began to stretch due to the northwest drag created by the Pacific Plate.

California's Earthquakes

The San Andreas Fault extends almost the full length of California, some 600 miles (965 km) from the Gulf of California northwest to Cape Mendocino. It is not the only fault in California but it is one of the most active. Each year, on average, the Pacific Plate moves 1–1.6 inches (2.5–4 cm) to the northwest. Earthquakes occur when this movement is resisted. Stresses build up and eventually they are released, causing an earthquake. Many of California's major earthquakes have occurred in the northern section of the fault. The terrible fire of 1906 that destroyed San Francisco was caused by an earthquake estimated at 7.8 on the Richter Scale. More recently, the earthquake of October 1989, south of San Francisco, killed 62 people and caused at least $6 billion worth of damage *(see p509)*. In 1994, the Northridge quake, magnitude R6.7, rocked Los Angeles and was felt in Las Vegas, Nevada. Scientists now predict that the next major earthquake, the "Big One," will hit Southern California.

The San Andreas Fault is one of the few sites on earth where an active plate boundary occurs on land.

Hayward Fault

1989 earthquake epicenter

1989 earthquake hypocenter

The 1906 earthquake confounded contemporary geologists and led to the "elastic rebound" theory of earthquake formation, which is still in use today.

The 1989 earthquake struck the Santa Cruz Mountains in central California.

1769 Members of Portolá's expedition are first Europeans to experience an earthquake in California	**1865** San Francisco hit by its first major earthquake on October 9 and another on October 23	**1872** Town of Lone Pine is destroyed and Sierra Nevada Mountains rise 13 ft (4m)	**1952** Kern County (R7.7) **1940** Imperial Valley (R7.1)	**1992** Yucca Valley outside LA (R7.4) **1989** Loma Prieta (R7.1) strikes San Francisco area

1750	1800	1850	1900	1950

Don Gaspar de Portolá

	1857 Fort Tejon earthquake (R8) is followed by smaller earth tremors in Bay Area	**1906** San Francisco earthquake (R7.8) causes a devastating three-day fire that leaves 3,000 dead and 250,000 homeless	**1994** Northridge (R6.7). At least 56 people killed, more than 7,000 injured, and 20,000 made homeless. Anaheim Stadium and several Los Angeles freeways are badly damaged	

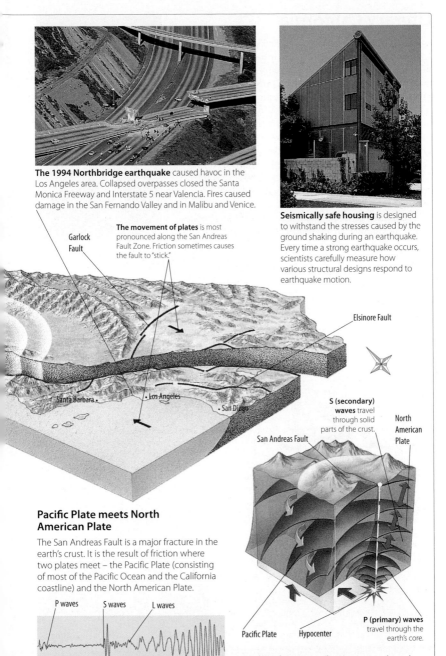

The 1994 Northbridge earthquake caused havoc in the Los Angeles area. Collapsed overpasses closed the Santa Monica Freeway and Interstate 5 near Valencia. Fires caused damage in the San Fernando Valley and in Malibu and Venice.

Seismically safe housing is designed to withstand the stresses caused by the ground shaking during an earthquake. Every time a strong earthquake occurs, scientists carefully measure how various structural designs respond to earthquake motion.

Garlock Fault

The movement of plates is most pronounced along the San Andreas Fault Zone. Friction sometimes causes the fault to "stick."

Elsinore Fault

Santa Barbara • Los Angeles • San Diego

S (secondary) waves travel through solid parts of the crust.

North American Plate

San Andreas Fault

Pacific Plate meets North American Plate

The San Andreas Fault is a major fracture in the earth's crust. It is the result of friction where two plates meet – the Pacific Plate (consisting of most of the Pacific Ocean and the California coastline) and the North American Plate.

P waves   S waves   L waves

It is possible to calculate the magnitude of an earthquake from a seismograph recording. Printouts show the intensity of earthquake vibrations graphically. The magnitude of the earthquake is registered on the Richter Scale (R).

Pacific Plate   Hypocenter

P (primary) waves travel through the earth's core.

Earthquake energy vibrations move through the earth's crust in waves. There are three types of wave: P or primary waves, S or secondary waves, and L or surface waves. The waves change as energy moves from the hypocenter to the earth's surface. Surface waves cause most of the damage associated with earthquakes.

Literary California

As journalist Carey McWilliams remarked in 1946, "What America is, California is, with accents, in italics." The chance to study the nation in microcosm has been especially appealing to authors. Many, such as Robert Louis Stevenson (1850–94), have simply passed through. He arrived in Monterey in 1879 and later based scenes in *Treasure Island* on the surrounding coastline. But California has not lacked for resident wordsmiths. This, after all, is where Henry Miller (1891–1980) blended erotic and verbal inventiveness and William Saroyan (1908–81) found his eccentric rural characters. Nobel prize-winning Eugene O'Neill (1888–1953) produced some of his best plays at Tao House in the Ramon Valley *(see p430)* and John Steinbeck (1902–68) based many of his novels on the people and places in Salinas. California is also where several major contemporary writers, such as Amy Tan (born in 1952), now chase their muse.

Robert Louis Stevenson, author of *Treasure Island*

The Pioneers

Much of the very early writing about California was unsophisticated, satisfying readers who simply wanted a taste of the frontier environment. But the Gold Rush *(see pp52–3)* created a market for prose that captured the poignancy, romance, and raw humor of life in the West. Bay Area literary journals such as *The Golden Era* and *The Overland Monthly* nurtured many local fiction writers. These included Bret Harte (1836–1902), the author of *The Luck of Roaring Camp*, essayist Henry George (1839–97), and bards ranging from Joaquin Miller (1837–1913) to Ina Coolbrith (the nation's first poet laureate in 1915).

Writer Samuel Clemens, alias Mark Twain

The literary journals also provided an apprenticeship for San Franciscan writer Samuel Clemens (1835–1910). His 1865 publication of the Gold Country yarn, "The Celebrated Jumping Frog of Calaveras County," introduced him to a national readership as Mark Twain.

The Social Critics

Ambrose Bierce (1842–1914) ranked among the first of many California writers who used their art to advocate wide-ranging political and social reforms. During the late 19th century, Bierce filled his *San Francisco Examiner* column with tirades against hypocrites and bureaucrats. His poisonous articles of biting criticism helped to trim the overweening influence of the vast Southern Pacific Railroad Company.

Frank Norris (1870–1902) attacked America's greed in his novel, *McTeague* (1899). In *The Octopus*, Norris also lashed out at the Southern Pacific, this time for its monopolistic mistreatment of ranchers in the San Joaquin Valley. Back from the Klondike Gold Rush (setting for *The Call of the Wild*), working-class author Jack London alternated between writing adventure novels and stories – such as *The Iron Heel* – that showed his faith in Marxism.

Upton Sinclair (1878–1968) had already published *The Jungle*, his exposé of the Chicago stockyards, when he moved to California after World War I. But it was in Pasadena that he wrote most of his novels, campaigning against poverty and inequality.

Social injustice was a frequent theme for Salinas-born novelist John Steinbeck (1902–68) *(see p521)*. *Tortilla Flat* (1935), about a band of Mexican-American outcasts, was his first success. It was *The Grapes of Wrath* (1939), however, that brought him the prestigious Pulitzer Prize for Literature. Steinbeck's book so powerfully portrayed the miseries endured by migratory laborers that it was banned from public libraries in some parts of the state.

Jack London at his Sonoma Valley ranch

Steinbeck on the Californian coast

The Crime Writers

Three California writers established the American school of private-eye fiction. The first of these was Dashiell Hammett (1884–1961), a tubercular former Pinkerton Agency detective and San Francisco resident. He began writing for *Black Mask* and other "pulp" crime-fiction magazines in the 1920s. He then went on to produce five novels, including *The Maltese Falcon* (1930). Hammett's work boasted a grim realism not found in either British whodunits or more venal tales by pulp writers lacking his investigative credentials.

Raymond Chandler (1888–1959) was less intimate with urban "mean streets," but was a more lyrical storyteller. Chandler was an oil company executive in Los Angeles until he was sacked for drunkenness. He went on to create the quintessential American detective – Philip Marlowe, star of seven novels, the best being

Poster for the film adaptation of Hammett's *The Maltese Falcon*

Farewell, My Lovely and *The Long Goodbye*. But it was Ross Macdonald (né Kenneth Millar) who finally rounded off his genre's rough edges and confirmed LA as its ideal setting. Macdonald was also the most prolific of this trio. He wrote 19 novels about sleuth Lew Archer, including *The Underground Man*.

Beat writers and friends, Jack Kerouac and Neal Cassady

The Beats

Protest against the political conservatism of President Eisenhower's America and against the conventions of society and art combined to produce San Francisco's "Beat Movement" of the 1950s. The Beats (or "Beatniks," as *San Francisco Chronicle* columnist Herb Caen labeled them) were led by the writers Allen Ginsberg (1926–97), Jack Kerouac (1922–69), and William Burroughs (1914–97). They extolled poetry made up of random word usages, produced stream-of-consciousness, drug-assisted narratives, and shunned social, literary, and sexual restraints.

The Beatniks' rebellion officially began in December, 1955, when Ginsberg gave a public reading of his poem "Howl," which was more like a shouting. Despite protests that "Howl" was obscene, it was subsequently

published by San Franciscan Lawrence Ferlinghetti, poet and owner of City Lights *(see p344)*, the first paperbacks only bookshop in the United States.

Two years later, Kerouac's novel *On the Road* spread the Beats' bohemian ethic nationwide. The most influential of the Beat writers, Kerouac also wrote *Desolation Angels* and *The Dharma Bums*, both novels set in California. By 1960 the Beat movement was waning, but not before it had paved the way for that decade's hippie movement.

The Moderns

Today, most best-seller lists feature at least one novel by a California author. The state has produced many distinctive voices, such as Ethan Canin (*The Palace Thief*, 1988), Michael Chabon (*The Wonder Boys*, 1995), and Ron Hansen (*Mariette in Ecstasy*, 1991). More established authors, such as Joan Didion (*A Book of Common Prayer*, 1977), Amy Tan (*The Joy Luck Club*, 1989, *The Bonesetter's Daughter*, 2001), and Alice Walker (*The Color Purple*, 1985 and *Possessing the Secret of Joy*, 1992), are still shining as brightly as ever. There are also many detective fiction writers here, including James Ellroy (*LA Confidential*, 1990), Dean Koontz (*Sole Survivor*, 2000), and Sue Grafton (*U is for Undertow*, 2009), all adding new depth to this genre.

Novelist Amy Tan

Art in California

In the wake of the Gold Rush *(see pp52–3)*, California became both a magnet and a breeding ground for artists. They generally eschewed native folk traditions, however, in favor of European aesthetics that, while making the most of this new land and its people, were not dramatically changed by it. Only after World War II did Californians – including painter Richard Diebenkorn and photographer Imogen Cunningham – shed subservience to Old World art movements in order to develop distinctive visual trends, which then spread internationally. Since the 1950s, Los Angeles has challenged San Francisco's cultural primacy, and California art has become a highly valued investment.

Figure on a Porch (1959) by Richard Diebenkorn

Painters

California's mountain and desert landscapes and dramatic ocean shores dominated painters' attention here during the late 19th century. Thomas Hill (1829–1908) was born in England and trained in Paris. He moved to California in 1861 and began to produce epic natural panoramas, especially of the stunning Yosemite Valley *(see pp492–5)*. His work not only attracted new visitors to the West Coast but also helped win Yosemite its national park status in 1890. Even more popular was William Keith (1838–1911), a Scotsman who spent 50 years portraying the state's virgin wilderness. At that time, cities and people may

have seemed comparatively pale inspirations. Yet Gilded Age California *(see pp54–5)* could not now be fully understood without such talents as William Hahn (1829–87), a German immigrant who captured life in nascent San Francisco; Grace Carpenter Hudson (1865–1937), renowned for her portraits of coastal natives; and William A Coulter (1849–1936), who recorded maritime scenes.

As early as 1900, the state's two halves displayed stylistically disparate growth. In the north, Xavier Martinez (1869–1943) and his fellow Tonalists filled canvases with the familiar hazy light and gray-brown hues of their environment. In the south, Guy Rose (1867–1925) led an

Impressionist school that used the region's vibrant colors and brighter light to produce Monet-like effects.

Prohibition-era Los Angeles flirted with the Synchromist style of Stanton Macdonald-Wright (1890–1973). San Francisco was enchanted by Cubist Realists such as Otis Oldfield (1890–1969). Another popular artist there was the great Mexican muralist Diego Rivera, who in 1940 composed *Panamerican Mind*, an enormous fresco that can be seen at the City College.

Modernism flowered fully in California after World War II. It was at that time that David Park (1911–60), Richard Diebenkorn (1922–93), and other members of the Bay Area Figurative School began to blend Expressionism with realistic imagery. In Southern California, Hard-Edge Abstractionists such as Helen Lundeberg (1908–99) and John McLaughlin (1898–1976) drew critical acclaim with their large-scale geometric shapes.

What is remarkable about contemporary California painters is not simply the worldwide recognition that they have earned, but their stylistic breadth. They range from Pop Artist Ed Ruscha (born in 1937) and urban landscapist Wayne Thiebaud (born in 1920), to cutting-edge British émigré David Hockney (born in 1937) and Arthur Carraway (1927–94), whose work celebrates his African-American heritage.

Afternoon in Piedmont (Elsie at the Window) by Xavier Martinez

Two Callas by Imogen Cunningham

Photographers

Many early California photographs were either portraits or straightforward documentary scenes done by surveyors. Some photographers, however, such as Eadweard James Muybridge (1830–1904), found photography no less powerful than painting in depicting nature. Others preferred to focus on human subjects. Allegorical nudes and other images by Anne Brigman (1869–1950) found fans even in New York City. Arnold Genthe (1869–1942) studied the Bay Area's Asian community, producing (with writer Will Irwin) a 1913 volume called *Pictures of Old Chinatown*.

In 1932, an Oakland group called "f/64" mounted a major exhibition at the de Young Museum in San Francisco *(see p370 and p371)*. Members of f/64, among them Ansel Adams (1902–84), Imogen Cunningham (1883–1976), and Edward Weston (1886–1958), believed photography should emphasize realism. This approach was riveting when used in close-ups of plants, or as Dorothea Lange (1895–1965) applied it in her portraits of Californians during the Great Depression.

The range of approaches now includes the snapshot aesthetics of Judy Dater (born in 1941) and photographs of Weimaraner dogs by William Wegman (born in 1943).

Sculptors

German-born Rupert Schmid (1864–1932) arrived in San Francisco in the 1880s. He soon became famous for figurative works employing western themes, such as *California Venus* (1895), his life-size female nude adorned with California poppies. More important still was Douglas Tilden (1860–1935), a sculptor from Chico who created impressive civic monuments. Arthur Putnam (1873–1930) also won notoriety with his sensual representations of wild animals in bronze, some of which are public monuments.

Schmid's *California Venus*

Californians have been expanding the parallel fields of sculpture and ceramics since the early part of the 20th century. Peter Voulkos (1924–2002) experimented in large-scale fired clay sculptures. Robert Arneson (1930–1992) abandoned more traditional vessel aesthetics to pursue startling and amusing Pop Art ceramics, while Bruce Beasley (born in 1939) and Michael Heizer (born in 1944) have created pieces that take on different dimensions depending on the weather.

Art Patronage in California

Private and public patronage have been essential to the vitality of California culture since the late 19th century. Had it not been for railroad baron Henry Huntington's money and interest in art treasures, there would be no Huntington Library, Art Galleries, and Botanical Gardens in Pasadena *(see pp162–5)*. The public would not have access to that institution's collection of 18th-century British art, including Thomas Gainsborough's *The Blue Boy* (c.1770) and many other masterpieces. Multimillionaire J Paul Getty brought together the world-famous collection of Greek and Roman antiquities housed in the J Paul Getty Villa in Malibu *(see p90)* and the painting, sculpture, and decorative arts collection occupying the J Paul Getty Center in Brentwood *(see pp86–9)*.

Another multimillionaire, Norton Simon, amassed the renowned selection of Goyas, Picassos, Rembrandts, and Van Goghs now on public display in the Norton Simon Museum *(see pp160–61)*.

Public financing, too, has enriched the state's art offerings. In the 1930s, the New Deal paid artists to paint the frescoes in San Francisco's Coit Tower *(see p347)* and embellish public structures throughout the state. More recently, city funds have been used to make Los Angeles one of the major centers of mural art in the world.

Henry Huntington

Architectural Styles in California

California's architectural history began with the arrival of the Europeans in the 18th century *(see pp50–51)*. Many of the late 18th- and early 19th- century Spanish missions were adaptations of Mexican Baroque architecture. The Spanish-Mexican influence continued to dominate until the mid-19th century. Later, this Hispanic vernacular merged with styles imported by settlers from the eastern US and Europe. Architects such as Henry Cleaveland, S & J Newsom, and Bernard Maybeck were influential in creating the state's unique Victorian style.

Hale House in Heritage Square, Los Angeles

Mission

Franciscan missionaries, arriving in California from Mexico, established a chain of 21 missions from San Diego to Sonoma as centers from which to colonize the area. They were all designed to be within a day's journey of their nearest neighbors. These provincial versions of Mexican churches and their communal buildings were designed by friars and built of adobe bricks and wood by unskilled Native American laborers. Over the years their crude constructions decayed and were shaken by earthquakes, but many have been carefully restored in the 20th century. Distinctive features include massive walls covered with white lime cement, small window openings, rounded gables, and tiered bell towers.

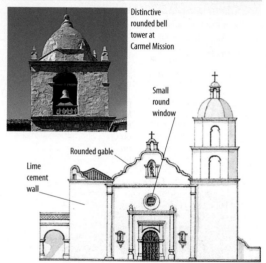
Distinctive rounded bell tower at Carmel Mission

Small round window

Rounded gable

Lime cement wall

Mission San Luis Rey (1811–51) was the 18th mission to be established and was so architecturally impressive that it was often referred to as a "palace" *(see pp266–7)*.

Monterey

In the 1850s and 1860s, East Coast settlers flooded into the newly declared 31st state, bringing with them styles that were already going out of fashion on the East Coast, such as Greek Revival. Monterey, the state capital under Mexican rule, gave its name to an architecture that is, in essence, a wooden Greek temple wrapped around a Mexican adobe. Features include two-story wooden porticoes supported by slim square posts, wood shingle roofs, and a chaste symmetry of plan and elevation.

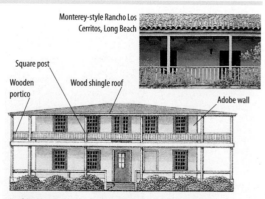
Monterey-style Rancho Los Cerritos, Long Beach

Square post

Wooden portico

Wood shingle roof

Adobe wall

Larkin House (1837), built by Thomas Larkin, was the first Monterey-style house, with its two stories of adobe brick.

Victorian

Three major styles emerged in California during the Victorian era: Italianate, most popular in San Francisco (see pp304–5), Queen Anne, and Eastlake. The two latter styles achieved a pinnacle of exuberance in California during the 19th century when they were brought to the state by migrants from the East Coast. The restrained Eastlake style, with its geometrically patterned facades and ornamentation, was often combined with the more extravagant Queen Anne style, notable for its gables, turrets, wraparound porches, and splendidly confused anthology of Classical details.

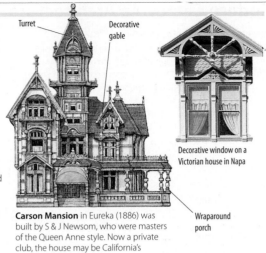

Turret

Decorative gable

Decorative window on a Victorian house in Napa

Carson Mansion in Eureka (1886) was built by S & J Newsom, who were masters of the Queen Anne style. Now a private club, the house may be California's ultimate Victorian folly.

Wraparound porch

Arts and Crafts

Pioneered by William Morris and Charles Voysey in England, the Arts and Crafts movement flourished briefly in California in the early 20th century. Also known as Craftsman style, its leading proponents included Bernard Maybeck and Charles and Henry Greene. Its emphasis is on simplicity and refinement on the outside and in the handcrafted interiors.

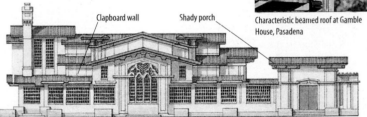

Clapboard wall

Shady porch

Characteristic beamed roof at Gamble House, Pasadena

The First Church of Christ Science in Berkeley (1907) is the finest example of Bernard Maybeck's Arts and Crafts designs.

Mission Revival

The Spanish-Mexican style was dormant during the second half of the 19th century. Decorative or pared-down versions were then enthusiastically revived in the early 20th century. The style is distinguishable by its rounded arches, harmonious proportions, and absence of ornamentation.

Red-tiled roof at the Beverly Hills Hotel

White stucco wall

Red-tiled roof

Rounded arch

The Women's Club (1913) in La Jolla was designed by Irving Gill, a pioneer of Modernism who used poured concrete and stucco to create elegant versions of the Mission style.

Modern California Architecture

In the early 20th century an architecture distinctive to
California emerged, after a brief return to the state's Hispanic
roots and an Art Deco style imported from Europe. This
California style borrowed post-and-beam construction and
wide porches from traditional Japanese buildings. Later,
during the postwar building boom of the 1950s, the whole
country was influenced by Cliff May's California ranch house,
with its fusion of indoor and outdoor living. In more recent
years, many architects, such as Craig Ellwood and Frank
Gehry, have helped to make LA a center of modern
architectural innovation (see pp76–7).

Mario Botta's 1995 San Francisco Museum of Modern Art building

Spanish Colonial

Ornate versions of traditional
Spanish architecture were first
given wide currency by the
Panama-California Exposition
in San Diego in 1915 (see
pp260–61), where many
buildings were decorated in
this style. Simplified versions
became the popular style for
houses and public buildings
throughout the 1920s.
Distinguishing features
included ornamental wood,
stone, and ironwork, used to
set off expanses of white
stucco, red pantiled roofs, and
lush gardens.

George Washington Smith,
the Montecito-based architect,
was a master of the style,
creating abstracted
Andalusian-style villages, such
as **Ostoff House** (1924) in San
Marino and Casa del Herrero
(1925), a private house in
Montecito. Another striking
example of this style is William
Mooser's **Santa Barbara
County Courthouse** (1929),
with its hand-painted ceilings,
murals, and sunken gardens.

Streamline Moderne

Art Deco made a brief appearance in California at the end
of the 1920s, with jazzy reliefs
and tile facades. It was
superseded by Streamline
Moderne, where sleek,
rounded forms are animated
by ribs, canopies, and reliefs.
Its inspirations were machine-
age imagery. The style is best
seen in movie theaters, such as
the **Academy Cathedral** (1939)
in Inglewood and Oakland's
Paramount Theater (Miller &
Pflueger, 1931).

PWA Moderne

This movement was named
after the Public Works
Administration, established
in the 1930s to fund public
buildings. It is a marriage
of Beaux-Arts formality
and the simplicity of
Modernism. It is notable for its
stone facades, pilasters, and
carved ornamentation. A good
example is the **Monterey
County Courthouse** (1937)
in Salinas.

Late 20th and Early 21st Century

A diversity of approaches by
leading architects has resulted
in some striking contemporary
buildings. Among the notable
achievements of the 1960s are
the ground-hugging, barnlike
structures of **Sea Ranch**. This
ecologically friendly vacation-
home community on the
Northern California coast began
as a cluster of condominiums by
Moore Lyndon Turnbull
Whittaker in 1965. In sharp
contrast is the **Salk Institute**, in
La Jolla (Louis Kahn, 1959–65).
State-of-the-art laboratories of
poured concrete flank a bare
travertine-paved plaza; a
symbolic meeting place that links
the continent and the ocean.

The **San Francisco Museum
of Modern Art**'s building,
designed by Swiss-Italian
architect Mario Botta in 1995,
has a cylindrical skylight
reaching up from stacked, top-
lit galleries. Snøhetta architects'
light-filled addition opened in
spring 2016, adjoining Botta's. It
rises up six stories, providing
increased exhibition space and
public areas.

Post-Modernism

Reacting to the impersonality
of corporate towers,
architects such as Michael
Graves, Venturi Scott-Brown,
and Robert Stern popularized

George Washington Smith's Casa del Herrero in Montecito (1925)

a more decorative approach to Modernism in the 1970s. Buildings such as **The Library** (1984) by Robert Stern in San Juan Capistrano make playful use of historical elements (columns, pediments, and pergolas) while employing colorful palettes.

Jon Jerde scrambles colors and architectural references with even greater abandon in his popular shopping centers, most notably **Westfield Horton Plaza** (1989) in San Diego. This multilevel outdoor shopping mall with domes and tilework echoes local Spanish-style buildings.

Post-Modern Westfield Horton Plaza

Programmatic Donut Hole in La Puente, east of Los Angeles

Programmatic Buildings

The automobile began to reshape California as early as the 1920s, and there was fierce competition to attract the attention of passing motorists on the commercial strips that linked scattered communities. An exuberant roadside architecture developed, in which travelers were invited to sleep in wigwam motels or have their shoes repaired inside a building in the shape of a huge shoe (Doschander's Shoe Repair Shop, Bakersfield, 1947). Most of these fantasies have been demolished, but a few remain in outlying areas, such as the drive-thru **Donut Hole** (1958) in La Puente.

Frank Lloyd Wright

Born in Wisconsin, Frank Lloyd Wright (1867–1959) lived in California in the 1920s and designed buildings in the state throughout his career. He began with **Hollyhock House** (1917–20) in Hollywood, and ended with the **Marin County Civic Center** in San Rafael, north of San Francisco, completed in 1972. Other notable buildings are the old VC Morris store (1949), now the **Xanadu Gallery** in San Francisco, and several LA "textile block" houses, inspired by Mayan temples.

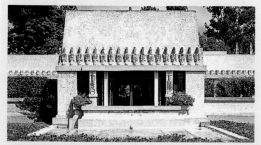
Frank Lloyd Wright's Hollyhock House in Hollywood

Where to Find the Buildings

Multicultural California

California is the most ethnically diverse state in the Union. In the 19th century, the discovery of gold, silver, and oil each brought an influx of migrants of many nationalities to California; the landscape and climate still attract farmers, fishermen, and vintners from all over the world. By the mid-21st century, many believe California will be a hybrid of cultures, with no clear ethnic majority. The concentration of races varies statewide: a greater number of Hispanics reside in the south, while the Silicon Valley and northern farmlands have attracted Asians and Europeans. Most ethnic communities still celebrate their cultures with lively festivals *(see pp40–3)*.

San Francisco's Chinatown

Performance of traditional Mexican dancing at the Cinco de Mayo festival in Los Angeles

entire areas of cities. Although many of the younger Chinese have now moved to middle-class areas, the Chinatowns of LA and San Francisco still attract tourists and visitors to their traditional shops and restaurants.

Native Americans

California has more resident Native Americans than any other state. The indigenous population grew in the 1960s when they gained more political rights. A few Native Americans still live on reservations, but the majority have opted for integration throughout the state.

Hispanic-Americans

You cannot go far in California without becoming aware of the state's Hispanic heritage. Spanish explorers who arrived in the 17th and 18th centuries *(see pp50–51)* established many of today's cities. As early as the 1940s the state was home to the largest population of Mexicans outside their own country. Political and economic troubles in Central and South America have continued to fuel Hispanic immigration. Today, almost every city has Mexican influences in its architecture, cuisine, and art. The Hispanics are also responsible for some of the brightest fiestas, including the extravagant *Cinco de Mayo* (May 5) *(see p40)*.

Chinese

Chinese immigrants first arrived in California during the Gold Rush *(see pp52–3)*. A further influx escaped the economic problems of their homeland in the 1860s to work as cheap labor building the transcontinental railroad *(see pp54–5)*. Following its completion, they remained in California, setting up laundries and other businesses, but were met with racial violence by activists claiming they were stealing "white jobs." In the 1880s Congress severely limited Chinese immigration, a law that was not repealed until 1943.

Such antipathy resulted in ghettolike Chinese communities, which dominated

Girl in Native American dress

African-Americans

African-Americans have been present in California since the days of Mexican rule. It was the increase in heavy industry during World War II, however, that led to the largest influx from the poorer southern

Rotchev House at Fort Ross

states. In the years that followed, low social standing and racism resulted in the growth of urban ghettos. Racial problems still persist in the US, but many African-Americans are making their mark in government, entertainment, and business. African festivals are celebrated in some cities, such as UMOJA in Oakland (see pp426–9).

Japanese

The Japanese arrived in California in the early 20th century. The majority of them were farmers who literally sowed the seeds of the state's agricultural industry. During World War II, however, Japanese-Americans were considered a risk to national security and were interned for the duration of the war. The succeeding generation has overridden these events, and Japanese businesses have continued to grow since the 1980s property boom.

Italians

Italians, predominantly fishermen, arrived in California in the late 19th century, and settled in North Beach, San Francisco (see pp344–7). The climate and soil also tempted Italian vintners, who founded what is now a highly respected wine industry.

Russians

Fur trappers from Russia and Alaska were among the first European settlers in California,

arriving in the early 1800s. For a short time, they established a successful settlement at Fort Ross (see p464), and today there is a Russian population of some 25,000 in and around San Francisco.

Irish

Fewer people of Irish descent reside on the West Coast than on the East Coast, and there are no distinct Irish districts in California. The Irish have largely integrated into a multicultural way of life, but their presence is still felt in the many Irish city bars, and particularly during the statewide parades on St. Patrick's Day (see p40).

Santa Monica English pub sign

Melting Pot

Over the last few decades there has been a steady rise in immigrants from Asia. Long Beach has the largest population of Cambodians outside Cambodia, and the district is known as "Little Phnom Penh." Wars in Korea and Vietnam brought natives of these countries to the liberal atmosphere of California in the 1950s and 1970s. Originally settling in the poorer areas of inner cities, they have now turned many of these into thriving communities. Fresno (see p520) has the second largest Hmong population outside Laos in the world.

The technological opportunities of Silicon Valley (see p432) have continued to attract Indians and Pakistanis to the region since the 1970s. Santa Monica is home to a large British contingent, complete with "authentic" pubs. The town of Solvang (see p223) was founded by immigrants from Denmark in 1911 and retains its Danish heritage. California also has the second largest Jewish community in the US, two-thirds of whom live in LA.

Danish windmill in Solvang

CALIFORNIA THROUGH THE YEAR

California generally enjoys a moderate climate *(see pp44–5)*, which explains how residents can schedule annual events without concern for the weather. The size of the state, however, means that a range of activities can be pursued in different locations: winter can be spent skiing in the north or soaking up the sun in the warmer south. Californians love to celebrate, and the calendar is full of parades and festivals. Many are related to the state's agricultural heritage; others have been inspired by its social history, such as the Gold Rush, or its ethnic diversity. There are also cultural events, including jazz and film festivals, and national sports fixtures.

Food & Wine Festival in Los Angeles

Spring

There is a clear sense of re-emergence in spring, when wildflowers carpet California's coastal headlands, gray whales swim north with their newborn offspring, and people start searching frantically for the sunglasses they tucked away the previous October. *Cinco de Mayo* (May 5) celebrations in Los Angeles and San Francisco, Hollywood's glamorous Academy Awards® ceremony, baseball games, and San Francisco's Bay-to-Breakers run are all familiar elements of the season.

March

Snowfest *(late Feb/early Mar)*, Tahoe City. The winter carnival features ski competitions, a "polar bear" (cold water) swim, parades, races, theater, and live music.
St. Patrick's Day Parade *(weekend nearest Mar 17)*, San Francisco. A parade down Market Street is usually followed by Irish coffee in the city's Irish bars.
Return of the Swallows *(Mar 19)*, Mission San Juan Capistrano *(see pp244–5)*. Crowds gather to see the birds fly back to the mission gardens from their winter homes in Argentina. Live music, food, and children's activities feature.

Swallows returning to Mission San Juan Capistrano

St. Patrick's Day shamrock

Redwood Coast Dixieland Jazz Festival *(end Mar)*, Eureka. Some of the world's finest Dixieland bands gather for this annual event.

April

Major League Baseball *(Apr–Sep)*. The San Francisco Giants, LA Dodgers, Anaheim Angels, Oakland Athletics, and San Diego Padres compete.
Toyota Grand Prix *(mid-Apr)*, Long Beach. The biggest street race in the US.
Agua Cahuilla Indian Heritage Festival *(mid-Apr)*, Palm Springs. Festivities honor the Native Americans who discovered the local hot springs.
Cherry Blossom Festival *(mid-Apr)*, San Francisco. Japanese dancing and martial arts displays are all part of this traditional annual event *(see p356)*.
San Francisco International Film Festival *(mid-Apr–early May)*. Independent films from around the world are shown in venues throughout the city.

May

Raisin Festival *(early May)*, Selma. A parade, art competitions and the crowning of the Raisin Queen.
Cinco de Mayo *(May 5)*, LA and San Francisco. The state's largest Mexican celebrations feature folk dancing and mariachi music.
Calaveras County Fair *(mid-May)*, Angels Camp. The famous

frog jumping contest (see p483) and a rodeo.

California Strawberry Festival (mid-May), Oxnard. Food booths, arts and crafts, and contests.

Bay-to-Breakers (third Sun), San Francisco. The world's largest fun run is 7.5-miles (12.5-km) from the Embarcadero to Ocean Beach.

Carnaval (last weekend), San Francisco. The Mission District turns Latin American, with salsa and reggae bands.

Sacramento Music Festival (last weekend). Classic jazz, swing, and other music.

Lesbian and Gay Pride parade in San Francisco

Mexican dancer at the Cinco de Mayo festival in Los Angeles

Summer

At no other time of year are the clichés of California so evident. Beaches are crowded with tanned, muscled bodies and daredevil surfers, and colorfully dressed gays and lesbians parade through San Francisco streets in June. Tourists flood into the state, attending its many outdoor music events, Wild West celebrations (such as Old Miners' Days in Big Bear Lake), and the renowned Gilroy Garlic Festival.

June

San Mateo County Fair (early Jun). Thousands of attractions include live music, a literary event, and horse shows.

Beaumont Cherry Festival (early Jun). Four days of music, games, parades, rides, food, and plenty of cherries.

Mainly Mozart Festival mid-Jun), San Diego. Leading orchestras perform Mozart.

Lesbian and Gay Pride Day (Sun in late Jun), San Francisco. Huge gay parade.

Lumber Jubilee (end Jun), Tuolumne. The history of California's lumber industry.

Juneteenth (end Jun), Oakland. African-American celebration, featuring jazz and gospel.

July

Fourth of July Fireworks Particularly good displays are at Disneyland and at the Rose Bowl.

Mammoth Jazz (first weekend after Jul 4). Some dozen world-class jazz bands perform.

California State Fair (mid-Jul), Sacramento. Everything from star-studded entertainment to pig races.

Obon Festival (mid-Jul), San Jose. Taiko drummers and dancers join in this Japanese-American party.

Carmel Bach Festival (mid-Jul–early Aug). Bach concerts and classes are held.

Gilroy Garlic Festival (end Jul). Enjoy garlic in all kinds of dishes.

Old Miners' Days (end Jul–mid-Aug), Big Bear Lake. The Gold Rush is recalled with a chili cook-off.

Festival of Arts (Jul–Aug), Laguna Beach.

International Surf Festival (late Jul/Aug). Body boarding and surfing events take place at various LA beaches.

August

San Francisco Marathon (late Jul or early Aug).

Outside Lands (early Aug), San Francisco. This popular festival with music, comedy, and food is held in the Golden Gate Park.

Old Spanish Days Fiesta (early Aug), Santa Barbara. Spanish markets and carnival.

Nisei Week (mid-Aug), Japanese festival in LA's Little Tokyo.

Pebble Beach Concours d'Elegance (mid-Aug). Classic automobile show.

Bigfoot Days (end Aug/early Sep), Willow Creek. A parade and ice-cream social at this homage to California's legendary hermit.

LA Food & Wine Festival (late Aug), Los Angeles. Four-day epicurean festival that showcases the best culinary talent in LA and from around the country.

Surfers at the International Surf Festival in Los Angeles

Mexican Independence Day parade in Santa Monica

Autumn

In the High Sierras, leaves of deciduous trees turn stunning shades of red and yellow. The Napa Valley wineries (see pp466–7) invite visitors to help celebrate their grape harvests with wine tastings and live music. All over the state, Oktoberfests serve up foamy mugs of beer and the "oompah-pah" of German bands, while rodeos dramatize California's frontier past.

September
Pro Football *(Sep–Dec)*. The San Francisco '49ers, Oakland Raiders, and San Diego Chargers take to the field.
Los Angeles County Fair *(whole month)*, Pomona. This vast county fair includes horse races, an operational farm, outdoor miniature railroad, and entertainment acts.
California State Gold Panning Championship *(early Sep)*, Foresthill. The 1849 Gold Rush is remembered with a gold panning competition.
Oktoberfest *(mid-Sep–mid-Oct)*, Torrance. The largest German beer festival in Southern California. Entry to the festival is for those aged 21 years and over only, except family day on Sunday. The event features German dancers, contests, and hearty food.
Mexican Independence Day *(Sep 16)*. Mexican dancing, music and food in Los Angeles, Calexico, and Santa Maria.
Monterey Jazz Festival *(third weekend)*. Running since 1958, this is the world's oldest continuously held annual jazz festival,

attracting over 500 top artists. All the greats have played here.
Danish Days *(mid-Sep)*, Solvang. Danish food stands and parades celebrate the city's Danish heritage *(see p223)*.
Sonoma County Harvest Fair *(late Sep/early Oct)*, Santa Rosa. A grape stomp and a 6-mile (10-km) run are highlights of this annual fair.
TARFEST *(late Sep)*. Three-day festival of film, music, and art in Los Angeles.

October
Black Cowboy Parade *(early Oct)*, Oakland. This festival and parade commemorates the part that African-Americans played in settling the American West.
Columbus Day Parade *(Sun nearest Oct 12)*, San Francisco. Bands and floats proceed down Columbus Avenue to Fisherman's Wharf.
San Francisco Jazz Festival *(end Oct–early Nov)*. All-star jazz performances throughout the city.
Pumpkin Festival *(mid-Oct)*, Half Moon Bay. The World Heavyweight Pumpkin Championship, pumpkin carving, and the opportunity to try pumpkin dishes.
Grand National Rodeo *(mid-Oct)*. Daly City. The largest two-day rodeo in the US features rodeo performances and a livestock exposition.
Craftsman Weekend *(mid-Oct)*, San Gabriel Valley. Largest celebration of the Arts and Crafts movement in western US, including architectural tours.

Halloween *(Oct 31)*, San Francisco. Dressed in scary costumes, residents parade through the city streets.
Butterflies *(end Oct–mid-Mar)*, Pacific Grove. Thousands of monarch butterflies migrate here from the north annually to shelter for the winter *(see p514)*.

Costumed participants in Pasadena's Doo Dah Parade

November
Dia de los Muertos/**Day of the Dead** *(Nov 1)*. LA's El Pueblo and San Francisco's Mission District. This is a Mexican religious festival, when the souls of the dead are said to visit their surviving relatives. The festival's origins date back thousands of years.
Death Valley '49ers Encampment *(early Nov)*. This festival has fiddle, banjo, mandolin, and guitar competitions, pioneer costume and horseshoe contests, cowboy poetry, and gold panning.
California Indian Center Powwow *(late Nov)*, Los Angeles. A celebration of Native American food and culture.

Mexican musicians at the *Dia de los Muertos* festival

Gray whale approaching a boat off Baja California

Public Holidays

New Year (Jan 1)

Martin Luther King Jr. Day (3rd Mon in Jan)

Presidents' Day (3rd Mon in Feb)

Memorial Day (last Mon in May)

Independence Day (Jul 4)

Labor Day (1st Mon in Sep)

Veterans' Day (Nov 11)

Thanksgiving (4th Thu in Nov)

Christmas Day (Dec 25)

Doo Dah Parade (late Nov), Pasadena. This fun costumed parody parade features irreverent satire.

Winter

Californians love bright lights, and this is most apparent at Christmas, when every building and public square seems to be draped in twinkling bulbs. Churches resound with Christmas carols, and film stars take part in seasonal parades. As Lake Tahoe's ski season gets under way, highways jam up with avid skiers traveling north.

December
Hollywood Christmas Parade (first Sun after Thanksgiving), Los Angeles. Hollywood and Sunset Boulevards are crowded with this celebrity-heavy extravaganza, held since 1931.

Newport Harbor during the Annual Newport Beach Christmas Parade

Newport Beach Christmas Boat Parade (mid-Dec). Carol singing takes place over five nights and almost a hundred glittering vessels light up the Newport waterfront.
International Tamale Festival (early Dec), Indio. Mexican dancing accompanies the tamale (spicy corn husk rolls) gluttony.
Whale-watching (end Dec–Apr). California gray whales, migrating south annually from the Bering Strait to Baja, can be sighted along the coast or from whale-watching boats out of many coastal cities (see p586).

January
Bald Eagles (Jan–Feb), Mount Shasta. The area fills with bald eagles who come here to nest.
Tournament of Roses Parade (Jan 1), Pasadena. A pageant, followed by the Rose Bowl football game (see p158).
Palm Springs International Film Festival (early–mid-Jan). Screenings and awards.
Gold Discovery Day (Jan 24), Coloma. Celebration of the anniversary of the first gold discovery (see p479).
Napa Valley International Mustard Festival (Jan–Mar), Mustard and wine tasting.

February
Academy Awards Ceremony (Feb), Los Angeles. Hollywood's finest gather to honor the year's best films and top actors.

Los Angeles Marathon (Feb). Taking place in the heart of the city, this offers more live entertainment than any other marathon.
AT&T Pebble Beach Pro-Am Golf Tournament (end Jan–early Feb). Pros and celebrities play golf together.
Dickens Festival (early Feb), Riverside. Writer Charles Dickens' life is celebrated in a re-creation of a mid-19th-century London marketplace.
Riverside County Fair and National Date Festival (mid–late Feb), Indio. Date dishes and camel and ostrich races.
Chinese New Year Festival (mid-Feb–early Mar), San Francisco. The nation's largest Chinese New Year festival.

Chinese New Year celebrations in San Francisco

The Climate of California

Apart from the extremes of the mountains and the deserts, the state's climate is neither oppressive in summer nor too cold in winter. The Northern Coastal Range is temperate, although wet in the winter. To the east, rain turns to snow on the Sierra Nevada Mountains. Central California and the Central Valley have a Mediterranean climate. The weather becomes drier and warmer toward the south with soaring temperatures in the desert during the summer.

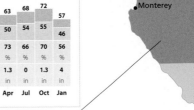

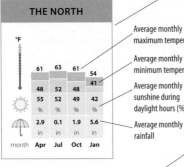

THE NORTH

°F				
	61	63	61	54
				41
	48	52	48	42
	55 %	52 %	49 %	42 %
	2.9 in	0.1 in	1.9 in	5.6 in
month	**Apr**	**Jul**	**Oct**	**Jan**

Average monthly maximum temperature

Average monthly minimum temperature

Average monthly sunshine during daylight hours (%)

Average monthly rainfall

WINE COUNTRY

°F				
	70	82	77	57
	43	52	48	37
	75 %	85 %	80 %	52 %
	1.6 in	0 in	1.6 in	5.4 in
month	**Apr**	**Jul**	**Oct**	**Jan**

SAN FRANCISCO AND THE BAY AREA

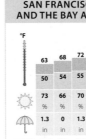

°F				
	63	68	72	57
	50	54	55	46
	73 %	66 %	70 %	56 %
	1.3 in	0 in	1.3 in	4 in
month	**Apr**	**Jul**	**Oct**	**Jan**

NORTH CENTRAL CALIFORNIA

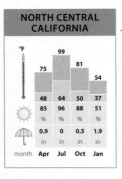

°F				
	75	99	81	54
	48	64	50	37
	85 %	96 %	88 %	51 %
	0.9 in	0 in	0.5 in	1.9 in
month	**Apr**	**Jul**	**Oct**	**Jan**

SOUTH CENTRAL CALIFORNIA

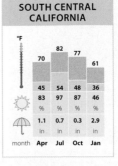

°F				
	70	82	77	61
	45	54	48	36
	83 %	97 %	87 %	46 %
	1.1 in	0.7 in	0.3 in	2.9 in
month	**Apr**	**Jul**	**Oct**	**Jan**

Eureka

Redding

Chico

Tahoe City

Santa Rosa

Sacramento

Stockton

San Francisco

Modesto

San Jose

Monterey

San Luis Obispo

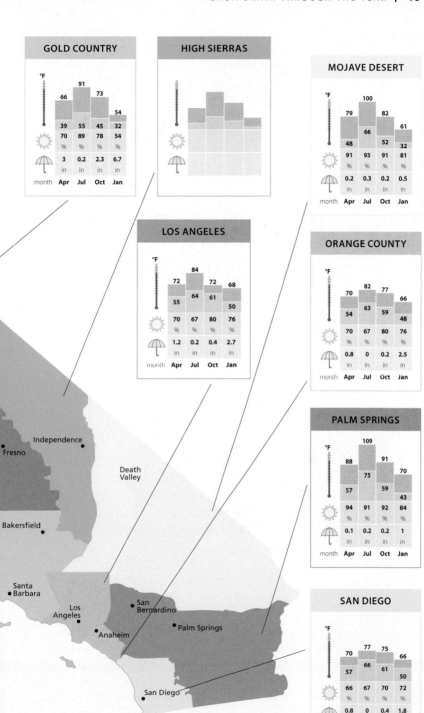

GOLD COUNTRY

°F	Apr	Jul	Oct	Jan
	66	91	73	54
	39	55	45	32
%	70	89	78	54
in	3	0.2	2.3	6.7
month	Apr	Jul	Oct	Jan

HIGH SIERRAS

MOJAVE DESERT

°F	Apr	Jul	Oct	Jan
	79	100	82	61
	48	66	52	32
%	91	93	91	81
in	0.2	0.3	0.2	0.5
month	Apr	Jul	Oct	Jan

LOS ANGELES

°F	Apr	Jul	Oct	Jan
	72	84	72	68
	55	64	61	50
%	70	67	80	76
in	1.2	0.2	0.4	2.7
month	Apr	Jul	Oct	Jan

ORANGE COUNTY

°F	Apr	Jul	Oct	Jan
	70	82	77	66
	54	63	59	48
%	70	67	80	76
in	0.8	0	0.2	2.5
month	Apr	Jul	Oct	Jan

PALM SPRINGS

°F	Apr	Jul	Oct	Jan
	88	109	91	70
	57	75	59	43
%	94	91	92	84
in	0.1	0.2	0.2	1
month	Apr	Jul	Oct	Jan

SAN DIEGO

°F	Apr	Jul	Oct	Jan
	70	77	75	66
	57	66	61	50
%	66	67	70	72
in	0.8	0	0.4	1.8
month	Apr	Jul	Oct	Jan

Independence · Fresno · Death Valley · Bakersfield · Santa Barbara · Los Angeles · San Bernardino · Anaheim · Palm Springs · San Diego

THE HISTORY OF CALIFORNIA

An early 16th-century chivalric Spanish novel, *Las Sergas de Esplanadían (The Exploits of Esplanadían)*, first gave the name *California* to a mythical island, plump with natural wealth and ruled by Calafía, a pagan queen. By 1542, when the Portuguese navigator Juan Rodríguez Cabrillo (João Rodrigues Cabrilho) sailed north from Mexico on Spain's behalf and discovered what he believed to be an island, the name California was already familiar enough for him to use it in his journal. Two centuries would pass, however, before Spain made a real claim on the land, sending Father Junípero Serra in 1769 to establish Franciscan missions across California.

The Gold Rush

Still, the territory remained remote until 1848; the same year that Mexico ceded California to the US, gold was found in the Sierra Nevada foothills. By 1849, hordes of fortune seekers had arrived in Northern California. The Gold Rush, followed by silver finds in the western Sierras and the completion of the transcontinental railroad in 1869, brought prosperity to the whole state. But the changes caused social rifts: whites charged Chinese immigrants with "stealing" their jobs, and by the beginning of the 20th century, economic divisions left over from the time of plenty had helped to create powerful labor unions. By 1860 California's native population was reduced by more than two-thirds due to Old World diseases that the natives were not immune to, poverty, and other historical factors.

20th-Century California

San Francisco's earthquake in 1906 convinced many that California's heyday was over. However, during the next 90 years, Hollywood drew international attention with its movie-making. Oil wells serviced the needs of increasingly car-dependent residents, and by 1937 orange groves had become a symbol of the state's fertile future. With the signing of the UN charter in San Francisco in 1945, it was clear that California was finally a player at center stage.

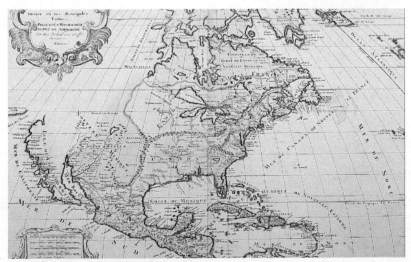

Early map of the United States, showing California as an island

◀ Mural at the Santa Barbara County Courthouse showing Cabrillo's landing in California

Early California

It is estimated that, at the time of European discovery, between 100,000 and 275,000 natives lived in California, with a way of life largely unchanged over thousands of years. They were not warlike, nor did they have much in the way of government. Only on the Colorado River did they practice agriculture; most relied on hunting, fishing, or the gathering of staples such as acorns for food. Their religion and medical beliefs were bound together in the person of a shaman, said to be in direct communication with the spirit world. They congregated in villages of 100 to 150 inhabitants generally living in conical or dome-shaped dwellings. Social classes were almost nonexistent, but there were great language divisions between different tribes.

Tcholovoni People
Various tribes, including these Tcholovoni people, settled in small villages on the shores of San Francisco Bay.

Money Box
Natives of Northern California used dentalium shells for money, held in ornately carved boxes.

Gift baskets, such as this Miwok example, were often decorated with beads.

Jewelry
This necklace, made of abalone and clamshells, is thought to be one of the earliest artifacts of Native California life.

Quail feathers and geometric dancers decorate this basket of the Yokut people.

Eel trapper

Headdresses
This headpiece, made out of black and white magpie feathers, derives from the native Miwok people.

Basketry

Basket-weaving was the primary native activity. They used a wide range of materials, which were twined or coiled into imaginative or symbolic designs. Baskets were used in all areas of life, including hunting, storage, cooking, and eating.

3,400,000 BC Volcanic ash from Mount St. Helens creates the Petrified Forest at Calistoga *(see p465)*		**200,000 BC** Early inhabitants, possibly predecessors of *Homo sapiens*, live near what is now Calico *(see p289)*	*Early flint stone tool*
3,400,000 BC	**2,000,000 BC**	**200,000 BC**	
3,000,000 BC Plate movements form Redrock Canyon in Death Valley *(see pp294–7)*	*Sabre-toothed tiger skeleton from La Brea Tar Pits*		**40,000 BC** Mammoths, tigers, and other Pleistocene epoch creatures are trapped in Los Angeles' La Brea Tar Pits

Kule Loklo People
These early Bay Area inhabitants were depicted by
Anton Refregier in his mural in the foyer of the Rincon
Center (see p321).

(see p321)

Where to See Early California

The Page Museum at the La Brea Tar Pits
(see p122) includes fossil reconstructions of
creatures recovered from the nearby tar
pits. The Chumash Painted Cave State
Historic Park (p223) has rare pictographs
executed by the Chumash people. LA's
Historic Southwest Museum (p157) and the
California Academy of Sciences in San
Francisco (pp374–5) both feature Native
American artifacts.

Painted caves dating back thousands of
years have been carefully preserved in the
Chumash Painted Cave State Historic Park
in Southern California.

Storage baskets
were made in a
variety of shapes,
designs, and
materials.

Water basket

Ladles were tightly woven
to hold a large amount of
water.

Ceremonial Costumes
Aprons made of animal skins and
tails were worn by participants
in the traditional White
Deerskin Dance.

Woodpecker traps were made out
of willow branches.

8,000 BC Climate is warm
enough to support cone-
bearing trees

1,000 BC Ubehebe
Crater formed in
Death Valley (see
pp294–6)

*Native
American
dwelling*

10,000 BC	6,000 BC	1,000 BC	AD 100

10,000–8,000 BC
Pleistocene epoch (Ice
Age) ends. First Native
American people settle in
California area

6,000 BC Climate is warm
enough to support
deciduous trees

AD 100 Devil's Golf
Course in Death Valley
formed by an evaporated
lake (see pp295)

The Colonial Period

Although the Spanish "discovered" California in 1542, they did not colonize the area until the 18th century. Their rule was enforced through a trio of institutions – the mission (church), the *presidio* (fort), and the pueblo (town). Of these, the mission was the most influential. Beginning at San Diego in 1769, Franciscan friars founded 21 missions at approximately 30-mile (48-km) intervals along *El Camino Real* ("the Royal Road"). Missionaries wanted to bring religion to the "benighted Indian," but they also used natives as cheap labor. European colonists committed a more serious crime by bringing with them diseases that would reduce the native population to about 16,000 by 1900.

- San Francisco de Solano (1823)
- San Rafael Arcangel (1817)
- San Francisco de Asis (1776)
- San Jose (1797)
- Santa Clara de Asis (1777)
- Santa Cruz (1791)
- San Juan Bautista (1797)
- Nuestra Señora de la Soledad (1791)
- San Carlos Borromeo de Carmelo (1770)
- San Antonio de Padua (1771)

El Camino Real

- San Miguel Arcangel (1797)
- San Luis Obispo de Tolosa (1772)
- La Purisma Concepcion (1787)
- Santa Ines (1804)
- Santa Barbara (1786)
- San Buenaventura (1782)

Sir Francis Drake
The English navigator landed in California in 1579 to make repairs to his ship, the *Golden Hind*. He named the land "Nova Albion" and claimed it for Queen Elizabeth I.

Father Junípero Serra
Originally from the Spanish island of Mallorca, Father Junípero Serra led the Franciscan expedition to establish a chain of missions in California.

Jedediah Smith
In 1828, a fur-trapper, Jedediah "Strong" Smith, was the first white man to reach California overland across the Sierra Nevada Mountains, from the eastern United States.

1524 Hernán Cortés, conqueror of Mexico, encourages the Spanish King Charles V to seize control of the "California Islands"

1579 English privateer Francis Drake anchors his *Golden Hind* near Point Reyes *(see p416)*

1500

1600

1650

1542 Juan Rodríguez Cabrillo (João Rodrigues Cabrilho) sails north from Mexico to San Diego harbor, making him the official discoverer of California

Juan Rodríguez Cabrillo

1595 Portuguese navigator Sebastián Rodríguez Cermeño discovers Monterey Bay

1602 Spanish merchant-adventurer Sebastián Vizcaíno sails up the California coast, naming landmarks as he goes – including San Diego, Santa Barbara, Point Concepción, and Carmel

Mission San Gabriel Arcángel
Ferdinand Deppe's 1832 work is thought to be the first painting of a mission. It depicts the central role of the mission in the community, surrounded by Native American dwellings.

Where to See Colonial California

Mission-era artifacts can be found at San Francisco's Mission Dolores (see p365), the Oakland Museum of California (pp428–9), the Carmel Mission (pp516–17), and the Mission Santa Barbara (pp226–7). Most of the 21 missions offer public tours.

Restored living quarters are displayed at the Santa Barbara Mission Museum.

US Victory
On July 9, 1846, 70 US sailors and marines marched ashore at San Francisco (then Yerba Buena) and claimed it for the US.

Mission Artifacts
The Franciscan friars brought many items from Spain and Mexico to California. As well as decorative objects, some, such as these prayer bells, had practical purposes.

• **San Fernando Rey de España (1797)**

• **San Gabriel Arcangel (1771)**

• **San Juan Capistranol (1776)**

• **San Luis rey de Francia (1798)**

• **San Diego de Alcalá (1769)**

El Camino Real

The 21 missions along El Camino Real, from San Diego to Sonoma, were planned so that each was one day's journey on horseback from the next.

701 Father Eusebio Francesco Kino proves that Baja California is a peninsula, not an island

1776 Captain Juan Bautista de Anza reaches San Francisco and sites a new presidio (see pp380–81)

1781 Pueblo of Los Angeles founded

1822 Mexican Revolution ends Spanish rule of California

1835 English entrepreneur William Richardson founds Yerba Buena, later renamed San Francisco

| 1700 | 1750 | 1800 |

18th-century presidio cannon

1769 Gaspar de Portolá discovers San Francisco Bay. California's first mission is founded at San Diego (see p264)

1777 Monterey becomes capital of Mexican California

1804 California's first orange grove is planted at San Gabriel Mission

John C Frémont

1846 John C Frémont leads Bear Flag Revolt (see p468). US troops claim California from Mexico

The Rush for Riches

In 1848 newspaperman Sam Brannan brandished nuggets that had been found in the Sacramento Valley, shouting "Gold! Gold! Gold from the American River!" Most of the prospectors who thereafter stampeded California's Mother Lode did not find fortune. But the gold-seeking hordes changed the area forever – especially San Francisco. Between 1848 and 1850, the town's population shot from 812 to 25,000. Food and property prices skyrocketed and crime thrived. In 1859, after the Gold Rush had ended, silver ore (the Comstock Lode) was exposed on the eastern Sierras, and Northern California boomed again.

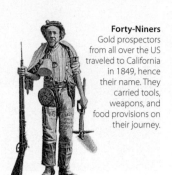

Forty-Niners
Gold prospectors from all over the US traveled to California in 1849, hence their name. They carried tools, weapons, and food provisions on their journey.

Pickaxes were used to loosen hard rock ready for the sluice.

Barbary Coast Saloon
Gambling and prostitution were rife in San Francisco's Barbary Coast region, and men were often pressed into naval service.

State Capital
Once little more than farmland, Sacramento grew into a bustling city within two years of the Gold Rush. It became the state capital in 1854.

The sluice was a long trough with wooden bars. As water was flushed along, gold particles were trapped behind the bars.

1848 California is annexed by the US. Gold discovered at Sutter's Mill *(see p479)*

1849 Almost 800 ships leave New York, full of men bound for the gold fields

Sign from the Flying Cloud *clipper ship*

1854 Sacramento becomes California state capital

| **1848** | **1850** | **1852** | **1854** |

1850 California becomes 31st state in the Union

1851 San Francisco vigilante movement hangs several lawbreakers. Clipper ship *Flying Cloud* sails from New York to San Francisco in a record 89 days

1853 Levi Strauss lands in the Bay Area and begins selling his canvas trousers *(see p347)*

John Sutter (1802–1880)

Count Agoston Haraszthy
The Hungarian was the first vintner to plant European grapevine cuttings in California.

Hydraulic mining blasted away rock with water to uncover gold underneath.

Gold Mining Techniques
As the rush for gold increased, ways of extracting the ore became more sophisticated. What began as an adventure became a highly developed industry.

Where to See the Gold Rush Era

Many of the settlements that were once thronged with gold miners have since disintegrated into ghost towns, such as Bodie (p498) and Calico (p289). But you can still get a feel for the times at Columbia State Historic Park (pp484–5), a restored Mother Lode town. The Wells Fargo History Museum in San Francisco (p318) has mementos of the Gold Rush. The Jackson Square Historical District (p318) was once part of the Barbary Coast.

Old schoolhouse at Calico ghost town

Comstock Lode Silver
Between 1859 and the mid-1880s, 400 million dollars worth of silver was extracted from mines in the High Sierras.

Gold panning involved swirling dirt and water around a flat-bottomed pan until only gold residue remained.

Emperor Norton
Self-proclaimed Emperor of the United States and Protector of Mexico, the eccentric Joshua Norton printed his own currency and gave advice to Sacramento legislators.

1855 Vigilante justice is enforced in Los Angeles

1856 Street-murder of newspaper publisher James King of William sparks San Francisco's second vigilante uprising; William T Sherman leads militia campaign to restrain them

1859 Prospector James Finney discovers silver deposits, the Comstock Lode

1860 Bankrupt grain merchant Joshua Norton declares himself Norton I, Emperor of the United States until his death in 1880

1856   **1858**   **1860**

1857 Agoston Haraszthy, father of California's wine industry, founds the Buena Vista estate in the Sonoma Valley (see p469)

San Francisco vigilante medal

1861 California swears allegiance to the Union. The first oil well is drilled

Humboldt County oil well

The Gilded Age

For California's *nouveaux riches*, the smartest address during the late 19th century was on Nob Hill in San Francisco *(see p334)*, where grand mansions were built. This was a time of ostentation but also of expansion, thanks to train connections with the East and South. California oranges could now be exported easily to New York markets; taking the return trip were European immigrants and others hoping for a better life on the West Coast. Land prices increased in LA County, and by 1900 San Francisco's population exceeded 300,000.

Victorian Decor
Windows in the Winchester Mystery House *(see pp434–5)* are typically ornate.

Transcontinental Railroad
On May 12, 1869, the final spike was driven for the new railroad, linking the East and West Coasts.

Bathroom, with original bath tub and tiles

Front parlor

Dining room

The "Big Four"
Charles Crocker, Leland Stanford, Collis Huntington, and Mark Hopkins made millions investing in the transcontinental railroad.

1863 Construction begins on the Central Pacific Railroad

1871 Racial violence in LA leaves about 20 Chinese dead

1873–5 Orange planting begins in Riverside

1876 Southern Pacific Railroad reaches Los Angeles

California oranges

1884 Sarah Winchester embarks on her 38-year house-building project in San Jose *(see pp434–5)*

1870

1875

1880

1869 Transcontinental railroad is completed

1873 Andrew Hallidie tests San Francisco's first cable car

San Francisco's first cable car

1877 San Franciscans torch Chinese stores and laundries to protest against cheap labor

1882 US Congress passes the Chinese Exclusion Act, limiting Chinese immigration

Sutro Baths
The largest swimming pool in San Francisco stood from 1896 until the 1960s.

Where to See Gilded Age California

Public tours are held at the Haas-Lilienthal House (*see p352*) and the first cable car is on display at the Cable Car Museum (*p335*), both in San Francisco. The "golden spike" from the transcontinental railroad is displayed, along with Big Four mementos, at the Cantor Arts Center at Stanford University (*p431*). Train buffs will also enjoy the California State Railroad Museum in Sacramento (*p477*).

Yosemite National Park
Made a national park in 1890, Yosemite also became California's first tourist attraction and a popular image for advertisers.

The California State Railroad Museum is a celebration of rail travel on the West Coast.

Chinese Immigrants
The "coolies" who helped build the transcontinental railroad stayed and set up businesses, such as laundries and restaurants, but were met with racism.

The living room
was originally the master bedroom.

Porch

Hall, with Victorian corner sofa

Haas-Lilienthal House

Grocer William Haas built this elaborate Queen Anne-style house in 1886, one of many in San Francisco. Today it is a museum, and shows how a wealthy family would have lived at the end of the 19th century (see p352).

1890 Yosemite wins national park status (*see pp492–5*)

Stanford University seal

1893 San Andreas Fault discovered by University of California geologist Andrew Lawson

1896 Comstock tunnel builder Adolph Sutro opens the world's largest indoor saltwater swimming center in San Francisco

1885 | **1890** | **1895**

1888 Hotel del Coronado opens in San Diego (*see p259*)

1891 Stanford University opens (*see p431*); future president Herbert Hoover is in the first graduating class

1894 West Coast's first world's fair is held in San Francisco's Golden Gate Park

1897 San Francisco merchants prosper by outfitting gold miners traveling to Canada's Klondike River

The Rise of Hollywood

In 1887, Kansas prohibitionist Harvey Henderson Wilcox wanted to call his farm and the LA suburb surrounding it "Figwood," after his chief crop. His wife chose instead a name she had overheard on a train: "Hollywood." By the 1920s, the film industry was making the town famous and offering Americans entertainment to help them escape the reality of World War I, Prohibition, and later, the Great Depression. Silent film stars such as Mary Pickford and Charlie Chaplin were succeeded by icons of a more glamorous Hollywood, such as Mae West and Errol Flynn. Wall Street bankers were quick to realize their potential and invested heavily in the film industry.

Panama Canal
Two world fairs celebrated the completion of the canal in 1915 *(see p353).*

San Francisco Earthquake and Fire
After the 1906 disaster, many buildings had to be demolished.

Clara Bow, dubbed the "It" girl, was one of Hollywood's first sex symbols.

Actors were chosen for their looks and often had little stage experience.

Hollywood's Silent Era
The movie industry grew rapidly and soon large corporate studios emerged. Mantrap (1927) was one of hundreds of silent movies made each month.

Los Angeles Aqueduct
The vast aqueduct was built at a cost of $24.5 million to irrigate the arid south with melted snow from the High Sierras.

1905 Tobacco magnate Abbot Kinney opens his many-canaled resort of Venice *(see p80),* west of LA. Excavations begin on La Brea Tar Pits *(see p119)*

1907 San Francisco political "boss" Abraham Ruef pleads guilty to extortion and brings down Mayor Eugene Schmitz

1913 Opening of Owens Valley–Los Angeles aqueduct improves LA's access to water

1900

1905

1910

1901 A three-month waterfront labor strike affects San Francisco business; four men die and 300 are injured in hostilities

1906 San Francisco is struck on April 18 by the worst ever US earthquake, at an estimated 8.3 on the Richter scale: 3,000 die and 25,000 are left homeless

Early Hollywood film camera

1911 *The Law of the Range,* shot by William and David Horsley, is the first film made in Hollywood

Prohibition (1920–33)
Los Angeles became a popular port of entry for smugglers bringing illegal alcohol into the United States from Mexico during the nationwide ban.

Studios operated like factories, filming different movies on adjacent sets.

Cameramen used 35 mm cameras, operating at 24 frames per second.

Directors aslo found fame and fortune in the new industry.

Orchestras were often hired to play in the background of a scene during filming to create the right mood for the actors.

Where to See Classic Hollywood

The likenesses of numerous movie stars are displayed at Madame Tussaud's Hollywood™ (p114). The Hollywood Heritage Museum (p116), once Cecil B De Mille's offices, now exhibits movie mementos. Some 200 stars have cemented their fame in front of TCL Chinese Theatre (p114).

The TLC Chinese Theatre has handprints, footprints, and autographs of film stars cemented in its forecourt.

Paramount Studios are the only studios now located in Hollywood and are still a magnet for would-be stars (p117).

Aimee Semple McPherson
In 1923 the controversial evangelist and spiritualist opened her Angelus Temple in LA where she held regular spiritual revivalist meetings.

1916 The Lockheed brothers start building airplanes in Santa Barbara

WR Hearst

1924 LA eclipses San Francisco as the most important port on the West Coast

1929 Stock exchange crash causes national Depression. Actor Douglas Fairbanks, Sr. hosts the first Academy Awards' presentation

1915

1920

1925

1915 San Francisco and San Diego both hold Panama-Pacific Expositions

1917 The US enters World War I

1919 WR Hearst begins construction of his magnificent castle at San Simeon (see pp206–9)

Norma Talmadge

1927 Actress Norma Talmadge is the first star to cement her footprints at TCL Chinese Theatre (see p114)

1928 Cartoonist Walt Disney creates character of Mickey Mouse

The California Dream

Movies and the new medium of television made California *the* symbol of America's postwar resurgence – suddenly everybody wanted the prosperous middle-class existence they believed was common here. The airplane industry, shipyards, and agriculture had burgeoned during the war, and a sense of prosperity lasted through the 1950s. Suburbs sprang up to meet the needs of returning soldiers, while new highways were laid to make them accessible. Yet at the same time, state schools lacked funds, African- and Mexican-Americans faced discrimination and violence, and Hollywood found itself attacked by politicians as a hotbed of Marxist Communism.

Olympic Games 1932
Los Angeles won the bid to hold the 1932 games and built Exposition Park for the event *(see pp168–9)*.

Kitchen units became more practical, with Formica counters.

Longshoreman's Strike
On July 5, 1934, police opened fire on dockers striking for better conditions, killing two.

Hoover Dam
In 1936 Hoover Dam was built on the Colorado River to supply electricity.

Household appliances became more widely available, easing domestic duties.

1932 LA hosts its first Olympic Games	**1934** Alcatraz Island becomes a maximum security penitentiary *(see pp342–3)*	**1936** Hoover Dam begins supplying Southern California with much-needed electricity	**1940** Los Angeles opens its first freeway – Arroyo Seco Parkway	**1942** Japanese-Americans sent to relocation camps for "war security reasons" *(see p49)*

1930   **1935**   **1940**

1933 Prohibition ends. "Sunny Jim" Rolph, a popular San Francisco mayor turned California governor, shocks supporters by praising a lynch mob in San Jose

"Sunny Jim" Rolph

1937 The Golden Gate Bridge opens

1939 San Francisco's third world's fair, the Golden Gate Exposition, is held on Treasure Island

1941 Japan attacks US fleet at Pearl Harbor

1943 California becomes nation's leading agricultural state

Golden Gate Bridge
On May 28, 1937, an official convoy of black limousines were the first vehicles to cross the bridge, which links San Francisco with Marin County.

Where to See the California Dream

LA's Petersen Automotive Museum celebrates California's love affair with the car *(see p122)*. All aspects of the Californian obsession with surf, from the evolution of surfing's unique culture to developments in board technology, are covered at the Santa Cruz Surfing Museum *(p511)*. A trip to the Sleeping Beauty Castle at Disneyland® Resort in Anaheim is the ultimate California Dream experience *(p237)*.

The Petersen Automotive Museum displays many classic models. This 1959 Cadillac epitomizes California cars.

Land of Plenty
California's agricultural industry boomed in the 1940s, and its farmland was the most productive in the US.

Large refrigerators, stocked with food, were a symbol of the California "good life."

The California Home
Eduardo Paolozzi's image is a pastiche of California's white, middle-class lifestyle in the 1950s. Nuclear families, ranch houses, and outdoor living were all part of the "dream."

San Francisco Giant
Willie Mays was part of the first team to bring professional baseball to California in 1958.

1945 End of World War II. International delegates meet at San Francisco April 25–June 25 to found the United Nations

1955 Disneyland® opens in Anaheim. Actor James Dean, 24, dies in a car accident near Paso Robles

James Dean

| 1945 | 1950 | 1955 |

1953 Beginning of Cold War is a boost to California defense industry

1958 New York Giants baseball team moves to San Francisco, finally bringing Major League baseball to the West Coast

United Nations flag

California Today

Since 1962, when California surpassed New York as the most populous state in the Union, it has become the focus of many of the country's most significant issues. UC Berkeley was home to America's Free Speech Movement during the 1960s, and Haight Ashbury in San Francisco was the mecca for the "hippie" movement. Silicon Valley leads high-tech development in the US, and California benefits commercially from its proximity to the Far East. However, the state is still at risk from earthquakes and its dry climate has led to wildfires and the threat of drought in recent years.

1984 LA hosts its second Olympic Games

1968 Democratic presidential candidate Robert Kennedy is assassinated at LA's Ambassador Hotel on June 5 after announcing his victory in the California primary

1967 Haight Ashbury is swamped by half a million young people celebrating the "Summer of Love" (see p362)

1978 Apple Computer produces its first personal computer

1962 Actress Marilyn Monroe dies in Hollywood, at age 36, from an overdose of sleeping pills

1970s Huey Newton, a founder of Oakland's Black Panther Party, is arrested in 1967 and becomes a symbol of resistance during the 1970s

1987 Film director Steven Spielberg starts his own studio, Dreamworks

1960   **1970**   **1980**

1960   **1970**   **1980**

1960 Winter Olympic Games are held at Squaw Valley near Lake Tahoe

1966 LA becomes the most populous county in the nation, with more than 7 million inhabitants

1969 American Indian Movement occupies Alcatraz Island (see pp342–3) to publicize its differences with the Bureau of Indian Affairs

1978 San Francisco Mayor George Moscone and his deputy Harvey Milk are assassinated at City Hall on November 27 by former policeman Dan White

1968 Richard Nixon becomes the first native-born Californian to be elected President. Facing certain impeachment, he was the only president to resign, leaving office in 1974 (see p242)

1976 French judges award California the top two prizes for wine at a blind tasting

1960s Surfing becomes a popular sport in California

NIXON'S THE ONE!

1989 The Bay Area endures its second worst earthquake, measuring 7.1 on the Richter Scale; 67 people die, another 1,800 are left homeless

1992 Riots in LA follow the acquittal of four white police officers who were videotaped beating a black motorist, Rodney King

2004 Iconic, Austrian movie star and former bodybuilder Arnold Schwarzenegger, married to news journalist Maria Shriver, is elected as the 38th governor of California

2006 San Francisco congresswoman Nancy Pelosi is the first woman to become elected speaker of the United States House of Representatives

1994 An earthquake measuring 6.8 on the Richter scale strikes LA, killing more than 60 people, injuring 9,000, and destroying freeways

2011 Massive power cut causes blackouts in California, Arizona, and Mexico; over 5 million people affected. Jerry Brown is elected 39th governor of California

2013 Gay marriage is officially legalized in California, 2 years ahead of nationwide legalization

1990	2000	2010	2020

1990	2000	2010	2020

2001 An energy crisis grips the state, with rolling blackouts affecting all major cities

1996 After 15 years as the speaker of the California Assembly, Democrat Willie Brown is sworn in as San Francisco's first black mayor

1995 The world-famous America's Cup yacht race, in which five countries compete, is held in San Diego from January to May

1991 AIDS becomes San Francisco's number one killer of men

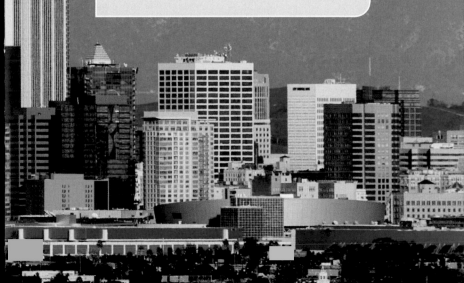

LOS ANGELES

Los Angeles at a Glance

Metropolitan Los Angeles is made up of 88 different towns, with a total population of more than 12.8 million and covering more than 4,800 sq miles (12,500 sq km). In this book, LA has been divided into six areas. Downtown is a cultural melting pot, juxtaposing Hispanic El Pueblo, Chinatown, Little Tokyo, and the Business District. The glamor of the movies is just one aspect of Hollywood and West Hollywood, which today is a vibrant area of museums and galleries. Beverly Hills, Bel Air, and Westwood are still the playgrounds of the stars. Beaches and ports in the coastal regions of Santa Monica Bay, Palos Verdes, and Long Beach show the importance of the sea to Angelenos. Around Downtown covers some of the outlying towns and areas of the city, including Pasadena.

Locator Map

AROUND DOWNTOWN (See pp144–69)

BEVERLY HILL BEL AIR, AND WESTWOOD (See pp92–103)

SANTA MONICA BAY (See pp78–91)

Sunset Boulevard (see pp106–11) is one of the most famous roads in the world. Lined with clubs and hotels, the section known as Sunset Strip is the center of LA's nightlife.

The J Paul Getty Museum at the Getty Center (see pp86–9) is situated on a hill and has stunning views across Los Angeles and the Santa Monica Mountains. Included in its world-class collection is Joseph Nollekens' marble statue of Venus (1773).

0 kilometers 5

0 miles 5

LACMA (see pp118–21) has been located in Hancock Park since 1965, and has expanded west along Wilshire Boulevard.

◀ Los Angeles skyline with snowy mountains in the background

At Universal Studios Hollywood[SM] *(see pp150–53)*, just north of Hollywood, visitors can see working film sets on the Studio Tour. A series of thrilling rides, based on the studios' movies, includes Jurassic Park – The Ride.

Huntington Library, Art Collections, and Botanical Gardens *(see pp162–5)* in Pasadena have a wealth of treasures. The North Vista is one of the gardens' loveliest views.

HOLLYWOOD AND WEST HOLLYWOOD
(See pp104–23)

DOWNTOWN LOS ANGELES
(See pp124–33)

FREEWAY

GLENDALE FREEWAY

PASADENA FREEWAY

HOLLYWOOD FREEWAY

FREEWAY

SAN DIEGO FREEWAY

HARBOR FREEWAY

LONG BEACH FREEWAY

HARBOR FREEWAY

SAN DIEGO FREEWAY

LONG BEACH AND PALOS VERDES
(See pp134–43)

El Pueblo *(see pp130–31)*, in the heart of Downtown Los Angeles, is the site of the city's first settlement. The area's Mexican population throngs its churches, plaza, and colorful markets, especially at festival time.

The Queen Mary *(see pp138–9)*, one of the most famous liners in the world, is now permanently docked in Long Beach. The ship is still in use as a tourist attraction and luxury hotel. Many of its Art Deco features remain intact.

The Shape of Los Angeles

The city of Los Angeles sits in a broad, flat basin, facing the Pacific Ocean and enclosed by mountains. The San Gabriel Mountains and the Traverse Range come from the north, meeting the Santa Ana Mountains east of the city. The Santa Monica Mountains and the Hollywood Hills in the northwest split the basin, dividing the city center from the San Fernando Valley in the north. The shoreline varies from the rocky cliffs of Palos Verdes to the sands of Santa Monica Bay. Downtown, with the impressive skyscrapers of the Business District, sits in the center of the basin. Hollywood, Beverly Hills, and Santa Monica lie to the west.

Hollywood *(see pp104–23)* is the birthplace of the modern film industry. Its famous sign *(see p149)* stands out like a beacon above Tinseltown.

The San Fernando Valley *(see p148)*, the city's great suburban sprawl, is home to the Mission San Fernando Rey de España.

San Gabriel Mountains

Burbank

Hollywood Hills

Santa Susana Mountains

San Fernando Valley

Mulholland Drive

Santa Monica Mountains

Sunset Boulevard

Malibu *(see pp90–91)* is an area of fine surfing beaches, wildlife havens, and private beach colonies nestled below rugged mountains.

Santa Monica *(see pp80–83)*, perched on palm-lined bluffs overlooking the Pacific Ocean, is a small independent city with LA's most accessible beaches. It has all the traditional seaside attractions, such as a pier and amusement park. Santa Monica is also known for its excellent restaurants, boutiques, exciting nightlife, and vibrant arts scene.

Beverly Hills *(see pp92–101)* is home to the rich and famous of Los Angeles. Their lifestyle is epitomized by the exclusive shops that line Rodeo Drive.

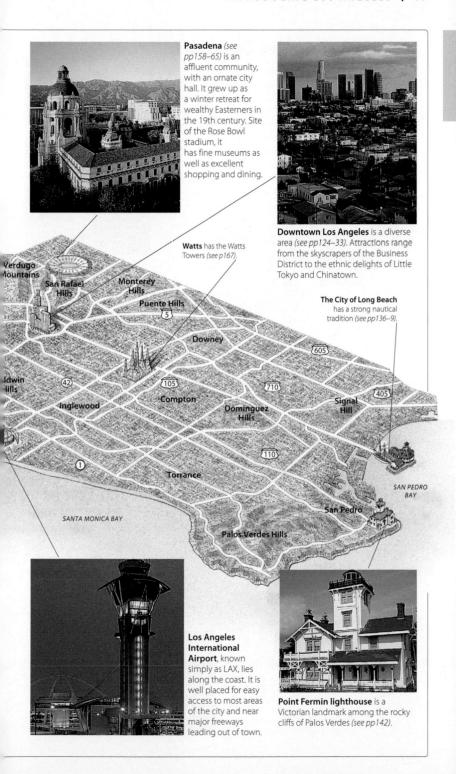

Pasadena *(see pp158–65)* is an affluent community, with an ornate city hall. It grew up as a winter retreat for wealthy Easterners in the 19th century. Site of the Rose Bowl stadium, it has fine museums as well as excellent shopping and dining.

Downtown Los Angeles is a diverse area *(see pp124–33).* Attractions range from the skyscrapers of the Business District to the ethnic delights of Little Tokyo and Chinatown.

Watts has the Watts Towers *(see p167).*

The City of Long Beach has a strong nautical tradition *(see pp136–9).*

Los Angeles International Airport, known simply as LAX, lies along the coast. It is well placed for easy access to most areas of the city and near major freeways leading out of town.

Point Fermin lighthouse is a Victorian landmark among the rocky cliffs of Palos Verdes *(see pp142).*

North Los Angeles Coastline

Each year more than 30 million people visit the beaches around Los Angeles, making them the most popular destination on the West Coast. The Malibu headland, from Point Dume to Malibu Lagoon, alternates between rocky shorelines and beaches. Farther south, the shoreline becomes a long sandy strand leading to the renowned beaches at Santa Monica and Venice. Inland, the terrain of the Santa Monica Mountains is rugged and largely unspoiled, with plenty of hiking trails leading to panoramic views of the Pacific Ocean. The waters off the Malibu Pier, Leo Carillo, and Topanga state beaches are considered to be the best for surfing.

Castro Crest is characterized by large areas of exposed reddish purple sandstone and oak woodland. The park's hiking trails offer magnificent views inland of the Santa Susana mountains and, offshore, the Channel Islands.

Cold Creek Canyon Preserve was set up in 1970 to protect the rich diversity of fauna and flora found in the Santa Monica Mountains, including the bobcat, the Pacific tree frog, and the stream orchid.

① ★ **Leo Carrillo State Beach**
At low tide it is possible to explore the wide variety of life in the rock pools around Sequit Point.

⑤ ★ **Surfrider County Beaach**
One of California's finest surfing beaches, Surfrider has featured in many surfing films. Malibu Pier is a good place from which to watch the action.

② Zuma County Beach

The white sands of Malibu's largest beach are very popular during the summer. There is good surfing and swimming, but be careful of the hazardous rip tides.

③ Point Dume County Beach

Surf fishing, diving, sunbathing, and exploring the rock pools beneath Point Dume are all popular activities on this sandy, sheltered beach.

④ Paradise Cove

This privately owned cove was featured in the TV series *The Rockford Files*. The pier is a good place for surf fishing, and the beach is ideal for sunbathing and swimming.

Locator Map

Key

🟫 Freeway
🟥 Major road
⬚ Minor road
🌊 River

⑥ Topanga State Beach

This narrow sandy beach is popular with windsurfers. It is divided in two by the mouth of Topanga Creek.

⑩ Marina del Rey Harbor

This is one of the world's largest artificial harbors *(see p84)*. The quaint Fisherman's Village, next to Basin H, has shops, cafés, and restaurants.

⑨ ★ Venice Beach

Backed by picturesque Venice *(see p84)*, Venice Beach offers an eclectic mix of street performers, skaters, and body builders, working out on Muscle Beach.

⑦ ★ Will Rogers State Beach

Named after the Hollywood actor *(see p85)*, this is a good beach for body surfing.

⑧ ★ Santa Monica State Beach

This is one of Santa Monica's *(see pp80–83)* most popular beaches. The group of houses at the western end of the beach are known collectively as "the Gold Coast."

South Los Angeles Coastline

The coast between Dockweiler State Beach and Torrance County Beach boasts shallow waters and wide stretches of sand, which are ideal for families. The two main communities, Manhattan Beach and Redondo Beach, have some of the cleanest waters in the area. Farther down the coast, the rocky bluffs of the Palos Verdes Peninsula shelter coves with rock pools teeming with marine life. Beyond the commercial and cruise port at San Pedro, the coastline turns into a vista of white sand and rolling waves bordering Long Beach. Belmont Shores is popular with anglers. Windsurfers, sea kayakers, and jet-skiers frequent Alamitos Bay, home to the man-made canals and islands of Naples.

② ★ Manhattan State Beach
Backed by the coastal cycle path, this long wide beach is good for swimming, surfing, and fishing.

③ ★ Hermosa City Beach
This family beach is ideal for all types of beach sports, as well as being popular with anglers who fish the surf for perch.

The Port of Los Angeles, with its 28 miles (45 km) of waterfront, includes an oil terminal, cruise ship, and cargo port. It is also home to the country's second largest fishing fleet.

⑤ ★ Torrance County Beach
Popular with surfers, swimmers, anglers, and divers alike, this beach marks the end of the Santa Monica Bay coastal cycle path (see p182).

④ ★ Redondo State Beach
A bronze bust commemorates George Freeth, who introduced surfing to California in 1907 at Redondo Beach.

① Dockweiler State Beach
The north end of Dockweiler, beyond the harbor entrance, includes a nesting area for the rare California least tern.

⑥ Cabrillo Beach
Split in two by the breakwater, Cabrillo has a fishing pier on the ocean side and a protected stretch of sand within San Pedro Bay.

⑦ Long Beach City Beach
At the western end of Long Beach Strand, as it is also known, stands the old clapboard lifeguard headquarters, now a lifeguard museum.

⑧ Belmont Shores
Belmont Pier, situated at the northern end of the beach, is used by anglers fishing for halibut, bonito, and perch. It is also a roosting site for the endangered California brown pelican. The beach stretches south as far as the mouth of the San Gabriel River.

Locator Map

⑨ Alamitos Bay
Windsurfing, waterskiing, and swimming are all popular activities in the protected waters of the bay.

DOWNTOWN LOS ANGELES

DOWNTOWN LOS ANGELES

Alameda Street

WILMINGTON

Long Beach Blvd

LONG BEACH

Ocean Blvd

ANAHEIM

SAN PEDRO

Port of Los Angeles

HUNTINGTON BEACH

Point Fermin

| 0 kilometers | 5 |
| 0 miles | 5 |

Key
 Freeway
 Major road
 Minor road
 River
 Viewpoint

Palos Verdes Peninsula rises 1,300 ft (400 m) above the rocky shoreline, which is home to many wading birds. Steep trails connect the shore to the clifftop with its panoramic views.

The Movies in Los Angeles

When people refer to Los Angeles as an "industry town," they invariably mean the movie industry. Its great fantasy factories employ more than 60,000 people and pump about $4 billion into the LA economy every year. Hollywood Boulevard has sadly lost much of its glamour over the years; some film companies have decamped to cheaper movie-making places. But the air of Hollywood as a dream-maker, a place where a secretary named Ava Gardner or college football player John Wayne could be "discovered" and go on to earn million-dollar salaries, still persists.

Film crews shooting location scenes for various Hollywood movies are a regular sight on Los Angeles' streets.

The Griffith Observatory *(see p154)* was the setting for the teenage school trip and dramatic car race at the climax of the legendary film *Rebel Without a Cause* (1955). The film catapulted James Dean to stardom, but he was to die in a car crash later the same year aged only 24.

Writers in Hollywood

Hollywood novels have been a literary feature since the 1930s. Some writers, such as Nathaneal West (1903–1940) and F Scott Fitzgerald (1896–1940), worked in Hollywood, only to turn against the town and publish novels that exposed its shallow and often cruel sides. West's *The Day of the Locust* (1939) is still considered the classic literary put-down of the film industry. Fitzgerald's posthumous *The Last Tycoon* (1941) sentimentalizes the career of Irving Thalberg, one of the most influential producers during Hollywood's "Golden Age." More recent is James Ellroy's *LA Confidential* (1997), a retro, atmospheric story of corruption and redemption in 1950s Los Angeles.

F Scott Fitzgerald

The Last Action Hero, Arnold Schwarzenegger's 1993 blockbuster, filled this LA street with the excitement of controlled explosions, car chases, and stuntmen flying through the air.

LA Locations

As well as utilizing the man-made sets erected on the backlots of the major studios in the 1940s and 1950s, film directors now regularly turn to the local landmarks of Los Angeles as locations for their films, often disguising them as other towns and cities. As a consequence, many of these places have become familiar to moviegoers all over the world.

Million-dollar contracts have been a feature of Hollywood since Charlie Chaplin's eight-picture deal in 1917. Top Hollywood actors and actresses earn colossal amounts every year, with Robert Downey, Jr., Leonardo DiCaprio, Bradley Cooper, Sandra Bullock, Angelina Jolie, and Jennifer Lawrence earning anywhere between $50 and $75 million. Studio executives justify the salaries by saying that big stars attract a large enough audience to recoup the high production costs.

Leonardo DiCaprio   Angelina Jolie

The Venice district *(see p84)* saw actress Sarah Jessica Parker dancing around Steve Martin, in his 1991 hit film *LA Story*. The colorful buildings and characters of the area make it a popular film location.

Santa Monica Pier *(see p82)* should be familiar to fans of the gangster film *The Sting* (1973), starring actors Robert Redford and Paul Newman.

Stargazing is enjoyed by both visitors and locals in LA's many glamorous venues. Good opportunities to spot actors, directors, and film executives can be found at Wolfgang Puck's trendy Spago *(see p550)* and the Polo Lounge at the Beverly Hills Hotel *(see p528)*.

Top Grossing Films

Critics gush over *Citizen Kane* (1941), and *Casablanca* (1943) is the most popular Hollywood love story ever made. Yet neither of these films is on trade paper *Variety*'s list of the US film industry's highest-grossing films of all time:

1 *Avatar* (2009)
2 *Titanic* (1997)
3 *Jurassic World (2015)*
4 *Marvel's The Avengers* (2012)
5 *Furious 7* (2015)
6 *The Avengers: Age of Ultron* (2015)
7 *Harry Potter and the Deathly Hallows: Part II* (2011)
8 *Frozen* (2013)
9 *Iron Man 3* (2013)
10 *Minions* (2015)

The only films that were made in or before 1980 on the top 100 list are *The Empire Strikes Back* (1980), at No. 57, and *Jaws* (1975), at No. 71.

Film poster for the top grossing film *Avatar*

Los Angeles's Best: Museums and Galleries

The museums of LA reflect the great diversity of the city. Collections ranging from natural history to Native American artifacts and from cowboy heritage to the history of the Holocaust educate and inspire the visitor. The city also contains many museums of art. Some of these display the private collections of the wealthy, such as Norton Simon, J Paul Getty, Eli Broad, and Henry and Arabella Huntington, and feature internationally acclaimed Old Masters, Impressionist paintings, and European and Asian works of art. "Museum Row" on Wilshire Boulevard has five museums, including the renowned LACMA.

Ceci n'est pas une pipe.

LACMA is one of the top US art museums. Its collection includes *La Trahison des Images (Ceci n'est pas une pipe)*, painted by René Magritte in around 1929 *(see pp118–21).*

FOOTHILL FREEWAY

SAN FERNANDO VALLEY FRWY

GOLDEN STATE FREEWAY

SAN DIEGO FREEWAY

VENTURA FREEWAY

HOLLYWOOD FREEWAY

AROUND DOWNTOWN

BEVERLY HILLS, BEL AIR, AND WESTWOOD

J Paul Getty Museum has an extraodinary collection of Impressionist works, including *La Promenade* (1870) by Pierre-Auguste Renoir *(see pp86–9).*

SANTA MONICA BAY

SANTA MONICA FR

SAN DIEGO FREEWAY

Museum of Tolerance aims to promote understanding between peoples. This sculpture of President Sadat of Egypt, with President Carter of the United States and Prime Minister Begin of Israel, illustrates that aim *(see p97).*

0 kilometers   5

0 miles   5

Historic Southwest Museum
exhibits thousands of artifacts of the native cultures of the Americas. It is currently undergoing renovation, but is open on Saturdays when highlights of the collection are on display *(see p157)*

Autry National Center is dedicated to preserving the history of the American West by exploring the connections among the area's varied Native American and Western cultures. Wax models, such as this one of outlaw Billy the Kid, are on display *(see p155)*.

Norton Simon Museum of Art was built in 1969. It houses a superb collection of European, Indian, and Southeast Asian art that spans more than 2,000 years *(see pp160–61)*.

VENTURA FREEWAY

GLENDALE FREEWAY

GOLDEN STATE FREEWAY

PASADENA FREEWAY

HOLLYWOOD AND WEST HOLLYWOOD

DOWNTOWN LOS ANGELES

HARBOR FREEWAY

LONG BEACH FREEWAY

CENTURY FREEWAY

Huntington Library, Art Collections, and Botanical Gardens are in Pasadena. Roger van der Weyden's 15th-century *Madonna and Child* is one of the treasures on display *(see pp162–5)*.

Natural History Museum of Los Angeles County is one of three museums in Exposition Park. The exhibits include this eight-million-year-old skeleton of a short-legged rhinoceros *(see p168)*.

Twentieth-Century Architecture in Los Angeles

For more than a century after it was founded in 1781, LA remained a small town of modest adobe buildings. It was not until the late 19th century that settlers from the East and Midwest introduced the Victorian styles of building they had grown up with. When the transcontinental railroad reached LA in 1887 there was a building boom, and the city has been expanding ever since. In the 20th century, LA's finest contributions to architecture were the inventive reworkings of past styles. Architects have also remodeled dilapidated commercial buildings to create lively, fashionable structures.

Beverly Hills Civic Center (1990) Designed by Charles Moore, this building has a mixture of Spanish Revival, Art Deco, and Post-Modern styles *(see p96)*.

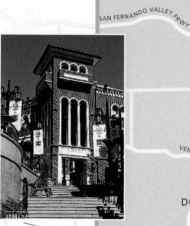

2 Rodeo (1990) This pastiche of European architecture, including a replica of Rome's Spanish Steps, is part of the famous shopping district *(see p98)*. This area has Victorian-style street lamps and a cobblestone street.

AROUND DOWNTOWN

BEVERLY HILLS, BEL AIR, AND WESTWOOD

SANTA MONICA BAY

Eames House (1949) This steel-framed house and studio were designed by Charles and Ray Eames as one of 36 projects commissioned by *Arts & Architecture* magazine.

The Binoculars Building (1991) Frank Gehry, one of LA's leading architects, designed this striking building, now the LA headquarters of Google *(see p82)*.

Michael D Eisner Building (1991)
Housing the executive offices of Walt Disney®
Studios, Michael Graves' Post-Modern building in
Burbank includes a classically inspired pediment
supported by 19-ft (5.7-m) statues of the Seven
Dwarfs. Inside, chairs incorporate Mickey Mouse
in their design *(see pp148–9)*.

Ennis House (1923)
The base, plan, and textured interiors of this
house are typical of Frank Lloyd Wright's
"textile block" houses.

Gamble House (1908)
This is the finest example
of Charles and Henry
Greene's turn-of-the-
century Arts and
Crafts bungalows. Its
expansive eaves,
outdoor sleeping
porches, and elegant
interior are characteristic
of the brothers'
style *(see p158)*.

GLENDALE FRWY

PASADENA FREEWAY

OLLYWOOD
AND WEST
OLLYWOOD   **DOWNTOWN
LOS ANGELES**

EWAY

HARBOR FREEWAY

CENTURY FREEWAY

Union Station (1939)
The last of the great American
railroad terminals combines
Mission Revival and Streamlines
Moderne styles in its vaulted
concourse, arches, waiting
room, and patios *(see p132)*.

**Eastern Columbia
Building** (1930)
This Art Deco building,
designed by Claude
Beelman, is one of the most
impressive of its kind in LA.

Enticing sweep of Will Rogers State Beach, Santa Monica

Sights at a Glance

Districts
1 Santa Monica pp80–83
2 Venice
3 Marina del Rey
11 Malibu Colony

Museums
4 Museum of Flying
5 J Paul Getty Museum at the Getty Center pp86–9
8 The Getty Villa
9 Adamson House and Malibu Lagoon Museum

Parks and Beaches
6 Will Rogers State Historic Park
7 Topanga State Park
10 Malibu Lagoon State Beach
12 Malibu Creek State Park

SANTA MONICA BAY

With its warm sun, cool sea breezes, long stretch of sandy beaches, excellent surf, and world-class museums, Santa Monica Bay epitomizes the best of California. The area was inhabited by the Chumash and Tongva/Gabrielino peoples for 2,500 years before the arrival in 1542 of the Portuguese explorer Juan Cabrillo, who sailed here on behalf of the Spanish Empire *(see p50)*. In the early 19th century, Santa Monica Bay was divided into several land grants, including Rancho San Vicente y Santa Monica and Rancho Topanga Malibu Sequit. In 1875, Nevada senator John Percival Jones bought control of the former, hoping the port of Los Angeles would be built there. Thankfully, that honor went to San Pedro *(see pp142–3)* and the beach resort sections of Santa Monica and Venice were developed in its place. These areas have remained two of the most attractive and lively parts of Los Angeles.

Farther along the coast, the Rancho Topanga Malibu Sequit was bought in 1887 by Frederick and May Rindge. The Rindge family fought with the state for many years to keep their property secluded. Eventually failing, they sold much of Malibu to the rich and famous. Large mountain areas backing Santa Monica Bay have remained undeveloped, however. The vast Topanga and Malibu Creek state parks help to improve Los Angeles's air quality and offer a large number of hiking trails.

Locator map

For keys to symbols *see back flap*

❶ Street-by-Street: Santa Monica

Santa Monica's fresh sea breezes, mild climate (on average, the sun shines 328 days a year), and pedestrian-friendly streets make it one of the best places in LA to go for a stroll. The city is perched on a high cliff overlooking Santa Monica Bay and miles of broad, sandy beach. Running along the cliff edge is palm-shaded Palisades Park, a narrow, 26-acre (10-ha) garden offering spectacular views, especially at sunset. A stairway leads down to Santa Monica's famous beach and pier. A few blocks inland from the hotel-lined seafront is Third Street Promenade – a great place to sit outside a café or restaurant and people-watch.

View from Palisades Park
The cliff top park offers panoramic views of Santa Monica Bay. Looking northward, you can see all the way to Malibu.

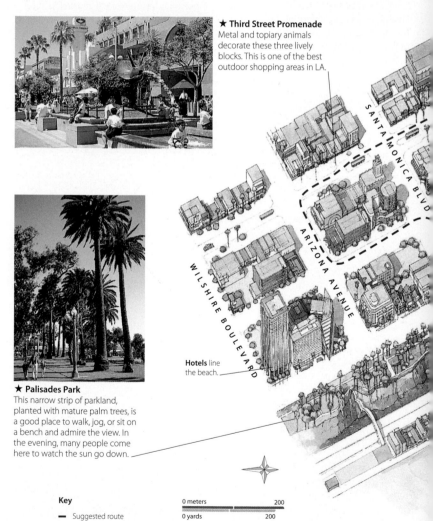

★ Third Street Promenade
Metal and topiary animals decorate these three lively blocks. This is one of the best outdoor shopping areas in LA.

SANTA MONICA BLVD

ARIZONA AVENUE

WILSHIRE BOULEVARD

Hotels line the beach.

★ Palisades Park
This narrow strip of parkland, planted with mature palm trees, is a good place to walk, jog, or sit on a bench and admire the view. In the evening, many people come here to watch the sun go down.

Key
— Suggested route

0 meters	200
0 yards	200

Santa Monica Place
This lively shopping mall, designed by architect Frank Gehry in 1979, has since undergone a major renovation. The modern, open-air complex features upscale stores and rooftop dining.

Locator Map

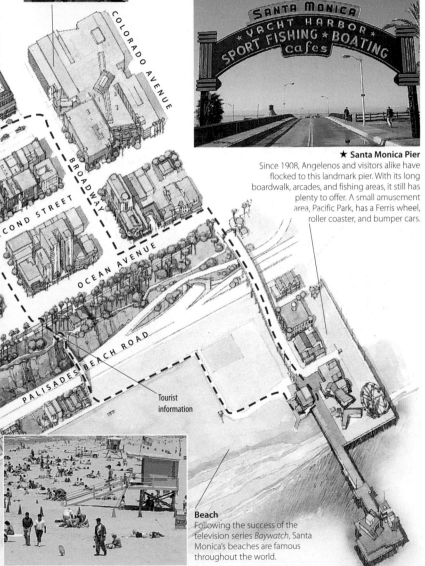

★ Santa Monica Pier
Since 1908, Angelenos and visitors alike have flocked to this landmark pier. With its long boardwalk, arcades, and fishing areas, it still has plenty to offer. A small amusement area, Pacific Park, has a Ferris wheel, roller coaster, and bumper cars.

COLORADO AVENUE

BROADWAY

COND STREET

OCEAN AVENUE

PALISADES BEACH ROAD

Tourist information

Beach
Following the success of the television series *Baywatch*, Santa Monica's beaches are famous throughout the world.

Exploring Santa Monica

Santa Monica has been the star of LA's coastline since the 1890s, when trolleys linked it to the city, and beach parties became the rage. In the early days, it lived a dual life as a sleepy coast town and the headquarters for offshore gambling ships. In the 1920s and 1930s, movie stars such as Cary Grant and Mary Pickford bought land here, creating "the Gold Coast." The beach and pier are still major attractions, but the city is now also famous for its restaurants *(see p554)*. Santa Monica offers many outdoor shopping areas and an active arts scene and has the cleanest air in LA. Bergamot Station and the Edgemar complex on Main Street have a range of galleries.

The Binoculars Building, Google's LA headquarters, designed by Frank Gehry

Around Santa Monica

Grassy parks dot the city's landscape, with none quite as beautiful or revered as **Palisades Park** on the bluff overlooking the ocean. Stretching 1.5 miles (2.5 km) along the cliff's edge, this narrow, well-manicured park is one of the best spots to watch the sun go down. For the quintessential California experience, take a walk or jog along the paths, with the ocean as a backdrop and the towering palms overhead. The landscaping is beautiful, with semitropical trees and plants. At the northern end, the aptly named Inspiration Point has great views of the bay, stretching from Malibu to Palos Verdes.

Inland, between Wilshire Boulevard and Broadway, is **Third Street Promenade**. Once a decaying shopping street, this boulevard has undergone a major face-lift and is now one of the liveliest places in Los Angeles. Its three pedestrian blocks are lined with shops, coffee houses, restaurants, bookstores, and cinemas. At night the mood is especially festive. Street performers entertain passers-by with music, dance, puppet shows, and magic tricks. Nearby, on Arizona Avenue, the farmers' market held on Saturdays and Wednesdays is one of the best in the city.

Santa Monica's other major shopping area is **Main Street**, which runs south toward Venice *(see p84)*. At the turn of the 20th century, Main Street was the commercial district for Pacific Ocean Park, an amusement park, baths, and pier. By the early 1970s, however, the majority of the neighborhood's attractions had been demolished, and Main Street itself had become a slum.

Today, this revitalized street abounds with a wide range of shops, superb restaurants, and first-rate art galleries.

There are many examples of public art displayed along Main Street.

Chain Reaction by Paul Conrad

Sculptor Paul Conrad's *Chain Reaction* (1991) is a stainless-steel and copper-link chain statement against nuclear war. It stands next to the Civic Auditorium. *Ocean Park Pier* (1976), a mural by Jane Golden and Barbara Stoll, is situated at the junction with Ocean Park Boulevard and depicts the Pacific Ocean Park in the early 1900s.

A lovely example of Spanish Colonial architecture remains at the northwest corner of Main Street and Pier Avenue. Nearby, the Binoculars Building, designed in 1991 by Frank Gehry and shaped like a giant pair of binoculars, dominates the street *(see p76)*.

🚇 Santa Monica Pier

Colorado & Ocean Aves.
Tel 310-458-8901. Looff Carousel:
Tel 310-394-8042 (call for hours)
Arcade: **Open** (310) 451-5133
(call for hours). Pacific Park:
Tel (310) 260-8774 (call for hours).
📷 🌐 santamonicapier.org

This popular 1909 landmark is the West Coast's oldest amusement pier, with popcorn, cotton candy, bumper cars, and an amusement arcade. At the western end, Pacific Park has a Ferris wheel rising 11 stories high. Nearby, the 1922 Looff Carousel, similar to that in Santa Cruz *(see p510)*, with 44 handcrafted horses, was featured in George Roy Hill's 1973 film *The Sting* *(see p73)*. You can fish without a permit from the balconies on the pier's lower deck. On Thursday evenings during the

Beach apartments along the front of Palisades Park

summer, there is free dancing and live music (see p177).

🏛 Bergamot Station

2525 Michigan Ave.**Tel** 310-453-7535.
Open 10am–6pm Tue–Fri, 11am–5:30pm Sat. ♿

Bergamot Station is a 5.5-acre (2-ha) arts complex that stands on the site of an abandoned Red Line trolley station. The crude buildings are constructed from aluminum siding, with an added touch of high-tech styling. More than 25 galleries and a small museum showcase the latest works in contemporary and radical art, including painting, sculpture, photography, and glass, plus collectibles and African art. Bergamot Station also houses some artists' studios.

An exhibit at Bergamot Station art gallery and cultural complex

🏛 California Heritage Museum

2612 Main St. **Tel** 310-392-8537.
Open 11am–4pm Wed–Sun.
Closed Jan 1, Jul 4, Thanksgiving, Dec 25. 🅿 ♿ 🆆 **california heritagemuseum.org**

The Queen Anne style museum building was built in 1894 by architect Sumner P Hunt as the home of Roy Jones, son of the founder of Santa Monica (see p79). On the first floor, the rooms depict the lifestyle of various periods in Southern California history: a Victorian dining room, an Arts and Crafts living room, and a 1930s kitchen. Upstairs, there are changing exhibitions on topics such as surfing (see pp202–3), the Hollywood Western, handmade quilts, and Monterey Rancho-style furniture.

Victorian facade of the California Heritage Museum

🏛 Angels Attic

516 Colorado Ave. **Tel** 310-394-8331.
Open noon–4pm Thu–Sat.
Closed major holidays.
🆆 **angelsattic.com**

The Angels Attic museum is housed in one of the last two preserved Victorian mansions in Santa Monica. Built in 1895 and restored to the original period, the heritage building is an attraction in its own right, featuring beautiful Queen Anne style architecture and a pretty garden.

VISITORS' CHECKLIST

Practical Information
Road map inset A.
ℹ Palisades Park, 1400 Ocean Ave, 310-393-7593. 🎊 Santa Monica Festival (May).
🆆 **santamonica.com**

Transport
✈ LAX 8 miles (13 km) SE of Santa Monica. 🚌 4th St & Colorado Blvd.

The museum features an impressive collection of antique and contemporary dolls, dollhouses, toys, and miniatures that appeal to both children and adults. Visitors can explore social history through the exhibits, which document the changing styles in fashion, architecture, interior design, paintings, and books, the evolution of the toy industry, across the seven galleries and many display cabinets.

Raymond Chandler

Novelist and screenwriter Raymond Chandler (1888–1959) set several of his works wholly or partly in Santa Monica, a city that he loathed and that he thinly disguised as sleazy Bay City in *Farewell, My Lovely*. There was some truth in Chandler's portrayal of Santa Monica. Corruption and vice in the 1920s and 1930s are well documented. Illegal gambling ships were anchored offshore, including the *Rex*, 5 miles (8 km) out in Santa Monica Bay, called the *Royal Crown* in *Farewell, My Lovely*.

Chandler's novels *Farewell, My Lovely*, *The Big Sleep*, *The High Window*, *The Little Sister*, and *The Long Goodbye* were made into films that portrayed the shadowy side of LA. With an elegant, dark style, he wrote vivid dialogue in the voice of the common man. His character Philip Marlowe was the definitive detective. A loner with a hard-boiled veneer often hiding a soft heart, Marlowe uttered tough one-liners, played by the rules, and usually didn't get the girl.

Film poster for *The Big Sleep* (1946)

❷ Venice

Road map inset A. **Tel** (310) 822-5425. **W** **venicechamber.net**

Since its inception, Venice has attracted a bohemian society, from the rowdy crowd who frequented its dance hall and bathhouse in the 1910s to beatniks in the 1950s. Today, the town features a vibrant array of shops, art galleries, restaurants, bars, and cafés.

The community was founded in 1905 by tobacco magnate Abbot Kinney as a US version of Venice, Italy. Hoping to spark a cultural renaissance in Southern California, he built a system of canals and imported gondolas and gondoliers to punt along the waterways. Unfortunately, Kinney did not take the tides into consideration when designing Venice, and the area was constantly dogged by sewage problems.

Today, only a few of the original 7 miles (11 km) of canals remain, the rest having been filled in during 1927. The traffic circle at Windward Avenue was the main lagoon, and Grand Boulevard, which runs southeast from there, was the Grand Canal. The best place to see the remaining canals is on Dell Avenue, where old bridges, boats, and ducks grace the waterways. Over the years, the circus atmosphere of Venice Beach has never faltered. On the boardwalk during weekends, semiclad men and women whiz past on bicycles and skates, while a zany array of street performers, like chain-saw jugglers and one-man bands, captivates the crowds. Muscle Beach, where Arnold Schwarzenegger used to work out, still attracts body builders.

The booming creative scene can be explored along Abbot Kinney Boulevard, which is lined with colorful shops and galleries. Regular art crawl events attract crowds.

Yachts moored in the harbor at Marina del Rey

❸ Marina del Rey

Road map inset A. **ℹ** 4701 Admiralty Ave, Marina del Rey, 310-305-9545. **W** **visitmarinadelrey.com**

Covering an area of just 1.3 sq miles (3.4 sq km), approximately half of which is water, Marina del Rey has the world's largest artificial small-craft harbor. Those attracted to this town tend to be young and single or with families, and enjoy outdoor activities such as skating, cycling, and water sports. Everything from paddle boats to yachts can be rented, or you can charter boats for deep-sea fishing or a luxury cruise.

Fisherman's Village, on Fiji Way, resembles a New England fishing town. It has a variety of shops, restaurants, and cafés, many of which offer fine views of the harbor.

❹ Museum of Flying

Road map inset A. 3100 Airport Ave. **Tel** (310) 398-2500. **Open** 10am–5pm Fri–Sun. **W** **museumofflying.com**

The Museum of Flying places heavy emphasis on the history of the Santa Monica Airport, where it is located, as well as the prominent role that the Douglas Aircraft Company played in the early development of commercial and military aviation.

The museum exhibits an impressive collection of aircraft, artifacts, aviation art, and memorabilia, plus educational offerings with hands-on, interactive exhibits.

Residence-lined canal in Venice

For hotels and restaurants in this area see p530 and p554

Nearly two dozen aircraft chronicle the history of flight, from a Wright Flyer replica to aircraft from the jet age.

Yellow Peril Boeing Stearman at the Museum of Flying

The Wildlife of Santa Monica Bay

Among the marine mammals that inhabit the waters of Santa Monica Bay are harbor seals, California sea lions, and bottle-nosed dolphins. From December to February gray whales can be seen migrating from Alaska to Baja California to calve. One of the best places in Los Angeles for whale-spotting is Point Dume. In the mountains, the range of wildlife is exceptional. The rare mountain lion can reach a size of 7 ft (2 m) in length and tends to live in the rockier, more remote areas. Its cousin the bobcat is smaller, with tufts of hair on the ends of its ears. Coyotes come out at dusk, often preying on the pets of people living in the hills. The bold, intelligent raccoon raids camp sites even when people are present. Mule deer, desert cottontail, and striped skunk also abound. Birds seen here include golden eagles and red-tailed hawks.

Raccoon (*Procyon lotor*)

❺ **J Paul Getty Center**

See pp86–9.

❻ **Will Rogers State Historic Park**

1501 Will Rogers State Park Road, Pacific Palisades. **Road map** inset A. **Tel** (310) 454-8212. **Open** 8am–sunset daily. **Closed** Jan 1, Thanksgiving, Dec 25. 🅿 🅘 lawn area. 🄲 🆆 **parks.ca.gov**

Will Rogers (1879–1935) started life as a cowboy and went on to become a film star, radio commentator, and newspaper columnist. Called the "Cowboy Philosopher," he was famous for his homespun humor and shrewd comments on current events, usually made while performing rope tricks. His show business career lasted from 1905 until his death. When his widow, Betty, died in 1944, she deeded the house and the surrounding land to the state, stipulating that nothing in the house be changed and that polo matches be held here on weekends (Rogers was an avid polo player).

Hiking trails lead up from the ranch, many of them originally cut by Rogers. The lawn just east of the house is an ideal setting for a picnic. Tours of the house include the living room where Rogers used to practice his roping skills.

❼ **Topanga State Park**

20825 Entrada Rd, Topanga. **Road map** inset A. **Tel** (310) 455-2465 & (805) 488-8147 for fire conditions in summer & autumn. **Open** 8am–sunset daily. 🅿 🅘 🆆 **parks.ca.gov**

Topanga State Park stretches from the Pacific Palisades to the San Fernando Valley (see p148). Topanga is thought to be an Indian term meaning "the place where the mountains meet the sea." The area was inhabited by the Tongva/Gabrielino and Chumash peoples 5,000 years ago. Today, its groves of sycamore and oak trees attract residents seeking a bohemian way of life.

The marked entrance to the 13,000-acre (5,300-ha) park lies just north of Topanga village, off Hwy 27 on Entrada Road. Most of the land falls within the LA city boundary, making it the largest city park in the US. As such, it vastly improves the region's air quality and provides ample space for hiking and riding.

As you ascend the Santa Monica Mountains, canyons, cliffs, and meadows give way to vistas of the ocean and the San Fernando Valley. Four trails begin from the park's headquarters at Trippet Ranch: a 1-mile (1.6-km) self-guided nature trail; the Dead Horse Trail; Musch Ranch Trail (which leads to a camp site); and East Topanga Fire Road, which connects with Eagle Junction. The 2.5-mile (4-km) Eagle Rock/Eagle Spring Trail from Eagle Junction is one of the most popular.

Bicycles are allowed on the park's dirt fire roads, and horses on all but one of the trails.

Hiking trails crossing the Santa Monica Mountains in Topanga State Park

❺ J Paul Getty Museum at the Getty Center

The Getty Center, which opened in December 1997, holds a commanding physical and cultural position in the city. It is situated amid the wild beauty of the Santa Monica Mountains, in the Sepulveda Pass, next to the San Diego Freeway (I-405). The complex houses not only the museum but also the Getty's research, conservation, and grant programs (the Getty Foundation). Getty made his fortune in the oil business and became an ardent collector of art. He wanted his collection, which focuses on European art from the Renaissance to Post-Impressionism, to be open to the public without charge. Works of art from the permanent collection are displayed on rotation. Greek, Etruscan, and Roman antiquities are exhibited at the Getty Villa in Malibu *(see p90)*.

Locator Map

 Illustrated area

Research, conservation, education, administration, restaurant, café, and auditorium buildings

Tram station

★ Irises (1889)
This work was painted by Vincent van Gogh while he was in the asylum at St-Rémy. Its graphic style reveals the influence of artists such as Paul Gauguin (1848 –1903) and the Japanese printmaker Hokusai (1760 –1849).

East Pavilion

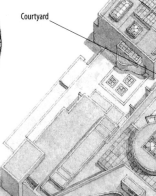

North Pavilion

Courtyard

Hispano-Moresque Deep Dish
This elaborately decorated earthenware dish was made in Valencia, Spain, in the mid-15th century. The use of lustrous colors was a specialty of Moorish potters at that time.

Entrance

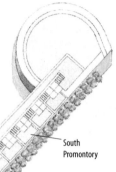

Cabinet on Stand
Attributed to the French master craftsman André-Charles Boulle, this 17th-century cabinet was made to celebrate the victories of Louis XIV.

South Pavilion

West Pavilion

South Promontory

Korean Man (c.1617)
This meticulous drawing in black and red chalk is by the Flemish artist Peter Paul Rubens.

★ **Wheatstacks, Snow Effect, Morning** (1891)
This is one in a series of works by Monet that shows the same landscape at different times of the day and year.

Temporary exhibitions
and the garden café are housed in this building.

Guide to the Getty Center

From below, the Getty Center (designed by architect Richard Meier) may look like a fortress, but once on top, the scale is intimate, with fountains, walkways, courtyards, and niches. An electric tram brings visitors from the parking area to the complex. The museum has a tall, airy foyer that opens onto a central courtyard. From here radiate five two-story pavilions. The Conceptualist artist Robert Irwin has created a garden to the west of the museum. Across the main plaza from the tram station there is a café and restaurant. Another café and a bookstore are located within the museum.

★ **The Abduction of Europa** (1632)
One of Rembrandt's few landscapes, this depicts the Roman god Jupiter, disguised as a bull, kidnapping Europa, princess of Tyre.

Exploring the Getty Museum

J Paul Getty (1892–1976) amassed a remarkable collection of antiquities, European painting, sculpture, and decorative arts, focusing on pre-20th-century artistic movements. Getty was a bold collector who enjoyed the pursuit of an object almost more than the possession of it. Since his death, the Getty Trust has strengthened the museum's holdings by purchasing works of the highest quality. New departments in related areas such as photographs (which includes 19th and 20th-century American and European photographs), drawings, and manuscripts have also been added.

Man with a Hoe, painted between 1860 and 1862 by Jean-François Millet

This painting, along with Claude Monet's *Wheatstacks, Snow Effect, Morning (see p87)*, Vincent van Gogh's *Irises (see p86)*, and Paul Gauguin's *The Royal End*, has helped elevate the museum's collection of Impressionists and Post-Impressionists.

European sculptures in the Getty date from the 16th century to the end of the 19th century. Pier Jacopo Antico's *Bust of a Young Man* (1520) was created at the end of the High Renaissance in Italy. The elongated body favored by the Mannerists can be seen in Benvenuto Cellini's *Satyr* (c.1542). Fine examples of Baroque sculpture are *Pluto Abducting Proserpine* (c.1693–1710) by François Girardon and Bernini's *Boy with a Dragon* (c.1614). Neo-Classical works include three statues by the British sculptor Joseph Nollekens.

European Paintings and Sculpture

The museum boasts a superb collection of European paintings, dating from the 13th century to the late 19th century. Italian works from the Renaissance and Baroque periods include *The Adoration of the Magi* (c.1495–1505) by Andrea Mantegna and *View of the Arch of Constantine with Colosseum* (1742–5) by Canaletto. Rembrandt's *The Abduction of Europa (see p87)* is a highlight from the Flemish and Dutch collections, which also include an oil sketch by Peter Paul Rubens (1577–1640) and a portrait by Anthony van Dyck (1599–1641).

Of the French artworks on display, *The Race of the Riderless Horses* (1817) is a key painting by the Romantic painter Théodore Géricault. In *Still Life with Apples* (1894) by Paul Cézanne, the artist's preoccupation with gradations of light and color reveals the progression in the late 19th century from the old, realistic style of painting, to a more modern, abstract approach.

Drawings

The purchase in 1981 of Rembrandt's red chalk study of *Nude Woman with a Snake* (c.1637) marked the beginning of the museum's drawings collection. Today, the collection contains more than 400 works in a wide range of media, spanning the 15th to the late 19th century. *The Stag Beetle* (1505) by Albrecht Dürer is an exquisitely detailed illustration in watercolor and gouache. By contrast, Leonardo da Vinci's *Studies for the Christ Child with a Lamb* (c.1503–6) is a looser pen-and-ink study.

Peter Paul Rubens' *Korean Man (see p87)* is one of several portrait drawings. The *Self-Portrait* (c.1857–8) by Edgar Degas, executed in oil on paper and showing the young artist on the threshold of his extraordinary career, is another.

Photographs

The museum launched its photographic department in 1984 with the purchase of several major private collections, including those of Bruno Bischofberger, Arnold Crane, and Samuel Wagstaff. The holdings focus on European and American photography up to the 1950s. Exceptionally rich in works from the early 1840s, the collection features many of the pioneers of

Cape Horn, Oregon (1881–3) by Carleton E Watkins

photography. In daguerreotypes, the identity of the sitter was often more important than that of the maker. The museum has one portrait of Louis-Jacques-Mande Daguerre himself, taken in 1848 by Charles R Meade.

Englishman William Henry Fox Talbot (1800–1877) was the first to make prints from negatives. A lovely example of his work is *Oak Tree in Winter* (1841). Other early practitioners on display include Hyppolyte Bayard (1801–87), portraitist Julia Margaret Cameron (1815–79), war photographer Roger Fenton (1819–69), Gustave Le Gray (1820–82), and Nadar (1820–1910).

Among the important early 20th-century artists represented are Edward Weston (1886–1958), who created beautiful still lifes, and Walker Evans (1903–75), who was a pivotal influence in American documentary photography.

Renaissance chalcedony, or agate, glass bowl, made in Venice, Italy, in around 1500

Applied Arts

Applied arts in the museum encompass pre-1650 European pieces and works from southern Europe from 1650 to 1900. They have been chosen to complement the Getty's extensive holdings of French decorative arts.

Highlights include glass and earthenware from Italy and Spain; metalwork from France, Germany, and Italy; and highly decorated furniture. An extravagantly inlaid display cabinet from Augsburg in Germany (c.1620–30) falls into this last category. All four of the piece's sides open to reveal numerous drawers and compartments for collectibles.

Sèvres porcelain basket, dating from the mid-18th century

Decorative Arts

Decorative arts were Getty's first love as a collector, after he rented a New York penthouse furnished with 18th-century French and English antiques. Originally, his collection focused on furnishings from the reign of Louis XIV to the Napoleonic era (1643–1815), encompassing the Regency, Rococo, and Empire periods.

The age of Louis XIV saw the development of French furniture reach great artistic heights, where appearances mattered more than function. The premier craftsman during that time was André-Charles Boulle (1642–1732), who was noted for his complex veneers and marquetry. The museum has several pieces attributed to Boulle from the French royal household. Two coffers on stands (c.1680–85), made for the Grand Dauphin, son of Louis XIV, probably held jewelry and valuable objects.

Several of the tapestries in the collection have remained in excellent condition, with their colors still vibrant. They include one woven by Jean de la Croix (active 1662–1712) for Louis XIV. The holdings also include ceramics, silver and gilded objects such as chandeliers and wall lights.

Pieces from Germany, Italy, and northern Europe have also been added. A Neo-Classical rolltop desk (c.1785), made by the German David Roentgen, has a weight-operated, concealed writing stand. This type of elaborate mechanical feature was Roentgen's trademark.

Manuscripts

The museum began collecting illuminated manuscripts in 1983 with the purchase of the Ludwig Collection of 144 works, which emphasized German and Central European texts. Tracing the development of illumination from the 6th to the 16th century, the collection today has masterpieces from the Byzantine, Ottoman, Romanesque, Gothic, and Renaissance periods.

Illuminated manuscripts were written and decorated entirely by hand. Initially, most were produced in monasteries, which were then the center of European intellectual life. Later, in the 12th century, they were also produced in the growing number of universities. Most books contained religious material, but some also preserved the philosophy, history, literature, law, and science of Western civilization. Kings, nobles, and church leaders commissioned these richly painted books, some of which were decorated with jewels and precious metals.

The manuscripts, as well as drawings and photos, are all rotated. Highlights include an Ottoman Gospel lectionary from either Reichenau or St. Gall (950–75); an English Gothic Apocalypse (1255–60); two Byzantine Gospel books; *The Visions of Tondal* (1475), in the Flemish holdings; and the *Hours of Simon de Varie*, illuminated by French artist Jean Fouquet in 1455.

Saint John the Evangelist (c.1120 – 40) from the German Abbey of Helmarshausen's Gospel book

❽ The Getty Villa

17985 Pacific Coast Hwy. **Road Map** inset A. **Tel** 310-440-7300. **Open** 10am–5pm Wed–Mon. **Closed** major holidays. Free admission; timed tickets required. ♿ 🅦 **getty.edu**

The Getty Villa is the home of the Antiquities collection of the J Paul Getty Museum (see pp86–9). Getty's vision – of a museum where his collection of antiquities could be displayed in a place where such art might originally have been seen – came to fruition in 2006. The museum displays around 1,200 works of ancient art from Greece, Rome, and Etruria, dating from 6,500 BC to AD 400, on both floors of the building.

The villa is based on the Villa dei Papiri, the country estate of a Roman consul. The Outer Peristyle garden is spectacular, with its large pool bordered by bronze statuary replicas and plants favored by the ancient Romans. The buildings combine authentic Roman detailing with modern technology.

Getty's original home on this property, and the site of the first Getty Museum, holds a research library, seminar room, classroom, reading room, conservation labs, and offices for scholars and staff. The outdoor amphitheater presents Greek drama and dance performances, and there is an upscale café.

Decorative facade and grounds of Adamson House

❾ Adamson House and Malibu Lagoon Museum

23200 Pacific Coast Hwy. **Road Map** inset A. **Tel** 310-456-9575. **Open** Tours: 11am–3pm Fri & Sat; Grounds: 8am–6pm daily. **Closed** Jan 1, Jul 4, Thanksgiving, Dec 25. 🅟 ♿ 📷 📹 last tour 2pm. 🅦 **adamsonhouse.org**

Adamson House was built in 1930 for husband and wife Merritt and Rhoda Adamson. Rhoda was the daughter of Frederick and May Rindge, the last owners of the Rancho Malibu Spanish land grant. Until 1928, the family owned 24 miles (39 km) of Malibu coastline. Situated on the beach, the idyllic house, designed by Stiles Clements, and its 6 acres (2.5 ha) of gardens overlook Malibu Pier and Malibu Lagoon. The Spanish Colonial style building is covered with vivid tiles from the Malibu

Potteries – a ceramics firm that was started by May Rindge and owned by the family. Hundreds of these individually designed tiles are featured throughout the house and grounds. The floors, walls, doorways, and fountains are all intricately decorated. The house's original 1920s furnishings are also on display.

Located in the converted garage of Adamson House is the Malibu Lagoon Museum, which is devoted to the history of Malibu. Artifacts, documents, and photographs tell the story not only of the Rindge family but also of the early Chumash population and José Tapia, who in 1802 became Malibu's first Spanish landowner.

❿ Malibu Lagoon State Beach

Road Map inset A. **Tel** 310-457-8143. **Open** 8am–sunset daily. 🅟 ♿ 🅦 **parks.ca.gov**

The Chumash people built Humaliwo, their largest village, on the shores of this lagoon. By the 16th century, about 1,000 people had their home here, making it one of the most populated Native American villages north of what is now Mexico.

The estuary supports a wide range of marine life and is an important feeding ground for up to 200 species of migratory and native birds. To the east of the lagoon, the 35-acre (14-ha)

The Getty Villa's Outer Peristyle garden

Exclusive beach houses in Malibu Colony

Surfrider County Beach is devoted to surfers. With its rare point break, Malibu is one of the finest surfing spots in southern California. The area closest to the pier is thought to have the best waves for longboarding.

View across Malibu Lagoon to the Santa Monica Mountains

⓫ Malibu Colony

Road Map inset A. 🛈 23554 Malibu Colony Rd.

In 1928, to raise money for an ongoing battle to keep Malibu in the family, May Rindge sold this section of shoreline to film stars such as Bing Crosby, Gary Cooper, and Barbara Stanwyck. Today, the colony is a private, gated compound, still favored by people working within the entertainment industry. Public access to the beach is difficult, but stars can often be spotted in the Malibu Colony Plaza, which is located near the entrance.

⓬ Malibu Creek State Park

Road Map inset A. **Tel** (818) 880-0367 or (800) 444-7275 for camp site reservations. **Open** dawn–dusk daily. 🅟 ♿ 🅿 🆆 **parks.ca.gov**

This 10,000-acre (4,000-ha) park was inhabited by the Chumash people until the mid-19th century. A varied landscape of forests, meadows, and rocky outcrops create the illusion of a vast wilderness, far away from civilization.

Some 2,000 acres (800 ha) of the park were once owned by 20th Century Fox, which made it a favorite location for movie-making *(see pp72–3)*. *M*A*S*H* (1970), *Butch Cassidy and the Sundance Kid* (1969), and *Planet of the Apes* (1968) were all filmed here. The state bought the land back from the film company in 1974.

The information center is close to the parking lot and has exhibits on the area's history, flora, and fauna. The stunning Gorge Trail starts from the center of the park and leads to a rock pool, which was used as a pseudo-tropical location to film the movies *South Pacific* (1958) and *Tarzan* (1959).

Off Crags Road, the marshy Century Lake harbors catfish, bass, bluefish, red-winged blackbirds, buffleheads, coots, and mallards. In spring the meadows are a riot of colorful wildflowers. Groves of live and valley oaks, redwood, and dogwood trees are scattered throughout the park.

Within the park there are 20 trails for hiking, cycling, or horseback riding; a nature center; and many picnic areas.

Rocky outcrop in Malibu Creek State Park

BEVERLY HILLS, BEL AIR, AND WESTWOOD

Beverly Hills is a city, independent of Los Angeles and with its own laws and regulations. Since the early 1920s it has been the entertainment industry's favorite residential address. Beverly Hills' Golden Triangle is the West Coast's answer to New York's Madison Avenue, with its array of restaurants, shops, and coffee bars. South of Bel Air's shady canyons, youthful Westwood Village brims with UCLA students. In the business-minded Century City, high-rises crowd the skyline. Together, these areas form part of the Westside region of Los Angeles.

Sights at a Glance

Historic Buildings
1 Beverly Hills Civic Center
8 The Beverly Hills Hotel
11 Hotel Bel-Air

Parks and Gardens
7 Greystone Park and Mansion
9 Virginia Robinson Gardens

Shopping Areas
3 *Rodeo Drive p98*
4 2 Rodeo
6 Century City

Tours
10 *Tour of the Stars' Homes pp100–101*

Museums
2 The Paley Center for Media
5 Museum of Tolerance

Universities
12 UCLA and Westwood Village

See also LA Street Finder maps 4, 5

0 kilometers 1
0 miles 0.5

◀ Doorway of Beverly Hills City Hall, Beverly Hills

Street-by-Street: The Golden Triangle

The area bordered by Santa Monica Boulevard, Wilshire Boulevard, and North Crescent Drive, known as the "Golden Triangle," is the shopping district of Beverly Hills. The shops, restaurants, and art galleries lining the streets are some of the most luxurious in the world. Cutting through the middle is Rodeo Drive, where many international designer boutiques are to be found. On Wilshire Boulevard, the cream of American department stores offer a heady mix of style and opulence. To the north are the beautifully manicured Beverly Gardens Park, the elegant Civic Center with its landmark City Hall, and the Paley Center for Media, formerly the Museum of Television and Radio.

❷ ★ The Paley Center for Media
A valuable addition to the Golden Triangle, this museum gives a comprehensive history of broadcasting.

The Electric Fountain in Beverly Gardens Park was built in 1930. The statue on the top is of a Native American praying for rain. Scenes from California history are depicted on the base frieze.

SANTA MONICA BOULEVARD

SANTA MONICA BOULEVARD

LITTLE SANTA MONICA BOULEVARD

NORTH CAMDEN DRIVE

NORTH BEDFORD DRIVE

NORTH ROXBURY DRIVE

BRIG

Saks Fifth Avenue is one of the four major department stores along Wilshire Boulevard.

The Creative Artists Agency building, with curving, mirrored glass and marble walls, was built in 1989 by architect IM Pei. (The CAA has since moved its offices.)

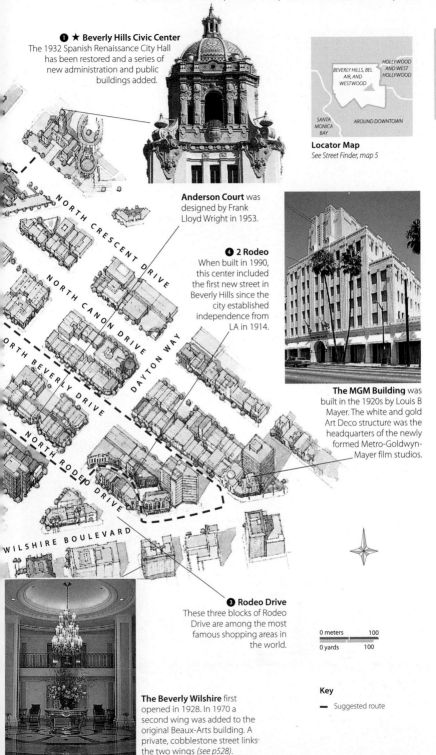

❶ ★ Beverly Hills Civic Center
The 1932 Spanish Renaissance City Hall has been restored and a series of new administration and public buildings added.

Locator Map
See Street Finder, map 5

Anderson Court was designed by Frank Lloyd Wright in 1953.

❹ 2 Rodeo
When built in 1990, this center included the first new street in Beverly Hills since the city established independence from LA in 1914.

The MGM Building was built in the 1920s by Louis B Mayer. The white and gold Art Deco structure was the headquarters of the newly formed Metro-Goldwyn-Mayer film studios.

❸ Rodeo Drive
These three blocks of Rodeo Drive are among the most famous shopping areas in the world.

0 meters   100
0 yards   100

The Beverly Wilshire first opened in 1928. In 1970 a second wing was added to the original Beaux-Arts building. A private, cobblestone street links the two wings *(see p528)*.

Key
— Suggested route

Beverly Hills Civic Center with City Hall in the background

❶ Beverly Hills Civic Center

455 N Rexford Drive. **Map** 5 F3.
Tel 310-285-1000. **Open** 7:30am–
5:30pm Mon–Thu, 8am–5pm Fri.
Closed public hols. ♿
Ⓦ beverlyhills.org

The Spanish Colonial City Hall,
with its majestic tower capped
by a tiled cupola, was
designed in 1932 by local firm
Koerner and Gage. Over the
years it has become a symbol
of the elegant, European-
inspired city of Beverly Hills.
In 1990, architect
Charles Moore linked the
building to a new
Civic Center by a
series of diagonal
landscaped and
pedestrianized
courtyards. On the
upper levels,
balconies and
arcaded corridors
continue the Spanish
Colonial theme. The
harmonious modern addition
houses a beautiful public
library as well as the local fire
and police stations.

Lucille Ball, the most
popular television star
during the 1950s

Billboards are banned in the
area, and a height restriction of
three stories or 45 ft (14 m) is
imposed on any new buildings,
leaving City Hall to dominate
the skyline.

❷ The Paley Center for Media

465 N Beverly Drive. **Map** 5 F3.
Tel 310-786-1091. **Open** noon–5pm
Wed–Sun. **Closed** public hols. ⬚ ♿
◨ Ⓦ paleycenter.org

Visitors to the Paley Center,
formerly the Museum of
Television and Radio, may
watch and listen to news
and a collection of
entertainment and
sports programs from
the earliest days of
radio and television
to the present.
Pop music fans can
see footage of the
early Beatles or a
young Elvis Presley
making his television
debut. Sports fans can relive
classic Olympic competitions.
Visitors can select up to four
extracts from the library's

computerized catalogue at
any one time. These are then
played on small private
consoles. The museum also
has a 150-seat theater, which
hosts major exhibitions,
seminars, and screenings on
specialized subjects and
selected actors or directors.
The collection of more than
75,000 television and radio
programs includes such
timeless classics as *I Love
Lucy* and *The Honeymooners*.
Favorite television and radio
commercials, encompassing
the industry's advertising
history, are also available.
The museum's holdings
duplicate those of New York's
highly successful Museum of
Television and Radio, which was
created in 1975 by the late
William S Paley, when he was
the head of CBS Television.

❸ Rodeo Drive

See p98.

Spanish Steps leading to 2 Rodeo

❹ 2 Rodeo

Map 5 F3. ℹ 268 N. Rodeo Drive,
310-247-7040. Ⓦ **2rodeo.com**

Developed in 1990 on the
corner of Rodeo Drive *(see p98)*
and Wilshire Boulevard, 2 Rodeo
is one of the most expensive
retail centers ever made. It looks

like a film set of a European street, complete with a public square and Victorian-style street lamps. Exclusive shops such as Versace and Jimmy Choo line Via Rodeo, the cobbled lane that bisects the center. Via Rodeo meanders to the Spanish Steps, which descend to Wilshire Boulevard.

History of racial prejudice displayed at the Museum of Tolerance

❺ Museum of Tolerance

9786 W Pico Blvd. **Map** 5 F5. **Tel** 310-553-8403. **Open** 10am–5pm Sun–Fri; until 9:30pm Thu. **Closed** Jan 1, Thanksgiving, Dec 25, and all major Jewish holidays. 🎨 🛗 📷 🎥
W museumoftolerance.com

This museum is dedicated to the promotion of respect and understanding among all people. Its two primary areas of focus are the history of racism and prejudice in the United States and the European Holocaust experience, examined in both historical and contemporary contexts.

The museum tour begins in the Tolerancenter, where visitors are challenged to confront racism and bigotry through interactive exhibits. A recreation of a 1950s diner has a menu of controversial topics focusing on personal responsibility, and a film on Bosnia and Rwanda and contemporary hate groups brings the displays on human rights violations up-to-date.

A 16-screen video wall depicts the 1960s civil rights struggle in America. Interactive video monitors ask visitors for their personal profiles and then challenge them on questions

of responsible citizenship and social justice. They also offer footage of the LA riots of 1992 *(see p61)*, with follow-up interviews.

At the beginning of the Holocaust section, each visitor is given the details and photograph of a child whose life was in some way altered by that period. Throughout the tour, the child's history is updated and, at the end, his or her fate is revealed. During the tour, visitors become a witness to events in Nazi Germany. Wax models in an outdoor café scene, set in prewar Berlin, seem to discuss the impending Nazi takeover of Germany. In a re-creation of the Wannsee Conference, the Third Reich leaders decide on the "The Final Solution of the Jewish Question." Videotaped interviews with concentration camp survivors shown in the "Hall of Testimony" tell of their harrowing experiences. Artifacts on display include Anne Frank's original letters and memorabilia from the camps.

Visitors must call ahead for reservations, as tickets are issued for allocated slots and specific exhibitions. There is a short orientation before a self-guided tour. Some of the exhibits, including the Holocaust portion, are not recommended for children under the age of 12.

Westfield Century City

❻ Century City

Map 5 D5. 🅸 2029 Century Park East, 90067, 310-553-2222.
W centurycitycc.com

This site used to be part of 20th Century Fox's backlot, famous for their

motion pictures. It was sold in 1961 to the developers of Century City, who designed a high-rise complex of offices, stores, and homes on the 180 acres (73 ha).

Today lawyers, agents, and production companies fill the office blocks. Despite this, the area has never developed a community feel and remains a corporate hub with some modern hotels and apartment blocks beginning to be built on the site.

The Westfield Century City Shopping Center, however, is a notable success and has become one of Northern California's premier shopping and dining destinations. Modeled around having indoor and outdoor shopping, the complex holds some 150 stores and restaurants, and a 15-screen cinema.

❼ Greystone Park and Mansion

905 Loma Vista Drive. **Map** 5 F1. **Tel** 310-550-4796 (call for park opening hours). Mansion: **Open** only for special events. 🛗 terrace & lower grounds.

In 1928 Edward L Doheny, an oil millionaire, built this 55-room mock-Tudor manor house for his son. Just three weeks after moving in with his family, Doheny's son was found dead in his bedroom with a male secretary, an apparent murder-suicide. His wife and children soon moved out, and since then the mansion has often been vacant.

Now owned by the city of Beverly Hills, Greystone has been used in films, such as the 2007 film *There Will Be Blood* and the house's staircase has appeared in numerous films becoming one of the most famous sets in Hollywood. It has also been the stage for music videos, and commercials. The house is closed to the public, but visitors can walk or picnic in the beautiful 18-acre (7-ha) terraced gardens, which offer views across Los Angeles.

❸ Rodeo Drive

The name Rodeo Drive is derived from *El Rancho Rodeo de las Aguas* ("the ranch of the gathering of waters"), the name of an early Spanish land grant that included Beverly Hills. Today, Rodeo Drive is one of the most celebrated and exclusive shopping streets in the world, with Italian designer boutiques, the best of French fashion, world-class jewelers, and some of the leading LA retailers. For those who enjoy celebrity-spotting, Rodeo Drive is a prime area.

Rodeo Drive's wide sidewalks, bordered by trees, help create a pleasant shopping environment.

Cartier, at No.370, is well known for its classic-style watches and diamond rings.

411 •

• 420

Barakat sells fine jewelry and also has an impressive collection of pre-Columbian and ancient Greek artifacts, at No. 405.

Gucci, at No. 347, is a leading Italian boutique. Best known for its leather accessories and colorful scarves, it also produces furnishings, such as this cushion.

BRIGHTON WAY

• 370

• 434

HERMÈS

R O D E O   D R I V E

• 317

Hammacher Schlemmer & Co

Lalique, at No. 238, is famous for its Art Deco and Art Nouveau glassware. The shop's frosted lamps are typical of Lalique's style.

Christian Dior, at No. 309, is one of the leading names in French *haute couture*. The founder of the house was responsible for the 1950s "New Look."

VAN CLEEF & ARPELS

DAYTON WAY

• 273

0 meters	50
0 yards	50

• 230

TIFFANY & CO

The landmark Beverly Hills Hotel

❽ The Beverly Hills Hotel

9641 Sunset Blvd. **Map** 5 D2. **Tel** 310-276-2251, (800) 283-8885. **Open** daily. 🚻 🅦 beverlyhillshotel.com
See Where to Stay p528.

Dubbed "the Pink Palace," this extravagant Mission Revival-style hotel was built in 1912 by developer Burton E Green. The hotel's 21 secluded bungalows, set in 12 acres (5 ha) of beautiful landscaped gardens, have been romantic hideaways for film stars such as Marilyn Monroe, Clark Gable, Richard Burton, and Elizabeth Taylor.

The Beverly Hills Hotel has undergone a massive $100 million program of renovations, reviving the style of Hollywood's glamorous heyday. Its legendary pool and cabanas have remained one of the places to be seen and heard in Los Angeles, and its famous restaurant, The Polo Lounge, is once more at the center of the movie industry's deal-making.

❾ Virginia Robinson Gardens

1008 Elden Way. **Map** 5 D1. **Tel** 310-550-2087. 🚻 🚻 🏷 9:30am–4pm Tue–Sat. Advance reservations required. 🅦 robinsongardens.org

In 1908, department-store heir Harry Robinson and his wife, Virginia, bought a plot of land in Beverly Hills. Three years later they completed the city's first house here and planted 6 acres (2.5 ha) of landscaped gardens set amid terraces, ponds, and fountains.

Bequeathed to LA County, the gardens were opened to the public in 1982. One of the most impressive sights is the 2.5-acre (1-ha) palm forest, where you can see the largest king palms outside Australia.

The organized tour includes part of the house, which still has its original furnishings. Be sure to make a reservation in advance as walk-up visits are not allowed.

❿ Tour of the Stars' Homes

See pp100–101.

⓫ Hotel Bel-Air

701 Stone Canyon Rd. **Map** 4 A1. **Tel** 310-472-1211, (800) 648-4097. **Open** daily. 🚻 🅦 hotelbelair.com

Considered by many to be one of the best hotels in the US, Hotel Bel-Air is located in a heavily wooded canyon, giving it an air of privacy and tranquillity. The 1920s Mission Revival-style buildings are set in 11 acres (4.5 ha) of beautiful gardens, interspersed with fountains and intimate courtyards.

Among the trees and shrubs rarely seen in Southern California are coastal redwoods, white-flowering bird of paradise trees, and a floss silk tree – the largest of its kind outside its native South America. The gardens are fragrant with roses, gardenias, jasmine, and orange blossoms. In fact, the Bel-Air is so perfect that one guest stayed for 40 years.

Pool at Hotel Bel-Air, surrounded by attractive gardens

For hotels and restaurants in this area see p528 & p531 and p550 & p556

⑩ Tour of the Stars' Homes

Beverly Hills has long been the symbol of success for those in the entertainment industry. When, in 1920, Mary Pickford and Douglas Fairbanks built their mansion, Pickfair, at the top of Summit Drive, everyone else followed – and stayed. Sunset Boulevard divides the haves from the have-nots: people who live south of it may be rich, but it is those who live to the north of the road who are considered to be the super-rich. A bus tour will take you around if you don't wish to drive yourself (*see p183*). Be aware that most of the addresses are the former homes of celebrities, who no longer live there.

⑬ Jimmy Stewart's former home at No. 918 Roxbury Drive

South of Sunset

Start at No. 714 Palm Drive, the elegant home of Faye Dunaway ①, who starred with Warren Beatty in *Bonnie and Clyde* (1967). Continue south and turn right on Elevado Avenue. The former home of Rita Hayworth ② is situated on the corner at No. 512 Palm Drive.

At Maple Drive, turn right. No. 720 is the white and green New England-style home of the late George Burns and Gracie Allen ③. Continue north and just before Sunset Boulevard make a sharp left onto Lomitas Avenue. Go two blocks and turn left onto Foothill Road. On the corner, at No. 701, is the unassuming house of Carroll Baker ④. This blonde-haired beauty made her debut in *Giant* (1956) with James Dean. At one time she was being groomed to be the next Marilyn Monroe.

Turn right onto Elevado Avenue, take the next right onto Alpine Drive, left onto Lomitas Avenue, and left at Crescent Drive. Doris Day's modest house ⑤ is at No. 713, hidden behind a tall hedge.

Turn right on Carmelita Avenue and right again at Cañon Drive. The pretty house ⑥ where Robert Wagner and Natalie Wood once lived can be seen through the low wall at No. 603. Continue north to the junction with Elevado Avenue. Just across the road, at No. 707 Cañon Drive, lush palm trees in the front of the estate mark the beginning of Kirk Douglas's walled and gated property ⑦.

Turn left onto Elevado Avenue. As you cross Rodeo Drive, look to your right. The lovely home of the late Gene Kelly ⑧ is at No. 725 Rodeo Drive. This renowned Hollywood icon performed in such classics as *An American in Paris* (1951) and *Singing in the Rain* (1952).

WEST SUNSET BOULEVARD

Key

•••• Tour route

Continue along Elevado Avenue, then turn right on Bedford Drive. The comedian and actor Steve Martin ⑨ has a home at No. 721. A modern block structure, it has no front windows and can be only partially glimpsed behind a bougainvillea hedge. Lana Turner's scandal-ridden house ⑩ at No. 730, on the corner of Bedford Drive and Lomitas Avenue, was where her

① Faye Dunaway's house at No. 714 Palm Drive

Locator Map

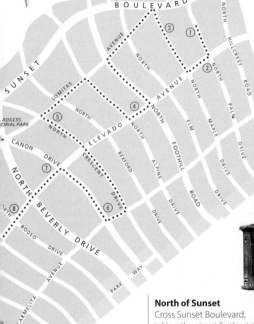

⑭ Gene Hackman's former home at No. 9906 Sunset Boulevard

house ⑪, which he occasionally used in his shows. His former neighbors at No. 1000 Roxbury Drive were Lucille Ball and Desi Arnaz ⑫. Their successful show *I Love Lucy (see p96)* reruns daily on television. Nearby, at No. 918, is the mock-Tudor former home of the much-respected Jimmy Stewart ⑬.

At Sunset Boulevard, turn right. Gene Hackman lived at No. 9906 ⑭, on the southwest corner of Sunset Boulevard, just past Greenway Drive. The actor became famous in the 1970s after his Academy-award winning role in *The French Connection*.

Turn right onto North Carolwood Drive. Just to the right, at No. 144 Monovale Drive ⑮, is one of rock-and-roll king Elvis Presley's former homes. Only the tennis courts can be seen from the street.

Continue along Carolwood Drive. Barbra Streisand ⑯ has lived at No. 301 on a heavily guarded estate. The singer and actress won an academy award in 1969 for her role as Fanny Brice in the musical *Funny Girl*. The late Walt Disney, who captured the world's imagination with his cartoon characters, used to live just north of here at No. 355 Carolwood Drive ⑰. His house is on a bend, behind a gate.

⑰ Walt Disney's mailbox

North of Sunset

Cross Sunset Boulevard, taking the street farthest to the left, which is now Benedict Canyon Drive. On the corner is the Beverly Hills Hotel, *(see p99)*, long a celebrity rumor mill. The private bungalows behind its pink facade saw many a romantic tryst, including, it is said, those between Marilyn Monroe and John and Robert Kennedy.

At Roxbury Drive, turn left and curve south with the road. At No. 1002 is the late Jack Benny's traditional-looking brick

gangster-lover Johnny Stompanato was stabbed to death with a kitchen knife by her daughter, Cheryl Crane.

Turn right onto Lomitas Avenue, then make a sharp left on Cañon Drive.

0 meters 500
0 yards 500

Tips for Drivers

Tour length: 5 miles (8 km).
Stopping-off points: Film stars' homes or former homes are private residences. Do not attempt to trespass or you may be arrested.

⑫ University of California Los Angeles, Westwood Village

A large university with a first-rate reputation, UCLA has a wide range of academic departments and professional schools, including the respected UCLA Hospital. Sited on 419 acres (170 ha), with more than 40,000 students, it is a city within a city. The original campus was designed in 1925 to resemble the Romanesque towns of southern Europe. The first four buildings followed this theme, but as the university expanded more modern architecture was favored. The disappointing mix of bland structures that resulted is redeemed by the beautiful landscaped grounds.

Romanesque-style facade of UCLA's Royce Hall

Exploring UCLA and Westwood Village

Since it was first developed in 1928, Westwood Village, at the foot of the UCLA campus, has been a meet and greet place for college students and anyone looking for a break from the city. This always lively enclave is chockablock with shops catering mostly to students, and restaurants of all kinds, plus the biggest lineup of movie theaters in LA. In fact, on any evening there is the possibility to see stars walking the red carpet at the Fox or the Bruin, since Hollywood favors these venerable theaters for its gala premieres.

▦ Royce Quadrangle

Dickson Plaza. **Tel** 310-825-2101. **Open** daily.

The four buildings that make up the Royce Quadrangle are the oldest on UCLA's campus in Westwood. Built of red brick in the Italian Romanesque style, Royce, Kinsey, and Haines halls, and Powell Library far surpass the other buildings at

UCLA in beauty. The best of them all is Royce Hall, which is based on the basilica of San Ambrogio in Milan, Italy. Its auditorium hosts professional music, dance, and theater shows throughout the year. Across the quad, Powell Library's grand rotunda was modeled on San Sepolcro in Bologna, Italy.

▦ Hammer Museum

10899 Wilshire Blvd. **Tel** 310-443-7000. **Open** 11am–8pm Tue–Fri, 11am–5pm Sat & Sun. **Closed** Jan 1, Jul 4, Thanksgiving, Dec 25. 🔊 📷 📷 W hammer.ucla.edu

The museum presents selections from the collection of businessman Armand Hammer (1899–1990). Works are largely by Impressionist or Post-Impressionist artists such as Mary Cassatt (1845–1926), Camille Pissarro (1830–1903), Claude Monet (1840–1926), John Singer Sargent (1856–1925), and Vincent van Gogh (1853–90). The collection also has some European old master paintings. Exhibits from

the Armand Hammer Daumier and Contemporaries Collection are also shown on a rotating basis and include paintings, sculptures, and lithographs by Daumier and his contemporaries. Displays are also drawn from the UCLA Grunwald Center for the Graphic Arts, which holds more than 35,000 works on paper dating from the Renaissance to the present day.

❏ Franklin D Murphy Sculpture Garden

Tel 310-443-7000. **Open** daily.

This is the largest sculpture garden on the West Coast with more than 70 20th-century sculptures. The highlights include Henry Moore's *Two-Piece Reclining Figure, No. 3* (1961) and Jacques Lipchitz's *Baigneuse* (*Bather*, 1923–5).

Entrance to UCLA's Hammer Museum

UCLA and Westwood Village

① Franklin D Murphy Sculpture Garden
② Fowler Museum at UCLA
③ Royce Quadrangle
④ Mildred E Mathias Botanical Garden
⑤ Westwood Village
⑥ Hammer Museum
⑦ Westwood Memorial Park

For hotels and restaurants in this area see p528 & p531 and p550 & p556

Automne (Autumn, 1948) by Henri Laurens in the Franklin D Murphy Sculpture Garden

New Wight Art Gallery

Franklin D Murphy Sculpture Garden ①

Royce Hall

Royce Triangle ③

Powell Library

Fowler Museum at UCLA ②

BRUIN WALK

Hilgard Bus Terminal

UCLA

Mildred E Mathias Botanical Garden ④

LE CONTE PLACE

Westwood Village ⑤

Hammer Museum ⑥

Westwood Memorial Park ⑦

BEVERLY HILLS HOLLYWOOD

BEVERLY HILLS

WILSHIRE BOULEVARD

0 meters 500
0 yards 500

VISITORS' CHECKLIST

Practical Information
Map 4 A3.
UCLA Campus: 📋 310-825-4321. 🔲 ucla.edu
Westwood Village: 📋 2990 S Sepulveda Blvd, (310) 481-0600.
🔲 westwoodvillageonline.com

Transport
🚌 20, 21, 22.

Mildred E Mathias Botanical Garden

Tel 310-825-1260. **Open** 8am–5pm Mon–Fri, 8am–4pm Sat & Sun. **Closed** public hols. ♿

Named after an acclaimed American botanist, this serene garden tucked away in a small shady canyon contains almost 4,000 rare and native species. Divided into 13 thematic sections, the gardens feature both subtropical and tropical plants. The trees are spectacular and include some outstanding Australian eucalyptus and some large specimens of dawn redwoods.

Fowler Museum at UCLA

Tel 310 825-4361. **Open** noon–5pm Wed–Sun (until 8pm Thu). **Closed** public hols. 📷 🔲 fmch.ucla.edu

This university museum is committed to enriching the community's understanding of the diverse cultures, peoples and religions of the world. Its exhibitions focus on the prehistoric, historic, and contemporary societies of Africa, Asia, the Americas, and Oceania. The collection of 750,000 artifacts makes it one of the nation's leading university museums.

Westwood Memorial Park

1218 Glendon Ave. **Tel** 310-474-1579. **Open** 8am–dusk daily. ♿

Off the beaten track, this small cemetery is located behind the iPic theaters and parking lot. The tranquil grounds are now the final resting place for celebrities such as Dean Martin, Peter Lorre, Buddy Rich, Natalie Wood, and Marilyn Monroe. For several decades after her death, Monroe's second husband, Joe DiMaggio, used to have six red roses placed on her tomb every week.

Tranquil Westwood Memorial Park, shaded by trees

Marilyn Monroe

Born Norma Jean Baker in the charity ward of Los Angeles General Hospital, Marilyn Monroe (1926–62) was placed in foster care by her mother when she was two weeks old. Her first marriage, at the age of 16, lasted four years, before she gave it up to pursue her dream of being an actress. In 1950, her career took off with *The Asphalt Jungle* and *All About Eve*. With films such as *The Seven-Year Itch* (1955) and *Some Like It Hot* (1959), she became the biggest sex symbol Hollywood has ever seen. In the latter part of her life, she struggled to escape the narrow confines of her on-screen persona.

MARILYN MONROE
1926   1962

Marilyn Monroe's memorial plaque

HOLLYWOOD AND WEST HOLLYWOOD

In 1887, Harvey Henderson Wilcox and his wife, Daeida, set up a Christian community, free of saloons and gambling, in a Los Angeles suburb and called it Hollywood. It is ironic that the movie business, with all its decadence, came to replace their Utopia. In 1913, Cecil B De Mille filmed *The Squaw Man* in a barn at the corner of Vine and Selma, and for several decades the studios were based here, generating wealth and glamor. During the 1980s and 90s the area fell into decline, but has since revived. Together with Sunset Boulevard, Hollywood is now the hub for Los Angeles nightlife. West Hollywood, with its large gay community, is also a lively area, while Wilshire Boulevard between La Brea and Fairfax Avenues is known as the Miracle Mile, or Museum Row.

Sights at a Glance

Museums

❷ Madame Tussaud's™ Hollywood
❼ The Hollywood Museum
❾ Hollywood Heritage Museum
⓮ *Los Angeles County Museum of Art pp118–21*
⓰ Petersen Automotive Museum
⓲ Page Museum at the La Brea Tar Pits
⓳ Craft and Folk Art Museum

Historic Streets and Buildings

❶ The Hollywood Roosevelt Hotel
❻ Walk of Fame

❽ Hollywood Bowl
⓬ Paramount Studios
⓯ Miracle Mile

Cemeteries

⓫ Hollywood Forever Cemetery

Cinemas and Theaters

❸ TCL Chinese Theatre
❹ Hollywood and Highland
❺ El Capitan Theatre
⓾ Pantages Theater
⓱ The Improv
⓴ Wiltern Theater

Shops and Markets

⓭ Farmers Market

See pp112–13

See pp106–8

See pp109–11

0 kilometers 2
0 miles 1

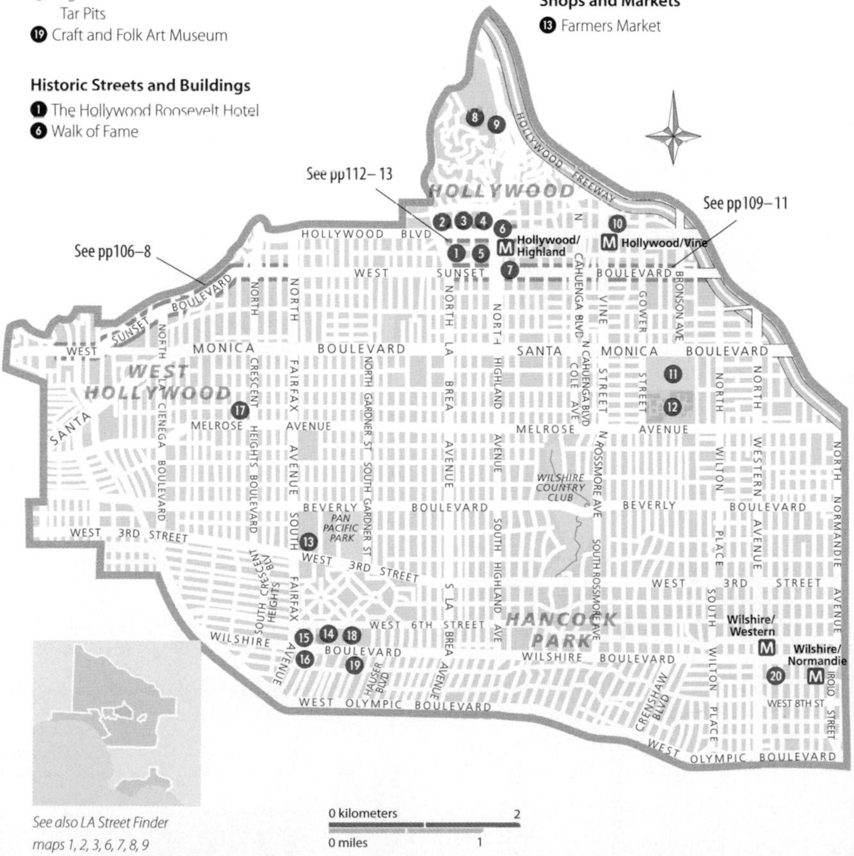

See also LA Street Finder maps 1, 2, 3, 6, 7, 8, 9

◀ TCL Chinese Theatre on Hollywood Boulevard

For keys to symbols *see back flap*

A View of Sunset Boulevard: Sunset Strip

Sunset Boulevard curves west for 26 miles (42 km) from downtown LA to the Pacific Coast Highway. Sunset has been associated with the movies since the 1920s, when it was a dirt track linking the burgeoning film studios in Hollywood with the hillside homes of the screen stars. Today, much of the boulevard is still lined with the mansions of the rich and famous *(see pp100–101)*. Sunset Strip is the liveliest and most historically rich stretch, filled with restaurants, luxury hotels, and nightclubs. The 1.5-mile (2.4-km) section was first paved in the mid-1930s. Its lack of local government made it a magnet for gambling and bootlegging. Famous nightclubs included the Trocadero, Ciro's, and the Mocambo – where young Margarita Cansino met studio boss Harry Cohen, who renamed her Rita Hayworth. Sunset Strip is still the center of LA's nightlife today.

Sunset Strip and the Santa Monica Mountains seen from Crescent Heights

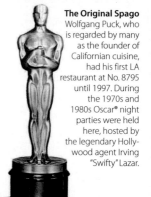

Rainbow Bar & Grill
The walls of this restaurant, at No. 9015, formerly the Villa Nova, are lined with wine casks and gold records. Vincente Minnelli proposed to Judy Garland here and, eight years later in 1953, Marilyn Monroe met Joe DiMaggio here on a blind date.

The Original Spago
Wolfgang Puck, who is regarded by many as the founder of Californian cuisine, had his first LA restaurant at No. 8795 until 1997. During the 1970s and 1980s Oscar® night parties were held here, hosted by the legendary Hollywood agent Irving "Swifty" Lazar.

The Roxy on Sunset
This trendy nightclub, at No. 9009, occupies the site of the old Club Largo.

The Viper Room, at No. 8852, is a popular live music club *(see p179)*, co-founded and once owned by the actor Johnny Depp. In October 1993 young film star River Phoenix, having taken a lethal cocktail of drugs, collapsed and died on the sidewalk outside.

CLARK ST

LARRABEE ST

HORN AVE

HAMMOND ST

HILLDALE AVE

SAN VICENTE BLVD

HOLLOWAY D

Andaz West Hollywood Hotel

Formerly known as the "Riot Hyatt," this hotel, at No. 8401 was often the chosen destination for visiting rock stars, including Jim Morrison *(see p531)*.

Sunset Tower Hotel

This hotel is an Art Deco high-rise. In Hollywood's heyday it was an apartment complex and home to Jean Harlow, Clark Gable, and other luminaries. *(See p531.)*

The Comedy Store

This is a world-famous spot for stand-up comedy, often enjoying television coverage. It stands on the site of the 1940s nightclub, Ciro's.

Cabo Cantina (The Source) at No. 8301

is where Woody Allen rants about LA in his film *Annie Hall* (1977).

0 meters   100
0 yards   100

N LA CIENEGA BLVD

OLIVE DRIVE

The Mondrian Hotel, at No. 8440

(see p531), was decorated with stripes as a tribute to artist Piet Mondrian when it was built, but has since been repainted.

The House of Blues

This tin-roofed blues bar, at No. 8430 *(see p178)*, has been transported from Clarksdale, Mississippi. It was co-founded by the actor Dan Ackroyd, who starred with John Belushi in the 1980 cult movie *The Blues Brothers*.

Sunset Plaza

This area is lined with chic stores and cafés. It is a good section to explore on foot.

Sunset Strip continued

Pink Taco, behind the big billboard to the west of the Chateau Marmont hotel, is popular with college crowds. It stands on the site of the Players Club, which was owned in the 1940s by movie director Preston Sturges.

Chateau Marmont
The hotel at No. 8221 *(see p531)* was modeled on a Loire Valley château. When it opened in 1929, it attracted actors such as Errol Flynn and Greta Garbo. Today's regulars have included Winona Ryder and Christopher Walken.

Directors' Guild of America
This is one of the many offices on Sunset Boulevard connected with the entertainment industry.

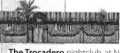

The Trocadero nightclub, at No. 8610, had Nat "King" Cole as its pianist in its heyday. Only three steps remain of the old building.

Schwab's
The former drugstore was a popular meeting place for film stars and columnists. Across Crescent Heights was the legendary Garden of Allah apartment complex whose residents included F Scott Fitzgerald and Dorothy Parker, and which was torn down in 1959.

LA's Hand-Painted Billboards

As in most city centers, mammoth stretch-vinyl advertisements crowd every available space along Sunset Strip. Los Angeles, however, has a special relationship with the art of the ad, having once been at the heart of the hand-painted billboard industry. Some of Hollywood's finest artists painted huge adverts, such as the colossal Marlboro Man, which towered over Sunset Strip for 16 years. Billboards were sometimes three-dimensional, a technique introduced in 1953 when Las Vegas's Sahara Hotel rented a billboard, erected a real swimming pool, and filled it with swimsuited models. During the 1960s the billboards were dominated by the music industry, with advertising space along Sunset Strip even being written into some rock stars' contracts.

The iconic Marlboro Man, dismantled in 1999, following the ban on tobacco advertising

A View of Sunset Boulevard: Old Studio District

During the first half of the 20th century, this 2-mile (3-km) stretch of Sunset Boulevard was the center of Hollywood's film industry. This historic district is located 1.2 miles (2 km) to the east of the fashionable nightlife and boutiques of Sunset Strip (see pp106–108). Major studios, including 20th Century Fox, RKO, Warner Bros., Paramount, and United Artists, were all in the vicinity, and the streets were filled with directors, actors, and would-be film stars. In the area known as Gower Gulch, low-budget outfits churned out Westerns by the score.

Sunset Boulevard during its heyday in the 1940s

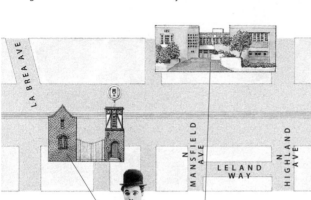

Jim Henson Company
These buildings, stretching from the southeast corner of Sunset Boulevard down La Brea Avenue, were constructed by Charlie Chaplin as homes for workers at his studio.

Crossroads of the World
Hollywood's first shopping mall, built in 1936, is located at No. 6621. Designed to resemble an ocean liner, with a globe-topped tower on its prow, it has now been converted into offices.

Hollywood High School
A long list of famous alumni have attended Hollywood High School, at No. 6800, including Lana Turner. The actress was first discovered in 1936 by director Mervyn LeRoy, sipping a soda in the now-defunct Top Hat Malt Shop. Its site, opposite the school, is now occupied by a garage.

Old Studio District continued

Hollywood Athletic Club
Stars of the 1930s and 1940s exercised here. *Flash Gordon* star Buster Crabbe trained here before winning a gold medal at the 1932 Olympics.

ArcLight Cinerama Dome
The distinctive dome of No. 6360 was the first wide-screen movie theater on the West Coast.

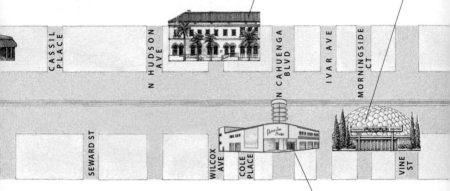

Time Capsule

In 1954 the Los Angeles Chamber of Commerce decided to preserve the history of Hollywood with a time capsule. A copy of Bing Crosby's hit record "White Christmas," released that year, a script of the most successful film made to date, *Gone With the Wind*, and various contemporary radio and television tapes were deposited under the sidewalk at the famous intersection between Sunset Boulevard and Vine Street. The time capsule was retrieved 50 years after it was planted, in 2004.

Singer Bing Crosby

A sidewalk plaque marking the site notes that the legend of Hollywood was born here in 1913 with the making of the first feature-length film, *The Squaw Man*, by Cecil B De Mille and Jesse Lasky. The actual location of their barn studio, now preserved on North Highland Avenue *(see p116)*, was farther up the block at No. 1521 Vine Street. Hollywood had also been incorporated as a town ten years earlier and numerous short films had been made here during that decade.

Poster of *Gone With the Wind* (1939)

Amoeba Music
The world's largest independent record store at No. 6400 is a Hollywood landmark. It houses a hugely diverse collection of music and movies.

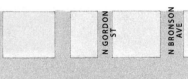

Hollywood Palladium
Norman Chandler, of the *Los Angeles Times* dynasty, built this theater and dance hall at No. 6215. It was opened by Lana Turner in 1940, when Frank Sinatra gave a concert here.

Warner Bros. Studio
The first talkie, Al Jolson's *The Jazz Singer* (1927), was made here at No. 5858. The following year the studio moved to Burbank *(see p149)*. The building now houses local radio stations.

Gower Gulch
In the 1930s, Gower Street earned the name "Gower Gulch" because of all the extras in cowboy costumes. Today, the Gower Gulch strip mall sits on the southwest corner of Sunset and Gower. An actual chuck wagon *(see left)* remains as a reminder of that era.

Sunset Boulevard Theatre
Showman Earl Carroll's Vanities Theater originally occupied this site at No. 6220 in the 1940s. It had the world's largest revolving stage, which held 60 dancers.

Visitors' Tip

This section of Sunset Boulevard, east of Vine St, was run down and frequented by drug dealers and prostitutes for many years. The gentrification of Hollywood has made a positive impact, however, and visitors need only observe the rules for safety as in any large city. Lock your car, keep your wallet in an inconspicuous place, and do not wear valuable jewelry.

A View of Hollywood Boulevard

Hollywood Boulevard is one of the most famous streets in the world, and its name is still redolent with glamor. Visitors wishing to recapture a Golden Age of film should visit the TCL Chinese Theatre and its autograph patio, and stroll down the Walk of Fame to spot the stars of icons such as Marilyn Monroe. World premieres of Disney films at the El Capitan Theatre often feature a live revue by the Magic Kingdom®'s favorite characters. Other attractions include Madame Tussaud's™, the Hollywood Guinness World of Records Museum, Ripley's Believe It or Not!®, and the Dolby Theatre, home of the Academy Awards®.

Locator Map
See Street Finder map 2

Madame Tussaud's™ has branches all over the world, and this site focuses on Hollywood stars. To create many of the figures, Tussaud's brought the celebrities in and measured them using computers, to make life-size, meticulously crafted wax figures, which are set up to make close-up viewing and photos easy.

The Dolby Theatre, home to the Academy Awards®, has hosted a range of stars including Celine Dion and Prince.

TCL Chinese Theatre

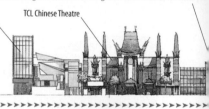

Hollywood Boulevard North Side

❻ ★ **Walk of Fame**
Marilyn Monroe's star is embedded in the sidewalk at No. 6776 Hollywood Boulevard. The camera symbol below her name indicates her career as a film actress.

MARILYN MONROE

Hollywood Guinness World of Records Museum uses models, videos, and special effects to bring record-breaking achievements alive. It is housed in the area's first movie theater.

Ripley's Believe It or Not!® is a museum devoted to the bizarre. The building, topped by a model *Tyrannosaurus rex*, contains more than 300 exhibits, such as shrunken heads and two-headed calves.

Hollywood Boulevard South Side

Key

►►►►►► North Side walking east

◄◄◄◄◄◄ South Side walking west

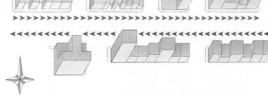

0 meters _____ 200
0 yards _____ 200

First National Bank marks the junction with Highland Avenue. Its tiered facade is decorated with stone reliefs of historical figures such as Christopher Columbus and Nicolaus Copernicus.

❹ **Hollywood and Highland** is great for retail shops and entertainment.

❸ ★ **TCL Chinese Theatre**
Stars' autographs fill the forecourt.

❶ **The Hollywood Roosevelt Hotel**
An image of the actor Charlie Chaplin (1889–1977) decorates the wall of this 1920s hotel.

❺ **El Capitan Theatre**
Neon lights welcome filmgoers to this beautifully restored Art Deco theater. Movies can be seen in old-fashioned comfort, but with state-of-the-art sound.

The old Masonic Hall is now a TV studio owned by Disney.

Sid Grauman's famous TCL Chinese Theatre

❶ The Hollywood Roosevelt Hotel

7000 Hollywood Blvd. **Map** 2 B4.
Tel (323) 856-1970, (844) 340-1927.
🚻 W **thehollywoodroosevelt.com**
See *Where to Stay p529*.

Named after US president Theodore Roosevelt, this hotel was opened in 1927 by joint owners Louis B Mayer, Mary Pickford, Marcus Loewe, Douglas Fairbanks, Sr., and Joseph Schenk. Marilyn Monroe, Ernest Hemingway, and Clark Gable were all visitors and, on May 16, 1929, the first Academy Awards® banquet was held in the Roosevelt's Blossom Room.

Renovations in 1986 revealed a Spanish Colonial design. The following year the pool was decorated by David Hockney *(see p32)*. The Hollywood Historical Review exhibition documents the area's history.

The Hollywood Roosevelt Hotel, locale for the first Academy Awards®

❷ Madame Tussaud's™ Hollywood

6933 Hollywood Blvd. **Map** 2 B4.
Tel (323) 798-1670. **Open** 10am–8pm daily (last admission 7pm); late May–early Sep: 10am–10pm (last admission 9pm). **Closed** Academy Awards® day.
🚻 W **madametussauds.com**

Madame Tussaud's™ Hollywood is the ninth location for the Madame Tussaud's franchise. The three-story structure features wax figures of hot Hollywood icons and stars including Johnny Depp, Nicole Kidman, Denzel Washington, Clarke Gable, James Dean, and Audrey Hepburn. Sports figures, pop stars, and movie characters are also represented. Over 80 figures are displayed in 11 themed areas, including The Red Carpet, and visitors can touch the figures and take photos with them.

❸ TCL Chinese Theatre

6925 Hollywood Blvd. **Map** 2 B4.
Tel (323) 461-3331. **Open** daily. 🚻
🚻 W **tclchinesetheatres.com**

One of the most famous sights in Hollywood has not changed much since it opened in 1927 with the gala premiere of Cecil B De Mille's *King of Kings*. The exterior is an ornate medley of Chinese temples, pagodas, lions, and dragons, reflecting the keen sense of showmanship of the theater's creator, Sid Grauman. Grauman also thought up one of the longest-running publicity stunts in Hollywood history: inviting movie stars to impress their handprints, footprints, and autographs in the cement courtyard of his theater. There are many versions of how this custom began. One tells of silent screen star Norma Talmadge accidentally stepping in the wet cement at the gala opening *(see p57)*. Another is that the French stonemason, Jean Klossner, put his hand in the wet cement for posterity. Whatever the precedent, Sid Grauman liked the idea and invited Norma Talmadge, Mary Pickford, and Douglas Fairbanks, Sr. to legitimately leave their mark in the cement on May 17, 1927.

Anyone can visit the courtyard, but only filmgoers can see the extravagant interior.

❹ Hollywood and Highland

6801 Hollywood Boulevard.
Map 2 B4. **Tel** (323) 467 6412.
Open 10am–10pm Mon–Sat, 10am–7pm Sun. 🅿 🚻
W **hollywoodandhighland.com**

Opened after a major refurbishment of this once-neglected area, this shopping and entertainment complex features restaurants, clubs, retail shops, a hotel, and a cinema. Visitors can also see a play or concert and take a tour of the **Dolby Theatre**, the home of the Academy Awards® ceremonies.

❺ El Capitan Theatre

6838 Hollywood Blvd. **Map** 2 B4.
Tel (818) 845-3110. **Open** daily.
🎦 **w** elcapitantheatre.com

Built in 1926 as a legitimate theater, El Capitan was later converted to a movie house. It was the venue for many premieres, such as Orson Welles's *Citizen Kane* (1941). In 1942 El Capitan was renamed the Hollywood Paramount and in 1991 it was bought by Disney and Pacific Theaters who restored the Art Deco interior. Today, Disney feature animations open here.

Some of the marble stars on The Walk of Fame

❻ Walk of Fame

Map 2 B4. ℹ️ 7018 Hollywood Blvd
Tel (323) 469-8311.
w walkoffame.com

The Walk of Fame is set with more than 2,000 polished marble stars. Since February 1960, celebrities from the worlds of film, radio, TV, theater, and music have been immortalized on Hollywood Boulevard and Vine Street. Each has to be sponsored and approved by the Chamber of Commerce, and pay a $25,000 installation fee. Among the most famous are Charlie Chaplin (No. 6751) and Alfred Hitchcock (No. 6506).

❼ The Hollywood Museum

1660 N Highland Ave. **Map** 2 B4.
Tel (323) 464-7776.
Open 10am–5pm Wed–Sun. ♿
w thehollywoodmuseum.com

This museum is housed in a restored 1930s Art Deco building, which was once make-up artist Max Factor's studios. Three floors display fabulous costumes worn in films by stars such as Marilyn Monroe, Judy Garland, Elizabeth Taylor, Humphrey Bogart, and Jodie Foster. The collectibles exhibition displays Sylvester Stallone's boxing gloves and WC Field's top hat among other oddities. The basement contains Hannibal Lecter's entire prison cell.

Tours of the museum are available by reservation only. Call (323) 464-7770 at least three days in advance to book a tour.

❽ Hollywood Bowl

2301 N Highland Ave. **Map** 2 B3.
Tel (323) 850-2000. **Open** late Jun–late Sep. 🎦 ♿ Box office:
Open 10am–6pm Tue–Sun.
Hollywood Bowl Museum: **Tel** (323) 850-2058. **Open** noon–6pm Tue–Sun.
w hollywoodbowl.com

Situated in a natural amphitheater, once revered by the Cahuenga Pass Gabrielino people, the Bowl is now sacred to Angelenos. Since 1922 it has been the summer home of the LA Philharmonic.

Thousands gather on warm evenings to picnic – often in high style – under the stars and listen to the orchestra. Jazz, country, folk, and pop concerts are also performed here while popular events include the Fourth of July concert with fireworks, the Easter Sunrise Service, and a Tchaikovsky Spectacular with cannons, fireworks, and a military band.

The shell-shaped stage was originally designed in 1929 by Lloyd Wright, son of architect Frank Lloyd Wright, and the Bowl and its privately-owned front-row boxes seat 18,000 people.

The Hollywood Bowl Museum explores the rich history of the Bowl, through videos, old programs and posters, and memorabilia of the artists who have come here to perform, from violinist Jascha Heifetz to The Beatles.

Hollywood Bowl, nestled in the Hollywood Hills

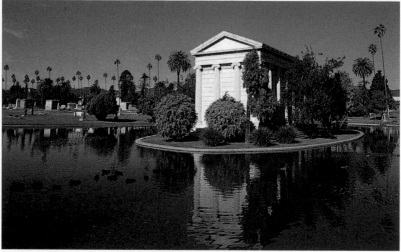

Mausoleum of William A Clark, Jr. in Hollywood Forever Cemetery

9 Hollywood Heritage Museum

2100 N Highland Ave. **Map** 2 B3.
Tel (323) 874-2276. **Open** noon–4pm
Wed–Sun. 🅿 ♿ 📷
🌐 **hollywoodheritage.org**

In 1913, Cecil B De Mille and
the Jesse L Lasky Feature Play
Company rented this barn, then
located on Vine Street, just north
of Sunset Boulevard. That year De
Mille used the building to make
The Squaw Man, the first feature-
length movie produced in
Hollywood. In 1935 the company
was renamed Paramount Pictures.

The barn was moved to its
present site, in the parking lot of
the Hollywood Bowl *(see p115)*,
in 1983. Thirteen years later
a fire prompted a major
renovation, and the barn was
turned into a museum,
displaying props, costumes,
photographs, and other
memorabilia from the early
days of filmmaking.

10 Pantages Theater

6233 Hollywood Blvd. **Map** 2 C4.
Tel (323) 468-1770. **Open** daily.
🅿 ♿ 🌐 **hollywoodpantages.com**

To attend a show at the
Pantages is to experience the
glory days of the 1930s movie
palaces. Built in 1929, the
marble and bronze Art Deco

theater catered to the comfort
of its audience, with a spacious
foyer and luxurious lounges.
It opened in 1930 with *The
Floradora Girl*, starring Marion
Davies, the mistress of WR
Hearst *(see p218)*. Between
1949 and 1959 the Academy
Awards Ceremony was also
held here.

Splendidly renovated in the
1980s, today Pantages is used
to stage Broadway musicals.
Only show ticket holders are
allowed into the breathtaking
interior, with its magnificent
chandeliers, vaulted ceilings,
and columns decorated with
geometric patterns.

Stylish Art Deco facade of the
Pantages Theater

11 Hollywood Forever Cemetery

6000 Santa Monica Blvd. **Map** 8 C1.
Tel (323) 469-1181. **Open** 8am–5pm
Mon–Fri; 8:30am–4:30pm Sat–Sun.
Closed public hols. ♿
🌐 **hollywoodforever.com**

The map of this cemetery
(available at the front office)
reads like a history of film.
Tyrone Power has a white
memorial overlooking a pond
on the eastern side. Next to him,
the mausoleum of Marion
Davies bears her family name of
Douras. Cecil B De Mille, Nelson
Eddy, and many others from
Hollywood's heyday are buried
here. Douglas Fairbanks Sr.'s
grave has a reflecting pool and
monument, reputed to have
been paid for by his ex-wife, the
silent film star Mary Pickford.
Inside the gloomy Cathedral
Mausoleum is the tomb of
Rudolph Valentino, still the
cemetery's biggest attraction.
Every year, on August 23, a
"Lady in Black" pays her respects
to the actor on the anniversary
of his death.

The back of Paramount
Studios forms the southern
wall of the cemetery, and
Columbia used to be to the
north. Columbia boss Harry
Cohn is said to have picked his
plot so that he could keep an
eye on his studio.

⑫ Paramount Studios

5555 Melrose Ave. **Map** 8 C1. **Tel** (323) 956-5000. Visitors' Center and Ticket Window: 860 N Gower St. **Tel** (323) 956-1777. **Open** for tours: 9am–6pm Mon–Fri (reservations only). **Closed** Jan 1, Easter Sun, Thanksgiving, Dec 25. **W** paramountstudiotour.com

The last major studio still located in Hollywood, Paramount was also the first in operation. Cecil B. De Mille, Jesse Lasky, and Samuel Goldwyn joined forces with Adolph Zukor in 1914 to form what became known as the directors' studio. The roster of stars was equally impressive: Gloria Swanson, Rudolph Valentino, Mae West, Marlene Dietrich, Gary Cooper, and Bing Crosby all signed with Paramount.

Aspiring actors still hug the wrought-iron gates at Bronson Avenue and Marathon Street. Seeking luck, they quote Norma Desmond's final line in *Sunset Boulevard*: "I'm ready for my close-up, Mr. De Mille."

Classics such as *The Ten Commandments*, *The War of the Worlds*, *The Greatest Show on Earth*, and the *Godfather Parts I, II*, and *III* were all made in Paramount's 63 acres (25 ha) of backlot and sound stages. Three available tour options include the Studio Tour, VIP Studio Tour, and Paramount After Dark Tour. These tours give visitors a behind-the-scenes view of the past and present legacy of the Paramount Studios.

Melrose Avenue

Once a bland avenue, Melrose burst onto the Los Angeles street scene in the mid-1980s with quirky shops and good restaurants. The prime area stretches for 16 blocks between La Brea and Fairfax avenues, providing a rare opportunity to walk and shop outdoors in the city. From Fifties to punk to classic, the clothing, shoe, and accessory boutiques offer a wide range of styles and goods and stay open until late *(see pp172–3)*. The same can also be said of the avenue's many restaurants, which represent the diverse ethnic flavors of Los Angeles. Mexican and Thai are two of the favorite cuisines, but pasta and pizza dominate the street, as they do the rest of the city.

Colorful shop window on Melrose Avenue

At the western end of Melrose, at San Vincente Boulevard, is the huge 600-ft (183-m) high blue-glass Pacific Design Center, known to the locals as the Blue Whale. Designed by César Pelli in 1975, this showcase for interior designers and architects is the largest on the West Coast. Although it caters mainly to trade, the center also welcomes the general public. Admission charges and purchasing policies may vary between individual showrooms.

⑬ Farmers Market

6333 W 3rd St. **Map** 7 D3. **Tel** (323) 933-9211. **Open** 9am–9pm Mon–Fri, 9am–8pm Sat, 10am–7pm Sun. **Closed** Jan 1, Easter Sun, Memorial Day, Jul 4, Labor Day, Thanksgiving, Dec 25. 🚻 **W** farmersmarketla.com

In 1934, during the Great Depression *(see p57)*, a group of farmers began selling their produce directly to the public in a field then at the edge of town. Since then, Farmers Market has become a favorite meeting place for Angelenos and tourists. There are stalls

Clock tower at the entrance to Farmers Market

selling fresh flowers, meats, cheeses, fruit, vegetables, breads, and gourmet foods. There are also more than 100 shops that sell everything from antiques to T-shirts and garden supplies. Among the best of the numerous cafés and restaurants are Bob's Donuts, Magee's Kitchen for roast or corned beef, turkey, and ham platters; and The Gumbo Pot, with sweet *beignets* (dough fritters) and traditional Cajun food. Next to the market complex is The Grove, a deluxe retail complex with shops, restaurants, and cinema.

Poster for Paramount's *The War of the Worlds* (1953)

⑭ Los Angeles County Museum of Art

The largest art museum west of Chicago, the Los Angeles County Museum of Art (LACMA) has one of the finest collections of art in the naiton and boasts the stunning Broad Contemporary Art Museum, built to exhibit the comprehensive private collection of contemporary art donated by its billionaire founder and art connoisseur Eli Broad. The world-renowned architect Renzo Piano designed the building and has been supervising the overhaul of the entire museum campus, which consists of nine museum venues along Wilshire Boulevard from the La Brea Tar Pits in Hancock Park to Fairfax Avenue. Due to ongoing updating, specific works of art may change location or be on loan to other galleries.

★ **In the Woods at Giverny**
This work of 1887, subtitled "Blanche Hoschedé at her easel with Suzanne Hoschedé reading," depicts the daughters of Monet's mistress.

★ **Soap Bubbles** (after 1739)
Parisian artist Jean-Baptiste-Siméon Chardin's work predominantly depicts small scenes of domestic life such as this.

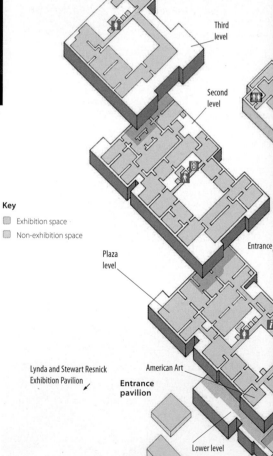

Third level

Second level

Key

▢ Exhibition space

▢ Non-exhibition space

Plaza level

Entrance

The Hope Athena
This marble statue is a 2nd-century AD Roman copy of the 5th-century BC Greek original.

Lynda and Stewart Resnick Exhibition Pavilion ↗

American Art

Entrance pavilion

LACMA West ↙

Lower level

Broad Contemporary Art Museum Building

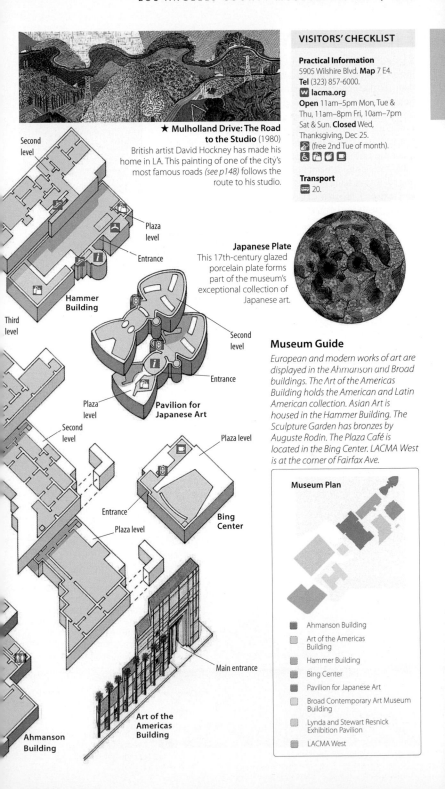

★ **Mulholland Drive: The Road to the Studio** (1980)
British artist David Hockney has made his home in LA. This painting of one of the city's most famous roads *(see p148)* follows the route to his studio.

VISITORS' CHECKLIST

Practical Information
5905 Wilshire Blvd. **Map** 7 E4.
Tel (323) 857-6000.
W lacma.org
Open 11am–5pm Mon, Tue & Thu, 11am–8pm Fri, 10am–7pm Sat & Sun. **Closed** Wed, Thanksgiving, Dec 25.
(free 2nd Tue of month).

Transport
20.

Japanese Plate
This 17th-century glazed porcelain plate forms part of the museum's exceptional collection of Japanese art.

Museum Guide

European and modern works of art are displayed in the Ahmanson and Broad buildings. The Art of the Americas Building holds the American and Latin American collection. Asian Art is housed in the Hammer Building. The Sculpture Garden has bronzes by Auguste Rodin. The Plaza Café is located in the Bing Center. LACMA West is at the corner of Fairfax Ave.

Second level
Plaza level
Entrance
Hammer Building
Third level

Second level
Entrance
Pavilion for Japanese Art
Plaza level

Second level
Plaza level
Entrance
Plaza level
Bing Center

Main entrance
Art of the Americas Building
Ahmanson Building

Museum Plan

- ■ Ahmanson Building
- □ Art of the Americas Building
- ■ Hammer Building
- ■ Bing Center
- ■ Pavilion for Japanese Art
- □ Broad Contemporary Art Museum Building
- □ Lynda and Stewart Resnick Exhibition Pavilion
- ■ LACMA West

Exploring LACMA

A tour of LACMA offers a comprehensive survey of the history of art throughout the world. The museum has more than 100,000 objects that represent many cultures, dating from prehistoric to modern and contemporary periods. Ancient art treasures encompass pre-Columbian finds as well as the largest Islamic art collection in the western United States. Decorative arts, which include European and American pieces from medieval times to the present, are exhibited alongside paintings and sculpture from the same period. The museum also has a superb collection of costumes and textiles. A program of world-class traveling exhibitions complements the permanent collection.

Magdalen with the Smoking Flame (c.1640) by Georges de la Tour

American Art

The collection of paintings traces the history of American art from the 1700s to the 1940s. Dating from the Colonial period are John Singleton Copley's *Portrait of a Lady* (1771) and Benjamin West's *Cymon and Iphigenia* (1773).

In the mid-1800s, American artists such as Edwin Church (1826–1900), Winslow Homer (1836–1910), and Thomas Moran (1837–1926) turned from portrait painting and Classical subjects to landscapes. The Realist painter George Bellows (1882–1925) depicted urban life in New York City in his paintings, such as *Cliff Dwellers* (1913). Notable Impressionist works include Childe Hassam's *Avenue of the Allies* (1918) and Mary Cassat's *Mother About to Wash her Sleepy Child* (1880). Decorative arts range from Chippendale and Federal-style furniture to lamps by Louis Comfort Tiffany (1848–1933).

Monument to Balzac, sculpted in the 1890s by Auguste Rodin

European Painting, Sculpture, and Decorative Arts

The collection of European works of art spans the 12th to early 20th centuries, beginning with medieval religious objects. Fine portraits by Lucas Cranach (1472–1553) and Hans Holbein (1497–1543) represent the Northern Renaissance. Religious paintings by Fra Bartolommeo (1472–1517) and Titian (c.1490–1576) date from the Italian Renaissance.

One of the European collection's strengths is its 17th-century Dutch and Flemish canvases. Rembrandt's *The Raising of Lazarus* (c.1630) and Anthony van Dyck's *Andromeda Chained to the Rock* (1637–8) are among the highlights. Works displayed from the French and Italian schools include Georges de la Tour's *Magdalen with the Smoking Flame,* painted around 1640, and Guido Reni's *Portrait of Cardinal Roberto Ubaldino,* which dates from before 1625. The French collections from the 18th and 19th centuries are also impressive, with works by Eugène Delacroix (1798–1863) and Camille Corot (1796–1875). The sculpture collection concentrates mostly on 19th-century French artists, with more than 40 works by Auguste Rodin (1840–1917).

Two highlights of the Impressionist and Post-Impressionist collection are *In the Woods at Giverny* by Claude Monet *(see p118)* and Edgar Degas' *The Bellelli Sisters* (1862–4). Others include paintings by Pierre Auguste Renoir (1841–1919), Vincent van Gogh (1853–90), and Paul Cézanne (1839–1906).

Among the finest decorative arts pieces are a Venetian enameled and gilded blue glass ewer, dating from about 1500, and a mid-16th-century Limoges plaque that depicts Psyche and Cupid.

The Cotton Pickers (1876) by Winslow Homer

Modern and Contemporary Art

The Broad Contemporary Art Museum on the LACMA campus is a bright, airy home for contemporary art displayed for its fullest impact, no matter what its size or shape. The building itself is a piece of art, funded by the Los Angeles philanthropist Eli Broad. It houses some 200 pieces from his own cutting-edge collection, plus LACMA's own growing assemblage of modern holdings, and visiting collections. Its span covers painting, sculpture, and installations ranging from 1945 to the present. Works include Richard Serra's *Band* (2006), John Baldessari's *Wrong* (1966–68), and Roy Lichtenstein's *Cold Shoulder* (1963).

Photography, Prints, and Drawings

The museum's outstanding photography holdings give a rare overview of the medium. Exhibits range from early 19th-century daguerreotypes and albumen prints to abstract mixed media images. A large group of works by Edward Weston (1886–1958) is filled with texture and sensuality.

LACMA's holdings of prints and drawings includes the Robert Gore Rifkind Collection of German Expressionist works. Erich Heckel's woodcut, *Standing Child* (1910), is just one of its outstanding prints.

Ancient and Islamic Art

The ancient art of Egypt, western Asia, Iran, Greece, and Rome make up an impressive collection of artifacts. Items include massive carved stone panels from a 9th-century BC Assyrian palace; a rare Egyptian bronze from the 25th Dynasty; and delicate Iranian figures, some dating from 3,000 BC. The Islamic art collection spans almost 1,400 years. Its Iranian and Turkish holdings are particularly strong.

Carved stone objects and ceramic vessels and statues from Central America and Peru comprise the pre-Columbian holdings. *Standing Warrior* (100 BC–AD 300), a Mexican effigy, is the largest known work of its kind.

Indian and Southeast Asian Art

With more than 5,000 works dating from the 3rd century BC, the museum has one of the most comprehensive collections outside Asia. It is especially strong in Indian arts, from splendid sculpture to intricate watercolors on cloth and paper. There are manuscripts and *thankas* (paintings on cloth) from Tibet and Nepal, and stone and bronze sculptures from Indonesia, Thailand, Sri Lanka, Cambodia, and Myanmar (Burma).

Pair of Officials (618–907), from the Tang dynasty, China

Far Eastern Art

This section includes fine ceramics, sculpture, screens, and scrolls from China, Japan, and Korea. The highlight, however, is the Shin'enkan Collection which features 200 screens and scroll paintings from the Edo period (1615–1868). These examples are considered to be the most outstanding in the Western world. Masterpieces include Ito Jakuchu's 18th-century hanging scroll, *Rooster, Hen and Hydrangea*, and Suzuki Kiitsu's 19th-century *Seashells and Plums*. The Bushell Collection of *netsukes* (carved toggles used to secure a small container), ceramics, sculpture, and wood-block prints is also impressive.

Costumes and Textiles

An encyclopedia of clothing and textiles, the collection boasts some 55,000 artifacts that represent more than 300 of the world's cultures. The oldest pieces are embroidered Peruvian burial shrouds that date from 100 BC and an Egyptian Coptic tunic from the 5th century AD. One of the most important pieces is the early 16th-century Iranian "Ardebil" carpet, named after a shrine in northwest Iran for which it was commissioned. A French noblewoman's gown, made from silk, gold, and silver, is one of only two complete 17th-century dresses in the US.

Dunes, Oceano (1936) by Edward Weston

⓯ Miracle Mile

Wilshire Blvd between La Brea & Fairfax Aves. **Map** 7 D4. ℹ 685 S Figueroa St (213) 689-8822; 6801 Hollywood Blvd (323) 467-6412.
w discoverlosangeles.com

In 1920, the developer A W Ross bought 18 acres (7.2 ha) of land along Wilshire Boulevard and built a shopping district aimed at the wealthy families living in nearby Hancock Park. With its Art Deco and Streamline Moderne buildings, wide sidewalks and streets built for cars rather than carriages, it earned the nickname "Miracle Mile." The suburban department stores were designed with parking lots, a convenience that attracted hordes of shoppers from the city. It was the start of LA's decentralization.

Today, this stretch of boulevard is still a shopping area, but grocery stores catering to various ethnic communities have replaced the department stores.

At the western end of the Miracle Mile, anchoring the corner of Fairfax Avenue, is the Streamline Moderne former May Company department store building, which is currently being converted into The Academy Museum of Motion Pictures, due to open in 2017. Due to LACMA *(see pp118–21)* and several other major museums in the vicinity, the area has become known as Museum Row.

Gold facade of the 1939 May Company building on Wilshire Boulevard

Round-door Rolls Royce at the Petersen Automotive Museum

⓰ Petersen Automotive Museum

6060 Wilshire Blvd. **Map** 7 D4. **Tel** (323) 930-2277. **Open** 10am–6pm Tue–Sun. **Closed** Jan 1, Thanksgiving, Dec 25. ♿ ♿ ♿ ♿
w petersen.org

Dioramas and temporary exhibitions illustrate the evolution of the United States' car culture *(see pp204–5)*. On the first floor there are highly detailed displays featuring cars such as the 1911 American Underslung "Stuck in the Mud" and Earl Cooper's 1915 "White Squadron" Stutz Racer. A 1922 Ford Model-T is shown in a scene from a Laurel and Hardy film, and a trio of beautiful vintage cars appear in a 1920s street setting.

Other displays include a 1920s garage; a 1930s car showroom, whose opulence defied the Depression; and a 1950s drive-in restaurant. A 1930s billboard shows how advertising was used to boost the popularity of the car.

Upstairs, five galleries showcase everything from hot rods and motorcycles to vintage classics and cars of the stars. Vehicles that fall into the last category are Rita Hayworth's 1953 Cadillac and Clark Gable's 1941 Cadillac Coupe.

⓱ The Improv

8162 Melrose Ave. **Map** 7 D1. **Tel** (323) 651-2583. **Open** 8pm Mon–Fri, 8:30pm & 10:30pm Sat & Sun. ♿ ♿ **w** hollywood.improv.com

When it opened in 1975, the Improv immediately became one of the finest comedy clubs in town, and today it is known throughout the world. Famous names such as Jay Leno, Richard Lewis, and Damon Wayans have appeared here and top comedians perform regularly. The club is also a great place to see talented newcomers, many of whom may have glittering careers ahead.

Food is available in the showroom and the restaurant, and the menu features burgers, pasta, steak, sandwiches, and more. A minimum of two items have to be ordered in the showroom.

Given the club's popularity, it is best to book a table well in advance.

Popular comedian Drew Carey performing at the Improv club

⓲ Page Museum at the La Brea Tar Pits

5801 Wilshire Blvd. **Map** 7 E4. **Tel** (323) 934-7243. **Open** 9:30am–5pm daily. **Closed** Jan 1, Jul 4, Thanksgiving, Dec 25. ♿ (free first Tue of month.) ♿ ♿ ♿ **w** tarpits.org

Opened in 1976, the Page Museum has a collection of more than one million fossils that were discovered at the La Brea Tar Pits. These include more than 500 types of mammals, birds, reptiles, plants, and

La Brea Tar Pits

The tar in the La Brea Pits was formed some 42,000 years ago by oil rising to the earth's surface and gelling. Animals entering the pits to drink the water became stuck in the tar and died. Their bones were then fossilized.

For centuries the tar was used by Gabrielino people to waterproof baskets and boats. Later, Mexican and Spanish settlers tarred their roofs with it. In 1906 geologists discovered the largest collection of fossils from the Pleistocene Epoch ever found in one place, and the pits began to attract greater attention. The land was deeded to the county in 1916.

Models at the La Brea Tar Pits depicting how animals were trapped

insects. Some of the pieces date back around 40,000 years. Among the highlights are mastodons, saber-toothed tigers, American lions, and an imperial mammoth. The display of more than 400 wolf skulls shows just how much variation can occur within a single species.

The only human skeleton to have been found in the pits is that of the "La Brea Woman." A hologram changes her from a skeleton to a fully fleshed person and back again.

Pit 91 has produced most of the fossils. During the summer, visitors on the viewing station can watch paleontologists at work. Inside the museum, a glass-walled laboratory allows observation of the cleaning and identification of the fossils.

⑲ Craft and Folk Art Museum

5814 Wilshire Blvd. **Map** 7 E4. **Tel** (323) 937-4230. **Open** 11am–5pm Tue–Fri, noon–6pm Sat & Sun. **Closed** Jan 1, Thanksgiving, Dec 25. 🚫 🎫 (Wed). ♿ 🌐 **cafam.org**

The museum's collection has more than 3,000 folk art and craft objects from around the world, ranging from 19th-century American quilts to contemporary furniture, to African masks. There are also regular exhibitions on subjects such as toys, glassware, and textiles.

Mexican artworks here include papier-mâché pieces made by Mexico City's Linares family.

A series of special exhibitions is held throughout the year, and regular art talks, workshops, and

other events are organized that appeal to people across different age groups.

African mask at the Craft Museum

⑳ Wiltern Theater

3790 Wilshire Blvd. **Map** 9 D4. **Tel** (213) 388-1400. **Open** performances only. 🚫 ♿ 🎫

Built as a movie theater in 1931, the Wiltern Theater was restored in 1985 and is a center for the performing arts. Its Art Deco tower and wings are faced with turquoise-glazed terra-cotta, and its main entrance is marked by a sunburst canopy. The sun motif continues in the auditorium, where rays of low-relief skyscrapers decorate the interior ceiling.

To see inside the Wiltern Theater visitors must buy a ticket to a show.

Mammoth skeleton at the Page Museum

DOWNTOWN LOS ANGELES

Considered a backwater a little over a hundred years ago, Downtown Los Angeles has confounded its critics by becoming a powerful worldwide influence. The city's Spanish roots are here, at El Pueblo, where the Avila Adobe and Old Plaza Church stand as reminders of Mexican frontier days, when *rancheros* and their *señoras* strolled through the streets. To the north of El Pueblo is Chinatown, with its numerous Asian shops and restaurants. To the south, Little Tokyo is the heart of the largest Japanese-American community in North America. Downtown's business district is centered around Bunker Hill, once a wealthy neighborhood where the city's Victorian elite lived. Today, office towers such as the First Interstate World Center and the Wells Fargo Center dominate the Downtown landscape. The district is also home to the Museum of Contemporary Art (MOCA) and the Music Center for the performing arts.

Sights at a Glance

Historic Districts and Buildings
1 Los Angeles Central Library
2 Angels Flight
3 Grand Central Market
5 Bradbury Building
8 El Pueblo pp130–31
9 Chinatown
10 Union Station
12 Los Angeles City Hall
13 Little Tokyo

Museums and Galleries
4 The Broad
6 Museum of Contemporary Art
11 Geffen Contemporary at MOCA
14 Japanese American National Museum
15 Fashion Institute of Design and Merchandising

Arts Complexes
7 Walt Disney Concert Hall

Churches
16 Cathedral of Our Lady of the Angels

See also LA Street Finder maps 10 & 11

| 0 meters | 500 |
| 0 yards | 500 |

e beautiful inlaid-tiled dome rotunda of Los Angeles City Hall

For keys to symbols see back flap

Street-by-Street: Business District

The 20th century saw LA expand west toward the ocean, temporarily relegating Downtown to a minor role in the city. All that has changed. Today a revitalized business district has developed around Flower Street, and the sidewalks are once more filled with tourists and Angelenos alike. California's banking industry has its headquarters here, housed in striking skyscrapers such as the Wells Fargo Center. The revival has continued eastward across Downtown, where the jewelry, toy, food, and garment wholesale industries are flourishing. A commitment to the arts has also borne fruit. The Museum of Contemporary Art (MOCA), Music Center, and Los Angeles Central Library have together encouraged a thriving cultural environment that has drawn people back to the city's center.

The Westin Bonaventure Hotel has external elevators with views of the business district.

The US Bank Tower, a 73-story office block designed by I M Pei, opened in 1989. At 1,017 ft (310 m) it is the tallest building in LA.

Fine Arts Building

7th Street/ Metro Center

Ⓜ

SOUTH FLOWER STREET

SOUTH HOPE STREET

WEST SIXTH STREET

WEST SEVENTH STREET

❶ ★ **Los Angeles Central Library**
The beautiful Beaux-Arts library is decorated with carvings and inscriptions based on the theme "the Light of Learning".

The James Oviatt Building (1925) is a marvelous example of Art Deco styling. René Lalique made some of the glass.

The Millennium Biltmore Hotel was one of LA's most luxurious hotels when it opened in 1923 *(see p528).*

❺ ★ Museum of Contemporary Art
Located off California Plaza, MOCA's sandstone building was greeted with acclaim when it opened in 1986. The collection gives an exciting overview of post-1940 art.

Locator Map
See Street Finder map 11

The Wells Fargo Center, the LA branch of this California company *(see p318)*, has a museum and sculpture court, with works by artists such as Jean Dubuffet.

❷ Angels Flight
The funicular runs from South Hill Street to California Plaza.

SOUTH GRAND AVENUE

SOUTH OLIVE STREET

SOUTH HILL STREET

WEST FOURTH STREET

WEST FIFTH STREET

SOUTH BROADWAY

Pershing Square
Metro station

❸ Grand Central Market
This indoor market lies at the heart of the movie theater district.

❹ ★ Bradbury Building
The atrium of this unassuming Victorian office block is one of the finest of its kind in the US.

Key
— Suggested route

Pershing Square was designated the city's first public park in 1866. The now-concreted square is still a popular meeting place and has been landscaped with trees, benches, and statuary.

| 0 meters | 500 |
| 0 yards | 500 |

Facade of the Los Angeles Central Library

❶ Los Angeles Central Library

630 W 5th St. **Map** 11 D4.
Tel (213) 228-7000. **Open** 10am–8pm
Mon–Thu, 10am–5:30pm Fri & Sat,
1–5pm Sun. **Closed** public hols.
🅰 🆆 lapl.org

Built in 1926, this civic treasure
was struck by an arson attack in
1986. It was closed for seven
years while a $213.9 million
renovation program was carried
out. Sympathetic to the
original architecture, the
improvements have
doubled the library's
capacity to more than
2.1 million books.

The original building
combines Beaux-Arts
grandeur with
Byzantine, Egyptian, and
Roman architectural
elements, inscriptions,
and sculpture on the
theme "the Light of
Learning." The murals in
the rotunda, painted by
Dean Cornwell (1892–
1960), depict the history
of California and are well
worth seeing.

The attention given to detail
in the Tom Bradley wing is
impressive. One example is the
three atrium chandeliers,
created by Therman Statom to
represent the natural, ethereal,
and technological worlds.

The Central Library's garden is
situated by the Flower Street
entrance. Weary sightseers
will appreciate its fountains,
sculptures, shaded benches,
and restaurant.

A varied program of arts events
takes place at the library, including prose and poetry readings,
lectures, concerts, and plays.

❷ Angels Flight

Between Grand, Hill, 3rd & 4th Sts.
Map 11 D4. **Tel** (213) 626-1901.
Closed check website for details.
🆆 angelsflight.org

Billed as the "shortest railway
in the world," Angels Flight
transported riders the 315 ft
(96 m) between Hill Street
and Bunker Hill for almost
70 years. Built in 1901, the
funicular quickly became
a familiar and much-loved
method of travel. But, by
1969, Bunker Hill had sadly
degenerated and was
considered an eyesore. The
city dismantled Angels
Flight, but promised to
reinstall the funicular once
the area had been re-
developed. It reopened
in 1996 but was closed
for almost a decade after
an accident. The funicular
is currently closed again
pending funding.

Statue, Central
Library

❸ Grand Central Market

317 S Broadway. **Map** 11 E4. **Tel** (213)
624-2378. **Open** 9am–6pm daily.
Closed Jan 1, Thanksgiving, Dec 25.
🅰 🆆 grandcentralsquare.com

Angelenos have been coming
to this vibrant indoor bazaar
since 1917. Today, more than

40 stallholders operate inside
the marketplace. Neatly
arranged mounds of bargain-
priced fresh fruits and
vegetables line the many
produce stands, and friendly
stallholders frequently offer
free samples of fruit.

Among the many cafés
and food stands in the market
is China Café, which has
been serving its popular
chow mein since the 1930s.
Mexican stalls, such as Ana
Maria, sell tacos and burritos,
which are filled with all
kinds of meat and seafood.
Visitors can enjoy watching
a rickety assembly-line
machine turn *masa* (corn flour
dough) into tortillas and then
partake of the free samples
on the counter.

Venturing from the market
onto Broadway, you will find
yourself on the main shopping
street of Los Angeles' Hispanic
community. Before World
War II, this was the movie
district, with extravagant
theaters and fashionable
shops. Today, most of the
theaters have either closed
down or are being used for
religious meetings conducted
in Spanish. The street has a
great deal of energy – the feel
is that of Mexico City or Lima,
Peru – but tourists should be
wary of pickpockets.

❹ The Broad

221 S Grand Ave. **Map** 11 D4.
Tel (213) 232-6200. **Open** 11am–
5pm Tue & Wed (to 8pm Thu & Fri),
10am–8pm Sat (to 6pm Sun).
🆆 thebroad.org

The Broad Museum features
almost 2,000 postwar and
contemporary artworks from
the collection of Eli and Edythe
Broad. The collection includes
works by Jasper Johns, Robert
Rauschenberg, Andy Warhol,
Ed Ruscha, Roy Lichtenstein,
Keith Haring, Jean-Michel
Basquiat, and Jeff Koons.
Stunning architecture and a
large public plaza with 100-
year-old Barouni olive trees
and an open lawn enhance this
addition to Grand Avenue.

For hotels and restaurants in this area see pp528–9 and p551

Atrium of the Bradbury Building

❺ Bradbury Building

304 S Broadway. **Map** 11 E4.
Tel (213) 626-1893. **Open** 9am–6pm
Mon–Fri, 9am–5pm Sat & Sun.
♿ from 3rd St.

The Bradbury Building was designed by architectural draftsman George Herbert Wyman in 1893. It is one of the few surviving Victorian structures in LA. Although the red facade is simple, the atrium is outstanding, with its lacework of wrought-iron railings, oak paneling, glazed brick walls, two open-cage elevators, and a glass roof. It is the only office building in LA to be designated a National Historic Landmark. Visitors may get a feeling of *déjà vu* – the building is a popular film location, with Ridley Scott's *Blade Runner* (1982) just one of the movies shot here.

❻ Museum of Contemporary Art

250 S Grand Ave. **Map** 11 D4.
Tel (213) 621-2766. **Open** 11am–5pm
Mon & Fri, 11am–8pm Thu, 11am–
6pm Sat & Sun. **Closed** Jan 1, Jul 4,
Thanksgiving, Dec 25. 📷 (free 5–
8pm Thu.) ♿ 🌐 **moca.org**

Rated by the American Institute of Architects as one of the best works of architecture in the US, the building of the Museum of Contemporary Art (MOCA) is as interesting as its collection. It is

an intriguing combination of pyramids, cylinders, and cubes, designed in 1986 by Japanese architect Arata Isozaki. Its warm native sandstone walls, which sit on a red granite foundation, are in pleasing contrast to the cool tones of the district's surrounding skyscrapers.

The gallery area lies off the sunken entrance courtyard and is reached via a sweeping staircase. Four of the seven galleries are naturally lit from pyramid-shaped skylights that punctuate the roofline.

Founded in 1979, MOCA has quickly amassed a respected selection of post-1940 work from artists such as Piet Mondrian, Jackson Pollock, Louise Nevelson, and Julian Schnabel. Added weight is given by the Panza Collection of 80 works of Pop Art and Abstract Expressionism by artists such as Robert Rauschenberg, Mark Rothko, and Claes Oldenburg.

In 1995, MOCA acquired the 2,100-print Freidus Collection of photographs, which traces the development of documentary photography in the United States from the 1940s through the 1980s. The collection includes works by Diane Arbus and Robert Frank.

MOCA stands at the northern end of the 11-acre (4.5-ha) California Plaza. This vast

Coca-Cola Plan (1958) by Robert Rauschenberg

development funded the creation of MOCA, donating 1.5 percent of its budget, as stipulated by LA law, to public art. The spectacular fountain at the center of the plaza repeats its synchronized program every 20 minutes. The finale drops a 10,000-gal (45,500-litre) wave that washes over the fountain edge.

❼ Walt Disney Concert Hall

135 N Grand Ave. **Map** 11 D3.
Tel (213) 972-7211. 📷 ♿ Dorothy
Chandler Pavilion box office:
Open 10am–6pm Thu–Sat.
Mark Taper Forum & Ahmanson
Theater box offices: **Open** noon–
8pm Tue–Sat, 11am–7pm Sun. Walt
Disney Concert Hall box office:
Open noon–5pm Tue–Sun.
🌐 **musiccenter.org**

The Music Center complex is one of the three largest performing arts venues in the US. The Walt Disney Concert Hall, designed by architect Frank Gehry, opened in 2003. This striking 2,265-seat venue is the home of the Los Angeles Philharmonic and Los Angeles Master Chorale. The Dorothy Chandler Pavilion is the venue for the Los Angeles Opera. The Ahmanson Theatre stages Broadway plays, while the intimate Mark Taper Forum presents innovative plays.

The Walt Disney Concert Hall designed by architect Frank Gehry

❽ Street-by-Street: El Pueblo

El Pueblo de la Reina de Los Angeles, the oldest part of the city, was founded in 1781 by Felipe de Neve, the Spanish governor of California. Today, El Pueblo is a State Historic Monument. The shops along Olvera Street sell colorful Mexican dresses, leather *huaraches* (sandals), *piñatas* (clay or paper-mâché animals), and snacks like *churros*, a Spanish-Mexican fried-dough pastry. During its festivals El Pueblo is ablaze with color and sound. The Blessing of the Animals (April), Cinco de Mayo (May 5), the Mexican Independence Day fiesta (September 13–15), and the candlelight procession of Las Posadas (December 16–24) are celebrated with passion *(see pp40–43)*.

★ Our Lady Queen of the Angels Church
The Annunciation (1981), a mosaic by Isabel Piczek, is on the city's oldest church's facade.

Pico House
California's last Mexican governor, Pío Pico, constructed the three-story Pico House in 1870. The colonial-style building was for many years the area's finest hotel. The ground floor is occasionally used for exhibitions and other events.

Site of the first cemetery in Los Angeles.

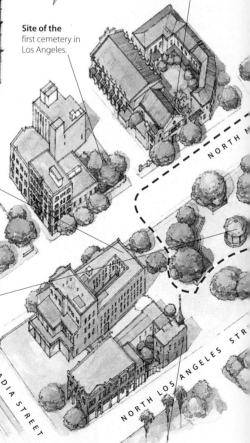

Plaza
A wrought-iron bandstand is set in the middle of the plaza. Nearby is a list of the first 44 settlers and a statue of Felipe de Neve.

NORTH M

NORTH LOS ANGELES STR

ARCADIA STREET

NORTH LOS ANGELES

Firehouse

Key

— Suggested route

★ **Avila Adobe**
The Avila Adobe is the oldest existing house in Los Angeles. It is furnished as it would have been in the late 1840s.

Locator Map
See Street Finder, map 11

David Alfaro Siqueiros' mural, *Tropical America*, was created in 1932.

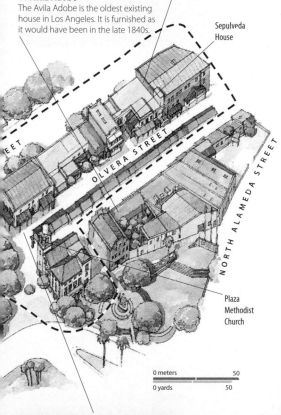

Sepulveda House

OLVERA STREET

NORTH ALAMEDA STREET

Plaza Methodist Church

| 0 meters | 50 |
| 0 yards | 50 |

Olvera Street
This pedestrian street was preserved in the 1930s as a Mexican marketplace following a campaign by local civic leader Christine Sterling.

⑨ Chinatown

Map 11 F2. ℹ️ 727 N Broadway, Suite 208 (213 680-0243).
Ⓦ chinatownla.com

The Chinese first came to California during the Gold Rush *(see pp52–3)* to work in the mines and build the railroads. Confronted by prejudice, they developed tightknit communities. LA's first Chinatown was established in 1870 on the present-day site of Union Station *(see p132)*. It was relocated about 900 yds (820 m) northward in 1938. Today it is the home of over 12,000 people, who live and work in this district.

The ornate East Gate on North Broadway leads into Gin Ling Way and the New Chinatown Central Plaza. This pedestrian precinct is lined with brightly painted buildings that have exaggerated pagoda-style roofs. Here, import shops sell everything from exquisite jade jewelry and antiques to inexpensive trinkets.

In the surrounding streets, the buildings are more bland, but tantalizing restaurants offer all manner of Chinese food, from dim sum (filled, steamed, or grilled dumplings), to spicy Szechuan dishes.

Although on a smaller scale than the celebrations in San Francisco *(see p43)*, LA has its own Chinese New Year Parade in early February. The festivities include dragon and lion dancers, who are accompanied by drums, cymbals, floats, and firecrackers.

Restaurant in Chinatown, topped by a pagoda

Unique blending of architectural styles on Union Station's facade

❿ Union Station

800 N Alameda St. **Map** 11 F3.
Tel (800) 872-7245. **Open** 24 hours
daily. ♿ 🖥 amtrak.com

Dating from 1939, this grand
railroad passenger terminal was
the last of its kind to be built in
the United States. The exterior
is a successful merging of
Spanish Mission, Moorish, and
Streamline Moderne styles
(see pp34–7). The tiles edging
the interior walls, the inlaid
marble designs of the floors,
and the filigree work over the
windows and doorways all
use Spanish motifs.

The vast concourse, with its
52-ft (15.8-m) high roof, will be
familiar to any fan of 1940s films
– stars were frequently photographed here arriving in Los
Angeles. It has been the
location for several movies,

including Sydney Pollack's *The
Way We Were* (1973) and Barry
Levinson's *Bugsy* (1991). Today
the station is quieter, but there
are still daily departures to
Chicago, Seattle, and San Diego.

⓫ Geffen Contemporary at MOCA

152 N Central Ave. **Map** 11 F4.
Tel (213) 626-6222. **Open** 11am–
5pm Mon & Fri, 11am–8pm Thu,
11am–6pm Sat & Sun. **Closed** Jan 1,
Jul 4, Thanksgiving, Dec 25. 🔲 (free
5–8pm Thu). ♿ 📷 🖥 moca.org

In 1983, this old police garage
was used as a temporary
exhibition space until MOCA's
California Plaza facilities were
completed *(see p129)*. Frank
Gehry's renovations in the

1980s were so successful that
the warehouse became a
permanent fixture. Exhibitions
often include highlights from
MOCA's collection as well as
more esoteric shows.

⓬ Los Angeles City Hall

200 N Spring St. **Map** 11 E4.
Tel (213) 485-2121. **Open** 8am–5pm
Mon–Fri. **Closed** public hols. ♿ from
Main St. 📷 advance booking; call
(213) 978-1995.

Until 1957, this 28-story
structure was the tallest in
Downtown – all others were
limited to 12 floors. When it was
built in 1928, sand from every
California county and water
from each of the state's 21
missions was added to the City
Hall's mortar.

Today City Hall is dwarfed
by surrounding skyscrapers,
but its distinctive tower is still
one of Los Angeles's most
familiar landmarks. Among
its many film and television
roles it has been the location
for the *Daily Planet*, Clark Kent's
place of work in the television
series *Superman*.

Inside, the rotunda has a
beautiful inlaid-tile dome and
excellent acoustics. The dome
is decorated with eight figures
showing the building's major
concerns: education, health,

Onizuka Street in Little Tokyo, looking toward Los Angeles City Hall

For hotels and restaurants in this area see pp528–9and p551

law, art, service, government, protection, and trust. Organized groups who take the 45-minute tour of the City Hall can ascend to an observation area in the tower, which has been restored after damage by the 1994 Northridge earthquake *(see p61)*. From here there are panoramic views across the city.

Rotunda of LA City Hall

⑬ Little Tokyo

Map 11 E4. **i** 244 S San Pedro St. (213) 628-2725. **w** **visitlittle tokyo.com**

Lying between First, Third, Los Angeles, and Alameda streets, the bustling area of Little Tokyo has a large number of visitors who throng its Japanese markets, shops, restaurants, and temples.

The first Japanese settled here in 1884. Today, the heart of the area is the Japanese American Cultural and Community Center at No. 244 South San Pedro Street, from which cultural activities and festivals such as Nisei Week *(see p41)* are organized. The center's fan-shaped Japan America Theater is often a venue for performers from Japan, such as the Grand Kabuki.

The Japanese Village Plaza at No. 335 East Second Street has been built in the style of a rural Japanese village, with blue roof tiles, exposed wood frames, and paths landscaped with pools and rocks. A traditional fire watchtower marks the plaza's First Street entrance. Stores include Nijiya Market and the Mikawaya Candy Store. Off San Pedro Street, Onizuka Street offers more upscale shops.

⑭ Japanese American National Museum

369 E 1st St. **Map** 11 F4. **Tel** (213) 625-0414. **Open** 11am–5pm Tue, Wed & Fri–Sun, noon–8pm Thu. **Closed** Jan 1, Thanksgiving, Dec 25. **w** janm.org

The former Nishi Hongwanji Buddhist Temple is now a museum. In 1925, architect Edgar Cline designed a building with a dual personality. The First Street entrance has an unremarkable brick facade, but the ceremonial entrance, on Central Avenue, mixes oriental and Egyptian motifs.

The museum is committed to preserving the history of Japanese-Americans in the US and has the largest collection of Japanese-American memorabilia in the world. Past exhibitions have covered the "Issei Pioneers," "America's Concentration Camps," and "Japanese-American Soldiers." Workshops are also offered.

⑮ Fashion Institute of Design and Merchandising Museum

919 South Grand Avenue. **Map** 10 C5. **Tel** (213) 623-5821. **Open** 10am–5pm Tue–Sat. **w** fidmmuseum. org

The Fashion Institute of Design and Merchandising Museum pays homage to the fashion, graphics, interior design, and entertainment industries. Ranging from the late 18th century to the

Central Avenue entrance to the Japanese American Museum

present day, there are some 12,000 pieces in the collection, from ready-to-wear garments to couture, film and theater costumes, bold textiles, ethnic fabrics, and accessories. World-renowned designers such as Commes des Garçons, Christian Dior, Issey Miyake, and Yves Saint Laurent are represented here. Many garments were worn by famous people, including Marlene Dietrich, Fred Astaire, and Carole Lombard.

⑯ Cathedral of Our Lady of the Angels

555 W Temple St. **Map** 11 E3. **Tel** (213) 680-5200. **Open** early morning–6pm daily.

LA's Catholic cathedral, dedicated in 2002, has drawn kudos and criticism ever since it opened. Designed by Spanish architect José Rafael Moneo, its modernist design of acute and obtuse angles is loved by some, yet scorned by others for its lack of stained glass and a steeple.

Costume display at the Fashion Institute of Design and Merchandising Museum

Pont Vincente Lighthouse on the cliffs lining the coast of Palos Verdes

LONG BEACH AND PALOS VERDES

The ocean is the unifying force of this disparate region, where waves crash against the cliffs of the Palos Verdes Peninsula and tankers head for the busy ports of Los Angeles and Long Beach. The peninsula, a magnificent stretch of coastline, is an affluent area, with mansions and stables set amid the rolling hills. On its southeastern side,

working-class San Pedro is home to the Port of Los Angeles as well as generations of fishermen. The big city in the area – the fifth-largest in the state – is Long Beach. Aptly named for its 5.5-mile (9-km) expanse of white sand, this community has long attracted those who love the ocean. Its most famous landmark is the ocean liner *Queen Mary*.

Sights at a Glance

Historic Buildings
2 Rancho Los Cerritos
3 Rancho Los Alamitos

Districts
1 Long Beach
4 Naples
8 Ports O'Call Marketplace
11 San Pedro

Historic Ships
6 *Queen Mary pp138–9*

Modern Architecture
12 Wayfarers Chapel

Parks and Gardens
10 Point Fermin Park
13 South Coast Botanic Garden

Museums
5 Aquarium of the Pacific
7 Los Angeles Maritime Museum
9 Cabrillo Marine Aquarium

0 kilometers 2
0 miles 2

Locator map

❶ Street-by-Street: Long Beach

With palm trees and the ocean as a backdrop, downtown Long Beach is a mixture of carefully restored buildings and modern glass high-rises. At its heart, Pine Avenue still retains the early midwestern charm that gave the city its nickname of "Iowa by the Sea." The trendy atmosphere attracts locals, who come to relax, enjoy a cup of espresso, and sample some of the best food in the area. Nearby, Long Beach Convention and Entertainment Center was once the site of the Pike Amusement Park, famous for its roller coaster. Now the Terrace Theater's respected music and dance programs draw the crowds. Along the ocean, the shops and restaurants in Shoreline Village offer views of the ocean liner *Queen Mary*.

Farmers and Merchants Bank Tower
When erected in 1922, this terracotta building was Long Beach's first skyscraper. Its hall is a fine example of period styling.

Transit Mall Metro station

Long Beach Municipal Auditorium Mural
This 1938 mural of a day at the beach was originally housed in the Municipal Auditorium. It was moved in 1979 when that building was demolished to make way for the Terrace Theater.

The Promenade is the site of Long Beach's farmer's market. Every Friday the street is filled with stands selling fruit, vegetables, and crafts.

The 1929 Mediterranean-style Ocean Center Building was the start of the Pike Amusement Park's Walk of a Thousand Lights.

★ **Pine Avenue**
The center of downtown Long Beach, Pine Avenue is lined with stores, cafés, and restaurants. Some of these businesses are housed in historic buildings, such as the 1903 Masonic Temple at No. 230.

Key

 Suggested route

For hotels and restaurants in this area see p529 & p530 and p552

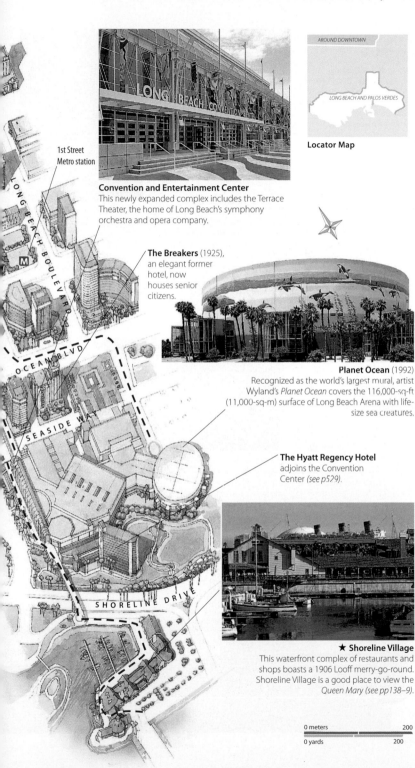

Locator Map

1st Street
Metro station

Convention and Entertainment Center
This newly expanded complex includes the Terrace
Theater, the home of Long Beach's symphony
orchestra and opera company.

The Breakers (1925),
an elegant former
hotel, now
houses senior
citizens.

Planet Ocean (1992)
Recognized as the world's largest mural, artist
Wyland's *Planet Ocean* covers the 116,000-sq-ft
(11,000-sq-m) surface of Long Beach Arena with life-
size sea creatures.

The Hyatt Regency Hotel
adjoins the Convention
Center *(see p529)*.

★ **Shoreline Village**
This waterfront complex of restaurants and
shops boasts a 1906 Looff merry-go-round.
Shoreline Village is a good place to view the
Queen Mary (see pp138–9).

0 meters		200
0 yards		200

❷ Rancho Los Cerritos

4600 Virginia Rd. **Road map** inset A.
Tel (562) 206-2040. **Open** 1–5pm
Wed–Sun. **Closed** Jan 1, Easter Sun,
Thanksgiving, Dec 25. 🚻 📷 1pm,
2pm, 3pm, 4pm Sat & Sun only.
🌐 rancholoscerritos.org

Rancho Los Cerritos was once part of a 300,000-acre (121,400-ha) land grant, given between 1784 and 1790 to Spanish soldier Manuel Nieto. Mission San Gabriel reclaimed nearly half of the property, and the rest was left to Nieto's children on his death in 1804.

In 1844 John Temple bought the ranch, built the adobe house, and later sold up to the firm Flint, Bixby & Co. The ranch was gradually sold off, but in 1955 the City of Long Beach bought the house and its 5 acres (2 ha). Today, it is a museum, focusing on those who lived here from 1840 to 1940. The Monterey-style house *(see p34)* is furnished to reflect the late 1870s.

❸ Rancho Los Alamitos

6400 Bixby Hill Rd. **Road map** inset A.
Tel (562) 431-3541. **Open** 1–5pm
Wed–Sun. **Closed** Jan 1, Easter Sun,
Thanksgiving, Dec 25. 🚻 📷
🌐 rancholosalamitos.com

Rancho Los Alamitos stands on a mesa inhabited since AD 500. In 1790 it formed part of the Manuel Nieto land grant. The house was built in 1806 and changed hands frequently until it was bought by the Bixby family firm in 1881. In 1968 the

Cactus Garden on the grounds of Rancho Los Alamitos

ranch was given to the City of Long Beach, and today the house is furnished as it was in the 1920s and 1930s. The grounds are a rare example of a pioneer garden.

❻ Queen Mary

Pier J, 1126 Queens Hwy.
Road map inset A. **Tel** (877) 342-0738.
Open 10am–6pm daily; restaurants
until 10pm. 🅿️ 🚻 📷
🌐 queenmary.com *See Where to Stay p529 and Where to Eat p552.*

Named after the wife of British King George V, this liner set new standards in ocean travel with its maiden voyage of May 27, 1936. The jewel in the crown of the Cunard White Star Line, the *Queen Mary* sailed weekly from Southampton, England to New York City. Although the second- and third-class quarters may look small next to the grandeur of the

Royal Jubilee Week, 1935 by AR Thomson, above the bar in the Observation Lounge

first-class rooms, they were considered chic and spacious for their time. On its five-day trips,

the liner carried an average of 3,000 passengers and crew. There were two swimming pools, two chapels, a synagogue, gym, ballroom, and children's playrooms. Anyone who was anyone sailed on the *Queen Mary*, from royalty to Hollywood stars.

From 1939 to 1946, the liner was converted into a troopship called the *Grey Ghost*, carrying

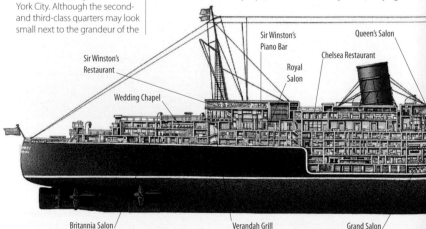

Sir Winston's Restaurant

Wedding Chapel

Sir Winston's Piano Bar

Royal Salon

Queen's Salon

Chelsea Restaurant

Britannia Salon

Verandah Grill

Grand Salon

❹ Naples

Road map inset A. 🚍 Long Beach.
ℹ️ One World Trade Center, Suite 300
(562 436-3645). Gondola Getaway:
5437 E Ocean Blvd (562 433-9595).
🌐 visitlongbeach.com

In 1903, developer Arthur
Parson began creating his own
version of the city of Naples in
Italy, complete with winding
streets and waterways (even
though the real Naples does
not have canals and gondolas).

Taking heed of the mistakes
made by Abbot Kinney in
Venice (see p84), Parson
designed his canals so that the
Pacific Ocean's tidal flows
would keep them clean.

Finished in the late 1920s,
this charming Long Beach
neighborhood is actually three
islands in the middle of

Alamitos Bay. An eclectic
architectural mix of shingled
Mission Revival, Victorian, and
Arts and Crafts houses (see
pp34–37) line the Italian-named
streets. The Rivo Alto Canal is
the largest in the network and
you can book a cruise on an
authentic Venetian gondola.

❺ Aquarium of the Pacific

100 Aquarium Way, Long Beach. **Road
map** inset A. **Tel** (562) 590-3100.
Open 9am–6pm daily. **Closed** Grand
Prix weekend at Long Beach, Dec 25.
🎟️ combined ticket packages
available (see website for details). ♿
📷 🖥️ 🌐 aquariumofpacific.org

Learn about the inhabitants
and ecosystems of the Pacific
Ocean in this, one of the

Canal in residential Naples, with boats
moored alongside the private jetties

largest aquariums in the US.
Over 500 species fill 19 major
habitats and 32 exhibits
which guide visitors on a
journey through the
Pacific's three regions:
Southern California,
the Tropical Pacific, and
the Northern Pacific.

more than 800,000 soldiers
during its wartime career.
At the end of the war,
it transported more
than 22,000 war
brides and children
to the US during
"Operation Diaper."

In 1967, after 1,001
transatlantic
crossings, the liner
was bought by the
City of Long Beach. It
was permanently docked for use
as a hotel and tourist attraction.
Today, visitors can view part of

Detail inside the ship's
Grand Salon

the original Engine Room,
examples of the
different travel
accommodations,
and an exhibition
on the war years.
Many of the
original Art Deco
features, created
by more than 30
artists, still decorate
the interior. Open
to the public for
dining, the Grand Salon and
Observation Lounge are fine
examples of period styling.

Dual set of brass steering wheels in the
Queen Mary's wheelhouse

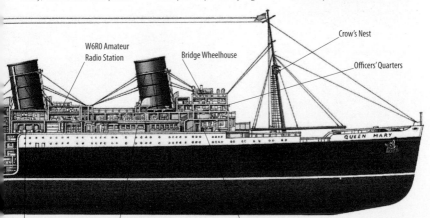

W6RO Amateur
Radio Station

Bridge Wheelhouse

Crow's Nest

Officers' Quarters

QUEEN MARY

Promenade Café and Bar

Piccadilly Circus

Observation Lounge

Cycling along Venice Beach, Los Angeles ▶

⑦ Los Angeles Maritime Museum

Berth 84, 6th St, San Pedro. **Road map** inset A. **Tel** 310-548-7618. **Open** 10am–5pm Tue–Sun. **Closed** Easter Sun, Thanksgiving, Dec 25. 🏛 ♿ 🅦 **lamaritime museum.org**

Housed in a restored ferry terminal building, the Los Angeles Maritime Museum contains an array of nautical paintings and memorabilia, including a wooden figurehead of British Queen Victoria. Highlights of the exhibition include its extensive model ship collection. Also on display is the bow and bridge of US Navy cruiser USS *Los Angeles*, and there are ever-changing temporary exhibitions. Early 20th-century fishing boats from Monterey (*see p513*) can be seen in the dock.

Figurehead of Queen Victoria

⑧ Ports O'Call Marketplace

Berths 75–79, San Pedro. **Road map** inset A. **Tel** 310-548-8076. **Open** 11am–7pm Sun–Thu, 11am–8pm Fri & Sat. 🅦 **sanpedro.com**

Ports O'Call Marketplace is a pastiche of many different seaports from all around the world. Building styles range from a 19th-century

Street scene in the picturesque Ports O'Call Marketplace

New England fishing village, to a Mediterranean harbor, to a Mexican town.

The village's quaint shops and restaurants are linked by charming cobblestone walkways. Seafood is a specialty here, and the restaurants all serve locally caught, delicious fresh fish. From the dockside boardwalk visitors can watch the huge cargo ships and cruise liners sail by. Daily harbor cruises tour the inner harbor, coastguard station, marina, freighter operations, and scrap yards. Helicopter rides offer a birds' eye view of the harbor, while in winter, whale-watching cruises leave from this area.

⑨ Cabrillo Marine Aquarium

3720 Stephen White Dr, San Pedro. **Road map** inset A. **Tel** 310-548-7562. **Open** noon–5pm Tue–Fri, 10am–5pm Sat & Sun. **Closed** Thanksgiving, Dec 25. 🏛 for parking only. ♿ 🅘 🅦 **cabrillomarineaquarium.org**

Designed by architect Frank Gehry and surrounded by a geometric chain-link fence, the Cabrillo Marine Aquarium houses one of the largest collections of Southern California marine life. Sharks, moray eels, and rays thrill thousands of visitors each year. The exhibition hall includes interpretive displays that explain the typical plants and animals of the region. It is divided into three environments – rocky shores, beaches and mudflats, and open ocean.

An outdoor rock pool tank contains sea cucumbers, sea anemones, starfish, and sea urchins that visitors are permitted to touch. This small museum also boasts 14,150 gallons (64,400 liters) of circulating sea water, as well as a tidal tank that allows viewers to see below a wave. Another exhibit shows how human activities have altered Los Angeles Harbor.

The beautifully maintained clapboard Point Fermin Lighthouse

⑩ Point Fermin Park

807 Paseo del Mar, San Pedro. **Road map** inset A. **Tel** 310-548-7705. **Open** daily. 🅦 **sanpedro.com**

This tranquil 37-acre (15-ha) park sits on a bluff overlooking the Pacific Ocean. Between January and March, migrating gray whales can be spotted offshore and, on a clear day, there are views of Catalina Island. The charming Eastlake-style lighthouse dates from 1874. Its bricks and lumber were shipped around Cape Horn. The lighthouse originally used oil lamps that emitted approximately 2,100 candlepower. They were replaced by an electric lamp in 1925.

⑪ San Pedro

Road map inset A. ✈ LAX, 15 miles (24 km) NW of San Pedro. 🚌 MTA. ℹ San Pedro Chamber of Commerce, 390 W 7th St, 310-832-7272. 🅦 **sanpedro.com**

Famous for the Port of Los Angeles, blue-collar pride, and a tradition of family fishermen, San Pedro ("San Peedro" to the locals) has a strong Eastern European and Mediterranean flavor. The harbor is the nation's busiest import-export site. The houses are tiny compared to those in Palos Verdes, but this is a very important center of industry. In Angels Gate Park, at

Korean Friendship Bell in Angels Gate Park, San Pedro

the end of Gaffey Street, there is a Korean Friendship Bell, given to the United States in 1976 by South Korea.

Steps leading to the hilltop Wayfarers Chapel

⓬ Wayfarers Chapel

5755 Palos Verdes Drive S, Rancho Palos Verdes. **Road map** inset A. **Tel** 310-377-1650. **Open** call ahead (frequently booked for weddings). Gardens: **Open** 8am–5pm daily. 🚻 **w** wayfarerschapel.org

This glass and redwood-framed chapel sits on a hilltop above the ocean. From the street below, all that can be seen is a thin stone and concrete tower rising from the greenery.

When the architect Lloyd Wright (son of Frank Lloyd Wright) designed the chapel in 1949, he tried to create a natural place of worship, surrounding it by trees. Today, its charm makes it a popular site for weddings.

The chapel is sponsored by the Swedenborgian church, which follows the teaching of Emanuel Swedenborg, the 18th-century Swedish theologian and mystic.

⓭ South Coast Botanic Garden

26300 S Crenshaw Blvd, Palos Verdes. **Road map** inset A. **Tel** 310-544-6815. **Open** 9am–5pm daily. **Closed** Dec 25. 🅿 🚻 📷 **w** southcoast botanicgarden.org

This 87-acre (35-ha) garden was created on top of some 3,175,000 tons of waste that were dumped here from 1956 to 1960. Prior to that, the area was the location of a mine for algae-rich diatomaceous earth. Today, gas formed underground as a result of the waste decomposing is collected and used to generate electricity.

The garden is a study in land reclamation, with an emphasis on drought-resistant landscaping. Specimens from all the continents except Antarctica are planted within the grounds.

In the Herb Garden plants are divided into three main categories: fragrant, medicinal, and culinary. The Rose Garden has more than 1,600 roses, including old-fashioned and miniature roses, floribundas, hybrid teas, and grandifloras.

One of the most innovative areas is the Garden for the Senses. Here, plants are chosen for their extraordinary qualities of color, smell, or touch.

Children's Garden in the South Coast Botanic Garden

AROUND DOWNTOWN

From the freeways, it is hard to appreciate the many treasures that lie within Los Angeles's sprawl. But a short drive beyond the central sights to nearby areas can be surprisingly rewarding. Up-scale Pasadena, with its delightful Old Town, also has the excellent Norton Simon Museum as well as the Huntington Library, Art Collections, and Botanical Gardens.

Northeast of Downtown are the Heritage Square Museum with its historic buildings, and Lummis House. Just north of Hollywood, hilly Griffith Park offers precious open spaces for picnicking, hiking, and horseback riding as well as the Los Angeles Zoo, Griffith Observatory, the outdoor Greek Theater, and Autry National Center.

Nearby, Universal Studios offers tours of its backlots as well as theme park rides. Universal is one of four major studios based in Burbank, which has replaced Hollywood as the headquarters for the film and television industries. Farther north in the broad, flat San Fernando Valley, Mission San Fernando Rey de España provides a historical insight into California's origins.

South of Downtown, the Natural History Museum of Los Angeles County and the California Museum of Science and Industry are among the top attractions at Exposition Park, along with the stately buildings of the University of Southern California.

For sheer scenic delight and outstanding views over the city and San Fernando Valley, twisting mountainous Mulholland Drive is hard to beat.

Tranquil Japanese Garden at the Huntington Botanical Gardens

◄ Stunning Beaux-Arts City Hall in the 1920s Civic Center, Pasadena

Exploring Around Downtown

The outlying areas of Los Angeles contain a vast range of museums, galleries, historic buildings, and parks. A little forward planning is necessary, however, to make the best use of time. The Heritage Square and Southwest museums are easily visited on the way to Pasadena. While Universal Studios needs a day to itself, other studio tours in Burbank can be combined with a trip to Griffith Park or to Mission San Fernando Rey de España. Get an early morning start at the Flower Market before tackling the three museums at Exposition Park, or take a trip east to see the Watts Towers in between museum visits.

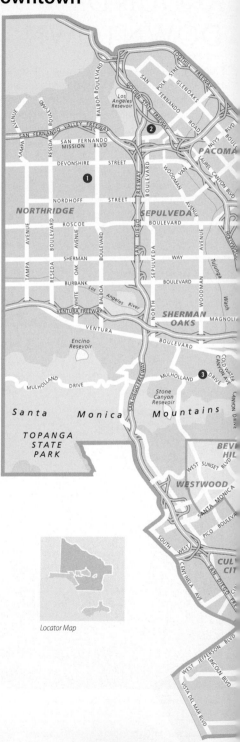

Locator Map

Sights at a Glance

Districts
1 San Fernando Valley
14 Pasadena pp158–65
20 LA Arts District

Historic Streets and Buildings
2 Mission San Fernando Rey de España
3 Mulholland Drive
7 Hollywood Sign
8 Hollyhock House
11 Heritage Square Museum
12 Lummis House
21 Watts Towers

Museums and Galleries
4 Los Angeles Police Museum
13 Historic Southwest Museum p157

Parks and Gardens
9 Griffith Park pp154–5
17 Exposition Park and University of Southern California pp168–9

Shopping Areas
15 El Mercado
16 Flower Market

Sports and Entertainment Venues
10 Dodger Stadium
18 LA Live
19 Staples Center

Film Studios
5 Burbank
6 Universal Studios Hollywood℠ pp150–53

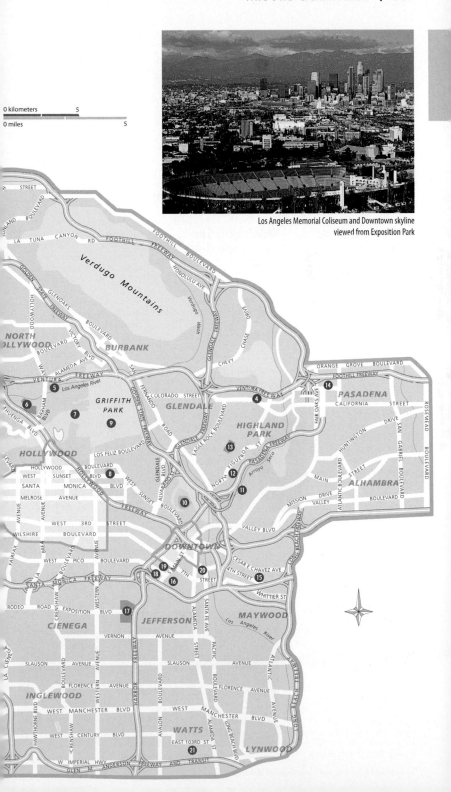

Los Angeles Memorial Coliseum and Downtown skyline
viewed from Exposition Park

0 kilometers   5

0 miles   5

STREET

SUNLAND
BOULEVARD

LA TUNA CANYON RD   FOOTHILL   FREEWAY   FOOTHILL   BOULEVARD

HONOLULU AVE

Verdugo Mountains

Verdugo Wash

GOLDEN STATE FREEWAY

GLENOAKS   BOULEVARD

VICTORY   BLVD

NORTH
HOLLYWOOD

BURBANK

ALAMEDA AVE

HOLLYWOOD   WAY

VENTURA   FREEWAY

Los Angeles River   **5**

BARHAM   BLVD

6

CAHUENGA   BLVD

7

GRIFFITH
PARK

9

SAN   FERNANDO

COLORADO   STREET

GOLDEN STATE FREEWAY

ROAD

GLENDALE

CHEVY   CHASE

GLENDALE   FREEWAY

EAGLE ROCK BOULEVARD

NAME

VENTURA FREEWAY   **4**

ORANGE   GROVE   BOULEVARD

FOOTHILL FREEWAY

FAIR OAKS AVE   **14**

PASADENA

CALIFORNIA   STREET

ROSEMEAD   BOULEVARD

HIGHLAND
PARK

PASADENA FREEWAY

NORTH FIGUEROA   ST

13

Arroyo Seco

12

11

HUNTINGTON   DRIVE

SAN   GABRIEL   BOULEVARD

HOLLYWOOD

LOS FELIZ BOULEVARD

HOLLYWOOD   BOULEVARD

HOLLYWOOD   BLVD

8

WEST   SUNSET   BLVD

SANTA   MONICA

MELROSE   AVENUE

SUNSET

WEST   3RD   STREET

WILSHIRE   BOULEVARD

FAIRFAX   AVENUE

WEST   PICO   BOULEVARD

WEST   BOULEVARD

WEST

ALVARADO   BLVD

GLENDALE   BLVD

FREEWAY

BOULEVARD

10

DOWNTOWN

MAIN   ST

19   7TH

18   **16**   STREET

20

4TH STREET

CESAR E CHAVEZ AVE

15

ALHAMBRA

MAIN   DRIVE

MISSION   DRIVE

VALLEY

BOULEVARD

ATLANTIC   BOULEVARD

VALLEY BLVD

WHITTIER ST

MAYWOOD

ALAMEDA   STREET

SANTA FE AVE

Los   Angeles   River

PACIFIC

LONG BEACH FREEWAY

LA   CIENEGA

RODEO   ROAD

CRENSHAW

SANTA   MONICA   FREEWAY

EXPOSITION   BLVD   **17**

CIENEGA   JEFFERSON   AVENUE

VERNON   AVENUE

SLAUSON   AVENUE

FLORENCE   AVENUE

HARBOR   FREEWAY

WESTERN   AVENUE

SLAUSON   AVENUE

FLORENCE   AVENUE

ATLANTIC   AVENUE

INGLEWOOD

HAWTHORNE BLVD

WEST   MANCHESTER   BLVD

CRENSHAW   BLVD

WEST   CENTURY   BLVD

AVALON   BOULEVARD

WEST   MANCHESTER   BLVD

ALAMEDA   ST

WATTS

EAST 103RD ST   **21**

LONG BEACH BLVD

LYNWOOD

W   IMPERIAL   HWY   ANDERSON   FREEWAY   AND   TRANSIT

GLEN M

View of San Fernando Valley from Mulholland Drive

❶ San Fernando Valley

Road map inset A. 🛫 Burbank-Glendale-Pasadena, 20 miles (32 km) SE of San Fernando. 🚌 MTA. ℹ️ 200 Magnolia Blvd, (818) 377-6388. 🌐 **thevalley.net**

The city of Los Angeles is split into two distinct halves by the Santa Monica Mountains (see pp66–7). To the north, the San Fernando Valley spreads out in an endless vista of neat houses, freeways, and shopping malls, such as the Sherman Oaks Galleria (see p170). Residents south of the mountains tend to dismiss "the Valley," as they call it, as it is more smoggy and noticeably hotter in the summer.

In the 19th century, the San Fernando Valley was made up of ranches, orange groves, and non-irrigated farms. With the completion of the LA Aqueduct in 1913 (see pp206–7), the city was insured a plentiful water supply. As a result, the Valley quickly developed into a mass of suburbs. Today, more than a million people live in this area of Los Angeles, which encompasses only 177 sq miles (460 sq km).

San Fernando Valley suffered a major earthquake in 1971 and an earthquake measuring 6.8 on the Richter scale in 1994, which caused extensive damage (see pp28–9). As a result, building legislation was revised to protect structures against such seismic events.

❷ Mission San Fernando Rey de España

15151 San Fernando Mission Blvd, Mission Hills. **Road map** inset A. **Tel** (818) 361-0186. **Open** 9am–4:30pm daily. **Closed** Thanksgiving, Dec 25. 🎫 ♿ grounds only. 📷 🌐 **missiontour.org**

One of 21 Franciscan missions in California (see pp50–51), San Fernando Rey de España was founded in 1797 and named after King Ferdinand III of Spain. The present church is an exact replica of the original, which was destroyed in the 1971 earthquake. The convento (living quarters) has a 21-arch portico and is the largest mission building still standing in California.

A tour of the complex explores the early days of Spanish rule, when the monks and converted Native Americans worked together to make the mission self-sufficient.

Mission altar detail

❸ Mulholland Drive

Off Hwys 1 & 27, from Hollywood Fwy to Leo Carrillo State Beach. **Map** 1 C2. ℹ️ Malibu Chamber of Commerce, 23805 Stuart Ranch Rd, Ste 100 (310) 456-9025.

Mulholland Drive, one of the most famous roads in Los Angeles, runs for nearly 50 miles (80 km) from north Hollywood to the Malibu coast (see pp68–9). As it winds along the ridge of the Santa Monica mountains, the route has spectacular views across the city, San Fernando Valley, and some of LA's most exclusive houses. Its spirit was captured in David Hockney's painting of the area, which hangs in LACMA (see p119).

The road was named after William Mulholland (see p206). Although better known for his work on the LA Aqueduct, he oversaw the completion of Mulholland Drive in 1924.

❹ Los Angeles Police Museum

6045 York Blvd. **Road map** inset A. **Tel** (323) 344-9445. **Open** 10am–4pm Mon–Fri, 9am–3pm third Sat of each month. 🌐 **laphs.org**

Located in the Highland Park police station built in 1925, this museum covers all aspects of the city's famous police force, the LAPD. Handcuffs, firearms, and uniforms are on display, along with old-fashioned patrol cars, some with bullet holes and shot-out windows. You can have your mugshot taken or sit in a holding cell, and kids will love taking the controls of the grounded LAPD helicopter.

Mission San Fernando Rey de España in the Mission Hills

Stage set at Warner Bros Studios in Burbank

❺ Burbank

Road map inset A. 🛫 Burbank-Glendale-Pasadena. 🚌 MTA. 🛈 200 W Magnolia Burbank (818 846-3111). 🔲 **burbankchamber.org**

Since 1915, when Universal Studios *see (pp150–53)* moved near here, Burbank has been competing with Hollywood as the true center of the Los Angeles film industry. Today there are four major studios: Universal, Disney, NBC, and Warner Bros. Disney's studios are closed to the public, but the fanciful building, designed by Michael Graves, can be seen from Alameda Avenue.

Warner Bros. offers an extensive tour that takes you behind the scenes of many popular television shows *(see p179)*, and a studio tour is included at the Universal Studios Hollywood℠ theme park *(see pp150–51)*.

❻ Universal Studios Hollywood℠

See pp150–53.

❼ Hollywood Sign

Mt Cahuenga, above Hollywood. 🛈 Hollywood Visitors Information Center, 6801 Hollywood Blvd (323) 467-6412. 🔲 **hollywoodsign.org**

The Hollywood Sign is an internationally recognized symbol of the movie business. Set high up in the Hollywood Hills, it is now a protected historic site. It is visible for miles from many parts of Los Angeles, but it is not possible for the public to reach the sign itself as there is no legitimate trail leading up to the 45-ft (13-m) tall letters.

Erected in 1923, it originally advertised the Hollywoodland housing development of the former *LA Times* publisher Harry Chandler. The "land" was removed in 1949. Nearly 30 years later, donors pledged $27,000 per letter for a new sign.

It has been the scene of a famous suicide – that of disappointed would-be actress Peg Entwhistle, who jumped off the "H" in 1932.

❽ Hollyhock House

4800 Hollywood Blvd. **Tel** (323) 913-4030. Park: **Open** 11am–3pm Thu–Sun. 📷 Wed–Sun (private tours). 🔲 **hollyhockhouse.net**

American architect Frank Lloyd Wright *(see p37)* designed a number of houses in LA. Hollyhock House was the first and remains one of the best known. An excellent example of Wright's infatuation with pre-Columbian styles, the hilltop house resembles a Mayan temple and is centered around a courtyard.

It was completed in 1921 for oil heiress Aline Barnsdall, who asked that her favorite flower, the hollyhock, be used as a decorative motif throughout the building. A band of stylized hollyhocks, fashioned in concrete, therefore adorns the exterior of the house. The flowers also feature as ornamentation inside, such as on the dining room chairs and other Wright-designed furnishings. The large Barnsdall Park, once the grounds of the estate, is now a public art park with galleries.

The Hollywood Sign, high above Los Angeles in the Hollywood Hills

❺ Universal Studios Hollywood^{SM}

Carl Laemmle bought a chicken ranch on this site in 1915 and moved his film studio here from Hollywood. He charged visitors 25 cents to see films being made, and guests could also buy fresh eggs. With the advent of the "talkies" in 1927, the sets needed quiet and the visits stopped. In 1964, Universal Studios Hollywood^{SM} was launched as a behind-the-scenes tram ride. The Studio Tour through Universal brings visitors face-to-face with soundstages and movie sets. Here, everything is, or looks like, a film set. The attractions, from *Shrek* to the latest virtual-reality thrill ride, create a world of magic and Hollywood glamor.

Locator Map
- ◼ Universal City
- ◻ Universal Studios

The Studio Tour takes in over 500 sets and facades on the backlot

Tackling the Park

Spread over 415 acres (168 ha) Universal Studios Hollywood^{SM} is the world's largest working movie and television studio and theme park. The complex is divided into three areas: the Entertainment Center, Studio Center, and the studio lots.

As soon as visitors walk through the gate, they stroll through the Streets of the World, which are actual working sets depicting anything from a 1950s America to a European village. The Studio Tour, boarded from the Entertainment Center, is the only way of seeing Universal's main television and movie stages, sets, and movie stars. Do not miss the Special Effects Stage and the spectacular show, Animal Actors. A futuristic escalator,

the Starway, links the upper and lower portions of the studio lot. The lower level is where the major thrill rides can be found, such as Revenge of the Mummy^{SM} – The Ride and Jurassic Park® – The Ride. Universal CityWalk connects the working studios, the theme park, and a 19-screen movie theater. There are also more than 65 different retail and entertain- ment venues.

Studio Tour

The original Universal Studios attraction, this classic Studio Tour gives visitors an up-close and personal view of the past, present, and future of Hollywood movie-making. Guests are ferried about in trolley buses fitted with state-of-the-art, high-definition monitors and digital playback systems. Comedian Jimmy

Fallon, the star of *Late Night with Jimmy Fallon*, is the video host of the tour and augments the live Studio Tour narration by introducing hundreds of clips of well-known films and hit TV shows. Guests see King Kong, Jaws, and plenty of dinosaurs, and survive a collapsing bridge, flash flood, earthquake, and avalanche. The tour passes the Bates Motel from *Psycho* (1960), the startlingly realistic Boeing 747 crash from *War of the Worlds* (2005), and Wisteria Lane from *Desperate Housewives*.

A favorite part of the tour is the "Before They Were Stars" montage and the special weather-effects demonstrations. The 35 different soundstages, various movie and TV sets, props, cameras, lights, and lots of action give guests a first-hand look into filmland's realities and illusions. Special installations of "The Mummy," "Earthquake – The Big One," "King Kong," and "Jaws Lake" let visitors experience the live action of each working set.

Set Locations on the Backlot

Guests on the Studio Tour will see these working sets for hundreds of movies and TV productions, many of which are instantly recognizable. Each tram has an LCD flat screen, audio system, and DVD player to put every set visited into context.

1 Courthouse Square: most frequently used set *(Back to the Future film series, To Kill a Mockingbird, Batman & Robin, Bruce Almighty, Dr Seuss' The Cat in The Hat)*.

2 Psycho House/Bates Motel: most famous set *(Psycho* original and the remake of the same movie).

3 Wisteria Lane: suburban idyll from the hit television series *Desperate Housewives*.

4 Denver Street: 7/8 scale to make actors look larger than life *(Winchester '73, Babe)*.

5 Falls Lake with Backdrop: most flexible set *(Apollo 13, Charlie's Angels, O Brother, Where Art Thou?, Van Helsing)*.

Witness live action and be part of the movie set on the Studio Tour

Universal Studios Hollywood^{SM} Tickets and Passes

General Admission: Tickets are either Adult or Child (3–9). Parking is extra.

1   2-Day Ticket: Valid for two visits for the same visitor within the same 30-day period. Includes all rides, games, and attractions.

2   Front of Line Pass: Allows one time front of line entry to all attractions and reserved seating at all shows.

3   Annual Pass: Unlimited park access for one year (contains 30 blackout days) and free guest pass Sep–Dec.

4   VIP: Admission, guided tour of studio backlot, front-of-line privileges, and escorted priority access to rides and shows.

5   SeaWorld Combo Pass: Admission to Universal Studios and SeaWorld San Diego. Valid for 14 days.

For more information, call 1-800-864-8377 or visit the website.

In spite of all the virtual-reality, thrill rides, and modern attractions, the Studio Tour is really what a visit to Universal Studios Hollywood^{SM} is all about. The tour is included in the general admission ticket.

Universal CityWalk

In 1993, American architect Jon Jerde designed a festive assortment of facades for the shops and restaurants that make up CityWalk's promenade. Now, with the addition of more than 30 new attractions, including bars, nightclubs, and theaters, Universal's CityWalk is being hailed as the entertainment mecca of Southern California. Designed to appeal to guests' sense of whimsy, a giant neon-lit baseball player swings his bat above a sports store. To enter an ice-cream store, visitors must walk under an upside-down pink convertible that has crashed through a Hollywood Freeway sign. Jillian's Hi-Life Lanes, a multimedia rock 'n' roll bowling alley, gives guests a chance to work off some extra energy; Howl at the Moon, a duelling piano bar, encourages audience participation; and the Samba Steakhouse and Lounge offers an authentic Brazilian experience with traditional cuisine and entertainment. Join the conga line around the restaurant or revel in the spontaneous performances and dances bringing the rhythms of Brazil to life.

The seven-story IMAX® 3-D theater shows the latest venture into knock-your-socks-off film, and the i-FLY Indoor Skydiving experience can be an antidote to the newest retail shops, name-brand outlets, and restaurants. This spectacular venture into California fantasy and entertainment is still one of the prime areas where you can buy Hollywood souvenirs and memorabilia.

VISITORS' CHECKLIST

Practical Information
Road map inset A.
100 Universal City Plaza,
Universal City. **Tel** (800) 864-8377.
W universalstudios
hollywood.com
Open Jun–Aug: 9am–8pm daily;
Sep–May: 10am–6pm daily. Times
can vary.

Transport
424.

Bright lights, big buildings, and prime entertainment in CityWalk

Rides and Special Effects

Thrill rides are what theme parks do best. Not only does Universal offer some of the most spectacular rides but, coupled with the special effects, it is the largest and only working studio and theme park. Revenge of the Mummy℠ – The Ride is a mix of high-speed roller coaster and space-age robotics, while many of the other attractions imitate the sense of movement by using flight-simulation technology and 3-D effects. In WaterWorld® the audience needs to be prepared for a soaking. Visitors can also see King Kong on the world's largest soundstage and may get the rare chance to get a sneak peek at one of dozens of the films currently in production. Each attraction here is a thrill ride in itself, where the excitement of movies literally comes alive.

A star of Animal Actors showing a talented paw

Entertainment Center

The entertainment center has dozens of themed souvenir shops and restaurants. The spectacular shows in this area of the park give visitors an insight into the stunts and special effects used to make a film.

Animal Actors

Animal stars, multi-media effects, human co-stars, and unique sketches from TV's Animal Planet Network offer warm family entertainment.

Transformers™: The Ride-3D

This ride is based on the popular movie franchise that spun out of the success of transforming robot toys. It uses 3-D effects and flight-simulation technology to provide an immersive, excitingly realistic experience. The adventure puts you in a war zone, and you must fight alongside the Transformers™ to save the human race from the Decepticons.

WaterWorld®

The audience is part of the action, and right in the middle of this thrilling, high-tech show, which packs dazzling pyrotechnics – a giant fireball that rises 50 feet (15 m) in the air – battle scenes, extraordinary stunts, and some wild jet-skiing into 16 minutes of daredevil action.

The attraction is based on the 1995 film, and starts where the movie left off, with stunts on water, land, and overhead, and a spectacular crash landing of the seaplane. Guests seated in the front Soak Zones can count on getting wet from the many special effects. The Splash Zones behind this area are a bit dryer, but will still get a few splashes.

Shrek 4-D™

This superb "multi-sensory" attraction continues Shrek's adventures in the "greatest fairytale never told." Picking up where the original DreamWorks movie left off, the Shrek 4-D™ features ground-breaking "Ogre Vision" animation.

The Simpsons Ride™

Homer, Marge, Bart, Lisa, and Maggie Simpson – stars of TV's longest running cartoon series – ride along with guests in this mega-attraction at Universal Orlando Resort and Universal Studios Hollywood℠. Guests are rocketed along with the Simpson family on a hysterical, almost unimaginable adventure. On the way they experience a side of Springfield previously unexplored, as they enjoy the ride's interpretation of the thrill rides, dark rides, and "live" shows that make up a fantasy amusement park dreamed up by the show's cantankerous Krusty the Clown.

King Kong 360 3-D

The King Kong 360 3-D is the first theme park attraction created by Peter Jackson, director of the Oscar-winning 2005 film upon which it is

Interactive action with Transformers™: The Ride-3D

based. Guests on the Universal tram are given 3-D glasses and enter into a world where the film and tram are tied into a motion simulator that creates a titanic struggle between the 30-ft- (9-m-) tall gorilla and a 35-ft- (11-m-) tall *Tyrannosaurus rex*. Surrounded by two curved screens, Studio Tour guests are completely swept up in the action. It is the first theme park attraction to win an award for "outstanding visual effect in a special venue project," from the Visual Effects Society.

Despicable Me Minion Mayhem

This simulator ride uses the latest 3-D HD animation to transport you into the Despicable Me world. Begin the journey sporting your Minion goggles (3-D glasses) and join Gru and his daughters as you are recruited as a minion. Take a trip through the laboratory and end up at a minion-inspired dance party.

Special Effects Stage

Join the audience – and perhaps go on stage yourself – to learn the secrets behind the special effects in today's blockbusters. An older, practical-effects expert and a younger, digital-effects master demonstrate CGI, stop motion, motion capture, and 3-D technology. Minions from *Despicable Me 2* make a special appearance to share behind-the-scenes clips on how the movie was made.

King Kong 360 3-D, beloved of filmgoers, on Universal's Studio Tour *(see p150)*

Studio Tour

The Starway, which links the upper and lower portions of Universal's working lots, offers some spectacular views. The Studio Tour on the lower lot has three super-thrilling rides and several other attractions that reveal the secrets of some of the studio's most successful films and television series. There are, of course, lots of photo opportunities around each corner, from the giant 24-ft (7-m) hanging shark to Universal's mascot Woody Woodpecker. Or you might bump into a host of characters, including Charlie Chaplin, Frankenstein, the Mummy, Dracula, or Marilyn Monroe.

Revenge of the Mummy^{SM} – The Ride

This is California's fastest indoor roller coaster, and uses some of the most advanced animatronics ever engineered, together with space-age robotics and technology to create a thrilling, scream-worthy ride. Light levels change from daylight to total darkness and do not forget to watch out for the skeleton warriors.

Jurassic Park® – The Ride

Based on one of the most successful films of all time, *Jurassic Park®* – The Ride takes visitors on a 5.5-minute trip through 6 acres (2.5 ha) of exotic prehistoric wilderness. Steven Spielberg's epic movie leaps and roars to life with the most sophisticated state-of-the-art computer and robotic technology ever designed. Guests are hurled into the

Jurassic Park® – The Ride roars to life

steamy world of Jurassic Park, where huge five-story dinosaurs swoop to within inches of riders' faces.

Tyrannosaurus rex with a mouthful of razorsharp teeth considers each rider part of his dinner. The ride ends with an 84-ft (25-m) drop into complete darkness.

The NBC Universal Experience

This attraction gives an extraordinary, close-up view of never-before-seen props, costumes, artifacts, and special effects items pulled from many of Universal's most celebrated productions, including hits and major motion pictures that have yet to be released. Highlights include the Oscar® statuette for *The Sting*, props and costumes from Guillermo del Toro's *Hellboy II: The Golden Army*, the Speak 'N Spell transmitter from *E.T.: The Extra-Terrestrial*, Gregory Peck's briefcase and glasses from *To Kill a Mockingbird*, and military props from *All Quiet on the Western Front*. Material from new movies and artifacts from the studio's archives update the displays on a regular basis.

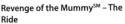
Jurassic Park® sign

❾ Griffith Park

Griffith Park is a 4,000- acre (1,600-ha) wilderness of rugged hills, forested valleys, and green meadows in the center of LA. The land was donated to the city in 1896 by Colonel Griffith J Griffith, a Welshman who emigrated to the United States in 1865 and made his money speculating in mining and property. Today, people come to Griffith Park to escape from the city crowds, visit the sights, picnic, hike, or go horseback riding. The park is safe during the day, but it should be avoided at night.

Griffith Observatory on Mount Hollywood

Exploring Griffith Park

The ranger station, located on Crystal Springs Drive, has maps of the park showing its numerous picnic areas and miles of hiking trails and bridle paths. There are two public 18-hole golf courses on the eastern side of the park and tennis courts on Riverside Drive and in Vermont Canyon.

In the hills just off Griffith Park Drive is a 1926 merry-go-round. Adults and children can still ride on its 66 carved horses and listen to its giant band organ. Across the street, an informal gathering of drummers has been meeting on Sundays since the 1960s.

Fern Dell, at the Western Avenue entrance, is a beautiful shady glen with a flowing stream and small waterfalls.

🏛 Griffith Observatory

2800 Observatory Rd. **Tel** (213) 473-0800. **Open** noon–10pm Tue–Fri, 10am–10pm Sat & Sun. 🎦 Planetarium.
W **griffithobservatory.org**

Situated on Mount Hollywood, Griffith Observatory commands stunning views of the Los Angeles basin below. The Art Deco observatory is divided into three main areas: the Hall of Science museum, the Planetarium theater, and the telescopes.

The planetarium has a seamless dome and the world's most advanced projector. In the Main Rotunda of the Hall of Science, the Foucault Pendulum demonstrates the speed of the earth's rotation. Above the pendulum are murals on a scientific theme, painted by Hugo Ballin in 1934. Characters

from Classical mythology are depicted on the domed ceiling.

Visitors are taken on a journey through space and time, as stars, moons, and planets are projected onto the ceiling. On the roof, the Zeiss Telescope is open to the public on clear nights.

🏛 Travel Town Museum

5200 W Zoo Drive. **Tel** (323) 662-5874. **Open** 10am–4pm Mon–Fri, 10am–5pm Sat & Sun. **Closed** Dec 25.
W **traveltown.org**

The spirit of the rails comes alive at this outdoor collection of vintage trains and cars. Children and adults can climb aboard freight cars and railroad carriages, or ride on a small train.

East of Travel Town, on Zoo Drive, miniature steam trains take people on rides during weekends.

🎭 Greek Theatre

2700 N Vermont Ave.
Tel (323) 665-5857. **Open** open for performances only. 🎦 for concerts.
W **greektheatrela.com**

Steam locomotive from 1922, one of 16 steam trains in Travel Town

Styled after an ancient Greek amphitheater, this open-air music venue has excellent acoustics. On summer nights, over 6,000 people can sit under the stars and enjoy performances by leading popular and classical musicians. Bring a sweater as evenings can be chilly.

🦁 Los Angeles Zoo

5333 Zoo Drive. **Tel** (323) 644-4200. **Open** 10am–5pm daily.
Closed Dec 25. 🎦 **W** **lazoo.org**

Map labels: Santa Barbara, 134, Ventura Freeway, Forest Lawn Drive, Griffith Park Drive, ①, Mulholland Highway, Western Canyon Road, Fern Dell Drive, Hollywood, Beverly H

Flamingos at Los Angeles Zoo

This 113-acre (46-ha) hilly compound has more than 1,200 mammals, reptiles, and birds living in simulations of their natural habitats.

Many newborn creatures can be seen in the Animal Nursery, including some from the zoo's breeding program for rare and endangered species. The Koala House is dimly lit to encourage the nocturnal creatures to be active. Adventure Island focuses on Southwestern animals and habitats. Visitors can also enjoy the Pachyderm Exhibit, the Rainforest of the Americas, and the Insect Interpretation Center. There are several animal shows that are aimed toward a young audience. Be prepared to walk long distances, or use the Safari Shuttle bus.

🏛 Autry National Center

4700 Western Heritage Way (opposite the zoo). Tel (323) 667-2000. Open 10am–4pm Tue–Fri, 10am–5pm Sat & Sun. Closed Thanksgiving, Dec 25. (free second Tue of month). theautry.org

The Autry National Center explores the many cultures that have shaped the American West. Artworks by such artists as Albert Bierstadt and Frederic Remington depict a romantic view of life in the region. Tools, firearms, tribal clothing, and religious figurines are some of the artifacts that show the diversity of the people who have lived here. Founded by the film star Gene Autry, "the singing cowboy," the museum also houses movie and television memorabilia. The museum is planning a major new facility in Burbank for 2020, and so some galleries and exhibits may be closed or not on show.

🐦 Bird Sanctuary

Vermont Canyon Rd (just N of Greek Theater). Tel (323) 913-4688. Open 10am–5pm daily.

Many trees and bushes have been planted in this secluded canyon to encourage local birds to nest here. Although you may not actually see many birds, you will definitely hear their song. Depending on the season, water may be running in the stream, adding to the serenity of the area.

San Fernando Valley
Ventura
Zoo Drive
Zoo Drive
Pasadena
134

Crystal Springs Drive
Golden State Freeway
Griffith Park Drive
North Trail
Del Valle Drive
Mineral Wells Trail
Vista Del Valle Drive
Fern Canyon Trail
Vermont Canyon Road
Coolidge Trail
Golden State Freeway
Crystal Springs Drive
Griffith Park Drive
Downtown Los Angeles

Griffith Park

① Travel Town Museum
② Los Angeles Zoo
③ Autry National Center
④ Merry-go-round
⑤ Bird Sanctuary
⑥ Greek Theatre
⑦ Griffith Observatory
⑧ Fern Dell

0 kilometers   1
0 miles   0.5

⓾ Dodger Stadium

1000 Elysian Park Ave (at Stadium Way). **Map** 11 F1. **Tel** (323) 224-1507. Tickets: **Tel** (323) 224-1471. **Open** for games and special events only. 🅿 ♿
ⓦ dodgers.com

This baseball stadium seats 56,000 spectators. Built in 1962 for the Brooklyn team which had moved to LA in 1958, the stadium has a cantilevered design that guarantees every seat an unobstructed view of the field.

From the stadium there are equally impressive panoramas of the city. To the south is Downtown LA, to the north and east are the San Gabriel Mountains. The stadium has undergone a multi-million-dollar renovation, resulting in a sleek, contemporary, and luxurious venue.

Queen Anne-style Hale House at Heritage Square Museum

⓫ Heritage Square Museum

3800 Homer St. **Tel** (323) 225-2700. **Open** late Mar–Oct: noon–5pm Fri–Sun; Nov–mid-Mar: 11:30–4:30pm Fri–Sun. 🅿 ♿ 🎴
ⓦ heritagesquare.org

Most Victorian buildings in Los Angeles were demolished during redevelopments, but some were saved by the Cultural Heritage Board and moved here. Dating from 1865 to 1914, they include a carriage barn, train depot, and church. Hale House, a Queen Anne-style building (see p35), has been authentically restored.

Restored interior of the 19th-century Lummis House

⓬ Lummis House

200 East Ave 43. **Tel** (818) 243-6488. **Open** 10am–3pm Sat–Sun. ♿ 🎴 donation

Also known as "El Alisal," Spanish for "Place of the Sycamore," this house was the home of Charles Fletcher Lummis (1859–1928), who built it out of concrete and rocks from the local riverbed. The structure's various design elements – Native American, Mission Revival, and Arts and Crafts – reveal the dominant influences of Lummis's life.

Constructed between 1898 and 1910, mostly by his own hands, the design reveals a creative, independent thinker.

Lummis was a newspaper editor, writer, photographer, artist, and historian. In 1885 he walked across the United States, from Ohio to LA, where he settled. He played a central role in the city's cultural life, editing the *Los Angeles Times*. As a co-founder of the California Landmark Club, he campaigned successfully for the preservation of the state's missions (see pp50–51). His collection of Native American artifacts was the basis of the holdings at the Southwest Museum.

Today, Lummis House is under the care of the LA Parks Department. Although few of Lummis's belongings remain in the house, there are some Native American artifacts. The built-in furnishings include a splendid Art Nouveau fireplace.

The garden was originally planted with vegetables and fruit trees. It was redesigned in 1985 and now grows a number of drought-tolerant and native Southern California plant species.

The Dodgers

The Dodgers originated in 1890 in Brooklyn, New York. They used to train by dodging the trolleys that traveled down that borough's streets, thus earning their name. Since moving to Los Angeles in 1958, they have become one of the most successful baseball teams in the United States. In 1955, they won the first of five world championships.

Over the years the team has had a number of outstanding players, notable examples include Sandy Koufax and Roy Campanella. In 1947, the Dodgers made headlines when they signed Pasadena-born Jackie Robinson, the first African-American to play in the major leagues.

Japanese star pitcher Hideo Nomo joined the Dodgers team in 1995, and created a sensation in his first season. During the playoffs, crowds brought Tokyo to a standstill as Nomo prepared to pitch on the other side of the Pacific Ocean.

Part of the victorious 1959 world championship team

Southwest Museum of the American Indian

Gallery Guide

Conservation of the museum's rare collection of Native American artifacts is in progress. Because of its small size, only two percent of the museum's 250,000 items are displayed at any one time. Two exhibitions are on show – one on Pueblo pottery, featuring more than 100 pieces of rare ceramics, and the other displaying highlights from the collection.

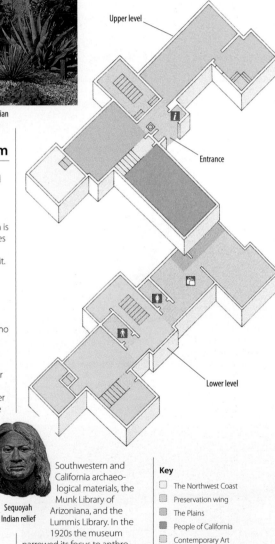

Upper level

Entrance

Lower level

⑬ Historic Southwest Museum

234 Museum Drive. **Tel** (323) 221-2165. **Open** 10am–4pm Sat. 📷 🏛
Ⓦ theautry.org

A part of the Autry National Center *(see p155)*, this museum is one of the oldest in Los Angeles and is officially named the Historic Southwest Museum Mt. Washington Campus. It was founded by Charles Fletcher Lummis, a photographer, amateur anthropologist, and prolific historian of the southwestern United States who helped popularize the idea of Los Angeles as a multicultural city. In 1884, Lummis walked from Ohio to California in a pair of knickerbockers and street shoes to take a job as a reporter for the *Los Angeles Times*. In the process he gained a national following as well as a deep appreciation for both the natural beauty and cultural diversity of the Southwest, where he remained for the rest of his life. In 1903, Lummis set out to create "a great, characteristic Southern California museum". When it opened in 1914, the museum included halls of conchology and Asian and European art, along with displays of

Sequoyah Indian relief

Southwestern and California archaeological materials, the Munk Library of Arizoniana, and the Lummis Library. In the 1920s the museum narrowed its focus to anthropology and its subject matter to the cultural history and prehistory of the indigenous peoples of the Americas.

Key

☐ The Northwest Coast
☐ Preservation wing
☐ The Plains
☐ People of California
☐ Contemporary Art
☐ People of the Southwest
☐ Non-exhibition space

⑭ Pasadena

With the completion of the Santa Fe Railroad in 1887, wealthy people from the East Coast began to spend the winter in the warmth and sunshine of Southern California. Many settled in Pasadena and were soon joined by artists and bohemians, who were also seeking the sun. This mix of creativity and wealth has resulted in a city with a splendid cultural legacy. The highlights of the area include the Huntington Library, Art Collections, and Botanical Gardens *(see pp162–5)*, and the outstanding collection of Old Masters and Impressionist paintings at the Norton Simon Museum *(see pp160–61)*.

Pasadena's city hall in the Beaux-Arts Civic Center

Exploring Pasadena

Just east of the Norton Simon Museum is **Old Pasadena**, once a decaying section of town. A dozen blocks of commercial buildings dating from the 1880s and 1890s have been restored and are now filled with stores, restaurants, and movie theaters. The mixture of Victorian, Spanish Colonial, and Art Deco architecture adds to the area's pleasant environment. The stately Beaux-Arts **Civic Center**, on Union Street at Garfield Avenue, was designed by Edward Bennett in the early 1920s. It includes the city hall, police station, post office, library, and civic auditorium. The neighborhood northeast of Gamble House has many examples of Arts and Crafts architecture *(see p35)*, most notably along tree-lined **Prospect Boulevard**.

Tiffany lamp in the Gamble House

🏟 Rose Bowl

1001 Rose Bowl Drive. **Tel** (626) 577-3101. 🚗 🌐 **rosebowlstadium.com**

Sited in a wealthy neighborhood, the stadium seats more than 100,000 people. It was built in 1922 for the annual Rose Bowl football game, which matches college teams from the Midwest and the West Coast. The first collegiate game played here was delayed for more than an hour when the visiting team was stuck in traffic, a fate that befalls many visitors today.

This is the home of UCLA's football team, the Bruins. Numerous Super Bowl games have also been played here as well as the World Cup Championships in 1994 and the 1984 Summer Olympics soccer competitions. There is also a flea market here every month.

🏟 Gamble House

4 Westmoreland Place. **Tel** (626) 793-3334. **Open** noon–3pm Thu–Sun. **Closed** public hols. 🚗 📷 obligatory. 🌐 **gamblehouse.org**

A masterpiece of the era, this wooden house epitomizes the Arts and Crafts movement, which stressed simplicity of design with superior craftsmanship. The dwelling was built in 1908 for David Gamble, of the Procter and Gamble Company. It is considered the crowning achievement of brothers Charles and Henry Greene, Boston-trained architects who visited Pasadena in 1893 and never left *(see p35)*.

Gamble House was tailor-made for LA's climate. Its terraces and open porches facilitate indoor-outdoor living, and broad overhanging eaves shade the house. At certain times of day, the sun illuminates the stained-glass front door, a dazzling sight.

🏛 Pacific-Asia Museum

46 N Los Robles Ave. **Tel** (626) 449-2742. **Open** 10am–6pm Wed–Sun. **Closed** public hols. 🚗 📷 🌐 **pacificasiamuseum.org**

Built in 1924 to a traditional northern Chinese design, the Pacific-Asia Museum houses a collection of Far Eastern art founded by art dealer and collector Grace Nicholson. Changing exhibitions on the arts of Asia and the Pacific Basin supplement the permanent collection. The museum's lovely courtyard garden is one of only a few authentic Chinese gardens in the United States.

A packed Rose Bowl during a football game

For hotels and restaurants in this area see p530 and p553

🏛 LA State and County Arboretum

301 N Baldwin Ave, Arcadia. **Tel** (626) 821-3222. **Open** 9am–4:30pm daily. **Closed** Dec 25. 🅿 ♿ 📷 (free third Tue every month).
🔲 **arboretum.org**

Situated on 127 acres (51 ha) east of Pasadena, the arboretum has more than 30,000 plant species displayed according to their geographical origin. The park includes a herb garden, a waterfall, lily ponds, and a tropical jungle. It was used as the backdrop for all of Johnny Weissmuller's *Tarzan* films (1932–48) and for some parts of Humphrey Bogart's *African Queen* (1951). Among the historical buildings in the grounds are *wickiups* (huts) used by the Gabrielino people and the reconstructed 1839 Hugo Reid adobe.

🏛 Kidspace Children's Museum

480 North Arroyo Blvd, Brookside Park. **Tel** (626) 449-9144. **Open** 10am–5pm daily (closed Mon in winter). **Closed** public hols. 🅿 ♿
🔲 **kidspacemuseum.org**

This museum engages children and families by sparking creativity and imagination through the 17 different indoor exhibits and 10 outdoor learning environments in the museum's Brookside Park location. There are also continually changing educational programs, as well as a café and a learning store.

The Rose Parade

In 1890 the Pasadena Valley Hunt Club decided to hold the first Tournament of Roses to celebrate – and advertise – the region's balmy winters. Little did they know that their horse-drawn carriages would be the start of this world-famous New Year's day extravaganza, with marching bands and riders and gigantic electronically animated floats covered in flowers, grasses or seeds.

Tropical landscaping in the LA State and County Arboretum

Rose Parade float

Pasadena City Center

① Rose Bowl
② Gamble House
③ Norton Simon Museum
④ Civic Center
⑤ Pacific-Asia Museum
⑥ Kidspace Children's Museum
⑦ Huntington Library, Art Collections, and Botanical Gardens

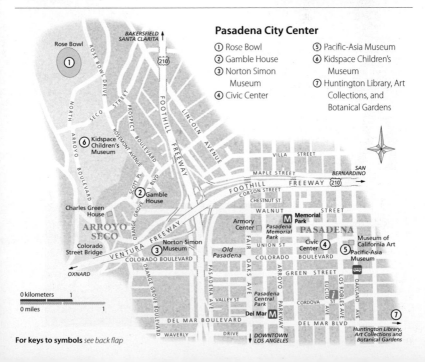

0 kilometers 1
0 miles 1

For keys to symbols *see back flap*

Norton Simon Museum

Norton Simon (1907–93) was a businessman who combined
running his multinational corporation with forming an
internationally acclaimed collection of works of art. From
the 1950s to the 1980s, he amassed, with the genius of a
connoisseur, masterpieces spanning more than 2,000 years
of Western and Asian art. Within the European holdings, the
Old Masters and Impressionist paintings are especially strong.
Renaissance, Post-Impressionism, German Expressionism, and
the modern period are also well represented. Sculptures from
India and Southeast Asia are among the finest outside the
region and offer an insight into the complex roles art and
religion play in these cultures.

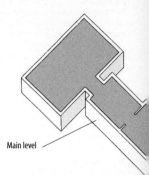

Main level

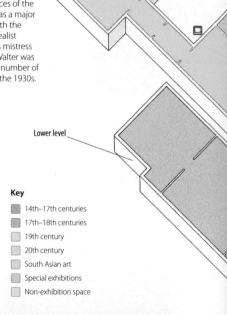

Sculpture Garden

★ Woman with a Book (1932)
Pablo Picasso, one of the
great artistic forces of the
20th century, was a major
influence on both the
Cubist and Surrealist
movements. His mistress
Marie-Thérèse Walter was
the subject of a number of
his paintings in the 1930s.

Lower level

**Little Dancer Aged
Fourteen** (1878–81)
This bronze is one
of more than 100
works by Edgar
Degas in the
museum. It features
one of the artist's
favorite subjects,
the ballet.

Key

- ■ 14th–17th centuries
- ■ 17th–18th centuries
- ▢ 19th century
- ▢ 20th century
- ■ South Asian art
- ■ Special exhibitions
- ▢ Non-exhibition space

**★ Still Life with Lemons,
Oranges and a Rose** (1633)
The Spanish painter Francisco
Zurbarán excelled at
contemplative still lifes. Many of
his works were exported to the
Spanish Americas, where they
influenced colonial painters.

Gallery Guide

The museum's galleries are on two floors. European paintings, prints, sculpture, and tapestries, dating from the Renaissance to the 20th century, as well as special exhibitions, are on the main level. The lower galleries showcase the Norton Simon's impressive collection of Indian and Southeast Asian works. Visitors can also enjoy the gallery's outdoor space, which takes the form of a huge sculpture garden with a natural pond in the center, inspired by the artworks of Claude Monet.

Saints Paul and Frediano (c.1483)
This is one of a pair of religious panels executed by Florentine artist Filippino Lippi. It shows the influence of Lippi's more famous father, Fra Filippo Lippi, and his other mentor, Botticelli.

Theater

Spiral staircase

Main entrance

Self-Portrait (c.1636–8)
Rembrandt painted nearly 100 self-portraits during his lifetime. This one shows the artist in his early thirties.

Buddha
This bronze was made in Kashmir in India in the 8th century. It is inlaid with silver and copper.

Spiral staircase

Huntington Library, Art Collections, and Botanical Gardens

Visitors and scholars alike are united in their love of the Huntington. The Beaux-Arts mansion was built between 1909 and 1911 for Henry Huntington (1850–1927), who made his fortune building a network of interurban trams in Los Angeles. In 1913 he married his uncle's widow, Arabella. Together they amassed one of the most significant libraries and collections of 18th-century British art in the world. An expansion has more than doubled the exhibit space for its growing American art collection.

Mausoleum
Designed by the architect John Russell Pope, this building in the form of a Greek temple is made of Colorado yule marble.

Main entrance

North Vista
Backed by the San Gabriel Mountains, the vista re-creates the feel of a 17th-century European garden, complete with an Italian Baroque fountain at one end.

★ Japanese Garden
Designed as a place for quiet contemplation, this typical Japanese garden includes a small lake, crossed by a curved moon bridge, and a traditional Japanese house.

Rose Garden
Nearly 1,200 rose varieties trace the development of the flower from the early blooms of classic antiquity to modern hybrids.

★ **Gutenberg Bible**
This Bible was printed on vellum around 1450–55 by Johannes Gutenberg in Mainz, Germany. It is the oldest printed book in the Huntington Library.

VISITORS' CHECKLIST

Practical Information
1151 Oxford Rd. **Tel** (626) 405-2100. **Open** Jun–Aug: 10:30am–4:30pm Wed–Mon; Sep–May: noon–4:30pm Mon, Wed–Fri; 10:30am–4:30pm Sat & Sun. **Closed** pub hols. 🅿 ♿ 📷 ✏
📷 🆆 **huntington.org**

Jungle Garden
The palms, ferns, gingers, and other plants in this garden are all typical of a tropical rainforest. The waterfalls add to the lush beauty of the garden.

★ **The Blue Boy** (c.1770)
Thomas Gainsborough's portrait of Jonathan Buttall, a merchant's son, is one of the collection's most famous paintings.

KEY

① Orange Grove

② The Munger Research Center

③ Dibner Hall of the History of Science

④ Huntington Library

⑤ Palm Garden

⑥ Desert Garden

⑦ Lily Ponds

⑧ Huntington Art Gallery

⑨ Subtropical Garden

⑩ Shakespeare Garden

⑪ Australian Garden

⑫ Zen Garden

⑬ Japanese House

⑭ Herb Garden

⑮ Boone Gallery

⑯ Chinese Garden

⑰ Virginia Steele Scott Galleries

⑱ Camellia Garden

⑲ Rose Hills Foundation Conservatory for Botanical Science

⑳ Children's Garden

Exploring the Huntington

In 1919 Henry and Arabella Huntington put their home and gardens into a trust, creating a nonprofit research institution. Today, the Huntington has undergone a $20 million renovation, adding an educational facility and cultural center, serving scholars and the public. The institution comprises one of the world's great research libraries, an outstanding art collection of 650 paintings and 440 sculptures, and over 130 acres (50 ha) of botanical gardens with plants from all over the world.

Diana Huntress (1782) by Jean-Antoine Houdon

Huntington Library

Built in 1920, the library specializes in British and American history and literature. It attracts nearly 2,000 scholars every year. The public can view key items and exhibits in the Library Exhibition Hall.

Among the 600,000 books and six million manuscripts are Benjamin Franklin's autobiography and the Ellesmere manuscript of Chaucer's *Canterbury Tales* (c.1410). The collection includes a Gutenberg Bible (c.1455) – one of only 12 surviving copies printed on vellum in the world.

There are first editions and manuscripts by noted authors, including Mark Twain, Charles Dickens, and Lord Tennyson, and early editions of Shakespeare's plays. Letters written by George Washington, Benjamin Franklin, and Abraham Lincoln are also part of the collection.

Pilgrim from *The Canterbury Tales*

Huntington Art Gallery

The Huntingtons' mansion houses the majority of the art collection, including British and French art from the 18th and early 19th centuries. The most famous works are the portraits in the Thornton Portrait Gallery, which provide an unrivaled opportunity to study British art. On display are Thomas Gainsborough's *The Blue Boy* (c.1770) and Thomas Lawrence's *Pinkie* (1794), as well as paintings by Constable, Romney, Reynolds, Van Dyck, and Turner.

The Large Library Room contains some outstanding 18th-century furnishings, which include two Savonnerie carpets made for Louis XIV, and five Beauvais tapestries. On the second floor of this palatial home, formerly occupied by the Huntingtons, are Renaissance paintings and bronzes and more choice pieces of French and British art.

Boone Gallery

The Boone Gallery displays temporary exhibitions of American and English art, rare books, and manuscripts, as well as items from the Huntington's permanent collection.

Built in 1911 as a garage for Mr Huntington's fleet of automobiles, the Neo-Classical building later fell into disrepair. Its restoration in 2000, funded by MaryLou and George Boone, provides 4,000 sq ft (370 sq m) of additional exhibition space.

Virginia Steele Scott Galleries of American Art

A major expansion added 16,379 sq ft (1,522 sq m) of gallery space that combines the old Virginia Steele Scott Gallery and the Lois and Robert F. Erburu Gallery. The space is one

Dibner Hall of the History of Science

How beautiful ideas in science have changed the world is the theme of this exhibit. The Burndy Library, formerly at the MIT, plus the Huntingdon's own history of science collection, are combined here in four galleries to present the findings of world-renowned scientists from Ptolemy to Einstein. Visitors will be able to make use of a reading room to study translations and modern editions of work in the collection.

French furniture in the Large Library Room

of the largest presentations in Southern California of American art from the colonial period through to the mid-20th century. Some of the most well-known works in the collection are *The Meeting of Lear and Cordelia* (1784), by Benjamin West (1738–1820); *Chimborazo* (1864), by Frederic Edwin Church (1826–1900); and *Breakfast in Bed* (1897), by Mary Cassatt (1844–1926). The gallery also features the marble sculpture *Zenobia in Chains* (1859), by Harriet Hosmer (1830–1908), which was discovered in a private collection after years of being presumed lost or destroyed. Other notable artists include Edward Hopper (1882–1967); and there is a group of seminal photographs by Edward Henry Weston (1886–1958).

Desert Garden

Botanical Gardens

In 1904, Henry Huntington hired landscape gardener William Hertrich to develop the grounds, which now contain 15 principal gardens.

The 12-acre (5-ha) Desert Garden has more than 4,000 drought-tolerant species from around the world. In the Rose Garden, a walkway traces the history of the species over 1,000 years, with 2,000 varieties. The oldest are found in the Shakespeare Garden.

One of the most popular areas is the Japanese Garden, with a moon bridge, Zen Garden, and Japanese plants.

Huntington Art Gallery

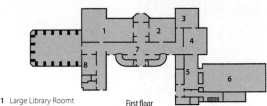

First floor

1 Large Library Room†
2 Large Drawing Room†
3 Small Drawing Room
4 Dining Room
5 Anteroom
6 Thornton Portrait Gallery
7 Hall
8 Small Library
9 European and Renaissance art
10 Ceramics
11 British art
12 Wedgwood vases
13 Silver
14 Miniatures and early 19th-century oil sketches
15 Morris and Co. stained glass window

Second floor

Dibner Hall of the History of Science

1 Astronomy
2 Natural History
3 Medicine
4 Light
5 Reading Room

Huntington Library

1 Medieval Manuscripts and Early Printing
2 English and American Literature
3 American History
4 Temporary Exhibitions

First floor

Virginia Steele Scott Galleries of American Art

1 20th century
2 19th century
3 Sculpture
4 18th century
5 17th century
6 Dorothy Collins Brown Wing
7 Susan and Stephen Chandler Wing: temporary exhibitions

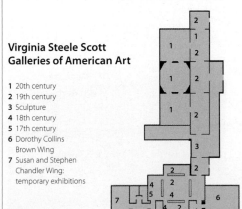

First floor

Cowboy boot stand at El Mercado

⓯ El Mercado

3425 E 1st St. **Tel** (323) 268-3451.
Open 10am–8pm daily.
W elmercadodelosangeles.com

East Los Angeles is the heart of the Mexican-American community *(see p38)*, and this marketplace caters to the locals. Its three levels bustle with taco vendors, *mariachis* (Mexican street musicians), and families out for a good meal. Unlike Olvera Street *(see p131)*, El Mercado is not designed as a tourist spot. The greatest attraction here is the authentic Mexican food and regional music.

On the main floor, stands offer everything from chilies to snack food. A *tortillaria* sells fresh, hot tortillas; bakeries display traditional Mexican breads and pastries; and delicatessens have meats you may never have seen before. To hear the *mariachis*, go to the mezzanine level, which is also where the cafeteria-style restaurants are located.

The Lakers and Basketball

Basketball originated in Springfield, Massachusetts in 1891 as a team sport that could be played indoors during the harsh winters. LA's winter may be warm, but people still love the fast-paced, high-scoring game. The city's team, the Lakers, has a huge following. Such illustrious players as Magic Johnson, Wilt Chamberlain, Kareem Abdul-Jabbar, Shaquile O'Neal, and Kobe Bryant have helped make the team one of the most successful in the National Basketball Association (NBA). The Lakers started out in Minnesota; in 1960 they came to LA; they won the NBA Championship four times in the 1980s, and now play in the state-of-the-art Staples Center (pictured below).

Magic Johnson

Brightly colored Mexican clothing, furniture, and crafts fill the shops in the basement, along with the sounds of Latin American salsa music. It gets particularly crowded on Sundays.

⓰ Flower Market

754 Wall St. **Tel** (213) 627-2482.
Open 8am–noon Mon, Wed, Fri, 6am–noon Tue, Thu, Sat.
W originallaflowermarket.com

In the early hours before sunrise the city's florists flock to this two-block long area to buy wholesale flowers and plants. Warehouses lined with tables and stands are laden with

brightly colored blossoms that contrast sharply with the gray surrounding buildings. An enormous range of flowers is offered, so that California varieties compete with plants from Columbia, New Zealand, France, and Holland.

Anyone can take advantage of the low prices (bargains are available after 8am). However, it is advisable to arrive early because supplies tend to sell out quickly.

⓱ Exposition Park and University of Southern California

See pp168–9.

⓲ LA Live

Downtown. **Map** 10 C5.
Tel (213) 763-5483. **W** lalive.com

Downtown LA has long been overlooked as a residential and shopping district but is rapidly changing with its abundance of trendy apartments, theaters, hotels, restaurants, and night clubs surrounding the Los Angeles Convention Center and the Staples Center *(see p167)*. All were part of the massive $1.7 billion LA Live sports and entertainment district development project that was completed in 2010.

The Staples Center, home to the LA Lakers and LA Clippers

For hotels and restaurants in this area see pp528–9 and p551

⓳ Staples Center

1111 S Figueroa St. **Map** 10 C5.
Tel (213) 742-7340 (Box office).
Open for events. 🖼 for events.
🅦 **staplescenter.com**

Home to three professional ball clubs, the LA Lakers, the LA Clippers (basketball), and the LA Kings (ice hockey), this stadium has revitalized downtown LA for sports fans. It also hosts the US Figure Skating Championships, major rock and pop concerts, WWF wrestling, and Hollywood awards events, as well as graduation ceremonies.

⓴ LA Arts District

East of Downtown. **Map** 11 F5.
🅦 **downtownmuse.com**

The flourishing Arts District, located roughly east of Little Tokyo and west of the LA River, has become one of the hippest destinations on the West Coast. Former factories and abandoned warehouses have been converted into stylish galleries, artists' studios, and trendy boutiques. Showcasing urban art, the exteriors of many of the former warehouses are painted with murals. The area is also dotted with specialty coffee roasters and some of the most fashionable and best bars and restaurants in the city. The neighborhood keeps growing and has emerged as a popular home for local artists and film and TV professionals.

Watts Towers, covered in shells, china, and glass

Guerilla Atelier, a luxury store and gallery on East 3rd Street in the LA Arts District

㉑ Watts Towers

1727 E 107th St, Watts. **Road map** inset A. **Tel** (213) 847-4646. 🕙 10am–4pm Wed–Sat, noon–4pm Sun. 🖼 Towers only. 🅰 Arts Center only.
🅦 **wattstowers.us**

Watts Towers is a masterpiece of folk art that embodies the perseverance and vision of Simon Rodia, an immigrant from Naples, Italy. It is the world's largest single construction created by one individual. Between 1921 and 1954, the tile-worker sculpted metal including steel rods and pipes, into a huge skeletal framework. The highest tower reaches 100 ft (30 m). Rodia adorned the cemented surface with seashells, tiles, china, and glass. He never gave a reason for building the towers and, upon finishing, he deeded the land to a neighbor and left Los Angeles.

Despite several attempts to have Watts Towers razed, it is now a State Historic Site. It stands as a symbol of hope in this area that, in 1965 was the site of the worst riots in Los Angeles.

Adjacent to the monument is the Watts Towers Arts Center. This complex displays temporary exhibitions of work by African-American artists in the community and hosts workshops for artists of all ages.

South Central Los Angeles, which includes the Watts area, is an impoverished and somewhat high-crime neighborhood. Visitors are recommended to visit only in the daytime and take commonsense precautions at all times.

⑰ Exposition Park and University of Southern California

Exposition Park began life in the 1880s as an area of open-air markets, carnivals, and horse-racing. By the end of the century, the district was rife with drinking, gambling, and prostitution. When Judge William Miller Bowen's nearby Sunday school pupils began skipping church to enjoy local temptations, he pushed for the transformation of the area into a cultural landmark that today includes three museums. The Exposition Park Rose Garden in their midst contains more than 19,000 rose bushes. Across the street, the University of Southern California (USC) covers 152 acres (62 ha) and is attended by almost 28,000 students. Founded in 1880, it is the oldest and largest private university in the western United States.

Bovard Administration Building

🏛 Doheny Memorial Library
Corner of Hoover Blvd and Childs Way, USC. **Tel** (213) 740-2924. **Open** daily.
A majestic building with Italian Romanesque, Egyptian, and Moorish design influences, USC's main reference library was built in 1932 in memory of Edward L Doheny, Jr., a trustee of the university. There is a monumental marble staircase at the entrance, and ornate stone and woodwork throughout.

🏛 Natural History Museum of Los Angeles County
900 Exposition Blvd. **Tel** (213) 763-3466. **Open** 9:30am–5pm daily. **Closed** Jan 1, Jul 4, Thanksgiving, Dec 25. 🅿 🚇 **W** nhm.org
This museum is one of the country's most significant natural and cultural history museums. A $135-million, seven-year renovation that began in 2006 has restored the Beaux-Arts 1913 building at its core, as well as a wing added to the museum in the 1920s. The buildings house the Age of Mammals exhibit and the Dinosaur Hall. The Nature Lab, and indoor-outdoor science

hub, are the latest additions. The collection aims to highlight Southern California's natural and cultural treasures.

🏛 Bovard Administration Building
Hahn Plaza, USC. **Open** daily.
This Italian Romanesque structure was named after USC's fourth president, George Bovard. The former bell tower has sculpted figures of John Wesley, Abraham Lincoln, Theodore Roosevelt, Cicero, and Plato. The Gothic Norris Auditorium seats 1,600 people. *Tommy Trojan*, a statue of a Trojan warrior by the main entrance, was sculpted in 1930 by Roger Nobel Burnham.

🏛 Los Angeles Memorial Coliseum
3911 S Figueroa St. **Tel** (213) 747-7111. **Open** for events. 🅿 🎥 by request. **W** lacoliseum.com
Built in 1928, this is the only facility in the world to host two

Natural History Museum in Exposition Park

Sights at a Glance
① Bovard Administration Building
② Tommy Trojan
③ Doheny Memorial Library
④ Mudd Memorial Hall
⑤ USC Fisher Museum of Art
⑥ Natural History Museum of Los Angeles County
⑦ Aerospace Museum
⑧ California African American Museum
⑨ California Science Center
⑩ Los Angeles Memorial Coliseum

Los Angeles Memorial Coliseum

Olympiads, two Super Bowls, and a World Series. Home court for the USC football team, it has also hosted numerous rock concerts, Nelson Mandela's triumphant return to the US in 1990, Pope John Paul II's Mass in 1987, and John F. Kennedy's 1960 acceptance speech as the Democratic party's candidate for president. The venue also benefits from a sound system and videoboards.

🏛 California Science Center

700 Exposition Park Drive. **Tel** (323) 724–3623. **Open** 10am–5pm daily. **Closed** Jan 1, Thanksgiving, Dec 25.
🌐 **californiasciencecenter.org**

One of the largest of its kind in the US, the California Science Center aims to make science accessible to people of all ages. The World of Life exhibit in the Kinsey Hall of Health explores how living things function, with Body Works, a 50-ft- (15-m-) long transparent human figure with illuminated organs, as its centerpiece. The Creative World area shows how people create what they need, following an idea from inception to production. Ecosystems invites visitors to explore eight different environments. The IMAX® Theater at the museum has a seven-story-high screen presenting nature-related movies. The **Aerospace Museum**, designed by Frank Gehry, has an F-104 Starfighter jet bolted to its facade. It features all kinds of winged craft, from a Wright Brothers' glider to a Gemini 11 space capsule. The space shuttle *Endeavour* is on display in the Samuel Oschin Pavilion.

🏛 USC Fisher Museum of Art

Harris Hall, USC. **Tel** (213) 740-4561. **Open** noon–5pm (4pm Sat) Tue–Fri. **Closed** public hols & summer.
🌐 **fisher.usc.edu**

Named after the gallery's benefactor, Mrs. Walter Harrison Fisher, the collection includes 19th-century French and American landscapes and works by Peter Paul Rubens.

🏛 California African American Museum

600 State Drive. **Tel** (213) 744-7432. **Open** 10am–5pm Tue–Sat, 11am–5pm Sun. **Closed** Jan 1, Thanksgiving, Dec 25.
🌐 **caamuseum.org**

This museum is a record of African American achievements in the arts, sciences, politics, religion, and sports. The permanent art collection includes works by artists such as Martin Pierré, Betye Saar, Noah Purifoy, and the 19th-century landscape painter Robert Duncanson. Frequent temporary exhibitions are held in the sculpture court.

🏛 Mudd Memorial Hall

Corner of Trousdale Parkway and Exposition Blvd, USC. **Open** daily.

The philosophy department's hall is predominantly pre-Renaissance Tuscan in style. Its bell tower is 146 ft (44 m) high and was used in the 1939 film *The Hunchback of Notre Dame*. Statues of great philosophers are detailed on the exterior, with the Cynic Diogenes placed over the entrance. The Hoose Library of Philosophy has more than 60,000 volumes and is considered to be one of the best in the country.

Italianate facade of the Mudd Memorial Hall

SHOPPING IN LOS ANGELES

Whatever money can buy can be found in Los Angeles, from Cartier necklaces to organic farm produce. LA's temperate climate also allows for many pleasant outdoor alternatives to the ubiquitous malls. Melrose Avenue *(see p117)* and Santa Monica's Third Street Promenade *(see p82)* are both vibrant areas. Upscale Rodeo Drive *(see p98)* and Golden Triangle *(see p94)* are famous for high couture houses and jewelers. Santa Monica's chic Montana Avenue is favored by both Hollywood wives and movie stars. The best areas for the latest in fashion and home decor are Robertson Boulevard near Burton Way, and Beverly Boulevard at Martel Avenue. Shopping is a pleasure in Old Pasadena *(see p158)*, which has many unique shops in restored, late 19th-century buildings.

Interior of the Westside Pavilion, just south of Westwood Village

Shopping Centers and Malls

Shopping centers in LA tend to outclass most other American malls. One of the newest outdoor malls in the city, **The Grove** offers a blend of shopping and entertainment venues. The street is popular with families and teens who, between all the stores, cinemas, and restaurants, find plenty to keep themselves busy. Also check out the adjacent Farmers Market *(see p117)*, where you will find many quaint souvenir shops, and inexpensive, yet excellent outdoor food stands.

For a smooth indoor mall experience, try the trendy **Beverly Center**, which boasts a selection of more than 160 stores. Surrounded by Century City's office towers and in an open-air setting, **Westfield Century City** shopping center has more than 120 shops. The newly built stadium-style cinemas and upmarket outdoor dining terrace make this mall a popular weekend hangout. Nearby, **Westside Pavilion** has an excellent array of clothing stores for children. A new cineplex adds to its appeal. **Santa Monica Place** *(see p81)* is a short walk from the beach, and is next door to the delightful Third Street Promenade. In the suburban San Fernando Valley, **Westfield Fashion Square** offers an eclectic shopping mix, with special appeal to families. One of the smaller malls, **Sherman Oaks Galleria** also boasts a fitness center and spa, in addition to its cineplex, shops, and restaurants.

Department Stores

Every shopping mall has at least one department store, all of which stock a wide variety of goods, from cosmetics and clothes to cutlery and crockery. The old favorites are **Bloomingdale's**, best known for its shop-within-a-shop boutiques, and **Macy's**, with its in-house clothing lines that offer reasonably-priced designer fashion. The Beverly Hills section of Wilshire Boulevard *(see pp94–5)* has come to be known as Department Store Row. Among its big-name retailers are **Barneys New York** and **Saks Fifth Avenue**. Barneys rooftop deli is packed at lunchtime with shoppers and crowds from the film industry. The shoe department at the high-end **Nordstrom** is legendary, as are its January and June half-price sales.

Shop logo on Melrose Avenue

Discount Stores

Many of LA's discount stores are part of national chains. A dollar goes a long way at such outlets, but it is strictly no-frills shopping.

Target is popular for household items, toys, camping gear, and casual clothes, while **Costco** vends everything from bulk food items to computers. Wine and liquor are especially well priced here. Some even sell gas, though an annual membership fee is required. Bargain hunters will delight in **99 Cents Only** stores. It is hard to predict what will be in stock, but items range from food to flower pots. **Nordstrom Rack**, the

Upscale shops on Rodeo Drive *(see p98)*

outlet for the chain, has top quality clothes, cosmetics, and lingerie. Again, the products in stock here vary by day and season. **Ross** and **Marshall's** stores carry the latest fashion with big discounts.

Food and Wine

Food markets in LA reflect the region's ethnic diversity and obsession with a healthy lifestyle. Downtown, Grand Central Market *(see p128)* sells produce and also has plenty of inexpensive food stalls. Farmers Market *(see p117)* offers fresh fruit, vegetables, and specialties such as freshly ground peanut butter. Dining alfresco here at vintage tables is a popular pastime. The market is also home to **Monsieur Marcel**, a gourmet French mini-market and deli, which specializes in cheeses, wines, and several other delicacies.

LA's homegrown food emporium, **Trader Joe's** sells an array of healthy foods, ready-to-eat meals, and wines. You can find everything from vitamins to fresh seafood here. **Whole Foods Market** also services the health-conscious, discerning customers. Prepared delights, from soups and salads to sushi, can be consumed on the spot at tables here, making it a great choice for a quick bite. **Bristol Farms** is the city's most upscale grocer and wine merchant. All of the branches are spectacular, with in-store sushi bars and cafés.

A paradise for cheese lovers, **The Cheese Store of Beverly Hills** has the widest selection of domestic and imported cheeses in LA. It also stocks luxuries such as truffles and truffle oils.

In Beverly Hills, **The Wine Merchant** keeps one of the most superb cellars in town. Specializing in California-grown estate wines, **Silverlake Wine** offers weekly tastings and friendly service.

There is no dearth of ethnic food and spices in LA, and you will find Mexican, Chinese,

A Gucci cushion

and Thai markets dotted around. A must-try among ethnic stores is **India Sweets and Spices**, which stocks all things Indian, and also serves vegetarian delicacies in its small cafeteria.

Clothes

Casual, of-the-moment styles dominate LA's fashion scene. The influence of Hollywood and its legion of slim actresses means that most trendy outlets stock breathtakingly small sizes. Unsurprisingly, custom-made haute couture is best in Beverly Hills, where you will find glitzy, red-carpet outfits throughout the shopping district. Rodeo Drive's tenants are among the who's who of the fashion world, from **Armani** to **Chanel** and **Versace**, all the most important fashion labels are within walking distance. These stores also offer sophisticated leather goods and signature fragrances. Prepare to be put on a waiting list for in-demand items. Also on Rodeo Drive is the architecturally magnificent huge **Prada**, which looks more like a museum than a retail store, with clothes, shoes, and purses that are must-haves for the upwardly mobile.

For unusual and trendsetting women's fashions at relatively affordable rates, **Anthropologie** is a fashionista's dream come true. **Eduardo Lucero** and **Trina Turk** are two of the city's most popular and original

Colorful stalls of produce in Grand Central Market *(see p128)*

designers, and both sell distinctive designs in their eponymous boutiques. **American Rag** features both new and second-hand clothes and shoes for men, women, and children.

In West Hollywood, **Fred Segal** is more a collection of individually owned hip boutiques than a single store, and is frequented by many celebrities and movie stars. **Maxfield** also attracts fashionable and well-heeled clients, who love the exciting and ultra-stylish range of women's and men's clothing labels available.

For men, **Ermenegildo Zegna** and **John Varvatos** have some of the finest menswear fashions in stock, while for the ultimate hip LA look, visit **Urban Outfitters**, the favorite of the college-aged and hipster crowd. If you' have left home without your bikini, try the trendy **Everything But Water**.

A Hollywood classic, Fred Segal boutique on Melrose Avenue

Children's Clothes

Seasonal styles sell quickly at big box retailer Target *(see p170)*, which offers good value for children's clothing. **Old Navy** has low-priced, trendy styles, and popular end-of-season sales, while **GapKids** can be found at most malls, selling the popular casual jeans and T-shirt look. Kids with a high-end brand sensibility can visit Bloomingdale's *(see p170)* for labels such as Guess and Juicy Couture.

For designer kids' clothes, be prepared to spend at speciality boutiques such as **Flicka** on Larchmont Avenue. **Rightstart** offers quality gear, toys, books, accessories, and safety items. For the baby who has everything, **James Perse** is the store for sophisticated all-cotton clothing that has won over many Hollywood moms.

Vintage Clothes

Vintage clothes in LA can be anything from hardly worn designer styles, clothes from decades past, or yesterday's cast-offs. Sifting through the racks takes time at charity-run thrift stores such as **NCJW/LA Council Thrift Shops** and **Goodwill**. You may well find treasures among the donated goods, but it is all hit-and-miss.

Hipsters and teens favor shops trading in funky recycled fashions. Try **Buffalo Exchange**, where customers bring clothes for cash or trade. **Lemon Frog** is the place of choice for boots, shoes, jewelry, sunglasses, belts, and other accessories in all price ranges, as well as a good selection of vintage dresses. **Wasteland** on Melrose Avenue has some of the most popular retro looks in stock. Do not be surprised by some of the high prices, as some vintage clothes are quite valuable.

reVamp produces new vintage-inspired clothing, focusing on fashions from between 1910 and 1950. Clothes that come straight from film and TV show wardrobe departments can be found in the Valley at **It's A Wrap!**.

Specialty Shops

Hollywood memorabilia is on sale throughout LA. **Fantasies Come True** sells only Disney-related items. Located in the heart of Hollywood, **Larry Edmund's Cinema Bookshop** is a cinephile's dream. It has new and used books, plus vintage posters. **Dark Delicacies** has everything for the horror fan, with some truly creepy items on sale. For unique, handmade items, **The Folk Tree** in Pasadena has

a superb selection of Latin American arts and crafts, while **New Stone Age** sells unusual artisan ceramics and jewelry.

Art and Antiques

Fine antiques shops are found everywhere in the city. Those in Beverly Hills and West Hollywood cater to buyers with deep pockets. **Richard Shapiro** is filled with wonderful museum-quality pieces. His vine-covered building is close to more than 25 other dealers such as **Rose Tarlow**, also known for fabrics and candles, and **Off the Wall**, which offers mid-century furniture and decor items. Window shopping in this neighborhood is a rarefied pleasure. On Sunset Boulevard, **Wells Antiques** has the city's best collection of vintage tiles and California pottery.

In addition to LA's diverse antiques shops, its art galleries run the gamut from the edgy grad-student work of Chung King Road, to the renowned contemporary artists at **Gagosian Gallery**. Bergamot Station *(see p83)* is home to several galleries, including top photograph dealer **Peter Fetterman**. Check newspaper listings for weekend gallery openings that bring out LA's art crowd.

DIRECTORY

Shopping Centers and Malls

Beverly Center
8500 Beverly Blvd.
Map 6 C2.
Tel 310-854-0070.

The Grove
189 The Grove Drive.
Map 7 D3.
Tel (323) 900-8080.

Santa Monica Place
395 Santa Monica Place,
Santa Monica.
Tel 310-394-5451.

Sherman Oaks Galleria
15301 Ventura Blvd,
Sherman Oaks.
Tel (818) 382-4100.

Westfield Century City
10250 Santa Monica Blvd,
Century City.
Tel 310-277-3898.

Westfield Fashion Square
14006 Riverside Drive,
Sherman Oaks.
Tel (818) 783-0550.

Westside Pavilion
10800 W Pico Blvd.
Tel 310-470-8752.

Department Stores

Barneys New York
9570 Wilshire Blvd.
Map 5 F4.
Tel 310-276-4400.

Bloomingdale's
Beverly Center, 8500
Beverly Blvd.
Map 6 C2.
Tel 310-360-2700.

Macy's
Beverly Center, 8500
Beverly Blvd.
Map 6 C2.
Tel 310-854-6655.

Nordstrom
Westside Pavilion, 10830
W Pico Blvd.
Tel 310-470-6155.

Saks Fifth Avenue
9600 Wilshire Blvd.
Map 5 E4.
Tel 310-275-4211.

Discount Stores

99 Cents Only
601 S Fairfax Ave.
Map 7 D4.
Tel (323) 936-3972.

Costco
2901 Los Feliz Blvd.
Tel (323) 644-5201.

Marshall's
2206 Sawtelle Blvd.
Tel 310-312-1266.

Nordstrom Rack
227 N Glendale Ave,
Glendale.
Tel (818) 240-2404.

Ross
6298 W 3rd St.
Tel 323-936-2864.

DIRECTORY

Target
7100 Santa Monica Blvd,
W Hollywood.
Map 7 F1.
Tel (323) 603-0004.

Food and Wine

Bristol Farms
9039 Beverly Blvd. **Map** 6
A2. **Tel** 310-248-2804.
w bristolfarms.com

The Cheese Store of Beverly Hills
419 N Beverly Drive,
Beverly Hills. **Map** 5 F3.
Tel 310-278-2855.
w cheesestorebh.com

India Sweets and Spices
3126 Los Feliz Blvd.
Tel (323) 345-0360.

Monsieur Marcel
Farmers Market, 6333 W
3rd St.
Map 7 D3.
Tel (323) 939-7792.
w mrmarcel.com

Silverlake Wine
2395 Glendale Blvd.
Tel (323) 662-9024.
w silverlakewine.com

Trader Joe's
7304 Santa Monica Blvd.
Map 7 F1.
Tel (323) 851-9772.
w traderjoes.com

Whole Foods Market
6350 W 3rd St.
Map 7 D3.
Tel (323) 964-6800.
w wholefoods.com

The Wine Merchant
228 N Canon Drive.
Map 5 F3.
Tel 310-278-7322.
w beverlyhillswine
merchant.com

Clothes

American Rag
150 S La Brea Ave.
Map 7 F2.
Tel (323) 935-3154.
w amrag.com

Anthropologie
320 N Beverly Drive,
Beverly Hills.
Map 5 F3.
Tel 310-385-7390.
w anthropologie.com

Armani
436 N Rodeo Drive,
Beverly Hills. **Map** 5 F3.
Tel 310-271-5555.
w armani.com

Chanel
400 N Rodeo Drive,
Beverly Hills.
Map 5 F3.
Tel 310-278-5500.
w chanel.com

Eduardo Lucero
7378 Beverly Blvd.
Map 7 E2.
Tel (323) 933-2778.

Ermenegildo Zegna
301 N Rodeo Drive,
Beverly Hills.
Map 5 F3.
Tel 310-247-8827.
w zegna.com

Everything But Water
Beverly Center, 8500
Beverly Blvd.
Map 6 C2.
Tel 310-289-1550.

Fred Segal
8118 Melrose Ave.
Map 7 D1.
Tel (323) 651-1935.

John Varvatos
8800 Melrose Ave.
Map 6 B2.
Tel 310-859-2791.

Maxfield
8825 Melrose Ave.
Map 6 B2.
Tel 310-274-8800.

Prada
343 N Rodeo Drive,
Beverly Hills.
Map 5 F3.
Tel 310-278-8661.
w prada.com

Trina Turk
8008 W 3rd St.
Map 6 C3.
Tel (323) 651-1382.
w trinaturk.com

Urban Outfitters
1440 Third St Promenade,
Santa Monica.
Tel 310-394-1404.

Versace
248 N Rodeo Drive,
Beverly Hills.
Map 5 F3.
Tel 310-205-3921.
w versace.com

Children's Clothes

Flicka
204 N Larchmont Blvd.
Map 8 B3.
Tel (323) 466-5822.

GapKids
6801 Hollywood Blvd.
Map 2 B4. **Tel** (323) 462-6124. w gap.com

James Perse
8914 Melrose Ave. **Map** 6
A2. **Tel** 310-276-7277.
w jamesperse.com

Old Navy
8487 W 3rd St. **Map** 6 C3.
Tel (323) 658-5292.
w oldnavy.com

Rightstart
2212 Wilshire Place,
Santa Monica.
Tel 310-829-5135.
w rightstart.com

Vintage Clothes

Buffalo Exchange
131 N La Brea Ave. **Map** 7
F3. **Tel** (323) 938-8604.

Goodwill
4575 Hollywood Blvd,
Hollywood. **Tel** (323) 644-1517. w goodwill.com

It's A Wrap!
3315 N Magnolia Ave,
Burbank. **Tel** (818) 567-7366. w itsawrapholly
wood.com

Lemon Frog
1202 N Alvarado St, Echo
Park. **Map** 10 C1.
Tel (213) 413-2143.

NCJW/LA Council Thrift Shops
360 N Fairfax Ave.
Map 7 D2.
Tel (323) 934-1956.

reVamp
834 S Broadway. **Map** 11
D5. **Tel** (213) 488-3387.
w revampvintage.com

Wasteland
7428 Melrose Ave. **Map** 7
E2. **Tel** (323) 653-3028.

Specialty Shops

Dark Delicacies
4213 Burbank Blvd,
Burbank. **Tel** (818) 556-6660. w darkdel.com

Fantasies Come True
4383 Tujunga Ave, Studio
City. **Tel** (818) 985-2636.
w fantasiescometrue.
com

The Folk Tree
217 S Fair Oaks Ave,
Pasadena. **Tel** (626) 795-8733. w folktree.com

Larry Edmund's Cinema Bookshop
6644 Hollywood Blvd.
Map 2 B4.
Tel (323) 463-3273.
w larryedmunds.com

New Stone Age
8407 W 3rd St. **Map** 6 C3.
Tel (323) 658-5969.
w newstoneagela.com

Art and Antiques

Gagosian Gallery
456 N Camden Drive,
Beverly Hills. **Map** 5 E3.
Tel 310-271-9400.
w gagosian.com

Off the Wall
737 N La Cienega Blvd.
Map 6 C2.
Tel (323) 930-1185.
w offthewallantiques.
com

Peter Fetterman
Bergamot Station 2525
Michigan Ave, Gallery A7,
Santa Monica.
Tel 310-453-6463.
w peterfetterman.com

Richard Shapiro
8905 Melrose Ave, W
Hollywood. **Map** 6 A2.
Tel 310-275-6700.
w rshapiroantiques.
com

Rose Tarlow
8540 Melrose Place, W
Hollywood. **Map** 6 C1.
Tel (323) 651-2202.
w rosetarlow.com

Wells Antiques
2162 Sunset Blvd.
Tel (213) 413-0558.
w wellstile.com

Many of the listings have
multiple branches. Shops
will be happy to provide
information of their
nearest branch.

Books and Music

Residents of LA buy more books than in any other city in the country. Some of the most popular independent bookshops are **Book Soup** and **Skylight Books**. Each of these old favorites regularly host readings by major writers. Also, the staff at these shops tend to be more knowledgeable about their merchandise than chain outlets. Book Soup has a great selection of art books and guidebooks devoted to California and LA, while **Hennessey & Ingalls** has one of the largest collections of art and architecture books on the west coast. **Children's Book World** stocks more than 80,000 titles for children, parents, teachers, and collectors.

Many large bookstore chains, such as **Barnes & Noble**, have coffee bars and stock music CDs as well. **Amoeba Music** *(see p110)*, located in Hollywood, is the city's largest independent music store with two floors of new and used records and CDs. The weekly in-store performances are free and fun.

Origami Vinyl is a record store that carries a curated selection of new, reissued, and used vinyls. They often host in-store performances by new indie bands.

Farmers' Markets

With 80 certified Farmers' Markets held in the city each week, there is no shortage of opportunities to see and taste Southern California's seasonal, newly harvested bounty. Each outdoor farmers' market has vendors selling a range of fresh produce, including organically grown fruits and vegetables straight from the fields. Many markets also feature stalls, which offer prepared food as well as arts and crafts. Check out the **Los Angeles Times Farmers Markets** website for exact times and locations of the various markets.

The popular **Santa Monica's Wednesday and Saturday Farmers' Market** at Arizona and Second Streets is the largest. The high quality of the produce

on sale is attested to by the well-known chefs who frequent the stalls. Savvy buyers prefer to start their shopping early. On Sunday mornings, visit Ivar Avenue's **Hollywood Farmers' Market**, which attracts a very hip crowd. Famous faces can often be spotted browsing amidst the crowd. **Santa Monica Sunday Farmers' Market** on Main Street is a favorite with families who line up for delicious, freshly made crêpes and omelets to picnic on in the busy street-side green.

Flea Markets

Most of LA's best-known flea markets take place on Sundays at varying locations. All are in the open, with hundreds, and sometimes thousands of vendors spreading out their wares over massive parking lots. Be prepared to spend more than a couple of hours browsing, bargaining, and walking. Comfortable shoes and a discriminating eye are a must. It is possible to find outstanding bargains for antiques, jewelry, vintage clothes, and assorted knick-knacks.

On the first Sunday of the month, the **Pasadena City College Flea Market** adds huge numbers of used records to the mix, while on second Sundays, the **Rose Bowl Flea Market**, one of the largest and best-loved markets in LA, sells hard-to-find collectibles. However, those who arrive early have to pay an extra entry fee. The **Long Beach Outdoor Antique & Collectible Market** runs on the third Sunday of every month and offers bargains galore.

Home Accessories

There's an entire universe of stores dedicated to outfitting LA's sprawl of homes and apartments. **IKEA** does basic home furnishings stylishly, and at extremely affordable prices. These items are generally home assembly and emphasis is more on looks than longlasting quality. **Pottery Barn** and **Crate & Barrel** serve those who do not mind spending more for

durability and good design. Both have several outlets, as does the home accessory superstore, **Bed, Bath & Beyond**. Look here for items such as kitchen gadgets, picture frames, towels, and clever decorative accessories.

Anthropologie *(see p173)* offers endearingly whimsical, flea market-style goods for the home. Glassware and crockery change palettes and styles with each season. **Shabby Chic** on Montana Avenue helped popularize the casual Southern California look, as is evident from its oversized, comfortable, and slip-covered sofas and chairs.

For both vintage as well as modern reproduction furnishings, survey the stores along Beverly Boulevard from La Brea west, to Crescent Heights. Shops such as **Modern One**, **Twentieth Design**, and **Modernica** feature the best of sleek, mid-20th-century design. **Grace Home Furnishings** is known for its eclectic new and retro furniture. Chic and tasteful, **Bountiful** sells period furniture along with luxurious bath and home products on Venice's charming Abbot Kinney Boulevard.

Gifts and Toys

Some of the best luxury gifts – from picture frames to fine jewelry – can be found in Beverly Hills' **Gearys**, a shop known for its opulent bridal and gift registry. At the other end of the price spectrum, **Wing Hop Fung** in Chinatown stocks all sorts of imported goods, from cheap toys to tea sets. Other smaller gift shops in the area are also within easy walking distance and are good for inexpensive shopping.

Sumi's in Silver Lake features local designers, as well as lines from around the world. Jewelry is the star here. **Compartes Chocolatier** sells handmade chocolates packaged in beautifully wrapped boxes. **Wacko** sells offbeat novelties, gifts, and pop-culture knick-knacks.

For toys, Target *(see p170)* and **Toys 'R' Us** have several branches selling many brands, games, and smaller sporting goods. **PuzzleZoo** has puzzles, games, and the most in-demand action figures.

Hair and Beauty

LA is the world's beauty capital. Credit goes to the youth-obsessed film and television business for the proliferation of high-quality soap-and-salve emporiums. Glossy skin care and make-up superstore **Sephora** displays dozens of product lines. Sales clerks here are helpful and offer many samples. **Aveda** adheres to organic principles in its fragrant, natural skin- and hair-care lines. Shoppers can ask for a brief, relaxing chair massage and tea. **Wilshire Beauty** was a laboratory for Rita Hayworth's colorist and Bette Davis's make-up artist, and stocks premier beauty products. **The Salon** at Fred Segal's Santa Monica branch specializes in what can be termed beauty couture. Fragrances can be made to order and make-up artists stand by for quick make-overs, using boutique brands such as Stilla.

Cost Plus World Market has bath products and candles at reasonable prices. Trader Joe's (see p171) has its own line of organic hair-and skin- care products, such as salt scrubs and lavender-scented shampoo. Many spas such as **Equinox Spa** sell higher-end skin-care lines and anti-aging regimes. Notable hair salons, including **Privé Salon**, also a spa, sells its own line of elegant hair care products. **MAC** is known for its seasonally changing color palette and alliances with top Hollywood make-up artists and stars.

DIRECTORY

Books and Music

Amoeba Music
6400 Sunset Blvd. **Map 2**
C5. **Tel** (323) 245-6400.

Barnes & Noble
1201 3rd St Promenade,
Santa Monica.
Tel 310-260-9110.

Book Soup
8818 W Sunset Blvd.
Map 1 A5.
Tel 310-659-3110.

Children's Book World
10580 1/2 W Pico Blvd,
West LA.
Tel 310-559-2665.

Hennessey & Ingalls
214 Wilshire Blvd, Santa Monica.
Tel 310-458-9074.

Origami Vinyl
1816 W Sunset Blvd.
Map 10 C1.
Tel (213) 413-3030.

Skylight Books
1818 N Vermont Ave.
Tel (323) 660-1175.

Farmers' Markets

Hollywood Sunday Farmers' Market
Ivar and Selma Aves.
Map 2 C4.
Tel (323) 463-3171.

Los Angeles Times Farmers Markets
For markets in your area see:
W projects.latimes.
com/farmers-markets

Santa Monica Sunday Farmers' Market
Ocean Park & Main St,
Santa Monica.
Tel 310-458-8712.

Santa Monica Wednesday and Saturday Farmers' Market
Arizona & 2nd Sts, Santa Monica. **Tel** 310-458-8/12.

Flea Markets

Long Beach Outdoor Antique & Collectible Market
Veterans Stadium, Faculty Ave & Conant St, Long Beach. **Tel** (323) 655-5703.

Pasadena City College Flea Market
1570 E Colorado Blvd,
Pasadena.
Tel (626) 585-7906.

Rose Bowl Flea Market
1001 Rosebowl Dr,
Pasadena.
Tel (323) 560-7469.

Home Accessories

Bed, Bath & Beyond
1557 Vine St. **Map 2** C5.
Tel (323) 460-4500.

Bountiful
1335 Abbot Kinney Blvd,
Venice.
Tel 310-450-3620.

Crate & Barrel
189 The Grove Drive. **Map** 7 D3. **Tel** (323) 297-0370.

Grace Home Furnishings
11632 Barrington Ct.
Tel 310-476-7176.

IKEA
600 N San Fernando Blvd,
Burbank.
Tel (818) 842-4532.

Modern One
7956 Beverly Blvd. **Map** 7 D2. **Tel** (323) 651-5082.

Modernica
7366 Beverly Blvd.
Map 7 F2. **Tel** (323) 933 0383.

Pottery Barn
300 N Beverly Drive.
Map 6 B3. **Tel** 310-860-9506.

Shabby Chic
1013 Montana Ave, Santa Monica.
Tel 310-394-1975.

Twentieth Design
8057 Beverly Blvd.
Map 7 D2.
Tel (323) 904-1200.

Gifts and Toys

Compartes Chocolatier
912 S Barrington Ave.
Tel 310-826-3380.

Gearys
351 N Beverly Drive,
Beverly Hills.
Map 5 F3.
Tel 310-273-4741.

PuzzleZoo
1411 3rd St Promenade,
Santa Monica.
Tel 310-393-9201.

Sumi's
1812 N Vermont Ave.
Tel (323) 660-0869.

Toys 'R' Us
11136 Jefferson Blvd,
Culver City.
Tel 310-398-5775.

Wacko
4633 Hollywood Blvd.
Tel (323) 663-0122.

Wing Hop Fung
725 W Garvey Ave,
Monterey Park.
Tel (323) 940-8000.

Hair and Beauty

Aveda
Beverly Center, 8500 Beverly Blvd. **Map** 6 C2.
Tel 310-659-5067.

Cost Plus World Market
6333 W 3rd St. **Map** 7 D3.
Tel (323) 935-5530.

Equinox Spa
2025 Ave of the Stars.
Map 5 D5.
Tel 310-556-2256.

MAC
133 N Robertson Blvd.
Map 6 B2.
Tel 310-854-0860.

Privé Salon
7373 Beverly Blvd. **Map** 7 E2. **Tel** (323) 931-5559.

The Salon
500 Broadway, Santa Monica.
Tel 310-394-8509.

Sephora
6801 Hollywood Blvd.
Map 2 B4.
Tel (323) 462-6898.

Wilshire Beauty
5401 Wilshire Blvd. **Map** 7 F4. **Tel** (323) 937-2000.

ENTERTAINMENT IN LOS ANGELES

As the center of the film industry, Los Angeles has dominated the world stage during much of the 20th and 21st centuries. It is therefore not surprising that the city sees itself as the Entertainment Capital of the World. LA's large and successful artistic community ensures that there is always plenty to do in the city, although only small areas tend to be lively after dark.

LA also has a huge number of theaters, which range from 1930s movie palaces to state-of-the-art multiplexes. Stage productions are also plentiful and diverse. The city has a well-respected symphony orchestra and opera company, which in the summer give outdoor concerts in places such as the Hollywood Bowl *(see p115)*. Jazz and blues bars and clubs are centered on Sunset Boulevard.

LA listings publications

Information

Various publications can help sift through the city's embarrassment of entertainment riches. The *LA Weekly* – a free paper available at bars, clubs, and corner stands across the city – has the most comprehensive entertainment and arts listings. It is aimed at the younger generation and outshines the *Los Angeles Times* in that respect, although the *Los Angeles Times* is also a reliable source of information.

The monthly publications include the popular *Los Angeles Magazine*, which lists all the main events in the city and also has good restaurant reviews. More up-to-date and reliable information, aimed at tourists, is provided in the monthly *Where Magazine*, which is available in most hotels.

Listings for the gay, lesbian and bisexual community include *Odyssey Magazine*, *Edge Los Angeles*, and the popular *Curve Magazine*.

The most convenient branch of the **Los Angeles Convention and Visitors Bureau** is in Hollywood, and it offers multilingual assistance. Their visitors' guide gives listings of restaurants, hotels, shops, and attractions, and there is a detailed calendar of events on their very useful website. The city's other main tourist information center is **Visit West Hollywood**. In addition, **laweekly.com** has useful information.

Buying Tickets

The most straightforward place to buy tickets to concerts, plays, and sports events in LA is **Ticketmaster**. You can order your tickets online using a credit card, or visit one of the outlets in selected Walmart stores. If you want to avoid Tickemaster's hefty service charges, try calling the venues direct, but keep in mind that most ticket sellers have an administration fee of some sort. You could also try online ticket reseller **StubHub** or another ticket agency such as **Prestige Tickets** or **Los Angeles Times Tickets**.

Theater productions and times are available by calling **LA Stage Alliance**'s information line.

Discount Tickets

Barry's Tickets promises premium seats for sports, music, and theater events. This service also sells half-price theater tickets online. Most are for short-run shows – do not expect the most popular shows to be discounted.

If you are looking for a bargain and are willing to gamble on the availability of seats a few hours before the show starts, then you can try telephoning the box office direct. Many places offer last minute "rush" discounts on unsold seats for performances.

Students who hold a valid ISIC card *(see p592)* may be able to get discounts to some concerts and plays. Try those places affiliated with Los Angeles's universities, such as UCLA's Geffen Playhouse *(see p179)*.

LACMA *(see pp118–21)*, a venue for free concerts

Hollywood Bowl, one of LA's premier concert venues *(see p115)*

Free Events

Most Los Angeles neighborhoods have local festivals, particularly in the summer, which often feature food and live music. The **Los Angeles Department of Cultural Affairs** publishes detailed listings of festivals in the city that you can download from their website. On Thursday nights in the summer, Santa Monica Pier has concerts featuring a variety of music styles *(see pp82–3)*.

Also in the summer, the LA Philharmonic allows visitors to listen to its mid-day concert rehearsals at the Hollywood Bowl *(see p115)*.

Some of Los Angeles's museums do not charge entrance fees. They include the California Science Center *(see p169)*, Travel Town in Griffith Park *(see p154)*, and the J Paul Getty Museum *(see pp86–9)*. Los Angeles County Museum of Art *(see pp118–21)* hosts concerts of jazz and chamber music on Fridays and Sundays in the museum plaza.

Facilities for the Disabled

As elsewhere in California *(see p592)*, almost all clubs, movies, and theaters in LA are wheelchair accessible and will provide special seating. Most establishments also have parking and toilets designed to facilitate the needs of people with disabilities.

Information about disabled access at events and attractions can be found on **discoverlos angeles.com**. **LA Tourist** is a website with information on most LA attractions, including whether or not they are wheelchair-accessible, have assisted-listening systems, sign-language interpreters, ramps, elevators, and handicapped parking.
AbilityTrip provides information about transportation and equipment rental, with links to useful websites. **Travelers Aid International** operates a website with links to many resources for disabled travelers throughout the United States.

Detail on a LA theater

DIRECTORY

Useful Numbers

Los Angeles Convention and Visitors Bureau
6801 Hollywood Blvd, Hollywood, CA 90028.
Map 2 B4.
Tel (323) 467-6412.
W discoverlosangeles.com

Los Angeles Department of Cultural Affairs
201 N Figueroa St, Suite 1400, Los Angeles, CA 90012.
Map 11 D3.
Tel (213) 202-5500.
W culturela.org

Visit West Hollywood
8687 Melrose Ave, Suite M-38.
Map 6 B5.
Tel (800) 368-6020.
W visitwesthollywood.com

Ticket Agencies

Barry's Tickets
Tel (866) 708-8499.
W barrystickets.com

LA Stage Alliance
Tel (213) 614-0556.
W lastagealliance.com

Los Angeles Times Tickets
Tel (866) 215-8463.
W tickets.latimes.com

Prestige Tickets
Tel (888) 595-6260.
W prestigetickets.com

StubHub
W stubhub.com

Ticketmaster
Tel (213) 381-2000.
W ticketmaster.com

Facilities for the Disabled

AbilityTrip
W abilitytrip.com

LA Tourist
W latourist.com

Travelers Aid International
1612 K St, NW, Suite 206, Washington, DC 20006.
W ustravability.org

Art Deco facade of Hollywood's Pantages Theater *(see p116)*

Entertainment Venues

As befits a city of its size and reputation, LA has a vast range of entertainment spots. Sophisticated restaurants, concert venues, and lounges are found throughout the city. Downtown's Grand Avenue is the main cultural corridor, and is graced by the prestigious Museum of Contemporary Art and by the Music Center *(see p129)*. Hollywood and West Hollywood abound with historic movie houses, theaters, and celebrity-owned nightclubs such as The Viper Room *(see p106)*. By day, visitors can join a TV studio audience or watch a game at one of the major sports arenas. Almost every weekend, a vibrant themed festival takes place somewhere in the city.

The Rooftop at the Standard Downtown Hotel

Bars

From traditional, old-school watering holes to the latest and trendiest hot spots, LA's diverse bar scene is always expanding. Enjoy yourself, but be aware of rigorously enforced anti-drinking-and-driving laws when planning your itinerary for the evening.

At **Musso and Frank Grill**, a historic Hollywood cornerstone, the cocktails and decor remain almost unchanged since the time when renowned author William Faulkner drank here. Specialty bars also abound. The kitschy yet hip **El Carmen** serves

more than 270 kinds of tequila along with authentic Mexican bar fare. European-style gastro-pub **Father's Office** in Santa Monica has 36 artisan beers on tap and a wonderful choice of estate wines. It serves some of the most outstanding bar snacks in town. Trendy **Covell** is another low-key wine and craft beer bar with inventive appetizers and comfort food. **Tom Bergin's Tavern** is a traditional Irish pub, with veteran bartenders who prepare the best Irish coffee in town. For star sightings, try **Polo Lounge** at Beverly Hills Hotel *(see p528)*, or **Windows Lounge** at Four Seasons Hotel. Both venues cater to tycoons, the very well-heeled, and celebrities. **The Rooftop** at Standard Downtown combines panoramic skyscraper views with alfresco lounging all year long. The bar is gently lit by lights from the office towers nearby, while an outdoor

Club sign on Sunset Boulevard

fireplace keeps the rooftop warm. The intimate and elegant **The Lounge**, right in the lobby of Hotel Casa del Mar, is cozily furnished with plush leather couches, and offers stunning ocean views.

Clubs

Trends change rapidly in LA's dynamic club scene, so check local listings to stay up-to-date. Also, be prepared to show ID, since the 21-and-over drinking law is strictly enforced.

For the best clubbing action in LA, head to Hollywood. **The Avalon** is one of the oldest and most beloved clubs in the area, often attracting world-famous DJs and performers. It also houses the stylish Spider Club, an intimate VIP lounge. For clubbing with a twist, try **CineSpace**, which shows films on screens placed throughout the lounge.

In Santa Monica, **Zanzibar** has the hippest DJs and decor. For rock and indie music, **Bar Chloe** and **Hotel Cafe** are best, often featuring live gigs by up-and-coming bands.

West Hollywood, with its sizeable gay population, has many discos such as **The Factory** for a fun night out. Both **The Mayan** and **The Conga Room** are hot venues for salsa, merengue, and rock *en español* music.

Comedy Clubs

For ample laughs, visit one of LA's many comedy clubs. Talented unknowns, as well as major names, perform at **The Comedy Store**, **The Improv**, and **Laugh Factory**.

Movie Theaters

Most visitors do not spend a lot of time watching movies in LA, even though current releases and countless classics are always being shown. The movie palaces themselves, however, draw huge crowds, with TCL Chinese and El Capitan

Hotel Casa del Mar's luxurious and popular lobby bar, Lounge at Casa

theaters *(see p114)* being the best known.

Multiplexes, such as **The Grove, ArcLight Cinemas,** and **AMC Universal CityWalk 19** offer state-of-the-art entertainment. Built as a silent film palace in 1922, **The Egyptian Theater** is old Hollywood at its best, run by American Cinematheque, it now shows a mix of cult and international films. For a nostalgia trip, visit **Silent Movie Theatre,** which shows classics from the 1920s. Screenings here are frequently accompanied by charming musical performances.

Studio Tours And TV Shows

Several of LA's television and film studios offer behind-the-scenes tours as well as tickets to tapings of popular shows. In the high-tech studios of **CBS-TV,** sitcoms and game shows are taped before live audiences. For tickets, write about six weeks before your trip, specifying the date and show you want to see. Audience members must understand and speak English. During production season, July through March, check the **TV Tickets** website for entrance to dozens of shows.

The **Warner Bros** tour is probably the truest look at modern-day film-making – the deluxe tour includes lunch at the studio commissary. Visitors on the **Paramount Studios** *(see p117)* tour must be at least 12 years old. Show tickets are also available.

Theater

With hundreds of professional plays staged each year, there is something for everyone in Los Angeles. Downtown's Music Center *(see p129)* is home to two of the city's leading theaters for drama – **Mark Taper Forum** and **Ahmanson Theatre.** Ahmanson and Pantages *(see p116)* in Hollywood attract the big Broadway musicals, while the intimate Mark Taper Forum is known for its experimental drama. Sunset Boulevard's

Dolby Theater (home to the annual Academy Awards® telecasts) and the new **Nokia Theatre** at LA Live downtown host numerous special events, variety shows, concerts, and dance events. Housed in striking Mediterranean-style theaters, **Geffen Playhouse** and **Pasadena Playhouse** both put on new works as well as old favorites. More alternative productions are performed at the city's smaller spaces, such as **The Actors' Gang** or the innovative **REDCAT Theater.** In summer, the popular **Theatricum Botanicum** stages Shakespeare's classics in its outdoor amphitheater.

Rock, Jazz, and Blues

Still rocking the world, Sunset Strip *(see pp106–8)* boasts the venerable **Whisky A Go-Go.** A rock'n'roll legend since the time it hosted performances by The Doors, it carries on the tradition by featuring gigs by many established artists. Nearby, perennial favorite **The Roxy** may be somewhat cramped, but that does not deter the big names in rock from performing there. **The Viper Room,** with its line-up of promising new bands, also remains hugely popular with the young Hollywood crowd.

LA's jazz scene is lively and characterized by cozy joints such as **The Baked Potato,** where there are weekly jam sessions, performances by well-known studio artists, and gourmet baked potatoes on the menu. A refined, classic

Music Center plaza and fountain leading to Mark Taper Forum

atmosphere defines the well-respected **Catalina Bar & Grill. Piano Bar** always has live jazz and blues, friendly service, and no cover charge.

Look for top soul and blues acts in **House of Blues,** and try its "Gospel brunch." The grungy **Troubadour** often hosts promising newcomers, while **McCabe's Guitar Shop** is frequented by musicians for its emphasis on music and performances.

The historic 1920s **Fonda Theatre** hosts a variety of performances and parties and has a rooftop area that overlooks the Hollywood Boulevard.

The biggest names perform at LA's arenas, including Staples Center *(see p167)*, Hollywood Bowl *(see p115)*, and Greek Theatre *(see p154)*. Expect stratospheric ticket prices and parking charges at these top venues.

Roxy sign on Sunset Boulevard

Paramount Studios' famous gates *(see p117)*

Opera, Dance, and Classical Music

The **LA Philharmonic**, which winters at the Walt Disney Concert Hall (see p129) is a world-class orchestra. During the season, performances range from classical favorites to avant garde, modern works. The Philharmonic's summer home, the idyllic outdoor Hollywood Bowl (see p115), is famous for its magical musical moments, and is a perfect spot for relaxed alfresco picnicking.

The **LA Opera**, under the direction of Plácido Domingo, performs at the Dorothy Chandler Pavilion (see p129) between September and June. Chamber groups perform at various places, such as the **Colburn School of Performing Arts**, throughout the city. Colburn also offers a season of free performances, including music, dance, and drama.

Glendale's historic **Alex Theater** offers concerts, dance, and drama. The acoustically outstanding Royce Hall is the main venue at the **Center for the Art of Performance at UCLA**. More than 200 performances are featured annually, and offer an eclectic mix of vanguard theater, spoken word, music, and dance, with appearances by many prominent international artists. At the **Ford Amphitheatre**, you can enjoy music, dance, and outdoor film screenings as you feast on a picnic under the stars.

Outdoor Activities

Los Angeles's beaches are a great natural resource and offer surfing, swimming, and volleyball. The 27-mile- (43-km-) long stretch of beaches, with their adjacent bike and skate paths, make for delightful and invigorating rides. Beachside bike and skate rental outlets are plentiful.

Griffith Park (see pp154–5) and Topanga State Park (see p85) offer miles of hiking trails. Griffith Park also has horse trails, two golf courses, and two tennis centers. Many city parks have free tennis courts.

Spectator sports include baseball at Dodger Stadium (see p156), professional soccer at the Galaxy's deluxe **StubHub Center**, and ice hockey and basketball at the Staples Center (see p167). Besides these, you can watch horse racing at the **Santa Anita Racetrack**, and polo at Will Rogers State Historic Park (see p85).

Children's Entertainment

A variety of family-friendly diversions are available in Los Angeles, ranging from the free seaside street theater of the Venice Beach boardwalk to IMAX® movies at the **California Science Center**. During the warmer months, a visit to the beach or the pool is a good idea. The **Under the Sea Indoor Playground** has a turbo slide, games and more. Children can romp at the expanded **Kidspace Children's Museum**, which blends science and fun in hands-on exhibits. An outdoor garden and waterway add much to the visit. Since 1963, **Bob Baker Marionette Theater** has kept kids spellbound with its traditional puppet theater. Musical theater at **Santa Monica Playhouse** is especially tailored for young audiences.

It is also worth checking newspaper listings pages (see p176), which provide details and contact information of upcoming seasonal festivals.

DIRECTORY

Bars

Covell
4628 Hollywood Blvd, Los Feliz. **Tel** (323) 660-3400.
W barcovell.com

El Carmen
8138 W 3rd St. **Map** 6 C3.
Tel (323) 852-1552.

Father's Office
1018 Montana Ave, Santa Monica.
Tel 310-736-2224.
W fathersoffice.com

The Lounge
Hotel Casa del Mar, 1910 Ocean Way, Santa Monica.
Tel 310-581-5533.
W hotelcasadelmar.com

Musso and Frank Grill
6667 Hollywood Blvd.
Map 2 B4.
Tel (323) 467-7788.

Polo Lounge
Beverly Hills Hotel, 9641 Sunset Blvd.
Map 5 D2.
Tel 310-276-2251.
W thebeverlyhillshotel.com

The Rooftop
Standard Downtown Hotel, 550 S Flower St.
Map 11 D4.
Tel (213) 892-8080.
W standardhotels.com

Tom Bergin's Tavern
840 S Fairfax Ave.
Map 7 D4.
Tel (323) 936-7151.
W tombergins.com

Windows Lounge
Four Seasons Hotel, 300 S Doheny Drive.
Map 6 A3.
Tel 310-273-2222.

Clubs

The Avalon
1735 Vine St. **Map** 2 C4.
Tel (323) 462-8900.
W avalonhollywood.com

Bar Chloe
1449 2nd St, Santa Monica. **Tel** 310-899-6999. W barchloe.com

CineSpace
6356 Hollywood Blvd.
Map 2 C4. **Tel** (323) 817-3456. W cine-space.com

The Conga Room
LA Live downtown, 800 W Olympic Blvd. **Map** 10 C5.
Tel (213) 745-0162.
W congaroom.com

The Factory
652 N La Peer Drive. **Map** 6 A2. **Tel** 310-659-4551.
W factorynight club.com

Hotel Cafe
1623/2 Cahuenga Blvd.
Map 2 C4.
Tel (323) 461-2040.
W hotelcafe.com

The Mayan
1038 S Hill St. **Map** 10 C5.
Tel (213) 746-4287.

Zanzibar
1301 Fifth St, Santa Monica.
Tel 310-451-2221.
W zanzibarlive.com

Comedy Clubs

The Comedy Store
8433 W Sunset Blvd. **Map** 1 A5. **Tel** (323) 650-6268.
W thecomedy store.com

The Improv
8162 Melrose Ave. **Map** 7 D1. **Tel** (323) 651-2583.
W improv.com

DIRECTORY

Laugh Factory
8001 W Sunset Blvd.
Tel (323) 656-1336.
W laughfactory.com

Movie Theaters

AMC Universal CityWalk 19
100 Universal City Plaza, Universal City.
Tel (818) 508-0711.
W amctheatres.com

ArcLight Cinemas
6360 W Sunset Blvd. **Map** 2 C5. **Tel** (323) 464-1478.
W arclightcinemas.com

The Egyptian Theater
6712 Hollywood Blvd.
Map 2 B4. **Tel** (323) 466-3456. W americancine
mathequecalendar.com

The Grove
189 Grove Drive. **Map** 7 D3. **Tel** (323) 692-0829.
W thegrovela.com

Silent Movie Theatre
611 N Fairfax Ave. **Map** 7 D1. **Tel** (323) 655-2510.
W cinefamily.org

Studio Tours and TV Shows

CBS-TV
7800 Beverly Blvd. **Map** 7 D2. **Tel** (323) 575-2345.
W cbs.com

Paramount Studios
5555 Melrose Ave. **Map** 8 C7. **Tel** (323) 956-4848.
W paramount
studios.com

TV Tickets
W tvtickets.com

Warner Bros
3400 Riverside Dr, Burbank. **Tel** (818) 972-8687. W wbsstudio
tour.com

Theaters

The Actors' Gang
9070 Venice Blvd, Culver City. **Tel** 310-838-4264.
W theactorsgang.com

Ahmanson Theatre, Mark Taper Forum
135 N Grand Ave. **Map** 11 E3. **Tel** (213) 972-7211.
W musiccenter.org

Dolby Theater
6801 Hollywood Blvd.
Map 2 B4.
Tel (323) 308-6300.
W dolbytheatre.com

Geffen Playhouse
10886 Le Conte Ave.
Map 4 A4.
Tel 310-208-2028.
W geffenplayhouse.
com

Nokia Theatre
776 Chick Hearn Ct.
Map 10 C5. **Tel** (213) 763-6030.
W nokiatheatrelalive.
com

Pasadena Playhouse
39 S El Molino Ave, Pasadena. **Tel** (626) 356-7529. W pasadenaplay
house.org

REDCAT Theater
631 W 2nd St.
Map 11 D3. **Tel** (213) 237-2800. W redcat.org

Theatricum Botanicum
1419 Topanga Canyon Blvd, Topanga.
Tel 310-455-2322.
W theatricum.com

Rock, Jazz, and Blues

The Baked Potato
3787 Cahuenga Blvd W, Studio City.
Tel (818) 980-1615.
W thebakedpotato.
com

Catalina Bar & Grill
6725 W Sunset Blvd.
Map 2 B5.
Tel (323) 466-2210.
W catalinajazzclub.
com

The Fonda Theatre
6126 Hollywood Blvd.
Map 2 B4.
Tel (323) 464-6269.
W fondatheatre.com

House of Blues
8430 W Sunset Blvd.
Map 1 A5.
Tel (323) 848-5100.
W hob.com

McCabe's Guitar Shop
3101 Pico Blvd, Santa Monica. **Tel** 310-828-4497. W mccabes.com

Piano Bar
6429 Selma Ave. **Map** 2 C4. **Tel** (323) 466-2750.
W pianobarhollywood.
com

The Roxy
9009 W Sunset Blvd.
Map 6 A1. **Tel** 310-278-9457.
W theroxyonsunset.
com

Troubadour
9081 Santa Monica Blvd.
Map 6 A2.
Tel 310-276-1158.
W troubadour.com

The Viper Room
8852 W Sunset Blvd.
Map 6 B1. **Tel** 310-358-1880. W viperroom.
com

Whisky A Go-Go
8901 W Sunset Blvd.
Map 6 B1. **Tel** 310-652-4202. W whiskyagogo.
com

Opera, Dance, and Classical Music

Alex Theater
216 N Brand Blvd, Glendale.
Tel (818) 243-2539.
W alextheater.com

Center for the Art of Performance at UCLA
340 Royce Drive. **Map** 4 A4. **Tel** 310-825-2101.
W cap.ucla.edu

Colburn School of Performing Arts
200 S Grand Ave. **Map** 11 D4. **Tel** (213) 621-2200.
W colburnschool.edu

Ford Amphitheatre
2580 E Cahuenga Blvd.
Map 2 B3.
Tel (323) 461-3673.
W fordamphitheatre.
org

LA Opera
135 N Grand Ave.
Map 11 E3.
Tel (213) 972-8001.
W laopera.com

LA Philharmonic
W laphil.org

Outdoor Activities

Griffith Park
4730 Crystal Springs Drive. **Map** 3 F2.
Tel (323) 913-4688.
W laparks.org

Santa Anita Racetrack
285 W Huntington Drive, Arcadia.
Tel (626) 574-7223, (800) 574-6401.
W santaanita.com

StubHub Center
18400 Avalon Blvd, Carson.
Tel 310-630-2000.
W stubhubcenter.com

Children's Entertainment

Bob Baker Marionette Theater
1345 W 1st St. **Map** 10 C3.
Tel (213) 250-9995.
W bobbaker
marionettes.com

California Science Center
700 State Drive.
Tel (213) 724-3623
W california
sciencecenter.org

Kidspace Children's Museum
480 N. Arroyo Blvd, Pasadena. **Tel** (626) 449-9144. W kidspace
museum.org

Santa Monica Playhouse
1211 4th St, Santa Monica. **Tel** 310-394-9779. W santamonica
playhouse.com

Under The Sea Indoor Playground
12211 W Washington Blvd, No. 120.
Tel 310-915-1133.
W underthesea
indoorplayground.com

GETTING AROUND LOS ANGELES

The sheer size of Los Angeles – a sprawling 467 sq miles (1,200 sq km) – may seem daunting to navigate. A vast network of freeways *(see pp184–5)* provides an accessible, if sometimes crowded, means of traveling in the area. The fastest method of touring the city is by car, although the public transportation system works well in Downtown Los Angeles and Hollywood. Los Angeles has a total of 200 bus lines that run on most of the main streets in the city. LA's growing rail system, the Metro, is useful when exploring Downtown. Some neighborhoods are best seen on foot. Taxis are usually ordered by telephone. They travel all over town, but can be expensive.

Driving toward Downtown Los Angeles on the freeway

Driving

Planning ahead is the key to making sure that driving in Los Angeles is less stressful and not overwhelming. First, refer to the map on pages 184–5 to see which freeway changes or exit you will need. Second, avoid rush hour on the freeways. The peak times are from Monday to Friday, 7am to 9:30am and 4pm to 6:30pm. Carpool lanes are reserved for cars with at least two passengers, and are much faster on the freeways.

When parking, always remember to read the posted signs for limitations and carry plenty of quarters for the parking meters. At night it is safer to valet park.

Walking

Even though the city is very spread out, some districts are pedestrian-friendly. Third Street Promenade and the beach and Main Street in Santa Monica *(see pp80–83)* are all pleasant areas for walking. Other areas include: the business district in Downtown Los Angeles *(see pp126–7)*, Old Pasadena *(see p158)*, Melrose Avenue *(see p117)*, the Golden Triangle in Beverly Hills *(see pp94–5)*, and Long Beach's Pine Avenue *(see p136)*. Do not walk alone at night unless the street is well lit and populated.

Cycling

The coastal bike path that runs for 25 miles (40 km) beside Santa Monica Bay is the best place to cycle. Other popular areas are Venice Beach, Griffith Park, and the Oceanside Bike Path in Long Beach. Note that bicycles are not allowed on the freeways. The **LA Department of Transportation** provides detailed route maps, and bikes and skates can be rented by the day or hour from **Perry's Café Bike Rentals** along Santa Monica beach and at several pizza stands.

Bus and Rail System

Greater LA is served by the **Metropolitan Transportation Authority (MTA)**. Bus stops display a metro sign. Buses run on main thoroughfares: Wilshire Blvd to Santa Monica Beach, Nos. 20 and 720; to Westwood and UCLA, No. 21; Santa Monica Blvd to the beach, No. 4; Sunset Blvd to Pacific Palisades, No. 2. The **DASH** shuttle provides travel within small areas, such as Downtown LA and Hollywood. The **Santa Monica Blue Bus Co.** and **Long Beach Transit** also service those areas.

The Metro light rail and Subway is a rail system that features five separate lines: Red, Purple, Blue, Green, and Gold. These lines serve 70 stations in and around Los Angeles. The rapid bus transit Orange and Silver Lines connects with the suburbs and the Metrolink rail system. The Metrolink is used mainly by commuters and serves Los Angeles and Southern California.

The Los Angeles rail network is expanding with further Metro light rails planned to create a

Cycling through Venice on the bike path

link between Downtown Los Angeles and Santa Monica.

The Metro system runs between 5am and 12:30am. A weekend service runs on public holidays. Single rides cost $1.75. A one-week pass is $25 for unlimited rides. The Trip Planner at metro. net is a great way to quickly plan your trip by bus or rail.

Taxis and Limousines

Two reliable taxi companies are **Yellow Cab** and the **Independent Cab Co**. Or for a luxurious alternative, rent a limousine from **Limousine Connection** and **Orange County Limo Rental**. **Uber** and **Lyft** are two popular ridesharing alternatives.

Guided Tours

Private bus lines such as **Guideline Tours** offer visitors tours around the city and to the major theme parks. You can view the homes of movie stars and local celebrities with **Hollywood Tours** and **Starline Tours**. The popular **Dearly Departed Tours** visits sites of famous crimes and scandals, while **Another Side of LA Tours** offers helicopter flights and Segway tours. If group tours do not appeal, the **LA Conservancy** provides free audio clips for self-guided walking tours of the downtown area of LA's historic district – a great way to view this area.

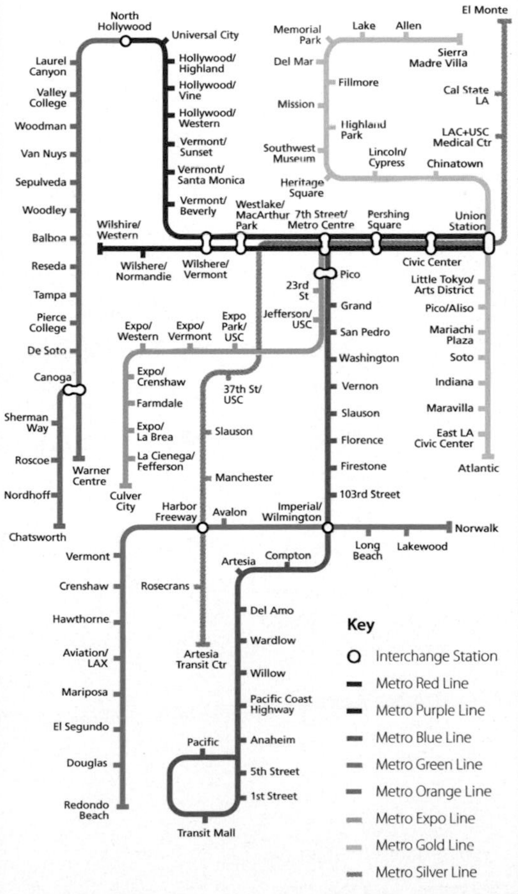

DIRECTORY

Cycling

LA Department of Transportation (LADOT)
100 Main St. **Tel** (213) 972-4962.
W ladottransit.com

Perry's Café Bike Rentals
1200 Palisades Beach Road, Santa Monica. **Tel** 310-458-3975.

Buses and Rail Systems

DASH
Tel (818) 808-2273.
W ladottransit.com

Long Beach Transit
Tel (562) 591-2301.
W lbtransit.com

Metropolitan Transportation Authority (MTA)
Tel (800) 266-6883. W metro.net

Santa Monica Blue Bus Co.
Tel 310-451-5444.
W bigbluebus.com

Taxis and Limousines

Independent Cab Co.
Tel (800) 521-8294.

Limousine Connection
Tel (800) 266 5466.

Lyft
W lyft.com

Orange County Limo Rental
Tel (888) 766-7433.

Uber
W uber.com

Yellow Cab
Tel (877) 733-3305.

Guided Tours

Another Side of LA Tours
Tel 310-289-8687.
W anothersideoflosangeles tours.com

Dearly Departed Tours
Tel (323) 466-3696.
W dearlydepartedtours.com

Guideline Tours
Tel (800) 604-8433.
W guidelinetours.com

Hollywood Tours
Tel (800) 789-9575.
W hollywoodtours.us

LA Conservancy
W laconservancy.org

Starline Tours
Tel (800) 959-3131.
W starlinetours.com

Metro Rail System

Key
O Interchange Station
— Metro Red Line
— Metro Purple Line
— Metro Blue Line
— Metro Green Line
— Metro Orange Line
— Metro Expo Line
— Metro Gold Line
— Metro Silver Line

Los Angeles Freeway Route Planner

A car is essential in Los Angeles and is the quickest way of getting around this vast city. All freeways are numbered but most also have names, such as the Golden State Freeway (I-5). Plan your trip carefully: freeway exits are marked by street name and direction rather than by area. It is advisable not to use the freeways during rush hour (7–9:30am and 4–6:30pm). For more details on getting around LA see pages 182–3.

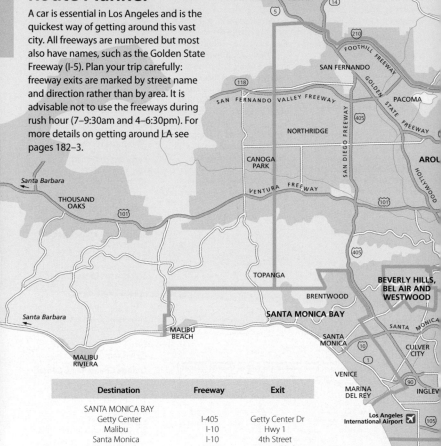

Destination	Freeway	Exit
SANTA MONICA BAY		
Getty Center	I-405	Getty Center Dr
Malibu	I-10	Hwy 1
Santa Monica	I-10	4th Street
Venice Beach	I-405	Venice Blvd
BEVERLY HILLS, BEL AIR, AND WESTWOOD		
Golden Triangle	I-405	Santa Monica Blvd
UCLA	I-405	Wilshire Blvd
HOLLYWOOD AND WEST HOLLYWOOD		
Hollywood Blvd	US 101	Hollywood Blvd
Sunset Blvd	US 101	Sunset Blvd
DOWNTOWN LOS ANGELES		
Business District	Hwy 110	6th Street
El Pueblo	US 101	Alameda Street
LONG BEACH AND PALOS VERDES		
Naples	I-405	Studebaker Rd
Queen Mary	I-710	Pico Avenue
San Pedro	I-110	Gaffey Street
AROUND DOWNTOWN		
Exposition Park	I-110	Exposition Blvd
Griffith Park	I-5	Zoo Drive
Pasadena	Hwy 110	Arroyo Parkway
Universal Studios	US 101	Cahuenga Blvd

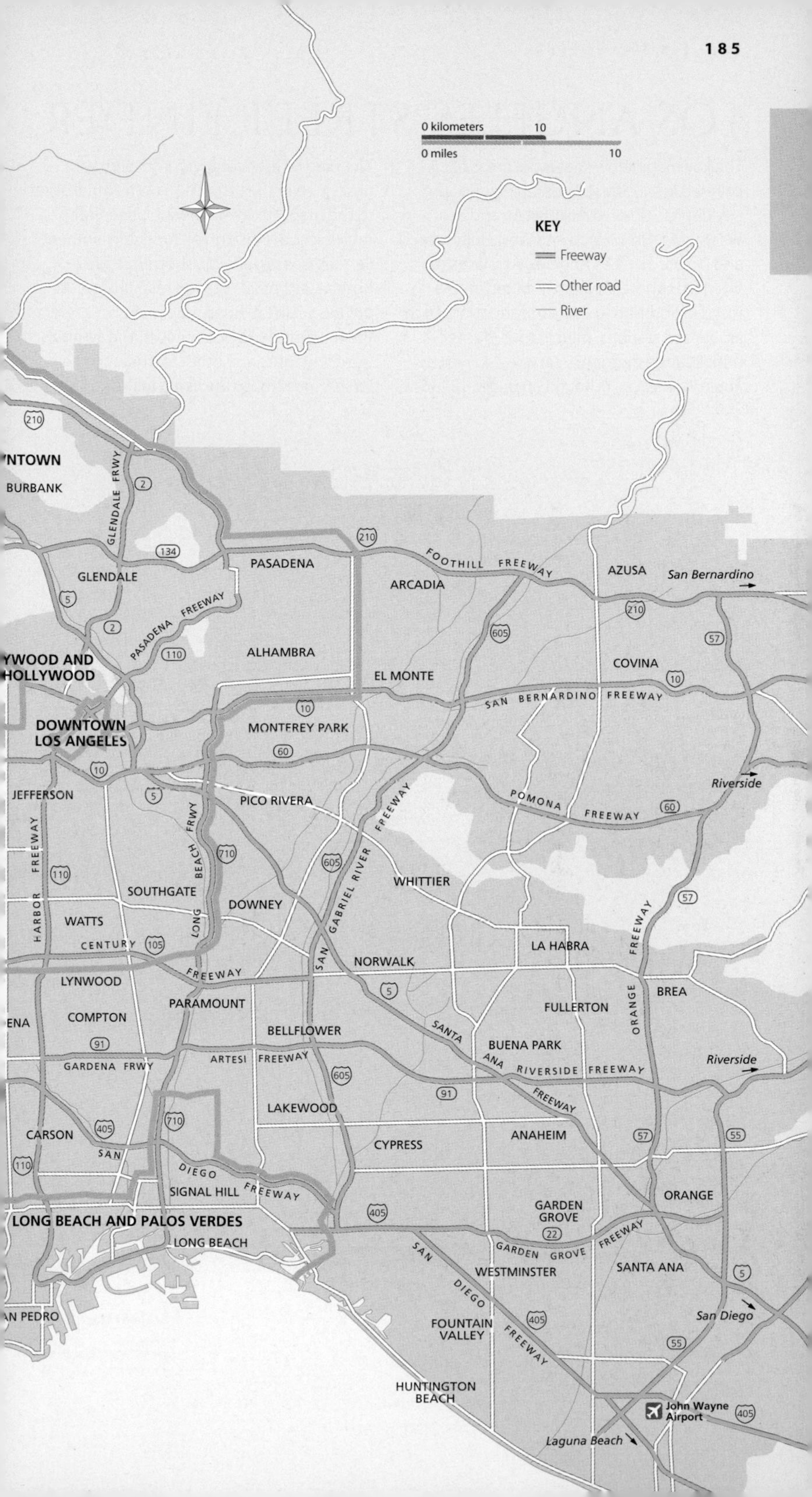

0 kilometers 10

0 miles 10

KEY

Freeway

Other road

River

210

NTOWN

BURBANK

GLENDALE FRWY

2

134

GLENDALE

PASADENA

ARCADIA

FOOTHILL FREEWAY

AZUSA

San Bernardino →

210

5

PASADENA FREEWAY

2

YWOOD AND
HOLLYWOOD

110

ALHAMBRA

EL MONTE

605

COVINA

210

57

10

SAN BERNARDINO FREEWAY

DOWNTOWN
LOS ANGELES

10

MONTEREY PARK

10

60

JEFFERSON

5

PICO RIVERA

POMONA FREEWAY

60

Riverside →

HARBOR FREEWAY

110

LONG BEACH FRWY

710

605

SAN GABRIEL RIVER FREEWAY

WHITTIER

LA HABRA

57

SOUTHGATE

DOWNEY

NORWALK

BREA

WATTS

CENTURY

105

FREEWAY

FULLERTON

ORANGE FREEWAY

LYNWOOD

PARAMOUNT

5

SANTA

BUENA PARK

COMPTON

91

ENA

BELLFLOWER

ANA

RIVERSIDE FREEWAY

Riverside →

GARDENA FRWY

ARTESI

FREEWAY

605

91

CARSON

405

710

LAKEWOOD

CYPRESS

ANAHEIM

57

55

SAN

110

DIEGO FREEWAY

SIGNAL HILL

22

ORANGE

LONG BEACH AND PALOS VERDES

405

GARDEN GROVE

GARDEN GROVE FREEWAY

LONG BEACH

SANTA ANA

5

AN PEDRO

SAN

DIEGO

WESTMINSTER

San Diego →

FREEWAY

405

FOUNTAIN VALLEY

55

HUNTINGTON BEACH

✈ John Wayne
Airport

405

Laguna Beach ↘

LOS ANGELES STREET FINDER

The key map below shows the areas of LA covered in the *Street Finder*. It includes the city districts of Beverly Hills, Bel Air and Westwood, Hollywood and West Hollywood, and Downtown Los Angeles. All places of interest in these areas are marked on the maps in addition to useful information, such as railroad stations, metro stops, bus terminals, and emergency services. A *Freeway Route Planner* can be found on pages 184–5.

The map references given with sights described in the LA section of the guide refer to the maps on the following pages. Map references are also given for entertainment venues *(see pp180–81)*, shops *(see p172–5)*, hotels *(see pp528–31)* and restaurants *(see pp550–56)* in LA. Road map references refer to the map inside the back cover. The symbols used for sights and other features on the *Street Finder* maps are listed in the key below.

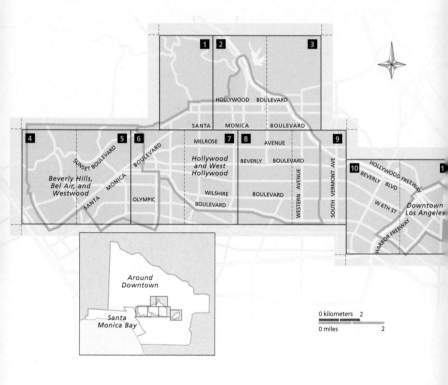

Key to Street Finder

- ▢ Major sight
- ▢ Place of interest
- Ⓡ Amtrak station
- Ⓜ Metro station
- 🚌 Bus terminal
- *i* Tourist information
- ➕ Hospital with emergency room
- 🚔 Police station
- 🏌 Golf course
- ═ Railroad line
- ═ Freeway
- ▬ Pedestrian street

0 kilometers 2
0 miles 2

Scale of Maps 1–11
0 meters 500
0 yards 500

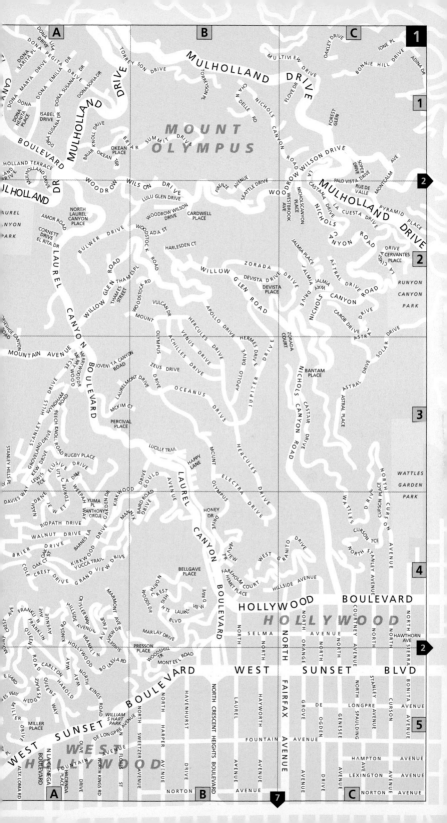

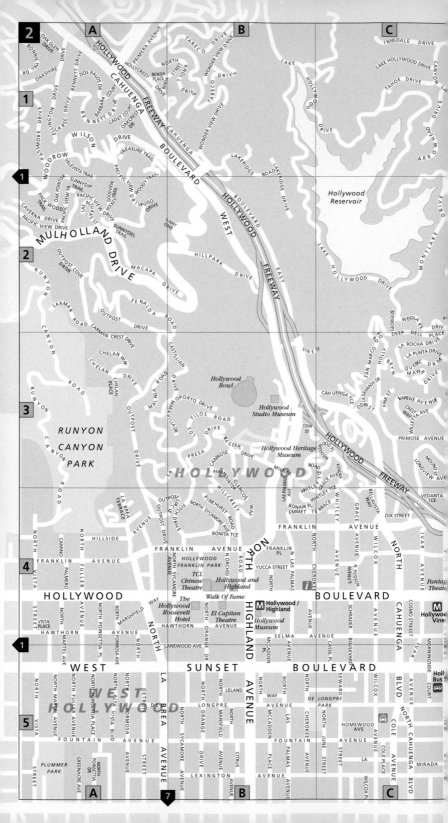

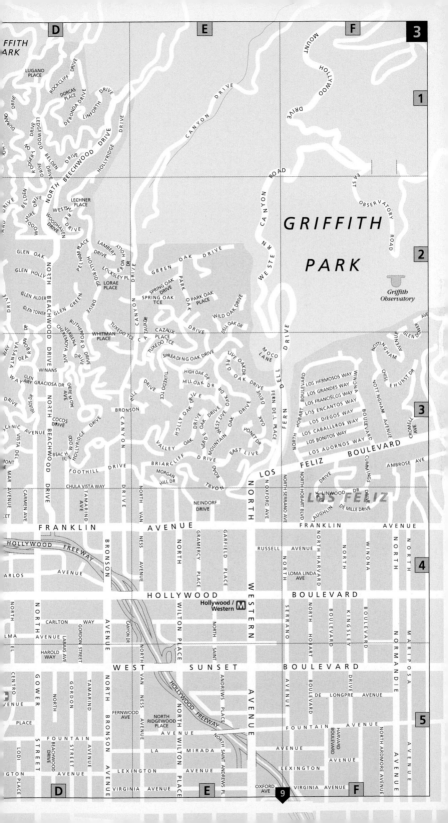

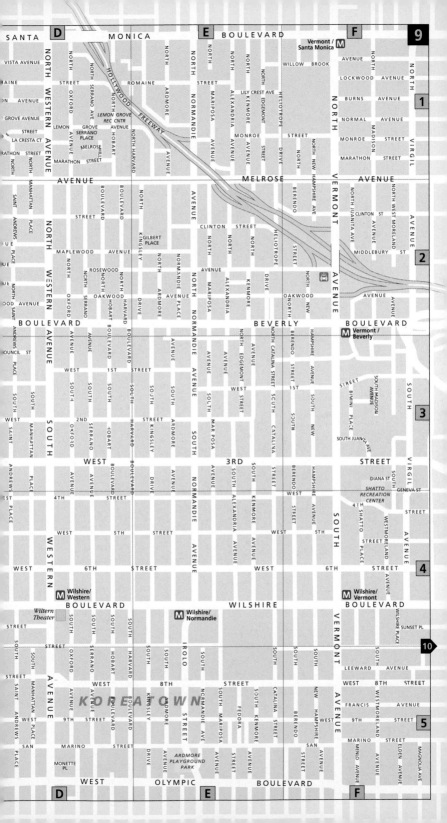

SOUTHERN CALIFORNIA

Southern California at a Glance

Southern California is a region of startling contrasts. Scorching deserts give way to snowcapped mountains, with views of the coast. It is possible to surf in the morning, ski in the afternoon, and play golf in the evening. From San Simeon to San Diego, the coast is lined with resorts, reflecting a shoreline that ranges from rugged bluffs to golden sands. Attractions along the way include historic missions, the charming cities of Santa Barbara and San Diego, and the theme parks of Orange County. Farther inland are two of the most startling desert areas in the United States: Death Valley National Park and the Joshua Tree National Park.

Locator Map

Santa Barbara Mission (see pp226–7) is the most visited mission in the state and is the only one in the chain of missions to have remained in continuous use since it was founded in 1786. The church facade is in Classical style, a theme continued inside the building.

Bakersfield

San Luis Obispo

SOUTH CENTRAL CALIFORNIA
(see pp208–29)

Mojave

Santa Maria

Lompoc

Santa Barbara

Ventura

Oxnard

Santa Monica

LOS ANGELES
(see pp63–197)

San Fernando

Los Angeles

Anaheim

ORANGE COUN
(see pp230–47)

Hearst Castle® (see pp216–19), on the south central coast, was built by publishing tycoon William R Hearst. In the 1930s and '40s he invited Hollywood stars and royalty here and entertained them lavishly. The Neptune Pool is particularly stunning.

Mission San Juan Capistrano (see pp244–5) in southern Orange County is known as the "Jewel of the Missions." Founded in 1776, its main buildings have been beautifully restored and feature historical exhibits.

◄ Lush gardens around the Mission San Juan Capistrano, Orange County

Death Valley National Park
(see pp294–7) in the Mojave Desert
encompasses one of the hottest
places on earth and the lowest point
in the Western Hemisphere. Within
Death Valley, which is 140 miles (225
km) long, lie dry lake beds, sand
dunes, and small outposts built
around springs. Despite the harsh
conditions, the area is rich in flora and
fauna. Sights of historical interest in
the park include Scotty's Castle.

oipe
ls

THE MOJAVE DESERT
(see pp284–97)

● Baker

● Barstow

Needles ●

Joshua Tree National Park *(see pp282–3)*,
with high and low desert areas, is famed for
its distinctive trees. Within easy reach of
the city of Palm Springs, it offers superb
views of the stark desert landscape
with its remarkable rock formations.

● San Bernardino

side

Palm
Springs ○   ● Indio

Blythe ●

● Temecula

**THE INLAND EMPIRE
AND LOW DESERT**
(see pp272–83)

eanside

● Escondido

N DIEGO COUNTY
(see pp248–71)

● El Centro

Balboa Park *(see pp260–63)* in San
Diego was the site of the Panama–
Pacific Exposition of 1915. The park is
now home to many museums, s
uch as the San Diego Museum of
Man, housed in the landmark
California Building and the famous
San Diego Zoo *(see p263)*.

0 kilometers   50

0 miles   50

Surfing and Beach Culture

If Southern Californians worship at the altars of youth, health, and beauty, then their churches are the beaches. Here, unbelievably beautiful men and women parade their surgically enhanced bodies beneath the ever-present sun. Favorite sports include skating and volleyball, but the ability to look good on a surfboard is the ultimate cool. Surfing was originally practiced by the Hawaiian nobility as a religious ceremony. It was introduced to California by Hawaiian George Freeth in 1907 *(see p70)* and popularized in the 1920s in Waikiki by Olympic swimmer Duke Kahanamoku. In 1961 the Beach Boys released "Surfin," and the sport took off around the world. Today surf culture is part of the mainstream consciousness. The loose-fitting clothes favored by surfers are reproduced on the catwalk, and surfing slang is used by many who have never been near the beach.

The Beach Boys sang of the joys of surfing despite the fact that only Dennis Wilson, the drummer, could surf.

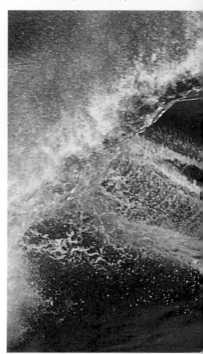

Films such as Gidget (1959), *Ride the Wild Surf* (1964), and *Beach Blanket Bingo* (1965), as well as the documentary *Endless Summer* (1966), helped to establish the cultural allure of surfing. Lengthy beach parties in the style of these films were highly popular during the 1960s.

Where to Learn to Surf

Beginners are advised to start by body surfing without a board. Boogie boarding, with a half-length board, is also far easier to master than surfing. Beaches with waves that break parallel to the beach (a surf break) are the most suitable. The best beaches on which to learn to boogie board include Santa Monica *(see p69)*, Carpinteria *(p213)*, and Del Mar *(p253)*. Beginners should avoid famous surfing beaches, such as Surfrider *(p68)*, San Clemente *(p234)*, and Huntington *(p234)*, as conditions can overwhelm the inexperienced.

Boys with boogie boards weighing up the surf

Lifeguards are stationed on most county and state beaches in California during the summer. Their distinctive gray huts have been made famous throughout the world by the television series *Baywatch*. Always follow their instructions on the beach, and ask if you are in doubt about the tidal conditions.

A **"tube"** is a cylindrical passage formed when a wave breaks and the crest curls over.

Surfing Highlights

One exhilarating surfing experience is to "beat the tube." The surfer rides beneath the crest, regulating his speed and position to stay just ahead of the falling wave. If he goes too fast he comes out of the wave; too slowly and he gets knocked off. The wave loses momentum as it nears the shore. At this point the surfer will shoot out of the tube, remaining upright.

By changing position a surfer can alter the speed and direction in which he or she is traveling. Crouching lowers the center of gravity and increases stability.

Other Beach Activities

Southern California's spectacular beaches are used by a wide variety of sports enthusiasts. Although the beaches are most popular in summer, activities are enjoyed year-round by hardy souls. Sailing is popular, with thousands of yachts of all sizes harbored in a string of marinas along the coast. Windsurfing and kite flying also take advantage of the prevailing onshore winds. Sea kayakers often explore the rocky coasts of the Channel Islands *(see p228)* and the mainland. Volleyball, once limited to friendly matches, is now a major professional sport with competitions held along the Southern California coast each summer.

Modern surfboards are made out of light, man-made materials, such as fiberglass, allowing surfers to reach much higher speeds. Their bright colors make them easy to see in the water.

The first boards came from Hawaii and were called coffin lids because of their distinctive shape. Made out of wood, they were heavy and unwieldy. Early surfboards can be seen at the Lighthouse Surfing Museum in Santa Cruz *(see p511)*.

Friendly volleyball game in Santa Monica

California Car Culture

It is difficult to understand Southern California without considering the influence of the car. The introduction of the freeway system in LA in 1940 *(see p58)* spawned an entirely new culture centered around the automobile. Owning a car became integral to the California identity, and the open desert road came to symbolize the freedom of the state. Customizing automobiles also made the car an art object. Drive-in movies led to the convenience of drive-in banks and fast-food restaurants. But there was a price to pay: smog, the result of car exhaust and sunlight, has become a fact of life in LA. Today, cars have cleaner exhausts, but LA has to cope with some 8 million cars on its increasingly "gridlocked" streets.

Los Angeles' freeways, begun in the 1950s, have expanded into a complex network, linking the city with the rest of the state.

Ford Thunderbird emblem

The canvas top could be lowered for sunny weather or raised in rain.

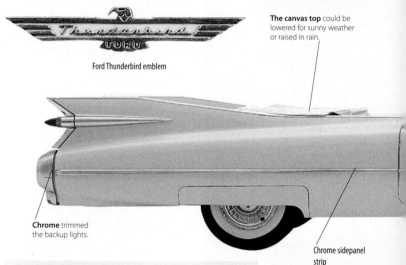

Chrome trimmed the backup lights.

Chrome sidepanel strip

Birthplace of the Motorcycle Gang

In the 1950s especially, California was home to rival gangs of "outlaw bikers." The most famous, the Hells Angels, began with a group of World War II veterans in San Bernardino in 1948. Their notorious reputation was immortalized in the 1953 film *The Wild One* with Marlon Brando. Today, the Hells Angels have around 2,500 members worldwide, who continue to symbolize defiance of authority.

Marlon Brando

Japanese cars, such as those imported through Worldport LA *(see p70)*, continue to be hot competition for American-made automobiles.

This car advertisement for Pontiac dates from 1950. As automobiles became more of a status symbol, manufacturers competed for customers with increasingly bright ads.

Where to See California Car Culture

Californians are very proud of their car culture and history; most towns have a parade or car show featuring vintage, classic, and customized automobiles. For information, inquire at the local visitors' center (see p591). One of the largest automobile events, the Automobile Club of Southern California NHRA drag race, is held each November at the LA County Fairgrounds. There are literally dozens of car shows and races throughout the year, particularly in Southern California, showcasing muscle cars, classics, and collectibles, and specific models, such as the Corvette. California also hosts several famous motor races, such as the Toyota Grand Prix Long Beach in April. There are several world-class automobile museums in the state, including the Petersen Automotive Museum (p122) in Los Angeles and the San Diego Automotive Museum (see p263).

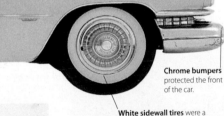

Tucker Torpedo, one of the cars on display at the Petersen Automotive Museum in LA

Chrome door lights were turned on from inside.

The wraparound windshield imitated aircraft designs.

Pink Cadillac

With its glamorous design and convertible roof, the 1959 pink Cadillac suited California's image and climate perfectly. However, the car's two-ton weight meant that its steering was heavy, and it soon gave way to more efficient designs.

Chrome bumpers protected the front of the car.

White sidewall tires were a popular option because of their expensive look.

The Model T Ford (affectionately known as the Tin Lizzie) first appeared in 1908. In 1913, Henry Ford introduced the assembly line and cars could be bought for as little as $500. This photograph of a 1924 beachside traffic jam shows that it took only a few years for Californians to become dependent on the car.

Recreational vehicles (RVs) became popular in the 1960s. Californians could now take to the open road and explore the state's wilderness without leaving any home comforts behind.

Deserts and Water Networks

Much of Southern California is desert, and before 1913, migrants to this area depended on wells for their water. The population grew extremely quickly and it soon became necessary to engineer what is now one of the most elaborate water networks on earth. This network has turned parts of what was once inhospitable desert into productive land, and made possible the desert resort of Palm Springs and the huge populations of the Southern Californian cities. However, the South's high rate of water consumption places a great demand on the region's major sources of water: the Colorado River and the Sierra Nevada Mountains. In 2015, the first statewide urban water restriction was enforced, aiming to spare cities and towns from drought.

The Sacramento/San Joaquin River Delta supplies water to the farms of the south. At peak times, pumping causes the river to flow in reverse, bringing salt water from San Francisco Bay.

Owens Lake *(see p499)* lies between the Sierra Nevada Mountains and the Mojave Desert, in Owens Valley. The Los Angeles Aqueduct diverted water from Owens River to LA and the 100-sq mile (260-sq km) lake gradually dried up.

The Los Angeles Aqueduct made the San Fernando Valley fertile *(see p148)*. Land speculators made their fortunes when the aqueduct was completed in 1914.

William Mulholland

As head of the Los Angeles city water department, William Mulholland (1855–1935) *(see p148)* and his colleague Fred Eaton designed an aqueduct and a series of tunnels to lead from Owens Valley to LA. Completed in 1914, it cost more than $24 million. By 1929 the supplies were no longer sufficient, and they had to divert water from Mono Basin and the Colorado River, 400 miles (645 km) away.

0 kilometers   75

0 miles   75

Key

- Populated areas
- Rivers
- Dry rivers
- Canals
- Aqueducts

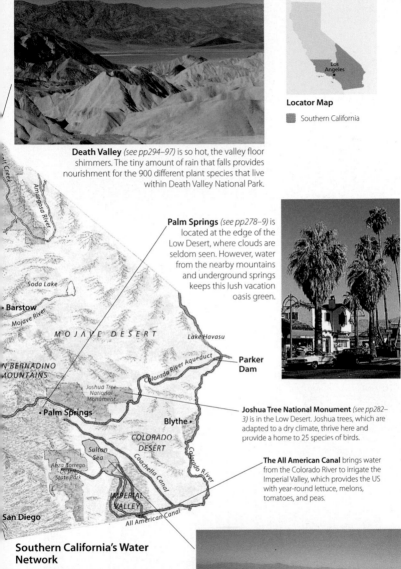

Locator Map

    Southern California

Death Valley *(see pp294–97)* is so hot, the valley floor shimmers. The tiny amount of rain that falls provides nourishment for the 900 different plant species that live within Death Valley National Park.

Palm Springs *(see pp278–9)* is located at the edge of the Low Desert, where clouds are seldom seen. However, water from the nearby mountains and underground springs keeps this lush vacation oasis green.

Parker Dam

Joshua Tree National Monument *(see pp282–3)* is in the Low Desert. Joshua trees, which are adapted to a dry climate, thrive here and provide a home to 25 species of birds.

The All American Canal brings water from the Colorado River to irrigate the Imperial Valley, which provides the US with year-round lettuce, melons, tomatoes, and peas.

Southern California's Water Network

Southern California has two main sources of water: ice-melt from the Sierra Nevada Mountains in the north, brought to LA via the LA Aqueduct, and the Colorado River to the southeast. The Colorado River Aqueduct system carries water 672 miles (1,080 km) from the Parker Dam via 395 miles (635 km) of pipes. Imperial Valley has a network of canals, making it fertile. The same canals irrigate the desert resort of Palm Springs.

The Salton Sea, formed in 1905, is now ravaged by algae; however, a giant restoration project is planned to bring it back to its pristine state (above).

SOUTH CENTRAL CALIFORNIA

South Central California is a land of lonely passes and wooded streams. Broad sandy beaches stretch along the gentle coast with empty, tawny hills as their only backdrop. It is a region of small and friendly towns, scattered farms and vineyards nestled in scenic valleys. Farther inland is Los Padres National Forest, where mountain lions roam freely, and eagles and condors soar overhead.

The region's Spanish heritage is highly visible, and no more so than in Santa Barbara. Here the area's most important garrison and the legendary structure that came to be known as "Queen of the Missions" *(see pp226–7)* can be found. The city's red tile Mission Revival-style architecture *(see p35)* has been imitated throughout the state.

Following the breakup of the wealthy missions during the 1830s, the land was divided into a handful of sprawling ranches, then the 1849 Gold Rush brought an influx of Easterners to California. The newcomers subdivided the large estates and set up small farming communities. They touted the land throughout the world as a "semitropical paradise," where the first season's crops would pay for the cost of the land.

In the early part of the 20th century the Central Coast was a popular vacation destination, drawing thousands of people each summer to seaside towns such as Pismo and Avila Beach. Farther north, at San Simeon, millionaire William Randolph Hearst built his own personal playground, the fabulous private museum now known as Hearst Castle®.

Today, South Central California provides a wealth of activities, from wine-tasting tours on horseback in the scenic Santa Ynez Valley to relaxation on empty beaches. The more active can try kayaking on the Kern River near Bakersfield. Offshore, the Channel Islands offer a unique view of the area's ecosystems and an opportunity to see the annual passage of the magnificent gray whales. The east of the region is dominated by the Los Padres National Forest, an area of breathtaking beauty with many hiking trails and drives through mountain scenery. Here, too, are signs of the Chumash people who once lived in thriving communities along the coast. Their enigmatic petroglyphs remain as silent reminders of their presence throughout these hills.

Seasonal produce on display in Morro Bay

◀ Casa Grande's elaborate twin-towered facade, Hearst Castle®

Exploring South Central California

South Central California's beaches and coastal plains are backed by low rolling hills covered with groves of oak. Beyond this, the Los Padres National Forest has hundreds of miles of mountainous hiking trails. Just north of Santa Barbara, the gentle countryside around Santa Ynez has proved perfect for growing vines. Along the coast of San Luis Obispo County, the seaside towns of Morro Bay and Pismo Beach are known for their fishing and clamming. In the northwest, Hearst Castle® is one of California's most popular tourist attractions.

Mission San Miguel Arcángel's campanario

Sights at a Glance

1. Mission San Miguel Arcángel
2. Hearst Castle® pp216–19
3. Cambria
4. Paso Robles
5. Atascadero
6. Morro Bay
7. San Luis Obispo
8. Pismo Beach
9. Lompoc Valley
11. Solvang
12. Mission Santa Inés
13. Chumash Painted Cave State Historic Park
14. Santa Barbara pp224–7
15. Ventura
16. Channel Islands National Park
17. Ronald Reagan Presidential Library
18. Ojai
19. Los Padres National Forest
20. Bakersfield

Tour

10. Santa Ynez Valley Wineries Tour p222

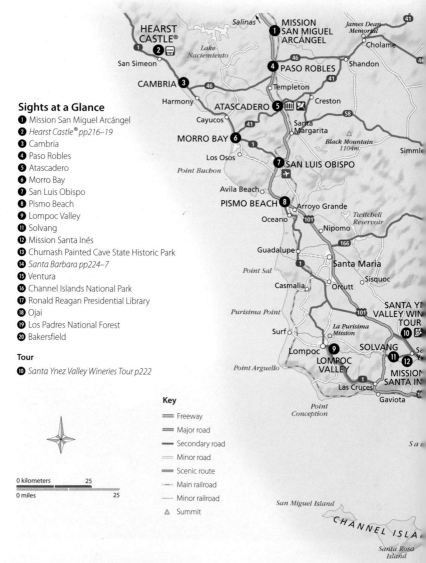

Key

═══ Freeway
─── Major road
─── Secondary road
····· Minor road
~~~ Scenic route
~~~ Main railroad
─── Minor railroad
△ Summit

0 kilometers 25
0 miles 25

Getting Around

I-101 and Hwy 1 follow the coast, passing through all the major sights. Amtrak runs a daily service, the Coast Starlight, from Los Angeles to San Francisco, stopping at Santa Barbara and San Luis Obispo. Greyhound buses also stop at these cities. There are roads through the Los Padres National Forest to Bakersfield, but the most common driving route to that city is I-5 from LA. Trips to the Channel Islands National Park leave from Ventura and Oxnard.

Rugged mountains in the vast Los Padres National Forest

Stearns Wharf, the recreation pier at Santa Barbara

For additional map symbols see back flap

California Coastline: South Central

The South Central coast offers accessible, broad, sandy beaches and some of the best surfing in the state. The water here is cooler than the ocean off the Los Angeles to San Diego coast, but these beaches offer privacy and solitude for swimming, sunbathing, and picnicking. The rugged mountain backdrop appears so close you can almost smell the pine and chaparral. Several South Central beaches are within state parks and have hiking and nature trails offering spectacular views. Visit www.parks. ca.gov/parkindex for more details.

③ ★ **Avila Beach**
This white, sandy beach, near a quiet seaside town, has a wooden fishing pier. It is popular in the summer for surfing and swimming.

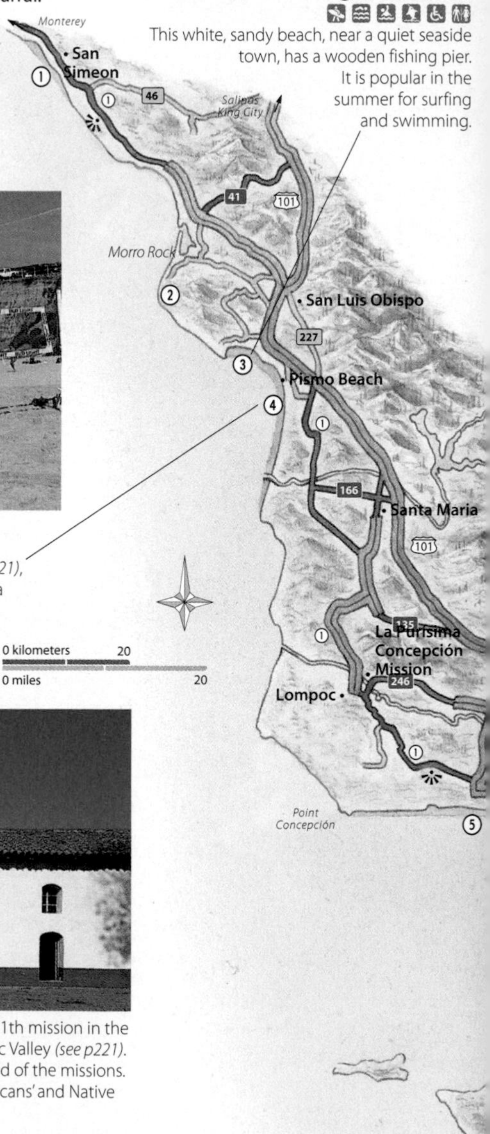

④ ★ **Pismo State Beach**
Known primarily for its clams (see pp220–21), the beach has compact sands making it a perfect surface for volleyball.

0 kilometers   20
0 miles   20

Monterey
San Simeon ①
46
Salinas King City
41 101
Morro Rock
②
San Luis Obispo
227
③ Pismo Beach
④ 1
166
Santa Maria
101
La Purísima Concepción Mission
246
Lompoc
1
Point Concepción
⑤

La Purísima Concepción Mission, the 11th mission in the chain (see pp50–51), is situated in Lompoc Valley (see p221). La Purísima is the most fully reconstructed of the missions. A visit gives a real insight into the Franciscans' and Native Americans' living conditions.

Locator Map

Morro Rock is one of South Central California's most distinctive landmarks. Used as a navigation point by the first Spanish explorers, it is best seen at sunrise or sunset *(see p220)*.

① William R Hearst Memorial State Beach

🎣 🏖 🏊 🎣 ♿ 🏨 ⛵

Situated below Hearst Castle® *(see pp216–19)*, this sheltered, crescent-shaped beach is a good spot for a picnic. Boats can be chartered from the pier for deep-sea fishing trips.

② Montana de Oro State Park

🎣 🏖 🏊 🥾 🏨 ⛺

The rocky beach is backed by 8,000 acres (3,250 ha) of park. Hiking trails wind through the hills and, in winter, monarch butterflies can be seen in the eucalyptus trees *(see p223)*.

⑦ ★ East Beach

🎣 🏖 🎣 🏊 ♿ 🏨

This sandy beach stretches for 1.5 miles (2.5 km) from Stearns Wharf, Santa Barbara's fishing pier. Children will enjoy the playground and paddling pool.

⑤ Gaviota State Park

🎣 🏖 🏊 🥾 🏨 ⛺ ⛵

This 5.5-mile (9-km) beach, in a sheltered cove, has a playground and fishing pier. It adjoins 2,800 acres (1,100 ha) of parkland with hiking trails.

⑥ El Capitan State Beach

🎣 🏖 🏊 🥾 🏨 ⛺ ⛵

El Capitan is a good place for spotting wildlife, both in the rock pools along the beach and in the woods behind. Gray whales pass close to the shore during the winter.

⑧ Carpinteria State Beach

🎣 🏖 🏊 🥾 ♿ 🏨 ⛺ ⛵

Backed by the Santa Ynez Mountains, this sheltered beach is one of the safest and most pleasant places to swim in Southern California.

⑩ Point Mugu State Park

🏖 🏊 🥾 ♿ 🏨 ⛺ ⛵

At the western end of the Santa Monica Mountains, the park is crisscrossed with hiking trails. Dolphins and California sea lions are often seen offshore.

⑪ Leo Carrillo State Beach North

🎣 🏖 🏊 🥾 ♿ 🏨 ⛺ ⛵

This stretch of Leo Carrillo State Beach *(see p68)*, which extends across the LA County border, is one of the classic spots for surfing in California.

⑨ ★ San Buenaventura State Beach

🎣 🏖 🏊 🥾 🏨 ⛵

Close to the center of Ventura *(see p228)*, this broad beach is sheltered by the harbor breakwater, making it a good area for swimming.

Los Padres National Forest

Santa Barbara

Ojai

⑦

⑧

Ventura

⑨

Oxnard

LOS ANGELES

CHANNEL ISLAND NATIONAL PARK

⑩

⑪

MALIBU

Key

🟰 Freeway

▬ Major road

▭ Minor road

〜 River

🔆 Viewpoint

Arched colonnade at the Mission San Miguel Arcángel

❶ Mission San Miguel Arcángel

775 Mission St, San Miguel.
Road map B5. **Tel** (805) 467-3256.
Open 10am–4:30pm daily.
W missionsanmiguel.org

This mission was the 16th in the Californian chain *(see pp50–51)*, and was founded in 1797 by Father Fermín de Lasuén, the successor to Father Junípero Serra *(see p50)*. Nine years later the original church was destroyed by fire and the present building, which was used as a parish church, was completed in 1819. A team of local Salinas Indians, working under the guidance of artist Esteban Munras, painted the frescos that can still be seen today.

In addition to growing grain and raising cattle, the padres made their own sacramental wine, and today the surrounding hills shelter over 30 wineries.

Following secularization in 1834, the mission was used as a warehouse and bar. In 1928 it was returned to the padres, and restoration was begun. The mission was badly damaged in the San Salinas earthquake of 2003. It reopened to the public in 2009 but retrofitting continues.

The six rooms in the mission's museum are furnished as they would have been in the early 19th century. There is also a gift shop and a pleasant courtyard.

❷ Hearst Castle®

See pp216–19.

❸ Cambria

Road map B5. 🚁 6,000. 🚌 **i** 767 Main St. **Tel** (805) 927-3624.
W cambriachamber.org

Situated between rugged seashore and pine-clad hills, and handy for Hearst Castle®, Cambria began as a mercury mining settlement in 1866. Later it became a center for dairy farming and lumber production, and today it is a popular location for artists and craftspeople.

The town is divided into two distinct districts: East Village, a charming colony of Arts and Crafts houses *(see p35)*, and West Village, which is more modern. Main Street, which joins the two, is lined with specialty shops, art galleries, and restaurants. Among the houses on Hillcrest Drive, just north of Main Street, is Nit Wit Ridge. It was built by local contractor Art Beal, who was known as "Captain Nit Wit." This whimsical abode was fashioned over six decades, starting in the 1930s, out of salvaged material, from sea shells to old tires. To the north

Statue of St. Michael the Archangel

of the town, on Moonstone Drive, is the Leffingwell Landing, which offers excellent views of the surf and occasionally sea lions, whales, and otters out at sea. At low tide it is also possible to climb down to the rock pools at the bottom of the cliffs. The area is also well equipped for picnickers.

❹ Paso Robles

Road map B5. 🚁 30,000. 🚌 **i** 1225 Park St. **Tel** (805) 238-0506.
W pasorobleschamber.com

Paso Robles, or "Pass of the Oaks," was once part of the 26,000-acre (10,500-ha) El Paso de Robles ranch. In 1857, a sulfurous hot spring, long used by Native Americans for its curative powers, was transformed into a health resort. With the arrival of the Southern Pacific railroad in 1886, the town quickly developed. Today, Paso Robles is ringed with horse ranches, vineyards, wineries, and more than 5,000 acres (2,000 ha) of almond orchards that bloom in early spring. The hot springs have now been capped – they were polluting the Salinas River – but the town still has much to offer. On Vine Street, between 12th and 20th streets, are several restored buildings from the 1890s, including **Call-Booth House Gallery**. Here works by mainly local artists are displayed in a Victorian setting.

Nit Wit Ridge in Cambria, made out of recycled materials

Wine festival event at the Eos Estate Winery in Paso Robles

Some of Paso Robles' many restaurants are also located in 19th-century buildings; for instance, Touch of Paso occupies a former post house on the Overland Stage Company route.

The Paso Robles Inn and Gardens, at 1003 Spring Street, stands on the site of the 1860 Hot Springs Hotel. The latter was replaced in 1891 with a three-story redbrick hotel designed by Stanford White. This building in turn was burned down in a fire in 1940. Visitors to the town may wander through the current hotel's landscaped gardens.

There are a number of moderately priced hotels in Paso Robles, which make convenient overnight stops when visiting nearby Hearst Castle®.

Two popular events are the California Mid-State Fair – a large agricultural and livestock fair in late July–early August with a reputation for top entertainment – and the Wine Festival in May, during which visitors can sample wines from 90 of almost 200 vineyards in the surrounding area.

Environs
Situated 17 miles (27 km) northwest of Paso Robles, off County Road G14, **Lake Nacimiento** is a local recreational spot. Set in a picturesque valley amid pine and oak trees, the lake offers fishing (bass and catfish are often caught here), camping, water sports, and picnicking.

At the second junction of Hwy 46 and Hwy 41, 24 miles (39 km) east of Paso Robles, is

the **James Dean Monument**. Set around a tree of heaven, it is a memorial to the film actor who died here, at the age of 24, when he crashed his silver Porsche 550 Spider on September 30, 1955. A metal plaque gives details of James Dean's short life.

🏛 **Call-Booth House Gallery**
1315 Vine St. **Tel** (805) 238-5473.
Open 11am–3pm Wed–Sun.
Closed public hols. 🐾

❺ Atascadero

Road map B5. 🚏 28,000. 🚉 San Luis Obispo. Dial-A-Ride (805 466-7433). 🚌 ℹ️ 6904 El Camino Real (805 466-2044). 🔳 atascaderochamber.org

Atascadero, which means "muddy place" in Spanish, was founded in 1913 by the publisher Edward G Lewis, who bought the 23,000-acre (9,300-ha) ranch to build his ideal town. Lewis's headquarters were in an attractive Italian Renaissance-style building, constructed in 1914 for almost half a million dollars. The building used to

house the Atascadero Historical Society Museum, which contained hundreds of photographs taken by Lewis's official photographer as well as artifacts that belonged to early settlers, but the building was damaged in a major earthquake in late 2003. Portions of the collection are on display at the Colony House until the building is restored.

Unfortunately, Lewis went bankrupt before Atascadero was finished. The town continued to grow steadily from the 1950s, however, as more people were attracted by its rural atmosphere. It became an official city in 1979.

Today's visitors frequent the town's antique shops, stylish boutiques, and its weekly farmers' market. There is a week-long Colony Days celebration in October, when the town remembers its early history with a parade and other festivities.

Just south of the town, off Hwy 41, Atascadero Park and Lake has pleasant walks and offers fishing, picnic areas, and a children's playground. Next door, the 3-acre (1-ha) **Charles Paddock Zoo**, named after the county park ranger who established the zoo in 1955, houses more than 100 animal species. These include monkeys, meerkats, grizzly bears, a pair of tigers, and a jaguar, which live in settings much like their natural habitats.

🐾 **Charles Paddock Zoo**
9305 Pismo Ave, Atascadero.
Tel (805) 461-5080. **Open** Apr–Oct: 10am–5pm daily; Nov–Mar: 10am–4pm daily. **Closed** Thanksgiving, Dec 25. 🐾 🎎 🎁
🔳 charlespaddockzoo.org

Ducks swimming on Atascadero Lake

❷ Hearst Castle®

Hearst Castle® perches on a hill above the village of San Simeon. The private playground and museum of media tycoon William Randolph Hearst is today one of California's top tourist attractions. Its three guest houses are superb buildings in their own right, but the highlight of the tour is the twin-towered Casa Grande. Designed by the Paris-trained architect Julia Morgan and built in stages from 1922 to 1947, its 115 rooms hold many artworks and epitomize the glamour of the 1930s and 1940s.

Facade
Casa Grande's poured concrete facade is in the Mediterranean Revival style. It is embellished with ancient architectural fragments.

Theater
The walls of Hearst's private cinema are lined with damask. Lamps held by gilded caryatids light the 50 seats.

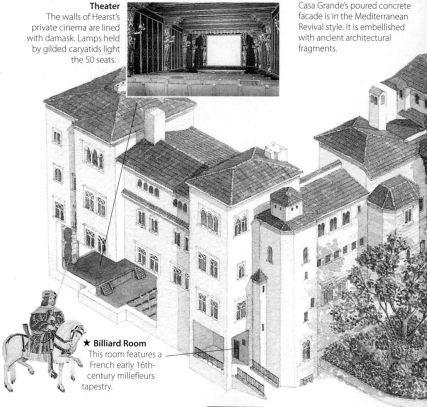

★ **Billiard Room**
This room features a French early 16th-century millefleurs tapestry.

1865 George Hearst buys 48,000 acres (19,425 ha) of land near San Simeon

1921 Casa del Mar completed

1924 Casa del Sol completed

16th-century wooden chest, depicting Christ Meeting St. Peter on the lid

1958 Hearst Castle® opens to public

1951 Hearst dies

1920	1930	1940	1950

1919 WR Hearst inherits family fortune. Plans a house on "Camp Hill"

1922 Work begins on Casa Grande

1928 Hearst moves into Casa Grande

1935 Neptune Pool completed

1947 Hearst has heart problems and leaves San Simeon

Classical Greek amphora dating from 3rd century AD

★ **Gothic Study**
When in San Simeon, Hearst ran his empire from the Gothic Study. He kept his books behind grilles.

VISITORS' CHECKLIST

Practical Information
750 Hearst Castle Rd. **Road map** B5. **Tel** (805) 927-2020; (800) 444-4445. **Open** 9am–4pm daily. **Closed** Jan 1, Thanksgiving, Dec 25. 🅿 🅰 call ahead. 📷 🎥 obligatory. 🆆 **hearstcastle.org**

Transport
🚌 to San Simeon.

Celestial Suite
The two Celestial Suite bedrooms are located high up in the north and south towers. They are linked by a spacious sitting room.

Main entrance

★ **Assembly Room**
A 16th-century French fireplace dominates the Assembly Room. Italian choir stalls line the walls, which are hung with Flemish tapestries.

★ **Refectory**
Tapestries, choir stalls, and colorful banners cover the walls of the massive dining hall. Its long tables are decorated with silver candlesticks and serving dishes.

Exploring Hearst Castle®

Visitors to Hearst Castle® must take one of half a dozen guided tours, all of which start from the Visitors' Center. The Grand Rooms Tour includes the first floor of the Casa Grande and is recommended for first-time visitors. The other tours cover the upper floors of the main house, two guest houses, the kitchen, the wine cellar, the gardens, and design specifics of "the enchanted hill". During spring and autumn, evening tours of the estate feature actors or "guests" in 1930s costume.

Gold and glass decor of the Roman Pool

Casa Grande: The Big House

Casa Grande is built from steel-reinforced concrete in order to withstand California's earthquakes. However, it has been designed to look like a masonry cathedral in the Mediterranean Revival style.

Houseguests stayed in one of 36 bedrooms, surrounded by works from the magnate's eclectic art collection. Hearst himself lived in the third-floor Gothic Suite. His bedroom was decorated with a 14th-century Spanish ceiling and a renowned *Madonna and Child* from the School of Duccio di Buoninsegna (c.1255–1318). A sitting room with ocean views linked it to his lover, Marion Davies' bedroom.

Across the hall, the Gothic Study housed Hearst's most prized books and manuscripts. It was from this room that he directed his media empire.

The Assembly Room, on the first floor, was designed around a massive 16th-century French fireplace. It came from the

d'Anglure family's Château des Jours in Burgundy. The high-ceilinged Refectory, next door, features a Renaissance dining table, misericord seats, and replica flagstones from Siena. Guests at the castle were required to attend their late evening meals here.

The Billiard Room, with its Spanish Gothic ceiling, showcases an early 16th-century tapestry of a stag hunt.

Adjoining this room is Hearst's private movie theater. Here, up to 50 guests would watch films. The screen could be removed, revealing a small stage, where famous actors and actresses would sometimes put on plays.

The exquisite indoor Roman Pool, entirely covered in mosaics of hammered gold and Venetian glass, is decorated with eight marble statues and was a favorite haunt among his guests.

The house was continually being developed in accordance with Hearst's ever-changing ideas. One supporting wall was moved at great cost to make room for a bowling alley that was never built. With scores of bedrooms and bathrooms, two pools, and a theater, Casa Grande was a gilded playhouse for all who came here.

The Grounds and Neptune Pool

Hearst transformed the rocky California hillside into a veritable Garden of Eden. Fan palms 15 ft (4.5 m) high and Italian cypresses were hauled up the dirt road at great expense, and thousands of flowers were planted each year.

Massive loads of topsoil were brought up to create flower-beds for the 127 acres (51 ha)

William Randolph Hearst

The son of a multimillionaire, WR Hearst (1863–1951) was an ebullient personality who made his own fortune in magazine and newspaper publishing. He married Millicent Willson, an entertainer from New York, in 1903. On his mother's death in 1919, Hearst inherited the San Simeon property. He began to build the castle and grounds as a tribute to his mother. On moving in, he installed his mistress, actress Marion Davies. The couple entertained royally at San Simeon over the next 20 years. When Hearst suffered problems with his heart in 1947, he moved to a house in Beverly Hills, where he died in 1951.

Portrait of WR Hearst, age 31

of gardens. Five green-houses supplied colorful plants throughout the year. To hide the water reservoirs on a distant hill, 6,000 Monterey pines were planted in holes blasted out of the rock. Many varieties of fruit trees were planted on the estate, providing an abundance of fresh fruit.

Ancient and modern statues were collected to adorn the terraces. Among the finest are four statues of Sekhmet, the Egyptian goddess of war. The oldest works date from 1560–1200 BC.

The *pièce de résistance* of the grounds is the 104-ft- (32-m-) long Neptune Pool. Made in white marble, it is flanked by colonnades and features Roman architectural elements and a temple facade. The latter is made from ancient columns and decorated with authentic friezes. The statues around the pool were carved in the 1930s by Charles-George Cassou, a Parisian sculptor.

A great lover of the outdoors, Hearst had a 1-mile- (1.6-km-) long pergola so that he could ride in all weather. Two tennis courts were also constructed above the indoor Roman Pool.

Hearst had a private zoo on "Camp Hill." The remains of enclosures, where lions, bears, elephants, pumas, and leopards were once kept can still be seen. Giraffes, ostriches,

Julia Morgan

Julia Morgan, the architect of Hearst Castle®, was 47 when she began her 30-year collaboration with Hearst. One of the first women graduates of engineering at the University of California, Berkeley, Morgan was the first woman to receive a certificate in architecture from the Ecole Nationale et Spéciale des Beaux-Arts in Paris. She was a multitalented architect and artist – she designed almost every aspect of Hearst Castle®, from tiles and windows to swimming pools and fountains – and a rigorous supervisor of the project's

Julia Morgan (1872–1957)

many contractors and artisans. Her relationship with Hearst was based on mutual respect but was often tempestuous. After spending long hours together finalizing a plan, Hearst would often telegraph Morgan with changes.

Tiered facade of Casa del Sol

zebras, and even a baby elephant were free to wander the grounds.

The Guest Houses

Until the mid-1920s, when Casa Grande became ready for occupancy, Hearst lived in the 20-room Casa del Mar, the largest of the three guest houses. He enjoyed his years in the smaller house, but on viewing the completed Casa Grande admitted, "If I had known it would be so big, I would have made the little buildings bigger." The "little buildings," however, are mansions in their own right.

Casa del Sol is built on three levels and has 21 rooms. It presents fabulous views of the sunset and has a broad terrace with a tall fountain topped with a cast bronze copy of *David* by Donatello. The smallest of the houses, Casa del Monte, faces the hills and has 12 rooms.

Neptune Pool, flanked by colonnades and Roman architectural elements

Fishing boats encircling Morro Rock in Morro Bay

❻ Morro Bay

Road map B5. 🏔 10,000. Dial-A-Ride (805) 772-2744. 🚌 ℹ 845 Embarcadero Rd, Suite D (805 772-4467). W **morrobay.org**

This seaside port was founded in 1870 to ship produce from the area's cattle-ranching and dairy-farming businesses. Today, tourism has become the town's main industry, and the waterfront is lined with galleries, shops, an aquarium, and seafood restaurants. Whale-watching trips, bay cruises, and a commercial fishing fleet also operate from here. A redwood stairway, celebrating the town's 100th birthday, descends from a stone pelican at clifftop level down to the Embarcadero where a giant chessboard sports redwood pieces up to 33 inches (84 cm) tall. The view from Black Hill Lookout is worth the hike from the parking lot to the top of the mountain.

The bay's principal feature is Morro Rock, a dome-shaped 576-ft- (175-m-) high volcanic peak – one of nine in the area. Named "El Moro" by Juan Rodríguez Cabrillo (João Rodrigues Cabrilho) in 1542, who thought it resembled a Moor's turban, it was connected to the mainland by a causeway in 1933. Between 1880 and 1969 it was used as a quarry, and a million tons of rock were blasted away for breakwater construction.

Today, Morro Rock is a wildlife preserve housing nests of peregrine falcons, while Coleman Park, at the rock's base, is a highly popular fishing spot.

❼ San Luis Obispo

Road map B5. 🏔 46,000. ✈ San Luis Obispo. 🚉 🚌 ℹ 895 Monterey St, (805) 781-2777. W **visitslo.com**

This small city, situated in a valley in the Santa Lucia Mountains, developed around the **Mission San Luis Obispo de Tolosa**. The mission was founded on September 1, 1772, by Father Junípero Serra *(see p50)*. Fifth in the chain of 21 missions built by the Franciscan Order, and one of the wealthiest, it is still in use as a parish church. Beside the church, the mission's museum displays Chumash artifacts, such as baskets, vessels, and jewelry; the padre's bed; and the mission's original altar.

In front of the church is Mission Plaza, a landscaped public square bisected by a tree-lined creek. During the 1860s, bullfights and bear-baiting took place in the park; today it is the site of many of the city's less bloody events. Just west of the plaza, at 800 Palm Street, is the Ah Louis Store. Founded in 1874 by a Chinese cook and railroad laborer *(see pp54–5)*, it became the center of a then thriving Chinatown, and was a post office, bank, and general store. It is now a gift shop, but is open on an irregular schedule.

🏛 **Mission San Luis Obispo de Tolosa**
751 Palm St. **Tel** (805) 781-8220. **Open** 9am–4pm daily (to 5pm Mar–Oct). **Closed** public hols.

❾ Pismo Beach

Road map B5. 🏔 7,800. ✈ San Luis Obispo. 🚉 San Luis Obispo. 🚌 ℹ 581 Dolliver St, (800) 443-7778. W **classiccalifornia.com**

Pismo Beach is famous for the Pismo clam. At the turn of the century up to 40,000 clams were harvested per day. In 1911 harvesters were limited to 200 clams per person; now, a fishing license is required and there are strict size and quantity

Pismo Beach, backed by rolling hills

restrictions. A clam festival is held in autumn.

The town's beach *(see p212)* stretches south for 8 miles (13 km) to the Santa Maria River. It offers campsites, boating, fishing, and picnic facilities. The sand is firmly compacted, so cars can go onto the beach via ramps at Grand Avenue in Grover Beach and Pier Avenue in Oceano. Extensive sand dunes shelter birdlife, sagebrush, wildflowers, verbena, and other seashore plants along with the occasional foxes, rabbits and coyotes. Shell mounds in the dunes, especially near Arroyo Grande Creek, identify sites where the Chumash people once lived.

During the 1930s and 1940s the dunes were the center of a cult of artists, nudists, and mystics. Filmmakers have also been drawn to these sands, which have been compared to the Sahara Desert. One of the many movies made here is *The Sheik* (1921) starring Rudolph Valentino *(see p116)*.

❾ Lompoc Valley

Road map B5. ✈ Santa Barbara. 🚌 Lompoc. ℹ️ 111 S I St, Lompoc, (805) 736-4567. 🌐 **lompoc.com**

Lompoc Valley is one of the world's major producers of flower seed. The hills and flower fields surrounding the valley are a blaze of color between late spring and mid-summer. Among the varieties grown are marigolds, sweet peas, asters, lobelia, larkspur, nasturtiums, and cornflowers. A map of the

Dune Ecology

Coastal dunes are the product of wind and, surprisingly, plants. Just above the high-tide line, dry sand is stabilized by sea lettuce. Behind it, beach grass and silver lupine trap more sand, creating small hummocks held in place by the plants' roots. Lupine compost mixes with the sand to produce soil, allowing other plants, such as dune buckwheat and haplopapus, to move in and overcome the lupine itself. Eventually, ice plant, verbena, and morning glory take root in the sandy soil. The plants provide food and protection for a broad range of insects and animals, from sand wasps and beetles to Jerusalem crickets and tiny mice. Most beach wildlife depends on the dew that drops from these plants into the sand below. If part of the fragile plant cover is destroyed by storms, high winds, or people, sand is dispersed farther inland, and a new dune is formed.

Ice plant growing among the coastal sand dunes

flower fields in the area is distributed by the town of Lompoc's Chamber of Commerce. The Civic Center Plaza, between Ocean Avenue and C Street, has a display garden in which all the many flowers are identified.

La Purísima Concepción Mission, 3 miles (5 km) northeast of the town, was the 11th mission to be founded in California *(see pp50–51)*. It was declared a State Historic Park during the 1930s. The early 19th-century buildings have now been authentically reconstructed, and the complex and grounds provide a real insight into the missionary way of life.

Visitors to the mission are able to view the priests' living quarters, furnished with authentic pieces, in the elegant residence building. The simple, narrow church is decorated with colorful stencilwork. In the adjacent workshops, cloth, candles, leather goods, and furniture were at one time produced for the mission.

La Purísima's gardens have been faithfully restored. The varieties of fruit, vegetables, and medicinal herbs that are grown here were all common in the 19th century. Visitors can also view the irrigation system that provided the mission with water.

🏛 **La Purísima Concepción Mission**
2295 Purísima Rd, Lompoc. **Tel** (805) 733-3713. **Open** 9am–5pm daily. **Closed** Jan 1, Thanksgiving, Dec 25. 🅿

La Purísima Concepción Mission in Lompoc Valley

⑩ Tour of the Santa Ynez Valley Wineries

Santa Ynez Valley is one of the newest and most distinctive wine regions in the state. The area experiences coastal fog, which produces microclimates according to shifts in altitude and distance from the sea. The area also has a longer growing season than Northern California. These unique conditions, coupled with varied soils, produce a selection of classic grape varieties.

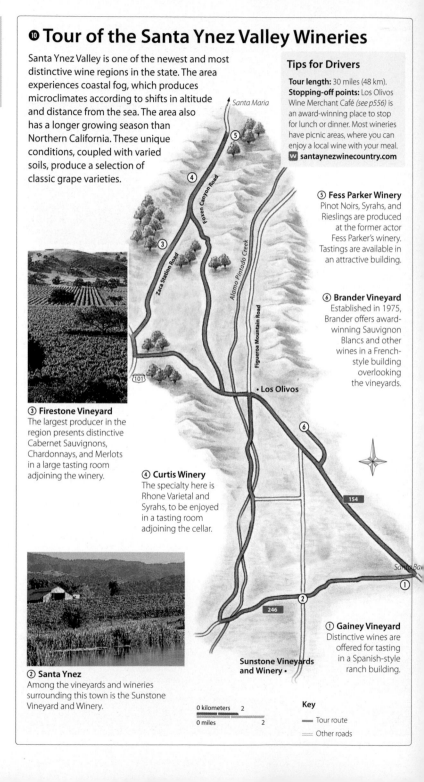

Tips for Drivers

Tour length: 30 miles (48 km).
Stopping-off points: Los Olivos Wine Merchant Café (*see p556*) is an award-winning place to stop for lunch or dinner. Most wineries have picnic areas, where you can enjoy a local wine with your meal.
Ⓦ santaynezwinecountry.com

⑤ **Fess Parker Winery**
Pinot Noirs, Syrahs, and Rieslings are produced at the former actor Fess Parker's winery. Tastings are available in an attractive building.

⑥ **Brander Vineyard**
Established in 1975, Brander offers award-winning Sauvignon Blancs and other wines in a French-style building overlooking the vineyards.

③ **Firestone Vineyard**
The largest producer in the region presents distinctive Cabernet Sauvignons, Chardonnays, and Merlots in a large tasting room adjoining the winery.

④ **Curtis Winery**
The specialty here is Rhone Varietal and Syrahs, to be enjoyed in a tasting room adjoining the cellar.

① **Gainey Vineyard**
Distinctive wines are offered for tasting in a Spanish-style ranch building.

② **Santa Ynez**
Among the vineyards and wineries surrounding this town is the Sunstone Vineyard and Winery.

Santa Maria

Foxen Canyon Road

Zaca Station Road

Alamo Pintado Creek

Figueroa Mountain Road

101

Los Olivos

154

Santa Ba

246

Sunstone Vineyards and Winery •

0 kilometers 2
0 miles 2

Key

— Tour route
═══ Other roads

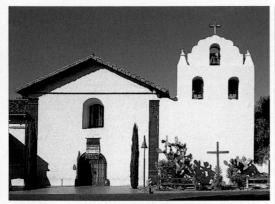

Mission Santa Inés church facade and campanile

⑪ Solvang

Map C5. 🏔 5,300. 🚌 𝒊 1639
Copenhagen Dr, (800) 468-6765.
W solvangusa.com

This Scandinavian-style town was established in 1911 by a group of Danish educators. They paid $360,000 for 9,000 acres (3,650 ha) of land on which to build a Danish colony and school. The original schoolhouse, a two-story frame structure on Alisal Road is today the the Bit o' Denmark Restaurant. Solvang's Bethnania Lutheran church, built in 1928 to a traditional Danish design, has a model sailing ship hanging from its ceiling. Visitors can tour the town in a horse-drawn streetcar, the *hønen* (hen), and see windmills, roofs with wooden storks, and gas streetlights. Restaurants serve *aebleskiver* (a type of Danish pancake), during the town's Danish Days festival *(see p42)*.

Statue of the Madonna

⑫ Mission Santa Inés

1760 Mission Dr, Solvang.
Road map C5. Tel (805) 688-4815.
Open 9am–5pm daily. Closed Easter, Thanksgiving, Dec 25. 🈂 🏛 ♿
W missionsantaines.org

Founded on September 17, 1804, Santa Inés was the 19th in the chain of California missions *(see pp50–51)*. In 1812

an earthquake destroyed the larger part of the church. It was rebuilt with 5-ft- (1.5-m-) thick walls and rededicated five years later. Before secularization in 1834 the mission was prosperous, with a herd of 12,000 cattle; afterward, it fell into disrepair and most of the Native Americans left. In 1843, the mission became the site of the state's first seminary. Restoration work began after World War II, including the campanile (financed by WR Hearst, *see p218*) and the church sanctuary. The mission also has a small museum, with period furnishings, parchment books, the vestments worn by early priests, and original murals by Native Americans. There is a landscaped garden.

⑬ Chumash Painted Cave State Historic Park

Painted Cave Road. Road map C5.
Tel (805) 733-3713. 🚌 from Santa Barbara. Parking limited to 2 vehicles.
W parks.cal.gov

In the Santa Ynez Mountains, 8 miles (13 km) northwest of Santa Barbara, are a number of remote and scattered caves with Chumash drawings. The most famous example is a 20 by 40 ft (6 by 12 m) cave just off Hwy 154. Inside, an egg-shaped cavity, covered in small ocher scratchings, is protected by a metal screen.

Some caves have primitive drawings that resemble lizards, snakes, and scorpions, executed in red, black, or white paint. Tribes are known to have traded different pigments with each other. Some experts believe the drawings are symbolic of the Chumash religion; others are of the opinion that they are random, with no significant meaning.

Native American paintings in the Chumash caves

Monarch Butterflies

Each year millions of monarch butterflies migrate from the western US and Canada to winter in Southern and Central California and Mexico. Starting their journey in October and November, the

butterflies cover up to 80 miles (130 km) a day at speeds approaching 30 mph (50 km/h). Along the central coast, they usually settle in eucalyptus groves. After the mating season in January and February, the butterflies attempt the journey back to their summer habitat. In season they can often be seen around Montana de Oro State Park *(see p213)*, Pismo Beach, and Ventura.

Monarch butterfly

⓮ Street-by-Street: Santa Barbara

To Santa Barbara Mission

Santa Barbara is a Southern Californian rarity: a city with a single architectural style. Following a devastating earthquake in 1925, the center was rebuilt according to strict rules that dictated Mediterranean-style architecture. The city was founded as a Spanish garrison in 1782 – four years before Santa Barbara Mission *(see pp226–7)*. During the 19th century Santa Barbara was a quiet pueblo, home to only a few hundred families and a center for the nearby cattle ranches. Remarkably, about a dozen adobes from that era have survived. Today, Santa Barbara is a favorite resort community with sand beaches, fine cafés and restaurants, boutiques, and art galleries.

FIGUEROA STREET

ANACAPA STREET

CARRILLO

★ Museum of Art
This outstanding regional art collection includes Asian art, antiquities, American art, prints, drawings, and photography. In the 19th-century French section is Jules Bastien-Lepage's *The Ripened Wheat* (1884).

★ County Courthouse
The 1929 Spanish Colonial-style courthouse is still in use. It is decorated with Tunisian tiles and wrought-iron metalwork. Murals by DS Groesbeck in the Mural Room depict California history *(see p46)*. There are panoramic views from the clock tower.

Paseo Nuevo
This colorful outdoor shopping and dining center complements an older arcade on the opposite side of State Street.

Key

— Suggested route

For hotels and restaurants in this area see p532 and pp556–8

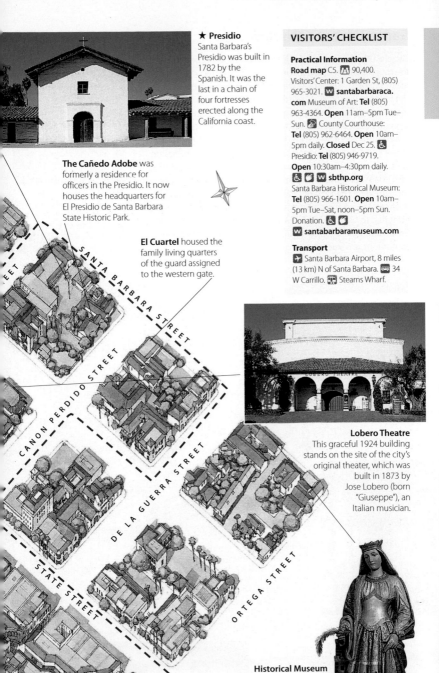

★ **Presidio**
Santa Barbara's Presidio was built in 1782 by the Spanish. It was the last in a chain of four fortresses erected along the California coast.

The Cañedo Adobe was formerly a residence for officers in the Presidio. It now houses the headquarters for El Presidio de Santa Barbara State Historic Park.

El Cuartel housed the family living quarters of the guard assigned to the western gate.

SANTA BARBARA STREET

CANON PERDIDO STREET

DE LA GUERRA STREET

STATE STREET

ORTEGA STREET

To East Beach

| 0 meters | 100 |
| 0 yards | 100 |

Lobero Theatre
This graceful 1924 building stands on the site of the city's original theater, which was built in 1873 by Jose Lobero (born "Giuseppe"), an Italian musician.

Historical Museum
The Historical Museum's collections are housed in two adobe buildings. Among the many artifacts is a statue of the 4th-century martyr St. Barbara.

VISITORS' CHECKLIST

Practical Information
Road map C5. 90,400.
Visitors' Center: 1 Garden St, (805) 965-3021. santabarbaraca.com Museum of Art: Tel (805) 963-4364. **Open** 11am–5pm Tue–Sun. County Courthouse: Tel (805) 962-6464. **Open** 10am–5pm daily. **Closed** Dec 25. Presidio: Tel (805) 946-9719. **Open** 10:30am–4:30pm daily. sbthp.org
Santa Barbara Historical Museum: Tel (805) 966-1601. **Open** 10am–5pm Tue–Sat, noon–5pm Sun. Donation. santabarbaramuseum.com

Transport
Santa Barbara Airport, 8 miles (13 km) N of Santa Barbara. 34 W Carrillo. Stearns Wharf.

Santa Barbara Mission

Labeled the "Queen of the Missions," Santa Barbara is the most visited mission in the state. Founded in 1786 on the feast day of St. Barbara, it was the tenth mission built by the Spanish *(see pp50–51)*. After the third adobe church on the site was destroyed by an earthquake in 1812, the present structure took shape and was completed in 1820. Its twin towers and mix of Roman, Moorish, and Spanish styles served as the main inspiration for what came to be known as Mission Style *(see p34)*. The mission was again hit by an earthquake in 1925, damaging the towers and facade of the church. These sections were repaired but, because of a chemical reaction between the alkalies and aggregates in the cement, the entire front had to be rebuilt in 1953, following the original design. Santa Barbara is the only California mission to have been in continuous use since it was founded.

Central Fountain
Palm trees tower above a central fountain in the Sacred Gardens.

Entrance

Arcaded Corridor
An open corridor fronts the museum rooms. Originally the living quarters, these now display a rich collection of mission artifacts.

Kitchen
The kitchen has been restored to show the typical cooking facilities of the early 1800s. Most of the food eaten was produced on the mission, which had fields and livestock.

★ **Sacred Gardens**
The beautifully landscaped Sacred Gardens were once a working area for Native Americans to learn Western trades. Workshops and some living quarters were located in the surrounding buildings.

VISITORS' CHECKLIST

Practical Information
2201 Laguna St. **Tel** (805) 682-4713. **Open** 9am–5pm daily (last tickets sold 4:15pm). 🎨 📷 11am Thu–Fri, 10:30am Sat. ♿ 📷
w santabarbaramission.org

Transport
🚌 22.

★ **Church**
The narrow church has a Neo-Classical interior. Imitation marble columns and detailing have been painted on the walls and doorways. The wooden reredos (altar screen), replaced after the 1915 earthquake, has carved wooden statues.

★ **Main Facade**
The church's Classical facade was designed by Padre Antonio Ripoll. Ripoll admired the Roman architect Vitruvius Pollio (active around 27 BC) and drew heavily on his ideas when building the church.

KEY

① **A missionary's bedroom** has been furnished as it would have been in the early 1800s.

② **The width of the nave** was determined by the height of the trees used as cross beams.

③ **The side chapel**, next to the altar, is dedicated to the Blessed Sacrament.

④ **The cemetery garden** contains the graves of some 4,000 Native Americans as well as friars.

San Buenaventura Mission's church in Ventura

⓵ Ventura

Road map C5. 🗺 108,000. 🚌 ℹ️
101 S California St, Suite C. **Tel** (805)
648-2075. **W** ventura–usa.com

All that remains of the **San Buenaventura Mission**, founded in 1782 and completed in 1809, is a church with a courtyard garden and tiled fountain. A museum at the mission details the buildings of the original complex.

Two mid-19th-century adobe houses survive in the city. The tiny **Ortega Adobe** reveals the harsh living conditions many experienced at that time. In contrast, the Monterey-style (see p34) **Olivas Adobe** is a two-story ranch hacienda, furnished in period style, with rose and herb gardens.

Today Ventura is largely an agricultural center. Ventura Harbor Village has shops, restaurants, a merry-go-round, and a community theater. Harbor fishing charters, and whale-watching cruises, as well as boats to the Channel Islands National Park, depart from here. You can also rent fishing equipment and kayaks.

🏛 **San Buenaventura Mission**
211 E Main St. **Tel** (805) 643-4318.
Open daily. **Closed** Jan 1, Easter,
Thanksgiving, Dec 25.
W sanbuenaventuramission.org

🏚 **Ortega Adobe**
215 W Main St. **Tel** (805) 648-2075.
Open daily. **Closed** Jan 1, Easter Sun,
Labor Day, Thanksgiving, Dec 25.

🏚 **Olivas Adobe**
4200 Olivas Park Drive. **Tel** (805) 658-4785. Grounds: **Open** daily. House:
Open Sat & Sun. **Closed** Jan 1, Easter,
Thanksgiving, Dec 25.

⓶ Channel Islands National Park

Road map C6. 🚂 Ventura. 🚌
Visitors' Center: 1901 Spinnaker Dr,
Ventura, (805) 658-5730.
Open daily. 🚢 Island Packers, 1867
Spinnaker Drive (805 642-1393).
W nps.gov/chis

The islands of Santa Barbara, Anacapa, San Miguel, Santa Cruz, and Santa Rosa together make up the Channel Islands National Park, a series of volcanic islands unpopulated by humans. Access to the islands is strictly monitored by park rangers, who issue landing permits from the Visitors' Center. Camping is allowed on all the islands, but visitors must make reservations at least two weeks in advance. They must also bring all their own food and water supplies, because there are none available on any of the five islands.

Depending on the island and the time of year, lucky visitors may spot dolphins, gray whales, and California brown pelicans on the passage across the Santa Barbara Channel. Wildlife on the small, picturesque islands is plentiful and includes cormorants, sea lions, elephant seals, and gulls.

Day trips to Anacapa, the nearest island to the mainland, offer an insight into this unique coastal ecosystem. Even more can be learned, however, by taking one of the various guided walks, conducted by park rangers, on all the islands. Visitors must stay on the designated trails, and pets are not allowed.

The rock pools on all of the islands are rich in marine life, and the kelp forests surrounding the islands provide shelter for more than 1,000 plant and animal species.

The islands' many sea caves make sea-kayaking a unique and exciting experience. The snorkeling and scuba diving in this area are superb.

⓷ Ronald Reagan Presidential Library

40 Presidential Drive, Simi Valley.
Road map C5. **Tel** (800) 410-8354.
Open 10am–5pm daily. **Closed** Jan 1,
Thanksgiving, Dec 25. 🎦 ♿
W reagan.utexas.edu

California brown pelican

President Reagan's papers are all archived in this Mission Revival-style structure. The library features a permanent exhibition documenting the life of Reagan and his wife, Nancy. There are also temporary exhibitions of gifts, costumes, works of art, and other objects related to his eight-year tenure in the White House, including a large piece of the Berlin Wall with its original graffiti. There is also an exact full-size replica of the Oval Office. In the Air Force One Pavilion, visitors can board the aircraft which was used by six presidents from 1973 to 2001.

Reconstruction of the Oval Office at the Reagan Presidential Library

Mission Revival arcade on Main Street, Ojai

⑱ Ojai

Road map C5. 🏔 7,500. 🚌
ℹ️ 150 W Ojai Ave, (805) 646-8126.
Ⓦ ojaichamber.org

Founded in 1874, this town was originally called Nordhoff after the author Charles Nordhoff, who wrote a book promoting California in the 1870s. In 1917 the town was renamed Ojai, a Chumash word for moon, a reference to the crescent-shaped valley where the town lies.

Ojai's Mission Revival arched arcade was funded by Edward J Libby, a glass-manufacturing millionaire, and was designed in 1917 by Richard Requa. Its tower was modeled on a campanile in Havana, Cuba. The arcade fronts two blocks of shops on the main street.

Barts Corner bookshop at No. 302 West Matilija Street has 25,000 volumes, many of which are displayed in bookcases outside. Late-night readers can browse and then pay for their finds through a slot in the door. Spiritual groups have been going on retreats in the Ojai Valley since the 1920s. Today several religious organizations and boarding schools are based here.

⑲ Los Padres National Forest

Road map C5. 🚌 Santa Barbara.
Visitors' Center: 6755 Hollister Ave, Suite 150, Goleta, (805) 968-6640.
Open 8am–4:30pm Mon–Fri.
Ⓦ fs.fed.us/r5/lospad:res

Los Padres National Forest covers almost 2 million acres (810,000 ha) of terrain that varies from desert to pine-clad mountains with peaks as high as 9,000 ft (2,700 m). Black bears, foxes, deer, and mountain lions are among the animals found here. Birds include golden eagles and giant condors. The latter are North America's largest birds with a wingspan of 9 ft (3 m).

Coastal redwood trees grow on the lower slopes, and the higher elevations are thick with firs bristling with pine cones. Temperatures in the summer can be scorching, and there is very little, if any, rain here between May and October.

The forest is crisscrossed by a huge number of hiking trails for experienced hikers, but there are few roads. Hwy 33 and Hwy 150 are two exceptions. Hwy 154 crosses one corner as it runs between Santa Ynez (see p222) and Santa Barbara (see pp224–7). On the way, it passes over Cold Spring Arch Bridge.

Scattered within Los Padres National Forest are 88 camp sites. Activities include fishing, horseback riding, and, on Mount Pinos, skiing.

⑳ Bakersfield

Road map C5. 🏔 363,600. 🚌 ℹ️
515 Truxton Ave, (866) 425-7353.
Ⓦ visitbakersfield.com

Bakersfield was named after Colonel Thomas Baker, a settler who planted a field of alfalfa here. The shrub fed the animals of early travelers who rested here before crossing the Tehachapi Mountains, the "border" that divides Northern and Southern California.

The town can be reached on the I-5 from San Francisco, before the ascent up Grapevine Canyon to LA. It can also be reached from Santa Maria or Ojai through the Los Padres National Forest.

Bakersfield's modern history began with the discovery of gold in the 1850s and several oil strikes in the following decades. Many people from Mediterranean countries settled on the fertile land, bringing agriculture to the area.

Today it is among the fastest growing cities in California, but still manages to retain a rural feel and is a recognized center for country music. There are also fine antique shops. The **Kern County Museum** has historical and oil industry exhibits. On the outskirts of Bakersfield is the Kern River for rafting and kayaking (see p584). Lake Isabella, 40 miles (65 km) east of the city, is a center for water sports.

🏛 **Kern County Museum**
3801 Chester Ave. **Tel** (661) 437-3330.
Open 10am–5pm Mon–Sat, noon–5pm Sun. **Closed** Jan 1, Thanksgiving, Dec 24, 25, 31. 🎫
Ⓦ kcmuseum.org

Cold Spring Arch Bridge, Los Padres National Forest

ORANGE COUNTY

A century ago, Orange County lived up to its name. This dry, sunny land, which stretches from the Santa Ana Mountains to the beautiful Pacific coastline, was indeed scattered with orange orchards and farms. Today, the region is a mass of freeways and suburban housing, but visitors to the county can explore a wide range of museums, sites of historical interest, and entertainment complexes.

In the mid-1950s, the roads leading to the county's theme parks still passed through extensive orange groves. At that time, Disneyland® was attracting its first enthusiastic crowds, and a local boy called Richard Nixon had become Vice President of the US. Today, orange groves have given way to urban development and fruit crate labels have become collectors' items. More than three million people live here, enjoying perennial sunshine and a high standard of living.

The coastline of Orange County is lined with wide, sandy beaches and a succession of legendary surfing haunts, marinas, and artists' enclaves. In the affluent coastal towns, few visitors can resist the temptation to seek out a clifftop bar and watch the sun set.

Inland lies a variety of cultural sights. Mission San Juan Capistrano, founded in 1776, is a reminder of the days of the Spanish Franciscan settlers. The Bowers Museum in Santa Ana houses superb examples of the art of indigenous peoples from all around the world. At Yorba Linda, the impressive Nixon Presidential Library and Museum commemorates the life of Orange County's most famous son.

Orange County is California's theme park capital. For visitors seeking family entertainment and roller-coaster thrills, there are the homey Knott's Berry Farm®, America's oldest theme park, the adjacent water park, Soak City, and the fantasy kingdom of Disneyland®, which is, as the saying goes, "the most famous people-trap ever built by a mouse."

Reflecting Pool at the Nixon Presidential Library and Museum

◀ Yachts moored at Avalon Bay, Catalina Island

Exploring Orange County

Much of Orange County's 798-sq mile (2,050-sq km) area is covered with sprawling urban communities linked by ever-busy freeways. Anaheim, home of Disneyland®, is its second largest city, after Santa Ana. The popular Knott's Berry Farm® theme park lies a short drive northwest at Buena Park, and together these cities form the tourist capital of the county. Most of the coastline is built up, but its communities have more variety and character than those around the theme parks. Inland, open spaces can be found where the county's eastern region encompasses part of the vast Cleveland National Forest and the Santa Ana Mountains.

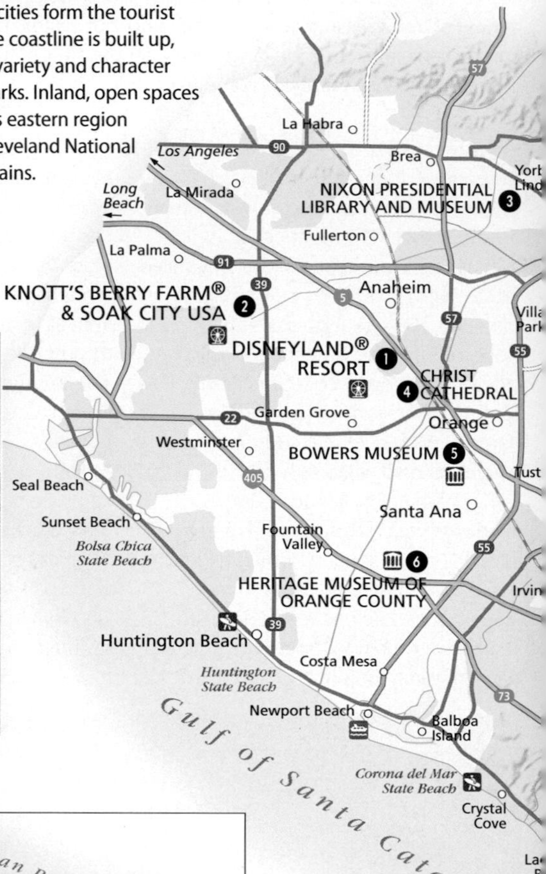

La Habra
Los Angeles
Brea
York Lind
Long Beach
La Mirada
NIXON PRESIDENTIAL LIBRARY AND MUSEUM ❸
Fullerton
La Palma
Anaheim
KNOTT'S BERRY FARM® & SOAK CITY USA ❷
Villa Park
DISNEYLAND® RESORT ❶
CHRIST CATHEDRAL ❹
Garden Grove
Orange
Westminster
BOWERS MUSEUM ❺
Tust
Seal Beach
Santa Ana
Sunset Beach
Bolsa Chica State Beach
Fountain Valley
HERITAGE MUSEUM OF ORANGE COUNTY ❻
Irvin
Huntington Beach
Costa Mesa
Huntington State Beach
Newport Beach
Balboa Island
Gulf of Santa Catalina
Corona del Mar State Beach
Crystal Cove
La

Catalina Island's Two Harbors

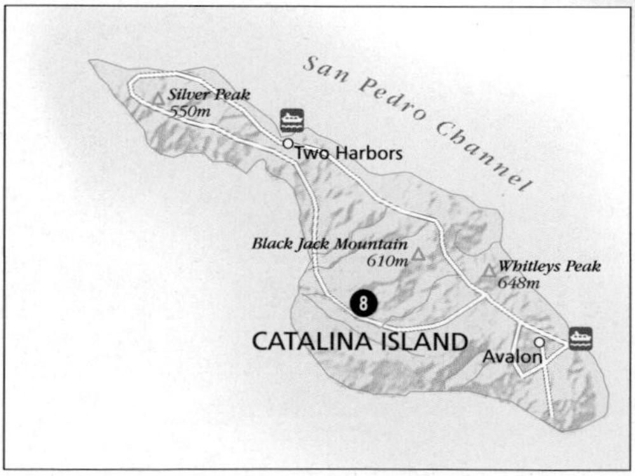

San Pedro Channel
Silver Peak 550m
Two Harbors
Black Jack Mountain 610m
Whitleys Peak 648m
❽
CATALINA ISLAND
Avalon
Santa Catalina

Key

━━ Freeway
━━ Major road
━━ Secondary road
····· Minor road
∘━∘ Main railroad
····· Minor railroad
△ Summit

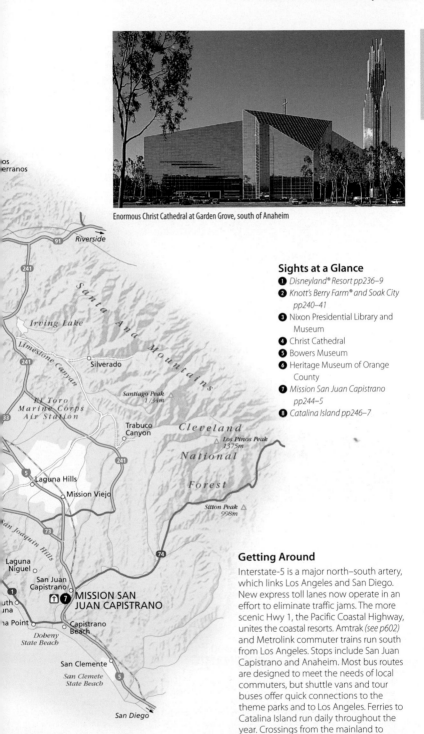

Enormous Christ Cathedral at Garden Grove, south of Anaheim

Sights at a Glance

❶ *Disneyland® Resort pp236–9*
❷ *Knott's Berry Farm® and Soak City pp240–41*
❸ Nixon Presidential Library and Museum
❹ Christ Cathedral
❺ Bowers Museum
❻ Heritage Museum of Orange County
❼ *Mission San Juan Capistrano pp244–5*
❽ *Catalina Island pp246–7*

Getting Around

Interstate-5 is a major north–south artery, which links Los Angeles and San Diego. New express toll lanes now operate in an effort to eliminate traffic jams. The more scenic Hwy 1, the Pacific Coastal Highway, unites the coastal resorts. Amtrak *(see p602)* and Metrolink commuter trains run south from Los Angeles. Stops include San Juan Capistrano and Anaheim. Most bus routes are designed to meet the needs of local commuters, but shuttle vans and tour buses offer quick connections to the theme parks and to Los Angeles. Ferries to Catalina Island run daily throughout the year. Crossings from the mainland to Avalon or Two Harbors take about an hour.

0 kilometers 5
0 miles 5

For additional map symbols *see back flap*

Orange County Coastline

Orange County's coast is Southern California at its most classic. The northern shoreline is flat and lowlying. South of the Balboa Peninsula, the coast features scenic cliffs and sheltered coves. Multi-million dollar homes, luxury marinas, constant sports activity, and a fashionable lifestyle reflect the wealth and vitality of its communities.

The Balboa Pavilion opened in 1905 as a terminal for the Pacific Electric Red Car Line from LA. Stars of the Big Band era, such as Count Basie, played here in the 1930s and 1940s. Today the wooden pavilion is a restaurant and center for sightseeing cruises around Newport Harbor.

③ ★ Huntington State Beach
California's Surf City USA®, Huntington Beach has a surfing museum, international competitions, and waters full of surfers whose exploits can be watched from the long pier.

Upper Newport Bay Ecological Preserve is a 1000-acre (405-ha) wedge of coastal wetland providing a refuge for wildlife and migratory birds. Facilities in the preserve include a bike path, fishing, and guided tours on foot and by kayak.

Key

- ▬ Freeway
- ▬ Major road
- ▭ Minor road
- ～ River
- ☆ Viewpoint

① Seal Beach
This is a quiet, 1-mile (1.6-km) long beach with level sand and some surfers. The wooden pier is popular with anglers. A walk along its 1,865-ft (570-m) length offers views northward to the high-rise buildings of Long Beach (see pp136–7).

② Bolsa Chica State Beach
The name Bolsa Chica means "little pocket" in Spanish. Flat, wilderness sands, oil extractors, and the protected wetlands of the 300-acre (120-ha) Bolsa Chica Ecological Reserve give this beach a unique atmosphere.

④ Newport Beach
Famous for its million-dollar homes and lifestyles to match, Newport Beach boasts a 3-mile (5-km) stretch of wide sand and two piers. Fresh fish, caught by the historic Dory fishing fleet, is sold beside Newport Pier at the northern end of the beach.

⑦ Aliso Beach
At the mouth of Aliso Creek lies this small, sandy beach. The 620-ft- (190-m-) long concrete pier is used by anglers. At the southern end of the beach is a marine life refuge with beds of giant kelp offshore.

⑧ Doheny State Beach
This sandy beach and marine life refuge is close to the mouth of San Juan Creek. The beach attracts a typically Southern Californian mix of swimmers, surfers, bird-watchers, anglers, cyclists, and campers.

⑨ San Clemente State Beach
The hillside community of San Clemente has a narrow, sandy beach at its foot. Near the railroad station there is a municipal pier. Farther south, the 100-acre (40-ha) State Beach has landscaped facilities including picnic areas and a camp site.

⑤ ★ **Corona del Mar State Beach**

Overlooked by cliffs lined with stylish houses and landscaped viewpoints, this is a family beach with good swimming, sandy coves, and rock pools to explore.

Locator Map

NEVADA

CALIFORNIA

Pacific Ocean

0 kilometers   5
0 miles   5

Los Angeles

Upper Newport Bay Ecological Reserve

• Balboa Pavilion

• Corona del Mar

• Laguna Beach

South Laguna •

San Juan Capistrano

Dana Point

San Clemente •

San Diego

Crown Valley Parkway

⑥ ★ **Laguna Beach**

With its clifftop promenades, small, sheltered beaches, and artistic community, Laguna courts the atmosphere of the Mediterranean Riviera. The ideal spot for a cocktail at sunset, Laguna is famous for its summer arts festival, the Festival of Arts *(see p41)*.

Dana Point headland is named after the author Richard Dana, whose 1840 book *Two Years Before the Mast* chronicled the early days of California. A replica of the contemporary brig, *Pilgrim*, is moored in the harbor.

❶ Disneyland® Resort

Disney's "Magic Kingdom" in Anaheim is not only the top tourist attraction in California, it is part of the American Dream. Now encompassing the original Disneyland® Park, Disney's California Adventure™ Park, and Downtown Disney®, plus three enormous hotels, the Resort has become the model for theme parks around the globe. Visitors to "The Happiest Place on Earth" find fantasy, thrill rides, glittering shows, and shopping in a brightly orchestrated land of long lines, fireworks, and Mickey Mouse, which is as American as apple pie.

Exploring the Resort

Spread over 107 acres (43 ha), the original Disneyland® Park is divided into eight theme areas, known as "lands." Transportation around the park is provided by the Disneyland® Railroad and monorail.

Disney's California Adventure™ Park has four theme areas *(see p239)*. Smaller in area than Disneyland® Park, Disney's California Adventure™ Park is easily covered by walking. This newest venture into nostalgia, impeccably executed in superb and stunning Disney-style, is suited to the interests and tastes of the whole family. In the heart of the Resort, between the two theme parks, lies Downtown Disney®. This lively area is full of restaurants, shops, and various innovative entertainment venues.

It takes at least three days to make the best of a visit, now that the Resort has grown so large. A joint ticket *(see box, p237)* can be bought for all the theme parks; it provides access to all the rides and shows, and includes a park map, and a schedule of the day's events. Both parks stay open late in the evening during the peak seasons; and the **Fireworks Show** that takes place in Disneyland® is well worth losing a little sleep for.

Main Street, U.S.A.®

This spotlessly clean, colorful street lined with turn-of-the-century buildings welcomes visitors to Disneyland®. The Town Square, near City Hall, is a good place to view the daily parade, which features cheerfully waving Disney characters and scenes from many of Disney's most famous movies. This is only one of the places where guests can meet and talk with many of the famous Disney cartoon characters. If you are lucky, you can find ample opportunities here for photographs and videos.

City Hall offers maps, dining and entertainment schedules, and general information about the park, while the **Main Street Cinema** screens early Disney silent films. Main Street itself has a large selection of attractions, shops, and places to eat.

Tomorrowland®

Visions of the future inspire the attractions here, which change regularly to keep ahead of technology and still retain a sense of fantasy. One of the first attractions in 1955 was **Autopia**, now completely redesigned and updated to take guests into a parallel universe from a car's point of view. The track winds through Tomorrowland®, as well as Fantasyland®.

Buzz Lightyear Astro Blasters

An interactive experience in which guests pilot their own Space Cruisers.

Finding Nemo Submarine Voyage

A truly unique experience where visitors go underwater accompanied by Nemo and his friends.

Star Tours©

Designed in collaboration with the *Star Wars*© genius, George Lucas, the use of flight-simulator technology makes this one of the most realistic rides in the park. The attraction recently added Odysseys in 3-D, with more than 50 story combinations.

Space Mountain®

A hands-down Disneyland® favorite and updated for the Millennium, this attraction provides a high-speed roller-coaster ride, 118 ft (36 m). Conducted almost entirely in darkness, the ride has meteoric flashes, celestial showers, and space-age music. Not suitable for very young children.

Mickey's Toontown®

All of Disney's favorite animated characters reside here. This is where visitors are most likely to

Shopping

The Disneyland® shops, particularly those along Main Street, U.S.A.®, are often busy late in the day, especially at closing time. If you can, it is worth making your purchases earlier in the day and then collecting them later from the Redemption Center. Although many of the goods on sale in the theme park bear the faces of Disney characters, each of the eight lands adds its own variations to what is on offer to buy. In Adventureland®, for example, you can buy Indiana Jones-style clothing, and Native American crafts are on sale in Frontierland®. The largest of all the shops within the Magic Kingdom® is the Emporium in Main Street, U.S.A®. If you are looking for Disney® characters or Disney merchandise, this is the first place to go.

Fairytale facade of Sleeping Beauty Castle in Fantasyland

and the constant crowds illustrate the enduring appeal of this area.

Matterhorn Bobsleds

This historic attraction and park icon has been providing "icy" roller-coaster rides since 1959. A copy of the famous peak near Zermatt in Switzerland, the Matterhorn Mountain towers 147 ft (45 m) above the park. Bobsleds carrying four passengers climb to the mountain's snow-capped summit, then drop into a steep, high-speed descent, zooming in and out of the hollow peak, passing glacier caves and waterfalls as they go. At the end of the trip, riders in the front seats are splashed as the sleds careen into a pond.

"It's a Small World"®

This show features dolls inspired by favorite Disney characters, but dressed in costumes from around the world. Colorful boats transport passengers through the attraction, which features nearly 300 singing-and-dancing Audio-Animatronics dolls, all in national costume.

find Mickey, Goofy, and other well-known characters having their pictures taken with guests.

The most popular celebrity residences are Mickey's house and Minnie's cottage, where subtle touches typify Disney's legendary attention to detail. Most of the attractions in this area are geared toward kids from age three up. **Chip 'n Dale Treehouse** is located in a giant Redwood, and the bustling interactive downtown area offers gentle excitement for this younger set.

Roger Rabbit's Car Toon Spin is Toontown®'s largest and most popular attraction. Its spinning cars provide a madcap taxi drive through a surreal cartoon world fraught with near-misses.

Fantasyland®

Dominated by the pink and gold towers of **Sleeping Beauty Castle** and a replica of the **Matterhorn**, Fantasyland®

is a shrine to children's dreams and adult nostalgia. Nursery heroes such as Peter Pan, Dumbo, and Snow White provide the themes for gentle fairytale rides in vehicles that range from flying galleons and canal boats to the Mad Hatter's giant spinning teacups. There are almost twice as many attractions to enjoy here as in most of the other lands,

Tickets and Tips

A basic one-day ticket to Disneyland® or Disney's California Adventure™ Park covers admission and most rides and attractions. Parking is extra, as are food and arcades. Multiday tickets for two to six days and Annual Passports allow unlimited admission and access to rides and attractions. Fastpass lets guests obtain a voucher with a computer-assigned boarding time for specific attractions or rides. This eliminates waiting in long lines. You can also save time at the front gate by buying your tickets in advance at any Disney Store or online at www.disneyland.com. To help you plan your day, there is updated information on showtimes, waiting times, and ride closures at the information board at the end of Main Street, U.S.A®, opposite the Plaza Pavilion, and on the website.

Mark Twain Riverboat navigating the Rivers of America

Frontierland®

This area is inspired by the adventurous days of the Wild West. Skirt-lifting song and dance take place on the **Golden Horseshoe** stage featuring Billy Hill and the Hillbillies. Every weekend at night the spectacular **Fantasmic!** show with fireworks, sound effects, and live performers light up the skies above Frontierland®.

Downtown Disney®

Located between the entrances to Disneyland® Park and Disney's California Adventure™ Park, Downtown Disney® is a lively walking street, offering guests some 300,000 sq ft (27,870 sq m) of innovative restaurants, shops, and entertainment venues. The fact that this area has no admission fee makes Downtown Disney® one of the more popular – but crowded – spaces. A 12-screen AMC Theatre®, ESPN Zone™, and a LEGO Imagination Center® are the top attractions here. The snack shops, top-notch restaurants, plus a vast range of retail and specialty shops and a travel center, create a total Disney experience.

The **Mark Twain Riverboat** offers visitors a 15-minute cruise on a paddle-wheel boat. While it crosses the Rivers of America, look out for the plastic moose and deer. Take time to visit the scary new **Pirate's Lair** on Tom Sawyer Island.

Thrill-seekers love the **Big Thunder Mountain Railroad** roller-coaster ride. Open ore trucks set off from the 1880s mining town of Big Thunder without a driver. The runaway train then speeds through the cavernous interior of Big Thunder Mountain, narrowly escaping boulders and waterfalls. Remember that this ride has height and age restrictions.

Critter Country

Built in a rustic style, based on the rugged American Northwest, Critter Country is a 4-acre (1.6-ha) area next to New Orleans Square. Home of Splash Mountain®, one of the most popular attractions in Disneyland®, and a quiet restaurant, the Hungry Bear.

Splash Mountain·

This is a winding, watery ride in hollowed-out logs. Brer Rabbit and Brer Fox are among the furry, singing characters from the 1946 film *Song of the South*,

who inhabit the mountain through which the ride passes. The ride culminates in a plummet down a steep waterfall. As on the Matterhorn ride, people in the front seats will get wet.

Davy Crockett's Explorer Canoes

Groups can take to the water and row downriver frontier-style. Guides provide lessons and ensure safety.

The Many Adventures of Winnie the Pooh

The world's most beloved bear and his stalwart friends go on a hunt for honey in this ride.

New Orleans Square

This charming town square is modeled on the French Quarter in New Orleans, as it was in that city's heyday in the 19th century. The buildings have wrought-iron balconies and house interesting French-style shops.

The Haunted Mansion·

Some of the visitors to this attraction, which promises 999 "ghosts and ghouls," are now so familiar with its introductory commentary that they join in as they descend into its spooky world of mischievous spirits and grave-diggers. The holographic figures, including a talking woman's head in a crystal ball, are very realistic. This show, which took 15 years to plan, has decor inspired by Tim Burton's *The Nightmare Before Christmas*. The show is exclusive to Disneyland® in California and provides a cool shelter inside on hot afternoons.

Pirates of the Caribbean*
This ride provides a floating tour through a yo-ho-ho world of ruffians and wenches who have been empowered with the gifts of song, dance, and heavy drinking by Audio-Animatronics. This technique, which brings toy figures to life using electronic impulses to control their sounds and actions, was perfected at Disneyland®.

Characters from the popular movie franchise have been added to the ride.

Adventureland*

The exotic atmosphere in Adventureland® offers dark, humid waterways lined with tropical plants. This is the smallest, but perhaps the most adventuresome, "land" in the park. **The Enchanted Tiki Room** showcases mechanical singing birds in a zany, musical romp through the tropics.

Indiana Jones™ Adventure
Inspired by the 1982 film trilogy, passengers set off on a jeep-style drive through the Temple of the Forbidden Eye. Theatrical props and scenery, a realistic

soundtrack, sensational film images, and the physical sensation of a roller coaster make this the ultimate experience created by Disneyland® to date.

Jungle Cruise
This safari-style boat ride through a jungle forest full of rampant apes and bloodthirsty headhunters is narrated by a real-life captain, who tells his captive audience terrible but amusing jokes during the ride through steamy waterways.

Tarzan™'s Treehouse
A climb-up, climb-through experience, starring Tarzan and Jane, with an interactive and musical play area at the base of the tree.

Disney's California Adventure™ Park

Disney's California Adventure™ Park is adjacent to Disneyland® and built on 55 acres (22 ha) of the old parking lot. Like its neighbor, Disney's California Adventure™ Park is also divided into "lands," each offering themed experiences that celebrate the California dream. The emphasis here is on adults and older teens, but there are still plenty of rides and attractions that appeal to all ages. Together with the original Disneyland® Park, Disney's California Adventure™ Park adds to the Disney legend.

Hollywood Pictures Backlot

The Backlot offers a great tongue-in-cheek view of the motion-picture industry. There are two blocks of facades and fakery, giving the visitor a Disney-eye view of Hollywood. Other attractions include **The Twilight Zone Tower of Terror™**, with a 13-story elevator drop, and **Monsters Inc. Mike and Sulley to the Rescue**, where visitors race around Monstropolis on a mission to return the adventurous little girl Boo home safely.

Golden State

A tribute to the state's topography and agriculture, the rock-carved Grizzly Peak stands as the landmark icon of Disney's California Adventure™ Park.

The centerpiece ride is **Soarin'™ Over California**, a simulated hang-glider ride that portrays the beauties of California's varied landscape on a huge wrap-around screen. There is no narrative, but guests can feel the wind currents and

smell the scent of orange blossoms as they soar 40 ft (12 m) aloft. **Grizzly River Run** will visitors down as they run the rapids on a rubber raft. **Bug's Land** features bug rides for children and a 3-D film starring Flik from *A Bug's Life*.

Paradise Pier

Lower-key than the thrill rides in the original park, Paradise Pier is the place where roller coasters and Ferris wheels rule. **California Screamin'** roller coaster, the giant **Mickey's Fun Wheel**, **Games of the Boardwalk**, and **King Triton's Carousel** are reminiscent of seaside boardwalk amusement parks of years ago.

Grizzly River Run, California Adventure™ Park's signature attraction

❷ Knott's Berry Farm® and Soak City

Knott's Berry Farm® has grown from a 1920s boysenberry farm to a 21st-century multi-day entertainment complex. America's first theme park offers more than 165 different rides and attractions, but its main charm lies in its emphasis on authenticity. The Old West Ghost Town at the heart of the park has original ghost town buildings and artifacts. Located in Buena Park in Orange County, 6 miles (10 km) from Disneyland®, Knott's offers five themed areas, dozens of live-action stages, thrill rides, shopping and dining, and a full-service resort hotel.

Ghostrider

Built in 1998, this mega-woodie has risen to the top of the "best coaster ride" list. With an initial drop of 108 ft (33 m) at speeds approaching 60 mph (97km/h), the 2.5-minute ride is a must for every visitor to the Old Ghost Town.

Old West Ghost Town

This 1880s Goldrush town has authentic century-old buildings. An 1880 steam train, the **Ghost Town & Calico Railroad**, circles the park, and a genuine **Butterfield Stagecoach** takes passengers on a trip into the past.

The **Gold Trails Hotel and Mercantile**, a restored Kansas school-house, and the **Western Trails Museum** are chock full of Wild West memorabilia. Visitors can join a line-dance at **Calico Square**. The **Timber Mountain Log Ride** floats visitors through a real 1880s sawmill before plunging down a waterfall.

At the heart of Ghost Town, the **Ghostrider** roller coaster towers over the park. **Silver Bullet** is Knott's first suspended coaster with spirals and corkscrews, and the **Pony Express** offers a horseback relay at speeds never imagined in the Old West.

Largest wooden coaster on the West Coast at 118-ft (36-m) high

4,533-ft (1,382-m) long track

An 1880 steam engine transporting visitors around the park

Camp Snoopy

Inspired by the majestic High Sierra, Camp Snoopy's 6-acre (2.4-ha) wonderland is an interactive participatory children's paradise. There are over 30 kid-tested attractions and pint-sized rides, hosted by the beloved *Peanuts* characters Snoopy, Lucy, and Charlie Brown. Children under 12 delight in the **Timberline Twister** roller coaster, the Red Baron's airplanes, and an old-fashioned Ferris wheel, where parents and kids can see wonderful views. The **Charlie Brown Speedway** appeals to little stock-car enthusiasts and their parents. **Woodstock's Airmail** is a child-sized version of Supreme Scream℠. Kids of all ages will want to come aboard **Lucy's Tugboat**, take a spin on **Sierra Side-winder**, or watch a show at the **Camp Snoopy Theatre**.

Fiesta Village

Celebrating California's Spanish legacy, Fiesta Village offers a collection of south-of-the-

Kids behind the wheel at the Charlie Brown Speedway

border adventures and high-energy thrills. **Casa Arcada** challenges the whole family to the latest arcade games, while a ride on the world's oldest **Dentzel Carousel** is a pleasant nostalgic treat. Two large roller coasters, the family-pleasing **Jaguar** and, for the more adventurous fun-seeker, **Montezooma's Revenge** provide exciting thrill rides.

Supreme Scream℠, a vertical ascending and descending thrill ride

Indian Trails

Intricate arts and crafts of Native Americans from the Pacific Northwest, Great Plains, South-west, and Far West are show-cased in this area. Totem poles and tepees from the Navajo, Cherokee, and Chumash tribes seen throughout Indian Trails were built to convey the beauty and diversity of Native American culture. Through participatory learning adventures and exquisite art-works, visitors will understand how the people lived, and how their beliefs, climate, and environment influenced their daily lives.

The Boardwalk

A continuous beach party is the theme here, where everything centers around Southern California's seaside culture. Beachside concessions and the most radical thrill rides rule: **Supreme Scream℠** simulates a rocket launch while the **Perilous Plunge** and **Xcelerator** are not for the nervous. Then, relax and take in a big-stage show at the **Charles M. Schulz Theater**.

Wild Water Wilderness

Experience the magic of the 1900s river wilderness with a raging white-water river, soaring geysers, and a giant waterfall – **Bigfoot Rapids** will fulfill your wildest dreams. The multi-sensory **Mystery Lodge** celebrates Native American culture, complete with a Native storyteller, music, and dance.

The **Ranger Station** has a resident naturalist who makes friends with Sasquatch, the California High Sierra creature also known as Bigfoot.

Soak City

Southern California's newest water adventure park has 21 awesome water rides – all themed to the 1950s and 1960s surfing culture.

Adjacent to Knott's main park, and separately gated, Soak City serves up 13 water-logged acres (5.3 ha), replete with tube and body slides, surfing pipelines, a six-lane super slide, and **Tidal Wave Bay**, a special pool with gentle to moderate wave

action. **Gremmie Lagoon** is a wet kid's playground with hands-on fun. **Pacific Spin**, the newest attraction, drops riders into a 75-ft (22-m) tunnel.

All rides have age and height requirements. Men's and women's changing rooms and lockers are also available.

Knott's Berry Farm® Resort Hotel

In addition to the rides and attractions at Knott's Berry Farm® and Soak City, and completing the whole experience, is the Knott's Berry Farm® Resort Hotel. Guests in the 321-room hotel can stay in Snoopy-themed suites and take advantage of the pools, sports facilities, fitness center, and children's activity area. Family-friendly restaurants such as Amber Waves add to the festive atmosphere. There are, of course, special rates for frequent guests, and value-added packages.

Spectacular water rides at Soak City

House in which Richard Nixon was born

❸ Nixon Presidential Library and Museum

Road map D6. 18001 Yorba Linda Blvd, Yorba Linda. **Tel** 714-993-5075. 🚉 to Fullerton. **Open** 10am–5pm Mon– Sat, 11am–5pm Sun. **Closed** Thanksgiving, Dec 25. 🅿️ 🅰️ 📷 🅦 nixonlibrary.gov

The life and achievements of the Republican politician Richard Nixon, president of the United States from 1969 to 1974, are celebrated in this museum and archive. In the immaculately landscaped grounds is the simple wooden house where the former president was born in 1913. Nearby are a Reflecting Pool and the graves of Nixon and his wife, Pat, marked by matching black granite tombstones.

In the museum, a walk-through exhibit provides a chronological account of Nixon's rise and fall, emphasizing his role as a peacemaker and international statesman. The Foreign Affairs gallery has a reconstruction of a Chinese pavilion housing an exhibit on Nixon's 1972 state visit to China. There is also a replica of St. Basil's Cathedral in Moscow, with a display on Nixon's trip to the Soviet Union that same year.

Do not miss the World Leaders' Room, where statues of famous politicians are surrounded by some of the many gifts that Nixon received while in office, such as a 6th-century BC statue of the goddess Isis from Anwar Sadat of Egypt, a Sonia Delaunay painting from Georges Pompidou of France, and a malachite jewelry box from Leonid Brezhnev of the Soviet Union.

Historic items exhibited in other galleries include a three-billion-year-old lump of rock from the moon, a 12-ft (3.5-m) section of the Berlin Wall, and dresses worn by the First Lady. Visitors are able to eavesdrop on the infamous "Watergate Tapes," which led to Nixon's resignation. In the Presidential Forum, a touch-screen exhibit using archive footage allows visitors to put questions to the late president. In additional galleries changing exhibitions are held.

These cover popular aspects of US presidential history, such as the visits paid to the White House by such pop stars as Elvis Presley.

❹ Christ Cathedral

12141 Lewis St, Garden Grove. **Tel** 714-971-4000. 🚌 45 N. **Closed** (scheduled to reopen in 2017). 🅰️ 🅦 christcathedralcalifornia.org

Constructed from an elaborate maze of white steel trusses covered with more than 10,000 panes of silvered glass, the Christ Cathedral (formerly the Crystal Cathedral) is a shimmering monument to the television-led evangelism that enthrals millions of Americans. The Crystal Cathedral was the main place of worship for R Schuller's Reformed Church of America which, after a lengthy evangelical crusade that began in 1955, filed for bankruptcy in 2010. The Roman Catholic Diocese of Orange bought the church in 2012 and is renovating the space, with plans to reopen as Christ Cathedral in 2017.

Designed in 1980 by Philip Johnson, the star-shaped cathedral is both a spiritual shrine and an architectural wonder. It

Vast interior of the Christ Cathedral in Garden Grove

could comfortably hold the 3,000 worshipers who would gather for the *Hour of Power*, the Schullers', (Christian televangelists) Sunday service that was broadcast live from the Crystal Cathedral on television every Sunday up until 2012. During the service, a huge glass door opened to enable the drive-in congregation outside to listen to the sermons without leaving their cars. A 15-ft- (4.6-m-) wide color video screen ensured everyone could see the proceedings, and the biggest pipe organ in the world provided the music. The organ has been dismantled and is being painstakingly refurbished in preparation for the grand opening of the building as Christ Cathedral.

Beside the church is a 236-ft (72-m) steeple, added in 1990 and adorned with polished stainless-steel prisms. The Reformed Church of America continues to run, and the *Hour of Power* is still produced from its new base at nearby Shepherd's Grove.

❺ Bowers Museum

2002 N Main St, Santa Ana.
Road map D6. **Tel** 714-567-3600. 🚆
to Anaheim. 🚌 45 S. **Open** 10am–
4pm Tue–Sun. **Closed** Jan 1, Jul 4,
Thanksgiving, Dec 25. 🅿 ♿ 📷
(Sat–Sun). 🌐 **bowers.org**

The Bowers has long been considered to be Orange County's leading art museum. Its serene Mission-style build-ings house rich permanent collections and high-profile temporary exhibitions. There is a stylish California café and a shop packed with ethnic crafts and art books.

The museum was founded in 1932. Its display of African masks, collected by Paul and Ruth Tishman and now on long-term loan from the Disney Corporation, is reason enough for a pilgrimage. Other galleries, with exhibitions of treasures from the pre-colonial cultures of Southeast Asia, Oceania, Mexico, and America, reflect the museum's commitment to art of indigenous peoples. Fascinating

Mission-style entrance arch leading to the Bowers Museum

examples of their crafts illustrate both the religious beliefs and the daily lives of these people. The upstairs galleries, decorated with 1930s murals and plaster work, cover the mission and rancho periods of California and Orange County history *(see pp50–51)*. One block away, a former bank has been converted into the companion **Kidseum**, where kids can enjoy arts-related activities and can try on masks and costumes from all over the world.

Mayan statuette (AD 800–950), Bowers Museum

🏛 Kidseum

1802 N Main St, Santa Ana. **Tel** (714) 480-1520. **Open** 10am–3pm Tue–Fri, 11am–3pm Sat & Sun. 🅿 ♿

❻ Heritage Museum of Orange County

3101 W Harvard St, Santa Ana.
Road map D6. **Tel** 714-540-0404. 🚆
to Anaheim. 🚌 45 S. **Open** 1–5pm
Fri, 10am–2pm Sat, 11am–3pm Sun.
Closed Jan 1, Easter Sun, Thanksgiving, Dec 25. 🅿 ♿ 📷
🌐 **heritagemuseumoc.org**

Victorian times in Orange County are brought to life in this curious three-story mansion, built in 1898 by a civil engineer, Hiram Clay Kellogg. Fascinated by ships, Kellogg incorporated several nautical design features into his Santa Ana residence. The oval, cabin-like dining room has an oak and walnut floor, laid in strips to resemble a ship's deck. Some of the drawers in the built-in wooden cabinets can also be opened from the kitchen, on the other side of the wall. Clusters of fruit are painted on the ceiling, and the room is overlooked by an elegant circular staircase with a mastlike central pillar.

The mansion now houses an exciting and child-friendly museum, which is also of historic and architectural interest to adults. Young visitors are given the opportunity to dress up in genuine antique clothing and experience life as it was at the turn of the century.

Upstairs, rooms are furnished with antique school desks, dolls' houses, and period games. In the master bedroom, now the textile room, a treadle sewing machine and spinning wheel are on display. Downstairs, visitors can investigate such instruments as a stereoscope and a hand-crank telephone, and see the old-fashioned kitchen that has an icebox and butter churn. Next door is an 1899 ranch house, carriage barn, and water tower. There is also an orchard of orange trees – now a rare sight in the county.

Implements for orange cultivation at the Heritage Museum Orange County

❼ Mission San Juan Capistrano

This beautiful "Jewel of the Missions" was founded in 1776, and its chapel is the only surviving building in California in which the famous Father Junípero Serra *(see p50)* preached. One of the largest and most prosperous in the whole chain, the mission was crowned by the Great Stone Church, completed in 1806. Six years later this was destroyed by an earthquake, leaving a ruined shell set amid a rambling complex of adobe and brick buildings. A restoration program, ornamental gardens, and many historical exhibits now enable visitors to imagine the mission's former glory.

★ Padres' Living Quarters
The fathers of Mission San Juan Capistrano lived in sparsely furnished rooms and slept on hard plank beds. Visitors enjoyed more comfortable accommodation.

KEY

① **A domed hut,** built from wooden poles, resembles the traditional dwellings of Native American villages at the time of the mission.

② **The kitchens** have corner ovens and displays of utensils.

③ **The Bodega,** or warehouse, where tallow, grains, woolens, and hides were stored.

④ **Ruins** are all that remain of the cruciform Great Stone Church, which was destroyed in an earthquake in 1812.

Sacred Garden Bells
The original four bells from the Great Stone Church now hang in the wall of a small garden. The larger pair date from 1796.

Junípero Serra
A statue of Father Serra and a Native American boy stands in a corner of the gardens.

★ Courtyard Gardens
This courtyard was at the heart of mission life. Surrounded by cloisters, it still has a fountain at its center and is today graced by mature trees and beautiful gardens.

Cloisters
Covered walkways with arches frame the mission's central courtyard. With their tiled walls, the cloisters provide a cool, shaded place in which to stroll or sit and contemplate the gardens.

★ Serra's Chapel
Built from cherry wood and covered with gold leaf, the 300-year-old altar in the mission's chapel was brought from Barcelona, Spain, in 1906.

Swallows at the mission

Every spring, thousands of migrating swallows return to San Juan Capistrano from South America. Their annual arrival is celebrated with a festival held on March 19, St. Joseph's Day *(see p40)*. The birds have been nesting in the tiled roofs and adobe walls of the mission for more than two centuries. They use mud pellets to build enclosed nests, in which four or five eggs are incubated. When autumn comes, the swallows fly south again.

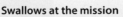

Migratory swallow at the mission

❾ Catalina Island

Just 22 miles (50 km) from the mainland, Catalina Island is the most accessible of California's Channel Islands. It was named Santa Catalina by the Spanish explorer Sebastián Vizcaíno when he landed here in 1602 on the feast day of St. Catherine of Alexandria. Much of the island's mountainous landscape remains unspoiled, and it has long been a favorite weekend and vacation destination.

Catalina's main town is the port of Avalon. The biggest buildings were constructed by the chewing-gum millionaire William Wrigley, Jr., who bought the island in 1919. Today most of Catalina's 76 sq miles (200 sq km) are owned by the Catalina Island Conservancy, which preserves the island's natural beauty.

Two Harbors
This low-lying isthmus backed by two bays is a popular anchorage for yachts. Facilities include a diving center, general store, B&B, and a restaurant.

West End
Two Harbors
Catalina Harbor
Little Harbor Road
Empire Landing Road
Little Harbor
BLACK MOU...
Middle Canyon
BULLRUSH CANYON
②
①

Little Harbor
This out-of-the way spot, located on the island's west shore, has a sheltered cove with a beach and a scenic harbor. There are also several hiking trails along the bay and a good camp site.

0 kilometers 5
0 miles 2

Catalina Wildlife

Over the centuries, Catalina has become a sanctuary for plants and animals that do not inhabit the mainland. Rare ironwood and Catalina Mountain mahogany trees, and the highly poisonous wild tomato are among endemic plants surviving on the island. Distinctive animal subspecies have also evolved, such as the small gray Catalina Island fox and the Catalina California ground squirrel. Many animals have been introduced to the island by settlers, whether intentionally or by accident. Catalina even has a population of bison, ferried over in 1924 for a film shoot and never rounded up.

One of the island's wild bison

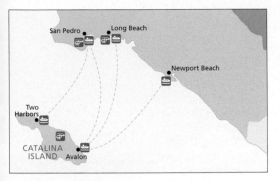

VISITORS' CHECKLIST

Practical Information
Map C6. **w** catalinainfo.com
w catalinachamber.com
i Foot of Green Pleasure Pier,
Avalon, 310-510-1520. 🎨
Catalina Arts Festival (mid-Sep).

Transport
🚁 Island Express Helicopter
Service: (800) 228-2566 from San
Pedro, John Wayne Airport &
Long Beach to Airport-in-the-Sky
and Nature Center. 🚢 Catalina
Express: (800) 481-3470; from San
Pedro, Long Beach & Dana Point
to Avalon or from San Pedro to
Two Harbors. Catalina Passenger
Service: (800) 830-7744 from
Newport Beach to Avalon.

★ **Avalon Casino**
Guided tours can be taken of this
1929 Art Deco jewel, which was
never a gambling venue but was
once a famous spot for big bands
and is now lovingly restored.

★ **Avalon Bay**
About 4,000 people live in Avalon, which has a pier,
restaurants, and hotels. Locals travel around in golf
carts, which visitors can rent.

Key

—— Minor road
═══ Road in poor condition
- - - Trail
- - - Trans Catalina Trail (TCT)
〜〜 River

KEY

① **Black Jack Mountain,** which
rises to 2,006 ft (610 m), is the
second-highest mountain on
Catalina Island and was mined
in the 1920s for lead, zinc,
and silver.

② **Airport-in-the-Sky and
Nature Center**

③ **Catalina Island Museum,**
near the center of Avalon, has
exhibits showing how the island
has been used for ranching,
mining, tourism, and as a
film location.

④ **Lovers Cove Marine Reserve**
is visited by glass-bottomed boats
that reveal the colorful marine life
existing around Catalina.

⑤ **Seal Rocks** tours, on which
colonies of migratory sea lions can
be seen, can be booked through four
fishing charter companies.

★ **Wrigley Memorial
& Botanic Gardens**
This 38-acre (15-ha)
park honoring William
Wrigley, Jr., has an
imposing memorial
and a collection of
plants endemic to
Catalina.

For additional map symbols *see back flap*

SAN DIEGO COUNTY

In San Diego, in 1769, the Spanish friar Junípero Serra laid down the first link in the chain of 21 missions that underpins the modern state of California *(see pp50–51)*. Blessed with a near-perfect climate and a magnificent natural harbor, his settlement has now become the eighth largest city in America. San Diego County has much to offer visitors, with its Pacific coastline, inland forests, and extensive state parks.

San Diego's character has always been determined by the sea. In the 19th century, gold prospectors, hide dealers, and whalers sailed into San Diego Bay. The United States Navy arrived in 1904, starting an enthusiastic courtship that has made San Diego the largest military establishment in the world. Aircraft carriers are a common sight in the bay, but so are cruise ships, fishing boats, yachts, and pleasure craft. San Diego is a city of sports and leisure. It has three times been host to the Americas Cup and is the home of the Padres baseball team and the Chargers football team. There are plenty of opportunities for surfing, sailing, golf, and water sports.

First-time visitors are always surprised by the sense of space and how much there is to enjoy. Few may realize that

San Diego is a fast-growing city, with shimmering new skyscrapers soaring beside the waterfront. Culturally, San Diego is rapidly gaining prestige, as its many museums and arts venues of Balboa Park flourish.

North of the city, the rugged Pacific Coast is lined with affluent beachside communities and wildlife preserves. Inland lie small towns, surrounded by peaceful countryside and fertile farmland. Deep forests and several state parks make the interior of San Diego County a paradise for hikers and campers escaping the frantic pace of city life. To the east, the region becomes increasingly mountainous, giving way to desert landscapes. And to the south, just a short train ride away from San Diego, is the Mexican border town of Tijuana.

Bazaar del Mundo in San Diego Old Town

◀ Bell Tower of the Museum of Man built in 1914, Balboa Park, San Diego

Exploring San Diego County

Covering more than 4,000 sq miles (10,350 sq km), San Diego County has a coastline of rocky cliffs, sandy beaches and wetlands, and a spacious, mountainous hinterland. The Anza-Borrego Desert *(see pp280–81)* forms a natural boundary to the east. San Diego city lies close to the border with Mexico, exploiting a large bay protected by two peninsulas. Stunning beaches and plentiful opportunities for leisure activities are the main attractions along the Pacific shoreline. A drive inland takes the visitor to the tranquillity of the Cleveland National Forest and the wilderness of state parks such as Palomar Mountain and Cuyamaca Rancho.

Cuyamaca Rancho State Park landscape

Shelter Island yacht harbor in San Diego Bay

0 kilometers   15'

0 miles   15

Margarita Peak
972m

Los Angeles

Riverside

Rainbow

Fallbrook

Camp Pendleton

Bonsal

**MISSION SAN
LUIS REY** 🏢 ⑧

Oceanside

Vista

LEGOLAND® ⑦

San Marco

Carlsbad

Leucadia

Encinitas

Cardiff-by-the-Sea

Rancho Santa F

Solana Beach

Del Mar

Torrey Pines State Beach

LA JOLLA ⑤

MI SAN DE A

Pacific Beach

MISSION BAY ④

SEAWORLD ③

Ocean Beach

Old

SAN DIEGO ①

Coronado
Nat

Point Loma

*Silver Strand
Beach*

**LIVING COA
DISCOVERY CENT**

**TIJUANA RIVE
NATIONAL ESTUARIN
RESEARCH RESERV**

Key

━━ Freeway

━━ Major road

━━ Secondary road

┄┄ Minor road

━━ Scenic route

╍╍ Main railroad

┄┄ Minor railroad

━━ International border

△ Summit

Sights at a Glance

1. *San Diego pp254–63*
2. Mission San Diego de Alcalá
3. SeaWorld
4. Mission Bay
5. La Jolla
6. San Diego Zoo Safari Park
7. Legoland®
8. Mission San Luis Rey
9. Palomar Observatory
10. Julian
11. Cuyamaca Rancho State Park
12. Lake Morena Park
13. Living Coast Discovery Center
14. Tijuana River National Estuarine Research Reserve
15. Tijuana (Mexico)

Cabrillo National Monument in San Diego

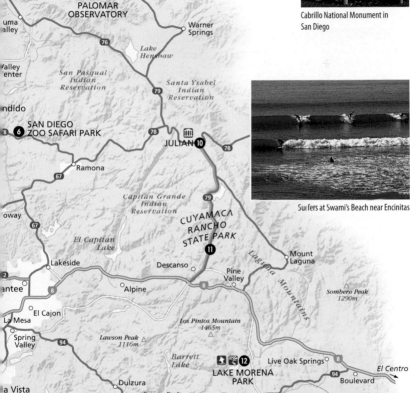

Surfers at Swami's Beach near Encinitas

Getting Around

The main transportation routes run from north to south – the coastal I-5 and Amtrak railway line both provide a fast connection with Los Angeles via the Orange County coast *(see pp232–3)*. The scenic Coaster train route serves stations between San Diego and Oceanside. A car is essential for exploring the county's inland areas. Within San Diego itself, public transportation is a viable option for the visitor *(see p270)*. The city has a comprehensive bus network, and the two lines of the efficient San Diego Trolley system extend east to El Cajon and south to the Mexican border.

For additional map symbols *see back flap*

San Diego County Coastline

Stretching from Orange County to the Mexican border, the coastline of San Diego County has 70 miles (112 km) of lovely sandy beaches, cliffs, coves, and seaside resorts. The beach culture is sophisticated, and the sports activity is frenzied. Peace can be found at Batiquitos Lagoon, Torrey Pines State Preserve, and the Living Coast Discovery Center (see p268), which are all sanctuaries for coastal wildlife. At Carlsbad, Legoland® California is a 128-acre family theme park for youngsters aged 2–12, with a castle, miniature lego cities, and an amusement park.

San Clemente

Batiquitos Lagoon lies between South Carlsbad and Leucadia State Beaches. Habitats include upland, intertidal, and open water, with abundant varieties of fish, saltwater plants, and birds such as the protected least tern and the snowy plover.

The Del Mar Racetrack was made famous in the 1930s by the singer Bing Crosby and other Hollywood stars. Its annual meetings remain a high point of the social calendar. San Diego's County Fair takes place at the adjacent fairground every June, and the racing season runs from late July to mid-September.

Torrey Pines State Reserve and Santa Rosa Island (see p228) are the only two places in the world where the Torrey Pine, or *Pinus torreyana*, survives. A remnant of pre-Ice Age forests, this tree is well adapted to this area's dry, sandy environment.

Key

- ▬ Freeway
- ▬ Major road
- ▬ Minor road
- ▬ River
- ◆ Viewpoint

0 kilometers 5
0 miles 5

① ★ **San Onofre State Beach**
🏄 🏖 🧍 🚶 🍴 ⛺ 🚻
Although close to the coastal San Onofre nuclear power plant and the vast Camp Pendleton military base, this popular beach is worth visiting to see serious California surfers in action.

③ **Swami's Beach**
🏄 🏖 🧍 🍴
This surfing beach is named after the founder of the Self-Realization Fellowship Temple, which overlooks the shore.

④ **Cardiff State Beach**
🏄 🏖 🧍 ♿ 🍴 ⛺ 🚻
On the south side of Encinitas, Cardiff offers swimming, surfing, and fine popular camp sites, as well as ocean-front dining on Restaurant Row at its north end.

⑥ **Torrey Pines State Beach**
🏄 🏖 🧍 🚶 🍴 🚻
This beach is popular for picnics and swimming. Just to the south is the Torrey Pines State Preserve, where several cliff-top hiking trails among the pine trees offer views over the ocean.

⑨ **Mission Beach**
🏄 🏖 🧍 🚶 ♿ 🍴
This is the liveliest beach in San Diego with plenty of opportunity for people-watching, plus the fairground attractions of Belmont Park (see p265).

⑩ **Ocean Beach**
🏄 🏖 🧍 🚶 ♿ 🍴
Ocean Beach's T-shaped pier, popular with pelicans, has good views of the coastline.

⑫ **Silver Strand Beach**
🏄 🏖 🧍 🚶 ♿ 🍴 ⛺ 🚻
This long, thin beach is sandwiched between areas of land reserved for naval training. It takes its name from the silvery shells in its sand.

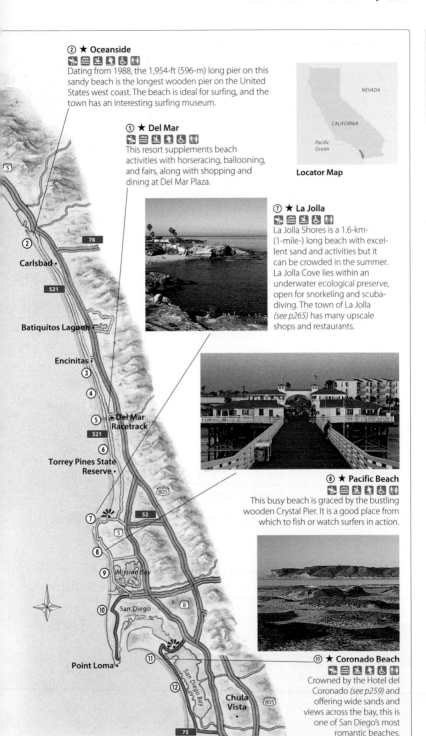

② ★ **Oceanside**

Dating from 1988, the 1,954-ft (596-m) long pier on this sandy beach is the longest wooden pier on the United States west coast. The beach is ideal for surfing, and the town has an interesting surfing museum.

⑤ ★ **Del Mar**

This resort supplements beach activities with horseracing, ballooning, and fairs, along with shopping and dining at Del Mar Plaza.

Locator Map

NEVADA

CALIFORNIA

Pacific Ocean

⑦ ★ **La Jolla**

La Jolla Shores is a 1.6-km- (1-mile-) long beach with excellent sand and activities but it can be crowded in the summer. La Jolla Cove lies within an underwater ecological preserve, open for snorkeling and scuba-diving. The town of La Jolla *(see p265)* has many upscale shops and restaurants.

⑧ ★ **Pacific Beach**

This busy beach is graced by the bustling wooden Crystal Pier. It is a good place from which to fish or watch surfers in action.

⑪ ★ **Coronado Beach**

Crowned by the Hotel del Coronado *(see p259)* and offering wide sands and views across the bay, this is one of San Diego's most romantic beaches.

Carlsbad

Batiquitos Lagoon

Encinitas

Del Mar Racetrack

Torrey Pines State Reserve

Mission Bay

San Diego

Point Loma

San Diego Bay

Chula Vista

Tijuana

❶ San Diego

Shaped like a hook and protected by the peninsula of Coronado (see p259), the 22 sq miles (57 sq km) of San Diego Bay form a natural deepwater harbor around which the second largest city in California has grown. The explorer Juan Rodríguez Cabrillo (João Rodrigues Cabrilho) arrived here in 1542, but colonization did not follow until 1769. In that year, the founding father of the mission chain, Junípero Serra, arrived in the region as part of a military expedition to secure Alta California (the part of California north of the Baja Peninsula) for Spain. Its commanders built a presidio and mission near the San Diego River, an area now known as Old Town (see pp258–9).

Shops in Seaport Village

Exploring Downtown San Diego

The growth of modern San Diego began in the 1870s, when Alonzo Horton, a San Francisco business-man, began to develop the waterfront areas. He laid down the grid of streets of the Gaslamp Quarter (see pp256–7), which, along with the Westfield Horton Plaza shopping center, has become the centerpiece of San Diego's rejuvenated Downtown.

The city's main street is Broadway, punctuated at its western end by the **Santa Fe Depot**. The towers and brightly tiled interior of this Spanish Colonial-style railroad station date from 1915. It was built to impress visitors to the Panama-Pacific Exposition in Balboa Park (see pp260–61).

Since the 1980s, Downtown San Diego has become the site of an ongoing architectural compe-tition. The tallest building in San Diego, the 34-story **America Plaza**, near the Santa Fe Depot, was built in 1991. On the waterfront, the galleon-like **San Diego Convention Center** overlooks San Diego Bay.

Three of the levels in the Westfield Horton Plaza shopping center

The promenades and piers of the **Embarcadero** waterfront pathway provide an intro-duction to San Diego's role as a major com-mercial and military port. At the northern end are the Maritime Museum's historic ships. A short stroll south is **Broadway Pier**, where visitors can join a harbor excursion. **Seaport Village**, a shop-ping and dining complex, has views across to the aircraft carriers of the **North Island United States Naval Air Station**.

🏬 Westfield Horton Plaza

Broadway, G St, 1st & 4th Aves.
Tel (619) 239-8180. **Open** daily.
Closed Easter, Thanksgiving, Dec 25.
Ⓦ westfield.com/hortonplaza

Opened in 1985, this innovatively designed shopping center has been a catalyst in the regener-ation of Downtown San Diego. The plaza is painted in festive pastel shades and built on inter-locking levels lined with 120 shops, the department stores Nordstrom and Macy's, and num-erous cafés. The architect, John Jerde, would go on to design the luxury Bellagio hotel in Las Vegas (see p293). Visitors can enjoy some evening shopping, close to the restaurants and historic buildings of the Gaslamp Quarter.

San Diego

① Cabrillo National Monument
② Junípero Serra Museum
③ Maritime Museum
④ Santa Fe Depot
⑤ Museum of Contemporary Art
⑥ Westfield Horton Plaza
⑦ Seaport Village
⑧ Embarcadero
⑨ The New Children's Museum
⑩ Gaslamp Quarter
⑪ Little Italy
⑫ Hotel del Coronado
⑬ USS Midway Museum

🏛 Maritime Museum

1492 North Harbor Drive. **Tel** (619) 234-9153. **Open** 9am–8pm daily, 9pm in summer. 🅿 **W** sdmaritime.com

The *Star of India*, an 1863 merchantman, and the San Francisco Bay passenger ferry, the *Berkeley* (1898), are moored here. Alongside them are the steam yacht *Medea* (1904) and the HMS *Surprise*, a replica of an 18th-century frigate from the film *Master and Commander*.

🏛 Museum of Contemporary Art

1001 & 1100 Kettner Blvd. **Tel** (858) 454-3541. **Open** 11am–5pm Thu–Tue. **Closed** Jan 1, Dec 25. **W** mcasd.org

This museum is the Downtown counterpart of the museum of the same name in La Jolla (see p265). The museum comprises two buildings, directly across from each other. The four galleries display changing exhibitions of new work by living artists, and selections from the museum's large permanent collection.

VISITORS' CHECKLIST

Practical Information
Road map D6.
🅐 3,200,000. 🛈 1040 1/3 West Broadway. 🎫 Street Scene Festival (Aug). **W** sandiego.org

Transport
✈ Lindbergh Field Airport, 3707 N Harbor Drive.
🚉 1050 Kettner Blvd.
🚌 120 West Broadway.

🏛 USS Midway Museum

910 North Harbor Drive. **Tel** (619) 544-9600. **Open** 10am–5pm daily. **Closed** Thanksgiving, Dec 25. **W** midway.org

Over 60 exhibits, including the crew's sleeping quarters, engine room, and pilots' ready rooms, are on display at this museum aboard one of America's longest-serving aircraft carriers.

🚉 Little Italy

Between W Laurel St and W A St, Pacific Hwy and Front St. 🛈 (619) 233-3898. **W** littleitalysd.com

Little Italy, sometimes known as Middletown, was originally a fishing neighborhood but has now gentrified, although it retains its bohemian character. Italian restaurants and hip cafés line the streets.

🏛 The New Children's Museum

200 W Island Ave. **Tel** (619) 233-8792. **Open** 10am–4pm Mon, Tue, Fri & Sat, 10am–6pm Thu, noon–4pm Sun. 🅿 **W** thinkplaycreate.org

This state-of-the-art museum was designed by Rob Wellington Quigley and is a premier family attraction. Children of all ages explore their creativity with hands-on projects.

0 kilometers 1
0 miles 1

Taking part in one of the many activities at The New Children's Museum

For keys to symbols *see back flap*

A Walk through the Gaslamp Quarter

During the boom years of the 1880s, the 16 blocks of San Diego's Gaslamp Quarter became known as the "Stingaree." It was an area notorious for prostitution, gambling, and drinking, where naïve customers could easily be "stung" by confidence tricksters. In spite of police clampdowns in the following decades and the growth of a close-knit Asian community, its streets remained in decline until the 1970s, when moves were made to revive its fortunes and protect its wealth of historic buildings. In 1980, the area was designated a National Historic District. As a result, the Gaslamp Quarter has emerged as the new heart of San Diego. It is now renowned as a place to shop, dine, and dance. Visitors can also admire the period buildings, ranging from a pie bakery and a hardware store to ornate office blocks and a Victorian hotel. The district is particularly attractive at night, when it is illuminated by graceful gaslamps that line its pavements.

Old City Hall
This 1874 Italianate office building once housed the entire city government.

The Lincoln Hotel at No. 536 was built in 1913. Its architecture has Chinese-influcenced style elements.

The Backesto Building office block at No. 614 dates from 1873.

FIFTH AVENUE WEST SIDE >>

★ Louis Bank of Commerce
Constructed in 1888, this was the first granite building in the city and housed the Bank of Commerce for just 5 years. It also housed an oyster bar and a brothel.

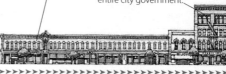

The Marston Building
This retail outlet on the corner of 5th Avenue and F Street dates from 1881. It was built by civic leader George Marston as a department store. The structur was remodeled in 1903 following fire damage.

FIFTH AVENUE EAST SIDE >>>

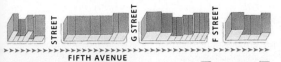

Key

➤➤ West side walking north

◄◄ East side walking south

The Gaslamp Quarter at night
In the evening the streets of the Gaslamp Quarter bustle
with people eating and drinking in its many restaurants
and bars, or simply strolling around.

Llewelyn Building
Dating from 1877, this structure
housed a shoe store until 1906 and
then a succession of hotels.

★ Yuma Building
Built in 1886, this commercial property
was one of the first brick buildings in
Downtown. In 1915, the Yuma Building
housed the first brothel to be closed
down during a police raid of the red-
light district.

```
0 meters                    10
0 yards                     10
```

Wyatt Earp
Lawman Wyatt Earp ran the Oyster
Bar on Fifth Avenue in the late 1800s.
In order to distance themselves from
the "Stingaree," the area's more
respectable businesses moved north
of Market Street.

Beyond Downtown

Four miles (6.5 km) north of the present Downtown lies the area now known as Old Town. Here, visitors can see San Diego's earliest buildings, many of which have been restored to their original state, and explore the fascinating Junípero Serra Museum. To the west of Old Town, the coast runs south to the end of the Point Loma Peninsula. From here, visitors have magnificent views of the Pacific Ocean and the city's waterfront across the bay. South of Point Loma, Coronado, with its numerous luxury hotels and popular sandy beaches, enjoys a privileged location at the end of a low-lying peninsula thrusting into San Diego Bay.

Victorian house in Heritage Park

Interior of Mason Street School in Old Town

Exploring Old Town

Until the 1870s the city of San Diego was centered around the presidio, the site of the original Spanish military outpost, in the area now known as Old Town. Today more than 20 historic buildings from this period have been restored or re-created to form the **Old Town San Diego State Historic Park**. At its center lies the grassy Plaza where parades and fiestas still take place. The **Robinson-Rose Building** at the western end of the Plaza now serves as the Historic Park headquarters and visitors' center.

Other buildings of historical interest include the **Colorado House** and **Mason Street School**, which dates from 1865. Mexican themes are evoked in the vibrant **Fiesta de Reyes** shopping center *(see p581)* in the north corner of the Plaza.

Old Town San Diego spreads far beyond the official limits of the park. Constructed in 1856, **Whaley House** at No. 2482 San Diego Avenue was the first two-story brick building in California and once functioned as a courthouse.

🏛 Junípero Serra Museum

2727 Presidio Drive. **Tel** (619) 232-6203. **Open** Sep–Jun: 10am–5pm Sat & Sun; Jun–Sep: 10am–5pm Fri, Sat & Sun. 🅿

Crowning Presidio Park, the whitewashed Junípero Serra Museum was built in 1929 in the Spanish Revival style *(see p35)* and is named after the founder of California's mission chain. Overlooking the San Diego River, the park occupies the site of the presidio fort and mission, which were built by the Spanish in 1769. The ruins of the presidio are still being explored by a team of archaeologists, and some of their finds, from fine china to cannonballs, can be seen in the museum. Its displays cover San Diego's early days and the city's successive Native American, Spanish, Mexican, and American residents. Of particular interest is a didactic painting, *La Madre Santísima de la Luz*, painted in Mexico by Luis Mena (c.1760), depicting Native Americans kneeling before the Virgin Mary. The painting is a rare surviving artifact from the time of the first mission, which moved to San Diego de Alcalá in 1774 *(see p264)*. Exhibits upstairs describe the first Spanish expedition to California, daily life in the presidio, and the changing face of San Diego.

🏛 Heritage Park

2450 Heritage Park Row. **Tel** (858) 565-3600. **Open** daily. **Closed** Thanksgiving, Dec 25. 🆆 sandiegocounty.gov/parks/heritage.html

On the east side of Old Town, Heritage Park is a collection of immaculately restored Victorian buildings from all over the city.

Junípero Serra Museum in Old Town San Diego

🏠 Casa de Estudillo

Old Town State Historic Park.
Tel (619) 220-5422. **Open** 10am–5pm
daily. **Closed** Jan 1, Thanksgiving,
Dec 25. Donation. 🅿️ 📷 ♿

Of the original adobe and
wooden buildings in Old Town
San Diego State Historic Park,
this is one of the most
impressive. It was constructed
by the commander of the
presidio, José María de Estudillo,
in 1829. The house has 13
rooms built around an internal
courtyard and has been
refurnished in the Mexican-
California style.

🏠 Seeley Stable

Old Town State Historic Park.
Tel (619) 220-5422. **Open** daily.
Closed Jan 1, Thanksgiving,
Dec 25. Donation.

The museum housed in this
reconstructed stable displays
a collection of horse-drawn
carriages and stagecoaches,
as well as some interesting Wild
West memorabilia.

Exploring Point Loma

The 156-acre (63-ha) **Cabrillo
National Monument** park
straddles the southern part of
the Point Loma Peninsula. The
monument was named after the
Portuguese explorer Juan
Rodríguez Cabrillo (also known
as João Rodrigues Cabrilho, *see
p50*), the first European to step
ashore in California in 1542. His
statue appropriately overlooks
the ships passing in and out of
San Diego Bay.

Between late December and
the end of February the nearby
Whale Overlook is a popular
place from which to watch
enormous gray whales
undertaking their annual
southward migration. Visitors
can also follow the 2-mile (3-km)
Bayside Trail around the Point,
with the aid of a highly
informative leaflet, and visit rock
pools on its western shore.

🏛 Cabrillo National Monument Visitor Center

Tip of Point Loma Peninsula.
Tel (619) 557-5450. **Open** 9am–5pm
daily. 🅿️ 📷 🌐 nps.gov/cabr
This excellent visitors' center
near the park entrance has a

Old Point Loma Lighthouse

small museum. A film recounts
Juan Rodríguez Cabrillo's 800-
mile (1,300-km) voyage along
the California coast.

🏠 Old Point Loma Lighthouse

Cabrillo National Monument Park.
Tel (619) 557-5450. **Open** 9am–5pm
daily. 🅿️ ♿ 📷
The lighthouse, a short walk
south from the Cabrillo statue,
sent its first beams into the
night in 1855 and operated for
36 years. Although its tower is
usually closed to the public,
lower rooms recreate the lighthouse keepers' living quarters
as they were in the 1880s.

Exploring Coronado

The city of Coronado, at the head
of a 4,100-acre (1,650-ha) peninsula in the middle of San Diego
Bay, is moneyed and self-
confident. Businessman Elisha
Babcock, Jr. bought the land in
1885 and set out to develop a
world-class resort. Coronado now
boasts San Diego's most exclusive homes, boutiques, hotels,
and restaurants. Its Pacific shore
is lined by a stunning beach *(see
p253)*, which is dominated at its
southern end by the landmark
Hotel del Coronado.

⛴ Coronado Ferry

1050 N Harbor Drive.
Tel (619) 234-4111. **Open** daily.
🅿️ 🌐 sdhe.com

Until the opening of the San
Diego–Coronado Bay Bridge
in 1969, the ferry provided the
area's principal link with the
mainland, a service that has
been revived for the benefit
of both tourists and locals.

The 15-minute trip between
the Broadway Pier on the
Embarcadero, or the San Diego
Convention Center, and the
Ferry Landing Marketplace is
breathtaking at sunset when
the sun illuminates the
skyscrapers of Downtown. From
the Ferry Landing, visitors can
take a bus or walk along Orange
Avenue to the Pacific shore.

🏨 Hotel del Coronado

1500 Orange Ave, Coronado.
Tel (619) 435-6611, (800) 468-3533.
Open daily. 🅿️ ♿ 📷
🌐 hoteldel.com

Opened in 1888 and given
National Historic Landmark
status in 1977, the "Del" *(see
p533)* is a lovingly preserved
grand Victorian seaside hotel.
It was built using both architects
and labor from the railroads –
a heritage that is most obvious
in the domed ceiling of the
Crown Room, which is built
from sugar pine without a single
nail. The list of illustrious guests
who have stayed here is
impressive – presidents from
Franklin D Roosevelt to Bill
Clinton and film stars from
Marilyn Monroe to Brad Pitt. The
hotel has been the setting for
several films, including *Some
Like It Hot*, the 1959 classic
starring Marilyn Monroe, Jack
Lemmon, and Tony Curtis.

Impressive turrets and gables of the exclusive Hotel del Coronado

Balboa Park and San Diego Zoo

Named after the Spanish explorer who first set eyes on the Pacific Ocean in 1513, Balboa Park was founded in 1868. Its beauty owes much to the dedicated horticulturalist Kate Sessions who, in 1892, promised to plant trees throughout its 1,200 acres (485 ha) in exchange for renting space for a nursery. In 1915 the park was the site of the city's Panama-California Exposition *(see p353)*, a world fair celebrating the opening of the Panama Canal. Several of the Spanish Colonial-style pavilions built in that year survive along El Prado (the park's main street), and the animals gathered for the exhibition formed the nucleus from which San Diego Zoo has grown *(see p263)*. Twenty years later the organizers of the California-Pacific International Exposition added more exhibition spaces around Pan-American Plaza. All these buildings now form a rich concentration of museums and performance venues.

Plaza de Panama
This plaza in the center of the El Prado thoroughfare was at the heart of the Panama-California Exposition.

★ **San Diego Museum of Man**
This historical museum is housed in the 1915 California Building. Designed in Spanish Renaissance style, its facade is decorated with statues representing famous Californians *(see p262)*.

Air and Space Museum
A child looks at the Apollo 9 exhibit in this museum devoted to the history of flight *(see p263)*.

KEY

① **Skyfari**

② **Tour bus**

③ **San Diego Zoo entrance**

④ **Timken Museum of Art**

⑤ **Casa del Prado**

⑥ **San Diego Natural History Museum**

⑦ **Reuben H Fleet Science Center**

⑧ **Casa de Balboa**

⑨ **Balboa Park Visitors Center**

⑩ **Plaza de Panama**

⑪ **Spreckels Organ Pavilion**

⑫ **Park Tram**

⑬ **Pan-American Plaza**

⑭ **San Diego Automotive Museum**

⑮ **El Prado**

⑯ **Old Globe Theater**

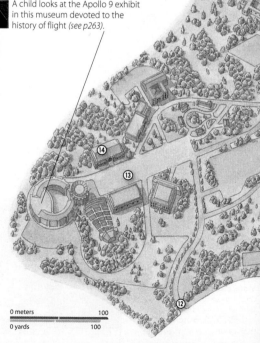

0 meters   100
0 yards   100

★ San Diego Zoo
Orangutans are among
the 4,000 animals that live in the
well-kept enclosures of this
world-famous zoo *(see p263)*.

Botanical Building
Constructed from thin strips of redwood,
this shaded sanctuary is full of tropical
and subtropical plants.

★ San Diego Museum of Art
A café and sculpture garden stand
next to the principal
art museum in the park.
Both North American and European
works are exhibited *(see p262)*.

Exploring Balboa Park and San Diego Zoo

Balboa Park, located at the heart of San Diego, is one of the city's most popular attractions. On the weekend, its pleasant, lush grounds and traffic-free promenades are crowded with strollers, joggers, cyclists, and street artists. In between museum tours, visitors can picnic in one of the shady picnic groves or play ball games on the grassy lawns. Just to the north of the museums and recreation grounds of Balboa Park lies San Diego Zoo, where 800 species from all over the world are housed in enclosures designed to resemble as closely as possible their natural habitat.

Sunday afternoon street entertainers in Balboa Park

🏛 San Diego Museum of Man

1350 El Prado. **Tel** (619) 239-2001. **Open** 10am–5pm Mon–Wed, 10am–8:30pm Thu–Sat. **Closed** Thanksgiving, Dec 25. 🅿 🆆 museumofman.org

The landmark pavilion of the Panama-California Exposition of 1915 *(see p260)*, also known as the California Building, houses an anthropological museum on the early history of mankind. Exhibits cover topics such as the cultures of ancient Egypt and the Mayans, and Native American crafts.

🏛 San Diego Museum of Art

1450 El Prado. **Tel** (619) 232-7931. **Open** 10am–5pm Tue–Sat (to 8pm Thu in summer), noon–5pm Sun. **Closed** Jan 1, Thanksgiving, Dec 25. 🅿 🆆 sdmart.org

This museum's large, varied art collection is boosted by a program of special exhibitions. European and American art from 1850 to the 20th century is shown in the first-floor galleries, along with exhibits from southern Asia, Japan, and China. The displays on the second floor feature work from 1300 to 1850, including *Coronation of the Virgin* (1508), by Luca Signorelli.

Ornate Colonial-style facade of the San Diego Museum of Art

🏛 Timken Museum of Art

1500 El Prado. **Tel** (619) 239-5548. **Open** 10am–4:30pm Tue–Sat, noon–4:30pm Sun. 🆆 timkenmuseum.org

Opened in 1965, the Timken exhibits a few exquisite works in an inviting space. On display are works by European masters such as Frans Hals (1581/5– 1666), François Boucher (1703–70), and Paul Cézanne (1839–1906). The Timken also has works by 19th-century American artists, including *The Yosemite Fall* (1864) by Albert Bierstadt, and a collection of Russian icons.

Portrait of a Man (1634) by Frans Hals in the Timken Museum of Art

🏛 Museum of Photographic Arts

1649 El Prado. **Tel** (619) 238-7559. **Open** 10am–5pm Tue–Sun (to 8pm in summer). **Closed** Dec 25. 🅿 🆆 mopa.org

This museum is located on the main floor of the ornate Casa de Balboa. It specializes in high-quality traveling exhibitions that demonstrate the art and power of photography. There is also a good bookstore.

🏛 San Diego History Center

1649 El Prado. **Tel** (619) 232-6203. **Open** 10am–5pm daily. **Closed** Thanksgiving, Dec 25. 🅿 🆆 sandiegohistory.org

Located in the Casa de Balboa, the museum showcases the region's unique and colorful history, exhibiting artifacts, costumes, textiles, art, furniture, and photographs. The Research Library has extensive archives of maps, architectural drawings, and one of the largest collections of photographs in the western US.

🏛 Reuben H Fleet Science Center

1875 El Prado. **Tel** (619) 238-1233. **Open** 10am–5pm Mon–Thu, 10am–6pm Fri–Sun. 🅿 call ahead for IMAX® show times. 🆆 rhfleet.org

Named after the man who founded the US airmail service, the Science Center's big attraction is the vast dome of the IMAX® cinema in the Space Theater, where films about the world around us are projected onto an enormous tilting screen. Planetarium shows are also staged.

The complex has a Science Center with over 100 hands-on exhibits that demonstrate the laws of science. There is also a café, and a shop selling books, games, and puzzles.

🏛 San Diego Natural History Museum

1788 El Prado, Balboa Park. **Tel** (619) 232-3821. **Open** 10am–5pm daily. **Closed** Jan 1, Thanksgiving, Dec 25. 🅿 🆆 sdnhm.org

The museum was founded in 1874 and is an active research

institution, dedicated to understanding the evolution and diversity of the Southern California-Baja California region. It features giant-screen films and a variety of programs for visitors of all ages. It is the oldest scientific institution in Southern California.

🏛 San Diego Air and Space Museum

2001 Pan American Plaza.
Tel (619) 234-8291.
Open 10:30am–4:30pm daily (to 5:30pm in summer). **Closed** Jan 1, Thanksgiving, Dec 25. 🅿
W sandiegoairandspace.org

The Air and Space Museum covers five centuries of aviation history, demonstrating the remarkable progress of flight. It has more than 60 aircraft and spacecraft on display (including both originals and full-scale reconstructions). The "Apollo 9 Has Landed" exhibit features the only display west of the Rockies of an Apollo Command Module flown in space. There is also a 3-D and 4-D cinema experience.

A 1948 Tucker Torpedo from the Automotive Museum's collection

🏛 San Diego Automotive Museum

2080 Pan American Plaza.
Tel (619) 231-2886.
Open 10am–5pm daily.
Closed Jan 1, Thanksgiving, Dec 25.
🅿 **W** sdautomuseum.org

Dream cars and motorcycles from both the United States and Europe shine on in this nostalgic museum. Because most of the cars are privately owned, the collection is constantly changing, but gleaming paintwork and whitewall tires are guaranteed. The library has a large collection of periodicals, manuals, and magazines.

San Diego Zoo

San Diego Zoo is one of the best-known zoos in the world, famous both for its conservation programs and as a highly educational source of family entertainment. With some 4,000 animals dispersed over 100 acres (40 ha), the best introduction is to take the 35-minute narrated bus tour that covers most of the zoo. The aerial Skyfari ride, which offers a trip across the south of the park in gondola cars 180 ft (55 m) up, is also rewarding. After these, visitors can track down their favorites in the animal world by following the paths and moving walkways. There is also a Children's Zoo, and in summer the zoo is open for nocturnal exploration.

Main entrance

Finding the Attractions

① Flamingo Lagoon
② Reptile House
③ Children's Zoo
④ Petting Paddock
⑤ Insect House
⑥ Wegeforth Bowl
⑦ Tiger Trail
⑧ Scripps Aviary
⑨ Monkey Trail
⑩ Owen's Rain Forest Aviary
⑪ Sun Bear Forest
⑫ Panda Canyon
⑬ Wings of Australasia
⑭ Gorilla Tropics
⑮ Hippo Trail
⑯ Lost Forest
⑰ Ituri Forest
⑱ Eagle Trail
⑲ Northern Frontier
⑳ Elephant Odyssey
㉑ Hunte Amphitheatre
㉒ African Rocks
㉓ Urban Jungle
㉔ Australian Outback

Sichuan takin calf resting in San Diego Zoo

The church at the Mission San Diego de Alcalá

❷ Mission San Diego de Alcalá

10818 San Diego Mission Rd, San Diego. **Road map** D6. **Tel** (619) 281-8449. 🚌 13, 20. **Open** 9am–4:30pm daily. **Closed** Jan 1, Thanksgiving, Dec 25. Donation. ✝ daily. ♿ **W** missionsandiego.com

Originally located at what is now the Junípero Serra Museum in Presidio Park *(see p258)*, San Diego's mission was moved to Mission Valley in 1774. The land surrounding the new site was more fertile and had a larger population of potential Native American converts. The name Diego refers to St. Didacus, born in Alcalá, Spain, in 1400.

The first mission in the California chain *(see pp50–51)* is today engulfed by freeways and urban development, but its harmonious buildings and gardens retain an atmosphere of peace. Early in the 20th century, the complex was restored to its appearance of 1813. The church retains some original materials, such as the timbers over its doorways, the floor tiles, and the adobe bricks in the baptistry. In the garden stands the Campanario (bell tower), and a statue of St. Francis. A small museum honors the state's first Christian martyr, Padre Luis Jayme, who was murdered when a gang of

Statuette at San Diego de Alcalá

600 Native Americans attacked the newly established mission in 1775.

❸ SeaWorld

500 SeaWorld Drive. **Road map** D6. **Tel** (800) 257-4268. 🚌 9. **Open** daily. 🍴 ♿ 🅿 **W** seaworld.com

One of California's numerous theme parks, San Diego's SeaWorld is a large marine life adventure park on Mission Bay offering thrill rides, whale and dolphin shows, and the chance to get close to many ocean creatures. A good starting point for a visit is the five-minute ride up the Skytower, a 320-ft (98-m) column with panoramic views. Another view is offered by the 100-ft- (30-m-) high Bayside Skyride in the park's northwest corner, where gondola cars take you in a 0.5-mile (1-km) loop over the waters of Mission Bay. Kids will particularly enjoy cavorting with Sesame Street characters and the exciting rides in the aquatic adventure park, whose largest attraction, Journey to Atlantis, includes a wet and wild thrill ride that ends with a 60-ft (18-m) plunge and a negative G-force drop. Another major ride is the Manta roller coaster.

The company has a rehabilitation program of rescuing stranded marine animals and, whenever possible, releasing them back into the wild. However, less positive aspects of SeaWorld have come to light since the release of the 2013 documentary film *Blackfish*, which questioned the ethics and highlighted the dangers of keeping killer whales in captivity. SeaWorld has since come under strong criticism for its treatment of its killer whales, seeing a downturn in public opinion and a drop in visitor numbers.

❹ Mission Bay

Road map D6. 🚌 from Downtown Mission Bay. Visitors' Center: **Tel** (619) 276-8200. **Open** 9am–5pm Mon–Sat, 9:30am–4:30pm Sun. **W** sandiego.gov

Mission Bay park is an area of 7 square miles (18 square kilometers) entirely given over to public recreational use. San Diegans come here to keep fit and relax in the well-tended parkland. The area was once a marsh, but systematic dredging and landscaping, begun in the 1930s, transformed it into a

The Giant Dipper at Belmont Park

Sailing on the peaceful waters of Mission Bay

recreational water park. The San Diego River has been corralled into a channel to the south, creating numerous sandy beaches, water-sports centers, and islands. Visitors can enjoy kite-flying, volleyball, golf, and cycling on designated paths. Along the shoreline, there is swimming, fishing, water-skiing, and sailing.

In the southwest corner of the bay is Mission Beach (see p252), one of the liveliest beaches in San Diego County. Its board-walk features surf stores, trendy beach bars, restaurants, and night clubs. Lovers of traditional seaside amusements will enjoy the historic beachfront **Belmont Park**, an amusement park whose Giant Dipper dates from 1925.

🎡 **Belmont Park**
3146 Mission Blvd. **Tel** (858) 228-9283. **Open** 11am–11pm Sun–Thu, 11am–midnight Fri & Sat.
W belmontpark.com

❺ La Jolla

Road map D6. 🚹 42,000. 🚌 from San Diego. 🛈 1162 Prospect St (858) 454-5718. W **lajollabythesea.com**

The origin of the name La Jolla (which is pronounced "La Hoya") is the subject of an on-going debate – while some people believe it to come from the Spanish *la joya*, meaning "jewel," others claim it was inspired by a Native American word, with the same pronunciation, which means "cave." Located 4 miles (6 km) north of San Diego's Mission Bay, La Jolla is an elegant, upscale coastal resort set amid beautiful cliffs and coves with lovely beaches, perfect for swimming, snorkeling, and scuba-diving (see p253). Its pretty streets are lined with gourmet chocolatiers, designer boutiques, and top-name jewelers. San Diegans and tourists alike come to enjoy the many art galleries and the chic restaurants promising a "Mediterranean" view.

A companion to the museum in Downtown San Diego (see p255), La Jolla's **Museum of Contemporary Art** occupies a prime oceanfront location. It displays works from its permanent collection of post-1950 art and houses a bookstore, café, and sculpture garden.

The town is also home to the University of California at San Diego and to the famous **Salk Institute for Biological Studies**, founded in 1960 by Dr. Jonas Salk, who developed the polio vaccine. Overlooking Scripps Beach is the Scripps Institution of Oceanography, with its magnificent **Birch Aquarium at Scripps**. The aquarium provides an insight into the fascinating world of oceanography, with exhibits, interactive displays, and feeding shows in the kelp tank. In the aquarium, visitors can observe sea life from the waters of the north Pacific as well as the tropics, including an Alaskan giant octopus.

🏛 **Museum of Contemporary Art**
700 Prospect St. **Tel** (858) 454-3541. **Open** 11am–5pm Thu–Tue. **Closed** Jan 1, Thanksgiving, Dec 25. 🅿 W mcasd.org

🏛 **Salk Institute for Biological Studies**
10010 N Torrey Pines Rd. **Tel** (858) 453-4100. **Open** Mon–Fri. **Closed** public hols. 🗓 noon. W **salk.edu**

🐚 **Birch Aquarium at Scripps**
2300 Expedition Way. **Tel** (858) 534-3474. **Open** 9am–5pm daily. **Closed** Jan 1, Thanksgiving, Dec 25. 🅿 W aquarium.ucsd.edu

Beautiful rocky shoreline of La Jolla cove

❻ San Diego Zoo Safari Park

Hwy 78, 15500 San Pasqual Valley Rd.
Road map D6. **Tel** (619) 231-1515.
🚌 Escondido. **Open** 9am–5pm daily.
🔲 🔲 ♿ 🔲 W sdzsafaripark.org

A rural counterpart to San Diego Zoo *(see p263)*, this wildlife park displays an encyclopedic variety of birds and mammals in its 1,800 acres (730 ha) of carefully landscaped grounds. Opened in 1972, the park was conceived as a breeding sanctuary for the world's endangered species and has remained at the forefront of the conservation race. As well as caring for its 3,200 residents, the park exchanges animals with zoological institutions around the world, with the ultimate goal of releasing endangered species back into the wild. Among the program's success stories is that of the California condor, a species once close to extinction.

A good way to begin a visit is to take the Journey Into Africa tour. This 25-minute, 2-mile (3-km) guided ride through African habitats visits giraffes, rhinos, and gazelles. It also stops at a waterhole where there are herons, ostriches, and many other birds. Another great trip is the Tethered Balloon Safari which rises to about 400 ft (120 m) and offers a panoramic view of the whole animal park including lions, giraffes, zebras, and cheetahs.

Visitors enjoy the California Coast Cruise boat ride at Legoland®

For many, the big animals, such as elephants, lions, and rhinos, are the stars. However, the park's various simulated natural environments, such as the Australian Rainforest and the Hidden Jungle, are also engrossing, and the Petting Kraal is popular with children. Before visiting the Safari Park, it is worth finding out the times of daily events.

Nairobi Village is a 17-acre (7-ha) area, where the park's amphitheaters and most of its facilities are to be found. Its many shops sell Africa-related books and souvenirs.

❼ Legoland®

1 Legoland Drive, Carlsbad. **Road map** D6. **Tel** (760) 918-5346. 🚌 S Carlsbad. **Open** daily, but check website for times. ♿ W legoland.com

This unusual 128-acre (744-ha) park is aimed mainly at families with children and offers more than 60 rides, shows, and attractions such as an aquarium with a LEGO-voyage to the ocean's depths, and a water park. For younger visitors, the DUPLO section showcases African wild-life such as giraffes and lions made of bricks.

The main attraction is the display of seven miniature areas of the United States, made using more than 20 million Lego bricks. Other areas of the park include Land of Adventure, transporting the visitor to 1920s Egypt, with rides such as Pharaoh's Revenge.

❽ Mission San Luis Rey

Hwy 76 (Mission Ave), Rancho del Oro Drive, San Luis Rey. **Road map** D6. **Tel** (760) 757-3651. 🚌 from San Diego. **Open** 9:30am–5pm Mon–Fri, 10am–5pm Sat–Sun. Donation. W sanluisrey.org

One of the largest and most prosperous estates in the California mission chain

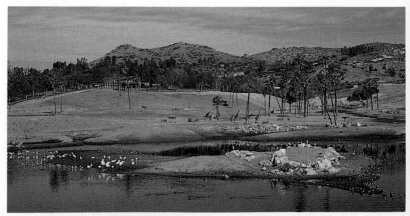
Animals roaming around freely in the San Diego Zoo Safari Park

Façade of Mission San Luis Rey

(see pp50–51), San Luis Rey de Francia was founded by the Spanish priest Padre Fermín Lasuén in 1798. The mission was named after the canonized 13th-century French king, Louis IX, and owed much of its success to the cooperation of the local Luiseño people. More than 3,000 Native Americans lived and worked in Mission San Luis Rey. They kept livestock and cultivated crops such as grain and fruit.

The majority of the mission's remaining buildings benefited from a long period of restoration in the early 20th century. Visitors are guided first into a **museum** outlining the history of the mission and the surrounding area. Of the vestments and religious artifacts on display, several have survived only because, after the church was secularized in 1833, some of its treasures were hidden by the Christian Native Americans. Their families returned the artifacts to the mission only when it was designated a Franciscan monastery in 1893.

The church at San Luis Rey has a cruciform shape as at San Juan Capistrano *(see p245)*, but it was the only one in the chain with a domed wooden ceiling. The wooden pulpit is original, and the painted designs are based on surviving stencils. The mission still functions as a

A statue in the church

church and retreat, and in its grounds are a partly restored laundry area, a cemetery, and California's oldest pepper tree, brought from Peru in 1830.

▥ Museum
Eastern Cloister. **Open** daily.
Closed Jan 1, Thanksgiving, Dec 25.
📷 ♿

❾ Palomar Observatory

Road map D6. 🚌 from Julian.

At the summit of Palomar Mountain is the surreal-looking white dome of the **Palomar Observatory**. Operated by the California Institute of Technology, this internationally renowned observatory first opened in 1948. It houses a computer-controlled Hale telescope with a 200-inch (510-cm) mirror capable of studying areas of the universe that are more than a billion light years away. From 1948 to 1956, the observatory's Oschin telescope was used to photograph the entire night sky.

A second survey began in 1985 and lasted until 2000, producing digital images. Currently, the Oschin is conducting a fully automated, wide-field survey of the sky as part of the Palomar Transient Factory systematic exploration project.

The observatory is now home to five telescopes that are used for a wide variety of astronomical research. Recent discoveries have included a new star orbiting the Big Dipper's Alcor, found in 2009, and a novel type of supernova first seen in 2011. Tours of the observatory cover historical and current scientific research, with an emphasis on the Hale Telescope.

Visitors are not permitted to look through the 540-ton telescope; however, an exhibition area and photo gallery explain how it functions.

▥ Palomar Observatory
35899 Canfield Rd, Palomar Mountain.
Tel (760) 742-2119. **Open** 9am–3pm daily. **Closed** Dec 24 & 25.
📷 10am–4pm Sat & Sun.
🌐 **astro.caltech.edu/palomar**

Dome of the Palomar Observatory at sunset

⑩ Julian

Road map D6. 🏔 1,500. 🚌 from San Diego. 🛈 2129 Main St (760 765-1857). 🖳 julianca.com

When San Diegans want to go for a pleasant drive or spend a romantic weekend in the "back country," they often head for the mountain town of Julian. Gold was discovered here in 1870, and the restored 19th-century wooden buildings that line the main street help to re-create the atmosphere of those pioneer days.

In autumn, the "Apple Days" of October attract hundreds of visitors, who come to taste Julian's famous apple pie and buy rustic souvenirs in the quaint gift shops. The delightfully cluttered **Julian Pioneer Museum** is packed with curiosities and photographs evoking the town's history. Visitors can also venture inside an original gold mine at the **Eagle and High Peak Mines**, which shows the tools and machinery of the early gold-diggers.

Apple pie store sign in Julian

For visitors wishing to stay overnight, there are plenty of homey hotels and bed-and-breakfast accommodation both in and around the town.

🏨 **Julian Pioneer Museum**
2811 Washington St. **Tel** (760) 765-0227. **Open** Apr–Nov: Fri–Sun; Dec–Mar: Sat & Sun. 🖼
🖳 julianpioneermuseum.org

🚇 **Eagle and High Peak Mines**
C St. **Tel** (760) 765-0036. **Open** daily, but call ahead. **Closed** Jan 1, Easter Sun, Thanksgiving, Dec 25. 🖼

⑪ Cuyamaca Rancho State Park

Road map D6. 🚌 🛈 (760) 765-0755. **Open** daily. 🖳 parks.ca.gov

Only an hour's drive east of San Diego, Cuyamaca Rancho State Park is a place to get away from it all. Almost half of its 25,000 acres (10,100 ha) are an officially designated wilderness that is home to skunks, bobcats, coyotes, mule deer, and mountain lions.

As well as horseback riding, camping, and mountain biking facilities, there are 130 miles (210 km) of hiking trails in the park. The Cuyamaca Peak Trail is an arduous but rewarding ascent by paved fire road. From the summit, hikers can enjoy fine views of the forested hills of northern San Diego County as far as Palomar Mountain *(see p267)*. At the northern end of the park lies the Stonewall Gold Mine. Once a 500-strong prospectors' town, it yielded over two million dollars' worth of gold in the 1880s.

🛈 **Park Headquarters and Museum**
12551 Hwy 79. **Tel** (760) 765-0755. **Open** daily. **Closed** public hols.

⑫ Lake Morena Park

Road map D6. 🚌 from San Diego. **Tel** (619) 478-5473.

This lush, oak-shaded park surrounding a large fishing lake forms an oasis in the dry

Shores of Lake Morena

southeastern corner of San Diego County. The park covers 3,250 acres (1,300 ha) of land. For those who come to fish or simply enjoy a peaceful afternoon on the lake, rental boats are available.

⑬ Living Coast Discovery Center

100 Gunpowder Point Dr. **Road map** D6. **Tel** (619) 409-5900. 🚌 E St, Bay. **Open** 10am–5pm daily. **Closed** public hols. 🖼 🖳
🖳 thelivingcoast.org

This remarkable zoo and aquarium beside San Diego Bay provides an opportunity to observe the wildlife of California's coastal wetlands. A free bus takes visitors to the Nature Center from a parking lot located by the I-5, and from the San Diego Trolley Station.

Here visitors can learn about the fragile environment of the 316 acres (130 ha) of protected land. Birds that can be seen all year round include herons, ospreys, and kestrels.

⑭ Tijuana River National Estuarine Research Reserve

301 Caspian Way. **Road map** D6. **Tel** (619) 575-3613. **Open** 10am–5pm Wed–Sun. **Closed** Jan 1, Thanksgiving, Dec 25. 🖳 trnerr.org

Encompassing 2,500 acres (1,010 ha) of coastal wetlands, this estuary is an important breeding, nesting, and feeding ground for over 370 species of native and migratory birds.

Horseback riding in the Cuyamaca Rancho State Park

For hotels and restaurants in this area see pp533–4 and pp560–62

ⓕ Tijuana

Traditionally, thousands of Americans would cross the border to Tijuana to enjoy its inexpensive shopping and lively nightlife. Reports of violence between rival drug cartels in 2008–9 and increased border control saw some decline in visitor numbers. Greater services and discounts are now on offer to attract tourists back. Contact the San Diego tourist office about any travel warnings before visiting.

Locator Map

--- International border
— San Diego Trolley line
⬛ Mexico

Exploring Tijuana
The border city of Tijuana is hardly representative of the fabled Mexico of Mayan art and Spanish colonial architecture, but it is interesting as a hybrid frontier town.

The city's futuristic **Centro Cultural Tijuana** was built on the banks of the Tijuana River in 1982. This cultural center has an OMNIMAX theater, where films about Mexico are shown on a giant tilting screen.

Sociedad de Historia de Tijuana is a cultural area with a museum, gallery, library, and computer center.

Most visitors come to shop and party – Tijuana has long been popular with young Americans taking advantage of laws permitting anyone over 18 to drink alcohol.

The best shopping is in the quiet bazaars situated in the lively Avenida Revolución. Painted pottery, leather boots, silver jewelry, and tequila are some favorite buys. Tourists are encouraged to

Bottles of liqueur on sale in a street bazaar in Tijuana

barter with the merchants. English-speaking staff at the **Tijuana Convention and Visitor's Bureau** can provide maps and free advice.

🏛 Centro Cultural Tijuana
Paseo de los Héroes. **Tel** 011-52 (664) 687-9600. **Open** daily.

ℹ Tijuana Convention and Visitor's Bureau
Ave Revolución (between 3rd & 4th). **Tel** 011-52 (664) 973-0430, (888) 775-2417 (from USA), (888) 025-0888 (from Mexico). **Open** daily. Tourist Assistance Hotline: dial 078.
w seetijuana.com

Tips for Travelers

Getting there: Since the San Diego Trolley (see p270) runs as far as the international border, the cheapest and simplest way to cross the border into Tijuana is on foot. Take a southbound trolley to San Ysidro and follow the crowds across the pedestrian bridges and walkways that lead to the city. You can also take a bus from San Ysidro across the border to downtown Tijuana, or book an excursion through the Tijuana Convention and Visitor's Bureau. Those taking a car or a motorcycle will need Mexican vehicle insurance. This is inexpensive and is available at the border.

Visas: Travel requirements change frequently and it is best to check on the latest documentation needed to cross the border before you travel. Citizens of the United States need a passport or a government-issued Nexus Card for re-entry into the US. Citizens of Australia, Canada, and the United Kingdom require passports but not visas to enter Mexico, unless they are planning to remain in the country for longer than six months. When crossing the border, non-American nationals must present a completed Mexican Tourist Card, which may be obtained directly at the port of entry. For further information, contact the Mexican consulate in your home country before departure. All travelers must ensure that they meet visa requirements.

Currency: Visitors on a short trip will rarely need to change money since US dollars and major credit cards are widely accepted.

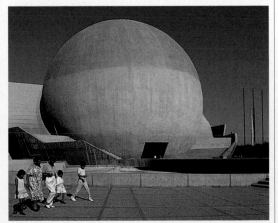

Facade of the Centro Cultural Tijuana

PRACTICAL INFORMATION

San Diego is an easy city to get to know, with a clean, efficient public transit system and a welcoming attitude toward visitors. The regeneration of the city's heart is evident in the growing number of shops, restaurants, and nightspots around Westfield Horton Plaza *(see p254)* and the Gaslamp Quarter *(see pp256–7)*. A variety of public transportation penetrates this Downtown area, where there are all the shops and entertainment spots you would expect in a vibrant California city. There are also regular connections to Old Town, Balboa Park, Coronado, and the Mexican border, while the best way to enjoy the waterfront of the Embarcadero *(see p254)* is on foot. Tourist information is available from excellent visitors' centers located in Westfield Horton Plaza and Balboa Park, as well as in Coronado.

An articulated San Diego MTS bus with a front-end bicycle rack

Getting Around San Diego

The three lines of the **San Diego Trolley**, the city's streetcar system, link Old Town East to Santee, and south to Downtown and the Mexican border. Another line links Downtown to Santee. Trolleys run every 15 minutes during the day and operate until around 1am. A comprehensive bus network runs throughout the city. The **Flagship San Diego Harbor Excursion** offers a regular service to the Coronado Peninsula *(see p259)*. Maps, timetables, and special one- to four-day Day Passes, valid for unlimited travel on any bus, trolley, or ferry, can be obtained from the **Transit Store**. **Old Town Trolley Tours** offer regular guided tours visiting all the principal sights.

The city's **Amtrak** station is housed in the beautiful Santa Fe Depot in Downtown. **San Diego International Airport** is located 3 miles (5 km) northwest of Downtown. Buses, taxis, and rental cars are all available from the airport.

The **Balboa Park Tram** provides free rides around the cultural park *(see pp260–61)*. All along San Diego Bay, the **San Diego Water Taxi** takes visitors to points of interest around the shoreline.

San Diego is also a bicycle-friendly city, well served with bike paths and bike rental shops. There is a gentle route from Mission Beach to La Jolla *(see p265)*, offering fine ocean views. Bikes can be carried on trolleys and buses for a small fee. Bicycle taxis are also widespread in the Downtown area.

It is generally safe to walk around the areas to the north and west of Downtown, even at night. However, the areas to the south of Downtown and, particularly, to the east of the Gaslamp Quarter, are best avoided after dark.

Mexican-style shopping in the Bazaar del Mundo

Shopping

If you intend to visit Tijuana *(see p269)*, avoid doing too much shopping before you go, since bargain goods are the main reason for crossing the border. The Fiesta de Reyes shopping mall *(see p258)* and **Bazaar del Mundo** in Old Town San Diego also have plenty of Mexican crafts and souvenirs.

Westfield Horton Plaza is the city's most colorful shopping center and can meet most tourists' needs, while the Paladion next door sells couture clothing. The oceanfront Seaport Village complex *(see p254)* is a good place to buy souvenirs and gifts to take home. Farther up the coast, Prospect Street in La Jolla has a selection of elegant stores. Del

A San Diego Trolley, offering a fast, frequent service to the Mexican border

Attractive shopping area of Seaport Village, on the waterfront

Mar and Carlsbad also have a good mix of boutiques, antique shops, and art galleries.

There are several factory outlet centers in San Diego County, where outlet stores sell well-known brand-name goods at considerably reduced prices *(see p579)*. The Las Americas Factory Outlet Center, located just before the Mexican border crossing in San Ysidro, is one of the largest and best in the region, with more than 120 factory outlet stores. Ask at the information desk in the large parking lot for a sheet of discount tokens, which allow you to obtain further reductions of up to 15 percent in many of the shops.

Here, as throughout the state, major credit cards are accepted, and the hours of most shops are 10am–6pm Monday to Saturday, with some stores open on Sundays as well. A local sales tax of 8.5 percent applies to all purchases. This is automatically added to the advertised price of the goods when you pay for them.

Entertainment

San Diego has a reputation for its cultural energy and has its own symphony orchestra, opera, and repertory theater companies. Listings of all the current cultural events can be found in the *U-T San Diego* and a range of free tourist magazines. *The Reader*, available free in cafés, bars, and bookstores, is a good weekly source for finding out about poetry readings, live music, and the alternative arts. Tickets for all these events can be bought from the **Times Arts Tix** office in Westfeld Horton Plaza.

The Gaslamp Quarter *(see pp256–7)* is the best area to go to for good restaurants and nightclubs. The nearby Lyceum and Spreckels theaters have regular stage performances. In Balboa Park, the Old Globe Theater *(see p260)* stages award-winning shows and is one part of a three-stage performing arts complex.

Like most Californians, San Diegans are also avid sports fans – the Chargers football team play in Mission Valley, and the Padres baseball team play downtown at Petco Park. If, however, you prefer participating in sports to watching them, Mission Bay *(see pp264–5)* offers a wide range of water sports, as well as beach games such as volleyball. San Diego County also has 90 excellent golf courses – ask at hotels or at local visitors' centers for information.

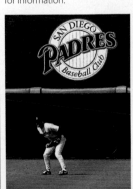

San Diego's own Major League Baseball team, the Padres

DIRECTORY

Getting Around

Amtrak
Santa Fe Depot, 1050 Kettner Blvd. **Tel** (800) 872-7245.
W amtrak.com

Balboa Park Tram
Tel (800) 310-7106.
W balboapark.org/maps/tram

Flagship San Diego Harbor Excursion
1050 N Harbor Dr. **Tel** (800) 442-7847. W flagshipsd.com

Metropolitan Transit System (MTS)
1255 Imperial Ave, #1000. **Tel** (619) 233-3004. W sdmts.com

Old Town Trolley Tours
4010 Twiggs St. **Tel** (888) 910-8687. W trolleytours.com

San Diego International Airport
Lindbergh Field.
Tel (619) 400-2404. W san.org

San Diego Trolley
Tel (619) 557-4555.
W sdmts.com/trolley.asp

San Diego Water Taxi
Tel (800) 442-7847.
W flagshipsd.com

Transit Store
102 Broadway. **Tel** (619) 234-1060.
W sdmts.com

Shopping

Bazaar del Mundo
4133 Taylor St. **Tel** (619) 296-3161.
W bazaardelmundo.com

Westfield Horton Plaza
G St & 1st Ave. **Tel** (619) 239-8180.
W westfield.com/hortonplaza

Entertainment

Times Arts Tix
Broadway Circle, Horton Plaza.
Tel (858) 381-5595.
W sdartstix.com

Tourist Information

Balboa Park
1549 El Prado. **Tel** (619) 239-0512.
W balboapark.org

Coronado
1100 Orange Ave.
Tel (619) 437-8788.
W coronadovisitorcenter.com

San Diego Visitors Bureau
West Broadway at Harbor Dr.
Tel (619) 232-3101.
W sandiego.org

THE INLAND EMPIRE AND LOW DESERT

The Inland Empire and Low Desert landscape is one of the most varied in California. The countryside changes from pine forests, cooled by gentle breezes, to searing desert. The contrast can be startling: passengers taking the Palm Springs Aerial Tramway make the transition between these two ecosystems in ten minutes.

The Anza-Borrego Desert State Park was the forbidding entry point to California for tens of thousands of hardy miners and settlers coming overland in the 1850s. Thirty years later communities in the northwest of the region, known as the Inland Empire, were transformed from a small collection of health resorts into the heart of a veritable economic empire based on the navel orange. The thick-skinned seedless Brazilian fruit, which traveled well, came to represent the sweet and healthy promise of California for millions of Americans. Many of the Victorian mansions built by citrus millionaires are still standing in the towns of Redlands and Riverside, but most of the fragrant orange groves have disappeared under asphalt and urban sprawl. Today Riverside is practically a suburb of Los Angeles.

At the heart of this region is Palm Springs, a favorite weekend retreat for Angelenos seeking relaxation and the desert sun. Just under two hours drive from Los Angeles, it has luxurious hotels, verdant golf courses, and a record number of pools and tennis courts.

Lying to the east of Palm Springs is the Joshua Tree National Park. This is a land of hot, dry days, chilly nights, tumbleweed, and creosote bushes. The stark and silent beauty of the rocky landscape evokes images of desperados, hardy pioneers in covered wagons, and leather-clad high plains drifters – visions of the Wild West of so many novels and movies.

When the desert becomes too hot, travelers can escape to one of the mountain resorts. The Rim of the World Tour is a spectacular drive in the heart of the San Bernardino Mountains.

Western film set in Pioneertown, near Yucca Valley

◀ Bent juniper tree and elongated boulder, Joshua Tree National Park

Exploring the Inland Empire and Low Desert

The Inland Empire is a region of vast scenic and climatic contrasts. In the northwest is the San Bernardino National Forest, with its cool mountain air and breathtaking views. Farther south lies the sun-baked Coachella Valley, ending in the steamy Salton Sea. Palm Springs, the largest of the desert resorts, is flanked by the stark Joshua Tree National Park and the mountain community of Idyllwild. The forbidding Anza-Borrego Desert State Park, in the southwest of the region, is the gateway to San Diego County.

A wild bighorn sheep in the Anza-Borrego Desert State Park

0 kilometers 20

0 miles 20

View across Desert Dunes golf course, near Palm Springs

Key

━━ Freeway

━━ Major road

━━ Secondary road

⋯⋯ Minor road

━━ Scenic route

┅┅ Main railroad

── Minor railroad

━━ State border

━━ International border

△ Summit

For hotels and restaurants in this area see pp534–5 and pp562–3

Sights at a Glance

Wind turbines in the Coachella Valley

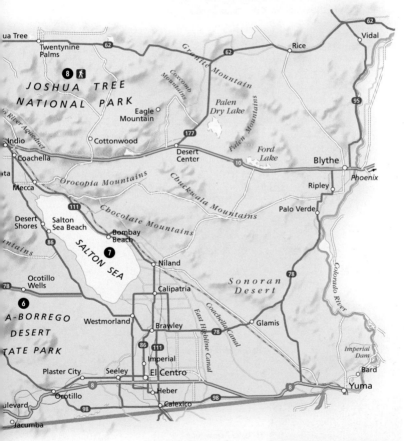

Getting Around

The easiest way to explore the desert areas is by car. The I-10 crosses the Inland Empire and Low Desert from east to west. Palm Springs, 107 miles (170 km) southeast of LA and 120 miles (190 km) northeast of San Diego, has a Greyhound bus terminal, an Amtrak station, and an airport, and is a good base for exploring the region.

For additional map symbols see back flap

❶ Rim of the World Tour

From San Bernardino this invigorating drive winds across the forested San Bernardino Mountains, offering spectacular views of the desert beyond. The altitude provides for distinct seasons, with warm, pine-scented air in the summer and brisk, cool days in the winter, when the snow-covered mountain trails are perfect for cross-country skiing. The tour passes through the resorts beside Lake Arrowhead and Big Bear Lake, both favorite destinations for those wanting to escape the heat and smog of LA. In Redlands visitors are offered a sense of the area's heady Victorian past, and yet another pleasure: the sweet smell of orange groves.

San Bernardino Mountain landscape

④ Heaps Peak Arboretum
A 1-mile (1.6-km) nature trail winds through this wooded hillside, planted with native and other trees. Species include dogwoods, Jeffrey pine, ponderosa pine, black oaks, live oaks, and white fir.

③ Big Bear Lake
A popular resort area, Big Bear Lake offers a range of sports including fishing, sailing, swimming, and, in the winter, skiing. Its two commercial centers are Big Bear City, to the east, and Big Bear Village, to the south.

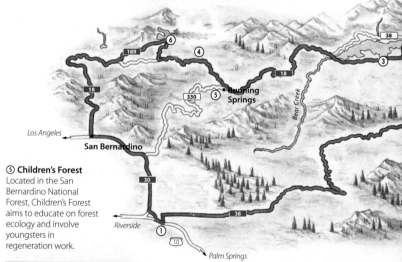

⑤ Children's Forest
Located in the San Bernardino National Forest, Children's Forest aims to educate on forest ecology and involve youngsters in regeneration work.

⑥ Lake Arrowhead
Lake Arrowhead Village, on the south shore, offers shops, restaurants and accommodation in both hotels and log cabins. Trips up the lake aboard the *Arrowhead Queen* also begin here. The north shore is almost exclusively residential.

① Redlands
This town is famous for its Victorian mansions, built at the end of the 19th century by those who made their fortunes growing navel oranges. Among the finest are Kimberly Crest House and Gardens, the Morey Mansion, and the Edwards Mansion.

ps for Drivers

ur length: 114 miles (183 km).
recautions: The mountain
ads wind considerably and
me areas are prone to falling
cks. Observe the maximum
eed recommendations marked
route and avoid night driving.
winter, snow chains should be
tached to tires. Some roads
ay be closed in bad weather.
topping-off points: The North-
oods Resort *(see p534)* is on Big
ear Lake and there are more
tels, cabins, and restaurants in
e villages of Big Bear and Lake
rrowhead. Redlands has plenty
amenities, including a number
restaurants *(see p563)*. Picnic
eas and camp sites are plentiful.

② Onyx Summit

At 8,443 ft (2,573 m), Onyx Summit
s the highest point on the Rim of
the World Tour. From a viewpoint
near the top there are stunning
views across the mountainous
San Bernardino National
Forest to the desert.

| 0 kilometers | 10 |
| 0 miles | 5 |

Key

▬ Tour route

__ Other roads

Ornate Mission Inn in Riverside

❷ Riverside

Road map: D6. 🔺 316,600. 🚌 ℹ️
3750 University Ave, (951) 222-4700.
🌐 **exploreriverside.com**

Some of the most elegant
architecture in Southern
California is to be found in
Riverside. During the late
19th century, the town was
the center of California's
citrus industry and by
1905 it had the highest
per capita income in the
US. One of the two
original orange trees
responsible for this great
success was planted in
1875 by early American
settlers Eliza and Luther
Tihbetts. The same orange tree
is still thriving in a small park at
the intersection of Magnolia
and Arlington avenues.

Pot at Hi-Desert
Nature Museum

Riverside's **Mission Inn Hotel
& Spa**, built in 1876 as a 12-room
adobe house, was expanded
early in the 20th century into a
275-room hotel *(see p535)*.
Architecturally, this ornate hotel
is an unusual mixture of Mission
Revival, Moorish, and Oriental
styles, with flying buttresses,
spiral staircases, and gargoyles.
The **Riverside Metropolitan
Museum** has exhibits on the
town's history and Native
American culture.

🚪 **Mission Inn Hotel & Spa**
3649 Mission Inn Ave. **Tel** (951) 784-
0300. 🚫 🌐 **missioninn.com**

🏛 **Riverside Metropolitan
Museum**
3580 Mission Inn Ave. **Tel** (951) 826-
5273. **Open** 10am–4:30pm Mon–Sat,
1–4:30pm Sun.

❸ Yucca Valley

Road map: D5. 🔺 21,000. 🚌
ℹ️ 56711 Twenty-nine Palms Hwy,
(760) 365-6323. 🌐 **yuccavalley.org**

Yucca Valley is a small town
located west of the Joshua Tree
National Park *(see pp282–3)*. On a
hillside, the **Desert Christ Park**
has more than 40 statues
depicting the life of Jesus,
sculpted by Antone
Martin in the 1950s. The
town's **Hi-Desert Nature
Museum** has various
exhibits on the region's
geology, crafts,
flora, and fauna.
Pioneertown, 4 miles
(6 km) north-west of Yucca Valley,
is a hamlet built in 1947 as a
Western film set.

🅿 **Desert Christ Park**
End of Mohawk Trail.
Tel (760) 364-0469. **Open** daily.

🏛 **Hi-Desert Nature Museum**
57090 Twenty-nine Palms Hwy.
Tel (760) 369-7212. **Open** 10am–5pm
Tue–Sat. **Closed** public hols.

Snow-white statue of Christ at the
Desert Christ Park

❹ Palm Springs

The Coachella Valley has been inhabited for 10,000 years, but it was only in 1853 that a government survey party came across a grove of palm trees surrounding a mineral pool bubbling up out of the desert sand. The area's first hotel was constructed in 1886, and by the turn of the century the city of Palm Springs was a thriving health spa. In the 1920s and 1930s the area become a fashionable winter resort, colonized by the rich and famous.

Exploring Palm Springs

The postwar building boom *(see p58)* brought rapid hotel and residential development to Palm Springs. Drawn by the city's growing popularity, developers later began opening up the empty desert lands eastward along the Coachella Valley. From 1967 to 1981, the resort cities of Cathedral City, Rancho Mirage, Palm Desert, Indian Wells, and La Quinta shot up between Palm Springs and the date-growing center of Indio, 22 miles (35 km) away. Desert Hot Springs, a spa just northeast of Palm Springs, also became a popular vacation destination. The extraordinary proliferation of luxury golf courses *(see p281)* dates from this period.

These towns are now gathered under the umbrella of Greater Palm Springs. Palm Desert, the most citified and home of luxury shopping, has long outstripped the actual town of Palm Springs in population, and these days the most luxurious resort hotels and estates are found in Indian Wells, Rancho Mirage, and La Quinta. An infinite choice awaits the millions of visitors who come to swim, golf, play tennis, relax, and enjoy the lifestyle, when they are not browsing through resale shops or playing the slot machines in the valley's numerous casinos.

Still, the city of Palm Springs with its long history of Hollywood glamor retains its attraction. Many celebrities still keep homes here, and several companies offer guided tours of their neighborhoods, pointing out landmarks associated with the stars past and present.

Old Shredded Wheat advertisement from Ruddy's in Village Green

🏛 Village Green Heritage Center

221 S Palm Canyon Drive. **Tel** (760) 323-8297. **Open** call for hours. **Closed** public hols. 🚶 walking tours available 9:45am Wed–Sat from McCallum Adobe. **W** **palmsprings.com**

This quiet enclave, in the heart of Palm Springs' shopping district, contains four historical buildings. Palm Springs' first white resident, John Guthrie McCallum, built the McCallum Adobe in 1884. Originally it stood near the Native American village of Agua Caliente, the site of the natural hot springs that inspired the town's name. The house was moved to its present location during the 1950s.

The Cornelia White House (1893) is built partly out of railroad ties. It is furnished with antiques dating from Palm Springs' pioneer era.

The heritage of the area's Cahuilla people is related through artifacts and photographs in the Agua Caliente Cultural Museum. There is also a collection of antique baskets that were handcrafted by Native American weavers.

Also in the Village Green Heritage Center is Ruddy's 1930s General Store Museum. Once the town's only druggist, Ruddy's is an immaculate and well-stocked replica of a Depression-era shop. Authentically packaged goods range from licorice to shoelaces.

🌊 Wet 'n' Wild Palm Springs

1500 Gene Autry Trail. **Tel** (760) 327-0499. **Open** late Mar & mid-May–Aug: daily; Apr–mid-May & Sep–mid-Oct: Sat & Sun. 🚶 **W** **wetnwildpalmsprings.com**

This state-of-the-art water park covers 16 acres (6.5 ha). Designed to evoke southern California beaches, the park boasts a variety of water rides and attractions, including an exciting 70-ft (20-m) free-fall slide and a 600-ft (180-m) artificial "river" for riding inflated inner tubes. There are special slides and pools for young children, like Kahuna's Beach House, which includes slides, hose jets, and water curtains. California's largest wave-action pool creates artificial waves suitable for surfing and boogie boarding. Surfboards and inner tubes can be rented from the park on either an hourly or a daily basis.

Kahuna's Beach House water ride for young children at Wet 'n' Wild Palm Springs

Palm Springs Aerial Tramway ascending to the Mountain Station

Palm Springs Aerial Tramway

1 Tram Way. **Tel** (760) 325-1391. **Open** daily. 🚫 🌐 pstramway.com

The Aerial Tramway's two revolving Swiss-built cars, each holding 80 passengers, are one of Palm Springs' most popular attractions. The trams depart from Valley Station, situated 6 miles (10 km) northwest of Palm Springs. The 2.5-mile (4-km) trip at a maximum angle of 42° takes about 10 minutes and ascends 5,900 ft (1,790 m) over spectacular scenery to the Mountain Station in the Mount San Jacinto State Park and Wilderness Area.

Passengers travel through five distinct ecosystems, ranging from desert to alpine forest, which is akin to traveling from Mexico to Alaska. The temperature changes dramatically during the journey. The heat of the valley floor sometimes differs as much as 40°F (4°C) from the temperature at the peak, so dress appropriately.

At the top there are 54 miles (85 km) of hiking trails, one of which leads to Idyllwild (see p280). The Adventure Center is open in the winter, with rentals available for cross-country skiing. There are also camp sites and picnic areas.

Observation decks perched on the edge of the 8,500-ft- (2,600-m-) high lookout offer views of the Coachella Valley, Palm Springs, and the San Bernardino Mountains. On a very clear day, it is possible to see for 50 miles (80 km) to the Salton Sea (see p281).

Both stations have gift shops, cocktail lounges, and snack bars. The Mountain Station also has a cafeteria and a fine dining restaurant.

Palm Springs Art Museum

101 Museum Drive. **Tel** (760) 332-4800. **Open** 10am–5pm Tue, Wed & Fri–Sun, noon–8pm Thu. **Closed** public hols. 🚫 🌐 psmuseum.org

The Palm Springs Art Museum focuses on painting and sculpture dating from the 19th century to the present day. Native American art, Mesoamerican artifacts, and photography are on display too. The museum also houses the extensive William Holden Collection, a gift from the estate of the late actor.

The adjoining Annenberg Theater is a 433-seat center for the performing arts, which features cabaret, pop, and contemporary entertainers, as well as dance, comedy, and theater. The lush gardens are enhanced by fountains and demonstrate that the desert need not be a barren place.

A trail leads out from the museum and enables visitors to explore the flora and fauna of this desert region. The 2-mile (3-km) Museum Trail climbs 800 ft (244 m) up into the Mount San Jacinto State Park. It joins the Lykken Trail at Desert Riders Overlook (a viewpoint from which to look out across Palm Springs and the Coachella Valley).

The Lykken Trail then continues for another 4 miles (6 km) to the mouth of the Tahquitz Canyon (see p280).

Exhibition inside the Palm Springs Art Museum

Palm Trees

Only one palm variety in Palm Springs is native to California, the desert fan palm (Washingtonia filifera), which crowds the secluded mountain oases. Unlike other palm varieties, the dead fronds do not drop off the trunk but droop down to form a "skirt" that provides a shelter for wildlife.

Date palms (Phoenix dactylifera) were introduced from Algeria in 1890 as an experiment. A mature date palm can produce up to 300 lb (135 kg) of dates a year. An annual ten-day National Date Festival in Indio features a cornucopia of dried and fresh dates (see p43).

Date palm grove in the Coachella Valley

🏜 Indian Canyons

38520 S Palm Canyon Dr. **Tel** (760) 323-6018. **Open** Oct–Jul: 8am–5pm daily; Jul–Sep: 8am–5pm Fri–Sun. 🅿 **w** indian-canyons.com

Approximately 5 miles (8 km) south of Palm Springs are four spectacular natural palm oases, set in stark, rocky gorges and surrounded by barren hills. Clustered along small streams fed by mountain springs, Murray, Tahquitz, Andreas, and Palm canyons are located on the land of the Agua Caliente Cahuilla people. Rock art and other traces of the area's early inhabitants can still be seen.

The 15-mile- (24-km-) long Palm Canyon is the largest of the gorges and contains many wild California fan palm trees and indigenous flora and fauna. Refreshments are available near the parking lot and from here it is a short but steep walk down to the main trail. There are also picnic tables beside a stream.

Desert fan palm oasis in the Indian Canyons

🦎 The Living Desert, Zoo and Botanical Garden

47–900 Portola Ave, Palm Desert. **Tel** (760) 346-5694. **Open** daily. **Closed** Dec 25. 🅿 **w** livingdesert. org

The Living Desert is a well-designed zoo and botanical garden representing the desert environments of North America and Africa. The park covers 1,200 acres (485 ha), but most of its major attractions can be seen in half a day. Broad paths lead visitors through 40 different gardens and 60 animal exhibits. The zoo houses 500 wild animals, and of special interest are golden eagles, mountain lions, a large

Flowering ocotillo in the Living Desert Wildlife and Botanical Garden

selection of nocturnal creatures, and a jaguar exhibit. The property also features various hiking trails, live animal shows, a model train exhibit, and camel rides. On winter days, walking through the park is a pleasure. During the summer, temperatures can exceed 100°F (37°C), so morning visits are recommended.

❺ Palms to Pines Highway

Road map D6. **w** visitgreaterpalmsprings.com

One of the most interesting drives in Southern California begins at the junction of Hwy 111 and Hwy 74 in Palm Desert. As you climb Hwy 74, you gradually leave behind the desert ecosystem with its palms, creosote, and desert ironwood trees and move into mountain scenery, made up of

pines, juniper, and mountain mahogany. The view from **Santa Rosa Summit**, just under 5,000 ft (1,500 m) high, is spectacular. Continue northwest on Hwy 74 to Mountain Center and the lush meadows of Garner Valley.

At Mountain Center, take Hwy 243 to the picturesque alpine village of **Idyllwild**, with its many restaurants, lodges, and camp sites. The renowned Idyllwild School of Music and the Arts holds regular classical music concerts during the summer. More active visitors can follow one of the many surrounding hiking trails, for which maps are available at the Ranger Station. One 8-mile (13-km) trek leads to the Mountain Station of the Palm Springs Aerial Tramway (see p279). This provides the quickest way back to the desert floor. Mule-pack rides may be available in the summer, and during the winter months there is cross-country skiing.

❻ Anza-Borrego Desert State Park

200 Palm Canyon Drive. **Road map** D6. **Tel** (760) 767-5311. 🚌 Escondido. Visitors' Center: **Tel** (760) 839-4777. **Open** daily year-round. **w** parks. ca.gov

Starting with the Gold Rush of 1849 (see pp52–3), the Southern Emigrant Trail, the only all-weather land route into California, brought tens of thousands of miners and early settlers through the Anza-Borrego Desert. Today, this former overland gateway is a

Picturesque mountain town of Idyllwild

Badlands in the Anza-Borrego Desert State Park

remote and pristine park, offering a rare insight into a unique desert environment.

The desert's well-equipped visitors' center is in **Borrego Springs**. This is the only major town in the otherwise undeveloped park. Nearby, the leisurely 1.5-mile (2.5-km) Palm Canyon Nature Trail leads to an oasis where the endangered bighorn sheep can occasionally be seen.

The **Box Canyon Historical Monument** is 31 miles (50 km) southwest of the visitors' center on County Road S2. Here you can view the old road once used by those miners who braved the desert climate on their way to the goldfields, which lay 500 miles (800 km) to the north.

The Anza-Borrego Desert is inhospitable for most of the year. Between March and May, however, following the winter rains, the burning land bursts into life. Cacti and desert flowers such as brittle-bush, desert poppies, and dune primroses produce a riot of color.

The desert's geology is as fascinating as its ecosystem. Over the millennia, a network of earthquake faults lifted and tilted the ground. Winter rains then carved through the shattered landscape, leaving multi-colored "layer-cake" bluffs, steep ravines, and jagged canyons such as the famous Borrego and Carrizo Badlands.

Much of the Anza-Borrego State Park, including its well-kept camp sites, is easily accessible via 100 miles (160 km) of surfaced and scenic highways. However, four-wheel drive vehicles are recommended for use on the park's 500 miles (800 km) of unsurfaced roads. Drivers of standard vehicles should contact the visitors' center in advance to check on current road conditions.

❼ Salton Sea

Road map E6. 🚉 Mecca. 🚌 Indio. Visitors' Center: **Tel** (760) 393-3052. **Open** daily. 🅦 desertusa. com/salton/salton.html

This manmade phenomenon has an interesting history, though for the next few years, you may choose not to visit unless interested in ecological reclamation.

Once a vibrant recreational area, the Salton Sea is currently experiencing rising salinity and selenium levels and is bogged down with algae in summer. Something of an ecological disaster, both fish and birds in adjoining marshland are fast disappearing. Governmental agencies have been working on restoration plans; however, no firm timetable has of yet been announced.

California's largest lake, the Salton Sea was created by accident in 1905 when the Colorado River flooded and flowed into a newly dug irrigation canal leading to the Imperial Valley. It took a team of engineers two years to stem the flow. By then, however, a 35-mile (55-km) inland sea had formed in the Salton Sink, 230 ft (70 m) below sea level.

On the east side of the sea there are hiking trails and camp sites set within the State Recreation Area. There is also a visitors' center.

Desert Golf

Thanks to irrigation with water supplied from underground sources, Palm Springs is now known as the golf capital of the United States. There are more than 100 courses in the region, most of which belong to private clubs or are attached to resorts or hotel complexes. Some courses are rugged, while others are more lush. Among the professional golf events held in the area each year are the Humana Challenge in January and the Women's Kraft Nabisco Golf Championship in late March to early April. A number of courses are open to the public, including the Desert Dunes course, noted for adding the desert terrain to its challenging layout. In the summer it is best to tee off early in the morning. November and December offer better value and cooler weather. Most courses are closed in October for reseeding.

Tahquitz Creek Golf Resort in Palm Springs

❽ Joshua Tree National Park

The Joshua Tree National Park was established in 1944 to preserve the groves of the unusual, spiny-leaved Joshua tree. The species was reportedly named in 1851 by early Mormon travelers, who saw in the twisted branches the upraised arms of the biblical Joshua. This large member of the agave family is unique to the area and can grow up to 30 ft (9 m) tall, living for 250–300 years. The 790,000-acre (319,700-ha) park offers uncommon vistas of the stark Californian desert, with its astounding formations of pink and gray rocks and boulders. A climber's paradise, Joshua Tree is also a fascinating area for hikers, who can discover lost mines, palm oases, and in the spring, a wealth of desert flowers. The Visitors' Center provides the latest weather report.

Joshua Trees
Large groves of Joshua trees thrive in the higher, wetter, and somewhat cooler desert areas of the park's western half.

Black Rock Canyon

Lost Horse

Hidden Valley

Keys View ①

Lost Horse Mine

Little San Bernardino Mountains

Yucca Valley

Joshua Tree

India Cove

Twentynine Palms

Fortynine Palms Oasis

Covington Flats

California Riding and Hiking Trail

Quail Springs Road

Scout Trail

La Contenta

Joshua Lane

Utah Trail

Hidden Valley
The gigantic boulders here formed natural corrals, making this a legendary hideout for cattle rustlers in the days of the Wild West.

0 kilometers 10
0 miles 10

KEY

① **Key's View** gives a sweeping view of the stunning valley, desert, and mountain terrain from its summit.

② **The arid wilderness** of the Colorado Desert (see p207) occupies the park's eastern half. This inhospitable region is difficult to reach.

③ **Cottonwood Spring** is a man-made oasis of palms and cotton-wood trees that attracts desert birds. There is a visitors' center nearby.

Lost Horse Mine
A 2-mile (3.2-km) trail leads to this historic gold mine, which was discovered by a cowboy searching for his lost horse. More than $270,000 in gold was extracted during the mine's first decade of operation.

Desert Wildlife

Despite the harshness of the arid desert environment, a variety of animals thrive here. In many cases, they have adapted to cope with lack of water. The kangaroo rat gets both its food and water from seeds alone, while its very large hind feet enable it to travel over the hot sand. Powerful legs, rather than wings, also serve the roadrunner, which gets its moisture from insects and small prey. The jackrabbit is born with a full coat of muted fur to camouflage it from large predators such as the coyote, bobcat, and eagle.

Coyote, wily denizen of the desert

VISITORS' CHECKLIST

Practical Information
Road map D5.
Tel (760) 367-5502.
w nps.gov/jotr
Oasis Visitors Center: 74485 National Park Drive, Twentynine Palms. **Tel** (760) 367-5500.
Open daily. **Closed** Dec 25.

Transport
Desert Stage Lines from Palm Springs to Twentynine Palms.

Lost Palms Oasis
A 4-mile (6.4-km) trail leads through attractive desert scenery to the largest group of palms in the park. It is one of the few areas where water occurs naturally near the surface.

Cholla Cactus Garden
A dense concentration of cholla cacti are the focal point of a short nature trail featuring desert flora and fauna. But beware – the cactus's fluffy-looking fingers are really sharp spines.

Key

— Freeway
— Major road
— Minor road
— Unsurfaced road
- - - Hiking trail
— National Park boundary

For additional map symbols see back flap

THE MOJAVE DESERT

The Mojave Desert is California's greatest secret, all too often missed by travelers who zoom through it on the interstate highway. The desert is a harsh environment – Death Valley is one of the hottest places in the United States. But this dry region supports a surprising amount of plant life and for a few weeks each year, when the wildflowers appear amid the arid rocks, it becomes hauntingly beautiful.

The Mojave Desert was a year-round overland gateway to California for much of the 19th century. Trappers, traders, and early settlers traveled hundreds of miles along the Old Spanish Trail from Santa Fe in New Mexico to Los Angeles. Passing through the towns of Barstow and Tecopa, the journey across the vast desert was both demanding and dangerous.

In the 1870s, gold, silver, borax, and various other precious minerals were discovered in the region, attracting large numbers of miners. Instant cities such as Calico sprang up, but when the mines became exhausted, many of the settlements were abandoned. In 1883 commercial mining became more viable when the Santa Fe Railroad was completed. Towns located along the route prospered, and the human population of the Mojave Desert increased. In the early 20th century a new breed of desert lovers emerged. Jack Mitchell settled in the empty expanses of the East Mojave Desert in the 1930s and turned the spectacular Mitchell Caverns into a popular tourist destination. Death Valley Scotty was another desert enthusiast. He spent much of his life in a castle built in the 1920s by his friend, Albert Johnson, near the hottest and lowest point in the western hemisphere. Death Valley National Park now attracts thousands of visitors each year, who come to explore the area's wealth of historical landmarks and impressive natural sights.

The main draw of the Mojave Desert region today, however, is Nevada's Las Vegas, a five-hour drive from Los Angeles. This center of entertainment and gambling is proof that people are still trying to strike it rich in the desert.

Death Valley's Moorish-style Scotty's Castle

◄ Highway 190 traveling straight through Death Valley with the Funeral Mountains looming behind

Exploring the Mojave Desert

Most of the Mojave Desert is at an altitude of over 2,000 ft
(600 m). It has cold winters and baking-hot summers.
Many of the region's rivers and lakes are dry during the
summer but are prone to flash floods. The desert is
home to an array of plant species and a range of
animals, from tortoises to foxes, which have evolved to
survive in this climate. Barstow, the largest town in the
Mojave region, caters to travelers to and from Las Vegas.
The northern Mojave is dominated by the Death Valley
National Park. To the east lie the resorts of Lake Havasu.

Sights at a Glance

1 Red Rock Canyon State Park
2 Edwards Air Force Base
3 Barstow
4 Calico Ghost Town
5 Kelso Dunes
6 Cinder Cone National Natural Landmark
7 Lake Havasu
8 Las Vegas
9 *Death Valley National Park pp294–7*

Key

━━━ Freeway
━━━ Major road
━━━ Secondary road
⋯⋯ Minor road
━━━ Scenic route
═══ Main railroad
─── Minor railroad
━━━ State border
△ Summit

Premises of a 19th-century ore smelter in
Calico Ghost Town

0 kilometers 25

0 miles 25

Sand dunes north of Furnace Creek in the Death Valley National Park

Getting Around

I-15 crosses the region. It links San Diego to Las Vegas, Nevada, via San Bernardino. This route follows the northern border of the East Mojave National Preserve, and I-40 skirts its southern border. The main south-north route across the desert is Hwy 127, from which Hwy 190 branches out, crossing the Death Valley National Park from southeast to southwest. In the west, US Hwy 395 leads south to LA. For safety reasons, it is vital that visitors to the desert obey posted signs and do not stray from main roads. Always carry water, a jack, a usable spare tire, a cell phone, and stay close to your vehicle if you break down. There is no public access to the area's clearly marked military zones (see p288).

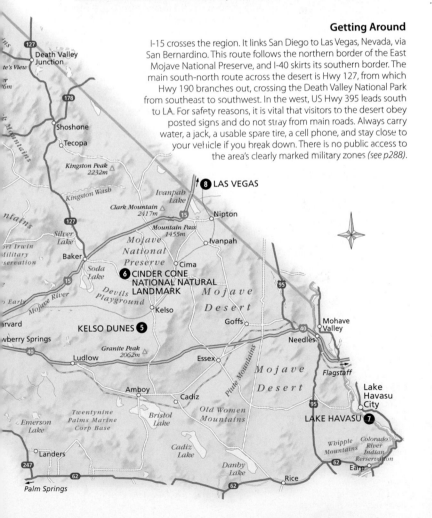

Stunning colors of Red Rock Canyon

❶ Red Rock Canyon State Park

Road map D5. 🚌 from Mojave, Ridgecrest. Visitors' Center: **Tel** (661) 946-6092. **Open** daily.
🆆 parks.ca.gov

Alternate layers of white clay, red sandstone, pink volcanic rocks, and brown lava are spectacularly combined in Red Rock Canyon. This beautiful state park is situated in the El Paso Mountains, which lie at the southern end of the Sierra Nevada Mountains. Like the High Sierras (see p488), Red Rock Canyon is the product of plate movements that pushed up the bedrock approximately 3 million years ago. The western side of the canyon slopes gently upward in stark contrast to the high, abrupt cliffs on its eastern side, which have been carved and crenellated by water and wind.

Three major desert ecozones overlap here, providing a wealth of plant and animal life. Eagles, hawks, and falcons nest in the cliffs. Coyotes, kit foxes, bobcats, and various reptiles, such as the desert iguana, are common. The landscape has been used as the backdrop for countless Westerns, advertisements, and science-fiction films, making it oddly familiar to many visitors.

❷ Edwards Air Force Base

Road map D5. **Tel** (661) 277-1110. 🚌 from Mojave, Rosamond. **Open** Mon–Fri. **Closed** public hols. 🅿 ♿ 📷 1st & 3rd Fri of month – by appt only.
🆆 edwards.af.mil

While it is famous around the world as the site of the West Coast space shuttle landings,

Edwards Air Force Base has been steeped in the history of America in flight since 1933. The 65-sq-mile (168-sq-km) flat expanse of Rogers Dry Lake provides an enormous natural runway that is perfect for emergency landings. The area's year-round fine and clear weather adds to its suitability for aircraft testing and the training of test pilots. It was here that the very first jet-propelled aircraft was tested in 1942. Here, too, Captain Chuck Yeager became the first to break the sound

Space shuttle Atlantis landing at Edwards Air Force Base

barrier on October 14, 1947, in a Bell XS-1 rocket plane. Fifty pilots still graduate each year from the Test Pilot School.

Edwards offers free guided tours of its NASA Dryden Flight Research Center and the space Aeronautics Center, by reservation (30 days in advance). Tours include a video on the history of aeronautics research and a visit to a hangar.

❸ Barstow

Road map D5. 🚗 23,000. 🚌 ℹ️ 681 North First Ave, (760) 256-8617.
🆆 barstowchamber.com

During the 19th century, this was a small settlement that served farmers as well as immigrants and miners on the Old Spanish Trail (see p285). In 1886 the new Barstow–San Bernardino rail line opened, linking Kansas City with the Pacific Coast. Barstow's original railroad station, the Casa del

The Military in the Mojave

The United States government has set aside vast areas of the Mojave Desert for military use. All such areas are strictly off-limits to civilians. During World War II, the Desert Training Center covered 17,500 sq miles (45,300 sq km) and was used by General Patton to train his forces. Today, smaller military preserves include the China Lake Weapons Center, north of Barstow, which is used for live bombing and artillery testing. Northeast of Barstow, the Fort Irwin National Training Center (NTC), which covers more than 1,000 sq miles (2,600 sq km), is an important US Army installation. The NTC has a population of 22,000, including civilian workers. Its desert terrain was used to prepare troops for the Gulf War in 1990–91, and is one of the main US training areas for tanks and weapons.

Talon high-altitude jet trainer at Edwards Air Force Base

Restored and reconstructed buildings in Calico Ghost Town

Desierto, has been restored. From 1937 to the late 1950s, Barstow was an important town along Route 66, the only surfaced road from Chicago to the West Coast. The town is best known today as being the midway point on I-15 between Los Angeles and Las Vegas. To the 41 million people who make this journey each year, it is a convenient stopping-off point. But many also come here in search of the precious minerals and gemstones to be found in the surrounding desert.

The **Desert Discovery Center**, in Barstow, has informative indoor displays on the Mojave Desert's flora and fauna. Maps of the area, and hotel and restaurant information are available.

ℹ Desert Discovery Center
831 Barstow Rd, Barstow. **Tel** (760) 252-6060. **Open** 11am–4pm Tue–Sat. **Closed** Jan 1, Dec 25, public hols.
w desertdiscoverycenter.com

❹ Calico Ghost Town

Road map D5. **Tel** (800) 862-5426. 🚌 Yermo. **Open** 9am–5pm daily. **Closed** Dec 25. 🅿 ♿
w calicotown.com

Calico Ghost Town, 12 miles (19 km) east of Barstow, is a late 19th-century mining town, which is part-authentic and part-reconstruction. Silver was found in the Calico Mountains on March 26, 1881, and soon hundreds of miners arrived. Some of the veins they struck were so rich that they produced 25 lb (11 kg) of silver per ton. Two years later, borax was discovered 3 miles (5 km) east of Calico, and the town's prosperity seemed assured. During the 1880s, Calico boasted a population of 1,200 and 500 working mines, but after the price of silver fell and the equally valuable borax gave out,

A flint tool from the Early Man Site

the miners left. By 1907, Calico was a ghost town.

Walter Knott, founder of Knott's Berry Farm® *(see p240)*, began the restoration process in the 1950s. Calico's isolation and desert setting reinforce the sense of a rough old mining town. Many of the original buildings remain, and visitors can take a ride in a mine train or explore tunnels in Maggie Mine, one of the most famous silver mines on the West Coast. Shows and tours are also held, including mock "shoot-outs," which are staged on the main street daily.

Environs
About 10 miles (16 km) west of Calico lies the **Calico Early Man Site**. Thousands of 200,000-year-old stone artifacts originally thought by some to be tools have been discovered here. That would put human habitation in North America over 150,000 years earlier than the earliest generally accepted date. The renowned archaeologist Dr. Louis Leakey was director of the site from 1964 to 1972. Self-guided tours start at the visitor center.

🏛 Calico Early Man Site
Off I-15 & Minneola Rd. **Tel** (760) 218-6931. **Open** noon–4pm Wed, 9am–4pm Thu–Sun. 🅿
w calicoarchaeology.com

Casa del Desierto, Barstow's historic railroad station

Salt flats at Badwater Basin, the lowest point in North America, Death Valley National Park ▶

❺ Kelso Dunes

Road map E5. 🚌 Baker. **Tel** Mojave National Preserve (760) 252-6100. **Open** daily. 🆆 nps.gov/moja

Kelso Dunes tower more than 600 ft (160 m) above the desert floor. Situated in the Mojave National Preserve, the dunes are formed from grains of golden rose quartz that have been blown from the Mojave River basin, 35 miles (56 km) to the west. Known as the "singing" dunes, they emit buzzing and rumbling sounds caused by the upper layers of sand sliding down the face of the dune, producing vibrations that are then amplified by the underlying sand.

The desert floor with the Kelso Dunes in the background

❻ Cinder Cones National Natural Landmark

Road map E5. **Tel** (760) 252-6100. **Open** open daily. 🆆 nps.gov/moja

The 32 cinder cones silhouetted against the horizon of Mojave National Preserve were designated a National

The original London Bridge, now located in Lake Havasu City

Natural Landmark in 1973. The hills of red and black volcanic rocks, and the black basalt lava flows surrounding them, are the result of volcanic activity that occurred about 7.6 million years ago. Cinder cones are formed when small streams of scorching lava are spewed through the cooler air, making the lava solidify and preserving small pockets created by escaping gases.

The light, cratered rocks created by the eruption accumulated around the vent to create captivating conical hills. The lava that did stream out across the desert ground created spectacular lava tubes, or tunnels.

The cinder cones that remain today form a serene landscape that tourists can either hike to or view from Kelbaker Road. One lava tube can be entered, although it is not maintained by the National Park Service, and cell phone service is unreliable, so visitors are advised to speak with park rangers for seasonal safety recommendations.

❼ Lake Havasu

Road map E5. 🚌 Las Vegas. **Tel** (928) 453-3444. 🆆 golakehavasu.com

Lake Havasu is a 46-mile (74-km) long reservoir, which was created in 1938 when the Colorado River was blocked by the Parker Dam *(see p207)*. Lake Havasu City, a resort town on the border between California and Arizona, was developed by the millionaire Robert McCulloch in the 1960s. McCulloch imported the historic London Bridge stone-by-stone to the newly created development. The bridge spans the Bridgewater Channel, which was dredged especially for it and leads from Lake Havasu to Thomson Bay.

The lake itself lies within a National Wildlife Refuge, which is frequented by bird-watchers and anglers. There are many camp sites and marinas that offer houseboats, boats, and water-sports equipment for rent. Several short boat tours around the lake are available. A daily three-hour excursion to Topock Gorge, at the northern end of Lake Havasu, offers a more leisurely introduction to the rugged Mojave desert setting.

Environs

Off Hwy 95, 20 miles (32 km) south of Lake Havasu City, lies the Colorado River Indian Reservation. Here, visitors can admire a collection of giant prehistoric figures, carved out of the rocks that form the desert floor. In both human and animal form, it is not known whether the figures were made for religious or artistic reasons.

The desert flora and barren hills of Cinder Cones National Natural Landmark

❽ Las Vegas

Las Vegas is in Nevada, 45 miles (72 km) from the California border. With the construction of the Hoover Dam in the 1930s, it grew into a major city. Gambling was legalized in Nevada in 1931. In 1946 the Flamingo Hotel and Casino were built on the outskirts on what is known as "The Strip." Similar places soon sprang up, and Las Vegas became a 24-hour oasis of gambling and entertainment.

The Las Vegas Strip, lit up at dusk

This colorful city has about 600,000 permanent residents (almost 2 million in the greater area), and its own museums and cultural institutions. However, it is the almost 40 million tourists a year who continue to fuel the amazing development of the US's gambling capital.

Hotels here provide more than food, lodging, and casinos. They are architectural marvels and attractions in their own right. The Mirage has an exploding volcano out front, while the opulent Bellagio has eye-popping floral displays in its Conservatory. Luxor, built on the same scale as the pyramids of Egypt, houses the largest atrium in the world, complete with animatronic camels, Egyptian decor, and high-tech laser shows. The nearby Venetian offers gondola rides on its own grand canal, while the Wynn has its own golf course.

Exploring Las Vegas

The gambling capital of the world, Las Vegas is fast becoming the restaurant and theater capital, too. Famed New York, San Francisco, and LA restaurateurs continue to open branches of their establishments along the Strip. Broadway hit musicals, Cirque de Soleil productions, and famed showgirl extravaganzas keep theaters filled.

After a failed experiment in attracting families with children, Las Vegas has returned to its old Sin City image.

VISITORS' CHECKLIST

Road map E4. **W** lvcva.com
🏙 603,000. 🛈 3150 Paradise Rd, (702) 892-0711. Mirage: 3400 Las Vegas Blvd S. **Tel** (702) 791-7111. **W** mirage.com Bellagio: 3600 Las Vegas Blvd S. **Tel** (888) 987-6667. **W** bellagio.com Luxor: 3900 Las Vegas Blvd S. **Tel** (702) 262-4000. **W** luxor.com The Venetian: 3355 Las Vegas Blvd S. **Tel** (702) 414-1000. **W** venetian.com Wynn Las Vegas: 3131 Las Vegas Blvd S. **Tel** (702) 770-7000. **W** wynnlasvegas.com

Transport
✈ McCarran Int. Airport, 4 miles (6.5 km) S of Las Vegas. 🚌 200 S Main St. 🚆 1 Main St.

⛲ Stratosphere Tower

2000 Las Vegas Blvd S. **Tel** (702) 380-7777. **W** stratospherehotel.com

At 1,149 ft (350 m), Stratosphere Tower is the tallest freestanding observation tower in the United States. At the top there is an incomparable view of Las Vegas from two observation decks (the views are best seen at night), a revolving restaurant and cocktail lounge, and three wedding chapels. The former world's highest roller-coaster ride has been replaced by the three highest thrill rides in the world.

🏙 Fremont Street Experience

Bordered by Charles & Stewart Sts. **W** vegasexperience.com

Las Vegas's first gaming license was issued on Fremont Street in the 1930s. Over the years, this downtown area became known as "Glitter Gulch," due to its profusion of neon signs and lights. Now five blocks of Fremont, stretching from Main Street to Las Vegas Boulevard, have been transformed into the Fremont Street Experience – a covered pedestrian promenade. Casinos line the street. A spectacular light and sound show is held hourly each evening, using over 12 million LED lights.

Environs

Lake Mead, which lies 25 miles (40 km) east of Las Vegas, was created by the construction of Hoover Dam, completed in 1936. The lake extends 110 miles (175 km) and has more than 500 miles (800 km) of shoreline. Scuba-diving, boating, water-skiing, and fishing facilities are all available. There are daily tours of the 726-ft- (220-m-) high dam and a visitors' center with exhibits on the region's natural history. The Valley of Fire State Park, 55 miles (88 km) northeast of Las Vegas, has stunning orange sandstone formations. Petroglyphs and other remains of an ancient Native American civilization can still be seen. Red Rock Canyon (not the same as the park on page 288), 15 miles (24 km) west of Las Vegas, has 3,000-ft- (900-m-) high escarpments and ridges, and trails for all levels of hikers.

Stratosphere Tower

⊙ Death Valley National Park

Throughout the summer months, Death Valley National Park has the highest mean temperature of anywhere on the planet. This is a land of wrenching extremes, a sunken trough in the earth's crust that reaches the lowest point in North America. The valley is guarded on both sides by ranges of rugged mountains. The range on the western side soars 11,000 ft (3,350 m) to form razor-sharp peaks. Even though it is inhospitable for half the year, Death Valley is also a place of subtle colors and polished canyons, of burning salt flats and delicate rock formations. It is now one of the most unique and popular tourist destinations in the state of California.

Central Death Valley

Furnace Creek, with its various provisions and accommodation centers, is located in the heart of Death Valley. Many of the most impressive sights in the park are within easy reach of this visitors' complex.

🐟 Salt Creek

Salt Creek supports the hardy pupfish. Endemic to Death Valley, the pupfish can live in water almost four times as salty as the sea and withstand temperatures of up to 111° F (44° C). The fish attract other wildlife, including great blue herons. Wooden walkways allow visitors to explore this unique site without disturbing the fragile habitat.

🏛 Borax Museum

Furnace Creek Ranch.
Tel (760) 786-2345. **Open** daily.
Borax was discovered in Death Valley in 1873, but mining did not begin until the 1880s when

Ruins of the Harmony Borax Works processing plant

crystallized borate compounds were taken to the Harmony Borax Works to be purified. They were then loaded onto wagons and hauled by teams of 20 mules the 165 miles (265 km) to Mojave Station. Each team of mules pulled two wagons carrying up to 10 tons of borax each. The wagons carried their heavy mineral loads from 1883 to 1888.

Used for producing glass that is heat-resistant, borax is more commonly used today as an ingredient in washing powder.

The Borax Museum has displays of mining tools and transport machinery used at the 19th-century refinery. On Hwy 190, 1 mile (1.5 km) north of the Death Valley Visitor Center, the eerie ruins of the Harmony Borax Works can still be seen.

🏛 Furnace Creek Visitor Center

Rte 190, Furnace Creek.
Tel (760) 786-3200. **Open** daily. 🅰
W nps.gov/deva
Interesting exhibits and a short film explain the natural and human history of Death Valley. Evening park-ranger programs and guided walks are available.

Furnace Creek

At Furnace Creek, millennia of flash floods have carved a natural gateway into Death Valley through the hills to the east. The springs here have drawn Shoshone people for thousands of years. Today, the same abundant springs make Furnace Creek a desert oasis and the de facto center of Death Valley. Shaded by date-bearing palms are restaurants and motels. The world's lowest golf course is also here, lying at 214 ft (65 m) below sea level. The Inn at Furnace Creek (see p535), a four-star hotel built in the 1920s, sits above the valley on a small mesa.

Historic Inn at Furnace Creek, set in spectacular surroundings

For hotels and restaurants in this area see p535 and pp563–4

Salt formations at the Devil's Golf Course

Southern Death Valley

Some of the valley's most breathtaking natural features are to be found in this area south of Furnace Creek.

Golden Canyon

Just over 3 miles (5 km) south of Furnace Creek on Hwy 178, a 1-mile (1500-m) hike leads into Golden Canyon and Zabriskie Point *(see p297)*. The mustard-colored walls, after which the canyon was named, are best seen in the afternoon. Native Americans used the red clay at the canyon mouth for ceremonies. The layers of rock were originally horizontal, but geological activity has tilted them to a 45° angle.

A paved road once led into the Golden Canyon, but it was washed out by a sudden storm in 1976. The battered state of the few remaining stretches of the road demonstrate the sheer power of fast-flowing water.

Devil's Golf Course

This expanse of salt pinnacles is located 12 miles (19 km) south of Furnace Creek, off Hwy 178. Until about 2,000 years ago, successive lakes covered this area. When the last lake evaporated, it left behind alternating layers of salt and gravel, at least 1,000 ft (305 m) deep and covering 200 sq miles (520 sq km). As surface moisture continued to evaporate, ridges and spires of crystallized salt formed. The ground is now 95 percent salt. Visitors can hear the salt expand and contract during changes of temperature. New crystals (with a whiter hue) are constantly forming.

Badwater

Temperature increases as elevation decreases, so the air at Badwater can reach 120° F (49° C). With the ground temperature 50 percent higher than the air temperature, it really is possible to fry an egg on the ground here. Rain is very rare, although flash flooding, caused by rainstorms, is common. In spite of its inhospitable environment, Badwater is home to several species of insect and to the endemic Badwater snail.

Northern Death Valley

This area includes Ubehebe Crater *(see p296)*, where only a few tourists venture, despite the beauty of the landscape. Scotty's Castle, which has more visitors per year than any other sight in the park, is also here.

Scotty's Castle

Hwy 267. **Tel** (760) 786-2392. Castle **Open** daily. Grounds: **Open** daily. **nps.gov/deva**

Albert Johnson began work on his "Death Valley Ranch" in 1922 after rejecting an original design by Frank Lloyd Wright. Materials were hauled from a railroad line 20 miles (32 km) away. When work ended in 1931, the castle covered more than 30,000 sq ft (2,800 sq m). Johnson died in 1948. "Death Valley Scotty" *(see p296)*, who lent his name to Johnson's ranch, was allowed to remain there until his death in 1954.

Western Death Valley

Sand dunes cover 15 sq miles (39 sq km) on this side of the park, not far from the second-largest outpost in Death Valley, Stovepipe Wells *(see p296)*.

Sand Dunes

A walk along the 14 sq miles (36 sq km) of undulating sand dunes, north of Stovepipe Wells, is one of the greatest experiences of Death Valley. Shifting winds blow the sand into the classic crescent dune configuration. Mesquite trees dot the lower dunes. A variety of wildlife feeds on the seeds of these trees, such as kangaroo rats and lizards. Included among the region's other, mainly nocturnal, creatures are the rattlesnake, the chuckwalla lizard, and the coyote.

Impressive sand dunes north of Stovepipe Wells

A Tour of Death Valley

The Native Americans called the valley Tomesha, referring to the ochre-colored rock in the surrounding hills. The valley is also the site of the highest recorded temperature in the United States: 134° F (57° C) in the shade, in July 1913. Death Valley stretches for some 140 miles (225 km) north to south and was once an insurmountable barrier to miners and emigrants. The valley and surrounding area were declared a National Park *(see pp294–5)* in 1994. It is now accessible to visitors, who can discover this stark and unique landscape by car and by taking short walks from the main roads to spectacular viewpoints. However, this remains the California desert at its harshest and most awe-inspiring.

⑧ Scotty's Castle

This incongruous Moorish-style castle was commissioned by Albert Johnson at a cost of $2.4 million. However, the people believed it belonged to Walter Scott, an eccentric prospector. The house remained unfinished after Johnson lost his money in the Wall Street Crash of 1929. In 1970 the building was bought by the National Park Service, who now hold hourly guided tours of the interior *(see p295)*.

⑦ Ubehebe Crater

This is one of a dozen volcanic craters in the Mojave area. The Ubehebe Crater is at least 2,000 years old. It is more than 900 yds (800 m) wide and 500 ft (150 m) deep.

Death Valley Wash

North Highway

Titus Canyon Rd

Sand Dunes

Death Valley Scotty

Walter Scott, would-be miner, beloved charlatan, and sometime performer in Buffalo Bill's Wild West Show, liked to tell visitors to his home that his wealth lay in a secret gold mine. That "mine" was, in fact, his friend Albert Johnson, a Chicago insurance executive, who built the castle where Scott lived and received visitors. Built during the 1920s by European craftsmen and local Native American labor, the castle represents a mixture of architectural styles and has a Moorish feel. Scott never owned the land or the building, and Johnson paid all his bills. "He repays me in laughs," said Johnson. Although Scott died in 1954, the edifice is still known as Scotty's Castle.

Panamint Springs

`190`

⑥ Stovepipe Wells

Stovepipe Village, founded in 1926, was the valley's first tourist resort. According to legend, a lumberjack traveling west struck water here and stayed. An old stovepipe, similar to the ones that were then used to form the walls of wells, marks the site.

Key

━━━ Tour route

══ Other roads

ℹ Tourist information

Grandiose Scotty's Castle

| 0 kilometers | 10 |
| 0 miles | 10 |

② Zabriskie Point

Made famous by Antonioni's 1960s film of the same name, Zabriskie Point offers views of the multicolored mud hills of Golden Canyon *(see p295)*. The spot was named after a former general manager of the borax operations in Death Valley *(see p294)*.

① Furnace Creek

The springs here are one of the few freshwater sources in the desert. They are thought to have saved the lives of hundreds of gold prospectors crossing the desert on their way to the Sierra foothills. The full-service visitors' complex here *(see p294)* is the valley's main population center.

③ Dante's View

At 5,475 ft (1,650 m), the view takes in the entire valley floor and is best seen in the morning. The name of the viewpoint was inspired by Dante's *Inferno*. In the distance is Telescope Peak in the Panamint Range.

Borax Museum •

Death Valley Museum and Visitor Center

Golden Canyon

Death Valley Junction

Furnace Creek Wash

DEVIL'S GOLF COURSE

Tecopa Hot Springs

④ Badwater

Badwater *(see p295)* is the lowest point in North America. It lies 282 ft (85 m) below sea level and is one of the world's hottest places. The water is not poisonous, but it is unpalatable, filled with sodium chloride and sulfates.

⑤ Artist's Palette

These multicolored hills of cemented gravels were created by mineral deposits and volcanic ash. The colors are at their most intense in the late afternoon sun.

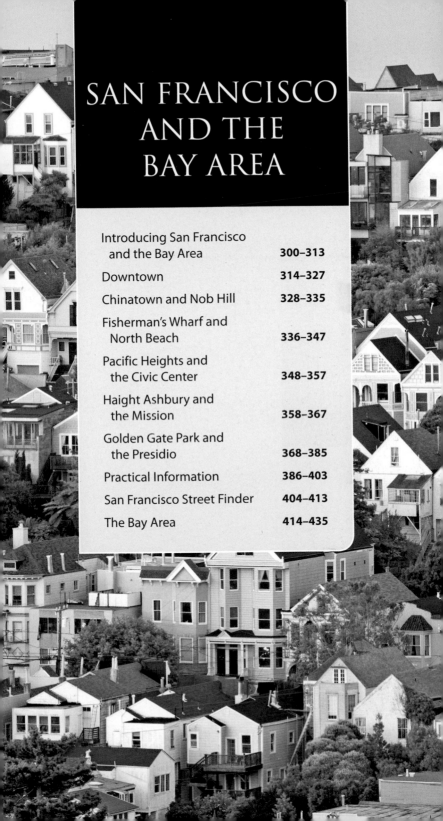

SAN FRANCISCO AND THE BAY AREA

San Francisco and the Bay Area at a Glance

San Francisco is a compact city and much of the central area can
be explored on foot. The many hills give rise to some strenuous
climbing, but are useful landmarks for orientation and offer
superb views. A rich ethnic mix adds a distinctive character to
the city's many neighborhoods. The smaller cities of Oakland
and Berkeley on the East Bay are reached via the Bay Bridge,
while to the north, Golden Gate Bridge links the peninsula to the
Marin Headlands and the Point Reyes National Seashore. To the
south are the burgeoning city of San Jose and rugged stretches
of coastline inhabited by a variety of flora and fauna.

LOCATOR MAP

Golden Gate Bridge
Built in 1937, the
bridge is as much
a part of the
landscape as the
craggy Marin
Headlands and
the idyllic bay
(see pp384–5).

GOLDEN GATE PARK
AND THE PRESIDIO
(see pp368–85)

Palace of Fine Arts
Built for the Panama-Pacific Exposition of
1915, this Neo-Classical monument was
fully restored in 1962 *(see p353).*

◀ The Victorian houses of San Francisco

Coit Tower
The 1933 tower is floodlit at night *(see p347)*.

Bay Area *pp414–35*

Novato
Larkspur
Concord
Berkeley
SAN FRANCISCO
(See main map)
Oakland
Hayward
San Mateo
Fremont
Palo Alto
San Jose
Pescadero
Santa Cruz

0 kilometers 25
0 miles 25

FISHERMAN'S WHARF
AND NORTH BEACH
(see pp336–47)

CHINATOWN
AND NOB HILL
(see pp328–35)

DOWNTOWN
(see pp314–27)

CIFIC HEIGHTS
AND THE
VIC CENTER
(see pp348–57)

Chinatown Gateway
This elaborate gate is the entrance to the city's historic Chinatown *(see p332)*.

GHT ASHBURY
THE MISSION
(see pp358–67)

City Hall
The building is the city's most imposing structure, with a vast rotunda displaying a wealth of architectural detail *(see p357)*.

Mission Dolores
The oldest building in San Francisco is one of the 21 Franciscan missions in California *(see p365)*.

0 kilometers 2
0 miles 2

The Shape of San Francisco

San Francisco, with its estimated 43 hills, sits at the tip of a peninsula, surrounded by the Pacific Ocean to the west and San Francisco Bay to the east. To the north, linked by the Golden Gate Bridge, are the rugged Marin Headlands and the protected wildlife area of the Point Reyes Peninsula. The Diablo Coast Range, with the 3,850-ft (1,170-m) Mount Diablo at its heart, forms a mountainous backdrop to the heavily populated cities of Richmond, Oakland, and Berkeley in the East Bay, and divides the region from the flat plains of the Central Valley. To the south, the coastal mountains enclose the industrial Silicon Valley *(see p432)* and run along the coastline toward Big Sur *(see pp518–19)*.

Vallejo
This town, in the north of the bay, is home to Six Flags Discovery Kingdom wildlife park and oceanarium, which includes dolphin displays *(see p419)*.

Sausalito
This former fishing community, across the Golden Gate Bridge, is lined with Victorian houses looking out toward the bay *(see p418)*.

Ferries

29

37

101

Richmond

Richmond Bridge

Tiburon

Sonoma Mountains

Mount Tamalpais

1

Mount Reyes National Seashore

Pacific Ocean

The Marin Headlands are part of the Golden Gate National Recreation Area. These green hills and quiet beaches offer perfect relaxation away from the city, with hiking, fishing, and bird-watching opportunities *(see pp420–21)*.

Point Reyes Peninsula
The rugged coastline of the peninsula, situated on the San Andreas Fault and only partly attached to the mainland, is abundant with wildlife and is home to a very productive dairy farming community *(see p418)*.

Downtown
One of the major financial districts in the United States is located in San Francisco's Downtown area. Its skyline is dominated by the Transamerica Pyramid *(see pp314–27).*

Livermore
This rural community is home to one of the world's largest wind farms, making use of the area's strong winds to produce natural energy *(see p430).*

Berkeley includes the University of California at Berkeley campus, once known for its radicalism *(see pp422–5).*

The Diablo Coast Range separates the East Bay from the Central Valley. Mount Diablo is at the heart of the range *(see p430).*

Bay Bridge

San Mateo Bridge

Golden Gate Bridge

Golden Gate National Recreation Area

San Bruno Mountains

San Jose was originally a Spanish colonial city, but is now California's third largest city. It is still home to a large Mexican–American population *(see pp432–3).*

Oakland
This busy city has a multicultural population and many historic landmarks. It is linked to San Francisco by the Bay Bridge *(see pp426–9).*

Palo Alto
This town was built up specifically to serve the Stanford University campus, which was created by railroad baron Leland Stanford in 1891 *(see p431).*

Victorian Houses in San Francisco

Despite earthquakes, fires, and the inroads of modern life, thousands of ornate, late-19th-century houses still line the streets of San Francisco. In fact, in many neighborhoods they are by far the most common type of houses. Victorian houses are broadly similar, in that they all have wooden frames, elaborately decorated with mass-produced ornamentation. Most were built on narrow plots to a similar floor plan, but they differ in the features of the facade. Four main styles prevail in the city, although in practice many houses, especially those constructed in the 1880s and 1890s, combine aspects of two or more styles.

Detail of Queen Anne-style gateway at Chateau Tivoli

Gothic Revival (1850–80)

Gothic Revival houses are the easiest to identify, as they always have pointed arches over the windows and sometimes, over the doors. Other features are pitched gabled roofs, decorated verge-boards (again, with pointed arch motifs), and porches that run the width of the building. The smaller, simpler houses of this type are often painted white, rather than the vibrant colors of later styles.

No. 1111 Oak Street is one of the city's oldest Gothic Revival buildings. Its front garden is unusually large.

The pitched roof over the main facade often runs lengthwise, allowing the use of dormer windows.

A gabled roof with ornate verge-boards is the clearest mark of Gothic Revival.

Gothic porch with cross bracing at No. 1978 Filbert Street

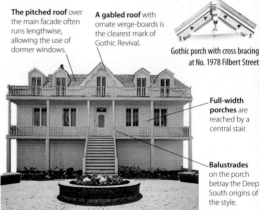

Full-width porches are reached by a central stair.

Balustrades on the porch betray the Deep South origins of the style.

Italianate (1850–85)

Italianate houses were more popular in San Francisco than elsewhere in the US, perhaps because their compact form was suited to the city's high building density. The most distinctive feature of the style is the tall cornice, usually with a decorative bracket, which adds a palatial air even to modest homes. Elaborate decoration around windows and doors is also typical of the style.

No. 1913 Sacramento Street displays a typical formal Italianate facade, modeled on a Renaissance *palazzo*. The wood boarding is made to look like stone.

Tall cornices, often with decorative brackets, conceal a pitched roof.

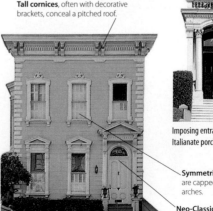

Imposing entrance with Italianate porch

Symmetrical windows are capped by decorative arches.

Neo-Classical doorways, sometimes with ornate pedimented porches, are a typical Italianate touch.

Stick (1860–90)

This architectural style, with its ungainly name, is perhaps the most prevalent among Victorian houses in the city. Sometimes also called "Stick–Eastlake" after London furniture designer Charles Eastlake, this style was intended to be more architecturally "honest." Vertical lines are emphasized, both in the wood-frame structure and in ornamentation. Bay windows, false-gabled cornices, and square corners are key identifying features.

Gabled roof with Eastlake windows at No. 2931 Pierce Street

Wide bands of trim often form a decorative truss, emphasizing the underlying structure of Stick houses.

Decorative gables filled with "sunburst" motifs are used on porches and window frames.

No. 1715–17 Capp Street is a fine example of the Stick–Eastlake style, with a plain facade enlivened by decorative flourishes.

Adjoining front doors can be protected by a single projecting porch.

Queen Anne (1875–1905)

The name "Queen Anne" does not refer to a historical period; it was coined by the English architect Richard Shaw. Queen Anne houses combine elements from many decorative traditions but are marked by their towers, turrets, and large decorative panels on wall surfaces. Many of the houses display intricate spindle-work on balustrades, porches, and roof trusses (see pp35).

Palladian windows were used in gables to give the appearance of an extra floor.

Queen Anne gable filled with ornamental panels at No. 818 Steiner Street

Queen Anne turret topped by a finial at No. 1015 Steiner Street

Round, square, and polygonal turrets and towers are typical of Queen Anne-style houses.

Gable pediments hold ornamental windows and decorative panels.

The curved window frame is not itself characteristic of Queen Anne style, but many houses include features borrowed from other styles.

The asymmetrical facade of No. 850 Steiner Street, together with its eclectic ornament, is typical of a Queen Anne house. Such features are often painted in various bright colors.

Where to Find Victorian Houses

San Francisco's Cable Cars

The cable car system was launched in 1873, and its inventor Andrew Hallidie rode in the first car. He was inspired to tackle the problem of transporting people up the city's steep slopes after witnessing a bad accident, when a horse-drawn tram slipped down a hill, dragging the horses with it. His system was a success, and by 1889 cars were running on eight lines. Before the 1906 earthquake *(see p28)*, more than 600 cars were in use. With the advent of the internal combustion engine, cable cars became obsolete, and in 1947 attempts were made to replace them with buses. After a public outcry the present three lines, using 17 miles (25 km) of track, were retained.

The Cable Car Museum garages the cars at night, and is a repair shop, museum, and powerhouse for the entire cable car system *(see p335)*.

The gripman has to be strong, with good reflexes. Only a third of candidates pass the training course.

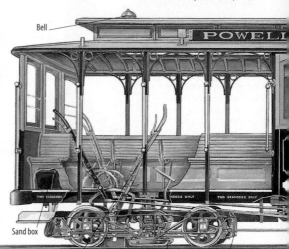

Bell

POWELL

Sand box

Grip handle

Center plate and jaws grip the cable

Emergency brake

Wheel brake

Cable

How Cable Cars Work

Engines in the central powerhouse wind a looped cable under the city streets, guided by a system of grooved pulleys. When the gripman in the cable car applies the grip handle, the grip reaches through a slot in the street and grabs the cable. This pulls the car along at a steady speed of 9.5 mph (15.5 km/h). To stop, the gripman releases the grip and applies the brake. Great skill is needed at corners where the cable passes over a pulley. The gripman must release the grip to allow the car to coast over the pulley.

Cable car grip mechanism

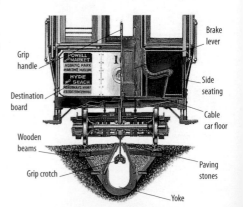

Grip handle

Destination board

Wooden beams

Grip crotch

Brake lever

Side seating

Cable car floor

Paving stones

Yoke

Hatch House is the name given to a four-story house that needed to be moved in its entirety in 1913. Herbert Hatch used a system of jacks and hoists to maneuver the house across the cable car line without causing any cessation of the service.

A cable car celebration was held in 1984 after a two-year-long system refurbishment. Each car was refitted, and all lines were replaced with reinforced tracks. The system should now work safely for the next 100 years.

A cable car bell-ringing contest is held at Union Square every July, when conductors ring out their most spirited rhythms. On the street, the bell signals a warning to other traffic.

Brake block   Brake shoe

The original San Francisco cable car, tested by Hallidie on Clay Street on August 2, 1873, is on display in the Cable Car Museum *(see p335)*. The cable car system has remained essentially unchanged since its invention.

Rebuilding the cable cars has to be done with attention to historical detail, since they are designated historic monuments.

Andrew Smith Hallidie

Andrew Smith was born in London in 1836 and later adopted his uncle's surname. He trained as a mechanic, emigrated to San Francisco in 1852, and formed a company that made wire rope. In 1873 he tested the first cable car, which soon became profitable by opening the hills of the city to development.

San Francisco's Best: Museums and Galleries

Museums and galleries in the city range from the encyclopedic de Young Museum and the Legion of Honor, to the San Francisco Museum of Modern Art with its huge collection of modern and contemporary works, and the Yerba Buena Center for the Arts. There are several excellent science museums, including the Exploratorium and the California Academy of Sciences. Other museums celebrate the city's heritage, including its ancestral Native American culture, and the people and events that made the city what it is today.

Legion of Honor houses a collection of ancient art through to the Middle Ages and the 19th century, including *Sailboats on the Seine* (c.1874) by Claude Monet *(See pp378–9)*.

GOLDEN GATE PARK AND THE PRESIDIO

de Young Museum has collections of American art, as well as art from Central and South America, the Pacific Islands, and Africa. It also has textiles and collections of ancient art and 20th-century European art *(See p371)*.

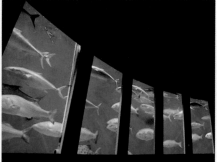

0 kilometers 2

0 miles 1

The California Academy of Sciences incorporates a planetarium, a natural history museum, and an aquarium in Golden Gate Park *(See pp374–5)*

Fort Mason Museums
house ethnic culture artifacts.
Muto by Mimo Paladino
(1985) is one of the many
exhibits *(See pp354–5).*

The Chinese Historical Society
administers one of the city's
smallest museums. Inside is a
unique collection that details
the history of California's
Chinese communities and their
participation in the development
of the state. Included among the
exhibits is this magnificent
dragon's head *(See p334).*

The Exploratorium
is one of the best
science museums
in the US. Here
visitors experiment
with *Sun Painting,* a
feast of light and
color *(See p347).*

FISHERMAN'S
WHARF AND
NORTH BEACH

CHINATOWN
AND
NOB HILL

DOWNTOWN

PACIFIC
HEIGHTS
AND THE
CIVIC CENTER

HAIGHT
ASHBURY
AND THE
MISSION

Wells Fargo History Museum is a small gallery
that displays the colorful history of California,
from the early days of the Gold Rush. This bronze
stagecoach (1984) is by M Casper *(See p318).*

**San Francisco
Museum of Modern
Art** has undergone a
major reconstruction.
It has a large collection
of painting, sculpture,
photography,
architecture and
design, and media arts
(See pp322–3).

The Asian Art Museum,
loacted in a beautiful 1917
Beaux Arts building, was once
the Old San Francisco Main
Library *(See p356).*

**Yerba Buena Center
for the Arts** is a
gallery that displays
diverse works of
contemporary art.
These change
regularly, since there
is no permanent
collection here
(See pp326–7).

San Francisco's Murals

San Francisco is proud of its reputation as a culturally rich and cosmopolitan city, qualities evident in the vivid elaborate murals that decorate walls and fences in several areas of the city. Many were painted in the 1930s, and many more in the 1970s, with some appearing spontaneously while others were commissioned. One of the best is the *Carnaval Mural* on 24th Street in the Mission District *(see p366)*; further examples are shown here.

503 Law Office at Dolores and 18th streets

Past and Present

Some of the best examples of San Francisco's historical mural art can be found inside Coit Tower, where a series of panels, funded during the Great Depression of the 1930s by President Roosevelt's New Deal program, is typical of the period. Many local artists participated in creating the work, and themes include the struggles of the working class and the rich resources of California. The city has since been decorated with a number of modern murals, most notably by the Precita Eyes Mural Arts Studio, as well as many others.

Detail from Coit Tower mural focuses on California's rich resources

Coit Tower mural showing life during the Depression years

Precita Eyes Mural Arts Association is a community-based organization that seeks to promote the mural arts through collaborative projects. They also sponsor new murals by established artists and run lively mural tours around San Francisco *(see box opposite)*.

Mosaic mural (2007) by Precita Eyes, Hillcrest school

Balloon Journey, Precita Eyes

This mural was designed and painted by AYPAL (Asian Pacific Islander Youth Promoting Advocacy and Leadership) students in 2007, in association with Precita Eyes. The association runs a number of community and youth workshops, which produce between 15 and 30 new murals every year. Visitors can see examples of these throughout the Bay Area.

Stop the Violence at 1212 Broadway #400, Oakland

Life Today

Life in the modern metropolis is one of the major themes of mural art in San Francisco, as much now as it was in the 1930s. In the Mission District particularly, every aspect of daily life is illustrated on the walls of banks, schools and restaurants, with lively scenes of the family, community, political activity and people at work and play. The Mission District contains around 200 murals, many painted in the 1970s, as part of a city program that paid young people to create works of art in public places. The San Francisco Arts Commission continues to foster this art form.

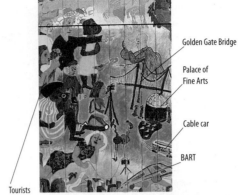

Golden Gate Bridge

Palace of Fine Arts

Cable car

BART

Tourists

This Balmy Alley mural is a view of the city as tourists see it. The alley, in the Mission District, is decorated with numerous vivid murals, some of the first painted by local children, artists and community workers in the 1970s. The works are now a major attraction.

The Learning Wall, Franklin St., depicting education and art

Positively Fourth Street, a weathered mural at Fort Mason

The Multicultural City

San Francisco's heritage of diversity and tolerance comes alive in the murals that enliven its ethnic neighborhoods. In Chinatown, Chinese-American artists evoke memories of the "old country." The Mission District is filled with art, some of it politically inspired, celebrating the struggles and achievements of its Mexican and Latin American population.

Mural in Washington Street encapsulating life in China

Mexican American dancer

Native American drummer

African American maracas player

Caucasian bass player

Multicultural San Francisco is celebrated at Park Branch Library in Haight Ashbury.

Where to Find the Murals

Balmy Alley, 24th & 25th Sts.
Coit Tower *p347*
Dolores and 18th St.
   Map 10 E3
Fort Mason *pp354–5*
Franklin Street. **Map 4 E1**
Oakland *pp427–7*
Park Branch Library
   1833 Page St. **Map 9 B1**
Precita Eyes Mural Arts &
   Visitor Center, 2981 24th St.
Washington Street. **Map 4 E3**

The 49-Mile Scenic Drive

Linking the city's most intriguing neighborhoods, fascinating sights and spectacular views, the 49-Mile Scenic Drive (79 km) provides a splendid overview of San Francisco. Keeping to the well-marked route is easy – just follow the blue-and-white seagull signs. However, some of these are hidden by overhanging vegetation, so you need to be alert. Set aside a whole day for this trip; there are plenty of places to stop to take photographs or admire the views.

㉕ The Palace of Fine Arts
The Palace's Beaux-Arts architecture and Neo-Classical buildings are surrounded by gorgeous grounds making it a lovely place for a picnic lunch or stroll.

⑤ Stow Lake
There is a waterfall and a Chinese pavilion on the island in this picturesque lake. Boats can be rented.

Key

— 49-Mile Scenic Drive

⑧ Sutro Tower
This distinctive orange and white tower is visible from all over the city.

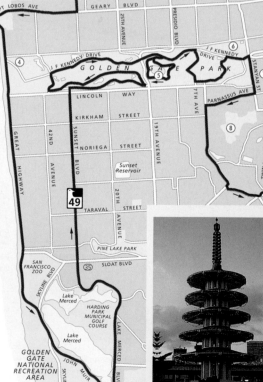

Five-tiered pagoda in Japantown

For keys to symbols see back flap

⑳ Coit Tower
Overlooking North Beach, Telegraph Hill is topped by this tower, which has fine murals and an observation deck.

0 kilometers 2
0 miles 1

㉔ Marina Green
This is an excellent vantage point from which to view or photograph Golden Gate Bridge.

⑱ Grace Cathedral
This impressive cathedral, based on Notre Dame in Paris, dominates the summit of the city's steepest hill, Nob Hill.

Tips for Motorists

Starting point: Anywhere. The circuit is designed to be followed in a counterclockwise direction starting and ending at any point.
When to go: Avoid driving during rush hours: 7–9am, 4–7pm. Most of the views are as spectacular by night as by day.
Parking: Use the parking lots that are situated around the Financial District, the Civic Center, Japantown, Nob Hill, Chinatown, North Beach, and Fisherman's Wharf. Elsewhere, street parking is usually easily available.

Finding the Sights

① Presidio pp380–81
② Fort Point p383
③ Legion of Honor pp378–9
④ Queen Wilhelmina Tulip Garden p373
⑤ Stow Lake p372
⑥ Conservatory of Flowers p372
⑦ Haight Street p362
⑧ Sutro Tower p367
⑨ Twin Peaks p367
⑩ Mission Dolores p365
⑪ Ferry Building p320
⑫ Embarcadero Center p318
⑬ Civic Center pp356–7
⑭ Cathedral of St. Mary of the Assumption p356
⑮ Japan Center p356
⑯ Union Square p324
⑰ Chinatown Gateway p332
⑱ Grace Cathedral p335
⑲ Cable Car Museum p335
⑳ Coit Tower p347
㉑ Exploratorium p347
㉒ San Francisco National Maritime Museum p341
㉓ Fort Mason pp354–5
㉔ Marina Green p354
㉕ Palace of Fine Arts p353

DOWNTOWN SAN FRANCISCO

Montgomery Street, now right in the heart of the Financial District, was once a street of small shops, where miners came to weigh their gold dust. Wells Fargo built the city's first brick building on the street during the Gold Rush *(see pp52–3)*. Today, old-fashioned banks stand in the shadow of modern skyscrapers. Union Square is the city's main shopping district and has a wealth of fine department stores. SoMa (South of Market) has become the city's "artists' quarter," with its old warehouses converted into studios, bars, and avant-garde theaters.

Sights at a Glance

Historic Streets and Buildings
2 Jackson Square Historic District
6 Union Bank of California
7 Merchant's Exchange
8 Pacific Coast Stock Exchange
10 Ferry Building
12 California Historical Society
23 Powell Street Cable Car Turntable
25 Old United States Mint

Shops
18 Crocker Galleria
19 Gump's
22 Union Square Shops
24 Westfield San Francisco Centre

Modern Architecture
1 Embarcadero Center
4 555 California
5 Transamerica Pyramid
11 Rincon Center
14 *Yerba Buena Gardens pp326–7*

Theaters
21 Theater District

Hotels
16 Palace Hotel

Museums and Galleries
3 Wells Fargo History Museum
13 *Museum of Modern Art pp322–3*
15 Museum of the African Diaspora
17 Contemporary Jewish Museum

Parks and Squares
9 Justin Herman Plaza
20 Union Square

See also San Francisco Street Finder maps 5 & 6

0 meters 400
0 yards 400

◀ Columbus Tower (Sentinel Building) with Transamerica Pyramid to the left

For keys to symbols *see back flap*

Street-by-Street: Financial District

San Francisco's economic engine is fueled predominantly by the Financial District, one of the chief commercial centers in the US. It reaches from the imposing modern towers and plazas of the Embarcadero Center to staid Montgomery Street, called the "Wall Street of the West." All the principal banks, brokers, and law offices are situated within this area. The Jackson Square Historical District, north of Washington Street, was once the heart of the business community.

❶ ★ Embarcadero Center
The center houses commercial outlets and offices. A shopping arcade occupies the first three tiers of the towers.

Hotaling Place is a narrow alley known for its many excellent antique shops.

❷ Jackson Square Historic District
This district, more than any other, recalls the Gold Rush era.

Bus stop (No. 41)

❺ ★ Transamerica Pyramid
This 853-ft (260-m) skyscraper is a landmark on the city's skyline.

The Golden Era Building was built during the Gold Rush and housed the paper *Golden Era*, for which Mark Twain wrote.

❻ Union Bank of California
This enormous bank is guarded by fierce stone lions carved by sculptor Arthur Putnam.

❼ Merchant's Exchange
Paintings of shipping scenes line the walls.

❸ Wells Fargo History Museum
An old stagecoach, evoking the Wild West days, is one of the exhibits in this transportation and banking museum.

❹ 555 California
Once the HQ of the Bank of America, this high-rise is one of the tallest in the city.

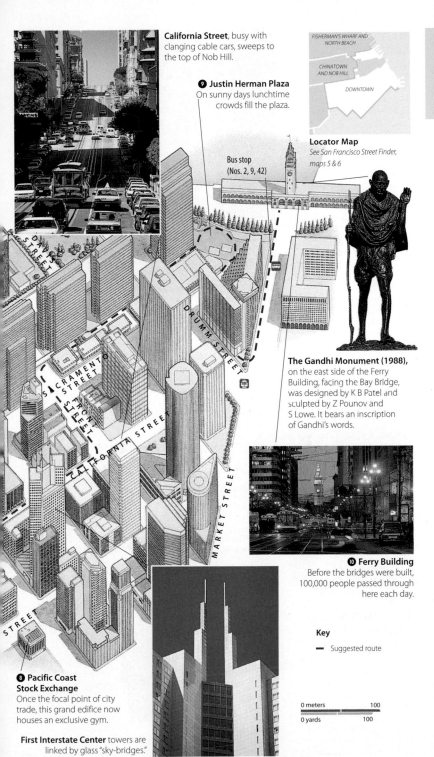

California Street, busy with clanging cable cars, sweeps to the top of Nob Hill.

⑨ Justin Herman Plaza
On sunny days lunchtime crowds fill the plaza.

Bus stop
(Nos. 2, 9, 42)

Locator Map
See San Francisco Street Finder, maps 5 & 6

The Gandhi Monument (1988), on the east side of the Ferry Building, facing the Bay Bridge, was designed by K B Patel and sculpted by Z Pounov and S Lowe. It bears an inscription of Gandhi's words.

⑩ Ferry Building
Before the bridges were built, 100,000 people passed through here each day.

Key
— Suggested route

0 meters   100
0 yards   100

⑧ Pacific Coast Stock Exchange
Once the focal point of city trade, this grand edifice now houses an exclusive gym.

First Interstate Center towers are linked by glass "sky-bridges."

❶ Embarcadero Center

Map 6 D3. **Tel** (415) 772-0700.
🚌 1, 32, 41. 🚋 J, K, L, M, N. 🚇
California St. *See Shopping pp386–91
and Entertainment Venues pp394–7.*
W embarcaderocenter.com

Completed in 1981 after a decade of construction, San Francisco's largest redevelopment project stretches from Justin Herman Plaza to Battery Street. Office workers and shoppers use its open spaces to relax in the sun and eat their lunch. Five high-rise towers reach 35 to 45 stories above the landscaped plazas and elevated walkways.

Adjacent to the fourth tower of the Embarcadero Center is the swanky Hyatt Regency Hotel, whose interior is just waiting to be admired. Its 17-story atrium contains an immense sculpted globe by Charles Perry, entitled *Eclipse*. Also housed in the center is a cinema screening an impressive array of independent and foreign films.

Lobby of the Hyatt Regency Hotel at the Embarcadero Center

Hotaling Place in Jackson Square

❷ Jackson Square Historic District

Map 5 C3. 🚌 12, 15, 41, 83.

Renovated in the early 1950s, this neighborhood contains many historic brick, cast-iron, and granite facades dating from Gold Rush days. From 1850 to 1910 it was known as the Barbary Coast, notorious for its squalor and the crudeness of its inhabitants. The old Hippodrome theater at No. 555 Pacific Street contains bawdy relief sculptures in the recessed front, which recall the risqué shows that were performed there. Today the buildings are used as showrooms, law offices, and fine antique shops; the best ones can be seen in Jackson Street, Gold Street, Hotaling Place, and Montgomery Street.

❸ Wells Fargo History Museum

420 Montgomery St. **Map** 5 C4.
Tel (415) 396-2619. 🚌 1, 3, 10, 41.
🚇 Montgomery St. **Open** 9am–5pm
Mon–Fri. **Closed** public hols. ♿
📷 **W** wellsfargohistory.com

Founded in 1852, Wells Fargo & Co. became the greatest banking and transportation company in the West and was influential in the development of the American frontier.

The company moved people and goods from the East to the West Coast, and between the mining camps and towns of California. It also transported gold from the West Coast to the East, and delivered mail,

placing mailboxes in convenient locations to enable the messengers to sort letters en route. The Pony Express was another mail venture in which Wells Fargo & Co. played a major role.

The splendid stagecoaches on display are famous, particularly for the legendary stories of their heroic drivers and the bandits who robbed them. The best-known bandit was Black Bart, who left poems at the scene of his crimes. He stalked the many lonely roads from Calaveras County up to the Oregon border from 1875 to 1883. In one holdup he mistakenly left behind his handkerchief. Its distinctive laundry mark revealed him as mining engineer Charles Boles *(see p483)*.

Museum visitors can experience how it felt to sit for days in a jostling stagecoach, and listen to the recorded diary of an immigrant called Francis Brocklehurst. Exhibits include Pony Express mail, photographs, early checks, and gold nuggets from the famous 1849 Gold Rush.

Black Bart, the poet bandit

❹ 555 California

555 California St. **Map** 5 C4.
Tel (415) 392-1697. 🚍 1, 41.
🚃 California St.

Completed in 1969, this red granite-clad building was the headquarters of the Bank of America up until it merged with Nations Bank in 1998. The skyscraper's 52 floors make it the second tallest building in San Francisco, just beaten by the Transamerica Pyramid. The Bank of America was originally the Bank of Italy, which was founded by AP Giannini in San Jose *(see pp432–3)*. It built up a huge clientele early in the 20th century by catering to immigrants and investing in the booming farmlands and small towns. In the great fire of 1906 *(see p56)*, Giannini personally rescued his bank's deposits, carrying them to safety by hiding them in fruit crates, so there were sufficient funds for the bank to invest in the rebuilding of the city.

Transcendence by Masayuki Nagari (1972) at 555 California

❺ Transamerica Pyramid

600 Montgomery St. **Map** 5 C3. 🚍 1, 10, 12, 30, 41. **Open** 8:30am–4:30pm Mon–Fri (lobby only); visitor center 10am–3pm. **Closed** public hols. ♿
🌐 thepyramidcenter.com

Capped with a pointed spire on top of its 48 stories, the pyramid reaches 853 ft (260 m) above sea level. It is the most widely recognized building in the city, and although San Franciscans disliked it when it opened in 1972, they have since accepted it as part of their city's skyline.

Designed by William Pereira & Associates, the pyramid houses over 1,500 office workers on a site that is historically one of the richest in the city. The Montgomery Block, which contained many important offices and was the largest building west of the Mississippi, was built here in 1853. In the basement was the Exchange Saloon, which was frequented by Mark Twain/Samuel Clemens. The Financial District was extended south in the 1860s, and artists and writers took up residence in the Montgomery Block. The Pony Express terminus, marked by a plaque, was opposite, at Merchant Street.

The spire is hollow, rising 212 ft (64 m) above the top floor. Lit from inside, it casts a warm, yellow glow at night. Its purpose is purely decorative.

The vertical wings of the building rise from the middle of the ground floor and extend beyond the frame, which tapers inward. The eastern wing houses 18 elevator shafts, and the western wing houses a smoke tower and emergency stairs.

The visitor center is situated on the ground floor. Here, a bank of monitors provides visitors with views beamed down from four cameras that revolve at the apex of the spire.

Earthquake protection is ensured by white precast quartz aggregate, interlaced with reinforcing rods at four places on each floor, that cover the exterior of the pyramid. Clearance between the panels allows for lateral movement in case of an earthquake.

The shape of the building tapers so that it casts a smaller shadow than a conventional design.

The 3,678 windows take cleaners an entire month to wash.

The foundations rest on a steel and concrete block, sunk 52 ft (15.5 m) into the ground and designed to move with earth tremors.

❻ Union Bank of California

400 California St. **Map** 5 C4. **Tel** (415) 705-7142. 🚌 1, 3, 10, 12, 41. 🚋 California St. Museum of Money of the American West: **Open** 9am–5pm Mon–Fri. **Closed** public hols. ♿

William Ralston and Darius Mills founded this bank in 1864. Ralston, known as "the man who built San Francisco," invested profitably in the Comstock mines (see p53). He used the bank and his personal fortune to finance many civic projects in San Francisco, including the city's water company, a theater, and the Palace Hotel (see p536). When economic depression struck in the 1870s, Ralston's empire collapsed.

The present colonnaded building was completed in 1908. In the basement, the Museum of Money of the American West displays gold, coins, old banknotes, and diagrams of the Comstock mines.

Neo-Classical facade of the Union Bank of California

❼ Merchant's Exchange

465 California St. **Map** 5 C4. **Tel** (415) 421-7730. 🚌 1, 4, 10, 12, 41. 🚋 Montgomery St. **Open** Banking Hall: 9am–5pm Mon–Fri. ♿ 🌐 merchantsexchange building.com

The exchange, designed by Willis Polk in 1903 survived the great fire of 1906 with little damage (see p56). Inside, William Coulter seascapes line the walls, depicting epic maritime scenes from the age of steam and sail. This was the focal point of San Francisco's commodities exchange in the early 20th century, when look-outs in the tower relayed news of ships

arriving from abroad. Now dwarfed by skyscrapers, it once dominated the skyline.

❽ Pacific Coast Stock Exchange

115 Sansome St. **Map** 5 C4. 🚌 3, 4, 15, 41. **Closed** to the public.

This was once America's largest stock exchange outside New York. Founded in 1882 it occupied these buildings, which were remodeled in 1930 by Miller and Pflueger from the existing US Treasury. The monumental granite statues that flank the Pine Street entrance were sculpted by Ralph Stackpole, also in 1930. The building is now closed, its once-frantic trading floor silent due to the emergence of electronic and Internet trading.

❾ Justin Herman Plaza

Map 6 D3. 🚌 many buses. 🚋 F, J, K, L, M, N. 🚋 California St.

Popular with lunchtime crowds from the nearby Embarcadero Center (see p318), this plaza is best known for its avant-garde Vaillancourt Fountain, built in 1971 by the Canadian artist Armand Vaillancourt. The fountain is modeled from huge concrete blocks, and some people find it ugly, especially when it is allowed to run dry during times of drought. However, you are allowed to climb on and through it, and with its splashing pools and columns of falling water, it is an intriguing public work of art when functioning as intended.

The area is often rented out to musicians during the lunch hour – the popular rock band U2 performed a lunchtime concert here in 1987, after which they spray-painted the fountain.

The Vaillancourt Fountain in Justin Herman Plaza

❿ Ferry Building

Embarcadero at Market St. **Map** 6 E3. 🚌 many buses. 🚋 F, J, K, L, M, N. 🚋 California St. 🌐 **ferrybuilding marketplace.com**

Constructed between 1896 and 1903, the Ferry Building survived the great fire of 1906 thanks to fireboats pumping water from the bay. The clock tower is 235 ft (71 m) high, inspired by the Moorish bell tower of Seville Cathedral, Spain. In the 1930s over 50 million passengers a year passed through the building – many were travelers from the transcontinental railroad terminal in Oakland; others were commuters using the 170 daily ferries between the city and their homes across the bay. With the opening of the Bay Bridge in 1936 (see pp426–7), the Ferry Building ceased to be the city's main entry point. Today it houses gourmet restaurants and shops. A few ferries still cross the bay, to Larkspur, Tiburon, and Sausalito in Marin County (see pp418–19), Alameda and Oakland in the East Bay (see pp426–7), and Vallejo in the North Bay (see p302).

The clock tower on the Ferry Building

⓫ Rincon Center

Map 6 E4. 🚌 14.
See Shopping pp386–91.

This shopping center, with its soaring atrium and its 90-ft (27-m) fountain, was added on to the old Rincon Annex Post Office Building in 1989. The Rincon Annex dates from 1940 and is well known for its murals by the Russian-born artist Anton Refregier, showing aspects of the history of San Francisco. Some of the works depict harsh images of important events and people of the city, which caused much controversy when first shown.

⓬ California Historical Society

678 Mission St. **Map** 5 C5.
Tel (415) 357-1848. 🚌 9, 30, 45.
🚋 Montgomery St. **Open** Museum: noon–5pm Tue–Sun; Library: noon–5pm Wed Fri. 🚫 📷 🆆 **california historicalsociety.org**

The California Historical Society is dedicated to preserving and interpreting Californiana. The Society offers a reference and research library, museum galleries, and a well-stocked bookstore. There is also an impressive photographic collection, more than 900 oil paintings and watercolors by American artists, and a unique costume collection.

⓭ Museum of Modern Art

See pp322–3.

Rincon Annex mural depicting the Spanish discovery of San Francisco

⓮ Yerba Buena Gardens

See pp326–7.

⓯ Museum of the African Diaspora

685 Mission St. **Map** 5 C5. **Tel** (415) 358-7200. 🚌 5, 6, 9, 14, 30. 🚋 J, K, L.
Open 11am–6pm Wed–Sat, noon–5pm Sun. 🚫 🆆 **moadsf.org**

One of the few museums in the world focused on African Diaspora culture, MoAD aims to educate visitors regarding the culture, history, and art of the African Diaspora. Founded in 2005, the museum explores the rich cultural artworks of the people of Africa and of African descendant cultures around the world. The exhibitions and programs trace the cultural, social and artistic evolution of the diaspora through music, dance, visual arts and crafts, and much more. Interactive features include iPad kiosks and slavery narratives.

⓰ Palace Hotel

2 New Montgomery St. **Map** 5 C4.
Tel (415) 512-1111. 🚌 7, 8, 9, 21, 31, 45, 71, 91. 🚋 J, K, L, M, N. *See Where to Stay p536.* 🆆 **sfpalace.com**

The original Palace Hotel was opened by William Ralston, one of San Francisco's best-known financiers, in 1875. It was the most luxurious of San Francisco's early hotels, with 7 floors, 700 windows, an inner courtyard, and exotic international decor. It was regularly frequented by the rich and famous. Among its patrons were the actress Sarah Bernhardt and writers Oscar Wilde and Rudyard Kipling. The celebrated tenor Enrico Caruso was a guest at the hotel at the time of the earthquake of 1906 when the hotel caught fire. It was rebuilt shortly after under the direction of the architect George Kelham, and reopened in 1909. The Garden Court glass dome contains about 63,000 pieces of iridescent glass and totals 12,000 sq ft (1,115 sq m), making it one of the largest expanses of colored glass on Earth.

Glass dome and chandeliers at the Garden Court, Palace Hotel

⓭ San Francisco Museum of Modern Art

This museum forms the nucleus of San Francisco's reputation as a leading center of modern art. Created in 1935, it moved into its current quarters in 1995, and in spring 2016 reopened after a major three-year $365 million expansion that doubled its capacity. Designed by the international architecture firm Snøhetta, the new 235,000-square-foot expansion is seamlessly integrated with Swiss architect Mario Botta's 1995 modernist building. The museum offers a dynamic schedule of special exhibitions and permanent collection presentations in its 130,000-sq-ft (12,075-sq-m) gallery space.

Expansion
The eastern facade of the new expansion, designed by Snøhetta, is inspired in part by the waters of the San Francisco Bay. Its ground level features free exhibition spaces.

Museum Guide

The ground floor welcomes visitors with free art-filled public spaces and galleries. The Koret Education Center and works from the permanent collection of painting and sculpture are on the second floor, as is a new gallery for works on paper and galleries dedicated to California art. The new 15,000 square-foot Pritzker Center for Photography is on the third floor. The Doris and Donald Fisher Collection, comprising more than 1,100 works, begins on the third floor with a gallery of works by Alexander Calder, and continues in the Fisher Galleries on the fourth, fifth, and sixth floors. The sixth floor also features spaces dedicated to architecture and design, while the seventh floor showcases contemporary works as well as galleries dedicated to media arts, and a two-story conservation lab and artist's studio.

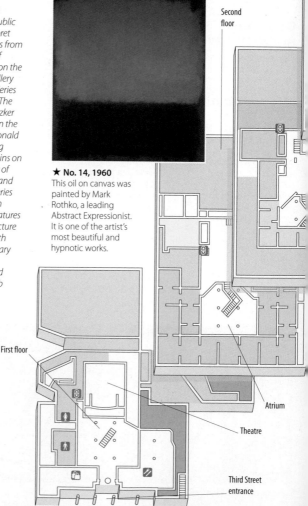

Second floor

★ No. 14, 1960
This oil on canvas was painted by Mark Rothko, a leading Abstract Expressionist. It is one of the artist's most beautiful and hypnotic works.

First floor

Atrium

Theatre

Third Street entrance

Key to Floor Plan

- Painting and sculpture
- Architecture and design
- Photography
- Media arts
- Koret Education Center
- Special exhibitions
- Roberts Family Gallery
- Sculpture Garden
- Contemporary Galleries
- Non-exhibition space

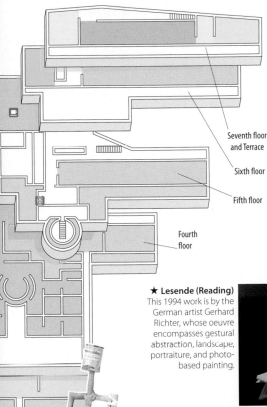

Seventh floor
and Terrace

Sixth floor

Fifth floor

Fourth
floor

Third floor

★ Lesende (Reading)
This 1994 work is by the
German artist Gerhard
Richter, whose oeuvre
encompasses gestural
abstraction, landscape,
portraiture, and photo-
based painting.

Koret Education Center
The reimagined Koret
Education Center houses
a resource library and
classrooms, serving
students, teachers
and lifelong learners.

★ California Art
Richard Shaw's sculpted
figure *Melodious Double
Stops* (1980) is a highlight
of the collection.

Country Dog Gentlemen
Bay Area artist Roy De Forest
painted this fantasy of a universe
guarded by animals in 1972.

Central plaza of the Crocker Galleria

⑰ Contemporary Jewish Museum

736 Mission St. **Map** 5 C5. **Tel** (415) 655-7800. 🚌 5, 6, 9, 14, 30. 🚋 J, K, L. **Open** 1–8pm Thu, 11am–5pm Fri–Tue. ♿ 🌐 thecjm.org

Housed in a stunning building designed by Daniel Libeskind, this museum presents wide-ranging exhibitions that celebrate and explore Judaism. The changing exhibits make innovative use of hands-on activities, art, historical objects, film, and music.

⑱ Crocker Galleria

Between Post, Kearny, Sutter, and Montgomery Sts. **Map** 5 C4. **Tel** (415) 393-1500. 🚌 2, 3, 4. 🚋 J, K, L, M, N. 🌐 thecrockergalleria.com
See Shopping pp386–91.

The Crocker Galleria was built in 1982. Inspired by Milan's Galleria Vittorio Emmanuelle, the building features a central plaza under an arched atrium. More than 50 shops and restaurants are housed here, with displays promoting the best of European and American designers.

⑲ Gump's

135 Post St. **Map** 5 C4. **Tel** (800) 882-8055. 🚌 2, 3, 4, 30, 38, 45. 🚋 J, K, L, M, N. 🚡 Powell–Mason, Powell–Hyde. **Open** 10am–6pm Mon–Sat, noon–5pm Sun. ♿ 🌐 gumps.com *See Shopping: pp386–9.*

Founded in 1861 by German immigrants who were once

mirror and frame merchants, this indigenous San Francisco department store has now become a local institution.

Gump's houses one of the largest collections of fine china and crystal in the United States, by prestigious designers such as Baccarat, Steuben, and Lalique.

The store is also celebrated for its oriental treasures, furniture, and rare works of art. The Asian art is particularly fine, especially the jade collection, which enjoys an international reputation. In 1949 Gump's imported a great bronze Buddha and presented it to the Japanese Tea Garden in Golden Gate Park *(see pp370–71).*

Gump's has a very refined atmosphere and is often frequented by the rich and famous. It is renowned for its extravagant window displays.

⑳ Union Square

Map 5 C5. 🚌 30, 38, 45. 🚋 J, K, L, M, N, T. 🚡 Powell–Mason, Powell–Hyde. 🌐 visitunionsquaresf.com

Union Square was named after the big, pro-Union rallies held here during the Civil War of 1861–5. The rallies galvanized popular support for the Northern cause, which was instrumental in bringing California into the war on the side of the Union. The original churches, gentlemen's clubs, and the synagogue have been replaced by shops and offices. This green square, lined with palm trees, is at the heart of the shopping district and marks the edge of the Theater District. On the west side is the luxurious Westin St. Francis Hotel. In the center, a bronze statue of the Goddess of Victory stands at the top of a 90-ft (27-m) Corinthian column. Sculpted by Robert Aitken in 1903, it commemorates Admiral Dewey's victory at Manila Bay during the Spanish-American War of 1898.

㉑ Theater District

Map 5 B5. 🚌 2, 3, 4, 38. 🚋 J, K, L, M, N, T. 🚡 Powell–Mason, Powell–Hyde. *See Entertainment pp392–5.*

Several theaters are located near Union Square, all within a six-block area. The two largest are on Geary Boulevard: the Curran Theater, designed in 1922 by Alfred Henry D Jacobs, which imports Broadway shows, and the Geary Theater, with its Edwardian facade. The Geary Theater is now home to the American Conservatory Theater (ACT), which shows classical and contemporary pieces. The city has a fine reputation for the variety of performances it offers and has always attracted great actors. Isadora Duncan, the innovative 1920s dancer, was born nearby at No. 501 Taylor Street, which is now marked by a plaque.

㉒ Union Square Shops

Map 5 C5. 🚌 30, 38, 45. 🚋 J, K, L, M, N, T. 🚡 Powell–Mason, Powell–Hyde. *See Shopping pp386–91.*

Many of San Francisco's largest department stores can be found around Union Square, including Macy's, Saks Fifth Avenue, and Gump's. The Neiman Marcus store, at the request of San

Department stores overlooking Union Square

Rotating a cable car on the Powell Street Turntable

㉔ Westfield San Francisco Centre

Fifth St and Market St. **Map** 5 C5.
Tel (415) 512-6776. 🚌 5, 8, 9, 14, 21,
71. 🚊 J, K, L, M, N. 🚋 Powell–Mason,
Powell–Hyde. **Open** 10am–8:30pm
Mon–Sat, 10am–7pm Sun.
🌐 **westfield.com/sanfrancisco**
See Shopping pp386–91.

Located in the heart of San
Franciso, near Union Square, the
Westfield San Francisco Centre
integrates the existing San
Francisco Centre with the
adjacent former Emporium
department store building
whose dome dates back to
1904 and is the centerpiece of
the project. The mall features
more than 200 shops,
restaurants, and cafés, along
with San Francisco's largest day
spa and a Century 9 cinema.

㉕ Old United States Mint

Fifth St and Mission St. **Map** 5 C5.
Tel (415) 537-1105. 🚌 14, 14L, 26, 27.
🚊 J, K, L, M, N. **Closed** to public.
🌐 **usmint.gov**

San Francisco's Old Mint produced
its last coins in 1937. It was built of
granite in the Classical style by AB
Mullet between 1869 and 1874,
hence its nickname, the "Granite
Lady." Its windows were fortified
by iron shutters and its basement
vaults impregnable. The building
was one of the few to survive
the 1906 earthquake *(see pp56)*.
Plans are under way to convert
The Mint into a history museum.

Franciscans, has preserved the
1900 rotunda and skylight from
the City of Paris. The latter was
the city's most elegant store at
the end of the 19th century but
was demolished in 1982. As well
as the larger stores, the area
houses many antiquarian
bookshops and smaller
boutiques. In 1947, Frank Lloyd
Wright *(see p37)* designed
140 Maiden Lane, which now
houses an Asian antiques shop,
Xanadu Gallery. This intimate
space incorporates an elegant
spiral ramp constructed before
the one at the Guggenheim
Museum in New York.

㉓ Powell Street Cable Car Turntable

Hallidie Plaza, Powell St at Market St.
Map 5 C5. 🚌 many buses. 🚊 J, K, M,
N. 🚋 Powell–Mason, Powell–Hyde.
🌐 **sfcablecar.com**

The Powell–Hyde and the Powell–
Mason cable car lines are the most
spectacular routes in San Francisco.
They start and end their journeys
to Nob Hill, Chinatown, and
Fisherman's Wharf at the corner of
Powell Street and Market Street.
Unlike the double-ended cable

cars that are found on the
California Street line, the Powell
Street cable cars were built to
move in one direction only –
hence the need for a turntable
at the end of each line.

After the last passengers
have disembarked, the car is
pushed onto the turntable
and rotated manually by the
conductor and gripman. The
next passengers for the return
journey wait for the half-circle
to be completed amid an
ever-moving procession
of street musicians, local
shoppers, and office workers.

The impregnable "Granite Lady" Old Mint

⑭ Yerba Buena Gardens

The construction of the Moscone Center, San Francisco's largest venue for conventions, heralded the start of ambitious plans for Yerba Buena Gardens. New housing, hotels, museums, galleries, shops, restaurants, and gardens have now been built to rejuvenate a once-depressed area. Access the center from Yerba Buena Lane, home to retail shops and a museum.

★ **Yerba Buena Center for the Arts**
The center is an arts forum, with galleries and regular screenings of contemporary films.

Esplanade Gardens
Visitors can wander along the paths or relax on benches.

Children's Creativity Museum
This museum is located at the Yerba Buena Children's Garden. It has an ongoing program of events and provides opportunities for youngsters and artists to collaborate in the design and creation of anything from airplanes, robots, and futuristic buildings to mosaics and sculptures.

KEY

① **The Martin Luther King Jr. Memorial** has words of peace in several languages.

② **East Garden**

③ **Moscone Ballroom** is part of San Francisco's extensive convention facilities. It is available for large conferences and symposia.

④ **The children's garden** has imaginative play equipment in a pleasant outdoor setting.

⑤ **Ice-skating rink**

⑥ **Bowling Center**

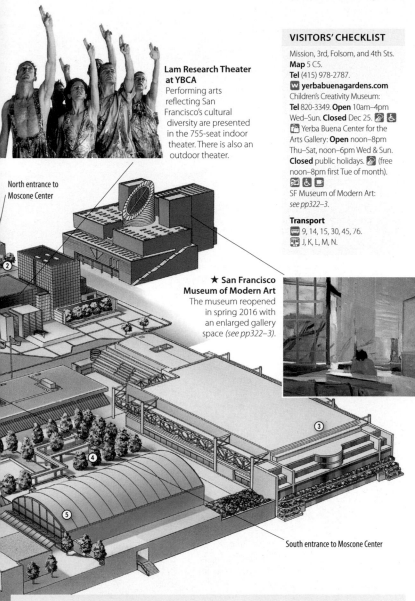

Lam Research Theater at YBCA
Performing arts reflecting San Francisco's cultural diversity are presented in the 755-seat indoor theater. There is also an outdoor theater.

North entrance to Moscone Center

② ④ ⑤ ③

★ **San Francisco Museum of Modern Art**
The museum reopened in spring 2016 with an enlarged gallery space (see pp322–3).

South entrance to Moscone Center

VISITORS' CHECKLIST

Mission, 3rd, Folsom, and 4th Sts.
Map 5 C5.
Tel (415) 978-2787.
W yerbabuenagardens.com
Children's Creativity Museum:
Tel 820-3349. **Open** 10am–4pm
Wed–Sun. **Closed** Dec 25. 🐾 ♿
📷 Yerba Buena Center for the
Arts Gallery: **Open** noon–8pm
Thu–Sat, noon–6pm Wed & Sun.
Closed public holidays. 🐾 (free
noon–8pm first Tue of month).
🐾 ♿ 🖥
SF Museum of Modern Art:
see pp322–3.

Transport
🚌 9, 14, 15, 30, 45, 76.
🚃 J, K, L, M, N.

Entrance foyer Ballroom Exhibition hall Ground-level rooftop Base of supporting arch

Moscone Center

Engineer T.Y. Lin found an ingenious way to support the rooftop garden above this huge underground hall without a single interior column. The bases of the eight steel arches are linked, like an archer's bow strings, by cables under the floor. By tightening the cables, the arches exert enormous upward thrust.

CHINATOWN AND NOB HILL

The Chinese settled around Portsmouth Square during the 1850s; wealthy San Franciscans moved further up Nob Hill where there was more room to build. Today the district recalls the atmosphere of a typical village in Guangdong, although the architecture, customs, and public events are distinctly American hybrids on a Cantonese theme. This densely populated neighborhood has been called the "Gilded Ghetto," because its colorful facades and lively markets stand in contrast to a harsher world where the poor live in undesirable conditions. Nob Hill is San Francisco's most celebrated hilltop, famous for its cable cars, plush hotels, and views. In the late 19th century, the "Big Four," who built the first transcontinental railroad, were among its richest tenants. In 1906, the earthquake and fire *(see p56)* leveled all but one of these houses, but today's luxury hotels still recall the opulence of the Victorian era *(see pp537–8)*.

Sights at a Glance

Historic Streets and Buildings
1 Chinatown Gateway
5 Chinatown Alleys
6 Grant Avenue
10 Nob Hill

Galleries and Museums
8 Chinese Culture Center
9 Chinese Historical Society of America
11 Cable Car Museum

Churches and Temples
2 Old St. Mary's Cathedral
3 Kong Chow Temple
4 Tien Hau Temple
12 Grace Cathedral

Parks and Squares
7 Portsmouth Square

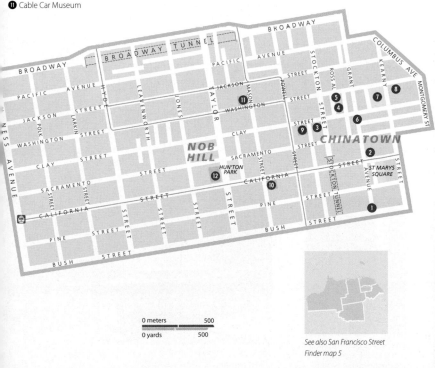

0 meters 500
0 yards 500

See also San Francisco Street Finder map 5

◀ Entering Grant Avenue through the Chinatown Gateway   **For keys to symbols** *see back flap*

Street-by-Street: Chinatown

Grant Avenue is the Chinatown for tourists, with dragon lampposts, Chinese pagoda-style roofs, and neighborhood hardware stores selling everything from kites to cooking utensils. Locals shop on Stockton Street, where boxes of vegetables, fish, and other produce spill over onto crowded sidewalks. In the alleys in between, look for temples and family-run restaurants.

❺ ★ Chinatown Alleys
Authentic sights and sounds of Asia echo in these busy alleys.

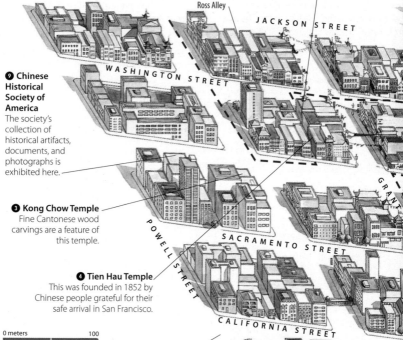

Ross Alley

JACKSON STREET

WASHINGTON STREET

❾ Chinese Historical Society of America
The society's collection of historical artifacts, documents, and photographs is exhibited here.

❸ Kong Chow Temple
Fine Cantonese wood carvings are a feature of this temple.

POWELL STREET

SACRAMENTO STREET

❹ Tien Hau Temple
This was founded in 1852 by Chinese people grateful for their safe arrival in San Francisco.

CALIFORNIA STREET

GRANT

STOCKTON S

| 0 meters | 100 |
| 0 yards | 100 |

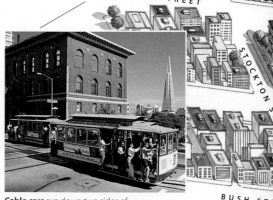

The Bank of Canton was home to Chinatown's telephone exchange until 1946. The operators spoke five Chinese dialects.

Cable cars run down two sides of Chinatown and are an essential part of the area's bustling atmosphere. Any of the three lines will take you there.

BUSH STR

For hotels and restaurants in this area see pp537–8 and p566

❼ Portsmouth Square
Laid out in 1839, this was the social center for the village of Yerba Buena. Today it is a place for children and players of cards and mahjong.

❻ ★ Grant Avenue
In the 1830s and early 1840s this was the main thoroughfare of Yerba Buena.

Locator Map
See Street Finder, map 5

FISHERMAN'S WHARF AND NORTH BEACH

CHINATOWN AND NOB HILL

PACIFIC HEIGHTS AND THE CIVIC CENTER

DOWNTOWN

Key

— Suggested route

❽ Chinese Culture Center
Housed in the elegant hotel Hilton San Francisco Financial District, the center contains an art gallery and a small crafts shop. It sponsors a lively program of lectures and seminars.

To buses nos. 30, 45

KEARNY STREET

CLAY STREET

SON, OBSERVE THE TIME AND FLY FROM EVIL. Ecc. IV. 23.

❶ St. Mary's Square is a quiet haven in which to rest.

❷ Old St. Mary's Church
The clock tower of this church, built while the city was still in its infancy, bears an arresting inscription.

PINE STREET

To bus nos. 31, 38

❶ ★ Chinatown Gateway
Also known as the "Dragons' Gate," this marks Chinatown's south entrance.

❶ Chinatown Gateway

Grant Ave at Bush St. **Map** 5 C4.
🚌 2, 3, 30, 45.

This ornate portal, opened in 1970, was designed by Clayton Lee as an arch over the entrance to Chinatown's main tourist street, Grant Avenue. It was inspired by the ceremonial entrances of traditional Chinese villages. The three-arched gateway is capped with green roof tiles and a host of propitiatory animals, all of glazed ceramic. The gate was erected by an American institution, the Chinatown Cultural Development Committee. The materials were donated by Taiwan (Republic of China).

It is guarded by two stone lions that are suckling their cubs through their claws, in accordance with ancient lore. Once through the gate, visitors can buy antiques, embroidered silks, and gems, though prices here can be aimed at tourists.

Stone lions decorating the Chinatown gateway

❷ Old St. Mary's Cathedral

660 California St. **Map** 5 C4. **Tel** (415) 288-3800. 🚌 2, 3, 8, 8AX, 8BX, 8X, 15, 30, 45. 🚋 California St. ✝ 7:30am, noon Mon–Fri, noon, 5pm Sat, 8.30am, 11am Sun. 📷
🌐 oldsaintmarys.org

San Francisco's first Catholic cathedral, Old St. Mary's, was consecrated on Christmas Day 1854 as the seat of the Roman Catholic bishop of the Pacific Coast. Until 1891 it served a largely Irish congregation, when the new St. Mary's Cathedral was built on Van Ness Avenue. Because of the unavailability of the right building materials in California, the bricks and iron for the church were imported from the East Coast, while the granite foundation stones came from China. The clock tower of the church bears a large inscription, "Son, observe the time and fly from evil," said to have been directed at the brothels that stood across the street. It was one of the few buildings to remain unharmed by the 1906 earthquake and retains its original foundations and walls. The graceful interior, with stained-glass windows and a balcony, was completed in 1909.

Entrance to Old St. Mary's Church below the clock tower and its inscription

❸ Kong Chow Temple

4th floor, 855 Stockton St. **Map** 5 B4. **Tel** (415) 788-1339. 🚌 30, 45. **Open** 9am–4pm daily. Donation ♿

From the top floor above the district's post office, the Kong Chow Temple looks out over Chinatown and the Financial District. Although the building itself dates from only 1977, the Taoist temple was founded in 1857 and the altar and statuary are thought to form the oldest Chinese religious shrine in the country. One altar was handcarved in Guangzhou (Canton), and shipped here in the 19th century. The main shrine is presided over by a carved wooden statue of Kuan Di, also dating from the 19th century. He is the deity most often found in shrines in Cantonese cities.

Kuan Di is also frequently seen in the city's Chinatown district: his highly distinctive face looks down from Taoist shrines in many of the area's restaurants. He is typically depicted holding

Carved statue of Kuan Di inside the Kong Chow Temple

a large sword in one hand and a book in the other. These are symbols of his unswerving dedication to both the martial and the literary arts.

❹ Tien Hau Temple

Top floor, 125 Waverly Pl. **Map** 5 C3. **Tel** (415) 986-2520. 🚌 1, 10, 12, 30, 41, 45. 🚋 Powell–Hyde, Powell–Mason. **Open** 9am–4pm daily. Donation.

This unusual temple is dedicated to Tien Hau, the Queen of Heaven and protector of seafarers and visitors, and is the oldest operating Chinese temple in the United States. The sanctuary was originally founded in 1852 by Day Ju, one of three Chinese immigrants who were the first to land in San Francisco. The temple was designed in 1911 and is now situated at the top of three steep, wooden flights of stairs, which are considered to place it closer to heaven. The narrow space is filled with the smoke from both incense and burned paper offerings, and is brightly decorated with hundreds of gold and red lanterns. It is lit by red electric light bulbs and burning wicks floating in oil. Gifts of fruit lie on the carved altar in front of the wooden statue of the temple's namesake deity.

The impressive facade of the Tien Hau Temple on Waverly Place

A view along Chinatown's main street, Grant Avenue

❺ Chinatown Alleys

Map 5 C3. 🚌 1, 30, 45.

Contained within a busy neighborhood, the Chinatown Alleys are situated between Grant Avenue and Stockton Street. These four narrow lanes intersect at Washington Street within half a block of each other. Of these, the largest is Waverly Place, known as the "Street of Painted Balconies" for reasons that are apparent to every passerby. Its other nickname, "15 Cents Street," derives from the cost of a haircut by the Chinese barbers trading here at the turn of the century. Nearby, Sun Yat-sen, first president and founding father of the Republic of China, spent many years in exile at No. 36 Spofford Alley.

The alleys contain many old buildings, as well as traditional shops and restaurants. There are also atmospheric, old-fashioned herbalist shops, displaying elk antlers, sea horses, snake wine, and other exotic wares in their windows. Numerous small restaurants, above and below street level, serve cheap and delicious home-cooked food.

❻ Grant Avenue

Map 5 C4. 🚌 1, 30, 45. 🚋 California St.

Grant Avenue is historically important for being the first street of Yerba Buena, the village that preceded San Francisco. A plaque at No. 823 marks the site of the first dwelling, a canvas tent that was erected on June 25, 1835. By 1836 the tent was replaced with a wooden structure and by 1837 with an adobe house. The street was then named Calle de la Fundacíon, the "Street of the Foundation."

An estimated 25,000 Chinese arrived in San Francisco during the Gold Rush era (see pp52–3). They settled in this area on the undesirable lower east slopes of Nob Hill, which were too steep for horse-drawn carriages. In 1885 the street was renamed Grant Avenue, in memory of Ulysses S Grant, the US president who died that year.

Most of the buildings on Grant Avenue were built after the 1906 earthquake in an Oriental Renaissance style. They now form the main tourist street in Chinatown.

Portsmouth Square, at the hub of Chinatown life

❼ Portsmouth Square

Map 5 C3. 🚌 1, 41.

San Francisco's original town square was laid out in 1839. It was once the social center for the village of Yerba Buena. On July 9, 1846, just after US rebels in Sonoma had declared California's independence from Mexico *(see pp468–9)*, Marines raised the American flag above the plaza, officially seizing the port as part of the United States. Two years later, Sam Brannan announced the discovery of gold in the Sierra Nevada Mountains *(see pp52–3)* here. In the 1850s the area was the hub of this new dynamic city, but in the 1860s the business district shifted to flatlands reclaimed from the bay and the plaza declined in civic importance.

Today Portsmouth Square is the social center of Chinatown. Children play, people practice *t'ai chi* or gather in the evening to play cards.

❽ Chinese Culture Center

750 Kearny St. **Map** 5 C3.
Tel (415) 986-1822. 🚌 1, 41.
Open 9:30am–6pm Tue–Fri,
10am–4pm Sat. ♿ 🌐 **c-c-c.org**

Founded in 1965, the Chinese Culture Center of San Francisco is located on the third floor of the luxurious hotel Hilton San Francisco Financial District. The vision of the center is to promote intercultural interests through art, education and a range of cultural events and exchange programs.

The Visual Arts Center at the site has rotating Chinese art exhibitions. The center is an ideal place for visitors to better understand and explore Chinese culture, festivals, and the Chinese zodiac.

❾ Chinese Historical Society of America

965 Clay St. **Map** 5 B4. **Tel** (415) 391-1188. 🚌 1, 30, 45. 🚋 Powell St.
Open noon–5pm Tue–Fri, 11am–4pm Sat. **Closed** public hols. 📷 📹 📱 free 1st Thu every month.
🌐 **chsa.org**

Among the exhibits in this museum are a ceremonial dragon costume and a "tiger fork." This triton was wielded in one of the battles during the reign of terror known as the Tong Wars. The tongs were rival Chinese clans who fought over the control of gambling and prostitution in the city in the late 19th century. Other objects, documents and photographs illuminate the daily life of Chinese immigrants in San Francisco. There is a yearbook of the neighborhood written in Chinese, and the original Chinatown telephone directory.

Dragon's head in the Historical Society

The contribution of the Chinese to California's development was extensive despite the antagonism and poor treatment they encountered. Chinese workers made the perilous voyage to California in their thousands to find gold and escape the economic difficulties of their homeland. Rich merchants used them as cheap labor in the gold mines, and later they were used to build the western half of the transcontinental railroad *(see pp55–5)*. They also constructed dikes in the Sacramento River delta, were pioneers in the fishing industry, and planted the first vines in many of California's early vineyards.

❿ Nob Hill

Map 5 B4.

Nob Hill is the highest summit of the city center, rising 338 ft (103 m) above the bay. Its steep slopes kept prominent citizens away until the opening of the California Street cable car line in 1878. The rich then flocked to build homes here, including the "Big Four" railroad barons *(see p54)*. Its name is thought to come from the Hindi word *nabob*, meaning governor. Sadly, all the mansions were burned down in the fire of 1906 *(see p56)*, except the home of James C Flood, now the Pacific Union Club.

Nob Hill still attracts the affluent to its splendid hotels, which benefit from spectacular views of the city.

A panoramic view of the city from a penthouse bar on Nob Hill

⓫ Cable Car Museum

1201 Mason St. **Map** 5 B3. **Tel** (415) 474-1887. ⬛ 1, 12, 30, 45, 83. ⬛ Powell–Mason, Powell–Hyde. **Open** 10am–6pm daily (Oct–Mar until 5pm). **Closed** Jan 1, Thanksgiving, Dec 25. ♿ mezzanine only. 📷 🌐 **cablecarmuseum.org**

This is both a museum and the powerhouse of the cable car system *(see pp306–7)*. Anchored to the floor are the wheels that wind the cables through the system of channels and pulleys beneath the city's streets. You can observe them from the mezzanine, then walk downstairs to see under the street. The museum also houses an early cable car and specimens of the mechanisms that control the movements of individual cars. The cable car system is the last of its kind in the world.

The entrance to the Cable Car Museum

⓬ Grace Cathedral

1100 California St. **Map** 5 B4. **Tel** (415) 749-6300. ⬛ 1. ⬛ California St. **Open** 7am–6pm Mon–Fri, 8am–6pm Sat, 7am–7pm Sun. ✝ Choral evensong: 5:15pm Thu, 3pm Sun; Choral Eucharist: 8:30am, 11am Sun. ♿ 📷 1–3pm Mon–Fri, 11:30am–1:30pm Sat, 12:30–2pm Sun. 📷 🌐 **gracecathedral.org**

Designed by Lewis P Hobart, Grace Cathedral is the mother church of the Episcopal Diocese of California and the third largest Episcopal Cathedral in the United States. Building started in 1928, but it did not near completion until 1964; the interior vaulting remains unfinished. Despite its modern construction, the building is inspired by Notre Dame in Paris, using traditional materials. The leaded windows were designed by Charles Connick, using the blue glass of Chartres as his inspiration. The rose window is made using 1-inch- (2.5-cm-) thick faceted glass, which is illuminated from inside the building at night. Other windows were executed by Henry Willet and Gabriel Loire. These include depictions of modern heroes such as Albert Einstein and astronaut John Glenn. Objects in the cathedral include a 13th-century Catalonian crucifix and a 16th-century Brussels tapestry. The entrance doors are cast from molds of Ghiberti's "Doors of Paradise," made for the Baptistry in Florence. There is an outdoor terrazo-stone labyrinth and an indoor one made of limestone.

Cast figure from the main entrance

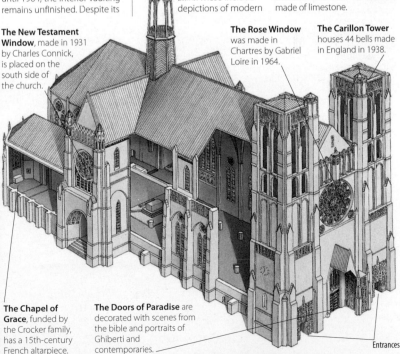

The New Testament Window, made in 1931 by Charles Connick, is placed on the south side of the church.

The Rose Window was made in Chartres by Gabriel Loire in 1964.

The Carillon Tower houses 44 bells made in England in 1938.

The Chapel of Grace, funded by the Crocker family, has a 15th-century French altarpiece.

The Doors of Paradise are decorated with scenes from the bible and portraits of Ghiberti and contemporaries.

Entrances

FISHERMAN'S WHARF AND NORTH BEACH

Fishermen from Genoa and Sicily first arrived in the Fisherman's Wharf area in the late 19th century and founded the San Francisco fishing industry. The district has slowly given way to tourism since the 1950s, but brightly painted boats still set out from the harbor on fishing trips early each morning. To the south of Fisherman's Wharf lies North Beach, sometimes known as "Little Italy." This lively part of the city has an abundance of delis, bakeries, and cafés, from which you can watch the crowds. It is home to many Italian and Chinese families, with a sprinkling of writers and bohemians; Jack Kerouac *(see p31)*, among others, found inspiration here.

Sights at a Glance

Museums and Galleries
- ❸ USS Pampanito
- ❹ Madame Tussauds™
- ❺ Ripley's Believe It or Not! Museum
- ❽ San Francisco Maritime National Historic Park
- ❿ San Francisco Art Institute
- ⓭ The Beat Museum
- ⓲ Exploratorium

Historic Streets and Buildings
- ❶ *Alcatraz Island pp342–3*
- ❷ PIER 39
- ❾ Lombard Street
- ⓫ Vallejo Street Stairway

Shopping Centers
- ❻ The Cannery
- ❼ Ghirardelli Square

Restaurants and Bars
- ⓬ Club Fugazi

Parks and Gardens
- ⓮ Washington Square
- ⓰ Telegraph Hill
- ⓱ Levi's Plaza

Churches
- ⓯ Saints Peter and Paul Church

◀ View of the crooked roads of Lombard Street

For keys to symbols *see back flap*

See also San Francisco Street Finder maps 4, 5, 6

Street-by-Street: Fisherman's Wharf

Italian seafood restaurants have now replaced fishing as the primary focus of the Fisherman's Wharf local economy. Both the expensive restaurants and the cheap outdoor crab pots serve San Francisco's celebrated Dungeness crab, in season from November to June. As well as sampling the seafood, visitors also enjoy taking in the many shops, museums, and other attractions for which Fisherman's Wharf is noted.

❸ ★ USS Pampanito
A tour gives an idea of the hardships endured by sailors in this World War II submarine.

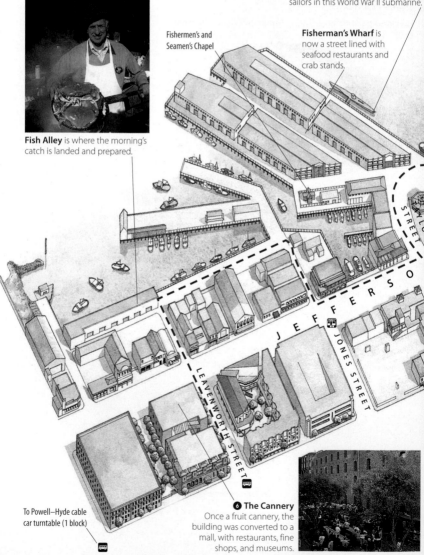

Fishermen's and Seamen's Chapel

Fisherman's Wharf is now a street lined with seafood restaurants and crab stands.

Fish Alley is where the morning's catch is landed and prepared.

JEFFERSON STREET

BEACH STREET

JONES STREET

LEAVENWORTH STREET

To Powell–Hyde cable car turntable (1 block)

❻ The Cannery
Once a fruit cannery, the building was converted to a mall, with restaurants, fine shops, and museums.

For hotels and restaurants in this area see p538 and pp566–7

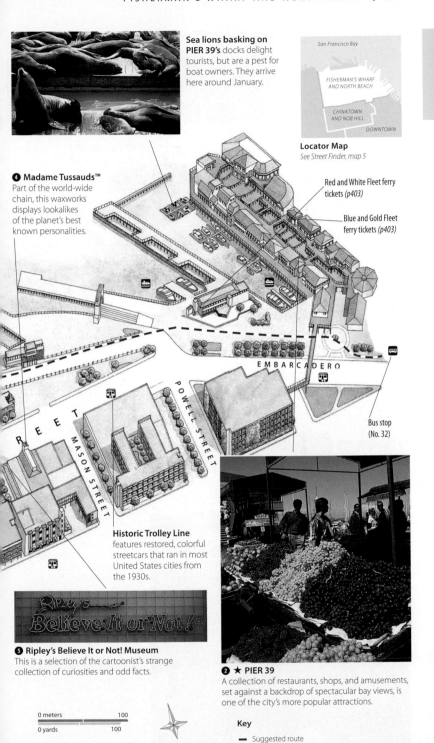

Sea lions basking on
PIER 39's docks delight
tourists, but are a pest for
boat owners. They arrive
here around January.

Locator Map
See Street Finder, map 5

San Francisco Bay

FISHERMAN'S WHARF
AND NORTH BEACH

CHINATOWN
AND NOB HILL

DOWNTOWN

❹ **Madame Tussauds™**
Part of the world-wide
chain, this waxworks
displays lookalikes
of the planet's best
known personalities.

Red and White Fleet ferry
tickets *(p403)*

Blue and Gold Fleet
ferry tickets *(p403)*

E M B A R C A D E R O

Bus stop
(No. 32)

POWELL STREET

R E E T

MASON STREET

Historic Trolley Line
features restored, colorful
streetcars that ran in most
United States cities from
the 1930s.

❺ **Ripley's Believe It or Not! Museum**
This is a selection of the cartoonist's strange
collection of curiosities and odd facts.

❷ ★ **PIER 39**
A collection of restaurants, shops, and amusements,
set against a backdrop of spectacular bay views, is
one of the city's more popular attractions.

0 meters   100
0 yards   100

Key

— Suggested route

❶ Alcatraz Island

See pp342–3.

❷ PIER 39

Map 5 B1. 25. **Open** 10am–10pm daily (but hours can vary). **W** **pier39. com** *See Shopping pp386–91.*

Refurbished in 1978 to resemble a quaint wooden fishing village, this 1905 cargo pier now houses souvenir shops and specialty stores on two levels.

The pier's street performers and amusements are popular and appeal particularly to families with children. You can ride on the two-level carousel, or visit the 7D Experience, which has a couple of exhilarating attractions.

The Dark Ride, a 20-seat theater, combines the thrill of a rollercoaster ride and the excitement of a state-of-the-art laser game. The other highlight is the Laser Maze Challenge, a game that allows visitors to test their reflexes and energy levels.

USS *Pampanito*'s torpedo room

❸ USS Pampanito

Pier 45. **Map** 4 F1. **Tel** (415) 775-1943. 8X, 47. F. **Open** 9am–6pm daily (stays open late some days; call ahead to check). **W** **maritime.org**

This World War II submarine fought in, and survived, several bloody battles in the Pacific, sinking six enemy ships and severely damaging others. Tragically for the Allies, two of its fatal targets were carrying British and Australian prisoners of war. The *Pampanito* managed to rescue 73 men, however, and carry them to safety in the US. A self-guided tour of the ship takes visitors from stern to bow

and includes visits to the torpedo room, the claustrophobic galley, and officers' quarters. In the days when the USS *Pampanito* was in service, it had a crew of 10 officers and 70 enlisted seamen.

❹ Madame Tussauds™

145 Jefferson St. **Map** 5 B1. 32. F. **Open** 10am–10pm Sun–Thu, 10am–11pm Sat; last admission 1 hour prior to closing. **W** **madametussauds. com/sanfrancisco**

After 50 years at Fisherman's Wharf, the Fong family finally closed-up their famous Wax Museum, handing the keys to the world-renowned Madame Tussauds™, which opened a fully revamped waxworks in 2014. The latest attraction is a fun, interactive, star-studded experience with numerous figures representing sports stars, music legends, TV icons, film characters, and local A-list celebrities.

The building is also home to the San Francisco Dungeon – a thrill-filled journey through the dark parts of the city's past – and the Rainforest Café with its waterfall and theme shops.

❺ Ripley's Believe It or Not! Museum

175 Jefferson St. **Map** 5 A1. **Tel** (415) 205-9850. 32, 39, 47. F. **Open** Sep–May: 10am–10pm Sun–Thu, 10am–midnight Fri & Sat; Jun–Aug: 9am–11pm Sun–Thu, 9am–midnight Fri & Sat. **W** **ripleys.com/sanfrancisco**

Californian native Robert L Ripley was an illustrator who collected peculiar facts and artifacts and earned his fame from syndicating his celebrated US newspaper cartoon strip, called "Ripley's Believe It or Not!" Among the 350 oddities on display are a cable car built of 275,000 matchsticks, a two-headed calf, tombstones with wry epithets, and a life-size replica of a man with two pupils in each eyeball.

The two-level Venetian Carousel on PIER 39

❻ The Cannery

2801 Leavenworth St. **Tel** (415) 771-3112. **Map** 4 F1. 🚌 19; 30. 🚋 Powell–Hyde. **Open** 10am–10pm Mon–Sat, 9am–10pm Sun. **Closed** Thanksgiving, Dec 25. ♿ *See Shopping pp386–91.*

The interior of this 1907 fruit-canning plant was redeveloped in the 1960s. It now incorporates footbridges, rambling passages, and sunny courtyards, with restaurants and shops selling clothing, collector dolls, and Native American arts and crafts.

Jack's Cannery Bar boasts a massive oak-paneled long hall, as well as a finely carved fireplace, both of which were brought from Europe to the United States by William Randolph Hearst in the 1920s. Of particular note is the incredible 13th-century Moorish ceiling (installed on the third floor), which came from the Palacio de Altamira in Toledo, Spain.

Ghirardelli Square

❼ Ghirardelli Square

900 North Point St. **Tel** (415) 775-5500. **Map** 4 F1. 🚌 19, 30, 47, 49. 🚋 F. **Open** 9am–11pm Sun–Thu, to midnight Fri–Sat. 🚋 Powell–Hyde. 🌐 **ghirardellisq.com** *See Shopping pp386–91.*

This former chocolate factory and woolen mill is the most attractive of the city's many refurbished sites, with shops and restaurants. The clock tower and roof sign from the original building still remain. The Ghirardelli Chocolate Manufactory on the plaza houses old chocolate-making machinery and sells the confection, but the chocolate bars are now made in San Leandro, across the bay. Fountain Plaza is a colorful focal point for shoppers, at any time of day and evening.

❽ San Francisco Maritime National Historic Park

900 Beach St at Polk St. **Map** 4 F1. 🚌 10, 19, 30, 47. 🚋 Powell–Hyde. Museum: **Tel** (415) 447-5000. **Open** 9:30am–5pm daily. 🚸 pier. ♿ pier and museum. 📷 Lectures, maritime demonstrations, activities: 🏠 🌐 **nps.gov/safr**

Resembling a beached ocean liner, the 1939 Aquatic Park Bathhouse building reopened as the Maritime Museum in 1951. On display is a collection of ship models, vintage nautical instruments, paintings, and photographs illustrating local

Hyde Street Pier

nautical history. In the lobby, visitors to the museum can also see colorful, historical murals depicting the underwater world. Moored at the

nearby Hyde Street Pier is the US's largest collection of National Historic Landmark ships. Among the most spectacular is the 1886 SS *Balclutha*, a three-masted square-rigger that rounded Cape Horn 17 times. Also at the pier is the 2,320-ton side-wheel ferryboat, *Eureka*, built in 1890 to ferry trains between Hyde Street Pier and the counties north of San Francisco Bay. It carried 2,300 passengers and 120 cars and was the largest passenger ferry of its day. In summer, the 1891 *Alma* offers 3-hour sailing ranger tours.

SS Balclutha

This ship is the star of Hyde Street Pier. Launched in 1886, she sailed twice a year between Britain and California, trading wheat for coal.

Mainmast

Mizzenmast

Quarterdeck

Foremast

Bowsprit

❶ Alcatraz Island

Alcatraz means "pelican" in Spanish and refers to the first inhabitants of this rocky, steep-sided island. Lying 3 miles (5 km) east of the Golden Gate, the windswept island's location is highly strategic. In 1859, the US Army established a fort here that guarded San Francisco Bay until 1907, when it became a military prison. From 1934 to 1963, it served as a maximum-security Federal Penitentiary. In 1969 the island was seized by members of the Native American Movement *(see p60)* claiming it as their land. They were expelled in 1971, and Alcatraz is now part of the Golden Gate National Recreation Area.

★ **Cell Block**
The cell house contains four cell blocks. No cell has an outside wall or ceiling. The dungeonlike foundation of the prison block shares the original foundation of the old military fortress.

Alcatraz Island from the Ferry
"The Rock" has no native soil. Soil was shipped from Angel Island to make garden plots.

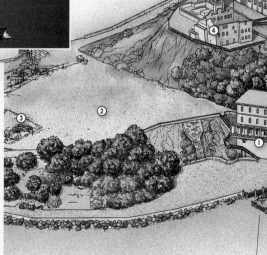

KEY

① **Barracks buildings**

② **Military parade ground**

③ **The officers' apartments** stood here.

④ **The Warden's House** was fire damaged during the 1969–71 siege.

⑤ **Alcatraz Hospital Wing**

⑥ **Metal detectors** checked prisoners when they passed to and from the dining hall and exercise yards.

⑦ **The Military Morgue** is tiny and cramped, and is not open to the public.

⑧ **Water tower**

⑨ **Prison workshops**

⑩ **Rose Terrace**

⑪ **The officers' club,** dating from the days of Fort Alcatraz, was a military store that also served as a recreation center.

⑫ **The Military Dorm** was built in 1933.

⑬ **The Officers' Row Gardens**

⑭ **The Information Center** is in the old barracks.

Alcatraz Pier
Most prisoners took their first steps ashore near this pier; no other wharf served the steep-sided island at the time. Now it is visitors that alight here.

★ **Exercise Yard**
Meals and walks around the exercise yard were the highlights of a prisoner's day. The walled yard featured in films shot at the prison.

VISITORS' CHECKLIST

Practical Information
Map 6 F1.
Tel (415) 981-7625 or online for tickets and schedules.
🌐 alcatrazcruises.com
Open daily. **Closed** Jan 1, Dec 25.
Night tours: (Thu–Mon) call (415) 561-4926. 🚻 📷 🎧 free with ticket. No restaurant or café.

Transport
🚢 from Pier 33

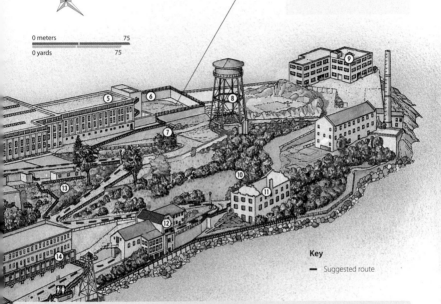

0 meters 75
0 yards 75

Key
— Suggested route

Famous Inmates

Al Capone

The Prohibition gangster, "Scarface" Capone was actually convicted in 1934 for income tax evasion. He spent much of his five-year sentence on Alcatraz in an isolation cell, and left the prison mentally unstable.

Robert Stroud

The original *"Birdman of Alcatraz"* spent all of his 17 years on The Rock in solitary confinement.

Carnes, Thompson, and Shockley
In May 1946, prisoners led by Clarence Carnes, Marion Thompson, and Sam Shockley overpowered guards and captured their guns. The prisoners failed to break out of the cell house, but three inmates and two officers were killed in what became known as the "Battle of Alcatraz." Carnes received an additional life sentence, and Shockley and Thompson were executed at San Quentin prison for their part in the insurrection.

Anglin Brothers

Brothers John and Clarence Anglin, together with Frank Morris, chipped through the walls of their cells, and hid the holes with cardboard grates. On June 11, 1962, they made their move. Leaving dummy heads in their beds, they climbed up the ventilation shafts on to the roof and paddled away in a handcrafted raft. They were never caught. Their story was dramatized in the film *Escape from Alcatraz* (1979).

Cars negotiating the steep and crooked section of Lombard Street

❾ Lombard Street

Map 5 A2. 🚌 45. 🚋 Powell–Hyde.

Banked at a natural incline of 27°, this hill proved too steep for vehicles to climb. In the 1920s the section of Lombard Street close to the summit of Russian Hill was revamped, and the severity of its gradient was lessened by the addition of eight curves.

Today it is known as "the crookedest street in the world." Cars can travel downhill at a speed of only 5 miles per hour (8 km/h), while pedestrians use steps. There are spectacular views of San Francisco from the summit.

❿ San Francisco Art Institute

800 Chestnut St. **Map** 4 F2.
Tel (415) 771-7020. 🚌 30, 45, 91.
Diego Rivera Gallery: **Open** 9am–5pm daily. **Closed** public hols. ♿ partial.
📷 🄳 🆆 **sanfranciscoart institute.org**

San Francisco's Art Institute dates from 1871 and once occupied the immense wooden

A 30-Minute Walk through North Beach

Settlers originally from Chile, and more recently Italy, have brought their enthusiasm for nightlife to North Beach, earning this quarter its vibrant reputation. Its café-oriented atmosphere has long appealed to bohemians, particularly the 1950s Beat Generation *(see p31)*.

The Beat Neighborhood

Start the walk from the southwest corner of Broadway and Columbus Avenue at City Lights Bookstore ①. Owned by Beat poet Lawrence Ferlinghetti, City Lights was the first bookshop in the US to sell paperbacks exclusively. The author Jack Kerouac, a friend of Ferlinghetti, coined the word "Beat," later referred to as "Beatnik."

One of the most popular Beat bars was Vesuvio ②, south of City Lights, across Jack Kerouac Alley. Welsh poet Dylan Thomas was a patron here, and it is still a favorite with poets and artists.

From here go south to Pacific Avenue, cross to the opposite side of Columbus Avenue and walk back toward Broadway, stopping at Tosca ③. The walls of this bar and café display murals of Tuscany, and a jukebox plays selections from Italian opera. A few steps north bring you to Adler Alley. Specs ④, a lively bar filled with memorabilia of the Beat era, is at No. 12. Walking back to Columbus Avenue, turn right into Broadway and at the corner of Kearny Street cross over to Naked Lunch ⑤.

Jack Kerouac

⑪ Columbus Café

The Strip

Naked Lunch, the inheritors of Enrico's Sidewalk Café's fêted space, is the best place from which to watch the action on The Strip ⑥, a stretch of Broadway noted for its "adult entertainment." At the junction with Grant Avenue is the former Condor Club ⑦, where the world's first topless stage show was performed in June 1964.

mansion built for the family of railroad baron Mark Hopkins on Nob Hill *(see p334)*, which burned down in the fire of 1906 *(see pp56)*. Today it is housed in a Spanish Colonial-style building that was constructed in 1926, complete with cloisters, a courtyard fountain, and bell tower. A modern extension was added at the rear of the building in 1969. The Diego Rivera Gallery, named after the famous Mexican muralist, sits to the left of the main entrance.

The Institute holds temporary exhibitions of works, from contemporary photography to design and technology.

Diego Rivera's *Making of a Fresco* (1931), San Francisco Art Institute

⓫ Vallejo Street Stairway

Mason St and Jones St. **Map** 5 B3. 🚌 30, 45. 🚃 Powell–Mason.

The steep climb from Little Italy to the summit of Russian Hill reveals some of the best views of Telegraph Hill, North Beach, and the bay. The street gives way to steps at Mason Street, which climb up through Ina Coolbrith Park.

Above Taylor Street, there are lanes, with several Victorian houses *(see pp304–5)*. At the crest of the hill is one of the rare parts of the city not destroyed in the earthquake of 1906 *(see pp56)*.

⓬ Club Fugazi

678 Beach Blanket Babylon Blvd. **Map** 5 B3. **Tel** (415) 421-4222. 🚌 8AX, 8BX, 10, 12, 30, 39, 41, 45. 🚃 Powell–Mason. **Open** Wed–Sun. 🔲 **beachblanket babylon.com** *See Entertainment 394–9.*

Built in 1912 as a North Beach community hall, the Club Fugazi is the venue for the musical cabaret

Beach Blanket Babylon. This is a lively show that has been running for more than two decades and has become an institution among San Franciscans. It is popular with locals and tourists alike, and is famous for its outrageous songs and the bizarre hats often worn by the performers.

⓭ The Beat Museum

540 Broadway **Map** 5 C3. **Tel** (800) 537-6822. 🚌 30, 41, 45. **Open** 10am–7pm daily. 🔲 **thebeatmuseum.org**

Celebrating the Beat Movement of 1950s San Francisco *(see p31)*, this "museum" showcases everyone and everything linked to the phenomenon. With references galore to Allen Ginsberg's *Howl* poem, including a warning of an emergency exit that will "howl" if opened, the museum's collection features letters, photos, magazine and newspaper clippings, books, and album covers.

Upper Grant Avenue
Turn right into Grant Avenue where you will find The Saloon ⑧ with its original 1861 bar. On the corner of Vallejo Street is Caffè Trieste ⑨, the oldest coffee house in San Francisco, and

a genuine Beat rendezvous since 1956. Very much a part of Italian-American culture, it offers live opera on Saturday afternoons. Follow Grant Avenue north past Maggie McGarry's Pub ⑩, now an Irish pub but formerly the Coffee Gallery, another of the Beat haunts. Turn left at Green Street and look for Columbus Café ⑪, whose

② Vesuvio, a popular Beat bar

exterior walls are decorated with attractive murals. Turning left again at Columbus Avenue, follow this main street of North Beach south past many more Italian coffee houses, to return to your starting point.

Tips for Walkers

Starting point: Corner of Broadway and Columbus Avenue.
Length: 1 mile (1.6 km).
Getting there: Muni bus No. 15 runs along Columbus Avenue.
Stopping-off points: All the bars and cafés mentioned are worth visiting for a drink and the atmosphere. Children are not usually allowed in bars.

Key

●●● Walk route

| 0 meters | 200 |
| 0 yards | 200 |

The facade of Saints Peter and Paul Church, Washington Square

a complex interior notable for its many columns and ornate altar. There are also statues and mosaics illuminated by stained-glass windows. The concrete and steel structure of the church, with its twin spires rising over the surrounding rooftops, was completed in 1924.

Cecil B DeMille filmed the workers laying the church's foundations and used the scene to show the building of the Temple of Jerusalem in his film *The Ten Commandments*, made in 1923.

The church is sometimes referred to as the Fishermen's Church (many Italians once earned their living by fishing), and there is an annual mass and procession from Columbus Avenue to Fisherman's Wharf to celebrate the Blessing of the Fleet in October. Masses in the church can still be heard in Italian, and also Cantonese.

⑯ Telegraph Hill

Map 5 C2. Coit Tower: Telegraph Hill Blvd. **Tel** (415) 362-0808. 🚌 39. **Open** 10am–6pm daily (until 5pm Nov–Apr). 🚫 ♿ murals only. 📷 🌐 **coittowertours.com**

Originally called Alta Loma by the Mexicans, then Goat Hill after the animals that grazed on its slopes, Telegraph Hill was renamed in 1850 after the semaphore installed on its crest. This alerted the city's merchants to the arrival of ships through the Golden Gate. On the eastern side, which, until 1914, was regularly dynamited to provide

⑭ Washington Square

Map 5 B2. 🚌 8BX, 8X, 30, 39, 41, 45, 91. 🚋 Powell–Mason.

The square consists of a simple expanse of lawn, surrounded by benches and trees, set against the twin towers of Saints Peter and Paul Church. It has an almost Mediterranean atmosphere, appropriate for the "town square" of Little Italy. Near the center of the square stands a statue of Benjamin Franklin. A time capsule was buried under the statue in 1979 and is scheduled to be reopened in 2079. It is said to contain some Levi's jeans, a bottle of wine, and a poem written by Lawrence Ferlinghetti, one of San Francisco's famous Beat poets *(see p31)*.

⑮ Saints Peter and Paul Church

666 Filbert St. **Map** 5 B2. **Tel** (415) 421-0809. 🚌 8X, 30, 39, 45. 🚋 Powell–Mason. **Open** 7:30am–4pm Mon–Fri daily. ✝ call or check website for mass times. ♿ 🌐 **sspeterpaulsf. org/church**

Still known by many as the Italian Cathedral, this large church is situated at the heart of North Beach, and many Italians find it a welcome haven when they first arrive in San Francisco. It was here that the local baseball hero, Joe Di Maggio, was photographed after his marriage to the actress Marilyn Monroe in 1957, although the actual wedding ceremony was held elsewhere. The building, designed by Charles Fantoni, has an Italianesque facade, with

Coit Tower mural showing Fisherman's Wharf in the 1930s

For hotels and restaurants in this area see p538 and pp566–7

Steps at the bottom of Filbert Street leading up to Telegraph Hill

rocks for landfill and paving, the hill falls away abruptly to form steep paths, bordered by leafy gardens.

The western side slopes more gradually into the area known as "Little Italy," around Washington Square, although in recent years the city's Italian population has begun to settle in the Marina District. In the past the hill has been a neighborhood of immigrants and struggling artists; these days, however, the quaint pastel clapboard homes are much sought after, and this is now one of the city's prime residential areas.

The 210-ft (64-m) reinforced concrete **Coit Tower** was built in 1933 at the top of the hill with funds left to the city by Lillie Hitchcock Coit, an eccentric San Franciscan pioneer and philanthropist. The encircling view around the North Bay Area from the observation platform (reached by an elevator) is quite spectacular.

In the lobby of the tower are absorbing murals (see pp310–11). These were sponsored in 1934 by a government-funded program designed to keep artists in employment during the Great Depression. Twenty-five artists worked together on the vivid portrait of life in modern California. Many of the faces in the paintings are those of the artists and their friends, along with local figures such as Colonel William Brady, the caretaker of Coit Tower. The work's political subject matter caused some public controversy and delayed its official unveiling.

⓲ Levi's Plaza

Map 5 C2. 🚌 10, 12, 39, 42, F.

This square is where the head-quarters of Levi Strauss & Co., the manufacturers of blue jeans, can be found. The square was landscaped by Lawrence Halprin in 1982, with the intention of recalling the company's long history in the state. The plaza is studded with granite rocks and cut by flowing water, symbolizing the Sierra Nevada canyon scenery in which the miners who first wore the jeans worked.

⓲ Exploratorium

Pier 15. Map 6 D2. Tel (415) 528-4444. 🚋 F. 🚇 Embarcadero. 🚢 Golden Gate Ferry. Open 10am–5pm Tue–Sun; 6–10pm Thu for over 18s. 🚭 ♿ 🌐 exploratorium.edu

Exploratorium, one of the most entertaining science museums in the United States, moved to Pier 15 on the Embarcadero in 2013, tripling its exhibition space. Opened in 1969 at the Palace of Fine Arts by physicist and educator Frank Oppenheimer (who worked alongside his brother J Robert Oppenheimer on the Manhattan Project), Exploratorium was a ground-breaking museum pioneering hands-on and experiential education and exhibits.

Today, Exploratorium keeps the original focus on interactivity, with more than 600 hands-on exhibits exploring biology, physics, cognition, the environment, and more. Exhibits include a chance to look through a research-grade microscope to consider stem-cell biology and other developments, and a monochromatic room where all color disappears. A whole gallery is dedicated to the art of tinkering – building playful contraptions and exploring mechanical systems. The museum's Outdoor Gallery considers the Bay, tides, and the urban habitat.

Levi Strauss and His Jeans

First manufactured in San Francisco in the days of the Gold Rush (see pp52–3), denim jeans have had a great impact on popular culture, and they are just as popular today as they were when they first appeared. Levi Strauss & Co., founded in the city in the 1860s, is still one of the leading producers of jeans.

The company's story started in 1853, when Levi Strauss left New York to establish a dry goods business with his brother-in-law in San Francisco. In the 1860s, though still primarily a seller of dry goods, he pioneered the use of a

Levi Strauss

durable, brown, canvaslike material to make work trousers, sold directly to miners. In the 1870s his company began to use metal rivets to strengthen the stress points in the garments, and demand increased. The company then expanded, and early in the 20th century it moved to 250 Valencia Street in the Mission District. Levi's jeans are now an institution, and are produced, sold, and worn all over the world.

The company that was first founded by Levi Strauss is still owned and managed by his descendants.

Two miners sporting their Levis at the Last Chance Mine in 1882

PACIFIC HEIGHTS AND THE CIVIC CENTER

Pacific Heights is an exclusive neighborhood, rising 300 ft (90 m) above the city. After cable cars linked it with the city center in the 1880s, it quickly became a desirable place to live, and fine Victorian houses now line its streets. To the north of Broadway, the streets drop steeply down to the Marina District, with its smart shops, fashionable cafés, and two prestigious yacht clubs. To the south of Pacific Heights is the Civic Center, which was built after the earthquake of 1906. It includes some of the best Beaux-Arts architecture in the city and was declared a historic site in 1987. The Civic Center is perhaps one of the most elegant city complexes built in the US.

Sights at a Glance

Historic Streets and Buildings
1 Haas-Lilienthal House
2 Spreckels Mansion
5 Palace of Fine Art
6 Wave Organ
8 Fort Mason
10 Cow Hollow
11 Octagon House
15 Asian Art Museum
16 Bill Graham Civic Auditorium
17 City Hall
19 Alamo Square
20 University of San Francisco

Shopping Areas
9 Chestnut Street
12 Fillmore Street
18 Hayes Valley

Modern Architecture
13 Japan Center

Churches
14 Cathedral of St. Mary of the Assumption

Parks and Gardens
3 Lafayette Park
4 Alta Plaza
7 Marina Green

See also San Francisco Street Finder maps 3, 4

◄ San Francisco's City Hall, built in Beaux-Arts style in 1915

For keys to symbols *see back flap*

Street-by-Street: Pacific Heights

The steep blocks between Alta Plaza and Lafayette Park are set in the heart of the exclusive Pacific Heights district. The streets here are quiet and tidy, lined with stylish apartment blocks and palatial Victorian houses. Some of these date from the late 19th century, while others were built after the great earthquake and fire of 1906 *(see pp56)*. To the north of this area, the streets drop steeply down toward the residential Marina District and offer outstanding views of San Francisco Bay. Wander through the two large landscaped parks and past the luxurious gardens of the private mansions in between, then visit one of the many fashionable bars, cafés, and restaurants along Fillmore Street.

The Webster Street Row houses have been declared a historic landmark. They were built for a middle-class clientele in 1878 and have since been restored to their original splendor.

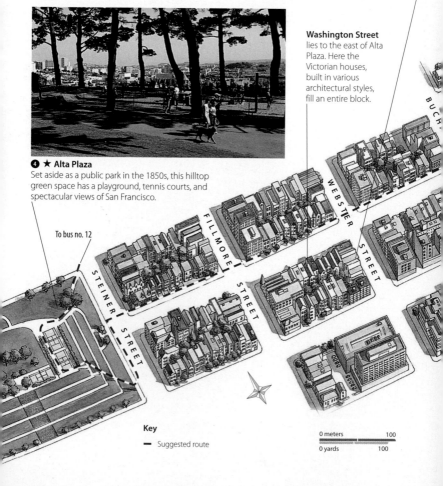

Washington Street lies to the east of Alta Plaza. Here the Victorian houses, built in various architectural styles, fill an entire block.

❹ ★ **Alta Plaza**
Set aside as a public park in the 1850s, this hilltop green space has a playground, tennis courts, and spectacular views of San Francisco.

To bus no. 12

Key

— Suggested route

0 meters 100
0 yards 100

❶ Haas-Lilienthal House
Furnished in Victorian style, this mansion is the headquarters of San Francisco Architectural Heritage.

Locator Map
See San Francisco Street Finder, maps 3, 4

To bus nos. 47, 76

No. 2151 Sacramento Street is an ornate French-style mansion. A plaque commemorates a visit by the author Sir Arthur Conan Doyle in 1923.

❸ Lafayette Park
This quiet park offers good views of the Victorian houses that surround it.

❷ ★ Spreckels Mansion
This impressive limestone building, constructed on the lines of a French Baroque palace, has been home to best-selling novelist Danielle Steele since 1990.

No. 2004 Gough Street, one of the more elaborate Victorian houses in Pacific Heights, was built in 1889.

The Haas-Lilienthal House, a Queen Anne mansion from 1886

❶ Haas-Lilienthal House

2007 Franklin St. **Map** 4 E3.
Tel (415) 441-3004. 🚌 1, 12, 19, 27, 47, 49, 76X, 83, 90. **Open** noon–3pm Wed & Sat, 11am–4pm Sun (times may vary so call ahead). 🚶 📷
W sfheritage.org/haas-lilienthal-house

This attractive Queen Anne-style mansion (see pp304–5) was built in 1886 for the rich merchant William Haas. Alice Lilienthal, his daughter, lived here until 1972, when it was given to the Foundation for San Francisco's Architectural Heritage. It is the only intact private home of the period in San Francisco, now open as a museum, and it is complete, with authentic furniture. A fine example of an upper-middle-class Victorian home, it has elaborate wooden gables and luxurious ornamentation.

A display of photographs in the basement describes the history of the building and reveals that this grandiose house was modest in comparison with some of the mansions destroyed in the great fire of 1906 (see p56).

❷ Spreckels Mansion

2080 Washington St. **Map** 4 E3.
🚌 1, 47, 49. **Closed** to the public.

Dominating the north side of Lafayette Park, this imposing Beaux-Arts mansion is sometimes known as the

"Parthenon of the West." It was built in 1912 for the flamboyant Alma de Bretteville Spreckels and her husband, Adolph, heir to the sugar fortune of Claus Spreckels (see p362). The house contains 26 bathrooms, and a large swimming pool in which Alma Spreckels swam daily until the age of 80. Her love of French architecture inspired the design. The architect of Spreckels mansion was George Applegarth, who in 1916 also designed the California Palace of the Legion of Honor in Lincoln Park (see pp378–9). The Palace was donated to the city by Alma and Adolph Spreckels in 1924.

Today Spreckels Mansion is privately owned. It occupies a whole block of Octavia Street, which is paved and landscaped in a similar style to curvy Lombard Street (see p344).

Facade of the impressive Spreckels Mansion

❸ Lafayette Park

Map 4 E3. 🚌 1, 10, 12, 47, 49.
W sfrecpark.org

One of San Francisco's prettiest hilltop gardens, Lafayette Park is a leafy green haven of pine and eucalyptus trees, although its present tranquillity belies its turbulent history. Along with Alta Plaza and Alamo Square (see p357) the land was set aside in 1855 as a city-owned open space. Then squatters and others, including a former City Attorney, laid claim to the land and began to build their houses on it. The largest of these houses remained standing at the center of the hilltop park until 1936, the squatter who had built it refusing to move. It was finally demolished after the city authorities agreed to swap it for other land on nearby Gough Street. Steep stairways now lead to the summit of the park and its delightful views.

In the streets surrounding Lafayette Park there are a number of other palatial Victorian buildings. Particularly ornate examples are situated along Broadway, Jackson Street, and Pacific Avenue going east–west, and Gough, Octavia, and Laguna streets going north–south.

❹ Alta Plaza

Map 4 D3. 🚌 1, 3, 10, 12, 22, 24.
W sfrecpark.org

Situated in the center of Pacific Heights, Alta Plaza is a land-scaped urban park, where the San Franciscan elite come to relax. Once the site of a quarry, Alta Plaza's nearly 12 acres (5 hectares) were purchased by the city in 1877. Although the park was established in 1888, nothing was done to improve the site and, like nearby Lafayette Park, it served as a campsite for refugees from the 1906 earthquake and fire. By 1910, John McLaren (see p373), superintendent of Golden Gate Park, had taken charge and was landscaping Alta Plaza. He added the terracing – much admired today – rather reluctantly, seeing no other way

Relaxing in the peaceful Alta Plaza park

to plant and stabilize the excessively steep slopes.

The stone steps rising up from Clay Street on the south side of the park offer good views of Haight Ashbury (see pp358–67), the Fillmore district, and Twin Peaks (see p367). The steps may be familiar to film buffs – Barbra Streisand drove down them in What's Up Doc? There are also tennis courts and a playground.

From the north side of the park some splendid Victorian mansions are visible, including Gibbs House, at No. 2622 Jackson Street, built by Willis Polk in 1894. Smith House, at No. 2600 Jackson Street, was one of the first houses in San Francisco to be supplied with electricity in the 1890s.

❺ Palace of Fine Arts

3601 Lyon St. **Map** 3 C2. **Tel** (415) 831 2700 (Palace Theatre). 🚌 22, 28, 29, 30, 43, 45, 47, 49. 🌐 **palaceoffine arts.org**

Sole survivor of the many grandiose monuments built as part of the 1915 Panama-California Exposition, the Palace of Fine Arts is a Neo-Classical folly that today houses an auditorium with capacity for 1,000 spectators. The Palace of Fine Arts was designed by the architect Bernard R Maybeck, who drew inspiration from the drawings of the Italian architect Piranesi and by the painting L'Isle des Morts by Swiss artist, Arnold Böcklin. Originally built of wood and plaster, the Palace eventually began to crumble, until one concerned citizen began to raise funds for its reconstruction in 1959. It was restored to its original splendor between 1962 and 1968 using reinforced concrete.

The central feature is the rotunda, perched on the edge of a landscaped, swan-filled lagoon. Its dome is decorated with allegorical paintings, all of which depict the defense of art against materialism. On top of the many Corinthian columns are nymphs with bent heads – symbolic of the "melancholy of life without art."

❻ Wave Organ

1 Yacht Rd. **Map** 4 D1. 🚌 30. 🌐 **exploratorium.edu**

Sitting at the tip of the breakwater that protects the Marina is the world's most peculiar musical instrument. Built by scientists from the Exploratorium (see p347), the Wave Organ consists of a number of underwater pipes that echo and hum with the changing tides. Listening tubes are imbedded in a mini-amphitheater that has views of Pacific Heights and the Presidio. The sounds you hear are more like gurgling plumbing than organ music.

Wave Organ acoustic sculpture

Classical rotunda of the Palace of Fine Arts

Panama-California Exposition

In 1915 San Francisco celebrated its successful recovery from the 1906 earthquake and fire with a monumental fair. Officially, it was intended to celebrate the opening of the Panama Canal, and was designed to be the most splendid world's fair ever held. Its grand structures were indeed described by one highly enthusiastic visitor as "a miniature Constantinople."

The halls and pavilions of the fair were constructed on land reclaimed from San Francisco Bay, on the site of today's Marina District. They were donated by all the states and by 25 foreign countries, and lined a concourse 1 mile (1.6 km) long. Many of the buildings were based on such architectural gems as a Turkish mosque and a Buddhist temple from Kyoto. The brilliant Tower of Jewels, at the center of the concourse, was encrusted with glass beads and lit by spotlights. To the west stands the beautiful Palace of Fine Arts, which visitors reached by gondola across a landscaped lagoon.

❼ Marina Green

Map 4 D1. 🚌 22, 28, 30.

A long thin strip of lawn running the length of the Marina District, Marina Green is popular with kite-flyers and picnickers, especially on the Fourth of July, when the city's fireworks display can be seen from here. Paths along the waterfront are the city's prime spots for cyclists, joggers, and skaters. Golden Gate Promenade leads from the west end of the green to Fort Point, or you can turn east to the Wave Organ at the end of the harbor jetty.

❾ Chestnut Street

Map 4 D1. 🚌 22, 28, 30, 43.

The main shopping and night-life center of the Marina District, Chestnut Street has a varied mix of movie theaters, markets, coffee houses, and restaurants, catering more to the local residents than to visitors. The strip stretches just a few blocks from Fillmore Street west to Divisadero Street, after which the neighborhood becomes residential in character.

❿ Cow Hollow

Map 4 D2. 🚌 22, 41, 45.

Cow Hollow is a shopping district along Union Street. It is so called because it was used as grazing land for the city's dairy cows up until the 1860s. It was then taken over for development and turned into a residential neighborhood. In the 1950s the area became fashionable, and chic boutiques, antique shops, and art galleries took over the old neighborhood stores. Many of these are in restored 19th-century buildings, lending an old-fashioned air to the district, in stark contrast to the sophistication of the merchandise on display.

Union Street itself has more than 300 boutiques, and open-air arts, crafts, and food fairs are held regularly in the area.

View from Fillmore Street, overlooking Cow Hollow

❽ Fort Mason

Map 4 E1. **Tel** (415) 441-3400. Events: 441-3400. 🚌 22, 28, 30, 42, 43. ♿ partial. 🌐 **fortmason.org**

Fort Mason reflects the military history of San Francisco. The original buildings were private houses, built in the late 1850s, which were confiscated by the US Government when the site was taken over by the US army during the American Civil War (1861–5).

The Fort was an army command post until the 1890s. It later housed refugees whose homes had been destroyed in the 1906 earthquake *(see p56)*. During World War II, it was the embarkation point for around 1.6 million soldiers.

The Fort was converted to peaceful use in 1972 although some of the white-painted mid-19th-century buildings still house military personnel. Other buildings, however, are open to the public. These include the original barracks, and the old hospital, which serves as

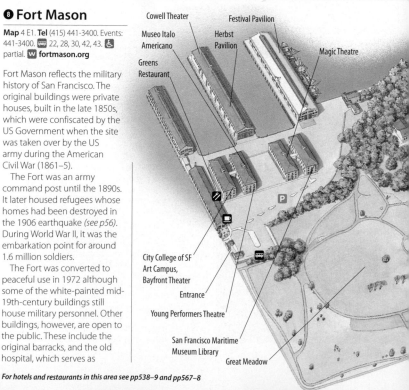

Cowell Theater

Festival Pavilion

Museo Italo Americano

Herbst Pavilion

Magic Theatre

Greens Restaurant

City College of SF Art Campus, Bayfront Theater

Entrance

Young Performers Theatre

San Francisco Maritime Museum Library

Great Meadow

For hotels and restaurants in this area see pp538–9 and pp567–8

⓫ Octagon House

2645 Gough St. **Map** 4 E2. **Tel** (415) 441-7512. 🚌 10, 41, 42, 45, 47, 49, 70, 80, 90. **Open** noon–3pm on 2nd Sun and 2nd & 4th Thu of the month, except Jan. Donation: ✉ ♿ limited.
🌐 **nscda-ca.org/octagon-house**

Built by William C McElroy in 1861, the Octagon House, with its eight-sided cupola, is a well-preserved example of a house style that was once popular throughout the United States. Now run by the Colonial Dames of America, the first floor has been opened up into one large room, and this and the second floor house a small but engaging collection of decorative arts as well as historic documents of the Colonial and Federal periods of the United States. Among the exhibits are furniture, paintings, porcelain, silver, pewter, samplers, playing cards from the American Revolutionary era, and signatures of 54 of the 56 signatories to the Declaration of Independence.

Octagon House's cupola ensures sunlight in each room

⓬ Fillmore Street

Map 4 D4. 🚌 1, 2, 3, 22, 24.

Fillmore Street managed to survive the 1906 earthquake and fire virtually intact, so for several years afterward it was forced to serve as the civic heart of the ruined city. Government departments, as well as several independent businesses, were housed in local shops, homes, and even churches. Today the main commercial district linking Pacific Heights and the Civic Center is located here, from Jackson Street to the outskirts of the Japan Center (see p356) around Bush Street. This area is filled with fine bookstores, fashionable restaurants, and exclusive boutiques.

San Francisco
Fisherman's
Wharf Hostel

Fort Mason
Officers' Club

Chapel

Visitors'
Center

Golden Gate National
Recreation Area
headquarters

a Visitors' Center and as the headquarters of the Golden Gate National Recreation Area (GGNRA). Besides being rich in history and culture, Fort Mason offers some of the city's finest views, looking across the bay toward Golden Gate Bridge (see pp384–5) and Alcatraz Island (see pp342–3). Starting from the west gate of the Fort, Golden Gate Promenade winds eastward to Aquatic Park and then to Fisherman's Wharf (see pp338–9).

Fort Mason Center

Part of the Fort is now occupied by one of San Francisco's major art complexes. The Fort Mason Center houses over 25 cultural organizations, which include art galleries, museums, and theaters, such as the Cowell Theater and BATS Improv at the Bayfront Theater. Italian and Italian-American artists display their works at the

Museo Italo Americano. The Magic Theatre is an experimental theater, and the Young Performers Theatre is a playhouse for children. The Maritime Library holds a wonderful collection of books, oral histories, and ships' plans. The Maritime Museum itself is located near Fisherman's Wharf (see p341).

The Fort Mason Center produces a monthly calendar of current events. Call the Events Line or visit their website for more information.

The SS *Balclutha*, at Hyde Street Pier, part of the Maritime Museum

For keys to symbols *see back flap*

The pagoda in the Japan Center's Peace Plaza

⓭ Japan Center

Geary, Post, Fillmore & Laguna Sts.
Map 4 E4. 🚌 2, 3, 38. **Open** 10am–
8pm Mon–Sat, 11am–7pm Sun
(restaurants stay open later).
🔲 sfjapantown.org

The Japan Center was built
as part of an ambitious 1960s
scheme to revitalize the Fillmore
District. Many blocks of aging
Victorian houses were demolished and replaced by the
Geary Expressway and the large
shopping complex of the Japan
Center. The neighborhood, now
known as Japantown, has been
the heart of the Japanese
community for some 75 years.

At the heart of the complex,
and centered upon a five-tiered,
75-ft (22-m) concrete pagoda,
is the remodeled Peace Plaza.
Taiko drummers and others
perform here at the Cherry
Blossom festival each April. Each
side of the pagoda is a mall with
shops, sushi bars, bathhouses,
and *Shiatsu* massage centers,
all modeled on Tokyo's Ginza
district. One of the city's best
movie theaters, the Sundance
Kabuki Cinema *(see p394)*, is also
here. More Japanese shops line
the open-air mall across Post
Street, flanked by twin steel
sculptures by Ruth Asawa.

⓮ Cathedral of St. Mary of the Assumption

1111 Gough St. **Map** 4 E4. **Tel** (415) 567-
2020. 🚌 2, 3, 31, 38. **Open** 8:30am–
5pm Mon–Fri, 9am–5:30pm Sat, 9am–
5pm Sun. 🕆 6:45am, 8am, 12:10pm
Mon–Fri, 6:45am, 8am, 5:30pm Sat,
7:30am, 9am, 11am, 1pm (in Spanish)
Sun. ♿ 🔲 stmarycathedralsf.org

Situated at the summit of
Cathedral Hill, St. Mary's is
one of San Francisco's most
prominent architectural
landmarks. Designed by Pietro
Belluschi and Pier Luigi Nervi,
it was completed in 1971.

The four-part arching
paraboloid roof stands out like
a white-sailed ship. The 200-ft-
(60-m-) high concrete structure,
which seems to hover
effortlessly above the nave,
supports the cross-shaped
stained-glass ceiling. A canopy
of aluminum rods sparkles
above the altar.

⓯ Asian Art Museum

200 Larkin St. **Map** 4 F5. **Tel** (415) 581-
3500. 🚌 5, 8, 19, 21, 26, 31, 47, 49.
🚋 F, J, K, L, M, N. 🚇 Civic Center.
Open 10am–5pm Tue–Sun (9pm
Thu). **Closed** public hols. 🎟 free 1st
Sun every month. ♿ 🗐 🏠 ▢
🔲 asianart.org

The Asian Art
Museum is located
in a building that
was the crown jewel
of the Beaux Arts
movement. The
former Main Library,
built in 1917,
underwent seismic
strengthening and
the original space
has been reused to
create the largest
museum outside
Asia devoted purely
to Asian art. The
museum's holdings
include 17,000 art
objects spanning
6,000 years of
history and
representing more
than 40 Asian

nations. Among the highlights
is a gilt-bronze Buddha, one of
the oldest Chinese Buddhas in
the world. The museum also
offers a diverse range of
programs for all ages.

⓰ Bill Graham Civic Auditorium

99 Grove St. **Map** 4 F5. **Tel** (415) 624-
8900. 🚌 5, 19, 21, 47, 49, 71. 🚋 J, K, L,
M, N. 🚇 Civic Center.

Designed in Beaux Arts style by
architect John Galen Howard,
the city's Civic Auditorium was
opened in 1915 and has since
become one of San Francisco's
major performance venues. It
was inaugurated by the French
pianist and composer Camille
Saint-Saëns. The building was
completed along with City Hall,
during the architectural
renaissance that followed the
great earthquake and fire of
1906 *(see p56)*. It was built,
together with the adjoining
Brooks Exhibit Hall, beneath the
Civic Center Plaza.

The civic auditorium now
serves as the city's main
conference center, and
seats 7,000 people. In 1964
its name was changed in
honor of Bill Graham
(see p363), the local rock
music impresario.

Grand staircase in the Asian Art Museum

The imposing facade of City Hall in San Francisco's Civic Center

⓱ City Hall

400 Van Ness Ave. **Map** 4 F5. **Tel** (415) 554-4000. 🚌 5, 8, 19, 21, 26, 47, 49, 71. 🚇 J, K, L, M, N. **Open** 8am–5pm Mon–Fri. ♿ 📷 🌐 **sfgov.org**

City Hall, completed in 1915, just in time for the Panama-Pacific Exposition *(see p353)*, was designed by the architect Arthur Brown at the height of his career. Its grand Baroque dome was modeled after St. Peter's Basilica in Rome and is higher than that of the United States Capitol in Washington, DC.

The renovated building stands at the heart of the Civic Center complex, and is a magnificent example of the Beaux Arts style. Allegorical figures evoking the city's Gold Rush past fill the pediment above the Polk Street entrance, which leads into the rotunda, one of the city's finest interior spaces.

⓲ Hayes Valley

Map 4 E5. 🚌 21, 22.

Situated west of City Hall, these few blocks of Hayes Street have become one of San Francisco's trendier shopping districts. After US 101 highway was damaged in the 1989 Loma Prieta earthquake *(see p509)* the road was demolished. The former highway had previously divided Hayes Valley from the wealthy power-brokers and theatergoers who frequented the rest of the Civic Center. A small number of adventurous cafés and restaurants, such as Ivy's and Mad Magda's Russian Tea Room, had already established themselves alongside Hayes Street's second-hand furniture and reject shops. Today an influx of art galleries, interior design shops, trendy cafés, and unique boutiques has made the area noticeably more stylish.

View from Alamo Square toward the Downtown skyscrapers

⓳ Alamo Square

Map 4 D5. 🚌 21, 22.

The most photographed row of Victorian houses in the city lines the eastern side of this sloping green square. It is set 225 ft (68 m) above the Civic Center, offering great views of City Hall and the Downtown skyscrapers. The square was laid out at the same time as the beautiful squares in Pacific Heights, but it developed later, with speculators building nearly identical houses.

The "Six Sisters" Queen Anne-style houses built in 1895 at 710–20 Steiner Street, on the east side of the square, appear on numerous postcards of San Francisco. The city has now declared the area to be a historic district.

⓴ University of San Francisco

2130 Fulton St. **Map** 3 B5. **Tel** (415) 422-5555. 🚌 5, 31, 33, 38, 43. **Open** 8am–5pm Mon–Fri. 🌐 **usfca.edu**

Originally founded in 1855 as St. Ignatius College, the University of San Francisco (USF) remains a Jesuit-run institution, though classes are now coeducational and non-denominational. The landmark of the campus is the St. Ignatius Church, completed in 1914. Its buff-colored twin towers are visible from the western half of San Francisco, especially when lit up at night. The campus and the surrounding residential area occupy land that was once San Francisco's main cemetery district, on and around Lone Mountain.

HAIGHT ASHBURY AND THE MISSION

To the north of Twin Peaks – two windswept hills rising 900 ft (274 m) above the city – lies Haight Ashbury. With its rows of Victorian houses *(see pp304–5)*, it is mostly inhabited by an eclectic mix of the middle classes, although this is where thousands of hippies lived in the late 1960s *(see p363)*. The Castro District, to the east, is the center of the city's gay community. Well known for its hedonism in the 1970s, the area has become far quieter in recent years, although its cafés and shops are still lively. The Mission District, even farther east, was first founded by Spanish monks *(see pp50–51)* and is home to many Latin Americans.

Sights at a Glance

Historic Streets and Buildings
③ (Richard) Spreckels Mansion
② Haight Ashbury
⑤ Lower Haight Neighborhood
⑧ Castro Street
⑩ Dolores Street
⑭ Noe Valley
⑮ Clarke's Folly

Churches
⑨ Mission Dolores

Landmarks
⑱ Sutro Tower

Parks and Gardens
① Golden Gate Park Panhandle
④ Buena Vista Park
⑥ Corona Heights Park
⑪ Dolores Park
⑯ Twin Peaks
⑰ Vulcan Street Steps

Museums and Galleries
⑫ Mission Cultural Center for the Latino Arts
⑬ Carnaval Mural

Theaters
⑦ Castro Theatre

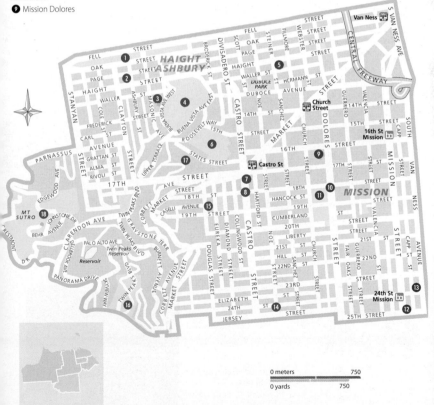

See also San Francisco Street Finder maps 9, 10

◀ Victorian houses painted in bright colors, Haight Ashbury

For keys to symbols *see back flap*

Street-by-Street: Haight Ashbury

Stretching from Buena Vista Park to the flat expanses of Golden Gate Park, Haight Ashbury was a place to escape to from the city center in the 1880s. It then developed into a residential area, but between 1930 and 1960 it changed dramatically from a middle-class neighborhood to the center of the "Flower Power" world, with a free clinic to treat hippies without medical insurance. It has now settled into being one of the liveliest and most unconventional places in San Francisco, with an eclectic mix of people, excellent book and music shops, and good cafés.

❷ Haight Ashbury
In the 1960s, hippies met at this crossroads, which gives the area its name.

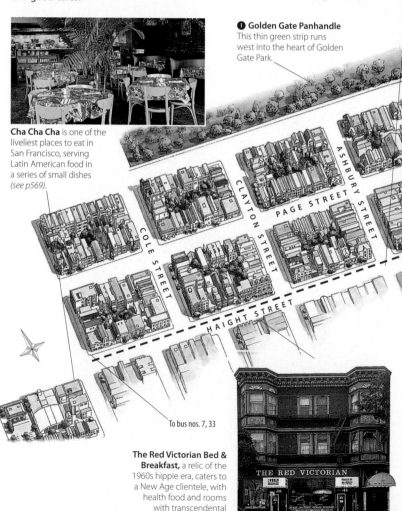

Cha Cha Cha is one of the liveliest places to eat in San Francisco, serving Latin American food in a series of small dishes *(see p569)*.

❶ Golden Gate Panhandle
This thin green strip runs west into the heart of Golden Gate Park.

To bus nos. 7, 33

The Red Victorian Bed & Breakfast, a relic of the 1960s hippie era, caters to a New Age clientele, with health food and rooms with transcendental themes *(see p539).*

THE RED VICTORIAN

No. 1220 Masonic Avenue is one of many ornate Victorian mansions built on the steep hill that runs down from Golden Gate Park Panhandle to Haight Street.

Locator Map
See Street Finder, map 9

Key

— Suggested route

OAK STREET

LYON STREET

CENTRAL STREET

❸ ★ **(Richard) Spreckels Mansion**
This grand home at No. 737 Buena Vista Avenue was built in 1887.

BUENA VISTA WEST

❹ ★ **Buena Vista Park**
Through its mass of twisting, matted trees, this dramatic park offers magnificent views over the city.

0 meters 100
0 yards 100

To bus no. 37

❶ Golden Gate Park Panhandle

Map 9 C1. 🚌 3, 5, 6, 21, 43, 66, 71.

This one-block-wide and eight-block-long stretch of parkland forms the narrow "Panhandle" to the giant rectangular pan that is Golden Gate Park (see pp370–73). It was the first part of the park to be reclaimed from the sand dunes that rolled across west San Francisco, and its eucalyptus trees are among the oldest and largest in the city.

The Panhandle's winding carriage roads and bridle paths were first laid out in the 1870s, and the upper classes came here to walk and ride. They built large mansions on the outskirts of the park, many of which can still be seen today. In 1906 the Panhandle was used as a refuge for families made homeless by the earthquake (see p56). Today the old roads and paths are frequented regularly by large crowds of joggers and cyclists.

The Panhandle is still remembered for its "Flower Power" heyday of the 1960s. The era's young hippies flocked to the park to listen to impromptu free concerts held here by the new psychedelic bands from Haight Ashbury. The area is still a popular spot for the city's street musicians and hippie guitarists.

Junction of Haight and Ashbury streets

❷ Haight Ashbury

Map 9 C1. 🚌 6, 7, 33, 37, 43, 66, 71. 🚃 N.

Taking its name from the junction of two major streets, Haight and Ashbury, this district contains alternative bookshops, large Victorian houses, and numerous cafés. Following the reclamation of Golden Gate Park (see pp370–73) and then the opening of a large amusement park called The Chutes, the area was rapidly built up in the 1890s as a middle-class suburb – hence the dozens of elaborate Queen Anne-style houses (see pp304–5) lining its streets. The Haight district survived the 1906 earthquake and fire (see p56), and then experienced a brief boom, which was followed by a long period of decline.

After the tram tunnel underneath Buena Vista Park was completed in 1928, the middle classes began their exodus to the suburbs in the Sunset district. The area reached its lowest ebb in the years after World War II. The big Victorian houses were divided into apartments and low rents attracted a disparate population. By the 1960s the Haight had become host to a bohemian community that was a hotbed of anarchy. A component of this "hippie scene" was the music of rock bands such as the Grateful Dead, but the area stayed fairly quiet until 1967. Then the "Summer of Love," fueled by the media, brought some 75,000 young people in search of free love, music, and drugs, and the area became the focus of a worldwide youth culture.

The Haight still retains some of its radical atmosphere, but now other problems have arisen with crime, drugs, and homelessness.

Late-Victorian mansion built for Richard Spreckels

However, from the cafés to the second-hand clothing shops, it still offers an "only in San Francisco" experience.

❸ (Richard) Spreckels Mansion

737 Buena Vista West. **Map** 9 C2. 🚌 6, 7, 37, 43, 66, 71. **Closed** to the public.

This house should not be confused with the grander Spreckels Mansion situated on Washington Street (see p352). It was, however, also built by the millionaire "Sugar King" Claus Spreckels, for his nephew Richard. The elaborate Queen Anne-style house (see pp304–5), built in 1887, is a typical late-Victorian Haight Ashbury home. It was once a guesthouse, whose guests included the acerbic journalist and ghost-story writer Ambrose Bierce, and the adventure writer Jack London, who wrote White Fang here in 1906 (see p30). The house is now in private hands.

❹ Buena Vista Park

Map 9 C1. 🚌 6, 7, 37, 43, 66, 71. 🌐 sfrecpark.org

Buena Vista Park rises steeply 570 ft (174 m) above the geographical center of San Francisco with views over the Bay Area. First landscaped in 1894, it is a pocket of land left to nature. Numerous overgrown and eroded paths wind up from Haight Street to the crest, but there is a paved route from Buena Vista Avenue. It is best to avoid the park at night.

❺ Lower Haight Neighborhood

Map 10 D1. 🚌 6, 7, 22, 66, 71. 🚃 K, L, M, N, T.

Halfway between City Hall and Haight Ashbury, and marking the southern border of the predominantly African-American Fillmore District, the Lower Haight is an area in transition. Unusual art galleries and boutiques, including the Used Rubber USA shop, which sells clothes and accessories made entirely of recycled rubber, began to open here in the mid-1980s. These were in addition to the inexpensive cafés, bars, and restaurants serving a bohemian clientele already in business in the area. This combination has created one of the most lively districts in San Francisco.

As in nearby Alamo Square *(see p357)*, the Lower Haight has dozens of houses known as "Victorians" *(see pp304–5)* built from the 1850s to the early 1900s, including picturesque cottages such as the Nightingale House at No. 201 Buchanan Street, built in the 1880s. The 1950s public housing blocks have discouraged wholesale gentrification. The area is safe during the day but, like Alamo Square, it can seem less than desirable after dark.

❻ Corona Heights Park

199 Museum Way. **Map** 9 D2. **Tel** (415) 554-9600. 🚌 24, 37. Randall Museum. 🚃 L, M. **Open** 10am–5pm Tue–Sat. **Closed** public hols. 🚻 limited. 🅿 donation. 🌐 **randallmuseum.org**

Corona Heights Park is a dusty and undeveloped rocky peak. Clinging to its side is the unusual Randall Museum for

View from Corona Heights across the Mission

children, with an extensive menagerie of rabbits, owls, snakes, and other animals, many of which children can handle and stroke. The emphasis of the museum is on participation, with many hands-on exhibits and workshops. Children also enjoy climbing on the craggy outcrops in the park. Corona Heights was gouged out by brick-making operations in the 19th century. It was never planted with trees, so its red rock peak has great views over the city. There is a good view of the winding streets of Twin Peaks *(see p367)*.

The Sounds of 1960s San Francisco

During the late 1960s, and most notably during the 1967 "Summer of Love," young people from all over the country flocked to the Haight Ashbury district. They came not just to "turn on, tune in, and drop out," but also to listen to bands such as Janis Joplin's Big Brother and the Holding Company, Jefferson Airplane, and the Grateful Dead, all of whom emerged out of a thriving music scene. They established themselves at the city's new music venues.

Premier Music Venues
The Avalon Ballroom on Van Ness Avenue first opened in 1968 and was the most significant venue. Run by Chet Helms and the Family Dog collective, the Avalon pioneered the use of colorful psychedelic posters by designers such as Stanley Mouse and Alton Kelly *(see pp444–5)*.

Fillmore Auditorium, facing the Japan Center *(see p356)* and a former church hall, was taken over by impresario Bill Graham in 1965, after whom the Civic Auditorium *(see p356)* is named. He put unlikely pairs such as Miles Davis and the Grateful Dead on the same bill, and brought in big-name performers from Jimi Hendrix to The Who. The Fillmore Auditorium was damaged in the 1989 earthquake but reopened in 1994.

By the time Bill Graham died in 1992 he had become the most successful rock music promoter in the US.

Janis Joplin (1943–70), hard-edged blues singer

❼ Castro Theatre

429 Castro St. **Map** 10 D2.
Tel (415) 621-6120. 24, 33, 35, 37.
F, K, L, M, T. **w** castrotheatre.com
See Entertainment pp394–5.

Completed in 1922, this brightly lit neon movie theater is a Castro Street landmark. It is the most sumptuous and best preserved of San Francisco's neighborhood film palaces, and one of the first commissions of the architect Timothy Pflueger. With its Arabian Nights interior, complete with a glorious Wurlitzer organ that rises from the floor between the screenings, it is well worth the price of admission. The ceiling of the auditorium is cast in plaster and resembles the interior of a large tent, with imitation swathes of fabric, rope, and tassels. The theater seats 1,500 and shows mainly revival classics.

❽ Castro Street

Map 10 D2. 24, 33, 35, 37.
F, K, L, M, T.

The hilly neighborhood around Castro Street between Twin Peaks and the Mission District is the heart of San Francisco's high-profile gay and lesbian community. Focused on the intersection of Castro Street and 18th Street, the self-proclaimed "Gayest Four Corners of the

Historic and ornate Castro Theatre

World" emerged as a homosexual nexus during the 1970s. Gays of the Flower Power generation moved into this predominantly working-class district and began restoring Victorian houses and setting up businesses. They also opened gay bars such as the Twin Peaks Tavern on the corner of Castro Street and 17th Street. Unlike earlier bars, where lesbians and gays hid in dark corners out of public view, the Twin Peaks installed large windows. Though the many shops and restaurants attract all kinds of people, the area's openly homosexual identity has made it a place of pilgrimage for gays and lesbians. Still the world's largest gay community, it symbolizes a freedom still

lacking in many other parts of the world.

One of the city's first openly gay politicians, Harvey Milk was known as the Mayor of Castro Street before his assassination on November 28, 1978. He and Mayor George Moscone were killed by an ex-policeman, whose lenient sentence caused rioting in the city. Milk is remembered with a plaza outside the Muni stop on Market Street and a candlelit procession from Castro Street to City Hall every year.

Over a quarter of a million people come to the area for the Castro Street Fair, which is held every year on the first Sunday in October. Arts, crafts, beer, food, and music are all provided, and proceeds go towards helping the local community.

AIDS Memorial Quilt on display in Washington, DC in 1992

The NAMES Project

The NAMES Project's AIDS Memorial Quilt was conceived by San Francisco gay rights activist Cleve Jones, who organized the first candlelit procession on Castro Street for Harvey Milk in 1985. Jones and his fellow marchers wrote the names of all their friends who had died of AIDS on placards, which they then taped to the San Francisco Federal Building. The resulting "patchwork quilt" of names inspired Jones to create the first panel for the AIDS Memorial Quilt in 1987. Public response to the quilt was immediate – both in the US and across the world – and it grew to over 48,000 panels, some sewn by individuals and others by "quilting bees" – friends and relatives who have come together to commemorate a person lost to AIDS. All panels are the same size – 3 by 6 ft (90 by 180 cm) – but each is different: the design, colors, and material reflect the life and personality of the person commemorated. The quilt is now warehoused at the NAMES Project Foundation headquarters in Atlanta. The last showing of the quilt in its entirety was in 1996, when it covered the entire National Mall in Washington, DC. The NAMES Memorial Quilt remains the largest community art project in the world (www.aidsquilt.org).

Mission Dolores

16th St and Dolores St. **Map** 10 E2.
Tel (415) 621-8203. 22, 33. J.
Open 9am–4:30pm
(to 4pm in winter).
Closed Thanksgiving,
Dec 25.
missiondolores.org

Preserved intact since
it was built in 1791,
Mission Dolores is the
oldest building in the city
and an embodiment of
San Francisco's religious
Spanish colonial roots *(see
pp50–51)*. The mission was
founded by Father Junípero
Serra and is formally known as
the Mission of San Francisco
de Asis. The name Dolores
reflects its proximity to

Figure of saint in
the mission

Laguna de los Dolores (Lake of
Our Lady of Sorrows), an ancient
insect-plagued swamp. The
building is modest by mission
standards, but its 4-ft-
(1.2-m-) thick walls have
survived the years
without serious decay
and Native American
paintings adorn
the ceiling.
There is a fine
Baroque altar
and reredos,
and a display
of historical
documents in
the small museum.
Most services are
now held in the
basilica, built next
to the mission in

1918. The cemetery contains
graves of San Franciscan
pioneers. A statue marking the
mass grave of 5,000 Native
Americans, most of whom died
in measles epidemics in 1804
and 1826, was later stolen. All
that now remains is a pedestal,
reading "In Prayerful Memory
of our Faithful Indians."

**The painted and gilded
altarpiece** was imported from
Mexico in 1780.

The statue of Father Junípero Serra is
a copy of the work of local sculptor
Arthur Putnam.

The ceramic mural was created by
Guillermo Granizo, a native San
Francisco artist.

Museum and
display

The ceiling paintings
are based on original
Ohlone designs using
vegetable dyes.

Entrance for the
disabled

**The mission
cemetery** originally
extended across
many streets. The
earliest wooden
grave markers have
disintegrated, but
the Lourdes Grotto
commemorates the
forgotten dead.

Statue of Our Lady of
Mount Carmel

**The mission
facade** has four
columns which
support niches
for three bells,
inscribed with their
names and dates.

Entrance and
gift shop

Spanish-American War memorial on Dolores Street

❿ Dolores Street

Map 10 E2. 🚌 22, 33, 48. 🚊 J.

Lined by lovingly maintained late Victorian houses (see pp304–305) and an island of palm trees, this street is one of the city's most attractive public spaces. The broad street runs parallel to Mission Street, forming the western border of the Mission District. It starts at Market Street, where a statue honoring soldiers of the Spanish-American War is quite overwhelmed by the Old Mint.

Mission High School, with the white walls and red tile roof typical of Mission-style architecture (see p34), and Mission Dolores (see p365) are both situated on Dolores Street. The street ends in the Noe Valley district.

⓫ Dolores Park

Map 10 E3. 🚌 22, 33. 🚊 J.
🌐 sfrecpark.org

Originally the site of San Francisco's main Jewish cemetery, Dolores Park was transformed in 1905 into one of the Mission District's few large open spaces. Ringed by Dolores, Church, 18th, and 20th streets, it is situated high on a hill with an excellent view of the city center.

Dolores Park is very popular during the day with tennis players, sunbathers, and dog walkers, but after dark it can draw drug dealers. Above the park to the south and west, the streets rise so steeply that many

turn into pedestrian-only stairways. Some of the city's finest Victorian houses can also be seen here.

⓬ Mission Cultural Center for Latino Arts

2868 Mission St. **Map** 10 F4.
Tel (415) 821-1155. 🚌 14, 22, 27, 48, 49. 🚊 J. 🚇 24th Street Mission.
Gallery: **Open** 10am–5pm Tue–Sat.
♿ 🌐 **missionculturalcenter.org**

This dynamic arts center, partly funded by the city, offers music and dance classes, concerts, theater, two art galleries, and a silk-screen print shop for the local Latino community. It also hosts the district's Day of the Dead (see p42) celebration.

Detail from the *Carnaval Mural*

⓭ Carnaval Mural

24th St and South Van Ness Ave.
Map 10 F4. 🚌 12, 14, 48, 49, 67.
🚊 J. 🚇 24th Street Mission.
🌐 sfmuralarts.com

One of the many brightly painted murals on the walls of the Mission District, the *Carnaval Mural* celebrates the diverse people who come together for the Carnaval festival (see p40). This annual spring event is the highlight of the year.

Guided tours of the other murals, some with political themes, are given by civic organizations. There is also an outdoor gallery with murals in Balmy Alley (see pp310–11).

⓮ Noe Valley

Map 10 D4. 🚌 24, 35, 48. 🚊 J.

Noe Valley is often referred to as "Noewhere Valley" by its residents, who remain determined to keep it off the tourist map. It is a pleasant, comfortable neighborhood, largely inhabited by young professionals. Its spotless streets and safe atmosphere seem at odds with the surrounding, densely populated Mission District.

The area was named after its original land-grant owner, José de Jesús Noé, justice of the peace of Yerba Buena, the Mexican village that eventually grew into San Francisco. The valley was first built up during the 1880s after a cable car line over the steep Castro Street hill was completed. The low rents attracted mostly working-class Irish families. Then, like so many other areas of San Francisco, this once blue-collar district underwent gentrification in the 1970s, raising the value of the properties and resulting in today's engaging mix of boutiques, bars, and restaurants. The Noe Valley Ministry, found at No. 1021 Sanchez Street, is a late 1880s Presbyterian church in the "Stick Style" (see pp304–5), the most prevalent architectural style in the city, with its emphasis on vertical lines. The ministry was converted into a community center in the 1970s.

Victorian facade of the Noe Valley Ministry on Sanchez Street

Nobby Clarke's Folly

⓯ Clarke's Folly

250 Douglass St. **Map** 10 D3. 🚎 33, 35, 37. **Closed** to the public.

This resplendent white manor house was at one time set in its own extensive grounds. It was built in 1892 by Alfred Clarke, known locally as Nobby. Clarke had worked for the San Francisco Police Department at the time of the Committee of Vigilance in 1851, when a group of local citizens attempted to control the city's growing lawlessness (see pp52–3). The house is said to have cost $100,000 to build, a huge sum in the 1890s.

Although it is now surrounded by other buildings, the house is a fine example of Victorian domestic architecture. The turrets and the gabled roof are typical of the Queen Anne style, while the shingled walls and front porch adopt the elements of Eastlake architecture (see pp304–5).

Today the house is divided into private apartments.

⓰ Twin Peaks

Map 9 C4. 🚎 33, 36, 37.

These two hills were first known in Spanish as El Pecho de la Chola, the "Bosom of the Indian Girl." They lie at the heart of San Francisco, and reach a height of 900 ft (274 m) above sea level.

At the top there is an area of parkland with steep, grassy slopes, from which incomparable views of the whole of San Francisco can be enjoyed.

Twin Peaks Boulevard circles both hills near their summits; there is a parking lot and viewing point that overlooks the city. Those who are prepared to climb up the steep path to the very top on foot can leave the crowds behind and get a breathtaking 360-degree view.

Twin Peaks are the only hills in the city left in their original state. The residential districts on the lower slopes have curving streets that wind around the contours of the hills, rather than the grid system that is more common in the rest of San Francisco.

⓱ Vulcan Street Steps

Vulcan St. **Map** 9 C2. 🚎 37.

Apart from a tiny figure of Spock standing on a mail-box, there is no connection between the cult television program Star Trek and this block of houses climbing between Ord and Levant Streets. However, the Vulcan Steps do feel light years away from the busy Castro District below. The small, picturesque gardens of the houses spill out and soften the edges of the steps, and a canopy of pines muffles the city sounds. There are great views of the Mission District and the southern waterfront.

⓲ Sutro Tower

Map 9 B3. 🚎 36, 37. **Closed** to the public.

Marking the skyline like an invading robot, Sutro Tower is 970 ft (295 m) high. It was named after the local philanthropist and landowner Adolph Sutro, and it carries antennae for the signals of most of San Francisco's TV and radio stations. Built in 1973, it is still much used, despite the rise of cable networks. The tower is visible from all over the Bay Area, and sometimes seems to float above the summer fogs that roll in from the sea. On the north side of the tower there are dense eucalyptus groves, first planted in the 1880s by Adolph Sutro.

View of the city and of Twin Peaks Boulevard from the top of Twin Peaks

GOLDEN GATE PARK AND THE PRESIDIO

The spectacular Golden Gate Park is one of the world's largest urban parks, created in the 1890s out of sandy wasteland. It houses three museums and a range of sports facilities. Land's End, the city's wildest region and scene of many shipwrecks, is accessible from the park.

To the north of Golden Gate Park, the Presidio, overlooking San Francisco Bay, was established as an outpost of Spain's New World empire in 1776, and for many years was a military base. In 1993 it became a National Park, and visitors can now stroll through its vast woodland full of wildlife.

Sights at a Glance

Historic Streets and Buildings
12 Clement Street
14 Presidio Officers' Club
18 Golden Gate Bridge pp384–5

Parks and Gardens
2 Shakespeare Garden
3 Japanese Tea Garden
5 Conservatory of Flowers
6 Strybing Arboretum
7 Stow Lake
8 Bison Paddock
9 Queen Wilhelmina Tulip Garden

Museums and Galleries
1 California Academy of Sciences pp374–5
4 de Young Museum
10 Legion of Honor pp378–9
15 Presidio Visitor Center
16 The Walt Disney Family Museum
17 Fort Point

Churches and Temples
11 Holy Virgin Cathedral
13 Temple Emanu-El

See also San Francisco Street Finder, maps 1, 2, 3, 7, 8, 9

◄ The Golden Gate Bridge, stretching across San Francisco Bay

For keys to symbols see back flap

Street-by-Street: Golden Gate Park

Golden Gate Park is 3 miles (5 km) long and almost 1 mile (1.6 km) across. It stretches from the Pacific Ocean to the center of San Francisco, forming an oasis of greenery and calm in which to escape from the bustle of city life. Within the park an amazing number of activities are catered to, both sporting and cultural. The landscaped area around the Music Concourse, with its fountains, plane trees, and benches, is the most popular and developed section. Here you can enjoy free Sunday concerts at the Spreckels Temple of Music. A total of three museums stand on either side of the Concourse, and the Japanese and Shakespeare gardens are within walking distance.

❹ ★ de Young Museum
This museum showcases collections from around the world. Exhibits include this mahogany chest, made in Philadelphia in 1780

The Great Buddha
reaches almost 11 ft (3 m) in height.

❸ ★ Japanese Tea Garden
This exquisite garden, with its well-tended plants and pretty lake, is one of the most attractive parts of the park

HAGIAWARA T

MARTIN LUTHER KING DRIVE

KEY

━ Suggested route

0 meters	80
0 yards	80

❷ Shakespeare Garden
This tiny garden holds more than 150 species of plants, all mentioned in Shakespeare's poetry or plays

For hotels and restaurants in this area see pp536–9 and pp569–70

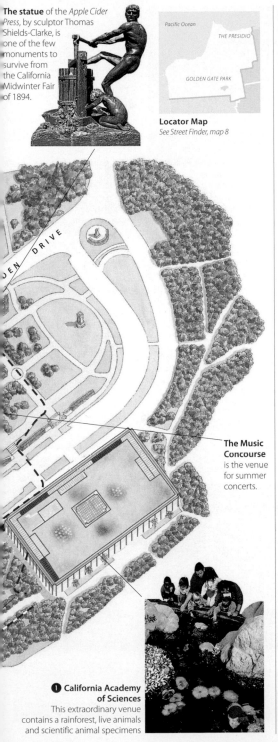

The statue of the *Apple Cider Press*, by sculptor Thomas Shields-Clarke, is one of the few monuments to survive from the California Midwinter Fair of 1894.

Locator Map
See Street Finder, map 8

The Music Concourse is the venue for summer concerts.

❶ California Academy of Sciences
This extraordinary venue contains a rainforest, live animals and scientific animal specimens

❶ California Academy of Sciences

See pp374–5.

❷ Shakespeare Garden

Music Concourse, Golden Gate Park. **Map** 8 F2. 44.

Gardeners here have tried to cultivate over 200 flowers and plants, including all those mentioned in Shakespeare's works. Relevant quotations are inscribed on plaques set in the wall at the back of the garden.

❸ Japanese Tea Garden

Music Concourse, Golden Gate Park. **Map** 8 F2. **Tel** (415) 752-4227. 5, 38, 44. **Open** Mar–Oct: 9am–6pm daily; Nov–Feb: 9am–4:45pm daily. **W japanese teagarden.sf.com**

Established by the art-dealer George Turner Marsh for the 1894 California Midwinter Fair, this garden was later tended by Japanese gardener, Makota Hagiwara. He and his family maintained and expanded the garden until 1942, when they were interned during World War II. The best time to visit is when the cherry trees blossom in April.

❹ de Young Museum

50 Tea Garden Drive, Golden Gate Pk. Map 8 F2. **Tel** (415) 750-3600. 5, 21, 44. **Open** 9:30am–5:15pm Tue–Sun (to 8:45pm Fri Apr–Nov). (free first Tue of month.) **W deyoungmuseum.org**

The de Young is a fine arts museum founded in 1895. In 1989 the original building was too damaged by an earthquake to be saved. The collection is now housed in a state-of-the-art facility with a copper exterior designed by Herzog & de Meuron. The museum contains a broad range of American art, and of pre-Columbian American, African, and Oceanic works.

❺ Conservatory of Flowers

100 John F Kennedy Drive, Golden Gate Park. **Map** 9 A1. **Tel** (415) 666-7001. 5, 33, 44. **Open** 10am–4:30pm Tue–Sun. (free 1st Tue of the month.) limited.
w conservatoryofflowers.org

This ornate greenhouse, inspired by the one in London's Kew Gardens, is the oldest building in the park. A property developer, James Lick, imported the frame from Ireland, but died before its erection in 1879. Ferns, palms, and orchids thrived for over a century until a hurricane in 1995 largely destroyed the conservatory. San Franciscans campaigned for its repair, and it reopened in 2003.

❻ Strybing Arboretum

9th Ave at Lincoln Way, Golden Gate Park. **Map** 8 F2. **Tel** (415) 661 1316. 44, 71. **Open** Apr–Oct: 7:30am–6pm daily; Nov–Mar: 7:30am–5pm daily. 1:30pm daily.
w sfbotanicalgarden.org

On display in the Botanical Garden are 7,500 species of plants, trees, and shrubs from around the world. There are Mexican, African, South American, and Australian gardens, and one that is

Garden of Fragrance in the Strybing Arboretum

devoted entirely to native California plants. Well worth a visit is the enchanting Moon-Viewing Garden. It exhibits Far Eastern plants in a naturalistic setting. Both medicinal and culinary plants are grown in the Garden of Fragrance, which is designed for blind plant-lovers. Here the emphasis is on the senses of taste, touch, and smell, and all the plants are identified in Braille.

Another area, with a stream winding through it, is planted with indigenous California redwood trees. This re-creates the flora and the atmosphere of a northern Californian coastal forest. There is also a New World Cloud Forest, with flora from the mountains of Central America. Surprisingly, all these gardens thrive in the Californian fogs.

There is a small shop selling seeds and books, as well as the Helen Crocker Horticultural Library, which is open to the public. A flower show and plant sale is held every spring.

❼ Stow Lake

Stow Lake Drive, Golden Gate Park. **Map** 8 E2. 28, 29, 44.

In 1895, the President of the Park Commission, WW Stow, ordered the construction of this artificial lake, the largest in the park. It was created encircling Strawberry Hill (named after the wild fruit that once grew here), so that the summit of the hill now forms an island in the lake. It is linked to the mainland by two stone-clad bridges. Stow Lake's circular stream makes an ideal course for rowing laps from the boathouse, although the tranquil atmosphere makes leisurely drifting seem more appropriate.

A Chinese pavilion on the island's shore was a gift to San Francisco from its sister city in Taiwan, Taipei. The red and green pavilion arrived in San Francisco by ship in 6,000 pieces and then was reassembled on the island. The millionaire railway baron Collis Porter Huntington *(see p54)* donated the money in

Chinese moon-watching pavilion on Stow Lake

1894 to create the reservoir and the waterfall that cascades into Stow Lake. These are known as Huntington Falls. Damaged in the 1906 earthquake *(see p56)*, it was restored in the 1980s and is now one of the park's most attractive features.

❽ Bison Paddock

John F Kennedy Drive, Golden Gate Park. **Map** 7 C2. 🚌 5, 29.

The shaggy buffalo grazing in this specially designed paddock are the largest of all North American land animals. Immediately recognizable by their short horns and humped backs, buffalo are the symbol of the American plains, and are more properly known as the American bison.

This paddock was opened in 1892, with the aim of protecting the species, then on the verge of extinction. The first herd, however, brought in from Wyoming, all died of a tuberculosis epidemic and had to be replaced. In 1902 William Cody, the American scout and showman "Buffalo Bill," traded one of his bulls for one from the Golden Gate Park herd. Both parties thought that they had rid themselves of an aggressive beast, but Cody's newly purchased bull jumped a high fence once it was back at his encampment and escaped. According to one newspaper, the *San Francisco Call*, it took 80 men to recapture it.

Queen Wilhelmina Tulip Garden and the Dutch Windmill

❾ Queen Wilhelmina Tulip Garden

Map 7 A2. 🚌 5, 18. Windmill: ♿

This garden was named after the Dutch Queen Wilhelmina, and hundreds of tulip bulbs are donated each year by the Dutch Bulb Growers' Association. In the spring, the area is carpeted with the flowers in full bloom. The Dutch Windmill, near the northwest corner of Golden Gate Park, was built in 1903. Its purpose, along with its companion, the Murphy Windmill, erected in the park's southwest corner in 1905, was to pump water from a source underground, in order to irrigate the park. The increasing volume of water required – about 5 million gallons, or 230 million liters per day – soon made the windmills obsolete, and they are no longer in use.

John McLaren

Although Golden Gate Park was designed by William Hammond Hall, the park's current status owes the most to his successor, John McLaren.

McLaren was born in Scotland in 1846 and studied botany before emigrating to California in the 1870s. He succeeded Hall as administrator in 1887, insisting there would be no "Keep off the grass" signs before accepting the position, and then devoted the rest of his life to the park.

An expert landscape gardener and botanist, McLaren succeeded in importing exotic plants from all over the world and making them thrive, despite the poor soil and foggy climate. He planted thousands of trees and chose the right shrubs to make sure the park was in full bloom all year long.

John McLaren Lodge, a sandstone villa situated on the park's east side, was built in 1896 as a home for McLaren and his family. As McLaren lay dying in 1943, he requested that the cypress tree outside the lodge be lit with Christmas lights, and his request was granted, despite a wartime blackout being in force. The tree is still referred to as "Uncle John's Christmas Tree" and is lit every December in his honor. He is buried in a tomb in the San Francisco City Hall. Golden Gate Park still remains true to his vision – a place in which to escape from city life.

American bison in the Buffalo Paddock

❶ California Academy of Sciences

The California Academy of Sciences is one of the largest natural history museums in the world. Completely rebuilt in 2008 in Golden Gate Park, the building houses the Steinhart Aquarium, Morrison Planetarium, and the Kimball Natural History Museum, combining innovative green architecture with flexible exhibition spaces. A large piazza is at the heart of the building, with excellent views overlooking Golden Gate Park.

A 2.5-acre (1-ha) living roof covers the building

Museum Guide

Steinhart Aquarium displays are spread throughout the museum, but most of the tanks can be found in the basement beneath the Piazza. An auditorium above the café holds traveling exhibits as well as special performances and programs. The back of the building holds the museum's collection of over 28 million scientific specimens along with staff offices and research laboratories.

The Swamp

Philippine Coral Reef (lower level)

Sharks and Rays (lower level)

Planetarium
State of the art exhibits and digital technology transform the ceiling here into a night sky.

Key to Floorplan

- African Hall
- Kimball Natural History Museum
- Planetarium
- Rainforests of the World
- Steinhart Aquarium
- Aquarium Tanks
- Non-exhibition space

African Hall
Realistic models of animals from Africa's deserts and savannas are displayed here, in lifelike dioramas.

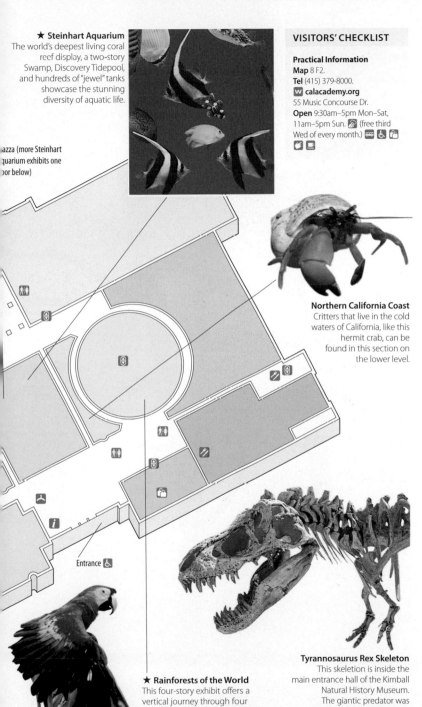

★ **Steinhart Aquarium**
The world's deepest living coral reef display, a two-story Swamp, Discovery Tidepool, and hundreds of "jewel" tanks showcase the stunning diversity of aquatic life.

VISITORS' CHECKLIST

Practical Information
Map 8 F2.
Tel (415) 379-8000.
W calacademy.org
55 Music Concourse Dr.
Open 9:30am–5pm Mon–Sat, 11am–5pm Sun. (free third Wed of every month.)

azza (more Steinhart
quarium exhibits one
oor below)

Northern California Coast
Critters that live in the cold waters of California, like this hermit crab, can be found in this section on the lower level.

Entrance

★ **Rainforests of the World**
This four-story exhibit offers a vertical journey through four different rainforest habitats. Real macaws and other exotic birds live in the canopy of this exhibit.

Tyrannosaurus Rex Skeleton
This skeleton is inside the main entrance hall of the Kimball Natural History Museum. The giantic predator was the most powerful carnivore ever to walk the earth.

Golden Gate Bridge from Lincoln Park golf course ▶

⑩ Legion of Honor

Inspired by the Palais de la Légion d'Honneur in Paris, Alma de Bretteville Spreckels built this museum in the 1920s to honor Californian soldiers who died in World War I, and to promote French art in California. Designed by the architect George Applegarth, it contains paintings by Monet, Rubens, and Rembrandt, more than 70 sculptures by Rodin, and over 4,000 years of ancient art. The Achenbach Foundation for Graphic Art, a famous collection of graphic works, occupies part of the gallery.

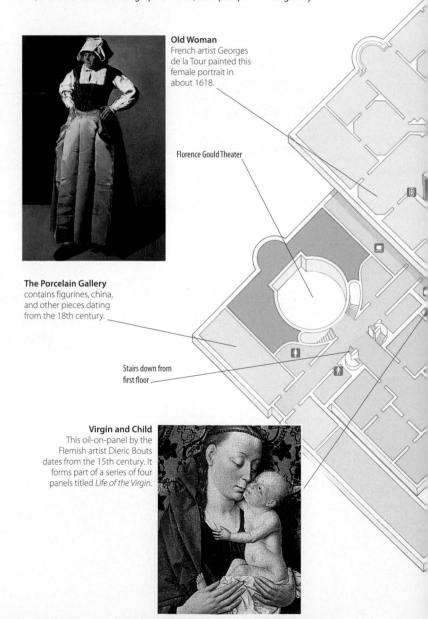

Old Woman
French artist Georges de la Tour painted this female portrait in about 1618.

Florence Gould Theater

The Porcelain Gallery
contains figurines, china, and other pieces dating from the 18th century.

Stairs down from first floor

Virgin and Child
This oil-on-panel by the Flemish artist Dieric Bouts dates from the 15th century. It forms part of a series of four panels titled *Life of the Virgin*.

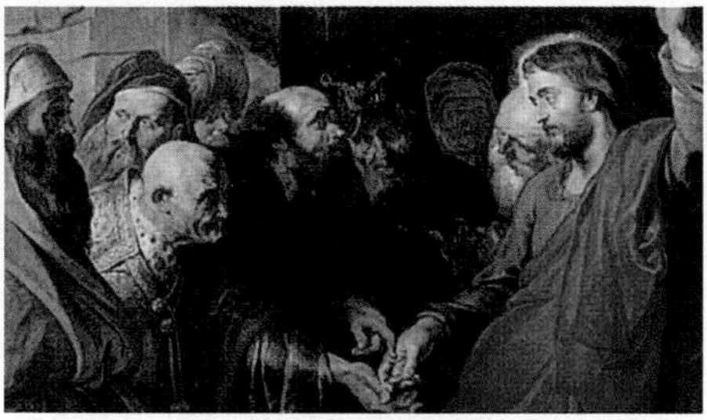

The Tribute Money (1612)
The use of primary colors in this oil-on-canvas is typical of the Flemish artist Peter Paul Rubens.

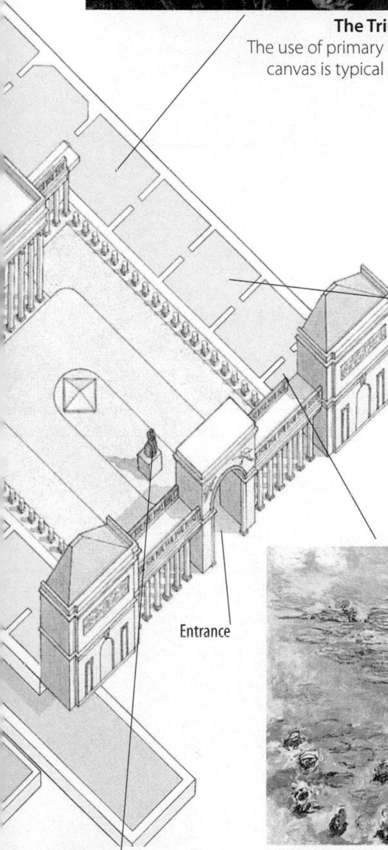

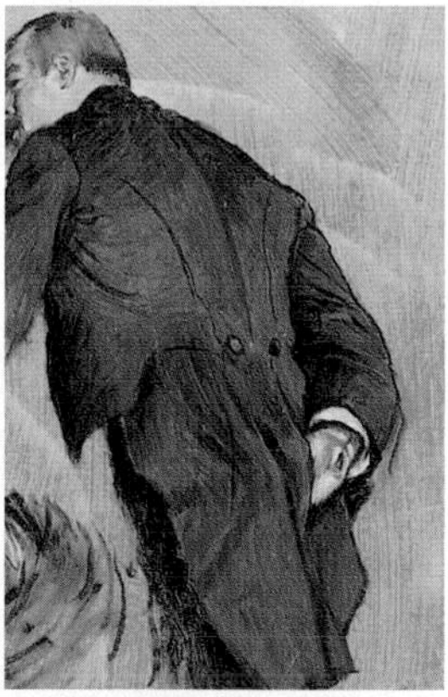

The Impresario
In this portrait from around 1877, artist Edgar Degas emphasizes the subject's size by making him appear too large for the frame.

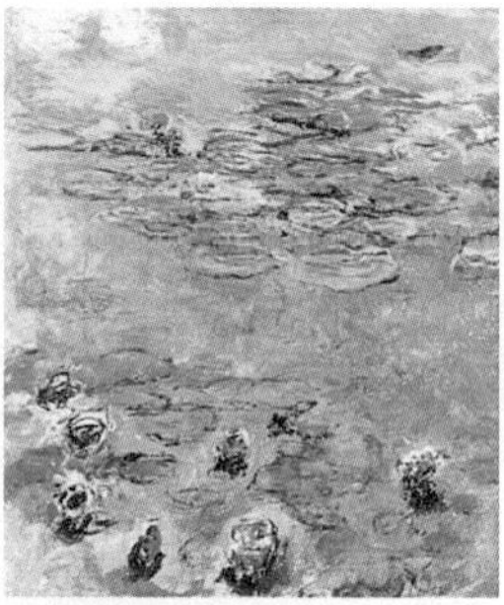

Gallery Guide

The museum's permanent collection of European and ancient art is displayed throughout the galleries on the first floor. Works are arranged chronologically, from the medieval period, left of the main entrance, through the Renaissance, and on to the 20th century. Temporary exhibitions, graphic art, and the porcelain collection are on the lower level.

Entrance

★ **Waterlilies**
Claude Monet's work from between 1914 and 1917 is one of a series depicting the lily pond in his gardens in Giverny, near Paris.

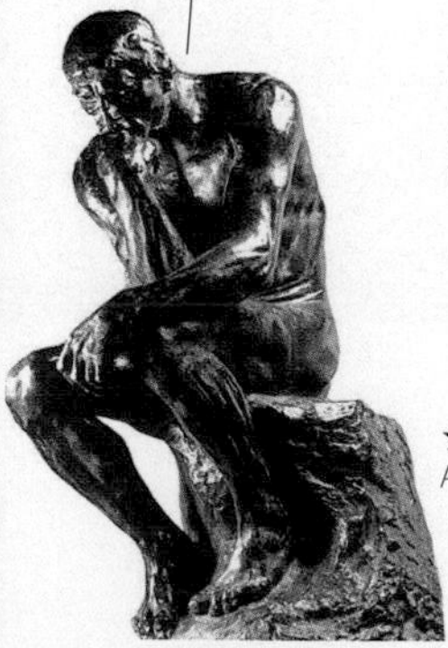

Key to Floor plan

- Permanent displays
- Achenbach Foundation Library
- Porcelain gallery
- Theater storage
- Special Exhibitions
- Non-exhibition space

★ **The Thinker**
An original bronze casting of Rodin's *Le Penseur* (1904) is at the center of the colonnaded Court of Honor. It is one of 11 castings of the statue in collections around the world.

The Presidio

The winding roads and lush green landscaping of the Presidio belie its long military history. This prominent site has played a key role in San Francisco's growth, and it has been occupied longer than any other part of the city. Remnants of its military past, including the well-preserved barracks, artillery emplacements, and cannons, can be seen everywhere, and there are many hiking trails, bike paths, beaches, and restaurants. The coastal path in Crissy Field is one of the most popular walks in the city. The Golden Gate Bridge crosses the bay from the northwest corner of the Presidio to Marin County.

⑯ Fort Point
This impressive brick fortress, now a national historic site, guarded the Golden Gate during the Civil War of 1861–5.

❷ ★ Golden Gate Bridge
Opened in 1937, the bridge has a single span of 4,200 ft (1,280 m).

Mountain Lake is a large spring-fed lake and a popular picnic spot. The original Presidio was established nearby in 1776 to defend the bay area and Mission Dolores (see p365).

Crissy Field was reclaimed from marshland for the 1915 Panama-Pacific Exposition *(see p353)*. It was used as an airfield from 1919 to 1936 and has been restored to wild open spaces.

Locator Map
See Street Finder, map 2 & 3

The San Francisco National Cemetary holds the remains of almost 30,000 American soldiers killed in action.

The Tidal Marsh is part of the restoration of the Presidio area at Crissy Field.

Arguello Gate
This decorative gate with its military symbols marks an entrance to the former army base, now a national park, open to the public.

🅖 **Presidio Visitor Center**
The visitor center serves as the gateway not only to the Presidio, but also to Fort Point Historic Site, Crissy Field, and Battery Chamberlain.

0 meters   500

0 yards   500

⓫ Holy Virgin Cathedral

6210 Geary Blvd. **Map** 8 D1. **Tel** (415) 221-3255. 🚌 2, 29, 38. **Open** 9:30–11:30am Tue & Wed. 🕒 8am, 6pm Mon–Sat, 7:30am, 9:45am, 6pm Sun.
W sfsobor.com

Shining gold onion-shaped domes crown the Russian Orthodox Holy Virgin Cathedral of the Russian Church in Exile, a startling landmark in the suburban Richmond District. Built in the early 1960s, it is generally open to the public only during services. In contrast to those of many other Christian denominations, the services in this cathedral are conducted with the congregation standing, so there are no pews or seats.

The cathedral and the many Russian-owned businesses surrounding it, such as the lively Russian Renaissance restaurant, are situated at the heart of San Francisco's extensive Russian community *(see p39)*. This has flourished since the 1820s, but it reached its highest population when immigrants arrived after the Russian Revolution of 1917. It boomed again in the late 1950s and late 1980s.

⓬ Clement Street

Map 1 C5. 🚌 2, 29, 44.

This is a bustling main thorough-fare of the otherwise sleepy Richmond District. Bookshops and small boutiques flourish here, and the inhabitants of the neighborhood meet together in a lively mix of bars, fast-food cafés, and ethnic restaurants. Most of these are patronized more by locals than by tourists.

Clement Street is surrounded by an area known as New Chinatown, home to more than one-third of the Chinese population of San Francisco. As a result, some of the city's best Chinese restaurants can be found here, and the emphasis in general is on Far Eastern cuisine, with Vietnamese, Thai, and Korean restaurants well represented. The area is also known for the diversity of its restaurants, and Peruvian and French establishments, among others, flourish here.

The street stretches from Arguello Boulevard to the north/south cross-streets that are more commonly known as "The Avenues." It ends near the Legion of Honor *(see pp378–9)*.

Interior of Temple Emanu-El, showing the Holy Ark

⓭ Temple Emanu-El

2 Lake St. **Map** 3 A4. **Tel** (415) 751-2535. 🚌 1, 1BX, 2, 33. **Open** by appointment only. 🕒 5:30pm, 7:30pm Fri, 10:30am Sat (call to verify times). 📷 during services. ♿
W emanuelsf.org

After World War I hundreds of Jews from Russia and Eastern Europe moved into the Richmond District and built major religious centers. Among these is the Temple Emanu-El, its dome inspired by that of 6th-century Hagia Sophia, Istanbul.

The temple was built in 1925 for the longest established congregation of Jews in the city, founded in 1850. The architect was Arthur Brown, who also designed City Hall *(see p357)*. The temple is an architectural hybrid: Mission style *(see pp34–5)*, Byzantine ornamentation, and Romanesque arcades.

⓮ Presidio Officers' Club

50 Moraga Ave. **Map** 3 A2.
Tel (415) 561-4400. 🚌 29.
Open 10am–6pm Tue–Sun.
Closed Mon & some public holidays.
W presidioofficersclub.com

Looking out across the original parade grounds of the Presidio, the Officers' Club was built in the Spanish Mission style *(see pp34–5)*. Although it dates from the 1930s, it was carefully built around the adobe (sun-dried brick) remains of the original 18th-century Spanish fort. A renovation in 2014 expanded the space to hold multi-media displays on the

The Russian Orthodox Holy Virgin Cathedral

For hotels and restaurants in this area see pp536–9 and pp569–70

Presidio's history, and cultural events and performances, including live music and dance, talks, and film screenings.

⓯ Presidio Visitor Center

36 Lincoln Blvd. **Map** 3 A2. **Tel** (415) 561-4323. **Open** 10am–4pm Thu–Sun.
W presidio.gov or **W** nps.gov/prsf

The Visitor Center provides useful information, maps, and brochures, and the staff can help with queries and suggestions. The exhibits at the center showcase the history of the Presidio. Displays focus on eyewitness accounts of the Presidio's evolution, from small, frontier military outpost to a major metropolis.

Two small cabins behind the Old Post Hospital are representative of the hundreds of shelters set up here after the earthquake of 1906 *(see p56)*.

⓰ The Walt Disney Family Museum

104 Montgomery St. **Map** 3 A2.
Tel (415) 345-6800. 🚌 28L, 43.
Open 10am–6pm Wed–Mon.
Closed Jan 1. 🚹 **W** waltdisney.org

Walt Disney is most often associated with the characters he created, from Mickey Mouse to Goofy, but less is known about Disney himself. This museum focuses on the life and times of

annon near the Old Post Hospital on the ounds of the Presidio

Golden Gate Bridge, seen from Fort Point

Walt Disney using photographs, documents, animation art, and an impressive range of interactive exhibits.

⓱ Fort Point

Long Ave & Marine Drive.
Map 2 E1. **Tel** (415) 556-1693.
Open 10am–5pm Fri–Sun (call for extra days open in summer). 🚹 partial. **W** nps.gov/fopo

Completed by the US Army in 1861, this fort was built both to protect San Francisco Bay from military attack and to defend ships carrying gold from the Californian mines *(see pp52–3)*. It is only the third system fort constructed along the Pacific coastline and is a classic example of a pre-Civil War brick-and-granite fortress. The building soon became obsolete when new rifled artillery came into use and its 8-ft- (2-m-) thick brick walls were not strong enough to stand up to continued bombardment. It was closed in 1900.

The fort's brickwork vaulting is unusual for San Francisco and may have saved the fort from collapse in the 1906 earthquake *(see p56)*. It was nearly demolished in the 1930s to make way for the Golden Gate Bridge, but it survived and is a good place from which to view the bridge. Restored in the 1970s, the fort now houses a museum displaying military uniforms and arms. Cannon-loading demonstrations and tours are available.

A History of The Presidio

In 1776 José Joaquín Moraga, one of the first Spanish settlers, founded a presidio. His aim in erecting this camp of adobe buildings on the edge of San Francisco Bay was to defend the Mission Dolores *(see p365)*. Following Mexican

The Presidio in the 19th century

independence from Spain, the site remained the northernmost fort of the shortlived republic until the United States took it over in 1847. The Presidio was used for military purposes until 1990.

From the 1850s to the 1930s, the adobe buildings were replaced, first with wooden barracks, and later with concrete Mission- and Georgian-style cottages for the officers and their families. These buildings remain.

The site covers 1,400 acres (567 ha), and its landscaped forests of eucalyptus and cypress trees are not found on any other army base in the world. The Presidio has now been declared an historic site and is a protected member of the Golden Gate National Recreation Area (GGNRA).

⑱ Golden Gate Bridge

Named after the entrance to the Strait of San Francisco Bay called "Golden Gate" by John Frémont in 1846, the bridge opened in 1937, connecting the city with Marin County. It took just over four years to build at a cost of $35 million. Breathtaking views are offered from this spectacular, world-famous landmark, which has six lanes for vehicles plus a free pedestrian walkway. It has the world's twelfth longest span between its two towers and, when it was built, it was the world's longest and tallest suspension structure.

KEY

① **The length** of the bridge is 1.7 miles (2.7 km), the span is 4,200 ft (1,280 m), and the roadway is 220 ft (67 m) above the water.

② **The roadway** is 220 ft (67 m) above water 318-ft (97-m) deep.

③ **The twin steel towers** rise to a height of 746 ft (227 m) above the water. The towers are hollow.

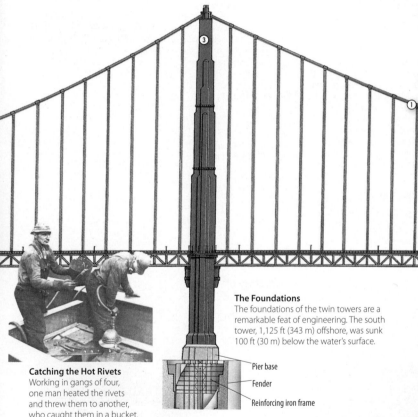

Catching the Hot Rivets
Working in gangs of four, one man heated the rivets and threw them to another, who caught them in a bucket. The other two fastened sections of steel with the hot rivets.

The Foundations
The foundations of the twin towers are a remarkable feat of engineering. The south tower, 1,125 ft (343 m) offshore, was sunk 100 ft (30 m) below the water's surface.

Pier base
Fender
Reinforcing iron frame

Toll Plaza
Between 100,000 and 120,000 cars cross the Golden Gate Bridge a day, passing through the eight automated toll lanes. Tolls are collected in the southbound direction only.

Joseph Strauss
Chicago engineer Joseph Strauss is officially credited as the bridge's designer, and he led the opening ceremony in April 1937. He was assisted by Leon Moisseiff and Charles Ellis. Irving F Morrow acted as consulting architect.

VISITORS' CHECKLIST

Practical Information
Map 2 E1.
Hwy 101, Presidio.
Tel (415) 923-2000.
Pedestrians/cyclists allowed, east walkway only. Toll Plaza: southbound Hwy 101 only.
🚻 observation area only.
Ⓦ goldengatebridge.org

Transport
🚌 2, 28, 76.

The Roadway
The original steel-supported concrete roadway was constructed from the towers in both directions, so that weight on the suspension cables was evenly distributed.

View from Vista Point
The best view of both the bridge and the San Francisco skyline is from the Marin County side.

The Bridge in Figures

• Every year more than 40 million vehicles cross the bridge; every day as many as 120,000 vehicles use it.
• The original coat of paint lasted for 27 years, needing only touch-ups. From 1965 to 1995, a crew stripped off the old paint and applied a more durable coating.
• The two great 7,650-ft (2,332-m) cables are more than 3 ft (1 m) thick, and contain 80,000 miles (128,744 km) of steel wire, enough to circle the earth at the equator three times.
• The volume of concrete poured into the piers and anchorages during the bridge's construction would be enough to lay a 5-ft-(1.5-m-) wide sidewalk from New York to San Francisco, a distance of more than 2,500 miles (4,000 km).
• The bridge can withstand 100 mph (160 km/h) winds.
• Each pier has to withstand a tidal flow of more than 60 mph (97 km/h), while supporting a 22,000-ton steel tower.

Painting the bridge

SHOPPING IN SAN FRANCISCO

Shopping in San Francisco is much more than simply making a purchase, it is a whole experience that allows a glimpse into the city's culture. It is the diversity of San Francisco that makes buying anything here an adventure. An enormous range of goods is available, from the practical to the more eccentric, but you can take your time in choosing, since browsers are generally made to feel welcome, particularly in the many small specialty shops and boutiques of the city. If you want convenience, the numerous shopping centers and department stores are excellent. For those in search of local color, every neighborhood shopping district has a charm and personality of its own, with each reflecting a different aspect of the city.

Malls and Shopping Centers

In contrast to a great many suburban shopping malls, those of San Francisco have character, and one or two of them are of considerable architectural interest. The Embarcadero Center (see p318) has more than 125 shops, in an area covering eight blocks. Ghirardelli Square (see p341) was a well-known chocolate factory from 1893 until 1953. It now houses a variety of shops and several restaurants, overlooking San Francisco Bay.

The Westfield San Francisco Centre (see p325) has nine levels and more than 200 shops. PIER 39 (see p340) is a marketplace on the waterfront, with restaurants, a double-decker Venetian merry-go-round, a marina, and many specialty boutiques. In The Cannery (see p341), located at Fisherman's Wharf, you will find a variety of charming small shops. The beautiful Crocker Galleria (see p324) is one of the city's most spectacular malls, with three floors set under a high glass dome built around a bright central plaza.

The Japan Center (see p356), complete with pagoda, offers exotic foods, goods, and art from the East, as well as a Japanese-style hotel and traditional baths. The Rincon Center (see p321), with a 90-ft (27-m) water column at its center, is an Art Deco haven for shopping and eating.

Department Stores

Most of San Francisco's major department stores are in or near Union Square (see p324). They are huge retail stores that offer their customers an outstanding selection of goods and services.

The **Bloomingdale's** chain opened its West Coast flagship store in San Francisco in late 2006 and is now one of the country's largest "Bloomies." The emphasis is on upscale fashion, as well as luxury accessories and housewares.

Macy's stocks an enormous range of goods and has a number of extra amenities, including currency exchange and an interpreting service. The men's department is particularly extensive.

Neiman Marcus is another stylish emporium. The huge stained-glass dome in its Rotunda Restaurant was part of the original building and is well worth coming to see.

Nordstrom, popular for its fashion and shoes, is also known as the "store-in-the-sky"; it is located in the top four floors of the innovative San Francisco Shopping Center.

Flags flying in front of the pagoda at the Japan Center

Shopping around Union Square

Serious shoppers should concentrate on the blocks bordered by Geary, Powell, and Post Streets, and on the surrounding blocks between Market and Sutter Streets. Here luxurious shops and inexpensive boutiques sell everything from designer bed linens to snow-globe souvenirs. Exclusive hotels, chic restaurants, and colorful flower stalls all add to the fashionable atmosphere.

Shops for a Good Cause

San Franciscans take great pleasure in shopping for a good cause. All purchases made at **The Pirate Store** benefit 826 Valencia, a non-profit organization dedicated to helping 6- to 18-year-olds with their writing skills, and to assisting teachers in creating curricula that will inspire their students to write. The **Warming Hut Bookstore** offers

Emporio Armani, Union Square

Flower stall on Union Square

eco-conscious gifts. Proceeds benefit environmental education at the Crissy Field Center. The **Community Thrift Store**, a non-profit organization, sells donated items and works with more than 200 charities in the Bay Area. The proceeds are disbursed for various causes. **Patagonia** offers plenty of outdoor gear made of recycled fibers. They also have fundraisers and donate clothes to non-profit groups.

Souvenirs

Many souvenirs, such as T-shirts, keyrings, and mugs are decorated with motifs symbolizing San Francisco at **Only in San Francisco** and the **Cable Car Store**. Souvenir and novelty hats are available at **Krazy Kaps**, while the store entrances on Grant Avenue *(see p333)* and Fisherman's Wharf *(see pp338–9)* are lined with baskets filled with bargain gifts.

Best Buys

Gourmet shoppers should look for seafood, one of the city's specialties. Wine from the Napa Valley *(see pp466–7)* is another good buy, as is the city's famous Ghirardelli chocolate. You will find jeans at competitive prices, also vintage clothing, ethnic art, books, and records particulary in the Mission District and the Haight-Ashbury.

Shopping Tours

Some tour companies may be able to arrange private shopping tours with a personalized guide service. The **San Francisco Travel Association** can provide information. Also, Macy's offers a VIP shopping day with shopping assistance and discounts.

Museums

Museum shopping offers exquisite gifts to suit all budgets. Among the city's best are the **Academy Store** in the California Academy of Sciences *(see p374)*, the **Museum Store** at the Legion of Honor *(see pp378–9)*, and **The Asian Art Museum Store** *(see p356)*. The San Francisco MOMA re-opened in 2016 with an impressive, new store *(see pp322–3)*.

Grant Avenue, Chinatown

DIRECTORY

Academy Store
California Academy of Sciences, Golden Gate Park, 55 Music Concourse Dr. **Map** 8 F2. **Tel** (415) 933-6154. W calacademy.org

The Asian Art Museum Store
200 Larkin St. **Map** 4 F5. **Tel** (415) 581-3600. W asianart.org

Bloomingdale's
845 Market St. **Map** 5 C4. **Tel** (415) 856-5300. W bloomingdales.com

Cable Car Store
PIER 39. **Map** 5 B1. **Tel** (415) 989-2040. W cablecarstore.com

Community Thrift Store
623 Valencia St. **Map** 10 F3. **Tel** (415) 861-4910.

Krazy Kaps
PIER 39. **Map** 5 B1. **Tel** (415) 296-8930. W pier39.com

Macy's
Stockton & O'Farrell Sts. **Map** 5 C5. **Tel** (415) 954-6271. W macys.com

Museum Store
Legion of Honor, Golden Gate Park. **Map** 1 B5. **Tel** (415) 750-3677. W deyoungmuseum.org

Neiman Marcus
150 Stockton St. **Map** 5 C5. **Tel** (415) 362-3900. W neimanmarcus.com

Nordstrom
San Francisco Shopping Center, 865 Market St. **Map** 5 C5. **Tel** (415) 243-8500. W nordstorm.com

Only in San Francisco
PIER 39. **Map** 5 B1. **Tel** (415) 397-0143. W pier39.com

Patagonia
700 North Point St. **Map** 5 A2. **Tel** (415) 771-2050. W patagonia.com

The Pirate Store
826 Valencia St. **Map** 10 F2. **Tel** (415) 642-5905. W 826valencia.org

San Francisco Travel Association
900 Market St. **Map** 5 C4. **Tel** (415) 391-2000. W sanfrancisco.travel

Warming Hut Bookstore
983 Marine Dr at Long Ave. **Map** 2 F2. **Tel** (415) 561-3043. W store.parkconservancy.org

San Francisco Specialties

Entrepreneurial spirit in San Francisco is strong and innovative, and the city's sophisticated image is very much deserved. Whether it is a small souvenir, a designer outfit, an antique, or a mouthwatering snack that is required, visitors will never be disappointed amid the shops and markets of San Francisco. The city is also home to many dedicated "foodies," gastronomes whose liking for fine wine and gourmet meals have resulted in unusual and delicious grocery stores. All this creates an environment that makes shopping in San Francisco an exciting experience.

Specialty Shops

If you are looking for whimsical art – either to wear or to display – head to **Kati Koos: A Gallery with Tongue in Chic**. Since Gold Rush days, **VIP Luggage**, a family-owned and operated shop for luggage, briefcases and small leather goods, has kept its reputation for excellence. You can describe the city's attractions on a designer card from **Flax Art and Design**, a sixty-year-old business offering a huge selection of handmade papers and artists' tools. The superstore of **Mac Cosmetics**, top global brand in beauty and makeup products, is a wonderland of a

The colorful exterior of Flax Art and Design on Market Street

contemporary and trendy range of cosmetics and beauty supplies. **Comix Experience** sells a large selection of comics and graphic novels. Exquisite Italian ceramics (majolica) are on display at **Biordi Art Imports** in North Beach, where handpainted dishware, vases, and platters are for sale. Those who would like to experience the authentic atmosphere of Chinatown will find it at **Ten Ren Tea Company**. At **Golden Gate Fortune Cookies**, descendants of Chinese immigrants allow their customers to taste samples

before buying the San Francisco fortune cookies that were a Chinatown invention.

Food and Wine

From abalone to zucchini, and from fresh California produce to imported specialty foods, the gourmet grocery **Whole Foods** carries a wide variety of items. **Williams-Sonoma** has jams, mustards, and gifts. **David's** is known for its lox (smoked salmon), bagels, and deli sandwiches. The Italian **Molinari Delicatessen** is famous for its fresh ravioli and tortellini, ready to throw into a saucepan. **Lucca Ravioli Company** has a friendly staff, who make their pasta on the premises. **Pasta Gina** caters to the young, fashionable crowd with freshly prepared pasta, pesto, and other sauces. It is well worth going to Chinatown (see pp320–21) for Far Eastern food products and produce. At **Casa Lucas Market** you will find a variety of Spanish and Latin American food

Fig jam, Williams-Sonoma

Ghirardelli Square, home to San Francisco's famous chocolate makers

specialties. A baguette of fresh sourdough bread from **Boudin Bakery** is a long-standing addiction with locals and a tradition with visitors. **La Boulange** brings Paris to San Francisco, with some of the best bread in the city. **Cheese Plus** sells fine cheeses and gourmet food items. Chocoholics are catered to at San Francisco's own **Ghiradelli Chocolate Factory**. San Franciscans are coffee connoisseurs, and there are many specialty houses. **Caffè Trieste** is the city's oldest coffee house and sells a range of custom-roasted and blended coffees, and a variety of brewing equipment. **Caffè Roma Coffee Roasting Company** and the **Graffeo Coffee Roasting Company** both sell excellent beans. The staff at the **California Wine Merchant**

Caffè Trieste on Vallejo Street, a North Beach landmark

makes good recommendations and are very knowledgeable about their affordable wines. The **Napa Valley Winery Exchange** features selections from the many Californian wineries, including the smaller local producers.

Locally grown fruit and vegetables arrive by the truckload at the regular farmers' markets in the center of the city. Stalls are erected for the day, and the farmers sell their goods directly to the public. The **Heart of the City** is open 7am to 5pm on Wednesdays, and to 5:30pm on Sundays. **Ferry Plaza Farmers' Market** is held Tuesdays and Thursdays (10am–2pm) and Saturdays (8am–2pm). Chinatown's produce stores have the feel of an exotic farmers' market and are open every day.

Books, Music, Art, and Antiques

Independent bookstores have had a hard time, with some landmark stores closing down. **Modern Times Bookstore**, which depends heavily on its local membership, carries a wide selection of best-sellers and classics, as well as unusual specialties. Beats once talked about the country's emerging 1960s social revolution at the **City Lights Bookstore** *(see pp334–5)*, which stays open late and is a famous San Francisco institution. **Green Apple Books & Music** has new and used books, and is open until 10:30pm, or 11:30pm on Fridays and Saturdays. **Adobe Books & Arts Cooperative** offers eccentric and rare books at discount prices. **William Stout Architectural Books** stocks books on art, architecture, furniture and interior design, and graphic and industrial design.

A wide selection of music is offered at various branches of **Rasputin Music** and **Best Buy**. More obscure music can usually be found at **Recycled Records**. **Amoeba Music** has the largest selection of CDs and tapes in the country. It has 500,000 titles,

Pinot Noir, a popular wine of the region

both new and secondhand, including jazz, international blues, and rock music. A music collector's paradise, this is the place to go if you are looking for hard-to-find music at low prices. Musical instruments and all types of sheet music can be found at the **Union Music Company**. Art lovers will find something to their liking in the city's hundreds of galleries. The **John Berggruen Gallery** has the city's largest collection of works by both emerging and more established artists. The **Fraenkel Gallery** is known for its collection of 19th- and 20th-century photography. **Xanadu Gallery** has masks, textiles, sculptures, and jewelry *(see p325)*.

Jackson Square is San Francisco's main area for antiques *(see p318)*. **49 Geary Street** is a veritable treasure-trove for art collectors, housing 20 galleries and four rare book shops. **Lang Antiques** has all kinds of antique jewelry. **Dragon House** sells Oriental antiques and fine art, while antique books, prints, and maps can be found at **Prints Old & Rare** – although you will need to make an appointment.

Clothing

San Francisco designer shops include **Diana Slavin** for classics, **Joanie Char's** for sportswear, and **Wilkes Bashford** for up-and-coming designs. For discount designer clothes, head to the trendy SoMa district. **Jeremy's** in

SoMa's swish South Park area, discounts formal clothing and designerwear for both men and women. Yerba Buena Square contains several kinds of outlets, including **Burlington Coat Factory**. Here you can find discounted lines from many local designers. **Upper Playground** sells playful, hipster attire, and a line of locally-inspired clothing. . **Buffalo Exchange** offers secondhand clothing with a history. **The Wasteland** in the Haight-Ashbury District is known for its vintage clothes. **Thrift Town**, at the heart of Mission District,

The Wasteland on Haight Street, a treasure of vintage garments

sells an assortment of good-quality secondhand merchandise and clothes, while **Mission Thrift** sells an eclectic mix of unusual finds.

Brooks Brothers is well known for its conservative men's suits and button-down shirts. Fashionable outdoor clothing is available from **Eddie Bauer**. For men's designer brands, sportswear, shoes, and accessories with a European influence, try **Rolo**. Many of the world's famous names in fashion are in San Francisco,

City Lights Bookstore *(see p334)* on Columbus Avenue

including **Chanel** and **Gucci**. **Salvatore Ferragamo** is in Union Square. **Prada** is famous for its extra-fine merino wool and cashmere clothes. **Marc Jacobs** carries men's and women's clothing, as well as high-end accessories. **Banana Republic** and **Guess** are well known for stylish, wearable clothes. **Uniqlo**, a popular Japanese brand, sells a collection of casualwear and accessories for men, women, and children at great prices. **Urban Outfitters** has bohemian retro clothes, and **Sui Generis Boutique** carries stylish, gently used designer clothing. **The Levi's Store** has been in business since 1853, offering a broad range of clothes, all of which

can be worn with their famous jeans (see p347).

Small Frys is the locals' favorite for cotton children's clothes. Top-quality footwear is available at **On The Run**. Best names in comfort are at **Ria's Shoes**, including Clarks, Ecco, Dansko, Timberland, and Sebago. **Nike** is a one-stop destination for sport clothing and sneakers, and **DSW Shoe Warehouse** offers discounted shoes.

Toys, Games, and Gadgets

Inside Exploratorium, San Francisco's fascinating science museum, is the **Exploratorium Store**. The store stocks a wide variety of science books, kits,

and games that make learning fun for children of all ages.

At **Puppets on the Pier** new owners are given puppetry lessons in the shop. **Ambassador Toys** sells a plethora of fun and educational toys – from colorful German trinkets to model train sets – for kids of all age groups. The **Chinatown Kite Shop** takes shopping to new heights, displaying an extraordinary assortment of flying objects. These range from traditional to World Champion stunt kites, all making attractive souvenirs. In **Brookstone** even the adult who has everything is sure to be intrigued by the high-tech wizardry of the gadgets and electronic goods on sale.

DIRECTORY

Specialty Shops

Biordi Art Imports
412 Columbus Ave.
Map 5 C3.
Tel (415) 392-8096.

Comix Experience
305 Divisadero St.
Map 10 D1.
Tel (415) 863-9258.

Flax Art and Design
1699 Market St.
Map 10 F1.
Tel (415) 552-2355.

Golden Gate Fortune Cookies
56 Ross Alley. **Map** 5 C3.
Tel (415) 781-3956.

Kati Koos: A Gallery with Tongue in Chic
500 Sutter St. **Map** 5 B4.
Tel (415) 362-3437.

MAC Cosmetics
45 Powell St. **Map** 5 B5.
Tel (415) 402-0658.

Ten Ren Tea Company of San Francisco
949 Grant Ave.
Map 5 C3.
Tel (415) 362-0656.

VIP Luggage
50 Post St.
Map 5 C4.
Tel (415) 391-2200.

Food and Wine

Boudin Bakery
4 Embarcadero Center.
Map 6 D3.
Tel (415) 362-3330.

La Boulange
2325 Pine St.
Map 4 D4.
Tel (415) 440-0356.

Caffè Roma Coffee Roasting Company
526 Columbus Ave.
Map 5 B2.
Tel (415) 296-7942.

Caffè Trieste
601 Vallejo St.
Map 5 C3.
Tel (415) 982-2605.

California Wine Merchant
2113 Chestnut St.
Map 4 D2.
Tel (415) 567-0646.

Casa Lucas Market
2934 24th St.
Tel (415) 826-4334.

Cheese Plus
2001 Polk St. **Map** 5 A3.
Tel (415) 921-2001.

David's
474 Geary St.
Map 5 A5.
Tel (415) 276-5950.

Ferry Plaza Farmers' Market
1 Ferry Building. **Map** 6 D3. **Tel** (415) 291-3276.
w ferrybuildingmarket
place.com

Ghiradelli Chocolate Factory
Ghirardelli Square.
Map 4 F1.
Tel (415) 474-3938.
44 Stockton St.
Map 5 B1.
Tel (415) 397-3030.

Graffeo Coffee Roasting Company
735 Columbus Ave.
5 B2. **Tel** (415) 986-2420.

Heart of the City Farmers' Market
1182 Market St,
No. 415.
Map 10 F1.
Tel (415) 558-9455.

Lucca Ravioli Company
1100 Valencia St. **Map** 10 F3. **Tel** (415) 647-5581.

Molinari Delicatessen
373 Columbus Ave. **Map** 5 C3. **Tel** (415) 421-2337.

Napa Valley Winery Exchange
415 Taylor St.
Map 5 B5.
Tel (415) 771-2887.
w nvwe.com

Pasta Gina
741 Diamond St.
Map 10 D4.
Tel (415) 282-0738.

Whole Foods
1765 California St.
Map 4 F4.
Tel (415) 674-0500.

Williams-Sonoma
340 Post St.
Map 5 C4.
Tel (415) 362-9450.

Books, Music, Art, and Antiques

49 Geary St
49 Geary St.
Map 5 C5.
Tel (415) 986-5826.

Adobe Books & Arts Cooperative
3130 24th St.
Map 10 F4.
Tel (415)
864-3936.**Amoeba Music**
1855 Haight St.
Map 9 B1.
Tel (415) 831-1200.

Best Buy
1717 Harrison St.
Map 6 D5.
Tel (415) 626-9682.

City Lights Bookstore
261 Columbus Ave.
Map 5 C3.
Tel (415) 362-8193.

DIRECTORY

Dragon House
455 Grant Ave.
Map 5 C4.
Tel (415) 781-2351.

Fraenkel Gallery
49 Geary St.
Map 5 C5.
Tel (415) 981-2661.

Green Apple Books & Music
506 Clement St.
Map 3 A5.
Tel (415) 387-2272.

John Berggruen Gallery
228 Grant Ave.
Map 5 C4.
Tel (415) 781-4629.

Lang Antiques
323 Sutter St.
Map 5 C4.
Tel (415) 982-2213.

Modern Times Bookstore
2919 24th St.
Map 10 E4.
Tel (415) 282-9246.

Prints Old & Rare
580 Crespi Drive,
Pacifica, California.
Tel (650) 355-6325.

Rasputin Music
69 Powell St.
Map 5 B5.
Tel (415) 834-0267.

Recycled Records
1377 Haight St.
Map 9 C1.
Tel (415) 626-4075.

Union Music Company
1710-B Market St.
Map 10 F1.
Tel (415) 775-6043.

William Stout Architectural Books
804 Montgomery St.
Map 5 C3.
Tel (415) 391-6757.

Xanadu Gallery
Frank Lloyd Wright Bldg,
140 Maiden Lane.
Map 5 B5.
Tel (415) 392-9999.

Clothing

Banana Republic
256 Grant Ave. **Map** 5 C4.
Tel (415) 788-3087.

Brooks Brothers
240 Post St.
Map 5 C4.
Tel (415) 402-0476.

Buffalo Exchange
1555 Haight St.
Map 9 C1.
Tel (415) 431-7733.
1210 Valencia St.
Map 10 F4.
Tel (415) 647-8332.

Burlington Coat Factory
899 Howard St.
Tel (415) 495-7234.

Chanel Boutique
155 Maiden Lane.
Map 5 C5.
Tel (415) 981-1550.

Diana Slavin
3 Claude Lane.
Map 5 C4.
Tel (415) 677-9939.

DSW Shoe Warehouse
400 Post St.
Map 5 B5.
Tel (415) 956-3453.

Eddie Bauer
Westfield San Francisco
Centre, 865 Market St.
Map 5 C5.
Tel (415) 343-0146.

Gucci
240 Stockton St.
Map 5 C5.
Tel (415) 392-2808.

Guess
865 Market St, Suite 206.
Map 5 C5.
Tel (415) 495-0200.

Jeremy's
2 South Park St, South
Beach. **Tel** (415) 882-4929.

Joanie Char
537 Sutter St. **Map** 5 B4.
Tel (415) 399-9867.

The Levi's Store
815 Market St
Map 5 C5.
Tel (415) 501-0100

Marc Jacobs
125 Maiden Lane.
Map 5 C4.
Tel (415) 362-6500.

Mission Thrift
2330 Mission St.
Map 10 F3.
Tel (415) 821-9560.

Nike
278 Post St.
Map 5 C4.
Tel (415) 392-6453.

On The Run
1310 9th Ave.
Map 8 F3.
Tel (415) 682-2042.

Prada
201 Post St.
Map 5 C4.
Tel (415) 848-1900.

Ria's Shoes
301 Grant Ave.
Map 5 C4.
Tel (415) 834-1420.

Rolo
2351 Market St.
Map 10 D2.
Tel (415) 431-4545.

Salvatore Ferragamo
236 Post St.
Map 5 C4.
Tel (415) 391-6565.

Small Frys
4066 24th St.
Map 10 D4.
Tel (415) 648-3954.

Sui Generis Boutique
2265 Market St.
Map 10 D2.
Tel (415) 437-2265.

Thrift Town
2101 Mission St.
Map 10 F3.
Tel (415) 861-1132.

Uniqlo
111 Powell St.
Map 5 B5.
Tel (877) 486-4756.

Upper Playground
220 Fillmore St.
Map 10 E1.
Tel (415) 861-1960.

Urban Outfitters
80 Powell St.
Map 5 B5.
Tel (415) 989-1515.

The Wasteland
1660 Haight St.
Map 9 B1.
Tel (415) 863-3150.

Wilkes Bashford
375 Sutter St.
Map 5 C4.
Tel (415) 986-4380.

Toys, Games, and Gadgets

Ambassador Toys
2 Embarcadero Center.
Map 6 D3.
Tel (415) 759-8697.

Brookstone
3251 20th Ave.
Tel (415) 731-8046.

Chinatown Kite Shop
717 Grant Ave.
Map 5 C3.
Tel (415) 989-5182.

Exploratorium Store
Pier 15.
Map 6 D2.
Tel (415) 528-4444.

Puppets on the Pier
PIER 39. **Map** 5 B1.
Tel (415) 781-4435.

Many of the listings have
multiple branches. Shops
will be happy to provide
information of their
nearest branch.

ENTERTAINMENT IN SAN FRANCISCO

San Francisco has prided itself on being the cultural capital of the West Coast since the city first began to prosper in the 1850s, and the entertainment offered is generally of high quality. The performing arts complex of the Civic Center, opposite the City Hall, is the principal venue for classical music, opera, and ballet. A vital part of the city's cultural life is the highly rated Center for the Arts Theater at Yerba Buena Gardens. Many international touring shows can be seen here. There are numerous repertory movie theaters offering filmgoers a wide range of programs, but theater, except for some of the "alternative" venues, is not the city's strongest suit. Popular music, in particular jazz and blues, is where San Francisco really excels, and you can hear good bands for the price of a drink or at the street fairs and music festivals that are held during the summer months. Facilities are also available for a wide variety of sports, from cycling to golf, tennis, and sailing.

Information Sources

Complete listings of what is on and where are given in the *San Francisco Chronicle* and *Examiner* newspapers. The *Chronicle*'s Sunday edition is very useful. Other good sources are the free weekly newspapers, such as the *San Francisco Weekly* (available in kiosks, cafés, and bars), which gives both listings and reviews, especially of live music, films, and nightclubs.

Visitors planning in advance will find the *San Francisco Book* very helpful. This is published quarterly by the San Francisco Travel Association and is available free at the **Visitor Information Center** at Hallidie Plaza. You can also phone the visitors' bureau's Events Line for recorded information or check their website. Look out for the numerous free magazines for visitors, such as **Where San Francisco**, which often have a useful associated website.

Buying Tickets

The international company **Ticketmaster** dominates the ticket sales industry in the US. You can order tickets for just about any performance or event through Ticketmaster online or over the phone. Note that service charges and other fees can add a significant amount to the price of your tickets.

Many venues have exclusive arrangements with Ticketmaster, but it is worth checking the venue's website in case you can buy from the venue, or relevant cultural organization, direct. Most venues will charge some kind of service fee on top of the price of a ticket. **Tix Bay Area** is another option, if you would

Storefront of San Francisco ticket agency

prefer not to buy from Ticketmaster.

You might also consider buying from one of the major online ticket resellers. **StubHub**, a subsidiary of eBay, enables anyone to sell their unwanted tickets online, and ensures the transaction is safe and secure. The price is set by the seller so will likely differ from the ticket's face value. Delivery fees are charged where applicable, plus there is a service fee.

Most box offices are not reliable sources for seats, as they usually do not open until just before the evening performance. If you are after a last-minute ticket and in the area, however, the box office is always worth checking. Keep in mind that to see productions by the reputable San Francisco Symphony, Ballet, and Opera companies, advance planning is essential.

Buying from the ticket scalpers invariably found outside sold-out events may be tempting, but is a risky undertaking. You will need to bargain hard, and then you may still find yourself in possession of a counterfeit ticket.

War Memorial Opera House, home to the San Francisco Ballet

Outdoor chess, popular in Portsmouth Plaza, Chinatown

Discount Tickets

Tix Bay Area is a nonprofit ticketing service selling full-price and discount tickets for almost every cultural show in San Francisco and the surrounding area. A substantial portion of Tix Bay Area's service charges goes to Theatre Bay Area, a performance art advocacy group that supports local artists.

Tix Bay Area runs a ticket booth on the east side of Union Square (see p324), open daily from 9am until 5pm (until 6pm on weekends), where you can pick up regular and discounted tickets to dance, theater, music, and film, and, if you are lucky, same-day half-price tickets to the best theater performances in town.

Free Events

In addition to San Francisco's many ticket-only events, a number of free concerts and performances are regularly staged all over the city. Many take place during the day and outdoors in the summer; they can offer a welcome change of pace from the usual standard fare. The San Francisco Symphony (see pp394) gives just one of the many musical performances in a series of free Sunday concerts from mid-June through August at Stern Grove, south of the Sunset District.

The San Francisco Opera stages a free full-scale performance in Golden Gate Park as a key event in the opera's first week of the season. Sponsored by the *San Francisco Chronicle*, this attracts 20,000-plus people each year. "Opera in the Park" is another popular annual event held in Dolores Park which also plays host to the San Francisco Mime Troupe. In the summer, Golden Gate Park is the place to be for the Shakespeare Festival and Comedy Celebration Day.

From May through October, Yerba Buena Gardens puts on popular and operatic music series, cultural festivals, dance performances, and more. Throughout the year dozens of free festivals and celebrations, such as Chinese New Year, provide plenty of fun (see pp40–43).

Facilities for the Disabled

California is a national leader in providing facilities for the handicapped. Most theaters and concert halls in San Francisco are therefore fully accessible and have open areas set aside for wheelchair-users. Some smaller venues may require the use of special entrances, or elevators to reach the upper tiers. Many cinemas offer amplifying headphones. Contact the venues themselves to ensure they are able to accommodate you.

The Presidio Cinema

AT&T Park, home of the San Francisco Giants (see p396)

Entertainment Venues

With a variety of entertainment options, San Francisco is one of the most enjoyable cities in the world for performing arts enthusiasts. Whatever your cultural preferences, what you see here is sure to be good. Besides housing the West Coast's best opera and ballet companies, it has a highly regarded symphony orchestra. The city also offers a wide range of jazz and rock music, diverse theater companies, and specialty movie houses. For the sports fan there are also plenty of opportunities to both watch and take part.

The ultramodern Louise M Davies Symphony Hall

Film and Theater

San Francisco has an avid film-going community. The **AMC Metreon** is a 16-screen complex plus IMAX with shops, restaurants, special programs, and other attractions. One of the city's best movie houses is the **Sundance Kabuki**, an eight-screen complex in the Japan Center *(see p356)*, which also hosts the **San Francisco International Film Festival** each May. Another popular venue for first-run films is the **Embarcadero Center Cinema**, which excels at indie films. Main venues for first-run foreign films include the **Clay Theatre** in Pacific Heights and **Opera Plaza**

Cinema. The **Castro Theatre** *(see p364)* shows Hollywood classics and other revivals, with a film program that changes daily. In the Mission District, **The Roxie** shows an eclectic mix of indie films and documentaries.

Many residents of San Francisco show apparent disdain for mainstream theater, which explains why it has a lower profile here than in other large cities. Mainstream theaters, which host a range of touring Broadway productions as well as those by local companies, are concentrated in the Theater District *(see p324)*. Three of the largest theaters are the **Golden Gate Theatre**, the **Curran Theatre**, and the **Orpheum Theater**, all part of the Best of Broadway performance series. The **Children's Creativity Museum** stages both student and professional productions, while musicals and comedy are staged at **The Marsh**. The most respected major company is the American Conservatory Theater (ACT). A variety of plays are performed during its October to May season at its longtime home, the historic **Geary Theater**.

Opera, Classical Music, and Dance

The main season of the **San Francisco Opera** runs from September to December; tickets can cost more than $100, but there is a summer season, with less expensive tickets.

The main venue for opera, classical music, and dance is the Civic Center performing arts complex on Van Ness Avenue. The **Louise M Davies Symphony Hall** located here is now San Francisco's principal location for fine classical music performances, and home to the highly regarded **San Francisco Symphony**, which give up to five concerts a week during its winter season. Guest conductors, performers, and touring orchestras perform additional special concerts. The **Herbst Theatre**, which usually hosts recitals by prominent performers, provides one of the city's most comfortable and intimate settings to attend a performance.

In addition to these big events, there are numerous less formal recitals and concerts in the Bay Area. The **Philharmonia Baroque Orchestra**, a period instrument ensemble, plays at various sites around the city, while the historic **Old First Presbyterian Church** has a series of chamber music and individual recitals on Friday nights and Sunday afternoons. In addition to educating the gifted musicians of tomorrow, the **San Francisco Conservatory of Music** hosts a plethora of classical performances, from faculty recitals to one-act operas, and the perenially popular

The landmark Castro Theatre

The Geary Theater *(see p314)*

Midsummer Mozart series. **Grace Cathedral** is a particularly striking setting for choral church music. The choir sings at Evensong on Thursdays at 5:15pm, while Choral Eucharist is celebrated on Sundays at 11am.

Founded in 1933, the **San Francisco Ballet** is the oldest professional ballet company in the US. Its season of classical and new works runs from mid-December to May at the splendid Beaux Arts **War Memorial Opera House**. Performances by local talent take place at the intimate **Z Space** and the **ODC Theater**, both located in the Mission District. The Yerba Buena Center for the Arts (see pp326–7) is home to **Alonzo King LINES Ballet**, while **Zellerbach Hall** across the Bay in Berkeley attracts the area's best touring productions.

Slim's, one of San Francisco's best rock venues

Rock, Jazz, and Blues

Two of the best rock clubs to hear live music are **Slim's** and **Bimbo's 365 Club**. Bimbo's hosts rock, jazz, country, and R&B – and attracts a similarly diverse crowd. Slim's is a bit more upscale, tending to feature established performers in its comfortable 436-seat room. Another popular place is the **Fillmore Auditorium**, which was the legendary birthplace of psychedelic rock during the 1960s (see p363).

There are a number of excellent places to hear live jazz in the city. The entertainment is usually free, if you buy dinner or drinks. For traditional Dixieland in an informal (and free) setting, visit the **Gold Dust Lounge**, in the heart of Fisherman's Wharf. Also try the piano bars located in downtown restaurants and hotels. For an interactive music experience, check out **Dueling Pianos at Johnny Foley's**,

where two pianists square off while working the crowd and playing requests. **SFJazz** is located in a state-of-the-art center built solely for, and dedicated to, jazz. The $50-million center hosts 200 performances per year, and it is the venue for some of SFJazz's signature activities, such as the annual SFJazz Festival (see p42) and SFJazz Hotplate. Many jazz fans plan trips to San Francisco to coincide with the world-famous **Monterey Jazz Festival**, which is held every September in Monterey, 2 hours south of San Francisco (see pp512–13).

Banner for the San Francisco Jazz Festival

Live blues is played somewhere in town every night of the week, in bars such as **The Saloon** and the **Boom Boom Room**. **Lou's Fish Shack**, on Fisherman's Wharf, has one or more blues bands on the bill almost every day, with special shows on weekends. The award-winning **Biscuits and Blues** has local blues spotlights on weekdays and special shows on weekends. The **Hemlock Tavern**, which mixes up the genres, is low-key and welcoming, with a free juke box and live music in the back room most nights of the week.

Clubs

Most of the larger clubs are located in the industrial South of Market (SoMA) area, and run from around 9pm until 2am. A few clubs stay open all night, especially on weekends, but all places stop serving alcohol at 2am. Always bring valid ID to prove you are over 21 or you will not be admitted.

One of San Francisco's popular clubs is **DNA Lounge** on 11th Street, with its multiple dance floors, flashy decor, great sound system, and fashionably mainstream clientele. R&B, hip-hop, and jazz are played at **Nickies** in Haight Ashbury. To dance to tunes spun by some of the best DJs in San Francisco, head to the **Chambers Eat & Drink**.

Some of the most popular clubs, such as **The Endup**, are primarily – though rarely exclusively – gay (see p398).

Clubbers flock to **Ruby Skye** to dance to superstar DJs or hang-out in the lounge upstairs. **The Parlor**, one of the only dance clubs near Fisherman's Wharf, has a cozy lounge, a pool table, a dance floor, and reasonably priced drinks.

Piano bars all have nightly live music that you can enjoy for the price of a drink. One of the best is the beautiful Art Deco-style **Top of the Mark** at the top of the Mark Hopkins InterContinental Hotel (see p537). **Forbidden Island**, a funky tiki lounge, offers a wide array of expertly-made, innovative drinks and snacks, and attracts partygoers across the bay to Alameda. The **Tonga**

The Saloon on Grant Avenue, North Beach

Room in the Fairmont Hotel is an elaborate cocktail bar where you can dance or just listen to jazz with a simulated rainstorm every half-hour.

Check local newspapers and websites for comedy club listings. Some of the best stand-up comedy shows take place at **The Marsh** in the Mission and **Cobb's Comedy Club** in Fisherman's Wharf.

Sports and Outdoor Activities

San Franciscans are sports enthusiasts, and there are plenty of activities to suit every taste. Popular spectator sports include football, baseball, and basketball. In 2014 the National Football League's, **San Francisco 49ers** moved from Candlestick, their homeground since 1971, to Levi's Stadium in Santa Clara.

The **Oakland Raiders** play at the O.co Coliseum in Oakland. Local colleges, including the **University of California at Berkeley** (see p422) and **Stanford University** (see p431), also have good football teams. Two professional baseball teams play in the Bay Area: the National League **San Francisco Giants** play their home games at the stadium at AT&T Park; the American League **Oakland Athletics** also play at the O.co Coliseum, just across the bay. The Bay Area's only NBA basketball team is the **Golden State Warriors**, who play at the Oracle Arena.

Large business hotels usually have health club facilities on the premises. Those that do not usually have an agreement with a private club that gives short-term membership to hotel guests. If neither of these options is available, choose from the upscale **San Francisco Bay Club**, near the Financial District, the **Pacific Heights Health Club**, or the **24-Hour Fitness Center**.

Golfers have a range of courses to choose from, including the municipal links in **Lincoln Park** and **Golden Gate Park**, and the beautiful **Presidio Golf Course**. The Presidio and Golden Gate Park area is also ideal for cycling. Rental shops here include **Stow Lake Boat & Bike Rentals**. In North Beach, **Blazing Saddles** also rents bikes. Most of the public swimming pools are on the suburban fringes: contact the **City of San Francisco Recreation and Parks District**. To swim in the chilly ocean, head out to China Beach, the only safe beach in the city.

DIRECTORY

Film and Theater

AMC Metreon
135 Fourth St.
Map 5 C5.
Tel (415) 369-6201.
w amctheatres.com

Castro Theatre
429 Castro St.
Map 10 D2.
Tel (415) 621-6120.
w castrotheatre.com

Children's Creativity Museum
221 4th St.
Map 5 C5.
Tel (415) 820-3320.
w creativity.org

Clay Theatre
2261 Fillmore St.
Map 4 D3.
Tel (415) 561-9921.
w landmark
theatres.com

Curran Theatre
445 Geary St.
Map 5 B5.
Tel (415) 551-2000.
w shnsf.com

Embarcadero Center Cinema
Embarcadero Center.
Map 6 D3.
Tel (415) 352-0835.
w landmarktheatres.
com

Geary Theater
415 Geary St.
Map 5 B5.
Tel (415) 749-2228.
w act-sf.org

Golden Gate Theatre
1 Taylor St.
Map 5 B5.
Tel (415) 551-2000.
w shnsf.com

The Marsh
1062 Valencia St.
Map 10 F3.
Tel (415) 826-5750
(theater), (415) 641-0235 (club).
w themarsh.org

Opera Plaza Cinema
601 Van Ness Ave.
Map 4 F5.
Tel (415) 267-4893.
w landmarktheatres.
com

Orpheum Theater
1192 Market St.
Map 4 F5.
Tel (415) 551-2000.
w shnsf.com

The Roxie
3117 16th St.
Map 10 F2.
Tel (415) 863-1087.
w roxie.com

San Francisco International Film Festival
Tel (415) 561-5000.
w festival.sffs.org

Sundance Kabuki
1881 Post St. **Map** 4 E4.
Tel (415) 346-3243.
w sundancecinemas.
com

Opera, Classical Music, and Dance

Alonzo King LINES Ballet
26 7th St.
Tel (415) 863-3040.
w linesballet.org

Grace Cathedral
1100 California St.
Map 5 B4.
Tel (415) 749-6300.
w gracecathedral.org

Herbst Theatre
401 Van Ness Ave.
Map 4 F5.
Tel (415) 392-4400.
w sfwmpac.org

Louise M Davies Symphony Hall
201 Van Ness Ave.
Map 4 F5.
Tel (415) 864-6000.
w sfsymphony.org

ODC Theater
351 Shotwell St.
Map 10 F3.
Tel (415) 863-6606.
w odcdance.org

Old First Presbyterian Church
1751 Sacramento St.
Map 4 F3.
Tel (415) 474-1608.
w oldfirstconcerts.org

Philharmonia Baroque Orchestra
180 Redwood St, Suite 200. **Map** 4 F5.
Tel (415) 252-1288.
w philharmonia.org

San Francisco Conservatory of Music
50 Oak St. **Map** 10 F1.
Tel (415) 503-6231.
w sfcm.edu

San Francisco Opera
301 Van Ness Ave.
Map 4 F5.
Tel (415) 864-3330.
w sfopera.com

San Francisco Symphony
201 Van Ness Ave. **Map** 4 F5. **Tel** (415) 864-6000.
w sfsymphony.org

DIRECTORY

War Memorial Opera House (San Francisco Ballet)
301 Van Ness Ave. **Map** 4 F5. **Tel** (415) 861-2000.
w sfballet.org

Z Space
450 Florida St.
Tel (415) 626-0453.
w zspace.org

Zellerbach Hall
UC Berkeley.
Tel (510) 642-9988.
w calperformances.org

Rock, Jazz, and Blues

Bimbo's 365 Club
1025 Columbus Ave.
Map 5 A2.
Tel (415) 474-0365.
w bimbos365club.com

Biscuits and Blues
401 Mason St.
Map 5 B5.
Tel (415) 292-2583.
w biscuitsandblues.com

Boom Boom Room
1601 Fillmore St.
Map 10 E1.
Tel (415) 673-8000.
w boomboomblues.com

Dueling Pianos at Johnny Foley's
243 O'Farrell St. **Map** 5 B5.
Tel (415) 954-0777.
w duelingpianosatfoleys.com

Fillmore Auditorium
1805 Geary at Fillmore St.
Map 4 D4.
Tel (415) 346-6000.
w thefillmore.com

Gold Dust Lounge
165 JeffersonSt.
Map 5 B1.
Tel (415) 397-1695.
w golddustsf.com

Hemlock Tavern
1131 Polk St. **Map** 4 F4.
Tel (415) 923-0923.
w hemlocktavern.com

Lou's Fish Shack
300 Jefferson St. **Map** 5 B1. **Tel** (415) 771-5687.
w lousfishshacksf.com

Monterey Jazz Festival
2000 Fairgrounds Rd at Casa Verde, Monterey.
Tel (831) 373-3366.
w montereyjazzfestival.org

The Saloon
1232 Grant Ave.
Map 5 C3.
Tel (415) 989-7666.

SFJazz
Franklin and Fell St.
Map 10 E1.
Tel (866) 920-5299.
w sfjazz.org

Slim's
333 11th St.
Map 10 F1.
Tel (415) 255-0333.
w slims-sf.com

Clubs

Chambers Eat & Drink
601 Eddy St.
Map 5 A5.
Tel (415) 829-2316.
w chambers-sf.com

Cobb's Comedy Club
The Cannery at Beach St, 915 Columbus Ave.
Map 5 A1.
Tel (415) 928-4320.
w cobbscomedyclub.com

DNA Lounge
375 11th St.
Tel (415) 626-1409.
w dnalounge.com

The Endup
401 6th St.
Tel (415) 646-0999.
w theendup.com

Forbidden Island
1304 Lincoln Ave, Alameda.
Tel (510) 749-0332.

Nickies
466 Haight St.
Map 10 E1.
Tel (415) 255-0300.
w nickies.com

The Parlor
2801 Leavenworth St.
Map 4 F1.
Tel (415) 775-5110.
w theparlorsf.com

Ruby Skye
420 Mason St.**Map** 5 B5.
Tel (415) 693-0777.
w rubyskye.com

Tonga Room
950 Mason St.
Map 5 B4.
Tel (415) 772-5278.
w tongaroom.com

Top of the Mark
Mark Hopkins InterContinental Hotel, 1 Nob Hill. **Map** 5 B4.
Tel (415) 616-6916.
w intercontinentalmarkhopkins.com

Sports and Outdoor Activities

24-Hour Fitness Center
Multiple locations.
w 24hourfitness.com

Blazing Saddles
1095 Columbus Ave.
Map 5 A2.
Tel (415) 202-8888.
One of seven branches.
w blazingsaddles.com

Golden Gate Park Golf Course
(Municipal 9 hole). **Map** 7 B2. **Tel** (415) 751-8987.
w goldengateparkgolf.com

Golden State Warriors
Oracle Arena.
Tel (888) 479-4667.
w nba.com/warriors

Lincoln Park
300 34th Ave.
Map 1 C5.
Tel (415) 221-9911.
w sfrecpark.org

Oakland Athletics
O.co Coliseum, 7000 Coliseum Way, Oakland.
Tel (877) 493-2255.
w oakland.athletics.mlb.com

Oakland Raiders
O.co Coliseum, 7000 Coliseum Way, Oakland.
Tel (510) 864-5000.
w raiders.com

Pacific Heights Health Club
2356 Pine St.
Map 4 D4.
Tel (415) 563-6694.
w phhcsf.com

Presidio Golf Course
300 Finley Rd. **Map** 3 A3.
Tel (415) 561-4661.
w presidiogolf.com

City of San Francisco Recreation and Parks District
Golden Gate Park, 501 Stanyan St.
Tel (415) 831-2700.
w sfrecpark.org

San Francisco 49ers
Levi's Stadium, 4900 Centennial Blvd, Santa Clara.
Tel (415) 464-9377.
w 49ers.com

San Francisco Bay Club
150 Greenwich St.
Map 5 C2.
Tel (415) 433-2200.
w bayclubs.com/sanfrancisco

San Francisco Giants
AT&T Park.
Tel (415) 972-2000.
w sfgiants.com

Stanford University Athletics
Stanford University.
Tel (650) 723-4591.
w gostanford.com

Stow Lake Boat & Bike Rentals
Golden Gate Park.
Map 8 E2.
Tel (415) 752-0347.
w stowlakeboathouse.com

UC Berkeley Athletics
UC Berkeley.
Tel (800) 462-3277.
w calbears.com

San Francisco's Bars

San Francisco has been a drinkers' town ever since the heady days of the Gold Rush *(see pp52–3)*, when there was a saloon for every 50 residents. The bawdy public houses of the mid-19th century no longer exist. Instead, today, you can drink with a view; grab a local brew; sip an elegant, sweet cocktail in a chic lounge; sample a fine local country vintage wine; mingle with cheering local fans at a sports bar; see satellite-broadcast matches from Europe and soak up charm and an occasional concert at an Irish Bar. Alternatively, join in the party atmosphere at one of San Francisco's many gay bars.

Rooftop Bars

Those with a head for heights and a craving to be above the hills can visit the bars at the top of the towers in the city center. **The View** at the Marriott Marquis *(see p537)* and **Top of the Mark** at the Mark Hopkins *(see p537)* offer splendid views and evening jazz along with dance music. Harry Denton's **Starlight Room**, 21 stories above the Sir Francis Drake Hotel *(see p536)*, is a traditional hotel bar, mixing old-school charm with unbelievable views of the city.

Enjoy authentic margaritas and Mexican food, along with views of the city skyline, from the rooftop bar at **El Techo de Lolinda**. **Jones** is just a few stories up but has a gorgeous, expansive outdoor deck.

Beer Bars

For a more down-to-earth experience, visit one of the city's many beer bars, popular gathering places for the after-work crowd and weekend revelers. The best of these specialize in beers brewed by West Coast breweries, including San Francisco's fine Anchor Steam and Liberty Ale.

One of the best, the English **Mad Dog in the Fog**, is situated on Haight Street. **Toronado**, also on Haight Street, has an unparalleled selection of rare craft beers, and lures beer lovers from across the world. **The Pig and Whistle** is another classic pub serving beer from around the world. **Magnolia Pub & Brewery**, in a 1903 Haight Victorian adobe, retains its original wooden bar and name from ex-dancer, Magnolia Thunderpussy. Both **Thirsty Bear Brewing Company**, known for

tapas, and **The City Beer Store & Tasting Bar**, where drinkers can peruse bottles as they sip from fine brews, make their own excellent beer on the premises. At the Pacific Ocean edge of Golden Gate Park, **Beach Chalet** combines brews with fine views.

Cocktail Bars

Traditional cocktail bars, with a chatty bartender holding court in front of rows of gleaming bottles, are great fun in San Francisco, and there are plenty of venues to choose from.

Those in the need-to-be-seen crowd are in the Clift Hotel **Redwood Room**, with a backlit bar and upper tier cocktail prices *(see p537)*. A lively bohemian crowd can be found along Columbus Avenue at **Specs'**, **Tosca Café**, and **Vesuvio** – a one-time beatnik hangout where a popular house drink is the Jack Kerouac (rum, tequila, orange/cranberry juice, and lime). Banquettes, cocktail tables, and Rat Pack-era decor mix with a relaxed North Beach crowd at **Tony Nik's Café**.

Across town in the Mission District, **Elixir** is a neighborhood bar with darts in a Victorian building that once had a bootblack on the premises. For a swinging night of live music and potent cocktails, head to **Bimbo's 365 Club** in North Beach. **Buena Vista Café** is the 1952 birthplace of Irish Coffee and serves 2,000 glasses a day. **Chambers Eat & Drink** is a groovy, glam-rock bar and gastropub, with cool cocktails, leather sofas, and neon lights. Hip, crowded **Rickhouse** in the Tenderloin sports a wood-paneled interior and a famous

punchbowl. In other bars, such as **Café du Nord**, in a former Prohibition speakeasy, and the award-winning **Biscuits and Blues**, live jazz is available.

Wine Bars

With the proximity to Northern California Wine Country, the **Ferry Plaza Wine Merchant Bar**, surrounded by artisan cheese-makers and bakers, is a fine spot to sample wines.

Champagne and candlelight create the atmosphere of the **Bubble Lounge**. Popular with locals, **Amelie**, an inviting, candle-lit lounge, offers an extensive wine list that pairs well with an assortment of cheese and charcuterie plates. **Ma'velous** harnesses the combined culinary resources of California to offer an establishment specializing in both the finest roasted coffees and boutique wines. Nearby, the well-reputed **Press Club**, in a cozy underground space beneath the Four Seasons Hotel, spotlights two wineries a month.

Themed Bars

Smuggler's Cove, with a nautical and pirate-themed decor, boasts exotic cocktails and one of the country's biggest rum lists featuring over 500 labels. Bring your own food or snacks to the drinks-only **The Greens Sports Bar**. **Edinburgh Castle Pub** offers indie music complete with fish 'n' chips, darts, and pool. Good Irish cheer and ample Guinness are quaffed at **The Irish Bank** and **The Chieftain**.

Gay Bars

Watering holes popular with the LGBT crowd range from fetish clubs to those favored by a particular clientele. The Castro, SoMa, and Mission Districts are magnet areas. **440 Castro** draws a Levi's and leather crowd. **AsiaSF** and **The Endup** keep drinks flowing with the dancing. In a city where few lesbian bars have survived, **Wild Side West** keeps the party going. **Divas Nightclub & Bar** is a well-known transgendered spot.

DIRECTORY

Rooftop Bars

El Techo de Lolinda
2518 Mission St.
Map 10 F3.
Tel (415) 550-6970.
[w] eltechosf.com

Jones
620 Jones St.
Map 5 B4.
Tel (415) 496-6858.
[w] 620-jones.com

Starlight Room
450 Powell St. **Map** 5 B4.
Tel (415) 395-8595.
[w] starlightroomsf.com

Top of the Mark
19th floor, Mark Hopkins
InterContinental Hotel,
1 Nob Hill. **Map** 5 B4.
Tel (415) 616-6916.
[w] intercontinental
markhopkins.com

The View
39th floor, Marriott Hotel,
55 4th St. **Map** 5 C5.
Tel (415) 896-1600.
[w] sfviewlounge.com

Beer Bars

Beach Chalet
1000 Great Hwy.
Map 7 A2.
Tel (415) 386-8439.
[w] beachchalet.com

**The City Beer Store &
Tasting Bar**
1168 Folsom St.
Tel (415) 503-1033.
[w] citybeerstore.com

Mad Dog in the Fog
530 Haight St. **Map** 10 E1.
Tel (415) 626-7279.
[w] themaddoginthe
fog.com

**Magnolia Pub &
Brewery**
1398 Haight St. **Map** 9 C1.
Tel (415) 864-7468.
[w] magnoliapub.com

The Pig & Whistle
2801 Geary Blvd.
Map 3 C5.
Tel (415) 885-4779.

**Thirsty Bear Brewing
Company**
661 Howard St.
Map 6 D5.
Tel (415) 974-0905.
[w] thirstybear.com

Toronado
547 Haight St.
Map 10 E1.
Tel (415) 863-2276.
[w] toronado.com

Cocktail Bars

Bimbo's 365 Club
1025 Columbus Ave,
North Beach.
Map 5 B2.
Tel (415) 474-0365.
[w] bimbos365club.com

Biscuits and Blues
401 Mason St. **Map** 5 B5.
Tel (415) 292-2583.
[w] biscuitsandblues.
com

Buena Vista Café
2765 Hyde St.
Map 4 F1.
Tel (415) 474-5044.
[w] thebuenavista.com

Café du Nord
2170 Market St.
Map 10 D2.
Tel (415) 861-5016.
[w] cafedunord.com

**Chambers Eat &
Drink**
601 Eddy St.
Map 5 A5
Tel (415) 8829-2316.
[w] chambers-sf.com

Elixir
3200 16th St (at
Valencia St).
Map 10 F2.
Tel (415) 552-1633.
[w] elixirsf.com

Redwood Room
Clift Hotel, 495 Geary St.
Map 5 B5.
Tel (415) 929-2372.
[w] clifthotel.com

Rickhouse
246 Kearny St.
Map 5 C4.
Tel (415) 398-2827.

**Specs' Twelve Adler
Museum Café**
12 William Saroyan Alley.
Map 5 C3.
Tel (415) 421-4112.

Tony Nik's Café
1534 Stockton St.
Map 5 B2.
Tel (415) 693-0990.
[w] tonyniks.com

Tosca Café
242 Columbus Ave.
Map 5 C3.
Tel (415) 986-9651.
[w] toscacafesf.com

Vesuvio
255 Columbus Ave.
Map 5 C3.
Tel (415) 362-3370.
[w] vesuvio.com

Wine Bars

Amelie
1754 Polk St.
Map 4 F3.
Tel (415) 292-6916.

Bubble Lounge
714 Montgomery St.
Map 5 C3.
Tel (415) 434-4204.
[w] bubblelounge.com

**Ferry Plaza Wine
Merchant & Wine Bar**
1 Ferry Building, Shop 23.
Map 6 E3.
Tel (415) 391-9400.
[w] fpwm.com

Ma'velous
1408 Market St.
Map 10 D2.
Tel (415) 626-8884.
[w] maveloussf.com

Press Club
20 Yerba Buena Lane.
Map 5 C5.
Tel (415) 744-5000.
[w] pressclubsf.com

Themed Bars

The Chieftain
198 5th St.
Tel (415) 615-0916.
[w] thechieftain.com

Edinburgh Castle Pub
950 Geary Blvd.
Map 5 A5.
Tel (415) 885-4074.

**The Greens Sports
Bar**
2339 Polk St.
Map 5 A3.
Tel (415) 775-4287.

The Irish Bank
10 Mark Ln (off Bush St).
Map 5 B4.
Tel (415) 788-7152.
[w] theirishbank.com

Smuggler's Cove
650 Gough St.
Map 4 F5.
Tel (415) 869-1900
[w] smugglercovesf.com

Gay Bars

440 Castro
440 Castro St.
Map 10 D3.
Tel (415) 621-8732.
[w] the440.com

AsiaSF
201 9th St.
Tel (415) 255-2742.
[w] asiasf.com

Divas Nightclub & Bar
1081 Post St.
Map 4 F4.
Tel (415) 474-3482.
[w] divassf.com

The Endup
401 6th St.
Tel (415) 646-0999.
[w] theendup.com

Wild Side West
424 Cortland Ave.
Map 10 F5.
Tel (415) 647-3099.
[w] wildsidewest.com

GETTING AROUND SAN FRANCISCO

San Francisco occupies a compact area, making it a sightseer's dream. Many of the sights featured on visitors' itineraries are only a short walk from each other. Cycling is also a popular way to travel around. The public transportation system is easy to use and efficient. Bus routes crisscross town and pass many attractions. MUNI Metro streetcars and BART lines serve downtown as well as the suburbs and outlying neighborhoods. Taxis are reasonably priced and recommended for trips after dark in certain areas. They can be hailed on the street or booked in advance by telephone. And, of course, no one can resist a cable car ride over the city's famed hills. Passenger ferries and boat trips run regularly east and north across the bay. If driving in San Francisco see page 605 for details on the city's parking laws.

Do not cross the street

You may cross the street

Walking

The best way to explore San Francisco is on foot. The main tourist areas are within 15 to 20 minutes of each other when walking at an average speed. The hills can be a struggle, but the views over the city and the bay make them well worth the climb.

Most road intersections are marked with a green and white sign bearing the name of the cross street, or names are imprinted in the concrete pavement at street corners.

Vehicles are driven on the right-hand side of the road and are allowed to turn right on a red light if the road is clear, so be careful when crossing at traffic lights. Never rely solely on a pedestrian "Walk" signal.

Jaywalking is common but illegal and crossing a street when the "Don't Walk" signal is showing can result in a hefty fine so wait for the "Walk" signal and proceed with caution. Pedestrian lights countdown to show how much time you have to cross.

Taxis

Taxis in San Francisco are licensed and operate 24 hours a day. You can catch a cab at a taxi stand, call for a pick-up, or hail a cab when its rooftop sign is illuminated. There is a flat fee ($3.50) for the first mile (1.6 km). This increases by about $2.75 for each additional mile or 45 cents a minute while waiting at an address or in heavy traffic. Add a 15 percent tip onto the fare. Mobile app cab services such as **Uber** and **Lyft** are available in the Bay Area.

Cycling

Cycling is a popular way to get around San Francisco. It is possible to find cycle lanes avoiding hills along the waterfront. Bikes can be rented from around $30 a day or $130 a week from hire outlets. Buses are equipped to carry bikes strapped to the front of the bus. **Bay Area Bike Share** provides bikes for hire from bike stations throughout the city. You need to purchase a 24-hour or 3-day membership. The first 30 minutes of each ride are included in the membership fee.

Other Ways to Get Around

Pedicabs and horse-drawn carriages can be found on The Embarcadero, especially near Fisherman's Wharf (see pp338–9).

A pedicab – an increasingly popular way of seeing the sights

Small, two-seater go karts are available to rent throughout the city as well, through **GoCar**. The small cars can drive up to 60 mph (97 kmh) and are pre-programmed with tours and GPS systems to guide you around the city. If you do not feel like driving, a fleet of motorized cable cars dash around the city giving guided tours of all the sights, allowing you to hop-on and off. Sight-seeing bus tours are offered as half- or full-day trips.

DIRECTORY

Taxis

Black & White Checker
Tel (415) 285-3880.

DeSoto
Tel (415) 970-1300.

Fog City Cab
Tel (415) 282-8749.

Yellow Cab
Tel (415) 626-2345.

Cycling

Bay Area Bike Share
W bayareabikeshare.com

Bay City Bike
2661 Taylor St, Fisherman's Wharf.
Map 4 F1. **Tel** (415) 346-2453.
W baycitybike.com

Blazing Saddles
2715 Hyde St. **Map** 5 A1.
Tel (415) 202-8888.
W blazingsaddles.com

Other Ways to Get Around

GoCar
Tel (800) 914-6227.
W gocartours.com

Traveling by Bus and Muni Metro Streetcar

San Francisco Municipal Railway (Muni) is the organization that runs the city's bus, cable car, and streetcar systems. You can use one interchangeable pass – Muni Passport – to travel on Muni buses, Muni Metro light rail streetcars, the F Market & Wharves historic streetcar line, and the three cable car lines. Bus routes and the seven lines of the Muni Metro streetcar system serve most tourist attractions and all neighborhoods.

Fares and Tickets

Buses, streetcars, and the metro cost $2.25 per ride. Since the **Muni** system has phased out paper tickets, visitors now need to buy either a Clipper card or Limited Use Muni tickets. The Clipper card is a reloadable fare card that is accepted on all Muni vehicles, as well as on BART, AC Transit, Caltrain, SamTrans, VTA, and Golden Gate Transit and Ferry. It can be bought at BART and Muni stations, as well as at many stores and costs $5. Visitors can buy a Limited Use Muni Ticket from machines in Muni stations for use on Muni only. Senior citizens over 65 and children aged five to 17 years pay reduced fares. Kids under five travel free.

A Muni Passport, valid for one, three, or seven days, allows unlimited travel on buses, streetcars, and cable cars. It is available from information kiosks at San Francisco International airport, the **San Francisco Travel Association**, and the cable car ticket booths at Powell & Market and Hyde & Beach Streets.

CityPass *(see p603)* is another option. For $94 ($69 for kids), you get unlimited Muni and cable car rides for seven of the nine days covered by the pass, plus entry to four attractions including the California Academy of Sciences.

Muni Metro streetcar, with its distinctive red and silver cars

Buses and Muni Metro Streetcars

Buses stop only at their designated bus stops every two or three blocks. The route number and the destination are found on the front and side of each bus. Those route numbers followed by a letter (L, EX, A, etc.) are limited-stop or express services.

Bus stops have signs displaying the Muni logo. The walls of the shelter list the route numbers of buses that stop there, and provide route maps and frequency guides. On boarding, put the exact change in the fare box or show your Muni Passport to the driver. To indicate that you want to get off at the next stop, pull the cord that runs along the windows or inform the driver. The "Stop Requested"

sign above the front window will light up.

Muni Metro streetcars and BART trains *(see p403)* share four of the seven under-ground stations along Market Street, marked by orange, yellow, and white illuminated signs. Once inside, look for the separate "Muni" entrance.

To travel west of the city, choose "Outbound"; to travel east, choose "Downtown." Electronic signs indicate which streetcar is about to arrive. Doors open automatically unless you are at a low-level or street-level station, in which case just push on the low bar beside the door. Stops above ground level are identified by an orange-and-brown flag or a yellow band around a pole, marked "Muni" or "Car Stop." Streetcar stops are wheelchair accessible and ramps are provided to board.

Sightseeing by Bus

The following are some popular bus routes for visitors: Route 38 runs to Japantown and the hills above Ocean Beach; Golden Gate Park *(see pp370–75)* is on Routes 5, 21, 28, 29, 44, 71, and N. For Chinatown and Nob Hill *(see pp328–35)* take Routes 1, 9X, 12, 30, 45. For Haight Ashbury *(see pp360–63)* take Route 6, 33, 37, 43, 71; Mission District *(see pp365–7)* is on Routes 14, 18, 22, 24, 33, 48, J. The rest of the Bay Area *(see pp414–35)* can be reached in about 30 to 45 minutes.

DIRECTORY

Muni Information
Tel (415) 673-6864.
Ⓦ sfmta.com

City Pass
Tel (888) 330-5008.
Ⓦ citypass.com

San Francisco Travel Association
Hallidie Plaza.
Map 5 C5. **Tel** (415) 391-2000.
Ⓦ 511.org

Destinations are shown on the front and side of the bus

Traveling by Cable Car, BART, and Ferry

San Francisco's cable cars are world-famous *(see pp306–7)* and every visitor will want to ride one at least once. San Francisco peninsula and the East Bay are linked by BART (Bay Area Rapid Transit), a 104-mile (114-km) light rail system with a high-speed, efficient fleet of trains, all wheelchair accessible. Boats and passenger ferries are also a favorite way to see the city's shoreline and to get around.

Nob Hill, where the Powell and California lines cross

The thrilling descent down Hyde Street to the bay

Using the Cable Cars

The city's cable car service operates 6:30am–12:30am daily with special schedules at weekends. There is a flat fare of $6 for a single trip with a discount for seniors and the disabled between 9pm and 7am. Kids of four and younger travel free. A $1 All-Day Passport gives you unlimited cable-car rides, plus unlimited Muni streetcar and bus rides. There are also three-day and seven-day unlimited tickets ($26 and $35 respectively).

Cable cars are reliable and run at 15-minute intervals. To catch a cable car, you should be prepared to jump on board quickly. Stops are marked by maroon signs that display the outline of a cable car in white, or by a yellow line painted on the road at right-angles to the track.

If you have not purchased a Muni Passport *(see p401)*, you can buy a ticket or a one-day pass from the conductor. Tickets are collected once you board. Muni passes, souvenir tickets, and maps are available at kiosks at Powell and Market streets and at Hyde and Beach streets, or at the San Francisco Travel Association *(see p401)*.

Cable cars run along three routes. The name of the line is displayed on the front, back, and sides of every car. The Powell–Hyde line is the most popular, starting at the Powell and Market turntable *(see p325)* and ending on Hyde Street, near Aquatic Park. The Powell–Mason line also begins at Powell and Market streets and ends at Bay Street. Sit facing east on the Powell lines and you will see the best sights as you travel. The California line runs from the base of Market Street, then through part of the Financial District and Chinatown, ending at Van Ness Avenue.

The city's hills present no problem to the cable cars and they tackle precipitous slopes effortlessly. The most thrilling descent is the final stretch of the Powell–Hyde line as it dips from Nob Hill to the bay.

Commuters also use cable cars, so try to avoid traveling during the rush hours 7am to 9:30am Mon–Fri and 4pm to 6:30pm Mon–Fri.

Traveling Safely in a Cable Car

If there is not a crowd, you can sit or stand inside, sit outside on a bench, or stand on a side running board. If you choose the latter, hold on tightly to the "hang on" poles that are provided.

Try not to get in the way of the gripman; he needs plenty of room to operate the grip lever. This off-limits area is marked by yellow lines on the floor. Use caution while on board. Passing other cable cars is exciting, but do not lean out too far because they get very close to one another. Be careful when boarding or getting off, as cable cars often stop at intersections, where you have to maneuver between the car and other vehicles.

Ferry Services and Bay Trips

Residents of the Bay Area adore their ferries, and they are used as much by local commuters as they are by tourists. Although these ferries do not provide audio tours to point out and describe the sights, they are a less expensive option than sightseeing cruises.

The Ferry Building *(see p320)* is the terminal

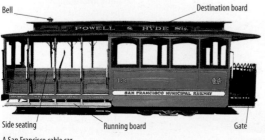

Bell — Destination board

Side seating — Running board — Gate

A San Francisco cable car

Making a Journey by BART

The BART logo

BART trains operate daily from early morning until midnight. During rush hours, 7am to 9am and 4pm to 7pm, they run at nearly full capacity. The trains are clean, well kept, and the service is highly efficient.

BART trains run each day from the International Terminal of San Francisco International Airport (SFO) into the heart of the city every 15–20 minutes. These trains stop at four central stations, all underneath Market Street – Civic Center, Powell, Montgomery, and Embarcadero. It costs $8.65 each way and takes 30 minutes. All eastbound trains

BART Route Map

— Richmond-Daly City

— Pittsburg/Bay Point-Daly city

— Fremont-Daly

— Fremont-Richmond

— Pleasanton-Millbrae

stop at downtown SF stations before heading for the East Bay via a dark, 4-mile (6-km) underwater tunnel. Transfers in the East Bay are best done at

MacArthur and 19th Street Oakland stations. Clipper cards (see p401) can be reloaded at the machines in all stations.

---

for Golden Gate Ferries. Bay sightseeing cruises from Fisherman's Wharf are operated by **Blue & Gold Fleet** and **Red & White Fleet**. Excursions offered include Angel Island and towns that lie on the north shore of the bay (see pp418–19). **Alcatraz Cruises** operates tours of Alcatraz island (see pp342–3). There are also combined boat and bus tours to Six Flags Discovery Kingdom and Muir Woods (see pp418–19).

You can dine and dance aboard one of several cruisers that ply the bay's waters.

Hornblower Dining Yachts offer lunch on Friday, brunch on weekends, and dinner daily on their cruises. Choose a bayside table for a spectacular view of the waterfront during your meal. The **Oceanic Society** offers trips with an onboard naturalist around the Farallon Islands, which lie 25 miles (40 km) off the coast of San Francisco (see p416). Whale-watching expeditions off the city's west coast (see p586) are also available, but you should check with individual operators for seasonal details.

DIRECTORY

Cable Cars

Cable Car Museum
(see p335 and also Muni, p401))

Ferries Services and Bay Trips

Alcatraz Cruises
Tel (415) 981-7625.
W alcatrazcruises.com

Blue & Gold Fleet
PIER 39. **Map** 5 B1.
Tel (415) 705-8200.
W blueandgoldfleet.com

Hornblower Dining Yachts
Pier 3. **Map** 6 D3.
Tel (888) 467-6256.
W hornblower.com

Oceanic Society
Tel (415) 256-9604.
W oceansociety.org

Red & White Fleet
Tel (415) 673-2900.
W redandwhite.com

Red & White Fleet ferry passing under the Golden Gate Bridge

1   **A**   **B**   **C**

SAN FRANCISCO
STREET FINDER

Map references given with sights,
entertainment venues, shops and Practical
Information addresses described in the San
Francisco section refer to the maps on the
following pages. Map references for hotels
and restaurants in the city *(see pp528–43 and
pp550–77)* also apply to these pages. The key

map below shows the area covered by the
Streetfinder, including the sightseeing areas
and other districts important for restaurants,
hotels, and entertainment venues. A large-
scale map of the city center appears on pages
5 and 6. The symbols used on the Street
Finder maps are listed in the key below.

Key to Street Finder

▢ Major Sight
▢ Places of interest
🚇 BART station
🚌 Bus terminus
🚋 Streetcar station
🚠 Cable car terminus
⛴ Ferry boarding point
ℹ️ Tourist information office
➕ Hospital with emergency unit
🏛 Police station
✝ Church
✡ Synagogue
☪ Mosque
☸ Buddhist temple
🛕 Hindu temple
⛳ Golf course
═ Railroad line
▬ Freeway
<<6600 House number (main street)

**Scale of Maps
1–4 and 7–10**

0 meters	500
0 yards	500

Scale of Maps 5 & 6

0 meters	500
0 yards	500

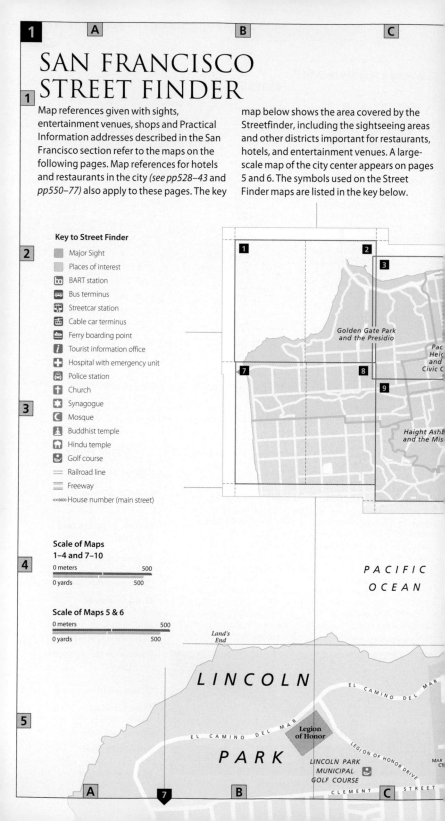

Golden Gate Park
and the Presidio

Pac
Heig
and
Civic C

Haight Ashl
and the Mis

PACIFIC
OCEAN

Land's
End

LINCOLN

EL CAMINO DEL MAR

EL CAMINO DEL MAR

Legion
of Honor

LEGION OF HONOR DRIVE

PARK

LINCOLN PARK
MUNICIPAL
GOLF COURSE

MAR
C

CLEMENT   **C**   STREET

A   **7**   **B**

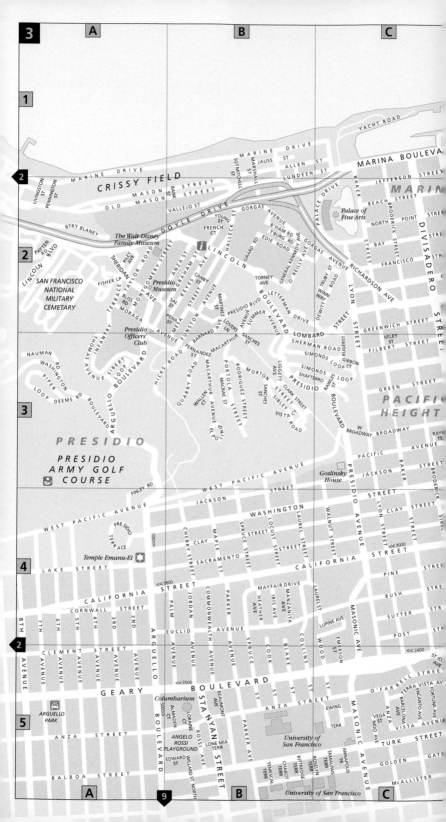

Sausalito,
Larkspur

1

Alcatraz
Island

PIER 23

PIER 19

PIER 17

PIER 15

Exploratorium

PIER 9

2

*San Francisco
Bay*

PIER 7

PIER 5

DAVIS STREET

THE

PIER 3

PIER 1

Oakland,
Alameda

3

EET

DAVIS STREET

DRUM

EMBARCADERO

KSON   STREET

ASHINGTON ST

MAKITIME
PLAZA

EMBARCADERO
PLAZA PARK

ST

JUSTIN
HERMAN
PLAZA

World Trade Center

PIER 2

LAY

*Embarcadero
Center*

ACRAMENTO

FRONT   ST

DAVIS   ST

*Hyatt
Regency Hotel*

Ferry Building

STREET

< 200

STREET

STREET

STEUART

Embarcadero

STREET

*Rincon
Center*

4

*Coast
Exchange*

*Amtrak
Terminal
Ticket Office*

MISSION

SPEAR

STREET

STREET

MAIN

STREET

PIER 24

SAN FRANCISCO-OAKLAND BAY BRIDGE

VENSON
ST

STREET

BEALE   STREET

FREMONT

**Greyhound
Bus Depot**

STREET

HOWARD

STREET

Folsom

STREET

PIER 26

omery St

**Transbay
Terminal**

1ST

STREET

MINNA STREET 100>>

FOLSOM

ELKHART
ST

350>>

PIER 28

*Pacific
Telephone
Building*

MALDEN

2ND

AL

TEHAMA STREET

CLEMENTINA

GROTE

GUY PL

CLEMENTINA
ST

LANSING ST

<<460

STREET

THE

PIER 30

PIER 32

*useum of
odern Art
enter for
he Arts*

HAWTHORNE

STREET

DOW PL

ESSEX
ST

STREET

STREET

1ST

STREET

EMBARCADERO

PIER 34

5

*scone
ntion
ater*

OM

HAMPTON
PL

HARRISON

VERONICA PL

STREET

300>>

STILLMAN ST

BRYANT

560>>

DE BOOM
ST

RINCON
ST

1ST

STREET

BRANNAN

STREET

Brannan

PIER 36

<<665

PIER 38

THE BAY AREA

Many of the settlements encircling San Francisco Bay were once summer retreats for the city's residents, but today they are sprawling suburbs or cities in their own right. Two of the most popular destinations in the East Bay are Oakland's museum and harbor and Berkeley's gardens and famous university. Farther south, San Jose has emerged as the region's newest commercial and cultural center, combining the technology of Silicon Valley with fine museums and preserved architecture of its Spanish Colonial past. Smaller towns such as Tiburon, Pescadero, and Sausalito, however, have managed to retain their village atmosphere, despite their closeness to the city. The area also has the advantage of its coastal landscapes: the cliffs of Point Reyes and the Marin Headlands, with their abundance of wildlife, offer perfect afternoon retreats away from the metropolis.

Sights at a Glance

Historic Towns
4 Sausalito
5 Tiburon
7 Benicia
9 *Berkeley pp422–5*
10 *Oakland pp426–9*
13 Livermore
16 Pescadero
17 *San Jose pp432–5*

Theme Parks
6 Six Flags Discovery Kingdom

Historic Buildings
11 Tao House
14 Stanford University
15 Filoli

Parks and Beaches
1 Point Reyes National Seashore
2 Muir Woods and Beach
3 *Marin Headlands pp420–21*
8 John Muir National Historic Site
12 Mount Diablo State Park

0 kilometers 25

0 miles 25

Key
Central San Francisco
Urban areas
Major road
Minor road

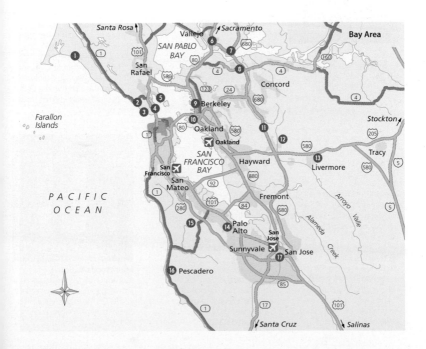

◀ UC Berkeley's Slather Tower at dusk

For keys to symbols *see back flap*

The Bay Area Coastline

The coastline around San Francisco varies a great deal, its rugged cliffs alternating with sandy beaches. Since the ocean water hovers around 60° F (15° C) all year, nobody swims or surfs without a wet suit, but for sun-bathing or aimless beachcombing strolls, the Bay Area beaches are hard to beat. Much of the coast is protected by a series of state and federal parks, such as the Point Reyes National Seashore, the Marin Headlands section of the Golden Gate National Recreation Area, and the many state beaches that line the Southern coast.

Santa

Tomales Road

① Point Reyes Station

Pacifica was once the agricultural outpost of Mission Dolores *(see p365)*. The two-story Sanchez Adobe in the town now houses a museum of 19th-century farming equipment.

① ★ Point Reyes National Seashore
This protected stretch of land is noted for its diverse ecosystems and its 360 species of birds *(see p418)*.

② Bolinas
Following the Gold Rush *(see pp52–3)*, Bolinas became a summer haven for San Franciscans, and some Victorian buildings still survive. The town is also a winter home to monarch butterflies.

④ Marin Headlands
The Marin Headlands benefit from stunning views of San Francisco as well as a wilderness rife with diverse birdlife *(see pp420–21)*.

⑥ Treasure Island
At the center of the Bay Bridge *(see pp420–21)*, the island was the site of the 1939 World's Fair. Connected to Yerba Buena Island, Treasure Island is now a residential community.

⑦ Fort Funston
The bluff overlooking this beach, which is also used as an observation site, is a favorite launch site for professional and amateur hang gliders.

⑧ Colma
This unusual town consists almost entirely of cemeteries, containing the graves of former San Franciscans and Bay Area residents. Cemeteries are prohibited within the city of San Francisco.

⑨ Pillar Point Harbor
This is the only naturally protected harbor located between San Francisco and Santa Cruz. In the late 19th century it was used as a whaling station.

⑫ ★ Farallon Islands
Twenty-seven miles (44 km) west of Point Bonita, the islands are the most important nesting site for sea birds and stopover point for migratory birds in California. They are also a breeding ground for elephant seals. There is no public access.

Muir Woods National Monument is the last remaining redwood forest in the Bay Area *(see p418)*. The others were cut down for lumber during the 19th century.

Mount Tamalpais, reaching a height of 2,604 ft (794 m), is the habitat of various flora and fauna, including the rarely sighted mountain lion. The Mountain Theater is set in a natural bowl overlooking the bay.

Locator Map

③ ★ Muir Beach

Redwood Creek drains down from Mount Tamalpais to the ocean at Muir Beach. It is home to silver salmon and crayfish. South of Muir Beach, Potato Patch Shoal is a low-tide area of turbulence and freak waves.

⑤ ★ Point Bonita

Point Bonita's lighthouse on this rugged clifftop was the last manually operated lighthouse in the state, only changing to automation in 1980. The lighthouse is reached via a tunnel carved through solid rock or over a surf-lashed bridge.

⑩ ★ Half Moon Bay

The soil here is ideal for growing artichokes, broccoli, and pumpkins. The town, the oldest in San Mateo County, holds a pumpkin festival each October in celebration of its prime crop.

⑪ ★ Pigeon Point

Following numerous shipwrecks in the area, including the *Carrier Pigeon*, which gave the area its name, a 115-ft (35-m) lighthouse was erected in 1872. Sea lions can often be spotted offshore.

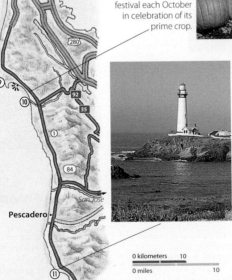

San Rafael · Berkeley · San Francisco · Pacifica · San Jose · Pescadero · Monterey

Key

- ▒ Freeway
- — Major road
- ⋯ Minor road
- ⇌ River
- ⚓ Viewpoint

0 kilometers 10
0 miles 10

For additional map symbols *see back flap*

Dairy farm at picturesque Point Reyes

❶ Point Reyes National Seashore

Road map A3. 🚌 from San Rafael Center (weekends only). Bear Valley Visitors' Center: 1 Bear Valley Rd, main entrance to National Seashore, Point Reyes. **Tel** (415) 464-5100. **Open** 9am–5pm Mon–Fri, 8am–5pm Sat & Sun. 🔤 **nps.gov/pore**

This triangular area of land, only half attached to the San Franciscan coastline, has been gradually drifting northward along the California coast for more than six million years. Situated due west of the San Andreas Fault, the peninsula moved a full 20 ft (6 m) north of the mainland during the 1906 earthquake (see pp28–9). A displaced fence on the Earthquake Trail near Bear Valley Visitor Center is evidence of its overnight movement. The visitors' center itself contains interesting displays on local geology and geography.

A notable feature of this stretch of coastline is its abundance of wildlife, including a herd of tule elk. The area has cattle and dairy ranches, and three small towns: Point Reyes Station, Olema, and Inverness. Drake's Bay is named after the English explorer Sir Francis Drake, who is believed to have anchored here in 1579. He named the land Nova Albion and briefly claimed it for England (see p50).

POINT REYES
NATIONAL SEASHORE

United States Department of the Interior
National Park Service

Signpost to Point Reyes

❷ Muir Woods and Beach

1 Muir Woods Road. **Road map** A3. 🚌 Mill Valley. Visitors' Center: Hwy 1, Mill Valley. **Tel** (415) 388-2595. **Open** summer: 8am–8pm, winter: 8am–5pm. 🌲 for the woods (beach is free) 🔤 **nps.gov/muwo**

Nestling at the foot of Mount Tamalpais (see pp417) is Muir Woods National Monument, one of the few remaining stands of old-growth coastal redwoods. Before the 19th-century lumber industry flourished, these tall trees (the oldest is at least 1,000 years old) once covered the coastal area of California. The woods were named in honor of John Muir, the 19th-century naturalist responsible for turning Yosemite into a national park (see pp492–5).

Redwood Creek bubbles out of Muir Woods and makes its way down to the ocean at Muir Beach, a wide expanse of sand popular with beachcombers and picnickers (see p417). Along the road to the beach is the incongruous Pelican Inn, a 16th-century-style English guesthouse. It is proud of its traditional English menu, with items such as roast beef, and offers a warm welcome.

Muir Beach is likely to be crowded at weekends, especially during the summer months, but visitors who are prepared to walk for 15 minutes or more along the sand are rewarded with peace and quiet.

❸ Marin Headlands

See pp420–21.

❹ Sausalito

Road map inset B. 🏔 7,060. 🚌 ⛴ ℹ 780 Bridgeway Ave (415 332-0505). 🔤 **sausalito.org**

In this small town that was once a fishing community, Victorian bungalows cling to steep hills rising from San Francisco Bay. Parallel to the waterfront, Bridgeway Avenue serves as a promenade for the weekend crowds that come to patronize the restaurants and shops and enjoy the views. The **San Francisco Bay Model Visitor Center** is the only operational hydraulic model in the US, which simulates the movement of the tides and currents in San Francisco Bay, and in the bay-delta system.

🏛 San Francisco Bay Model Visitor Center

2100 Bridgeway Ave. **Tel** (415) 332-3871. **Open** Sep–May: 9am–4pm Tue–Sat; Jun–Aug: 9am–4pm Tue–Fri, 10am–5pm Sat. **Closed** public hols. 🔤 **spn.usace.army.mil**

Harbor scene in Sausalito

❺ Tiburon

Road map inset B. 🏔 8,960. 🚌 ⛴ ℹ 96B Main St, (415) 435-5633. 🔤 **ci.tiburon.ca.us**

The main street of this elegant waterfront town is lined with fashionable shops and restaurants, some housed in "arks." These unique buildings are in fact houseboats from the early 20th century that have

Attractive main street of Tiburon

been pulled ashore and innovatively refurbished. They now stand in what is called "Ark Row." Less hectic than nearby Sausalito, Tiburon is a good town for walking. Parks are situated along the waterfront from which you can contemplate the bay and are a popular spot for hikers and cyclists.

❻ Six Flags Discovery Kingdom

1001 Fairgrounds Dr. **Road map** inset B. **Tel** (707) 643-6722. 🚃 🚢 from San Francisco. **Open** (check website for times). 🎡 🚻 📷 W **sixflags.com/discoverykingdom**

The most unique wildlife park, oceanarium, and theme park in Northern California, Six Flags Discovery Kingdom attracts 1.6 million visitors each year. Its lush 135-acre (55-ha) site is located along I-80 at Hwy 37 on the outskirts of Vallejo. There is equal emphasis on education and entertainment in the park, but the primary attractions are the shows featuring marine mammals. Arenas housing large pools showcase a killer whale, sea lions, and dolphins. In the Shark Experience, visitors enter by way of a transparent tunnel through a tank filled with large sharks and tropical fish.

Land animal attractions include shows featuring Bengal tigers, elephants exotic birds, and tropical butterflies.

❼ Benicia

Road map inset B. 🏔 27,000. 🚃 🚢 ℹ Benicia Chamber of Commerce, 601 1st St, (707) 745-2120. W **visitbenicia.com**

Set on the north side of the Carquinez Straits, the narrow waterway through which the Sacramento and the San Joaquin rivers flow from the Sierra Nevada to San Francisco Bay, Benicia is one of California's most interesting historic towns. From February 1853 until February 1854, Benicia served as an early state capital. The Greek Revival building that once housed the government has been preserved as a state historic park, complete with many original fixtures and furnishings. Next door to the former capitol, the Fisher-Hanlon House, a former Gold Rush hotel, has also been restored to its original condition as part of **Benicia Capitol State Historic Park**. At the other end of Main Street from the capitol complex is the Benicia waterfront, where ferries shuttled to Port Costa during the 1850s. The former Benicia Arsenal, which stored army weapons from the 1850s to the 1950s, has been converted to live-work studio spaces.

🏛 **Benicia Capitol State Historic Park** 115 West G St. **Tel** (707) 745-3385. **Open** 10am–5pm Sat & Sun. 📷 W **parks.ca.gov**

❽ John Muir National Historic Site

4202 Alhambra Ave, Martinez. **Road map** inset B. **Tel** (925) 228-8860. **Open** 10am–5pm daily. **Closed** Jan 1, Thanksgiving, Dec 25. ♿ 1st floor & grounds only. W **nps.gov/jomu**

Set amid the suburban neighborhood of Martinez, the John Muir National Historic Site preserves the home where the naturalist and writer lived from 1890 until his death in 1914. The 17-room Italianate house is typical of a late Victorian upper middle-class dwelling, conveying little of Muir's simple tastes and back-to-nature inclinations. Only the library, which Muir called his "scribble den," gives a real sense of the man. The house was once surrounded by 2,600 acres (1,052 ha) of fruit trees, only 9 acres (4 ha) of which survive. In season, rangers pick fruit for visitors to sample.

The Visitor Center, in keeping with Muir's own values of conservation, has eco-conscious features such as bamboo flooring and a recycled-redwood front desk. The Center includes exhibits on Muir that are used to educate the public about his life and achievements through conservation. There is also information for kids, allowing them to get involved and understand more about being a park ranger.

Nearby are 320 acres (130 ha) of hiking trails, which pass through fruit orchards and wildflower fields. Full Moon walks are also available.

John Muir (1838–1914)

❸ A 90-Minute Walk through the Marin Headlands

At its northern end, the Golden Gate Bridge is anchored in the rolling green hills of the Marin Headlands. This is an unspoiled wild area of windswept ridges, sheltered valleys, and deserted beaches, once used as a military defense post and now part of the vast Golden Gate National Recreation Area. From several vantage points there are spectacular views of San Francisco and vast panoramas of the sea, and, on autumn days, you can see migrating eagles and ospreys gliding past Hawk Hill.

Schoolchildren on a trip to the Marin Headlands

③ Rodeo Beach

Marin Headlands Visitor Center

Before starting this walk, pause a while at the steepled Visitors' Center ①, which was once the interdenominational chapel for Fort Cronkhite. It has since been refurbished and is now a museum and information center, with a natural history bookshop that specializes in books on birds. Here you can discover the history of the Marin Headlands and see a shelter made by the Coast Miwok people. The walk, which will take you around Rodeo Lagoon ②, begins at the gate on the west, ocean side, of the parking lot. Take the path to the left that leads to the sea. This part of the trail is thick with trees and shrubs, including poison oak, of which visitors should be aware. The songs of birds fill the air and around the edges of the lagoon you will see brown pelicans, snowy egrets, and mallards. A 15-minute walk will bring you to the sandy, wind-blown Rodeo Beach ③, and from here you can see Bird Island ④ lying offshore to

MARIN HEADLANDS
(GOLDEN GATE NATIONAL RECREATION AREA)

MITCHELL ROAD

⑥

⑤

③ Rodeo Beach

Rod

COAS

Battery Smith-Guth

PACIFIC OCEAN

④ Bird Island

MENDELL R

Batter Mende

Key
— Walk route

② Rodeo Lagoon

For hotels and restaurants in this area see pp539–40 and pp570–71

⑦ Seal at The Marine Mammal Center

that climbs a steep hill to The Marine Mammal Center ⑦. This was used as a missile defense site during the Cold War, but is now run by volunteers who rescue and care for sick or injured marine mammals. Sea lions and seals, including the rare elephant seals, are examined and treated here in

but on the separate footpath at the side. Before the guard rail ends, a path ⑨ plunges to the right into the dense shrubbery. From here, continue up the hill again, via a series of steps that will return you to the path at the end of the Marin Headlands Visitor Center parking lot. Walk across the lot and up the hill to a three-story wooden building, constructed at the turn of the century. This is listed on the National Historic Registry and has been officers' headquarters,

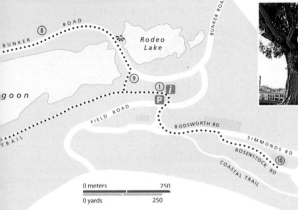

① Marin Headlands Visitor Center

a hospital, and a missile command center. It is now the Marin Headlands Hostel ⑩ for travelers. The Marin Headlands also offer a wide range of longer, more challenging walks. Wolf Ridge and Bobcat Trail are two popular routes you may want to try.

the south. Fishing boats may be seen bobbing out at sea, but the beach is mostly empty of people, although sometimes you might see groups of children working on coastal ecology programs. These are run by the Headlands Institute, which is based in the nearby clutch of former army barracks.

Barracks to The Marine Mammal Center

From the beach, turn inland again as you approach the tip of the lagoon, crossing a wooden footbridge ⑤. Here there are lavatories, and barracks ⑥ housing various offices, among them the Headlands District Office, the Raptor Observatory, and an energy and resources center. Walking past the barracks, continue along the path, then turn left at the road

specially designed pens. They are then returned to the sea when they have recovered. You can watch the vets at work and get a close view of the mammals, many of which are orphaned pups. There are also some displays of the marine ecosystem.

Lagoon to the Marin Headlands Hostel

Make your way back down the hill and return to the paved road ⑧ that runs past Rodeo Lagoon. There is a separate pathway beside the road for hikers, but you have to climb over a guard rail to get to it. Just before the road crosses a bridge, there is a large bench where you can view the water birds. There are plenty of birds to be seen in this brackish lagoon with its tall grasses. Cross the bridge, not on the roadway

Horse Trail

Bike Trail

Sign marking a trail

Tips for Walkers

Starting point: The Marin Headlands Visitor Center at Fort Cronkhite.
Length: 2 miles (3 km).
Getting there: San Francisco Muni bus 76 leaves from the intersection of Sutter Street and Sansome or Sutter Street and Van Ness Avenue on Sundays and some holidays. **Tel** (415) 673-6864. By car, drive across the Golden Gate Bridge, taking the Alexander Avenue exit. Turn under the freeway, following signs for the Headlands, Fort Cronkhite, and Fort Barry.
Stopping-off points: Water is available, but there are no refreshments or restaurants in the Marin Headlands. You will need to bring your own picnic lunch, which can be enjoyed at any number of tables dotted along the trails and the beaches.

For keys to symbols *see back flap*

❾ Berkeley

Berkeley began to boom following the earthquake of 1906 (*see pp56*), when many San Franciscans fled their ruined city and settled on the east side of the bay. Berkeley did not really find its own voice, however, until the birth of the Free Speech Movement and the student uprisings against the Vietnam War during the 1960s, earning itself the nickname "Beserkeley." Many stores and market stalls still hark back to the hippie era with their psychedelic merchandise, but in recent years Berkeley has begun to raise its profile. Stylish restaurants and cafés have emerged, as well as a reputation for fine food – it was here that the popular California cuisine was born. Today the city blends idealism and style in unique harmony.

Claremont Hotel Club & Spa

▦ University of California at Berkeley

Tel (510) 642-6000. Phoebe A Hearst Museum of Anthropology: **Tel** (510) 642-3682. **Open** 10am–4:30pm Wed–Sat, noon–4pm Sun. **Closed** public hols. Berkeley Art Museum and Pacific Film Archive: **Tel** (510) 642-0808. **Open** 11am–5pm Wed–Sun (to 9pm Fri). **Closed** public hols. 🖬 (free first Thu of month). 🚻 🚾 **berkeley.edu**

The reputation of UC Berkeley for counter-cultural movements sometimes eclipses its academic reputation, yet it is one of the largest and most prestigious universities in the world. Founded in 1868, Berkeley numbers at least ten Nobel laureates among its professors. The campus (*see pp424–5*) was laid out by the architect Frederick Law Olmsted. There are more than 30,000 students and a wide range of museums and cultural amenities, including the University Art Museum (*see p425*), Sather Tower (the Campanile), and the Hearst Museum of Anthropology.

Model of DNA at the Lawrence Hall of Science

▥ Lawrence Hall of Science

Centennial Dr, UC Berkeley. **Tel** (510) 642-5132. **Open** 10am–5pm daily. **Closed** public hols. 🚻 🚾 **W lawrencehallofscience.org**

Science is fun here. Hands-on exhibits tempt visitors to manipulate a hologram, track earthquakes, or plot stars in the planetarium. There are also changing exhibitions.

At night, the view of the lights around the northern Bay Area from the Hall's plaza is an extraordinary sight.

♨ Claremont Hotel Club & Spa

41 Tunnel Rd, Berkeley. **Tel** (510) 843-3000, (800) 551-7266. 🖬 🚾 **claremontresort.com**

The Berkeley hills form a backdrop to this half-timbered, fairytale castle. The enormous Claremont Hotel construction began in 1906 and ended in 1915. In the early years the hotel failed to prosper, partly due to a law that forbade the sale of alcohol within a 1-mile (1.6-km) radius of the UC Berkeley campus. In 1937 an enterprising student actually measured the distance and discovered that the radius line passed through the *center* of the building. The Terrace Bar was opened beyond the line, in the same corner of the hotel that it occupies today.

❂ University of California Botanical Garden

200 Centennial Dr, Berkeley Hills. **Tel** (510) 643-2755. **Open** 9am–5pm daily. **Closed** public hols. 🖬 limited. 🚾 (free first Thu of month). 🚾 **botanicalgarden.berkeley.edu**

More than 12,000 species from all over the world thrive in the Mediterranean-style climate of Berkeley's Strawberry Canyon. Although primarily used for research, the collections are arranged in thematic gardens linked by paths. Particularly noteworthy are the Asian, African, South American, European, and California sections. The Chinese medicinal herb garden, the orchid houses, cactus garden, and the carnivorous plants are also well worth a visit.

Wellman Hall on the University of California campus

🌳 Tilden Regional Park

Tel (510) 544-2747. Steam trains: run 11am–5pm Sat & Sun, and daily during summer. 🎠 Carousel: **Open** 10am–5pm Sat & Sun, 11am–5pm daily during summer. **Closed** public hols. 🌿 Botanical Garden: open 8:30am–5pm daily. ♿ limited.
W ebparks.org/parks/tilden

Though preserved for the most part in a natural wild condition, Tilden Park offers a variety of attractions. It is noted for the enchantingly landscaped Botanical Garden, specializing in California plants. Visitors can stroll from alpine meadows to desert cactus gardens by way of a redwood glen, and there are guided nature walks. If you have children, do not miss the carousel and the model steam train.

🏛 Magnes Collection of Jewish Art and Life

2121 Aliston Way, Berkeley. **Tel** (510) 643-2526. **Open** mid-Sep–mid-Dec & Feb–May 11am–4pm Tue–Fri. **Closed** Jewish and public hols. ♿ ground floor only. **W** magnes.org

Located in a sleek terracotta-colored building, the Magnes has been safeguarding the evidence of Jewish lives around the world since 1962. Comprised of nearly 15,000 items and

19th-century Jewish ceremonial dress,
Magnes Collection of Jewish Art and Life

dating back to 440 BCE, the collection serves as testimony to the contributions made by Jewish communities to world cultures. Ritual objects, ethno-graphic materials, fine art, and historical documents serve as powerful witnesses that connect generations to a shared history and sense of peoplehood. Exhibitions change regularly.

🚃 Telegraph Avenue

Berkeley's most fascinating street is Telegraph Avenue, especially the blocks between Dwight Way and the University. It has a plethora of

VISITORS' CHECKLIST

Practical Information
Road map inset B. 🗺 113,000.
ℹ 2015 Center St, (510) 549-7040, (800) 847-4823. 🎭 Taste of North Berkeley (May); Fourth of July Fireworks; Farmers' Market (check website for days); Salano Ave Stroll (Sep).
W visitberkeley.com

Transport
✈ Oakland, 12 miles (19 km) SW of Berkeley. 🚌 🚇 2160 Shattuck Ave.

coffee houses and cheap eateries, as well as clothing boutiques. The district was the center of student protest during the 1960s. It still swarms with students from dawn to dark, along with street vendors, musicians, protesters, and eccentrics.

🚋 Fourth Street

This gentrified enclave north of University Avenue is characteristic of Berkeley's fine craftsmanship and taste. Here you can buy everything from stained-glass windows and furniture, to organically grown lettuce and designer garden tools. There is also a handful of good restaurants (see p570).

Berkeley City Center

① University of California at Berkeley
② Lawrence Hall of Science
③ University of California Botanical Garden
④ Telegraph Avenue
⑤ Magnes Collection of Jewish Art and Life
⑥ Claremont Hotel Club & Spa

| 0 meters | 500 |
| 0 yards | 500 |

For keys to symbols *see back flap*

A 90-Minute Walk around the University of California Campus in Berkeley

This walk concentrates on a distinct area of Berkeley, the famous main campus of the University of California. It allows a stimulating glimpse into the intellectual, cultural, and social life of this vibrant university town *(see pp422–3)*.

West Entrance to Sather Tower

From University Avenue ①, cross Oxford Street and walk along University Drive past the Valley Life Sciences Building ②. Wellman Hall can be seen on the north fork of Strawberry Creek as you follow the road to the right, keeping California Hall ③ on your right. Take a left turn on Cross Campus Road ④. Wheeler Hall lies to the right, and ahead is the main campus landmark, the 307-ft (94-m) tall Sather Tower ⑤. Built by John Galen Howard in 1914, it was based on the campanile in the Piazza San Marco in Venice.

Before visiting the bell tower, go to the Doe Library ⑥ then the AF Morrison Memorial Library ⑦ in the north wing. The adjacent Bancroft Library houses the plate supposedly left by Sir Francis Drake in 1579, when he claimed California for England *(see p50)*.

Return to Sather Tower, open 10am–3:30pm Mon–Sat. There are fine views of the bay from the top of the tower. Across University Drive lies South Hall ⑧, the oldest building on campus.

Hearst Mining Building to the Greek Theater

Continuing north, walk past LeConte Hall then cross over University Drive to the Mining Circle. Here is the Hearst Mining Building ⑨, built by Howard in 1907. Inside are ore samples and pictures of old mining operations. Return to University Drive, turn left out of East Gate to the Hearst Greek Theater ⑩.

④ Students outside Wheeler Hall on Campus Road

HEARST AVENUE

Tolman Hall

HEARST AVENUE

Wellman Hall

(For k)

UNIVERSITY AVENUE

①

THE CRESCENT

OXFORD STREET

UNIVERSITY DRIVE

WEST CIRCLE

(North)

②

West Gate ⑲

ADDISON ST

Strawberry Creek

P

CENTER ST

FRANK SCHLESSINGER WAY

(South

SHATTUCK AVE

Downtown Berkeley

Alumni House

ALLSTON WAY

Evans Diamond

Haas Pavilion

Goldman Field

KITTREDGE STREET

P

BANCROFT

WA

FULTON ST

ELLSWORTH STREET

DANA STREET

P

DURANT

AV

| 0 meters | | 250 |
| 0 yards | | 250 |

Key

••• Walk route

⑤ The tall Sather Tower

Faculty Club to the Eucalyptus Grove

Follow Gayley Road, which straddles a major earthquake fault, and turn right down the first path past Lewis Hall and Hildebrand Hall, then left over a footbridge. The path winds between a log house and the Faculty Club ⑪. This rambling, rustic building was partly designed by Bernard Maybeck and dates from 1903. Faculty Glade ⑫ in front of the club is a favorite picnic and resting place with students and visitors alike.

The path now swings to the right, then sharp left. Take a look at Hertz Hall ⑬, then go down the diagonal walk that passes Wurster Hall to Kroeber Hall. Here you can visit the Hearst Museum of Anthropology (see p422). Included in the museum are artifacts made by Ishi, the last surviving member of the Yahi people who was brought by scientists to live on the campus from 1911 until his death in 1916. Cross Bancroft Way to the Caffè Strada ⑭ and then proceed to the University Art Museum ⑮, which includes Picassos and Cézannes among its exhibits (see p422). Continue along Bancroft Way to Telegraph Avenue ⑯, famous for the student riots of the 1960s and '70s (see p423).

The entrance to the university opposite Telegraph Avenue opens on to Sproul Plaza ⑰, which is often

⑮ *Within* (1969) by A Lieberman at UCB Art Museum

enlivened by street musicians. Step into the lower courtyard with its modern Zellerbach Hall ⑱, then, noting the state-of-the-art Harmon Gym, pass Alumni House and turn right. Cross over the south fork of Strawberry Creek at Bay Tree Bridge and bear left for the nature area to Eucalyptus Grove, which has some of the world's tallest eucalyptus trees, planted in 1882 ⑲.

Tips for Walkers

Starting point: The West Gate at University Avenue and Oxford Street.
Length: 2.5 miles (4 km).
Getting there: San Francisco–Oakland Bay Bridge, Hwy 80 north, University Avenue exit. By BART, Berkeley stop.
Stopping-off points: The upscale Caffè Strada, on Bancroft Way, is always crowded with students sipping cappuccinos or eating bagels and cakes. A few steps down the street, in the University Art Museum, is the Café Grace, which looks out on to the sculpture garden. You may want to browse in the bookstores on Telegraph Avenue that also have coffee shops, or try one of the food carts that crowd the entrance to Sproul Plaza. Here you could sample a smoothie or a wide selection of Mexican and Middle Eastern food. In the lower Sproul Plaza of the University, amid a phalanx of bongo drummers, there are several other cafés.

⑨ The Hearst Mining Building overlooking the Mining Circle

⑩ Oakland

At one time a small, working-class suburb of San Francisco, Oakland grew into a city in its own right when it became the West Coast terminus of the transcontinental railroad. With access to the town, businesses inevitably boomed, and it soon became one of the largest container ports in the United States. Many of the African-Americans who worked on the railroad then settled in Oakland, later followed by a Hispanic population, giving the city a multicultural atmosphere that continues to this day. Oakland's literary associations, including Jack London and Gertrude Stein, have also enhanced the area as a cultural center.

Facade and gardens of the Mormon Temple

🏛 Mormon Temple

4770 Lincoln Ave. **Tel** (510) 531-1475. 🚇 Fruitvale, then AC Transit 46 bus. Visitors' Center: **Open** 9am–9pm daily. Temple 🛗 💷 📷 🖥 **ldschurch temples.com/oakland**

Designed in 1963 and built on a hilltop, this is Northern California's only Mormon temple. Its full name is the Oakland Temple of the Church of Jesus Christ of Latter Day Saints. Floodlit at night, it can be seen all over Oakland and from San Francisco. The central ziggurat is surrounded by four shorter terraced towers, all clad with white granite and capped by glistening golden pyramids. From the temple there are magnificent views over the entire Bay Area.

VISITORS' CHECKLIST

Practical Information
Road map: inset B. 🗺 390,000.
ℹ 475 14th St, (510) 874-4800.
📷 Annual Holiday Parade
(1st Sat of Dec).
🖥 **visitoakland.org**

Transport
✈ Oakland, 5 miles (8 km) SW of
Oakland. 🚉 1245 Broadway St.

🌳 Lake Merritt

Formed when a saltwater tidal estuary was dredged, embanked, and partly dammed, Lake Merritt and its surrounding park form an oasis of rich blue and green in the urban heart of Oakland. Designated in 1870 as the first state game refuge in the US, the lake still attracts migrating flocks of birds. Boats can be rented from two boathouses on the west and north shores, and joggers and cyclists can circle the lake on a 3-mile (5-km) path. The north shore at Lakeside Park has flower gardens, an aviary, and a Children's Fairyland with pony rides, puppet shows, and nursery rhyme scenes.

🏙 Jack London Square

Author Jack London, who became famous for his adventure novels *The Call of the Wild* and *White Fang (see p30)*, grew up in Oakland in the 1880s and was a frequent visitor to the Oakland waterfront.

🌉 Bay Bridge

Map 6 E4

The compound, high-level San Francisco–Oakland Bay Bridge was designed by Charles H Purcell. It has two distinct structures, joining at Yerba Buena Island in the middle of the Bay, and reaches 4.5 miles (7.2 km) from shore to shore. Its completion in 1936 heralded the end of the age of ferry boats on San Francisco Bay by linking the peninsular city at Rincon Hill to the Oakland "mainland." Train tracks were removed in the 1950s, leaving the bridge for use by more than 250,000 vehicles a day. It is five traffic lanes wide and has two levels. The westbound traffic uses the top deck, eastbound the lower. The eastern cantilever is raised on more than 20 piers, climbing up from the toll plaza causeway in Oakland to 191 ft (58 m) above Yerba Buena Island.

Two suspension spans join at the central anchorage, which is sunk deeper in the water than that of any other bridge. Treasure Island *(see p416)*, the larger part of Yerba Buena Island, hosted the 1939–40 World's Fair to celebrate the

10 miles (16 km) of cable
holding up the bridge

2,310 ft (704 m)

The West Bay Crossing section of Bay Bridge

Oakland City Center

① Old Oakland
② Jack London Square
③ Oakland Museum of California
   (see pp428–9)
④ Lake Merritt

0 meters 500
0 yards 500

BERKELEY
WEST GRAND AVENUE
Greyhound Station
980
SAN PABLO AVENUE
STREET
Paramount Theater
20TH STREET
GRAND
Children's Fairyland
Oakland Ice Center
19th St (BART)
TELEGRAPH AVENUE
19TH STREET
PIEDMONT
Preservation Park
City Hall
AVENUE
Lakeside Park
BELLEVUE AVENUE
CASTRO
Federal Building
14TH STREET
P
Sailboat House
LAKESHORE AVENUE
12TH STREET
P
JEFFERSON STREET
SAN FRANCISCO
Old Oakland ①
12th St (BART)
LAKESIDE DRIVE
CLAY ST
HARRISON STREET
i
11TH STREET
④ Lake Merritt
SEVENTH STREET
BROADWAY
9TH STREET
NIMITZ FREEWAY
CHINATOWN
WASHINGTON
THIRD ST
OAK STREET
Oakland Museum of California ③
Ferry Terminal
SECOND STREET
EMBARCADERO
Amtrak Station
Chinese Garden
Lake Merritt (BART)
Mormon Temple
② Jack London Square
880
Airport 5 miles (8 km)

Today the area named after him is a bright promenade of shops, hotels, restaurants with outdoor tables, and pleasure boats. London's footsteps can be traced to the First and Last Chance Saloon, now sunken with age into the street, and the Yukon cabin, occupied by London in 1898.

Old Oakland
Farmers' Market Tel (510) 745-7100. **Open** 8am–2pm Fri.
w urbanvillageonline.com

Also known as Victorian Row, these two blocks were erected between the 1860s and 1880s and renovated in the 1980s. Crowds of shoppers visit the Farmers' Market on Fridays at Clay and 9th streets, where stalls sell fresh world-class produce, including fruit and vegetables, ranch eggs, cheeses, bakery goods, locally caught fish, and flowers, as well as delicious prepared foods, many of which are available to sample for free. There are also local handicrafts.

bridge's completion. This small island is now home to small parks and an upscale community.

In 1989 the bridge was closed for a month after the Loma Prieta earthquake *(see p509)* when a 50-ft (15-m) segment disconnected where the cantilever span meets the approach ramp from Oakland. At night, the bridge's exterior is illuminated by the Bay Lights, a light art installation.

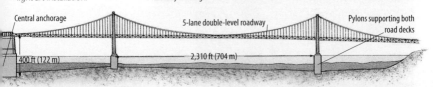

East Bay Crossing

Central anchorage
5-lane double-level roadway
Pylons supporting both road decks
400 ft (122 m)
2,310 ft (704 m)

For keys to symbols *see back flap*

Oakland Museum of California

California's only museum exclusively dedicated to documenting the state's art, history, and environment first opened in 1960 and has since undergone massive renovations and expansions. This includes the Art Gallery, History Gallery, and Oak Street entrance, with the Art Gallery offering over 4,000 sq ft (1,219 sq m) of gallery space. Check the website for details of the latest exhibits. Visitors can also enjoy interactive and digital features depicting the many people and stories of California.

Welcome to California
This display celebrates past and present-day life in California.

Museum Guide

Level 1 contains the shop and the Natural Sciences Gallery, illustrating the changes in the state's ecology from west to east. Artifacts in the Cowell Hall of California History on level 2 are arranged chronologically. Level 2 has the cafeteria, level 3 the Art Gallery.

Roof and gardens

The Great Hall is used for special exhibitions and functions.

Gallery of California Art
The modern art in this collection includes *Ocean Park No: 107* (1978) by Richard Diebenkorn.

Level 3

Level 2

10th Street entrance

★ **Barry McGee Installation**
This acrylic assemblage (2010) by San Francisco native Barry McGee reflects his interest in colorful geometric patterns.

For hotels and restaurants in this area see p539–40 and p570–71

Key to the Oakland Museum Levels

- Gallery of Californian Art
- Gallery of Californian Natural Sciences
- Gallery of Californian History

California Mud Wagon
Developed for rural life during the mid-19th century, this multipurpose vehicle could be converted easily from a field wagon to a stylish carriage.

Level 1

Railroad Exhibit
The construction of the railroad was crucial to the development of California, lifting the state out of isolation.

Sculpture Gardens host outdoor festivals and are also a popular spot for picnics.

★ Gallery of Natural Sciences
Explore California's conservation with dioramas of more than 2,000 different native species and seven major habitats.

Eugene O'Neill's beautiful Tao House, in Danville

⓫ Tao House

Road map inset B. Danville. **Tel** (925) 838-0249. **Open** 10am & 12:30pm Wed–Sun, by reservation only (no booking required on Sat). ♿ 🚻 10am & 2pm Wed–Fri, Sun. 🅦 nps.gov/euon

When the American playwright Eugene O'Neill (1888–1953) won the Nobel Prize for Literature in 1936, he used the stipend to build a home for himself and his wife in the then-rural San Ramon Valley at the foot of Mount Diablo. Tao House, a hybrid of Spanish Colonial and oriental styles, was completed in 1937. Over the next six years O'Neill worked in this house on what is now considered his best work, the semi-autobiographical series of tragic plays, including *The Iceman Cometh*, *A Moon for the Misbegotten*, and *Long Day's Journey Into Night*. In 1944, however, O'Neill was struck down with Parkinson's disease. The remote location of the house and the lack of available nursing staff due to the war forced the disabled O'Neill to abandon his beloved home. He died in a Boston hotel in 1953.

The surrounding valleys have now been developed into suburbs, but Tao House and its beautiful landscaped grounds have been turned into a National Historic Site, operated by the National Park Service. Both have been preserved in the condition the playwright left them in.

⓬ Mount Diablo State Park

Road map inset B. 🚌 🚇 Walnut Creek. ℹ️ Walnut Creek Visitor Center, (925) 837-6119. **Open** 8am–sunset daily. 🅦 parks.ca.gov

Rising voluminously over the inland suburbs, the 3,849-ft- (1,173-m-) high Mount Diablo dominates the East Bay region. Its summit offers one of the most impressive pano-ramas in North America. On a fine and clear day it is possible to see for more than 200 miles (320 km) in each direction, stretching from Mount Lassen *(see p457)* and the Cascade Mountains in the north to Mount Hamilton in the south, and from the Sierra Nevada mountains in the east to the Farallon Islands *(see pp416)* in the Pacific Ocean to the west. Almost 23,000 acres (9,000 ha) of land surrounding the summit have now been set aside as a state park, and there is a wide

Mask used in O'Neill's stage plays

range of hiking trails, as well as biking and horseriding. A twisting road takes car drivers within 50 ft (15 m) of the summit. The park's Visitors' Center at the summit offers information on the mountain's fauna and flora, including the wildflowers that cover the mountainside in spring.

⓭ Livermore

Road map inset B. 🚗 85,000. 🚌 🚇 ℹ️ 2157 First St. (925 447-1606). 🅦 livermorechamber.org

Founded in the 1870s as a cattle-ranching and grape-producing community, Livermore in recent years has grown into an outlying suburb of San Francisco. Still rural in feel and retaining a few ranches and vineyards, the town is now best known as the home of the Lawrence Livermore National Laboratory. This state-of-the-art technology research center is operated by the University of California on behalf of the United States Department of Energy. During the Cold War era the laboratory had primary responsibility for the design of the nation's nuclear weapons arsenal, but today it has diversified into civilian applications.

To the east of Livermore, along I-580 as it climbs over hilly Altamont Pass, are hundreds of shining high-tech windmills. This is the world's largest wind farm, producing natural, nonpolluting energy from the area's constant winds. The windmills are all privately owned and operated, with no

Windmills producing natural energy at Livermore's wind farm

government funding. They consist of two main types: the traditional propeller type, and the more unusual vertical axis windmills, which resemble giant egg-whisks.

⓮ Stanford University

Junípero Serra St. **Road map** inset B. **Tel** (650) 723-2560. Visitors' Center: 295 Galvez St. **Open** 8:30am–5pm Mon–Fri, 10am–5pm Sat & Sun. **Closed** university hols; call ahead. 📷 phone (650) 723-2560 for details. **W** stanford.edu

Among the most pleasant of the Bay Area suburbs, the town of Palo Alto grew up specifically to serve Stanford University, one of the most reputed centers of higher education in the country.

Founded by the railroad tycoon Leland Stanford *(see p54)* in honor of his son who died in 1885 at the age of 16, Stanford University opened in 1891. The campus occupies the former Stanford family farm, covering 8,200 acres (3,320 ha) – larger than the entire downtown district of San Francisco. It was designed in a mixture of Romanesque and Mission styles *(see pp34–5)* by the architect Frederick Law Olmsted, and its sandstone buildings and numerous arcades are capped by red-tiled roofs. At the heart of the university campus is the Main Quadrangle, where the Memorial Church is decorated with a gold-leaf and tile mosaic. Also on the campus is the Cantor Art Center. This small but intriguing museum holds one of the largest collections of sculptures by Auguste Rodin, including the impressive *Gates of Hell*.

⓯ Filoli

86 Cañada Rd. **Road map** inset B. **Tel** (650) 364-8300, ext 509. **Open** Feb–Oct: 10am–3:30pm Tue–Fri, 10:30am–3:30pm Sat, 11am–3:30pm Sun. **Closed** Federal and public hols. 📷 🚻 📷 **W** filoli.org

One of the most impressive mansions in Northern California open to the public, the Filoli estate was the home of gold-mining millionaire William Bourn, owner of the Empire Gold Mine *(see p474)*. It was designed in Palladian style by Willis Polk in 1916. The red-brick exterior resembles a Georgian terrace and encloses more than 36,000 sq ft (3,345 sq m) of living space on two fully furnished floors. The house is surrounded by 16 acres (6.5 ha) of formal gardens that provide blooms of varying colors through the year – one million daffodils and 75,000 tulips in spring, roses in summer, and maple leaves in the fall. The estate's name, Filoli, is an acronym for the motto "Fight for a just cause, Love your fellow man, Live a good life."

Picturesque church in the tiny village of Pescadero

⓰ Pescadero

Road map inset B. 🚍 640. 🅸 235 Main St, Half Moon Bay, (650) 726-8380. **W** halfmoonbaychamber.org

Only half an hour's drive from San Francisco to the north and the Silicon Valley *(see p432)* to the south, the tiny town of Pescadero seems light-years away from the surrounding modern world.

Pescadero is a sleepy little farming community that produces an abundance of vegetables such as asparagus and pumpkins. It contains little more than a whitewashed church (the oldest in the county), a general store, a post office, and the popular Duarte's Tavern *(see p571)* along its two main streets. Its many white-washed buildings follow a tradition that goes back to the 19th century, when a cargo of white paint was rescued from a nearby shipwreck.

Eight miles (13 km) south of town, the Pigeon Point Light-house is well worth a visit *(see p417)*. The lighthouse also operates as a hostel.

Facade of the Memorial Church at Stanford University

⑰ San Jose

The only other original Spanish Colonial town in California after Los Angeles, San Jose was founded in 1777 by Felipe de Neve and has grown to become the state's third largest city, its population exceeding that of San Francisco. Now the commercial and cultural center of the South Bay and civic heart of the Silicon Valley region, San Jose is a bustling and modern city that has only recently taken action to preserve its history. High-rise offices and high-tech factories now stand on what was only farmland in the 1950s, yet the city's fine museums and historic sites offer genuine attractions to the visitor, despite the suburban sprawl.

Statue outside the Egyptian Museum and Planetarium

Exploring San Jose

San Jose's colonial pueblo was situated on what is now Plaza Park, off Market Street. During 1849–50, California's first State Capitol was located in a hotel on the east side of the plaza, roughly on the site of the present Fairmont Hotel.

Other historic sites along Market Street include the San Jose Museum of Art and the birthplace of Amadeo P Giannini (see p319).

The well-known Winchester Mystery House (see pp434–5), is located on the town's outskirts.

🏛 Peralta Adobe

175 W St John St. **Tel** (408) 536-6000. **Open** 8am–5pm Mon–Fri. **Closed** public hols. 🎫 🏠 📷 ♿ first floor only.

One block to the left of Market Street is San Jose's oldest surviving building, the Peralta Adobe. Built in 1797, it is the sole remnant of the Spanish pueblo. Bars and cafés now fill the area.

⛪ Mission Santa Clara de Asis

500 El Camino Real. **Tel** (408) 554-4023. **Open** daily. 🌐 scu.edu

On the campus of the Jesuit University of Santa Clara, 5 miles (8 km) northwest of downtown San Jose, this mission church is a modern replica of the adobe original, first built in 1777 and reconstructed many times thereafter. Relics on display include bells given to the missionaries by the Spanish monarchy. The gardens adjacent to the church are carefully maintained in their original splendor.

Mission Santa Clara detail

🏛 Rosicrucian Egyptian Museum and Planetarium

Naglee & Park Aves. **Tel** (408) 947 3600. **Open** 9am–5pm Wed–Fri, 10am–6pm Sat & Sun. **Closed** Jan 1, Easter Sun, Thanksgiving, Dec 25. 📷 🌐 egyptianmuseum.org

This large museum displays the most extensive collection of ancient Egyptian artifacts west of the Mississippi. Housed in a complex of Egyptian- and Moorish-style buildings, each gallery represents a different aspect of Egyptian culture, from mummies, burial tombs, fertility figures, and canopic jars to domestic implements and children's toys. There are also replicas of the sarcophagus in which Tutankhamun was discovered in 1922, and of the Rosetta Stone.

The museum is operated by a nonsectarian organization known as the Rosicrucian Order, which is dedicated to combining modern science with the ancient wisdoms.

🏛 The Tech Museum of Innovation

201 S Market St. **Tel** (408) 294-8324. **Open** 10am–5pm daily; closing times vary, call ahead to check. 📷 🌐 thetech.org

Located in the heart of San Jose, this fascinating science museum has its eyes set on the future. The Tech Museum is crowded with hands-on exhibits, which encourage visitors of all ages to discover how various technological inventions work. Its main focus is on understanding the workings of computer

Silicon Valley

The world-famous center of the computer industry, Silicon Valley covers approximately 100 sq miles (260 sq km) from Palo Alto to San Jose. However, the term refers to myriad businesses rather than to a defined geographical location.

The name, based on the material used in the manufacture of semiconductors, was first used in the early 1970s to describe the area's expanding hardware and software industries. The seeds, however, were sown a decade earlier, at Stanford University and the Xerox Palo Alto Research Center, as well as in the garages of computer pioneers William Hewlett, David Packard, and later Steve Jobs and Stephen Wozniak, who invented the Apple personal computer.

Many world-class high-tech firms are based here, including Intel, Oracle, Apple, Facebook, and Google.

Silicon chip circuitry

hardware and software.
It is worth catching a show at
the IMAX Dome Theater.

🏛 San Jose Museum of Art
110 S Market St. **Tel** (408) 271-6840.
Open 11am–5pm Tue–Sun. **Closed**
Jan 1, Thanksgiving, Dec 25.
w sjmusart.org

This small but daring art museum
is known for some of the Bay
Area's most interesting and popular art exhibits. The permanent
collection focuses on well-known
contemporary California artists.

🏛 Children's Discovery Museum of San Jose
180 Woz Way. **Tel** (408) 298-5437.
Open 10am–5pm Tue–Sat, noon–
5pm Sun. **Closed** Jan 1, Dec 24–25.
w cdm.org

This large purple building,
designed by Mexican architect
Ricardo Legorretta, has
interactive exhibits and
programs for all the family. Both
arts and technology are featured
in this warm, inviting space.

🏛 de Saisset Museum at Santa Clara University
500 El Camino Real. **Tel** (408) 554-
4528. **Open** 11am–4pm Tue–Sun.
Donation. w scu.edu/desaisset

Next to the Santa Clara
Mission, this museum
exhibits artifacts from the
18th-century mission and

Trolley car on display at the
History San Jose

other eras of California history,
along with a collection of
paintings and photographs.

🏛 History San Jose
1650 Senter Rd. **Tel** (408) 287-2290.
Open noon–5pm Tue–Sun. **Closed**
Jan 1, Jul 4, Thanksgiving, Dec 25.
w historysanjose.org

In Kelley Park, 1 mile (1.5 km)
southeast of downtown San
Jose, more than two dozen
historic structures of the town
have been reassembled into an
outdoor museum. Highlights
include a trolley car, a gas station
from the 1920s, and 19th-century
business premises including a
doctor's office, a hotel, and the
original Bank of Italy. In the
future the museum aims to
have 75 structures, completing
this life-size model of San Jose
as it used to be.

California's Great America
4701 Great America Parkway. **Tel** (408)
988-1776. **Open** check website for
timings (varies by season).
w cagreatamerica.com

The best amusement park in
Northern California packs a wide
variety of attractions into its
100-acre (40-ha) site.

The park is divided into several
different areas, each one
designed to evoke various
regions of the United States.
These include Orleans Place,
Yankee Harbor, and the Yukon
Territory. Along with high-speed
roller coasters, such as the
Demon and the Tidal Wave,
many rides incorporate themes
from films and television shows
produced by Paramount Studios,
including *Top Gun* and *Star Trek*.
Pop concerts are often held in
the large amphitheater.

San Jose City Center

① de Saisset Museum
② Mission Santa Clara de Asis
③ Rosicrucian Egyptian Museum and Planetarium
④ Peralta Adobe
⑤ San Jose Museum of Art
⑥ The Tech Museum of Innovation
⑦ Children's Discovery Museum
⑧ Winchester Mystery House *pp434–5*

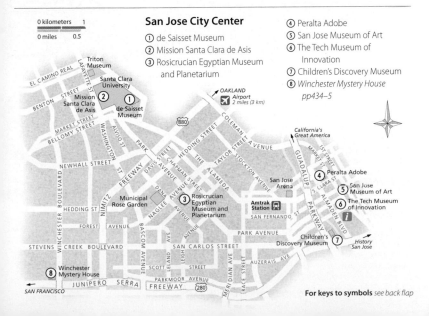

San Jose: Winchester Mystery House

Winchester Mystery House is a mansion with a remarkable history. Sarah Winchester, heiress of the Winchester Rifle fortune, moved from Connecticut to San Jose in 1884 and bought a small farmhouse. Convinced by a medium that its expansion would exorcise the spirits of those killed by the rifle, she kept builders laboring on the house 24 hours a day, 7 days a week, for 38 years, until her death in 1922. The result is a bizarre complex of 160 rooms, including stairs that lead nowhere and windows set into floors. The house has been refurbished with authentic 19th-century furniture while the Victorian gardens include statues and fountains.

VISITORS' CHECKLIST

Practical Information
525 S Winchester Blvd.
Map inset B.
Tel (408) 247-2101.
W winchestermystery
house.com
Open 9am–5pm daily; end Apr–
mid-Jun: 9am–5pm Sun–Thu,
9am–7pm Fri & Sat. **Closed** Dec
25. 🏠 ♿ gardens and firearms
museum. 📷 🛍 🖥

Transport
🚌 25, 60, 85.

Tiffany Stained-Glass Window
One of a set imported from Vienna, Austria for Mrs Winchester. They depict a lush garden of daisies (her favorite).

Facts and Figures

• The house contains 950 doors, 1,257 windows, 47 fireplaces, 40 bedrooms, and 17 chimneys.
• The number 13 is used superstitiously throughout – 13 bathrooms, 13 windows in a room, and 13 lights in the chandeliers.
• When the top of the house collapsed during the 1906 earthquake, building continued outward rather than upward.
• Mrs. Winchester's height of 4 ft 10 in (147 cm) explains hallways 2 ft (0.6 m) wide and doors only 5 ft (152 cm) high.
• Mrs. Winchester selected a new bedroom out of the 40 in the house each night, to confuse the spirits.

★ Grand Ballroom
This elaborate organ is one of the main features of the Grand Ballroom. Other features include artglass windows, a paneled ceiling, and hand-carved woodwork.

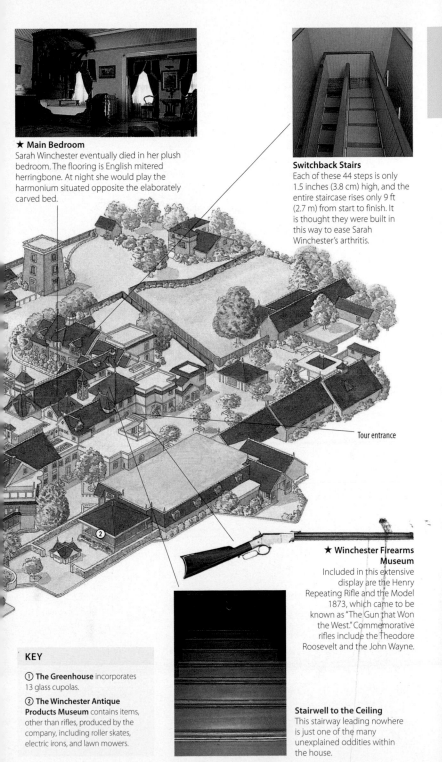

★ Main Bedroom
Sarah Winchester eventually died in her plush bedroom. The flooring is English mitered herringbone. At night she would play the harmonium situated opposite the elaborately carved bed.

Switchback Stairs
Each of these 44 steps is only 1.5 inches (3.8 cm) high, and the entire staircase rises only 9 ft (2.7 m) from start to finish. It is thought they were built in this way to ease Sarah Winchester's arthritis.

Tour entrance

★ Winchester Firearms Museum
Included in this extensive display are the Henry Repeating Rifle and the Model 1873, which came to be known as "The Gun that Won the West." Commemorative rifles include the Theodore Roosevelt and the John Wayne.

KEY

① **The Greenhouse** incorporates 13 glass cupolas.

② **The Winchester Antique Products Museum** contains items, other than rifles, produced by the company, including roller skates, electric irons, and lawn mowers.

Stairwell to the Ceiling
This stairway leading nowhere is just one of the many unexplained oddities within the house.

NORTHERN CALIFORNIA

Northern California at a Glance

Northern California stretches for more than 500 miles (800 km), from the sparsely populated border with Oregon to the high-tech urban civilization that marks the beginning of Southern California. Vast areas of wilderness cover the region, including volcanic landscapes and dense forests, imposing mountain ranges and rugged coastlines, proudly preserved by a series of national parks. Northern California also has a rich history, from the first European settlers in Monterey to the celebrated Gold Rush of 1849. Its natural beauty is enhanced by equally picturesque and significant towns, including the state's capital, Sacramento.

Locator Map

Crescent City

Yreka

THE NORTH
(see pp446–57)

Eureka

Weaverville

Red Bluff

Redwood National Park *(see p452)* is a protected landscape of dense, awe-inspiring redwood forests, including the world's tallest tree, named Hyperion, which reaches a height of 379 ft (115 m). The area is perennially popular with anglers, hikers, bird-watchers, and campers.

Mendocino

Ukiah

0 kilometers 50

0 miles 50

WINE COUNTRY
(see pp458–69)

Calistoga

Santa Rosa

Na

Sonoma *(see pp468–9)* was the site of the Bear Flag Revolt in 1846, when Americans rebelled against Mexican rule and tried to turn California into a republic. The vineyards of Sonoma County and the Napa Valley *(see pp466–7)*, benefiting from good soil and an ideal climate, produce world-class wines.

San Francisco

Oak

SAN FRANCIS
AND THE BAY
(see pp300–43

Santa Cruz

Monter

Carmel Mission *(see pp516–17)* was founded in 1770 by Junípero Serra and became the most important of all the 21 Franciscan missions, serving as the administrative center for Northern California. Today, restored to its original splendor, it is considered to be the state's most beautiful church.

◄ Deer grazing at the edge of Cathedral Lake, Yosemite National Park

Lassen Volcanic National Park *(see p457)* was formed in 1914, when more than 300 eruptions resulted in a new landscape of mudflows and sulfurous streams heated by molten lava. Mount Lassen, part of the Cascade Mountain Range, is considered to be still active.

Sacramento *(see pp476–9)* has been the state capital since 1854, and the Capitol is one of California's finest buildings. Old Sacramento preserves its historic structures from the 1860s and 1870s, when the town was the western terminus of the transcontinental railroad.

Yosemite National Park *(see pp492–5)* is an unforgettable wilderness of forests, alpine meadows, breathtaking waterfalls, and imposing granite rocks. In 1864 it became the first protected park in the US.

Alturas

Susanville

Quincy

ba City

South Lake Tahoe

Sacramento

GOLD COUNTRY AND THE CENTRAL VALLEY *(see pp470–85)*

Stockton

Modesto

Merced

Lee Vining

THE HIGH SIERRAS *(see pp486–501)*

Bishop

NORTH CENTRAL CALIFORNIA *(see pp502–21)*

Soledad

Fresno

Coalinga

Hanford

Tulare

Columbia State Historic Park *(see pp484–5)* was once the second largest town in California and is now the best preserved of the old gold mining centers.

Wildlife and Wilderness

Eons ago, most of Northern California was under water, until geological forces pushed up the floor of the Central Valley, causing the Pacific Ocean to recede. Diverse terrains and ecosystems then emerged and Northern California is now a land of peaks, canyons, and headlands. Unique flora grows here, such as giant sequoias in the High Sierras *(see pp500–1)* and Monterey cypress trees *(see p515)*. Black bears roam redwood groves and hawks hover above Yosemite Valley *(see pp492–5)*. Legend has it that Bigfoot, America's version of the Yeti, makes his home in these parts. In order to protect this landscape, the environment-friendly Sierra Club began here in 1892 and is still active today.

Prairie Creek State Park has a herd of protected Roosevelt elk, which roam the dunes of Gold Bluff Beach.

Redwood National Park *(see pp452–3)* contains the world's tallest redwood tree, reaching 379 ft (115 m). These evergreens soak up the winter's heavy rainfall and are kept moist in summer by fogs, which move in from the ocean. Woodpeckers, spotted owls, mule deer, squirrels, and banana slugs frequent the groves.

Point Reyes Peninsula *(see pp416 & 418)* is a small "island," almost separated from the mainland by the San Andreas Fault. Its forested ridges, littoral rocks, and rock pools are a prime habitat for crustaceans such as the Pacific rock crab.

The Sacramento National Wildlife Refuges protect the many birds that stop off on the Pacific Flyway.

The Farallon Islands *(see pp416)* are an important breeding ground for sea birds, including the puffin, and elephant seals. Visitors are not permitted on the islands.

Año Nuevo State Reserve *(see p508)* is occupied every winter by hundreds of breeding elephant seals.

The Monterey Peninsula *(see pp514–15)* is the winter home of the beautiful migratory monarch butterfly.

Map labels:
Crescent City
Six Rivers National Forest
Yreka
96
97
5
Klam Natio Fore
101
Trinity National Forest
Dunsmuir
Shasta National Forest
Clair Engle Lake
Eureka
Klamath
299
Black Butte
Reddir
Sacramento
3
Leggett
Sinkyone Wilderness
101
Mendocino National Forest
Chico
Eel
5
Mendocino
Ukiah
Clear Lake
Sut Nati Wilc Refe
Cache Creek
29
Lake Sonoma
101
Lake Barryessa
Bodega
Napa
San Francisco
San Jose
Big Bas Redwo State P
Santa Cruz
Mo
Point Lobos Reserve

Key
- ▢ National Park
- ▢ State Park
- ▢ National Forest
- ▢ Wildlife refuge
- ═ River

0 kilometers   50
0 miles   50

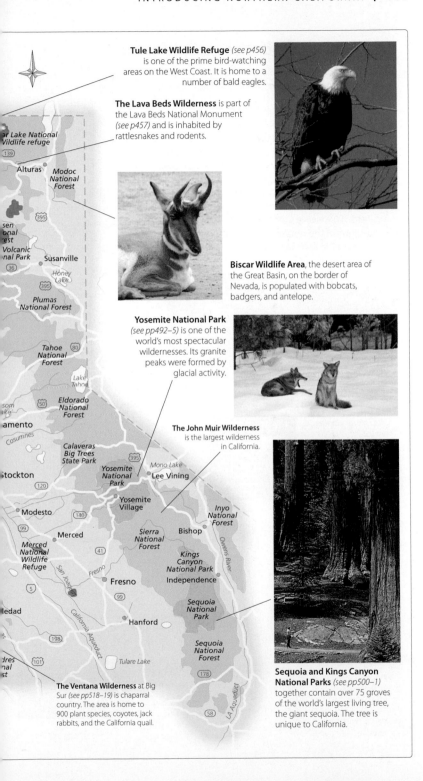

Tule Lake Wildlife Refuge *(see p456)* is one of the prime bird-watching areas on the West Coast. It is home to a number of bald eagles.

The Lava Beds Wilderness is part of the Lava Beds National Monument *(see p457)* and is inhabited by rattlesnakes and rodents.

Biscar Wildlife Area, the desert area of the Great Basin, on the border of Nevada, is populated with bobcats, badgers, and antelope.

Yosemite National Park *(see pp492–5)* is one of the world's most spectacular wildernesses. Its granite peaks were formed by glacial activity.

The John Muir Wilderness is the largest wilderness in California.

Sequoia and Kings Canyon National Parks *(see pp500–1)* together contain over 75 groves of the world's largest living tree, the giant sequoia. The tree is unique to California.

The Ventana Wilderness at Big Sur *(see pp518–19)* is chaparral country. The area is home to 900 plant species, coyotes, jack rabbits, and the California quail.

The Wines of Northern California

California is the most important wine-growing area in the United States, producing roughly ninety per cent of the nation's wine. More than 635,000 acres (216,140 ha) of the state's land is used for viticulture. Half of the grapes grown here are harvested from the fertile soil of the interior region, particularly the stretch of land bordered by the Sacramento Valley to the north and the San Joaquin Valley to the south. The north coast region accounts for less than a quarter of California's total wine-growing acreage, but many of the country's best Chardonnay, Sauvignon Blanc, Cabernet Sauvignon, and Merlot grapes are grown here. The north coast is also home to most of the state's 3,300 wineries. Chardonnay and Pinot Noir grapes are the mainstays of the central coast region, which extends from the San Francisco Bay Area to Santa Barbara.

Locator Map

Northern California wine region

Grape harvest at V. Sattui Winery near St. Helena in Napa Valley

Late Harvest Zinfandel from the Hop Kiln Winery is a red dessert wine made from grapes left on the vine longer than usual to increase their sweetness. The winery is housed in an historic hop kiln barn.

The Story of Zinfandel

The history of Zinfandel is one of the great success stories of California wine. This versatile grape is thought to have been brought to America from Croatia's Dalmatian coast. Zinfandel arrived in California in the 1850s, and is now the third-leading grape variety in the state. The Zinfandel reds, particularly those from the Dry Creek and Russian River valleys, are now in great demand. Some have oaky flavors, while others have strong, fruity flavors. The rosé White Zinfandel was created by winemakers to use up their surplus red grapes.

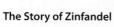

Beaulieu Vineyard's Private Reserve Cabernet Sauvignon is a medium-bodied red wine with ripe cherry and blackcurrant aromas. It has been produced since 1936 and was the first wine in the US to be called Private Reserve.

Saintsbury's Vin Gris is a Burgundy-style rosé wine, which is made from the juice of Pinot Noir grapes.

Map labels: Fel, Willits, Mendocino, Ukiah, Upper Lake, Navarro, Russian, Clear Lake, Point Arena, Cloverdale, Mid, Gualala, Healdsburg, Ca, Santa Rosa, N, V, Point Reyes, Richmo, San Francisco, San Mat

Key Facts about California Wines

Location and Climate
California's latitude, proximity to the ocean, and sheltered valleys create a mild climate. Winters tend to be short and mild, while the growing season is long and hot but cooled by summer fogs. Combined with fertile soil, these factors mean that large areas have ideal grape-growing conditions.

Grape Varieties
California's most widely planted grape variety is **Chardonnay**, used to make a dry wine with a balance of fruit, acidity, and texture. Other popular whites include **Sauvignon Blanc** (also known as **Fumé Blanc**), **Chenin Blanc**, **Pinot Blanc**, **Gewürztraminer**, and **Johannisberg Riesling**. California's red wines are typically dry with some tannic astringency and include the rich, full-bodied **Cabernet Sauvignon**, **Merlot**, **Syrah**, **Pinot Noir**, and **Zinfandel**.

Good Producers
Chardonnay: Acacia, Byron, Château Montelena, Ferrari-Carano, Kendall-Jackson, Kistler, Kunde Estate, Sonoma-Cutrer. *Cabernet Sauvignon*: Beaulieu, Beringer, Grgich Hills, Heitz, The Hess Collection, Jordan, Joseph Phelps, Silver Oak, Robert Mondavi, Stag's Leap, Wente, Whitehall Lane. *Merlot*: Clos du Bois, Duckhorn, Frog's Leap, Silverado, Sterling. *Pinot Noir*: Dehlinger, Etude, Gary Farrell, Saintsbury, Sanford. *Sauvignon Blanc:* Duckhorn, Glen Ellen, Kenwood, Matanzas Creek, J Rochioli. *Zinfandel*: Dry Creek, Lake Sonoma, De Loach, Hop Kiln, Ridge, Rosenblum, Sebastiani.

Good Vintages
(Reds) 2012, 2010, 2009, 2007, 2006, 2005, 2004, 2003, 2002, 2001, 2000, 1999, 1998, 1997. *(Whites)* 2012, 2010, 2009, 2007, 2006, 2005, 2004, 2003, 2002, 2001, 2000, 1999, 1998, 1997.

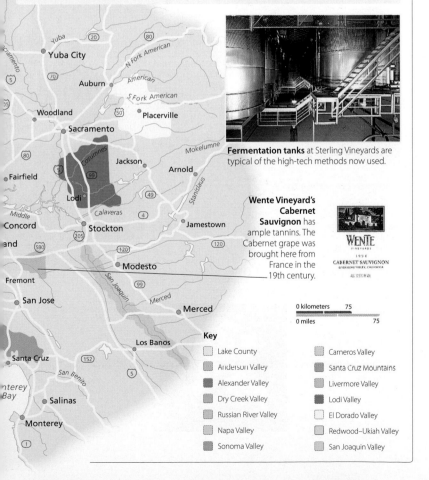

Fermentation tanks at Sterling Vineyards are typical of the high-tech methods now used.

Wente Vineyard's Cabernet Sauvignon has ample tannins. The Cabernet grape was brought here from France in the 19th century.

WENTE
VINEYARDS
1994
CABERNET SAUVIGNON
LIVERMORE VALLEY, CALIFORNIA
ALL 12.5% BY VOL

0 kilometers 75
0 miles 75

Key

- Lake County
- Anderson Valley
- Alexander Valley
- Dry Creek Valley
- Russian River Valley
- Napa Valley
- Sonoma Valley
- Carneros Valley
- Santa Cruz Mountains
- Livermore Valley
- Lodi Valley
- El Dorado Valley
- Redwood–Ukiah Valley
- San Joaquin Valley

The Bohemian North

Perhaps because the region attracted a wide range of people and enjoyed enormous wealth during the Gold Rush *(see pp52–3)*, Northern California has always tended to be nonconformist and somewhat hedonistic. This has caused some anguish over the years, as charlatans and crackpots have taken advantage of the region's broad-mindedness, but it has certainly made the area a colorful place. During the late 19th century, San Francisco's Barbary Coast was home to casinos, opium dens, and brothels *(see p318)*. Utopian communities, organized around humanitarian, religious, or dietary principles, have been another facet of Northern California life. In the 1960s, the area's air of liberality made it a haven for members of the "Make Love, Not War" generation *(see p363)*. It has since attracted everybody from nudists and hot-tub lovers, to religious gurus and the latter-day hippies who helped turn marijuana into a chief crop of Humboldt County.

Spiritual guidance became popular during the 1850s, and 1860s. San Francisco attracted many spiritualist "mediums," who held regular seances. There are still a few spiritualist churches operating in the Bay Area.

Sally Stanford, born in 1903, was a virtual pariah in Sausalito when she took over the Valhalla (now the Gaylord India), the town's oldest restaurant, in 1950. Local citizens did not approve of her previous occupation as a San Francisco madam. But Sally's personality eventually won the town over, and she served one term as the town's mayor (1976–8). She died in 1982.

Utopian Communities

From the 1850s to the 1950s, more Utopian communities were founded in Northern California than in any other place in the nation. William Riker's Holy City was established in 1918 in the Santa Cruz Mountains. Riker, a pro-Nazi and forecaster of apocalypses, called his totalitarian community the "headquarters for the world's perfect government." It eventually died out because the community was celibate.

Fountain Grove was a Utopian outpost north of Santa Rosa, founded in 1875 by New York mystic Thomas Lake Harris. He identified himself with Christ and as a bisexual "Divine Man-Woman". Under attack for alleged sexual and financial abuses, Harris was forced to close his commune in 1892.

William Riker

Young and old lived and traveled together in communties.

Bright colors and childlike designs were influenced by the lights and patterns experienced during drug-induced hallucinatory "trips."

Psychedelic Pop Art posters of the 1960s were distinctive for their inflated, crammed typeface, developed by artist Wes Wilson.

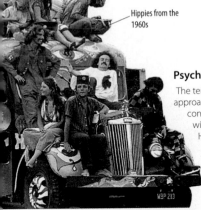

Hippies from the 1960s

Jim Jones and the People's Temple

The Reverend Jim Jones (1931–78) was a popular cult leader in the Bay Area during the 1970s, preaching an amalgam of racial and religious egalitarianism, political empowerment, doomsday visions, and sexual freedom. He was alternately a fundamentalist, supposedly "healing" people through touch, and a modern minister, with his services accompanied by music and dance. But he was also a self-proclaimed messiah. After building up a congregation of some 20,000 at his People's Temple in San Francisco, in 1978 he moved almost 1,000 of them to an isolated agricultural mission in Guyana, South America. After rumors of physical abuse and weapons caches at the colony brought international scrutiny, Jones ordered a mass suicide. Investigators later found hundreds of his followers' corpses in the jungle; they had all drunk a cyanide-laced fruit drink, and the despotic reverend had been shot in the head.

Jim Jones

Psychedelia

The term "psychedelic" originally referred to ideas or approaches that were somehow outrageous, non-conformist, or "mind-expanding." But after San Francisco witnessed the opening of the Psychedelic Shop on Haight Street in 1966 *(see p362)*, the word became associated with the hallucinatory drugs popular among the region's hippie generation. Psychedelia then turned into a symbol of an entire lifestyle: young hippie communities rejecting conformity and traveling from one gathering to another on brightly painted buses, taking drugs, and preaching peace.

The Esalen Institute *(see p518)* became famous in the 1960s as the center of the "human potential movement," a philosophy emphasizing individual responsibility for both the good and bad events in life. Today it is an expensive retreat where former flower children and stressed corporate executives all discuss spiritual insights while reclining in hot springs overlooking the Pacific Ocean.

THE NORTH

Ranging from deserted beaches strewn with giant driftwood logs to dense forests at the foot of alpine peaks, the far north of California is the state at its most wild and rugged. The landscape is as diverse as any continent – lush redwood groves, the volcanic Cascade Mountains, the arid plains at the edge of the Great Basin – yet all this is confined within one-quarter of the state.

Native Americans settled in extreme Northern California around 10,000 BC. They coexisted peacefully with each other and with the earth, leaving behind few signs of their existence apart from discarded sea shells and pictographs on cave walls. When the Europeans arrived in the area in the 19th century, the Native American population declined rapidly due to exposure to diseases they were not immune to and reduction in food supply.

The first settlers to come were fur trappers, in search of beavers, sea otters, and other pelts. Soon afterward gold seekers descended upon the region's rivers, hoping for similar riches to those found in the Sierra Nevada (see pp52–3). Some gold was found, but the real wealth was made at the end of the century when lumber companies began to harvest the forests of coastal redwoods. These giant redwood trees *(Sequoia sempervirens)* are the region's defining feature. The finest forests have been protected by state and national parks and exude a palpable sense of history.

Inland, an even more ancient sight confronts visitors to the strange volcanic areas of Mount Lassen and the Lava Beds National Monument. Millions of years worth of geological activity has formed a stunning landscape that is devoid of civilization.

Far Northern California is sparsely populated, with a few medium-sized towns, such as Redding and Eureka. The prime attractions are natural, and life here, for visitors and residents, revolves around the great outdoors.

Lost Creek in Redwood National Park

◀ Steam rising from sulfurous pools at Bumpass Hell, Lassen Volcanic National Park

Exploring the North

Rugged, wild, and sparsely populated, California's northern extremes have more in common with neighboring Oregon and Washington than they do with the rest of the state. Dense forests of pine, fir, and redwood trees cover more than half the landscape, and two parallel mountain ranges, the Coast Range and, farther inland, the Sierra Nevada Mountains, divide the north into two very different sections. Along the coast, Cape Mendocino makes a good base for exploring the often deserted beaches and coastal redwood groves. Inland, the Sacramento Valley provides access to the beautiful snow-capped Mount Shasta, the volcanic spectacles of Lassen Volcanic National Park, and the Lava Beds National Monument.

Patrick's Point State Park in Humboldt County

Sights at a Glance

❷ Arcata
❸ Eureka
❹ Samoa Cookhouse
❺ Ferndale
❻ Willow Creek
❼ Avenue of the Giants
❽ The Lost Coast
❾ Weaverville
❿ Shasta Dam
⓫ Shasta State Historic Park
⓬ Mount Shasta
⓭ Tule Lake National Wildlife Refuges
⓮ Lava Beds National Monument
⓯ Lassen Volcanic National Park

Tour

❶ Redwood National Park
pp452–3

Getting Around

A car is essential for visiting northern California. Two north–south routes run parallel up and down the region, but the only comfortable route through the mountains east–west is Hwy 299. Bisecting the north, I-5 runs through the Sacramento Valley, while to the west US Hwy 101 runs through the lush valleys of the Russian and Eel Rivers. Public transportation is limited to Greyhound buses along the two main highways and a daily train service through the Sacramento Valley to Seattle.

For hotels and restaurants in this area see pp540–41 and p572

Key

▬▬ Freeway
▬▬ Major road
▬▬ Secondary road
⋯⋯ Minor road
▬▬ Scenic route
⤛⤛ Main railroad
——— Minor railroad
▬▬ State border
△ Summit

Impressive peak of Mount Shasta

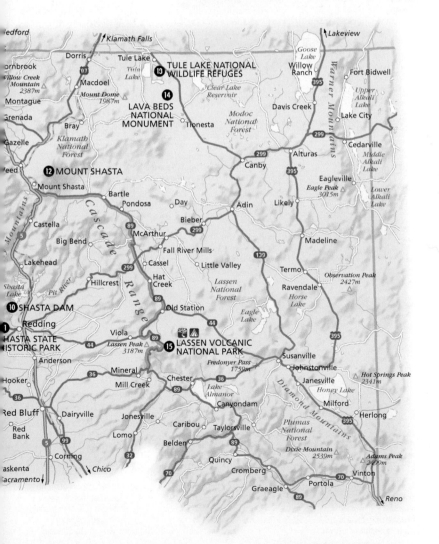

❶ Redwood National Park

See pp452–3.

❷ Arcata

Road map A2. 🏘 17,200. 🚌 ✈
Arcata/Eureka Airport, 8 miles (13 km)
N of Arcata. 🅸 1635 Heindon Rd, (707)
822-3619. 🆆 **arcatachamber.com**

Arcata is a small town and its life revolves around Humboldt State University, in the hills above. Arcata's main square, with palm trees and a statue of President McKinley (1843–1901), is filled with bookstores and cafés. The town is a pleasant base for exploring the redwood region. The forests east of Arcata are thought to be the stomping grounds of Bigfoot, the US equivalent to the Himalaya's Yeti. No one has yet proved its existence, but footprints larger than those of the biggest bear have been found.

❸ Eureka

Road map A2. 🏘 27,600. 🚌 ✈
Arcata/Eureka Airport, 15 miles
(24 km) N of Eureka. 🅸 2112
Broadway, (707) 442-3738, 800 356-
6381. 🆆 **eurekachamber.com**

Eureka was founded by gold miners in 1850, who were so excited by their find that they proudly named it after the new

Redwoods and the Lumber Industry

The tallest tree on earth, the coniferous coastal redwood (*Sequoia sempervirens*) is unique to northern California and southern Oregon, although it is also related to the giant sequoia (*Sequoiadendron gigantea*) of the High Sierras and the *Metasequoia glyptostrobiodes* species, native to China. Redwoods can live for 2,000 years and reach 350 ft (107 m), despite roots that grow up to 200 ft (61 m) horizontally but only 4–6 ft (1–2 m) deep.

The redwood's fast growth and resistance to disease makes it ideal for commercial use. By the 1920s, logging had destroyed 90 percent of the groves. The Save the Redwoods League was formed, buying land now protected in state parks. However, some groves are still owned by lumber companies, and their future is a major issue on both local and national levels.

Stacked redwood lumber

state's ancient Greek motto meaning "I have found it." It has since expanded into the northern coast's largest industrial center, with extensive logging and fishing operations surrounding the state protected natural harbor.

West of US 101, between E and M streets along the waterfront, is Eureka's interesting Old Town. Its restored 19th-century buildings, many with cast-iron facades, are now converted into cafés, bars, and restaurants.

Situated at M and Second streets is the extravagant Victorian architecture of Carson Mansion *(see pp35)*. It was built in 1885 for millionaire lumber baron William Carson. Its whimsical Gothic design is enhanced by its redwood construction typical of the area, painted to resemble the more expensive medium of stone. Carson Mansion is now a club and is closed to the general public.

Ornate Carson Mansion in Eureka

❹ Samoa Cookhouse

79 Cookhouse Ln & Samoa Rd, Samoa.
Road map A2. **Tel** (707) 442-1659.
Open daily. **Closed** Thanksgiving, Dec
25. 🅴 🆆 **samoacookhouse.net**

The Samoa Cookhouse was built in 1890 as a dining room for workers at the adjacent Louisiana Pacific pulp mill, one of many lumber mills standing on the narrow Samoa Peninsula. It was opened to the public in the 1960s, when automation in the mills had reduced the size of the workforce and the need for on-site dining facilities. The restaurant has retained its rustic decor and its giant-sized portions of traditional American dishes. Antique logging equipment adds to the unique ambience.

❺ Ferndale

Road map A2. 🏘 1,400. ✈ Arcata/
Eureka Airport, 40 miles (64 km)
N of Ferndale. 🅸 PO Box 325,
Ferndale, 707 786-4477.
🆆 **victorianferndale.com**

Located on a flood plain near the mouth of the Eel River, Ferndale is a pastoral respite from the wilderness of California's northern coast.

The town was founded in 1852 by Danish, Swiss-Italian, and Portuguese immigrants who together established a lucrative dairy industry here. In 1992, Ferndale was hit by one of the worst earthquakes in California's recent history, measuring 7.1 on the Richter scale, but damage was limited. Exhibits of the town's history can be seen in the **Ferndale Museum**.

The town is perhaps best known as the host of the annual Kinetic Sculpture Race, during which contestants ride their self-made vehicles from Arcata to Ferndale, finishing the race on Main Street.

Ⓜ Ferndale Museum
Shaw & 3rd St. **Tel** (707) 786-4466.
Open Feb–May & Oct–Dec:
11am–4pm Wed–Sat, 1–4pm Sun;
Jun–Sep: 11am–4pm Tue–Sat,
1–4pm Sun. **Closed** Jan.
Ⓦ ferndale-museum.org

Gingerbread Mansion, one of Ferndale's Victorian houses

❻ Willow Creek

Road map A2. ⓜ 1,700.
🚌 ✈ Arcata/Eureka Airport,
44 miles (71 km) E of Willow Creek.
ⓘ PO Box 704, Willow Creek
(530) 629-2693. **Ⓦ willowcreek
chamber.com**

An hour's drive east from the coast, the tiny town of Willow Creek attracts nature lovers and enthusiasts with its pristine scenic beauty and excellent fishing.

The town is perhaps best known for being home to the **Willow Creek – China Flat Museum**. The museum features the Bigfoot Collection, the world's largest assortment of curios related to the legendary hominid. The term

"Bigfoot" was coined in 1958 by the local newspaper after giant footprints and sightings of the fabled man-beast were reported by locals. Kids will love persuing the unique collection of Bigfoot pictures, footprint casts, maps, and other exhibits at the museum.

Sightings are all but guaranteed at the annual Bigfoot Days festival each Labor Day weekend.

Ⓜ Willow Creek – China Flat Museum
38949 CA-299 Willow Creek.
Tel (530) 629-2653.
Open May–Sep: 10am–4pm Wed–Sun; Oct: noon–4pm Fri–Sun.
Ⓦ bigfootcountry.net

❼ Avenue of the Giants

Road map A2. 🚌 Garberville.
ⓘ Weott (Nov–Apr: 10am–4pm daily;
May–Oct: 9am–5pm daily, (707) 946-2263. **Ⓦ avenueofthegiants.net**

The world's tallest redwood trees and the most extensive primeval redwood groves stand along the banks of the Eel River in the impressive 50,000-acre (20,200-ha) Humboldt Redwoods State Park. The best overall sense of these trees can be seen by driving along the 33-mile (53-km) Avenue of the Giants, a winding two-lane highway running parallel to US 101 through the park. For the best experience, however, leave your car in one of the many

Large wooden statue of Bigfoot outside the Willow Creek – China Flat Museum

parking areas and walk around the groves, taking in the full immensity and magnificence of the trees.

The tallest individual specimen, the 364-ft (110-m) Dyersville Giant, was blown over during a storm in the winter of 1991, but its size is perhaps even more astounding now, lying on its side in Founder's Grove at the north end of the park. Currently the tallest and largest trees stand within the Rockefeller Forest above the west bank of the river.

The visitors' center, halfway along the Avenue of the Giants on US 101, exhibits displays on the natural history of these mighty forests. It also supplies maps and detailed information on the many hiking, camping, picnicking, swimming, and biking facilities available within the park.

Avenue of the Giants, in Humboldt Redwoods State Park

❶ A Tour of Redwood National Park

Redwood National Park protects some of the largest original redwood forests in the world, stretching along the coastline of Northern California. Established by President Johnson in 1968 to promote tourism to the area, the 58,000-acre (23,500-ha) park includes smaller areas that had already been established as state parks. A tour of the area takes one full day, although two days allows time to walk away from the roads and experience the tranquillity of these majestic groves.

Coastal redwood trees

③ Del Norte Coast Redwood State Park
This park became the first protected area in 1926. Part of the old Redwood Highway has been maintained as a hiking trail. In spring, wildflowers cover the hillsides.

④ Trees of Mystery
A major tourist attraction of the area is marked by giant fiberglass statues of the fictional lumberjack Paul Bunyan and his ox, Babe. The two characters were popularized in early 20th-century folklore stories about their journey from Maine to California.

⑤ Tall Trees Grove
One of the world's tallest trees, a 379-ft (115-m) giant, stands in the aptly named Tall Trees Grove, at the southern end of the park. The park provides a habitat for one of the world's last remaining herds of Roosevelt elk.

⑥ Gold Bluffs Beach
This 11-mile (18-km) beach is rated by many as the most beautiful in Northern California.

⑦ Humboldt Lagoons State Park
Big Lagoon, a freshwater lake stretching for 3 miles (5 km), and two other estuaries form Humboldt Lagoons State Park.

⑧ Patrick's Point State Park
In winter, the headlands are a good place to watch for migrating gray whales. Rock pools abound with smaller marine life.

Fort Dick · D4 · 197
D3
Parkway Drive ①
②
101
③
Klamath ④ Klamath River
101
Alder Camp Road ⑥
Davidson Rd ⑤
101
Orick
Stone Lagoon
⑦
Big Lagoon
⑧

0 km   1
0 miles   1

① Jedediah Smith Redwoods State Park
Found among the 9,200 acres (3,720 ha) of this park are the most awe-inspiring coastal redwoods. The park was named after the fur-trapper Jedediah Smith, the first white man to walk across the US. He explored this region in 1828 *(see p50)*.

② Crescent City
This northern town is the site of the headquarters and main information center for Redwood National Park.

Key
▬▬▬ Tour route
═══ Other roads

Tips for Drivers

Tour length: Arcata to Crescent City is 78 miles (125 km). US 101 is the quickest route.

Duration of trip: One could drive the entire route in under two hours one-way, but to experience a more satisfying and relaxing visit to the Redwood National Park area, allow at least a full day.

When to go: September and October are ideal months to travel. Spring and summer can be foggy, but the best flowering plants are on view during these months. Winter is often rainy but is best for whale-watching. Summer is the prime tourist season, although crowds are rarely a problem in this remote area of the state.

Where to stay and eat: Tourist services are comparatively few and far between in this region. However, there is a limited range of restaurants and motels available in Orick and Klamath, while a much wider range of facilities is available in Crescent City and Arcata or Eureka *(see pp540–41 and p572)*, south of the park .

Visitor information: Crescent City Information Center, 111 Second St. **Open** Mar–Oct: 9am–5pm daily; Nov–Feb: 9am–4pm daily. **Closed** Jan 1, Thanksgiving, Dec 25. **Tel** (707) 464-6101. **W** redwoods.info

The Lost Coast, near Crescent City

❽ The Lost Coast

Road Map A2. 🚌 Garberville.
ℹ️ 782 Redwood Drive, 707 923-2613, 800 923-2613. **W** garberville.org

Covering a small section of coastline so craggy and wild that no road could reasonably be built along it, the so-called Lost Coast is the largest remaining stretch of undeveloped shoreline in California. Protected by the government within the Sinkyone Wilderness State Park and the King Range National Conservation Area, the Lost Coast region stretches for more than 40 miles (64 km).

The salmon-fishing port of Shelter Cove, tucked away within a tiny bay, is at the center of the Lost Coast. Its remote location has kept the village small, but it remains a good base for hikers and wildlife enthusiasts. Sixteen miles (25 km) of hiking trails, inhabited only by fauna such as black bears, deer, mink, and bald eagles, run along the clifftops, interspersed with free camp sites. Shelter Cove is accessible only via a winding but well-maintained road.

A good feel for the Lost Coast can be had by taking Hwy 211 west of US 101 and then following the scenic road between Humboldt Redwoods State Park and Ferndale *(see p450)*. This beautiful 50-mile (80-km) road runs to the edge of the Pacific Ocean around Cape Mendocino, the westernmost point on the coast of California.

❾ Weaverville

Map A2. 🏔 3,500. ✈️ Redding Municipal Airport, 40 miles (64 km) E of Weaverville. ℹ️ 215 S. Main St, 530 623-6101, 800 487-4648.
W weavervilleinfo.org

This small rural town, set back in the mountains between the coast and the Central Valley, has changed little in the 150 years since it was founded by gold prospectors.

At the heart of the small commercial district, which boasts the state's oldest drugstore, is the **Jake Jackson Museum and History Center**, which has displays tracing the history of Weaverville and its surrounding gold-mining and lumber region. Adjacent to the museum, the Joss House State Historic Site is the oldest and best-preserved Chinese Temple in the country. Built in 1874, it serves as a reminder of the Chinese immigrants who arrived in the US to mine gold and stayed in the state as cheap labor building the California railroads *(see pp54–5)*.

North of Weaverville, the Trinity Alps, part of the Salmon Mountain Range, rise up at the center of a beautiful mountain wilderness. They are popular with hikers and backpackers in the summer and with cross-country skiers during the winter months.

🏛 **Jake Jackson Museum and History Center**
780 Main St. **Tel** (530) 623-5211.
Open Apr: noon–4pm daily; May–Oct: 10am–5pm daily; Nov–Mar: noon–4pm Tue & Sat. Donation.
W trinitymuseum.org

Freight train below the snow-bound peaks of Mount Shasta ▶

Shasta Dam, controlling the North's water supplies

❿ Shasta Dam

Road map A2. 🚃 Redding. Redding Convention and Visitors' Bureau: 844 Sundial Bridge. **Tel** (800) 874-7562.
W visitredding.com

In order to provide a steady supply of water for agriculture, a cheap source of electricity for manufacturers, prevent flooding in the valley, and offer jobs for workers who had been left unemployed by the downturn in local mining industries, the US government funded the Central Valley Project. This was a network of dams, canals, and reservoirs, set up during the Depression of the 1930s and centered upon the 602-ft- (183-m-) high, 3,460-ft- (1,055-m-) long Shasta Dam. With a spillway three times as high as Niagara Falls, the dam is an impressive civil engineering achievement.

⓫ Shasta State Historic Park

Road map A2. 🚃 Redding. Visitors' Center: **Tel** (530) 225-2065. **Open** 10am–5pm Wed–Sun.
W parks.ca.gov

During the 1850s, Shasta was one of the largest gold mining camps in the state and the base of operations for prospectors working along the Trinity, Sacramento, McCloud, and Pit Rivers. As the Gold Rush faded, the town faded too, especially after the railroad was rerouted through the town of Redding, 5 miles (8 km) east.
Shasta is now a ghost town, but in the early 1920s the state of

California, realizing its historical importance, took over and began to restore it. Numerous old brick buildings are preserved in a state of arrested decay, and the **Shasta Courthouse** has been restored to its original condition. Exhibits at the small visitors' center traces the town's history.
One mile (1.5 km) west of Shasta town, the land around Lake Whiskeytown forms the smallest parcel of the three-part Shasta-Whiskeytown-Trinity National Recreation Area, a forest preserve surrounding the three reservoirs. Lake Shasta is the largest of the three. Trinity Lake is also known as Clair Engle Lake, in honor of the local politician who helped make this ambitious reclamation project a reality. All three lakes are popular with fishermen, water-skiers, houseboat owners, and other recreational users.

🏛 **Shasta Courthouse and Visitors' Center**
Main St. **Tel** (530) 243-8194. **Open** 10am–5pm Wed–Sun.

⓬ Mount Shasta

Road map B1. 🚃 Dunsmuir. 🚌 Siskiyou. 🚌 Shasta. Visitors' Center: 300 Pine St. **Tel** (530) 926-4865, (800) 926-4865. **Open** daily.
W visitmtshasta.com

Mount Shasta reaches a height of 14,162 ft (4,316 m) and is the second highest of the Cascade Mountains, after Mount Rainier in Washington State. Visible more than 100 miles (160 km) away and usually covered with snow, the summit is a popular destination for mountaineers.

Mount Shasta, towering over the town of Shasta below

⓭ Tule Lake National Wildlife Refuges

Road map B1. 🚃 Klamath Falls. Visitors' Center: 4009 Hill Road. **Tel** (530) 667-2231.
W fws.gov/refuge/Tule_Lake

Six refuges on both sides of the California–Oregon border form one of the most popular

Interior of the preserved Shasta Courthouse

bird-watching spots in the western US. Centering upon Tule Lake and the Lower Klamath River, much of the region has been set aside as wildlife refuges *(see pp440–41)*, popular with bird-watchers. In the fall the refuges attract hundreds of thousands of wildfowl as they migrate south, from Canada to the Central Valley and beyond. Tule Lake is also the winter home to as many as 1,000 bald eagles.

⓮ Lava Beds National Monument

Road map B1. 🚌 Klamath Falls. Visitors' Center: 1 Indian Wells. **Tel** (530) 667-8100. **Open** daily. 🅦 **nps.gov/labe**

The Lava Beds National Monument spreads over 46,500 acres (18,800 ha) of the Modoc Plateau, the volcanic tableland of northeastern California, and preserves an eerie landscape of lava flows and cinder cones. Beneath the lava beds are more than 500 lava tube caves – cylindrical tunnels created by exposed lava turning to stone.

The greatest concentration of caves can be visited via the Cave Loop Road, 2 miles (3 km) south of the park's visitors' center. From here, a short trail leads down into Mushpot Cave, the only one with lights and a paved floor. The name derives from splatters of lava found near the entrance.

Other caves along the road are also named for their main feature: Crystal Cave contains sparkling crystals, and Catacombs Cave requires visitors to crawl through its twisting passages. To visit any of the caves, wear sturdy shoes, carry a flashlight, and be sure to check first with the visitors' center.

The park is also notable as the site of the Modoc War of 1872–3, the only major war between the US and the Native Americans in California. After being removed from the area to a reservation in Oregon, a group of Modoc Indians returned under the command of Chief Kientpoos, or "Captain Jack." For six months they evaded the US Cavalry, but

Captain Jack's Stronghold in Lava Beds National Monument

Captain Jack was eventually captured and hanged, and the rest were forced into a reservation in what is now Oklahoma. Captain Jack's Stronghold is along the park's north border.

⓯ Lassen Volcanic National Park

Road map B2. 🚌 Chester, Red Bluff. Visitors' Center: 38050 Hwy 36 East, Mineral. **Tel** (530) 595-4444. **Open** daily. 🅦 **nps.gov/lavo**

Prior to the eruption of Mount St. Helens in Washington in 1980, the 10,457-ft (3,187-m) high Lassen Peak was the last volcano to erupt on the mainland United States. In a series of nearly 300 eruptions between 1914 and 1917, Lassen Peak laid waste to 100,000 acres (40,500 ha) of the surrounding land. The area was set aside as Lassen Volcanic National Park in 1916.

The volcano is the southernmost in the Cascade Mountain range and is considered to be still active. Numerous areas on its flanks show clear signs of the geological pro- cesses. Bumpass Hell was named after an early tour

guide, Kendall Bumpass, who lost his leg in one of the boiling mudpots in 1865. This boardwalk trail leads past a series of steaming, sulfurous pools of boiling water, heated by molten rock deep underground. Bumpass Hell is one of the park's most interesting stops and is located along Hwy 89, 5 miles (8 km) from the Southwest Entrance Station.

In winter, Hwy 89 across the park is closed because of weather conditions. In summer, the road winds through the park, climbing more than 8,500 ft (2,590 m) high, up to Summit Lake. The road continues across to the Devastated Area, a bleak gray landscape of rough volcanic mudflows, ending at Manzanita Lake in the northwest corner of the park. Here the **Loomis Museum** displays a photographic record of Lassen Peak's many eruptions.

The park contains more than 150 miles (240 km) of hiking trails, including a very steep 2.5-mile (4-km) route up the side of Mount Lassen to the ashen gray summit.

🏛 Loomis Museum
Lassen Park Rd, North Entrance. **Tel** (530) 595-3399. **Open** late May– Oct (call for opening times).

Sulfur springs in Lassen Volcanic National Park

WINE COUNTRY

Famous throughout the world for its superlative wines, the Wine Country interior has a temperate climate, huge stretches of vine-covered rolling hills, and spectacular architecture. There are over 600 wineries in Napa and Sonoma counties. To the west lie the dramatic, rocky landscapes of the Sonoma and Mendocino coastlines. Throughout the region, a wide choice of excellent food and, of course, premium wine is available, making this an ideal place for a relaxing retreat.

California's wine industry was born in the small, crescent-shaped Sonoma Valley, when, in 1823, Franciscan fathers planted grape vines to produce sacramental wines. In 1857, the flamboyant Hungarian Count Agoston Haraszthy brought winemaking in California to a new level: using imported European grape varieties, he planted the state's first major vineyard at Sonoma's revered Buena Vista Winery. Haraszthy made a name not only for himself (he is known as the "father of California wine") but also for this previously unrecognized wine-producing region.

Over the years, many wine producers have followed in the count's footsteps, most of them favoring the rich, fertile soil of the Napa Valley. Hundreds of wineries now stand side by side along the length of the valley floor. Most of them offer tours of their facilities and wine tastings. Many are also of architectural interest, including such gems as the Mission-style Robert Mondavi Winery and the bright-white Greek-style architecture of Sterling Vineyards, which is perched on a volcanic bluff. Nearby, the stunning modern winery of Clos Pegase is distinguished by rows of imposing russet- and earth-colored columns and towers.

Nestled at the northernmost edge of the Napa Valley is the small town of Calistoga, famous for its restorative mud baths, enormous geysers, and hot mineral-water tubs. West of the valley, the Russian River which is bordered by the Sonoma and Mendocino coastal areas flows into the Pacific Ocean. These wild stretches of shoreline provide perfect opportunities for bird-and whale-watching and beachcombing.

Goat Rock Beach at the mouth of the Russian River

◀ Grand chateau of Francis Ford Coppola's Inglenook Winery near Rutherford in the Napa Valley

Exploring the Wine Country

The sheltered valleys of the coastal ranges provide the best conditions for planting vines, particularly within the Russian River, Sonoma, and Napa valleys. To the west of these famous wine-producing areas, quaint coastal towns, such as Mendocino, Jenner, and Bodega Bay, are surrounded by pristine, secluded beaches and small rock pools. Inland, visitors can explore the ancient redwood groves on foot, horseback, or by train. For those who prefer to have a bird's-eye view of the region, trips are available in hot-air balloons that soar gracefully above the vineyards. A short drive away are several immense state historic parks, with dense forests and unique architecture. Nearby, a wide variety of water-sports is offered at Clear Lake, California's largest freshwater lake, and Lake Berryessa, which is the second largest artificial lake in the state.

Gerstle Cove, site of a marine preserve at Salt Point

Getting Around

The majority of visitors explore the Wine Country and the areas along the Sonoma and Mendocino coasts by car. From San Francisco, Hwy 1 follows the coast; Hwy 101 runs south–north through the center of the region and into Humboldt County. Route 20 links Nevada City and the Wine Country, joining Hwy 101 north of Lake Mendocino. Public transportation services in the area are limited, although bus tours from San Francisco are available, and train tours of the Napa Valley (see pp466–7) and of the northern redwood forests (see p463) run regularly. The closest international airports are Sacramento, San Jose, San Francisco and Oakland (see pp600–1).

Key

≡ Freeway
▬ Major road
▬ Secondary road
∷∷ Minor road
▬ Scenic route
— Minor railroad
△ Summit

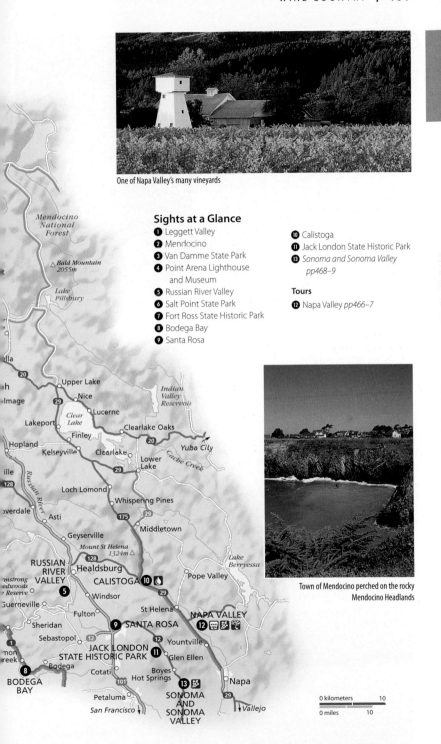

One of Napa Valley's many vineyards

Sights at a Glance

1. Leggett Valley
2. Mendocino
3. Van Damme State Park
4. Point Arena Lighthouse and Museum
5. Russian River Valley
6. Salt Point State Park
7. Fort Ross State Historic Park
8. Bodega Bay
9. Santa Rosa
10. Calistoga
11. Jack London State Historic Park
13. *Sonoma and Sonoma Valley pp468–9*

Tours

12. Napa Valley *pp466–7*

Town of Mendocino perched on the rocky
Mendocino Headlands

| 0 kilometers | 10 |
| 0 miles | 10 |

For additonal map symbols *see back flap*

❶ Leggett Valley

Road map A2. ▦ to Leggett.
ℹ 70400 Hwy 101.

This lush, green valley, separated from the Pacific Ocean by the King Mountain Range, is famous in California for its majestic giant redwoods. In the 1930s a hole was cut in the trunk of one enormous redwood to allow motorists to drive through the tree.

Hikers come to Leggett Valley and the surrounding area to enjoy the atmospheric redwood forest trails (part of the forest here was used to film scenes for George Lucas's science-fiction epic, *Star Wars*). The local wildlife population includes raccoons and deer, and golden eagles can often be seen soaring above the trees, searching the forest floor for unsuspecting prey.

South Fork Eel River, which is rich in salmon and steelhead trout, attracts many birds, including herons. The river is also popular with anglers and, in summer, swimmers.

❷ Mendocino

Road map A3. ▦ 900. ▦ ℹ 2175 Main St, Fort Bragg, 707 961-6300.
ⓦ visitmendocino.com

The settlers of this fishing village came to California from New England in 1852. They built their new homes to resemble as closely as possible those they had left behind on the East Coast, with pointed gables and decorative wooden trims. As a result, the Mendocino coastline is often referred to as "California's New England Coast." Perched on a rocky promontory high above the Pacific Ocean, Mendocino has retained the picturesque charm of its days as a major fishing and logging center. Although tourism is now its main industry, the town remains virtually untarnished by commercialism. It is a thriving arts center and has a large number of artists and writers. Visitors can stroll around the many boutiques, bookshops, galleries, and cafés. Those who prefer the attractions of nature can admire the migrating gray whales and the stunning ocean vistas.

Giant ferns lining the beautiful Fern Canyon Trail in Van Damme State Park

❸ Van Damme State Park

Road map A3. Comptche Ukiah Rd. **Tel** (707) 937-5804. ▦ from Point Arena. **Open** daily; Apr–Oct: reservations needed for camping. ▦
♿ ⓦ parks.ca.gov

This beautiful 2,200-acre (890-ha) preserve has some of California's most scenic forest trails, shaded by immense redwoods and giant ferns, and accompanied by meandering creeks. The coastal areas of the park are popular with abalone divers. For visitors who want to enjoy a hike or jog through gorgeous countryside, the lush Fern Canyon Trail is one of the best in the park, which also has several cycle trails.

Visitors also come to Van Damme to contemplate the peculiar Pygmy Forest, an eerie grove of old, stunted trees. Due to a combination of poor soil and bad drainage, these trees grow no taller than about 4 ft (1.2 m). Situated 3 miles (5 km) north of the park, it is accessible on foot or by car.

❹ Point Arena Lighthouse and Museum

45500 Lighthouse Rd. **Road map** A3. **Tel** (707) 882-2777, (877) 725-4448. ▦ from Point Arena. Lighthouse and Museum: **Open** 10am–3:30pm daily (to 4:30pm Jun–Aug). ▦
♿ museum only. ▦
ⓦ pointarenalighthouse.com

One mile (1.6 km) north of the Point Arena fishing village stands this impressive 115-ft (35-m) lighthouse. Erected in 1870, the original brick building was destroyed in the earthquake of 1906 *(see p28)*. The present reinforced concrete structure was produced in San Francisco by the Concrete Chimney Company.

A climb up the 145 steps to the top of the lighthouse

Mendocino overlooking the ocean from the bay's rocky headlands

provides a stunning view of the coast – the effort is particularly worthwhile on fog-free days. Tours of the lighthouse (available all year round) offer a chance to see its huge original Fresnel lens close-up. Built in France, it measures over 6 ft (1.8 m) in diameter, weighs more than 2 tons, and floats in a large pool of mercury.

The adjacent fog signal building, which dates from 1869, now houses a museum. Exhibits include compressed-air foghorns and displays on the history of the lighthouse.

Point Arena Lighthouse overlooking the Pacific Ocean

❺ Russian River Valley

🚌 from Healdsburg. 🛈 16209 First St, Guerneville, 707 869-9000. 🔲 russianriver.com

Bisected by the Russian River and its tributaries, the area known as the Russian River Valley is so vast that it contains several smaller valleys, some dominated by hillsides planted with grapevines and apple orchards, others by redwood groves, family farms, and sandy river beaches. About 60 wineries, many of which are open for wine tastings, are scattered throughout the valley.

At the hub of the valley is the small town of Healdsburg, where visitors often congregate around the splendid Spanish-style town square, with its shops, cafés, and restaurants.

Southwest of Healdsburg lies the tiny, friendly town of

The Skunk Train

Since 1885, the Skunk Train has been running from Fort Bragg, a coastal logging town north of Mendocino, into the heart of the redwood groves. Thanks to the odoriferous mix of diesel and gasoline once used to fuel the locomotive, waiting passengers could always smell the train before they could see it, hence its name. Today, locomotive lovers can ride on one of the steam, diesel, or electric trains for a half-or full-day tour through the forests.

Skunk Train and its smoke cloud

Guerneville, a summertime haven for San Francisco Bay Area residents, particularly gay men and women. Every year in September, Guerneville plays host to the very popular Russian River Jazz Festival at Johnson's Beach. Johnson's is also a good place from which to take a canoe or rafting trip down the gentle Russian River, where turtles, river otters, and great blue herons are often sighted. Hikers and equestrians flock to Guerneville to visit the 805-acre (330-ha) **Armstrong Redwoods State Reserve**, which is the site of one of the few remaining old-growth redwood forests in California. Among the mighty redwoods in the park is a 308-ft (94-m) giant – a 1,400-year-old tree named Colonel Armstrong.

🌲 Armstrong Redwoods State Preserve

17020 Armstrong Woods Rd, Guerneville. **Tel** (707) 869-2015, 865-2391. **Open** daily. 🔲 parks.ca.gov

❻ Salt Point State Park

Road map A3. Hwy 1. **Tel** (707) 847-3221, 847-3465. 🚌 from Santa Rosa. **Open** Visitors' Center: Apr–Oct: 10am–3pm Sat & Sun. 🅿 ♿ 🔲 parks. ca.gov

Within this forested 6,000-acre (2,400-ha) seaside park are several rocky coves, frequented by abalone divers and surf fishers. Salt Point also includes Gerstle Cove Marine Reserve, where divers admire protected sea anemones, starfish, and various rock fish.

Numerous bridle paths and hiking trails wind through Salt Point's pines, redwoods, and flower-filled meadows. In April and May, the most popular park attraction is the route that leads through the 317-acre (130-ha) Kruse Rhododendron State Reserve, where rhododendrons with pink and purple blooms grow up to 30 ft (9 m).

Gerstle Cove in Salt Point State Park

Cannon on display in front of the Russian Orthodox chapel at Fort Ross

❼ Fort Ross State Historic Park

1900 Coast Hwy 1, Jenner. **Road map** A3. **Tel** (707) 847-3286. 🚌 from Point Arena. **Open** sunrise–sunset daily. Visitors' Center & Bookstore: 10am–4:30pm daily. **Closed** Thanksgiving, Dec 25. 🅿️ ♿ 🌐 **parks.ca.gov**

On a windswept headland, 12 miles (19 km) north of Jenner, stands the grand Fort Ross State Historic Park. A well-restored Russian trading outpost, the fort was founded in 1812 and was occupied until 1841 (the name "Ross" is a derivative of the Russian word "Rossyia," meaning Russia).

The Russians were the first European visitors to the region, serving as representatives of the Russian-American Company, which had been established in 1799. Although it was the presence of Russian fur hunters in the North Pacific that induced Spain to occupy Alta California in 1769, the Russians never tried to expand their territory in California. After 30 years of peaceful trading, they abandoned the fort.

Built in 1836, the original house of the fort's last manager, Alexander Rotchev, is still intact today, and several other buildings have been painstakingly reconstructed within the wooden palisade. The most impressive structure in Fort Ross is the Russian Orthodox chapel, which was constructed from local redwood in 1824.

Every year, a living history day is held on the last Saturday of July. More than 200 costumed participants re-create life at the outpost in the 1800s.

❽ Bodega Bay

Road map A3. Hwy 1. 🅰️ 1,300. 🚌 ℹ️ 850 Hwy 1 (707 875-3866). 🌐 **bodegabay.com**

In 1963, the coastal town of Bodega Bay, with its white clapboard houses, appeared in Alfred Hitchcock's classic film, *The Birds*. In the tiny neighboring town of Bodega, visitors can still see the Potter Schoolhouse, which was in the film.

Bodega Head, the small peninsula sheltering Bodega Bay, is one of California's best whale-watching points. Other favorite pastimes here include golfing, bird-watching, digging for clams, and deep-sea fishing. In the evening, visitors can watch the fishing fleets unload their day's catch at Tides Wharf dock on Hwy 1.

The northern end of Bodega Bay marks the start of the Sonoma Coast State Beach, a 10-mile (16-km) stretch of ten beaches, separated by rocky bluffs. At the northernmost tip

A harbor seal on Goat Rock Beach, Bodega Bay

of this chain of beaches sits the charming little town of Jenner. Here, the wide Russian River spills into the Pacific Ocean, and hundreds of gray harbor seals bask in the sun and breed on Goat Rock Beach. The most rewarding time to watch the seals is during their "pupping season," which begins in March and lasts until late June.

❾ Santa Rosa

Road map A3. 🅰️ 174,000. ✈️ Sonoma County Airport, 6 miles (10 km) N of Santa Rosa. 🚌 ℹ️ 9 4th St (707 577-8674; 800 404-7673). 🌐 **visitsantarosa.com**

Santa Rosa, which is one of the fastest-growing cities in California, is best known for its past and present residents, most notably the horticulturist Luther Burbank (1849–1926). Burbank lived here for more than 50 years and became world famous for creating 800 new plant varieties, including fruits, vegetables, and ornamental flowers. Self-guided tours explore the one-acre (0.5-ha) site of the **Luther Burbank Home and Gardens**, which includes a rose garden, and an orchard. The Victorian garden features plants often found in domestic gardens in the 1880s.

In a restored historical post office dating from 1909 is the **Sonoma County Museum**. It illustrates the history of Sonoma County through rare historical

Fishing boats at North Beach Jetty Marina in Bodega Bay

Spring flowers in bloom at Luther Burbank Home and Gardens

photographs, documents, and artifacts. Another famous resident of Santa Rosa was the late Charles Schulz, creator of the "Peanuts" series. Fans of his cartoon characters can visit **Snoopy's Gallery and Gift Shop**, which stocks the widest range of Snoopy, Charlie Brown, and "Peanuts" products in the world.

🐦 Luther Burbank Home and Gardens
204 Santa Rosa Ave. **Tel** (707) 524-5445. Gardens: **Open** 8am–dusk daily. Home: **Open** Apr–Oct: 10am–4pm Tue–Sun. 🖼 🆆 lutherburbank.org

🏛 Sonoma County Museum
425 7th Street. **Tel** (707) 579-1500. **Open** 11am–5pm Tue–Sun. 🆆 sonomacountymuseum.org

🏠 Snoopy's Gallery and Gift Shop
1665 West Steele Lane. **Tel** (707) 546-3385. **Open** 10am–6pm daily. **Closed** public hols. 🆆 snoopygift.com

❿ Calistoga
Road map A3. 👥 5,100. 🚌 🛈 1133 Washington St, 707 942-6333. 🆆 calistogavisitors.com

Visitors have had mineral or mud baths here since this little spa town was founded in the mid-19th century by the state's first millionaire, Sam Brannan (1819–89). Today, crowds are still drawn here by its specialized spa treatments and good Wine Country cuisine. The town also has a range of pleasant accommodations and small boutiques selling everything from handmade soaps to

European home furnishings. Two miles (3 km) north of the town, the **Old Faithful Geyser** spouts jets of boiling mineral water 60 ft (18 m) into the sky about once every 40 minutes. To the west lies the **Petrified Forest**. Here hikers can see huge redwoods turned to stone by a volcanic eruption over three million years ago (see p466).

Many visitors who prefer to hike among living redwoods travel east to the Robert Louis Stevenson State Park, where the author of *Treasure Island* (see p30) and his wife, Fanny Osbourne, spent their honeymoon in 1880. Those who climb the 5 miles (8 km) from the park to the summit of the 4,343-ft (1,325-m) Mount St. Helena, the Wine Country's highest peak, are rewarded by a breathtaking view of the vineyards below. To enjoy the view without making the rigorous ascent, it is worth taking a trip in a glider or hot-air balloon. These are available at the gliderport in nearby Calistoga.

🐦 Old Faithful Geyser
1299 Tubbs Lane. **Tel** (707) 942-6463. **Open** daily. 🖼 🆆 old faithfulgeyser.com

🐦 Petrified Forest
4100 Petrified Forest Rd. **Tel** (707) 942-6667. **Open** 10am–dusk daily. **Closed** Dec 25. 🖼 🆗 limited. 🆆 petrifiedforest.org

⓫ Jack London State Historic Park
London Ranch Rd, Glen Ellen. **Road map** A3. **Tel** (707) 938-5216. **Open** Park: 9:30am–7pm daily (summer), 10am–5pm (winter). Museum: 10am–5pm daily. **Closed** Jan 1, Thanksgiving, Dec 25. 🖼 🆗 museum only. 🖼 🆆 **jacklondonpark.com**

In the early 1900s, the world-famous author of *The Call of the Wild*, *The Sea Wolf*, and more than 50 other books (see p30) abandoned his hectic lifestyle to live in this tranquil 800-acre (325-ha) expanse of oaks, madrones, California buckeyes, and redwoods. London (1876–1916) aptly named this territory the Beauty Ranch, and it still contains his stables, vineyards, and the cottage where he lived and died. Also here are the eerie ruins of London's dream home, the Wolf House, which was mysteriously destroyed by fire just before its completion. The park is ideal for a quiet picnic and a hike.

After London's death, his widow, Charmian Kittredge (1871–1955), built a magnificent home on the ranch, called the House of Happy Walls. The house is now a museum displaying London memorabilia. The author's writing desk and early copies of his work are exhibited.

Old Faithful Geyser spurting hot water into the sky

⑫ Napa Valley Tour

The sliver of land known as Napa Valley is 35 miles (56 km) long and lies at the heart of Northern California's wine industry *(see pp442–3)*. More than 350 wineries are scattered across its rolling hillsides and fertile valley floor, some dating from the early 19th century. Most of the wineries hug the scenic Silverado Trail and Hwy 29, two major arteries that run the length of the valley and through the towns of Yountville, Oakville, Rutherford, St. Helena, and Calistoga *(see p465)*. Many of Napa Valley's popular wineries offer visitors free tours of their facilities, while some charge a small wine-tasting fee.

⑦ Sterling Vineyards
An aerial tramway provides access to this large, white, Mediterranean-style winery, which is perched on a hill overlooking the valley and vineyards.

⑥ Clos Pegase
Renowned architect Michael Graves designed this Post-Modern winery, which is well known for its distinctive art collection and fine wines.

Food and Wine in the Napa Valley

In addition to a number of superior wines, the Wine Country is well known for its fresh produce and prestigious chefs. Produce stalls and farmers' markets line the valley roads, selling organic vegetables and fruit and freshly squeezed juices. Restaurants in most small towns serve excellent meals, prepared with the freshest ingredients. Classic Wine Country cuisine includes dishes such as Sonoma leg of lamb with fresh mint pesto, creamy risotto with artichoke hearts and sun-dried tomatoes, wild-mushroom sauté in herb-garlic phyllo pastry, and salmon sautéed and served with a Pinot Noir sauce.

⑤ Petrified Forest
This forest is the home of the largest petrified trees in the world *(see p465)*.

④ Bale Grist Waterwheel
Built in 1846, this waterwheel still grinds grain into meal and flour on weekends.

③ Robert Mondavi Winery
Beautiful sculptures and paintings are on display throughout this huge, Mission-style winery. Guided tours are available year-round.

Restaurant terrace at Domaine Chandon in Yountville

Key
▬▬ Tour route
═══ Other roads
⁙ Viewpoint

Napa Valley vineyard in the late-afternoon sunlight

Tips for Drivers

Tour length: 40 miles (64 km), including the scenic Petrified Forest detour.
Stopping-off points: There are several bed-and-breakfast inns and hotels in the towns of St. Helena and Calistoga. For an excellent meal, visit French Laundry or Mustards Grill in Yountville, or Solbar in Calistoga. For details and other more affordable options, *see pp572–4.*

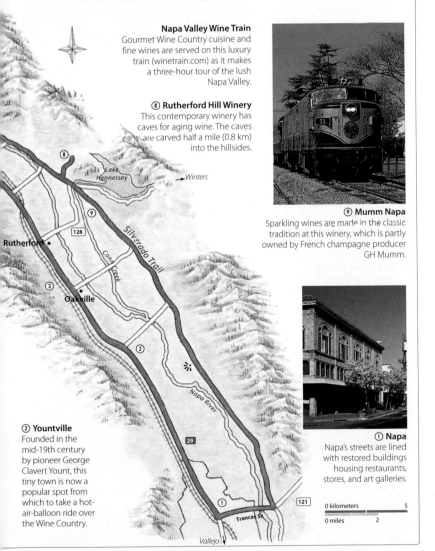

Napa Valley Wine Train
Gourmet Wine Country cuisine and fine wines are served on this luxury train (winetrain.com) as it makes a three-hour tour of the lush Napa Valley.

⑧ Rutherford Hill Winery
This contemporary winery has caves for aging wine. The caves are carved half a mile (0.8 km) into the hillsides.

⑨ Mumm Napa
Sparkling wines are made in the classic tradition at this winery, which is partly owned by French champagne producer GH Mumm.

① Napa
Napa's streets are lined with restored buildings housing restaurants, stores, and art galleries.

② Yountville
Founded in the mid-19th century by pioneer George Clavert Yount, this tiny town is now a popular spot from which to take a hot-air-balloon ride over the Wine Country.

Lake Hennessey
→ Winters
Rutherford
Conn Creek
Silverado Trail
Oakville
Napa River
Vallejo ↓
Trancas St.

0 kilometers 5
0 miles 2

⓭ Sonoma and Sonoma Valley

Nestling in the narrow, 17-mile- (27-km-) long Sonoma Valley, cradled by the Mayacama Mountains to the east and by the Sonoma Mountains to the west, are 6,000 acres (2,400 ha) of vineyards *(see pp442–3)*. At the foot of the valley lies the tiny town of Sonoma with its 8-acre (3-ha) plaza, a grass-covered town square designed in 1835 by Mexican General Mariano Vallejo (1808–90).

In the early 1840s, American settlers arriving in the area discovered that land ownership was reserved for Mexican citizens. On June 14, 1846, about 30 armed American farmers took General Vallejo and his men prisoner, seized control of Sonoma, and declared California an independent republic. The rebels' flag was adorned with a red star and stripe and a crude drawing of a grizzly bear. Although the republic was abolished 25 days later, when the United States annexed California *(see p51)*, the state legislature adopted the Bear Flag design as the official California flag in 1911.

Sonoma City Hall at the center of the historic Sonoma Plaza

🏛 General Joseph Hooker House

414 1st St East, El Paseo. **Tel** (707) 938-0510. **Open** 1–4pm Sat–Mon. 🅿 🅲
ⓦ sonomaleague.org

This 1855 gabled house belonged to Civil War hero "Fighting Joe" Hooker, who later sold it to settlers Pedro and Catherine Vasquez. The house is now the headquarters of the Sonoma League for Historic Preservation. Various historical exhibits and information on Sonoma walking tours are available here.

🏛 Toscano Hotel

20 E Spain St. **Tel** (707) 938-5889. **Open** 10am–5pm daily. 🅿 🅲 only.

Located on the north side of the plaza, the restored Toscano Hotel is now a historic monument. The two-story wood-frame building dates from the 1850s, when it was used as a general store and library. It was converted into a hotel for gold miners in 1886 and now belongs to the state.

Exploring Sonoma

Sonoma's main attractions are its internationally renowned wineries and the attractive area immediately surrounding the Spanish-style **Sonoma Plaza**. The well-shaded plaza is lined with dozens of meticulously preserved historical sites. Many of the adobe buildings around the square house wine shops, charming boutiques, and chic restaurants serving excellent California and Wine Country cuisine. At the very center of the town's plaza stands the **Sonoma City Hall**, a stone Mission Revival building *(see p35)* designed in 1908 by the San Francisco architect AC Lutgens. Close to the plaza's northeast corner is the bronze **Bear Flag Monument**, which serves as a memorial to the group of American settlers who rebelled against the ruling Mexican government in 1846.

Sonoma Town Center

① Sonoma Plaza
② City Hall
③ Bear Flag Monument
④ General Joseph Hooker House
⑤ Mission San Francisco Solano de Sonoma
⑥ Sonoma Barracks
⑦ Toscano Hotel
⑧ Sonoma Cheese Factory
⑨ Lachryma Montis

0 meters   250
0 yards   250

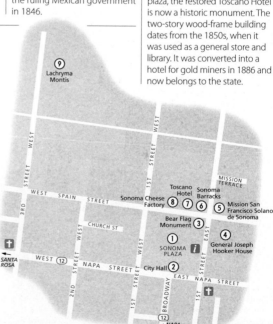

🏛 Sonoma Cheese Factory

2 W Spain St. **Tel** (707) 996-1931, (800) 535-2855. **Open** 9:30am–5:30pm daily. 🖥 **sonomacheesefactory.com**

The famous Sonoma Jack cheese has been produced in the enormous vats in this factory since 1931. Visitors can sample the main varieties of the cheese for free and the cheese can be purchased in the factory shop or deli.

⊞ Lachryma Montis

W Spain & W 3rd Sts.
Tel (707) 938-9559. **Open** daily.
Closed Jan 1, Thanksgiving, Dec 25.
🌿 🖥 **parks.ca.gov**

Visitors can glimpse the lavish lifestyle of Mexican General Mariano Vallejo by exploring Lachryma Montis, his former home. This Gothic Revival house was built of redwood in 1852. It features an eclectic array of Vallejo memorabilia, which ranges from the general's silver epaulettes and a cattle brand to his favorite books.

The name of the house is Latin for "mountain tear," a reference to a mineral spring on the property.

Lachryma Montis, once home to Mexican General Mariano Vallejo

⊞ Mission San Francisco Solano de Sonoma

114 E Spain St. Tel (707) 938-1519.
Open 10am–5pm daily. **Closed** Jan 1,
Thanksgiving, Dec 25. 🌿

Named after a Peruvian saint, this beautifully restored old mission (commonly called the Sonoma Mission) was the last of the historic chain of 21 Franciscan missions built in California (see p50). Father José Altimira of Spain founded the mission in 1823 at a time when California was under Mexican

Facade of the Mission San Francisco Solano de Sonoma

rule. Today, all that survives of the original building is the corridor of Father Altimira's quarters. The present adobe chapel was built by General Vallejo in 1840 to be used by the town's families and soldiers.

⊞ Sonoma Barracks

20 E Spain St. **Tel** (707) 938-1519.
Open 10am–5pm daily. **Closed** Jan 1,
Thanksgiving, Dec 25. 🌿
🖥 **sonomaparks.org**

Native American labor was used to build this two-story

adobe structure between 1836 and 1840, when it served as the headquarters for General Vallejo and his troops. After the 1846 Bear Flag Revolt, the barracks became an outpost for the United States Army for about a decade. After being purchased by the state in the late 1950s, the building was restored. It is now a California Historical Landmark.

Sonoma Valley Wineries

The Sonoma Valley has a rare perfect combination of soil, sun, and rain for growing superior wine grapes. In 1824, Father José Altimira planted Sonoma's first grapevines, in order to produce sacramental wine for the masses held at the Mission San Francisco Solano de Sonoma. When, in 1834, the ruling Mexican government secularized the mission, General Vallejo replanted grapevines on its land and sold the wine he produced to San Francisco merchants. In 1857, Hungarian Count Agoston Haraszthy (see p459) planted the nation's first European varietals at Sonoma's Buena Vista Winery, now the oldest premium winery in the state.

The arms of the Sebastiani Vineyards

The Sonoma Valley encompasses the Sonoma Valley, Carneros, and Sonoma Mountain wine-growing regions. The climate varies slightly in each region, creating different environments suitable for producing particular grape varieties, including Cabernet Sauvignon and Chardonnay. Today, Sonoma Valley is home to more than 300 wineries, which have 55,000 acres (22,258 ha) of grape plantations. Some of the valley's most notable wineries are Sebastiani Vineyards, Sonoma's largest premium-variety winery; Benziger Family Winery; Gundlach-Bundschu Winery; and Château St. Jean. Most of the wineries offer picnic areas, though most charge for tastings.

Vineyards in the Sonoma Valley

GOLD COUNTRY AND THE CENTRAL VALLEY

Located at the geographical heart of California, the Gold Country is also central to the state's allure as the land of overnight success. Long before the gilded world of Hollywood took shape, this was a real-life El Dorado, where a thick vein of solid gold, known as the Mother Lode, sat waiting to be discovered.

The Gold Country is largely rural, despite being the birthplace of modern California with the Gold Rush of 1849 and the designation of Sacramento as state capital.

Before the miners arrived, this quiet region, located on the far fringes of the Spanish colonial empire, was sparsely populated by members of the Miwok and Maidu peoples. With the discovery of gold flakes in January 1848, however, the region turned into a lawless jamboree, and by 1852 an estimated 200,000 men from all over the world were working in the mines. But by 1860 most of the region had fallen silent again, as the mining boom went bust *(see pp52–3)*.

A few years after the Gold Rush, the region experienced another short-lived boom. The transcontinental railroad was constructed through the Sierra Nevada Mountains by low-paid laborers, many of whom were Chinese *(see pp54–5)*. In the early 20th century, the Central Valley became the heart of the state's thriving agricultural industry, which today exports fruit and vegetables worldwide.

Stretching for more than 100 miles (160 km) north to south, the region's landscape is ideal for leisurely hikes or afternoon picnics. The Gold Country also offers one of California's best scenic drives along Hwy 49 which passes through historic mining communities. The route climbs up and down rocky ridges between pastoral ranch lands, lined with oak trees and crossed by fast-flowing rivers. Many of the picturesque towns it passes through, such as Sutter Creek, have survived unchanged since the Gold Rush.

Malakoff Diggins Historic Park, preserving the heyday of the Gold Rush

◄ The bright green slopes of the Sacramento Valley

Exploring the Gold Country

The Gold Country ranges from flat delta flood plains to the rugged, river-carved foothills of the Sierra Nevada Mountains. At the heart of the region is Sacramento, the state capital and largest Gold Country city, which has the highest concentration of sights. But the real attraction of this area is in traveling along its many scenic routes. The rural landscape is dotted with small historic towns. Some are still thriving communities, while others are ghostly memorials to their past. The Central Valley, along I-5, is scattered with picturesque farming towns. Larger towns, such as Nevada City and Sutter Creek, make excellent bases for a Gold Country tour, and visitors are welcomed and well taken care of everywhere.

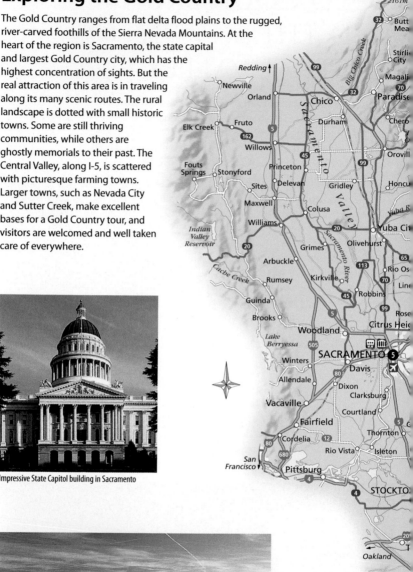

Impressive State Capitol building in Sacramento

Parrots Ferry Bridge over the New Melones Lake along Hwy 49 in Tuolumne County

For hotels and restaurants in this area see p542 and pp574–5

Sights at a Glance

❶ Malakoff Diggins Historic Park
❷ Grass Valley
❸ Empire Mine State Historic Park
❹ Nevada City
❺ *Sacramento pp476–9*
❻ Marshall Gold Discovery State Historic Park
❼ Folsom
❽ Placerville

❾ Sutter Creek
❿ Volcano
⓫ Chaw'se Indian Grinding Rock State Historic Park
⓬ Jackson
⓭ Mokelumne Hill
⓮ San Andreas
⓯ Murphys
⓰ Angels Camp

⓱ Moaning Cavern
⓲ Sonora
⓳ *Columbia State Historic Park pp484–5*
⓴ Jamestown
㉑ Stockton

MALAKOFF DIGGINS ❶
HISTORIC PARK

VADA CITY ⟨20⟩
❹
Reno

❷ ❸ EMPIRE MINE STATE
RASS HISTORIC PARK
ALLEY

Foresthill

Auburn

MARSHALL GOLD
❻ DISCOVERY STATE
HISTORIC PARK
Coloma ⟨50⟩

FOLSOM ❽ PLACERVILLE

Grizzly Flat
cho Cosumnes River
ieta Cooks Station
VOLCANO ⟨88⟩
Plymouth ❿ ⓫ CHAW'SE INDIAN
GRINDING ROCK
TTER CREEK ❾ STATE HISTORIC PARK
JACKSON ⓬
Camanche ⓭ MOKELUMNE
Reservoir HILL
Arnold
SAN ANDREAS ⓮ ⟨4⟩
ockeford MURPHYS ⓯ ⓱ MOANING CAVERN
ANGELS CAMP ⓰ ⓳ COLUMBIA STATE
aterloo Copperopolis HISTORIC PARK
⓲ SONORA
⟨4⟩ JAMESTOWN ⓴
Farmington
Valley Home ⟨108⟩
nteca ⟨120⟩ ⟨120⟩
laus River Oakdale Don Pedro
Reservoir Coulterville Yosemite
⟨99⟩ La Grange ⟨132⟩
Modesto
ayson Waterford Lake ⟨140⟩
McClure Midpines
Turlock Snelling Hornitos Mariposa
Patterson Catheys Valley
Winton Ahwahnee
Newman Merced ⟨140⟩
Gustine San Joaquin River ⟨99⟩ Le Grand
Chowchilla
⟨152⟩ Los Banos ⟨152⟩
i Luis Fresno
ervoir

Replica dwelling in the Chaw'se Indian Grinding Rock State Park

Getting Around

A car is essential for exploring the California Gold Country. Most sights are located along the Gold Rush Highway, Hwy 49. This makes the best and most scenic driving route as it undulates along the foothills through the most interesting Gold Country towns. Public transportation is severely limited, with only two long-distance bus services along the two main highways, I-80 and US 50, and several daily trains over the mountains from Sacramento. The area's main international airport is in Sacramento.

Key

▬▬ Freeway
▬▬ Major road
▬ Secondary road
⋯⋯ Minor road
▬ Scenic route
⊶⊶ Main railroad
── Minor railroad
△ Summit

For additional map symbols *see back flap*

The man-made canyon created by hydraulic mining at Malakoff Diggins

❶ Malakoff Diggins Historic Park

Road map B3. **Tel** (530) 265-2740. 🚌 from Nevada City. **Open** daily. Museum: 10am–4pm daily. **Closed** buildings Oct–Apr. 🏛 ♿ 📷 🌐 **malakoffdigginsstatepark.org**

As the original gold mining techniques became less rewarding in the late 1850s, miners turned to increasingly powerful and destructive ways of extracting the valuable ore. When the more easily recoverable surface deposits disappeared, the miners began to strip away the soil with powerful jets of pressurized water. Spraying more than 200,000 gal (115,000 liters) of water per hour, the jets washed away entire mountainsides in search of gold, a process known as hydraulic mining *(see pp52–3)*. In 1884 the California legislature forbade the dumping of gravel into streams, but huge swathes of land had already been ruined and the rivers had been clogged up with debris. The largest of these hydraulic mining operations was at Malakoff Diggins, 27 miles (45 km) northeast of Hwy 49, in the mountains above Nevada City. The eroded hillsides created a canyon that now forms an eerily beautiful historic park, with several preserved buildings from the 1870s mining town of North Bloomfield.

A nugget of gold set inside quartz crystal

❷ Grass Valley

Road map B3. 🏔 12,900. 🚌 ℹ 248 Mill St (530) 273-4667. 🌐 **grassvalleychamber.com**

Long the largest and busiest town in the northern Gold Country, Grass Valley served the Empire Mine and other nearby hard rock gold mines.

In the 1870s and 1880s Grass Valley welcomed workers from the tin mines of Cornwall, England, who were known as "Cousin Jacks." Their expertise enabled the local mines to recover underground ore deposits and so remain in business after the rest of the area had fallen quiet *(see pp52–3)*. Grass Valley also has one of California's best mining museums. The **North Star Mine Powerhouse and Pelton Wheel Museum** is situated in the powerhouse of the former North Star Mine. Surrounding the entrance are the giant Pelton wheels that increased production in the region's underground mines. Displays include a stamp mill (a giant pulverizer used to crush ore), a Cornish pump (used to filter out underground water), and various artifacts relating to the Cornish background of the local miners.

🏛 **North Star Mine and Pelton Wheel Museum**
Mill St at Allison Ranch Rd. **Tel** (530) 273-4255. **Open** May–Oct: 10am–5pm daily. Donation. 🌐 **nevadacountyhistory.org**

❸ Empire Mine State Historic Park

Road map B3. **Tel** (530) 273-8522. 🚌 from Nevada City. **Open** daily. **Closed** Jan 1, Thanksgiving, Dec 25. 🐾 ♿ Grounds & Empire Cottage. 📷 📹 🌐 **empiremine.org**

One of the longest surviving and most lucrative gold mining operations in the state, the Empire Mine was in business until 1956. It has now been preserved by the state as a historic park. Starting with surface workings in the 1850s, the Empire Mine grew to include 365 miles (585 km) of underground tunnels, from which pure gold estimated at 5.8 million ounces (16.5 million grams) was recovered.

Head frames, which held the mine's elevator shafts and other mining equipment, are scattered over the park's 785 acres (318 ha), but for a real sense of how much money was made here you should visit Empire Cottage.

Designed by San Franciscan architect Willis Polk in 1897 for the mine's owner, William Bourn, the granite and red-brick exterior resembles an English manor house, while the redwood interior gives an air of casual affluence. The gardens next door to the cottage contain nearly 1,000 rose bushes and a large greenhouse.

More exhibits on the history of the Empire Mine and on hard-rock gold mining are on display in the visitors' center, along with samples of the precious metal.

Original stamp mill used to crush ore at the Empire Mine

Firehouse Number 1's facade, a Nevada City landmark

❹ Nevada City

Road map B3. 🏔 3,100. 🚌
ℹ️ 132 Main St (800 655-6569)
🅦 nevadacitychamber.com

With Victorian houses and commercial buildings lining its steep streets, picturesque Nevada City deserves its reputation as "Queen of the Northern Mines." Located at the northern end of the Mother Lode gold fields, Nevada City

thrived until gold mining peaked in the 1860s, then it faded into oblivion. Nearly a century later, the city was resurrected as a tourist destination, with galleries, restaurants, and inns re-creating Gold Rush themes.

Hwy 49 takes visitors arriving in Nevada City to the foot of Broad Street. Looking up the street, the large building on the left is the **National Hotel**. One of the oldest hotels in California, it first opened in the mid-1850s.

A block east of the hotel is **Firehouse Number 1 Museum**, one of the region's most photographed facades. Dainty balconies and a white cupola decorate the exterior, and inside, a small museum displays artifacts by the local Maidu people, pioneer relics, including some relating to the tragic Donner Party *(see p490)*, and the altar from a Gold Rush Chinese temple. Antique mining devices are displayed in the park opposite, and several plaques on the city's walls commemorate events from its past.

Back on Broad Street, the arcaded brick facade marks the historic **Nevada Theater**, which has been in use as a performance venue since 1865. A block to the south is the **Miner's Foundry**, an old metalworks where the innovative Pelton wheel was first developed and produced. A block to the north is the Art Deco facade of the city's **County Courthouse**, one of the city's few 20th-century works of architecture.

🏛 **Firehouse Number 1 Museum**
214 Main St. **Tel** (530) 265-5468.
Open times vary, call first. Donation.
🅦 nevadacountyhistory.org

Nevada Theater, used as a playhouse since 1865

Nevada City Center

① National Hotel
② Firehouse Number 1 Museum
③ Nevada County Courthouse
④ Nevada Theater
⑤ Miner's Foundry

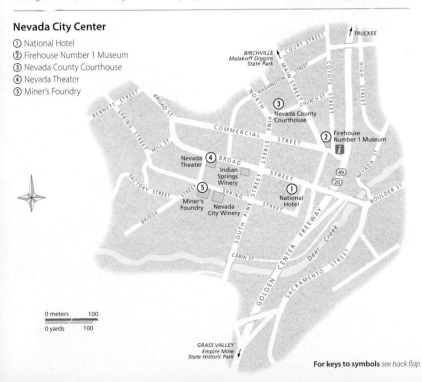

0 meters 100
0 yards 100

For keys to symbols *see back flap*

❺ Street-by-Street: Old Sacramento

Covering six blocks between the river and the modern city, Old Sacramento preserves many historic buildings within a precinct of shops, restaurants, and museums. Some of the structures protected here were built to serve the gold miners of 1849 *(see pp52–3)*, but most date from the 1860s and 1870s, when Sacramento confirmed its position as the link between rural California and the commercial centers along the coast *(see pp478–9)*. The Pony Express and transcontinental railroad both had their western terminus here, with paddle-wheel riverboats providing the connection to San Francisco. A handful of museums trace the area's historic importance, and the riverfront location is ideal for walking and cycling.

Delta King Riverboat
One of the last Sacramento Delta riverboats still afloat, this moored paddle-wheel steamer is now a hotel and restaurant.

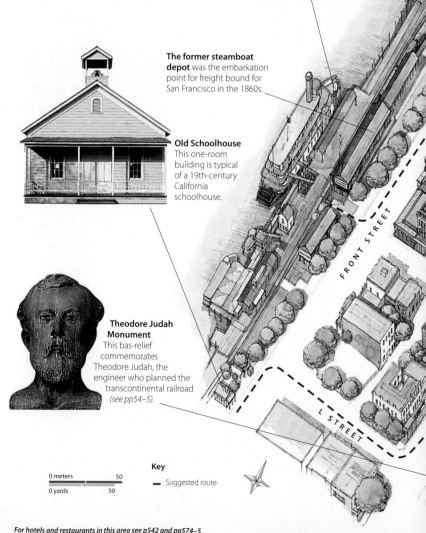

The former steamboat depot was the embarkation point for freight bound for San Francisco in the 1860s.

Old Schoolhouse
This one-room building is typical of a 19th-century California schoolhouse.

Theodore Judah Monument
This bas-relief commemorates Theodore Judah, the engineer who planned the transcontinental railroad *(see pp54–5)*.

FRONT STREET

L STREET

Key

— Suggested route

| 0 meters | 50 |
| 0 yards | 50 |

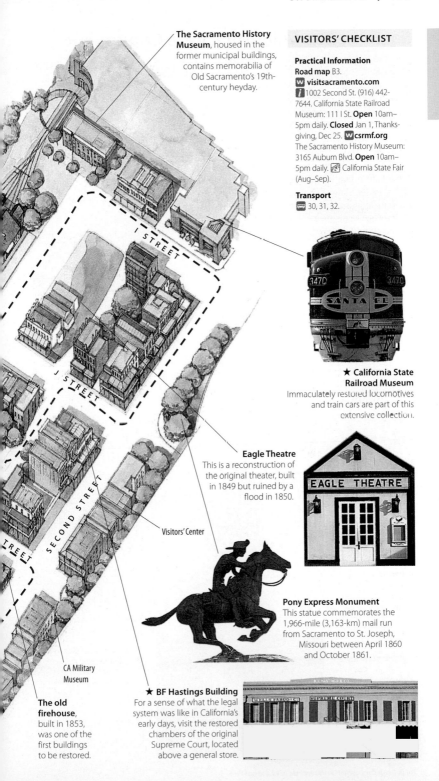

The Sacramento History Museum, housed in the former municipal buildings, contains memorabilia of Old Sacramento's 19th-century heyday.

★ **California State Railroad Museum**
Immaculately restored locomotives and train cars are part of this extensive collection.

Eagle Theatre
This is a reconstruction of the original theater, built in 1849 but ruined by a flood in 1850.

Visitors' Center

EAGLE THEATRE

Pony Express Monument
This statue commemorates the 1,966-mile (3,163-km) mail run from Sacramento to St. Joseph, Missouri between April 1860 and October 1861.

CA Military Museum

The old firehouse, built in 1853, was one of the first buildings to be restored.

★ **BF Hastings Building**
For a sense of what the legal system was like in California's early days, visit the restored chambers of the original Supreme Court, located above a general store.

Sacramento: California State Capitol

Standing at the center of a vast, landscaped park, the California State Capitol is Sacramento's primary landmark and one of the state's handsomest buildings. It was designed in 1860 by Reuben Clark and Miner F Butler in grand Greek Revival style, with Corinthian porticos and a tall central dome. The building was completed in 1874 after almost 15 years of construction and expenses totaling $2.5 million. The Capitol was expanded in the 1920s and 1950s and completely renovated and restored in the 1970s. The Governor of California operates from his Capitol office, but the building also stands as a shining example of the Golden State's proud past. Along with the chambers of the state legislature, which are open to visitors even when they are in session, the Capitol serves as a museum of the state's political and cultural history.

VISITORS' CHECKLIST

Practical Information
10th St & L St., Capitol Mall, Capitol Park. **Road map** B3. **Tel** (916) 324-0333. **Open** 8am–5pm Mon–Fri, 9am–5pm Sat & Sun. **Closed** Jan 1, Thanksgiving, Dec 25. 🅿 🛗 first floor only. 📷 ✏
📧 🆆 capitolmuseum.ca.gov

Transport
🚍 from LA & San Francisco.
🚌 30, 31, 36, 38, 61, 62.

Original 1860 statuary

★ **Capitol Rotunda**
The impressive rotunda was restored to its original 19th-century splendor in 1975. The copper ball on top of the dome is plated in gold.

Entrance

The Historic Offices on the first floor contain a few government offices restored to their turn-of-the-century appearance.

★ **State Senate Chamber**
The mezzanine gallery is open all year, but it is most interesting when the legislature is in session, making speeches and holding votes on issues of importance.

A portrait of George Washington, the first US president, occupies the focal point on the Chamber wall.

🏛 Crocker Art Museum

216 O St. **Tel** (916) 808-7000.
Open 10am–5pm Tue–Sun (to 9pm
Thu). **Closed** Jan 1, Thanksgiving, Dec
25. 🅿 🅒 (free public hols.)
🔲 crockerartmuseum.org

Founded in 1873, this is the
oldest public art museum west
of the Mississippi. The collection
includes Victorian painting and
sculpture from Asia, Europe, and
the US, but its real strength is the
California art and photography,
and the touring shows.

Another prime attraction is
the Italianate Victorian building
itself, designed by the architect
Seth Babson. The gallery includes
polychrome tiled floors, intricately
carved woodwork, and a graceful
central staircase. The Crocker also
houses the 125,000-sq-ft
(11,610-sq-m) Teel Family
Pavilion – a classic, contemporary
design that complements
the historic structures.

Foyer of the Crocker Art Gallery

🎴 Sutter's Fort State Historic Park

2701 L St. **Tel** (916) 445-4422.
Open 10am–5pm daily. **Closed** Jan 1,
Thanksgiving, Dec 25. 🅿
🔲 suttersfort.org

Now somewhat marooned amid
the suburban streets of the
modern state capital, Sutter's
Fort in its heyday was one of the
most important and populous
sites in early California history.

Established by John Sutter in
1839, the fort became the
cultural and economic center of
northern California in the years
leading up to the Gold Rush.
Apart from the 21 Spanish
missions along the coast, it was
then the only European
settlement in California.
Throughout the 1840s, new
immigrants following the
overland trails from the eastern
states stopped here for the fort's
blacksmith shop, grain mill, and

Reconstructed 19th-century kitchen at Sutter's Fort

many other facilities. The three-
story central building is all that
survives of the original fort. The
rest of the complex has been
reconstructed to give a picture
of frontier life. A courtyard,
surrounded by 18-ft (5.5-m) walls,
houses various historical exhibits
along a self-guided audio tour.
These include a prison, a bakery,
and a blacksmith's. This is one of
the few official sites in California
where the Mexican flag still flies.

🏛 State Indian Museum

2618 K St. **Tel** (916) 324-0971.
Open 10am–5pm daily.
Closed Jan 1, Thanksgiving, Dec 25.
🅿 🔲 parks.ca.gov

This area of California was once
occupied by the Maidu people.
This small but fascinating
museum, set in a park adjacent
to Sutter's Fort, explores the
different Native American
cultures that existed in the state
before the 16th-century arrival
of the first Europeans (see pp48–
9). Displays of handicrafts focus
on the beautiful reed baskets
that held both a practical and
spiritual value to the Maidu,
and a series of dioramas
re-create the look and feel of
tribal reservations. Slide shows,
tape recordings, and films
document other aspects of
tribal culture, from language to
agricultural skills.

Special programs, generally
held on weekends, celebrate
the survival of ancient Native
American traditions into the
present day.

John Sutter

The story of the early California entrepreneur John Sutter is
a classic real-life rags to riches to rags adventure. Following
bankruptcy in his native Switzerland, Sutter emigrated to
California in 1839. Only a year after his arrival, he was granted
Mexican government, which he patriotically named New
Helvetia (New Switzerland).In 1843 Sutter went into debt
once again in order to buy Fort Ross on the northern coast
from its Russian owners (see p464). For the next five years his
land and recovered wealth made him virtual lord and master
over most of northern California.

However, the discovery of gold
flakes by his employee James
Marshall at his mill in 1848
(see p480) spelled the end of
his vast empire. Thousands of
miners swarmed to the region
and almost immediately took
over his land. Sutter spent the
rest of his life in Washington, DC,
hoping for compensation from the
US government, but he died almost
penniless in 1880.

John Sutter (1802–80)

Reconstructed Sutter's Mill, where gold was first discovered

❻ Marshall Gold Discovery State Historic Park

310 Back St, Coloma. **Road map** B3. **Tel** (530) 622-3470. 🚌 from Placerville. **Open** 8am–sunset daily. **Closed** Jan 1, Thanksgiving, Dec 25. 🅿 ♿ 🍴 **W** marshallgold.com

Covering some 250 acres (101 ha) along the banks of the American River, this peaceful state park protects and interprets the site where gold was first discovered in January 1848. James Marshall spotted shiny flakes in the water channel of a sawmill he and his fellow workmen were building for John Sutter *(see p479)*, and the rest is history.

Within a year, some 10,000 miners had turned Coloma into a thriving city, but with news of even richer deposits elsewhere the boom went bust as quickly as it began, and little remains from this era.

A reproduction of Sutter's Mill stands on the original site, and a statue of James Marshall sits on a nearby hill to mark the spot where he is buried. The park's visitors' center includes the small **Gold Country Museum** with Native American artifacts, films, and other displays on the discovery of gold, as well as memorabilia relating to James Marshall.

🏛 **Gold Country Museum**
601 Lincoln Way, Auburn. **Tel** (530) 889-6500. **Open** 10am–4pm daily (to 3pm Sep–Mar). **Closed** Jan 1, Thanksgiving, Dec 25. 🅿 **W** placer.ca.gov

❼ Folsom

Road map B3. 🏠 72,000. 🚌
ℹ 200 Wool St, 916 985-2698.
W folsomchamber.com

Folsom is now a pleasant Sacramento suburb, despite being the site of the state penitentiary made famous by Johnny Cash's 1970s song "Folsom Prison Blues."

It played an important role as the last station on the Pony Express and transcontinental railroad. Folsom is now one of the few remaining trans-continental railroad sites, as documented in the local **Folsom History Museum**. Antique shops line the Wild West-style Sutter Street, set amid boxcars and other railroad memorabilia.

At the foot of Riley Street, behind Folsom Dam, there is also a large lake, which is a popular summer vacation spot for boating and fishing.

🏛 **Folsom History Museum**
823 Sutter St. **Tel** (916) 985-2707. **Open** 11am–4pm Tue–Sun. **Closed** public hols. Donation. **W** folsomhistorymuseum.org

❽ Placerville

Road map B3. 🏠 10,300. 🚌
ℹ 542 Main St, 530 621-5885.
W visit-eldorado.com

During the Gold Rush, Placerville was a busy supply center for the surrounding mining camps. Still located on one of the main routes to Sacramento, Placerville has retained its importance as a transportation center, although the stagecoaches have long since given way to cars and trucks along US 50.

The downtown business district preserves a handful of historic structures and sites, but the best sense of Placerville's past comes from the **Placerville History Museum** on Main Street and the **El Dorado County Historical Museum**. The displays range from old mining equipment and a replica of a 19th-century general store to artifacts from the Chinese settlement and other local historical exhibits.

🏛 **El Dorado County Historical Museum**
104 Placerville Dr. **Tel** (530)621-5865. **Open** 10am–4pm Wed–Sat, noon–4pm Sun. **Closed** public hols. Donation. **W** museum.edcgov.us

Gold Rush general store in Placerville's El Dorado County Historical Museum

❾ Sutter Creek

Road map B3. 🏠 2,000. 🚌
ℹ 71-A Main St, 209 267-1344.
W suttercreek.org

Named after John Sutter *(see p479)*, Sutter Creek is one of the prettiest Gold Country towns, full of antique shops and whitewashed country inns. It grew up around 1860 to service the Old Eureka Mine, which was owned by Hetty Green, reputedly the "Richest Woman in the World." Leland Stanford, one of the "Big Four" railroad barons *(see pp54)*, made his fortune in Sutter Creek. He put $5,000 into the town's Lincoln Mine, which turned into a multimillion-dollar investment. He used the money to become a railroad magnate and then, governor of California.

An attractive drive in the region is along Sutter Creek Road to Volcano, past remains of former mining equipment.

❿ Volcano

Road map B3. 🚷 150. 🚌 ℹ️ 115 Main St, Jackson, 209 223-0350. 🌐 **amadorcountychamber.com**

For a taste of the Gold Rush without the tourist trappings, visit Volcano, a picturesque ghost of a mining town containing a wealth of historic sights.

During the Gold Rush, the town had an unusual reputation for sophistication and culture, creating the state's first library and its first astronomical observatory. The old jail, stagecoach office, brewery, and a cannon dating from the Civil War are among the preserved buildings and artifacts on display around the four-block town. The most attractive Victorian building is the former historic **St. George Hotel**, covered in Virginia creeper.

Springtime visitors to the region should also follow the signs to Daffodil Hill, 3 miles (5 km) north of Volcano, when more than 300,000 naturalized daffodil bulbs come into full bloom on the hillside.

🏨 **St. George Hotel**
16104 Main St, off Volcano Rd. **Tel** (209) 296-4458. 🌐 **stgeorgevolcano.com**

⓫ Chaw'se Indian Grinding Rock State Historic Park

🚌 from Sacramento. 🚂 from Sacramento. 🚌 from Jackson. Museum: 14881 Pine Grove, Volcano Rd, (209) 296-7488. **Open** 11am–3pm Mon–Fri, 10am–6pm Sat & Sun. 🌐 **parks.ca.gov**

Tucked away amid the oak trees in the hills above Jackson, this 136-acre (55-ha) park protects one of the largest and most complete Native American sites in the country. The area was once home to the Miwok people and the park is dedicated to their past and future. The aim of this comprehensive museum is to increase understanding of Native American life, centering on the Californian foothill peoples. Exhibits include an array of basketry, dance regalia, and ancient tools.

Hundreds of mortar holes form the main focus of the park. These limestone pockets were formed by generations of Miwok grinding meal from acorns. There are also many rock carvings and replica Miwok dwellings.

St. Sava's Serbian Orthodox Church outside Jackson

⓬ Jackson

Road map B3. 🚷 4,700. 🚌 ℹ️ 115 Main St, 209 223-0350. 🌐 **amadorcountychamber.com**

Located at the crossroads of two main Gold Rush trails, Jackson was once a bustling gold mining community and has continued to thrive as a commercial center and lumber mill town since 1850.

The town center features a number of old Gold Rush buildings, but the most interesting stop is the **Amador County Museum**, located on a hill above the town. Here visitors can view working models of stamp mills *(see p474)* and a variety of other old mining equipment.

North of the town, in a small park off Hwy 49, are the massive tailing wheels from the Kennedy Mine, one of the deepest in the US. Reaching 58 ft (18 m) in diameter, these wheels were used to dispose of leftover rocks after the gold had been extracted. St. Sava's Serbian Orthodox Church, built in 1894 with a delicate white steeple, is also in the park. It is a testament to one of many cultures that contributed to the history of the Gold Country.

🏛️ **Amador County Museum**
225 Church St, Jackson. **Tel** (209) 223-6375. **Open** 11am–3pm Fri–Sun. **Closed** public hols. Donation. 🌐 **amadorgov.org**

Miwok ceremonial roundhouse replica, Chaw'se Indian Grinding Rock State Historic Park

Headstone on "Moke Hill"

⑬ Mokelumne Hill

Road map B3. 🏛 1,200. 🛈 1192 S Main St, Angels Camp, (209) 736-0049, (800) 225-3764. **W** gocalaveras.com

Bypassed by Highway 49, Mokelumne Hill is one of the most intriguing old Gold Country towns. A handful of old buildings, including the Hotel Leger and the old Wells Fargo stagecoach station, form a one-block business district. But the sleepy ambience of "Moke Hill," as it is commonly known, belies the town's unsavory and violent history.

Although much of the town has fallen into picturesque decay, during the Gold Rush era the hotels and saloons were packed with rowdy miners, whose drunken fights resulted in an average of one killing per week. Many of the victims ended up in the hilltop Protestant Cemetery – a short walk to the west of town. Here the multilingual headstones are now all that remain of the international population who came here in search of gold.

⑭ San Andreas

Road map B3. 🏛 1,500. 🛈 1192 S Main St, Angels Camp, (209) 736-0049). **W** gocalaveras.com

San Andreas is now a small, bustling city, home to the Calaveras County government. During the Gold Rush era, however, it was a gritty mining

camp, originally built in 1848 by Mexicans who were later forcibly removed by white Americans after rich deposits of gold were found *(see pp52–3)*. In 1883 the legendary outlaw Black Bart was captured here.

Very little now remains from the Gold Rush days, although San Andreas does house one of the Gold Country's best museums, the **Calaveras County Historical Museum**, in the old courthouse just north of Hwy 49. Along with exhibits tracing gold mining history from 1848 to the 1930s, the collection includes Miwok artifacts and the courtroom where Black Bart was tried and convicted. His prison cell during the trial, situated behind the museum, is now surrounded by a pleasant, if somewhat incongruous, garden of indigenous plants and trees.

🏛 **Calaveras County Museum & Archives**
30 N Main St. **Tel** (209) 754-1058. **Open** 10am–4pm daily. **Closed** Jan 1, Thanksgiving, Dec 25. 🅿
W calaverascohistorical.com

⑮ Murphys

Road map B3. 🏛 2,000. 🛈 1192 S Main St, Angels Camp, 209 736-0049. **W** gocalaveras.com

With mature sycamores, elms, and locust trees lining its quiet streets, Murphys is among the prettiest towns in the southern Gold Country. It offers a quiet break from the frantic tourism of many of the other Mother Lode towns and sights in the area.

Having played host to such luminaries as Ulysses S Grant, Mark Twain, and Will Rogers, the restored Murphys Hotel, built in 1855, is now the town landmark. Across the street, the **Old-Timers' Museum** houses a quirky collection of Gold Rush memorabilia. The outside wall displays a series of humorous plaques detailing the town's history.

🏛 **Old-Timers' Museum**
450 Main St. **Tel** (209) 728-1160. **Open** noon–4pm Fri–Sun. **Closed** Jan 1, Thanksgiving, Dec 25. 🅿
W murphysoldtimersmuseum.com

⑯ Angels Camp

Road map B3. 🏛 3,000. 🛈 1211 S Main St, 209 736-0049. **W** angelscamp.gov

Angels Camp is a former gold mining town that was best known as the real-life location of Mark Twain's classic short story "The Celebrated Jumping Frog of Calaveras County" *(see p30)*. Today the town has grown into a commercial center for the surrounding area.

A few historic structures, including the Angels Hotel where Twain heard the story of the jumping frog, still line the steep streets of the compact downtown area, which comes alive every May for a popular reenactment of the frog-jumping competition.

Two huge 19th-century locomotives stand on Hwy 49 in front of the **Angels Camp Museum**, which contains a standard array of old mining

Picturesque main street of the gold mining town, Angels Camp

equipment. There is also a large collection of Native American artifacts and exhibits on Mark Twain and the jumping frog.

🏛 Angels Camp Museum
753 S Main St. **Tel** (209) 736-2963. **Open** Mar–mid-Nov: 10am–4pm Thu– Mon; mid-Nov–Feb: 10am–4pm Sat & Sun. **Closed** Thanksgiving, Dec. 🎫 **W** angelscamp.gov

⓱ Moaning Cavern

5350 Moaning Cave Rd, Vallecito. **Road map** B3. **Tel** (209) 736-2708, (866) 762-2837. **Open** daily. 🎫 **W** caverntours.com

One of the largest limestone caverns in the area, Moaning Cavern took its name from the groaning sound emitted by the wind flowing out of the entrance. Unfortunately the sound was destroyed when the cavern was enlarged to improve public access. One-hour guided tours focus on the main "room," which is about 165 ft (50 m) high. Visitors can descend into the caves using the stairs or, if they dare, by rappelling down a rope.

A guided tour of Moaning Cavern

⓲ Sonora

Road map B3. 🚉 4,900. 🚌 ℹ 542 Stockton Rd, (209) 532-4212. **W** yosemitegoldcountry.com

Outstripping Columbia (see pp484–5) for the seat of county government during the Gold Rush, Sonora is now the Tuolumne County seat and a busy commercial center and logging town. Its sedate main street shows little sign of the town's once-violent reputation

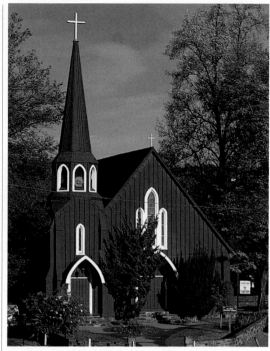

Nineteenth-century St. James Episcopal Church in Sonora

during the second half of the 19th century. Many of its historic buildings have been preserved, including the St. James Episcopal Church on Washington Street. There are also a number of interesting Victorian houses.

Sonora's old jail was built in 1857 and renovated after being destroyed by fire in 1866. It is now home to the **Tuolumne County Museum and History Center**. It houses a collection of Gold Rush artifacts, including gold nuggets and a number of 19th-century photographs.

🏛 Tuolumne County Museum and History Center
158 W Bradford Ave. **Tel** (209) 532-1317. **Open** 10am–4pm Mon–Fri, 10am–3:30pm Sat. **Closed** Jan 1, Dec 25. **W** tchistory.org

Black Bart

Famous for his politeness to his victims and his habit of leaving doggerel poetry at the scene of his crimes, the outlaw known affectionately as Black Bart has become one of the state's best-loved legends.

After holding up stagecoaches between 1877 and 1883, he was caught when the laundry mark on his handkerchief was traced to San Francisco. Black Bart turned out to be Charles Boles, a mining engineer.

After being tried and convicted in San Andreas, he spent five years in San Quentin prison. He disappeared from public view after his release in 1888.

The outlaw Black Bart

⓳ Street-by-Street: Columbia State Historic Park

At the height of the Gold Rush, Columbia was one of the largest and most important towns in the Gold Country. Most of California's mining camps were abandoned; they quickly disintegrated and disappeared after the gold ran out in the late 1850s. Unusually, Columbia remained active. It was proudly kept intact by its remaining residents until 1945, when the California government turned the entire town into a state historic park. A few of the buildings have been reconstructed, but the majority of them have been preserved in their original state.

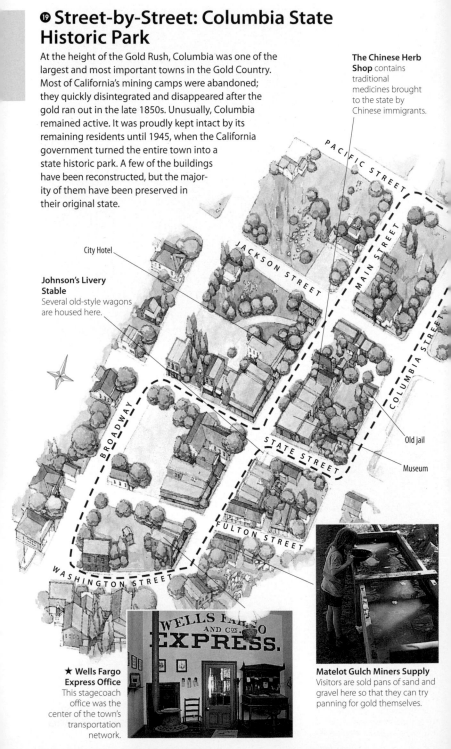

The Chinese Herb Shop contains traditional medicines brought to the state by Chinese immigrants.

PACIFIC STREET

JACKSON STREET

MAIN STREET

COLUMBIA STREET

City Hotel

Johnson's Livery Stable
Several old-style wagons are housed here.

BROADWAY

STATE STREET

Old jail

Museum

FULTON STREET

WASHINGTON STREET

★ **Wells Fargo Express Office**
This stagecoach office was the center of the town's transportation network.

Matelot Gulch Miners Supply
Visitors are sold pans of sand and gravel here so that they can try panning for gold themselves.

For hotels and restaurants in this area see p542 and pp574–5

VISITORS' CHECKLIST

Practical Information
Hwy 49. **Map** B3.
🌐 **parks.ca.gov**
ℹ️ 22708 Broadway, (209) 588-9128. 📷 🚫 📧 Wells Fargo Express Office: **Open** 10am–4pm daily (Jun–Aug until 6pm).
Closed Thanksgiving, Dec 25.
Columbia Schoolhouse:
Open 10am–4pm daily (Jun–Aug until 6pm).
Closed Thanksgiving, Dec 25.

★ **Columbia Schoolhouse**
The building was last used as a school in 1937, but in 1960 it was restored with the help of funds raised by California schoolchildren.

Key

— Suggested route

```
0 meters        100
0 yards         100
```

Historic antique store, The Emporium, on Main Street, Jamestown

🏛 Jamestown

Road map B3. 🏔 3,400. 🚌 ℹ️ 222 South Shephard St, Sonora, (209) 532-4212. 🌐 **jamestown-ca.com**

Jamestown was home to the largest gold mine in operation until 1993. Some of the historic town was destroyed by fire in 1966, but Main Street still has many picturesque buildings.
Railtown 1897 State Historic Park, north of downtown, preserves the steam locomotives and historic carriages of the Sierra Railroad. Rides are offered on weekends (April to October).

🏛 **Railtown 1897 State Historic Park**
5th Ave & Reservoir Rd. **Tel** (209) 984-3953. **Open** daily. **Closed** Jan 1, Thanksgiving, Dec 25. 🎫 (included in train ticket). 🌐 **railtown1897.org**

🏛 Stockton

Road map B3. 🏔 301,000. 🚌 ℹ️ 445 W Weber Ave, Suite 220, (877) 778-6258 🌐 **visitstockton.org**

Stockton is an inland port and a transportation hub for Central Valley farms. It is set on the eastern edge of the delta at the confluence of the Sacramento, American, and San Joaquin Rivers. Stockton's history is told at the Haggin Museum, which includes Native American crafts, 19th-century storefronts and works by Renoir. It also traces the development by a local inventor of the Caterpillar track.

🏛 **Haggin Museum**
1201 N Pershing Ave. **Tel** (209) 462-4116. **Open** 1:30–5pm Wed–Fri, noon–5pm Sat & Sun. **Closed** Jan 1, Dec 23–25, 30, 31. 🎫 (free 1st Sat every month).

Joaquin Murieta: The California Bandit

Little documentary evidence exists about Joaquin Murieta, the Gold Country criminal portrayed as everything from a 19th-century Gold Rush Robin Hood to a murderous outlaw.

His legend can be traced to the writer John Rollins Ridge, who published a novel called *The Life and Adventures of Joaquin Murieta, Celebrated California Bandit* in 1854. Ridge drew on the criminal exploits of five outlaws, all named Joaquin. The Governor of California offered a $1,000 reward for the capture of any of these men. In 1853 a man named Harry Love delivered the head of one Joaquin Murieta, which had been pickled in a glass jar. Ridge's novel was published the following year, and the Murieta legend was born.

THE HIGH SIERRAS

Forming a towering wall along the eastern side of central California, the densely forested Sierra Nevada mountains rise to over 14,000 ft (4,270 m) and include many of the most impressive peaks in the mainland United States. Known as the High Sierras, these rugged mountains make up one of the state's most popular recreation areas of lakes, meadows, towering trees, waterfalls, and ski trails, preserved by a series of splendid national parks.

The character of the High Sierras is defined by its geology and ecology. The mountains' granite base was formed deep underground more than 100 million years ago. However, the range started to rise roughly 4 million years ago as glaciers eroded to expose the granite and form stunning mountains and cliffs. The California Gold Rush took place from 1848 through 1855 in the range's western foothills, but due to the challenging nature of the terrain, the range was not fully explored until 1912. The most popular High Sierras destination is Yosemite National Park, one of the world's most spectacular natural sights. Waterfalls, ranging from delicate cascades to raging torrents, drop steeply down the granite walls of this alpine valley. Rock-climbers, photographers, and sightseers come from all over the globe to experience the park first-hand. South of Yosemite, the Sequoia and Kings Canyon National Parks preserve more of the state's high country scenery, including groves of sequoia, the tallest living trees on earth.

To the north, Lake Tahoe has been a year-round recreational haven for over a century. It offers hiking, camping, and water sports on one of the turquoise-bluest bodies of water in the US. In winter, the region is a skier's paradise, with Olympic-class resorts.

East of the Sierra Nevada's granite spine lies a less-visited but equally compelling region. The ghost town of Bodie is preserved as it was when gold miners abandoned it in 1882. Nearby, Mono Lake is an eerie sight of limestone towers and alkaline water. The eastern slope of the High Sierras merits exploration, including the 14,500-ft (4,420-m) Mount Whitney, the highest peak on the US mainland, and the bristlecone pines of the White Mountains, some of which are more than 4,000 years old.

Bodie State Historic Park, a preserved ghost town to the east of the Sierras

◄ Magnificent giant sequoia redwood trees, Sequoia National Park

Exploring the High Sierras

The highest peaks, the tallest trees, and some of the most impressive natural scenery in the United States are found in California's Sierra Nevada. This region includes one of the best-known wonders of the world, Yosemite National Park, as well as countless other remarkable examples of nature's prowess. North of Yosemite, the tuquoise-blue waters of Lake Tahoe are set within an alpine valley at the highest point of the High Sierras, while to the south stand the immense groves of Sequoia and Kings Canyon National Parks. Other than the resorts encircling Lake Tahoe, there are no large towns in the High Sierras. East of the mountains, however, near the shores of the eerily beautiful Mono Lake, the best ghost town in the state, Bodie, is immaculately preserved.

Sights at a Glance

1 Donner Memorial State Park
2 Truckee
4 Yosemite National Park pp492–7
5 Bodie State Historic Park
6 Mono Lake
7 Devil's Postpile National Monument
8 White Mountains

9 Owens Valley
10 Mount Whitney
11 Sequoia and Kings Canyon National Parks pp500–1

Tour
3 Lake Tahoe p491

How the Sierras were Made

The Sierras were formed approximately 4 million years ago when a giant granite batholith (igneous rock), approximately 6 miles (10 km) deep, lifted up the earth's surface and tilted it from a tectonic "hinge" beneath California's Central Valley. The effects of this uplift are most clearly visible on the steep eastern slopes, typical of mountains on the earth's faults. The western slopes are more gradual, made up of sedimentary, volcanic, and metamorphic rock, mixed together over the epochs.

Granite peaks of the High Sierras

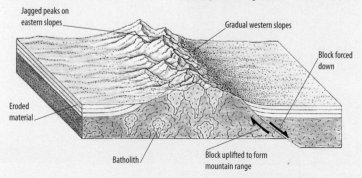

Jagged peaks on eastern slopes

Gradual western slopes

Block forced down

Eroded material

Batholith

Block uplifted to form mountain range

Yosemite Valley in Yosemite National Park

Getting Around

There are no roads across the mountains for more than 150 miles (240 km) between Yosemite and Kings Canyon, so it is essential to plan your route well ahead. Most visitors approach the mountains from the west, on the highways climbing up from the San Joaquin Valley. The eastern face of the High Sierras, Bodie, and Mono Lake can all be reached via Hwy 395 through Owens Valley. Public transportation is limited, but there is a daily bus service from Merced to Yosemite National Park.

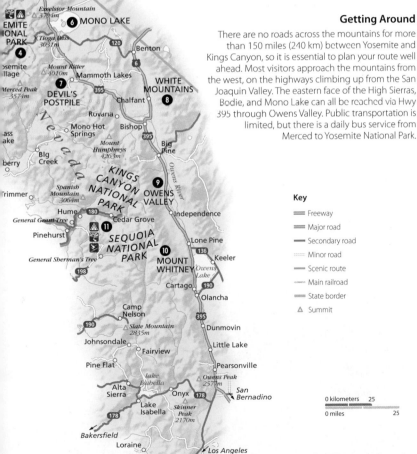

Coleville
Walker
Mount Patterson
3559m
ls Gate
2292m
⑤ **BODIE STATE**
HISTORIC PARK
Bodie

Excelsior Mountain
3784m
EMITE
IONAL
PARK
⑥ **MONO LAKE**
Tioga Pass
3031m
Benton
120
④
semite
llage
Mount Ritter
4010m Mammoth Lakes
6
Merced Peak
3574m
⑦ **DEVIL'S**
POSTPILE
395
WHITE
MOUNTAINS
Chalfant
⑧
ass
ake
Rovana
Mono Hot
Springs Bishop
berry
Big
Creek
Mount
Humphreys
4263m
395
Big
Pine
KINGS
CANYON
NATIONAL
PARK
Spanish
Mountain
3064m
⑨ **OWENS**
VALLEY
Trimmer
Hume
180
Cedar Grove
Independence
General Grant Tree
Pinehurst
⑪
SEQUOIA
NATIONAL
PARK
Lone Pine
136
General Sherman's Tree
⑩
MOUNT
WHITNEY *Owens*
Lake
Keeler
198
Cartago
190
Olancha
Camp
Nelson
Slate Mountain
2835m
Dunmovin
190
Johnsondale
Fairview
Little Lake
Pine Flat
Pearsonville
Alta
Sierra
lake
Isabella
Onyx
Owens Peak
2577m
San
Bernardino
Lake
Isabella
178
Skinner
Peak
2170m
178
Bakersfield
Loraine
Los Angeles

Key

━━ Freeway
━━ Major road
━━ Secondary road
┈┈ Minor road
━━ Scenic route
╴╴╴ Main railroad
━━ State border
△ Summit

0 kilometers   25
0 miles   25

For additional map symbols *see back flap*

❶ Donner Memorial State Park

Road map B3. **Tel** (530) 582-7892. **Open** call for hours. 🚌 Truckee. **W parks.ca.gov**

This tranquil 350-acre (140-ha) park, to the south of I-80, marks the site of one of the most tragic episodes of the volatile United States frontier era.

In the winter of 1846–7 a group of 89 California-bound emigrants from Independence, Missouri, were trapped by heavy snowfall. Known as the Donner Party because two of the families shared that surname, the group was one of the many wagon trains bound for the West Coast from the Midwest, along the Oregon Trail. Halfway into their journey, the Donner families, and another family headed by James Reed, decided to leave the established trail and try a shortcut recommended by the contemporary adventurer Lansford Hastings. This turned out, however, to be a far more difficult route, and added three weeks to what was already an arduous journey. The Donner Party finally arrived at the eastern foot of the Sierra Nevada Mountains in October 1846, having lost the majority of their cattle and belongings.

After resting for a week they were caught by an early winter storm. A few members decided to struggle on foot across the snowy mountains to seek help from Sutter's Fort *(see p479)*, but the rest of the party, now trapped by the heavy snow and with insufficient supplies, were forced to resort to cannibalism in order to survive. By the time rescuers were able to reach them in mid-February 1847, 42 of the 89 pioneers had already died.

A statue of this heroic pioneering family, standing atop a 22-ft (6.7-m) pedestal indicating the depth of the snow they encountered, now marks the site. The park's **Emigrant Trail Museum** details the Donner Party's harrowing story, as well as describing the natural history of the High Sierras.

🏛 Emigrant Trail Museum
12593 Donner Pass Rd. Tel (530) 582-7892. **Open** 9am–4pm daily. **Closed** Jan 1, Thanksgiving, Dec 25.

Facade of the 19th-century Old Truckee Jail, now a museum

❷ Truckee

Road map B3. 🚹 16,200. 🚌 🚍 **ℹ** 10065 Donner Pass Road, (530) 587-2757, (530) 546-5253 winter weather hotline. **W truckee.com**

One of the highest and coldest towns in California, Truckee is thought to have gotten its name when a native Paiute greeted the first white Americans with "Trokay," meaning "peace."

Truckee is situated along the main highway (I-80) and rail route across the Sierra Nevada Mountains. Its history as a transportation center goes back to 1863, when it was founded as a changeover point for railroad crews along the transcontinental railroad *(see pp54–5)*. The Southern Pacific Depot still serves rail and bus passengers as well as operating as a visitors' center.

Much of the town's Wild West character and history as a lumber center survives, especially along Commercial Row in the heart of town, where a line of old brick and wooden buildings faces the tracks. Many of these have now been converted into atmospheric shops, restaurants, and cafés.

Another evocative survivor of the town's past is the **Old Truckee Jail**, built in 1875. It is a small museum depicting the wilder side of frontier life.

Located only 25 miles (40 km) from Lake Tahoe, Truckee is also a popular base for winter skiers and summer hikers.

🏛 Old Truckee Jail
Jibboom & Spring Sts. **Tel** (530) 582-0893. **Open** times vary, call to check. **Closed** public hols. 🐾
W truckeehistory.org

Skiing around Lake Tahoe

The peaks surrounding Lake Tahoe, particularly on the California side, are famous for their ski resorts. The world-class Alpine Meadows and Squaw Valley are where the Winter Olympics were held in 1960. The largest ski area, Heavenly Valley, is above the city of South Lake Tahoe, with many more around the lake and at Donner Pass, west of Truckee, along I-80. There are also cross-country ski areas with groomed trails. The Lake Tahoe area receives more than 10 ft (3 m) of snow each winter and is the state's major center for winter recreation from November to March.

Lake Tahoe's Alpine Meadows resort

❸ A Tour of Lake Tahoe

The most beautiful body of water in California, Lake Tahoe is 1,645 ft (501 m) at its deepest point and is surrounded by forested peaks. The area began to develop as a tourist resort after the construction of the first road here in 1915 made it more accessible. Casinos opening on the Nevada border in the 1930s and the Winter Olympics in 1960 established its popularity.

View of Lake Tahoe from Heavenly Valley

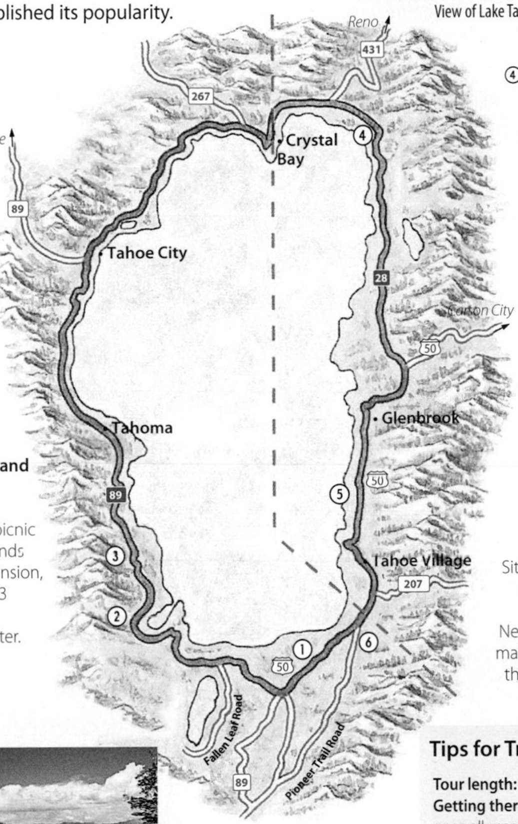

④ **Ponderosa Ranch**
Near the northeast shore of the lake, this ranch was formerly an amusement park based on the cult 1960s Wild West TV show, *Bonanza*.

⑤ **Cave Rock and Cave Rock Tunnel**
Lake Tahoe's east shore is so rugged that part of the highway is tunneled through solid granite.

⑥ **Stateline**
Situated on the border of California and the more liberal state of Nevada, Stateline is the main gambling town of the Lake Tahoe region.

③ **DL Bliss State Park and Ehrman Mansion**
A popular picnic area surrounds Ehrman Mansion, built in 1903 and now a visitors' center.

② **Emerald Bay State Park and Vikingsholm**
The beautiful inlet of Emerald Bay is the most photographed part of the lake. Vikingsholm, built as a summerhouse in the 1920s, is an incongruous reproduction of an old Nordic castle.

① **South Lake Tahoe**
The largest town in the area, South Lake Tahoe caters for visitors to Nevada's casinos.

Map labels: Reno, 431, Truckee, 267, Crystal Bay, 89, Tahoe City, 28, Incline City, 50, Tahoma, Glenbrook, 89, 50, Tahoe Village, 207, 1, 5, 6, 50, Fallen Leaf Road, Pioneer Trail Road, 89

0 kilometers 10
0 miles 10

Key
━━ Tour route
══ Other roads

Tips for Travelers

Tour length: 65 miles (105 km).
Getting there: I-89 and US 50 are open all year-round. Amtrak trains operate to Truckee. Greyhound buses and limited flights from San Francisco and Oakland serve South Lake Tahoe.
When to go: Peak tourist seasons are July, August, and winter. Spring and autumn are less crowded, but some facilities may be closed.
Stopping-off points: Many cafés and restaurants have views of the lake *(see pp575–6)*.
Tourist information: Lake Tahoe Visitors' Authority, South Lake Tahoe. **Tel** (800) 288-2463.
Ⓦ visitinglaketahoe.com

❹ Yosemite National Park

A wilderness of evergreen forests, high meadows, and sheer granite walls, much of Yosemite National Park is accessible only to experienced hikers or horseback riders. The spectacular Yosemite Valley, however, a good base from which to explore the park, is easily reached by car and there are 200 additional miles (320 km) of paved roads providing access to more remote areas. Soaring cliffs, plunging waterfalls, gigantic trees, rugged canyons, mountains, and valleys all combine to lend Yosemite its incomparable beauty.

Yosemite Museum
The history of the Miwok and Paiute people is displayed here, along with works by Yosemite artists.

Lower Yosemite Falls
Yosemite Creek drops 2,425 ft (740 m), to form the highest waterfall in the US (see p494).

To Upper Yosemite Falls

Yosemite Creek

Yosemite Falls Trail

Yosemite Village

ℹ

②

Sunnyside

P

• **Yosemite Lodge**

Northside Drive

P

P

Lower River

Upper

Merced River

Southside Drive

Sentinel Creek

Four-Mile Trail

Staircase Falls

ℹ P

SENTINEL ROCK
▲
7,038 ft (2,145 m)

Sentinel Falls

①

Point Road

Ahwahnee Hotel
Rustic architecture, elegant décor, and beautiful views make this hotel one of the most renowned in the country (see p495).

Yosemite Chapel (1879)
This tiny wooden church is all that is left of Yosemite's 19th-century Old Village.

Mirror Meadow
Park rangers no longer interfere with nature by dredging the lake, so the water at the foot of Half Dome *(see p494)* is now silting up and forming a meadow.

VISITORS' CHECKLIST

Practical Information
Road map C3. **Tel** (209) 372-0200. **W** nps.gov/yose **i** PO Box 577, Yosemite. **Open** daily.

Transport
to Yosemite Valley. to Merced, then YARTS shuttle to Yosemite Valley.

Key

— Major road
— Minor road
-- Paths and trails
'' Shuttle bus
►◄ Bike route
～ Rivers

NORTH PINES

LOWER PINES

UPPER PINES

rry lage

0 meters   1000
0 yards   1000

Merced River

KEY

① **Sentinel Dome** can be reached via the the trail from Glacier Point.

② **Valley Visitor Center**

③ **Washington Column**

④ **Half Dome** juts 5,000 ft (1,520 m) above the valley floor; the climb to the summit is formidable *(see p494).*

⑤ **At Vernal Fall**, the Merced River pours 317-ft (97-m) into the canyon below.

Merced River
This beautiful river can be appreciated along both the Mist Trail and the Panorama Trail. Anglers enjoy fishing for brown trout in its waters.

For additional map symbols *see back flap*

Exploring Yosemite National Park

Some of the world's most beautiful mountain terrain is protected within the 1,170 sq miles (3,030 sq km) of Yosemite National Park. Hundreds of thousands of visitors descend upon the park each year to admire its breathtaking views, formed by millions of years of glacial activity. Each season offers a different experience, from the swelling waterfalls of spring to the rustic colors of autumn. The summer months are the most crowded, but during the snowbound winter months several roads are inaccessible. Bus tours and well-maintained cycle paths, hiking trails, and roads are all aimed at leading visitors from one awe-inspiring panoramic scene to another.

Upper Yosemite Fall, swollen with ice-melt in the spring

ꕔ Half Dome
Eastern end of Yosemite Valley.
Open daily late May–mid-Oct (pending weather).

Standing nearly 5,000 ft (1,520 m) above the valley floor, the silhouette of Half Dome has become a symbol of Yosemite. Its curved back rises to a wave-like lip, before dropping vertically to the valley below.

Geologists believe that Half Dome is about three-quarters of its original size, rather than a true half. It is thought that as recently as 15,000 years ago, glacial ice floes moved through the valley from the Sierra crest, scything off rock and depositing it downstream.

The 8,840-ft (2,695 m) summit of Half Dome offers an unsurpassed view. Follow the 9-mile (14-km) trail from Happy Isles trailhead to reach the peak.

ꕔ Yosemite Falls
North Yosemite Valley. **Open** daily.
Yosemite Falls are the highest waterfalls in North America and tumble from a height of 2,425 ft (740 m) in two great leaps, Upper Yosemite and Lower Yosemite falls. One of the most recognizable features of the park, the cascades are visible all over the valley.

The top of Upper Yosemite Fall, by far the longer and more elegant of the pair, can be reached via a strenuous 7-mile (11-km) round-trip trail. The Lower Fall is easier to visit, via a short trail that starts next to Yosemite Lodge and frames an unforgettable view of both falls.

As with all the park's waterfalls, Yosemite Falls are at their peak in May and June, when the winter snows melt and fill the creek to capacity. Conversely, by September the falls often dry up and disappear altogether, their presence marked only by a dark stain on the granite wall.

ꕔ Vernal and Nevada Falls
Eastern end of Yosemite Valley.
Open daily May–Nov.
A popular half-day hike in Yosemite National Park is the Mist Trail, which visits these two waterfalls.

The first fall visited on this 7-mile (11-km) round-trip is Vernal Fall, which plunges 317 ft (97 m) and spreads its spray across the trail. The trail then continues for 2.7 miles (4.3 km) to the top of Nevada Falls, which drops an impressive 594 ft (180 m). At the top of Nevada Falls the Mist Trail joins the John Muir Trail, which runs

Sheer drop of El Capitán

For hotels and restaurants in this area see pp542–3 and p575–6

around the back of Half Dome all the way south to the summit of Mount Whitney *(see p499)*.

⚄ Glacier Point

Glacier Point Rd.
Open May–Oct: daily.

The great Yosemite panorama can be experienced from Glacier Point, which rests on a rocky ledge 3,215 ft (980 m) above the valley floor. Most of the waterfalls and other features of Yosemite Valley are visible from here, but the dominant feature is Half Dome. The panorama also includes much of the surrounding landscape, a beautiful area of alpine peaks and meadows.

Glacier Point can be reached only during the summer. The road is blocked by snow during winter at Badger Pass, which was developed in 1935 as California's first commercial ski resort. Another summer route is the Four-Mile Trail, which begins at the western side of the valley. Summer bus services also allow hikers to ride up to Glacier Point then hike down to the valley.

⚄ Mariposa Grove

Visitors' Center Hwy 41, South Entrance. **Open** mid-May–Oct: daily.

At the southern end of Yosemite, this beautiful grove was one of the main reasons the park was established. More than 500 giant mature sequoia trees

Giant sequoia trees in Mariposa Grove

Tunnel View, looking across Yosemite Valley

can be seen here, some of which are more than 3,000 years old, 250 ft (75 m) tall and more than 30 ft (9 m) in diameter at their base. A series of hiking trails winds through the grove, and open-air trams make a 5-mile (8-km) circuit along roads constructed during the early years of Yosemite tourism.

⚄ Tunnel View

Hwy 41 overlooking Yosemite Valley.
Open daily.

One of the most photographed views of Yosemite can be had from this lookout on Hwy 41 at the western end of the valley. Despite the name, which is taken from the highway tunnel that leads to Glacier Point Road, the view is incredible, with El Capitán on the left, Bridalveil Fall on the right and Half Dome at the center.

⚄ El Capitán

Northwestern end of Yosemite Valley.

Standing guard at the western entrance to Yosemite Valley, the granite wall of El Capitán rises more than 3,593 ft (1,095 m) from the valley floor. One of the world's largest monoliths, El Capitán is a magnet to rock-climbers, who spend days on its sheer face to reach the top. Less adventurous visitors congregate in the meadow below, watching the rock-climbers through binoculars. Named by US soldiers, who in 1851 were the first white Americans to visit the valley, El Capitán is the Spanish phrase for "captain."

⚄ Tuolumne Meadows

Hwy 120, Tioga Rd.
Open daily late May–Oct.

In summer, when the snows have melted and the wildflowers are in full bloom, the best place to experience the striking beauty of the Yosemite landscape are these sub-alpine meadows along the Tuolumne River. Located 55 miles (88 km) from Yosemite Valley via Tioga Pass Road, the meadows are also a base for hikers setting off to explore the area's many granite peaks and trails.

Black-tailed deer roaming Yosemite's meadows

⌂ Ahwahnee Hotel

Yosemite Valley. **Tel** (866) 875-8456.
Open daily. *See Where to Stay p543.*
W yosemitepark.com

A building that comes close to matching Yosemite's natural beauty, the Ahwahnee Hotel was built in 1927 at a cost of $1.5 million. It was designed by Gilbert Stanley Underwood, who used giant granite boulders and massive wood timbers to create a rustic elegance that is in tune with its surroundings. Fire was a real concern in this remote location, so much of what appears to be wood is actually made of poured concrete, including parts of the facade. The interior of the Ahwahnee Hotel also emulates the natural setting, decorated in a Native American style. The hotel also has a high-quality restaurant *(see p576)*.

View of El Capitán and the stunning scenery of Yosemite National Park ▶

Abandoned wooden buildings in Bodie State Historic Park

❺ Bodie State Historic Park

Road map C3. 🚗 10. 🚌 from Bridgeport. 🅸 End of Hwy 270, (760) 647-6445. **Open** 8am–6pm daily. 🆆 parks.ca.gov

High up in the foothills of the eastern Sierra Nevada, Bodie is the largest ghost town in California.

Now protected as a state historic park, Bodie was, during the second half of the 19th century, a bustling gold mining town, with a population that topped 8,000 in 1880. Named after the gold prospector Waterman S Bodey, who first discovered placer deposits (surface gold) here in 1859, Bodie boomed with the discovery of hard rock ore in the mid-1870s. Soon many different mines had been established in the area, but it all came to an end when the gold ran out in

1882. Later, a series of fires destroyed much of the town. Only the Standard Mine remained in business, but it closed in 1942 because of a wartime ban on mining.

The state acquired the entire town in 1962, and has maintained the 170 buildings in a condition of "arrested decay." The result is an evocative experience of empty streets lined by deserted wooden buildings. The Miners' Union Hall has been converted into a visitors' center and museum.

❻ Mono Lake

Road map C3. 🚆 Merced. 🅸 Hwy 395 & 3rd St, (760) 647-6595. 🆆 monolake.org

One of the strangest looking places in the United States, and possibly one of the oldest lakes in the world, Mono Lake is a 70-sq mile (180-sq km) body of

alkaline water at the eastern foot of the Sierra Nevada Mountains, set between two volcanic islands. The lake has no natural outlet, but evaporation in the summer heat combined with water diversion to LA has caused it to shrink to one-fifth of its original size. The result is extremely brackish water, three times saltier than sea water. It has also exposed a number of contorted tufa spires. These were formed when calcium from underground springs came into contact with carbonates in the lake water, forming limestone. The tufa formations once sat under water, but are now arrayed along the lakeside.

In recent years, Mono Lake has also been the subject of a heated political and environmental debate, part of an on-going battle over water rights. The City of Los Angeles purchased a large amount of land in the eastern Sierras and Owens Valley in 1905, and began diverting the streams and rivers through a system of aqueducts to LA in 1941 *(see pp206–7)*. This has accelerated the lake's shrinkage and put local wildlife, particularly the state's large seagull population, which breeds on the lake's islands, in danger. In 1994 the California State Government ruled that LA must preserve the lake and its surrounding ecosystem at 6,392 ft (1,950 m) above sea level.

Tufa spires rising out of Mono Lake

7 Devil's Postpile National Monument

Road map C4. **Tel** (760) 934-2289. shuttle from Mammoth Mountain Inn. **Open** mid-Jun–Sep: daily. **nps.gov/depo**

On the west of the Sierra Nevada crest, but most easily accessible from the eastern resort town of Mammoth Lakes, Devil's Postpile National Monument protects one of the most impressive geological formations in the state.

A wall of basalt columns, in varying geometrical shapes, predominantly pentagons and hexagons, cover a 545 sq yard (652 sq m) area and are more than 60 ft (18 m) tall. The columns were formed around 100,000 years ago, when molten lava cooled and fractured. Set at the heart of an 800-acre (320-ha) park, they resemble a tiled floor seen from above. The monument is covered in snow most of the year and is only accessible in summer via shuttle bus.

Rainbow Falls, 2 miles (3 km) from the Postpile, are named after the refraction of sunlight in their spray.

8 White Mountains

Road map C4. 798 N Main St, Bishop, (760) 873-2500.

Rising along the eastern side of Owens Valley, the White Mountains, at 12,000 ft (3,660 m), are almost as high but far drier than the 13,000-ft (3,960-m) parallel range of Sierra Nevada. Lack of water has kept the peaks rugged and largely free of vegetation, but the few trees that do survive here, the bristlecone pines *(Pinus aristata)*, are among the oldest living things on earth.

These gnarled pine trees seem to thrive on the adverse conditions, which batter them into strange, contorted shapes. The species is found only on the lower slopes of the White Mountains and on a few of the mountains in neighboring

Bristlecone pines on the slopes of the White Mountains

Nevada. Extremely slow growing, they seldom reach more than 50 ft (15 m) in height, despite living for more than 4,000 years – 1,000 years longer than the oldest sequoia tree *(see pp500–1)*.

9 Owens Valley

Road map C4. Lone Pine. 126 S Main St, Lone Pine (760 876-4444). **lonepinechamber.org**

Owens Valley has more in common with Nevada than with the rest of California. It is sparsely populated but ruggedly beautiful, the valley being wedged between the White Mountains and the Sierra Nevada. Once covered with farms and ranches, the land here was bought secretly in 1905 by agents working for the City of Los Angeles. Los Angeles needed to secure a water supply, and the aqueducts still drain the valley, destroying local agriculture.

In 1942 a detention camp was established at Manzanar for 10,000 Japanese-American men, women, and children, who were deemed a threat to national security and imprisoned for the duration of World War II. Exhibits on this and other aspects of Owens Valley can be seen at the **Eastern California Museum**, in the town of Independence.

Eastern California Museum
155 N Grant St, Independence.
Tel (760) 878-0364. **Open** 10am–5pm daily. **Closed** Jan 1, Easter Sun, Thanksgiving, Dec 25. Donation:
inyocounty.us

10 Mount Whitney

Road map C4. (760) 876-6200. Merced.

The highest peak in the lower 48 states of the US, Mount Whitney rises to a height of 14,496 ft (4,420 m), forming a sheer wall above the town of Lone Pine. A steep 11-mile (18-km) trail leads from Whitney Portal Road to the summit, offering a panorama over the High Sierras. A permit is required to hike the trail. The mountain, named after the geologist Josiah Whitney, was first climbed in 1873.

Mount Whitney borders the beautiful Sequoia National Park *(see pp500–1)*, and the surrounding alpine meadows are ideal for backpacking in the summer months.

Owens Valley, backed by the White Mountains

⓫ Sequoia and Kings Canyon National Parks

These twin national parks preserve lush forests, granite peaks, and glacier-carved canyons. Breathtaking scenery complements a habitat rich with wildlife. The parks embrace 34 separate groves of the giant sequoia tree, the earth's largest living species. America's deepest canyon, the south fork of the Kings River, cuts a depth of 8,200 ft (2,500 m) through Kings Canyon. Along the eastern boundary of Sequoia is Mount Whitney *(see p499)*, the highest summit on the US mainland.

Roads serve the western side of the parks; the rest is accessible only to hikers or with rented pack-trains of horses or mules. Winter visitors can ski cross-country over both marked and unmarked trails.

Road "tunnel" formed by a felled giant sequoia in Sequoia National Park

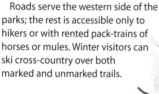

Wilsonia

Cedar Brook

REDWOOD MOUNTAIN GROVE

Redwood Creek

North Fork Kaweah River

Sequoia National Park

Yucca Creek

M465

180

198

General Grant Tree
The third-largest sequoia is known as the "Nation's Christmas Tree."

Big Stumps
The sequoia's unyielding nature makes it uneconomical for lumber, as these tall stumps, left by loggers in the 1880s, prove.

Key

━━ Major road

═══ Minor road

- - - Paths and trails

──── National Park boundary

〜〜 River

Moro Rock
A staircase carved into the rock takes visitors to the top of this granite monolith and affords a 360° view of the High Sierras and the Central Valley.

General Sherman's Tree
The world's largest living thing is 275 ft (84 m) tall, with a trunk measuring 36 ft (11 m) around its base. The tree still grows 0.4 inches (1 cm) every ten years.

KEY

① **Tharp's Log**, a hollowed-out sequoia, was home to Hale Tharp, a 19th century farmer who was introduced to the area by Native Americans.

② **Giant Forest** contains one of the largest groves of living sequoias in the world.

③ **Crystal Cavern**, one of the few caves open to visitors, is filled with stalagmites and stalactites.

Kings Canyon National Park

BIG MEADOWS

Stony Creek

• **Stony Creek**

Boulder Creek

Dorst Creek

LOST GROVE

Clover Creek

MUIR GROVE

Marble Fork Kaweah River

Lodgepole

③

198

①

②

0 kilometers 2
0 miles 2

Crescent Meadow
An array of sequoias border this area, which is more of a marsh than a meadow and too wet at its heart for the trees to survive.

For additional map symbols *see back flap*

NORTH CENTRAL CALIFORNIA

With a rugged shoreline rising from the Pacific Ocean and dense forests covering coastal mountains, North Central California marks the visual transition between the north and south of the state. The landscape holds an embarrassment of riches, with golden beaches, splendid wilderness, and inland valleys that include some of the world's most productive agricultural regions.

The natural beauty of the area, combined with a wealth of cultural history, makes this one of the state's most engaging regions. Native Americans lived along the coast and in the inland valleys for centuries prior to the arrival of Europeans in the 17th century. More than a century later the first European settlement was established at Monterey on June 3, 1770, marking the beginning of today's California. Monterey remained the capital of Upper California until the United States took formal control in 1848. The city still retains a unique character, with its many historic buildings now protected and restored.

North Central California has also inspired some of the state's most significant literature, from the poetry of Robinson Jeffers to the novels of Nobel prize-winner John Steinbeck. Many of the world's best photographers, including Ansel Adams and Edward Weston, have lived and worked here.

For all its culture and history, the region also abounds in recreational activities. Visitors can enjoy the historic amusement park at Santa Cruz, play golf on the world-famous courses at Pebble Beach, or simply walk around the many nature preserves, including the state's most beautiful stretch of coastline, the majestic Big Sur.

Writer John Steinbeck's house in Salinas

◀ Wildflowers blooming on the cliffs of the stunning Big Sur coast

Exploring North Central California

Monterey, the Spanish colonial capital of California, is at the heart of North Central California and the best base from which to explore the region. The wealthy resorts of Pacific Grove and Carmel stand on a rugged peninsula just outside the town. Farther south is the wildest length of coastline in the state, Big Sur, where otters and whales can be spotted offshore. To the north is Santa Cruz, a lively beach town, backed by densely forested mountains. Inland, the Salinas and San Joaquin valleys give a taste of California's productive agricultural areas.

Pfeiffer Burns State Park at Big Sur

Looking out across Big Sur along Hwy 1

Sights at a Glance

Elephant seals at the Año Nuevo State Reserve

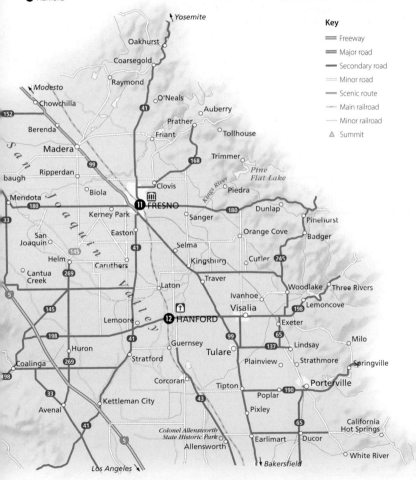

Key

═══ Freeway

━━━ Major road

━━━ Secondary road

┉┉┉ Minor road

━━━ Scenic route

⊶⊶⊶ Main railroad

──── Minor railroad

△ Summit

Getting Around

Hwy 1, which runs along the coast south from Monterey to Big Sur, is one of the world's most beautiful drives and a must on any tour of California. A car, or a bicycle and strong legs, is the best way to get around, although there is a skeletal network of buses centering upon Monterey. Inland from the coast, Hwy 101 and I-5 run north–south through the predominantly agricultural region, but there are very few roads between the coast and inland valleys.

For additional map symbols *see back flap*

The North Central Coastline

The beaches of North Central California are varied, from long, thin stretches to tiny coves at the foot of coastal bluffs. In summer, sun-worshipers and volleyball players congregate on the sands, and while the water is generally too cold for swimming, surfers don wet suits to brave the chilly waves. With almost no commercial developments along this stretch of coastline, these beaches are also ideal for leisurely walks, searching for driftwood or seashells. You may also catch a glimpse of the area's abundant wildlife, which ranges from shore birds and tidepool-dwellers to elephant seals and migrating gray whales.

San Francisco
Pacifica
①
Boulder Creek
Scotts Valley
9
Santa Cruz
Wilder Ranch State Park
②
③

Moss Landing is a colorful harbor and the home port for most of Monterey Bay's commercial fishing boats. It has many good seafood restaurants along its wharves.

③ ★ Santa Cruz Beach
With free volleyball courts and barbecue pits backed by the popular Boardwalk Amusement Park *(see p510)*, this broad golden expanse is the area's most popular beach.

0 kilometers   5
0 miles   5

② Lighthouse Field State Beach
This rugged 36 acres (14 ha) of shoreline is well suited to surfing or simply admiring the sculpted 40-ft (12-m) sandstone headlands. It is also a good place to spot sea otters, brown pelicans, and the occasional whale offshore.

④ Capitola Beach
A wooden railway trestle bridges the small creek that meets the ocean at this sandy beach. Next to the beach is Capitola Wharf, with restaurants, shops, and observation decks. The Capitola Bluffs are an important paleontological site, and the prehistoric shells can be seen at low tide.

⑤ Marina State Beach
Backed by sand dunes, this beach was once a part of a US Army base and is now part of a university campus.

Key
━━ Freeway
━━ Major road
--- Minor road
〜 River

① Waddell Creek Beach
This golden strand of beach is part of the Big Basin Redwoods State Park *(see p508)* and is a favorite spot for picnickers, anglers, and windsurfers.

Wilder Ranch State Park, at the northern edge of Santa Cruz, is a historic coastal dairy farm. Complete with ranch house and barns dating from the 1890s, it has been preserved as a state park.

Locator Map

Elkhorn Slough, halfway along Monterey Bay, is one of the prime bird-watching areas along the North Central coastline.

⑦ ★ **Asilomar State Beach**

This broad, rocky beach is an ideal place for watching migrating gray whales as they pass offshore every winter on their way south.

⑥ ★ **Lovers' Point**

Originally called Lovers of Jesus Point, the headlands form a natural amphitheater that was used for religious revivals in the 1880s. It is one of the few sandy beaches on the northern Monterey Peninsula.

⑧ ★ **Carmel City Beach**

Bright white sand and brilliant blue water are the distinguishing characteristics of this long beach, which sits at the foot of central Carmel's popular shopping and restaurant district (see p514).

Elephant seals ashore at Año Nuevo State Reserve

❶ Big Basin Redwoods State Park

Road map B4. 🚩 Santa Cruz, Boulder Creek Golf Course. Visitors' Center: 21600 Big Basin Way, Boulder Creek. **Tel** (831) 338-8860. **Open** Park: sunrise–sunset daily. 🅦 parks.ca.gov

In the year 1900 a group of environmentalists formed the Sempervirens Club with the aim of preventing the logging of redwoods. This resulted in Big Basin Redwoods State Park, California's first state park, being established in 1902. It covers 16,000 acres (6,475 ha) and protects the southernmost groves of the coastal redwood tree *(see p450)* and forests of Douglas fir and other conifers. It is also home to wildlife such as black-tailed deer and the mountain lion.

Trails lead through redwood groves to the park's many waterfalls, including the popular Berry Creek Falls. There are also more than 100 miles (160 km) of other routes, including the Skyline-to-Sea Trail, which drops down to the Pacific Ocean at Waddell Creek *(see pp506–7)*.

❷ Año Nuevo State Reserve

Road map B4. 🚌 Santa Cruz, Waddell Creek. 🛈 (650) 879-2025, 879-0227 (recorded info). **Open** daily. 🅦 parks.ca.gov

The Año Nuevo State Reserve, 60 miles (96 km) north of Monterey, has as its main point of interest the breeding grounds of the Northern elephant seal, one of the world's most fascinating creatures. A short stretch of sandy beach and a small offshore island are populated each winter by hundreds of these giant mammals, which arrive here from all over the Pacific Ocean to mate and give birth.

Elephant seals were hunted almost to extinction in the 19th century because of their valuable oil-bearing blubber. A few survivors found refuge off the coast of Mexico and made their way back to California in the 1950s. The first pups were born at Año Nuevo in 1975. There are now some 120,000 elephant seals off the coast of California.

The seals are named after the dangling proboscis of the male, which resembles an elephant's trunk. Male seals can reach 20 ft (6 m) in length and weigh upward of 2 tons. Ungainly on land, elephant seals can perform incredible feats in the sea – remaining under water for up to 20 minutes at a time and diving to more than 4,000 ft (1,220 m) beneath the surface. Each December, the male seals arrive here and begin the battle for dominance, engaging in violent fights. Only a handful of the most powerful males are able to mate, but one male can father pups with as many as 50 different females in one season. After spending most of the year at sea, the females arrive in January to give birth to young conceived the previous winter. Mating follows soon after, although conception is delayed for up to four months while the female recovers from giving birth.

The name Año Nuevo ("New Year") was given to the island by explorer Sebastián Vizcaíno, who sailed past the area on January 1, 1603 *(see pp50–51)*. The park is open all year, but during the winter when the elephant seals are present, visitors are allowed only on guided tours. Tickets are available through the California State Parks reservation service, *(see p587)*.

❸ Roaring Camp Railroads

Road map B4. **Tel** (831) 335-4484. 🚂 Santa Cruz. **Open** Sat & Sun. **Closed** public hols. 🅿 ♿ 🕚 11am, 12:15pm, 2pm. 🅦 roaringcamp.com

High up in the Santa Cruz Mountains, near the town of Felton, a pair of historic logging railroads have been kept in

Roaring Camp and Big Trees Railroad

Facade of Mission San Juan Bautista

operation as the focus of a family-orientated theme park devoted to the late 19th-century and early 20th-century logging town, complete with general store, one-room school house, and opera house. A narrow-gauge train with open-top cars, usually pulled by a steam engine, departs on a 6-mile (10-km) round-trip through the adjacent forests of Henry Cowell Redwoods State Park. From April through early fall, the standard-gauge Big Trees, Santa Cruz, and Pacific Railroad sets off from Roaring Camp on an hour-long trip through the mountains and down to Santa Cruz. There is a two-hour stopover, during which passengers can enjoy the beach and Boardwalk Amusement Park (see pp510–11) before the return journey. The trip can also be taken as a round-trip from Santa Cruz.

❹ Santa Cruz

See pp510–11.

❺ San Juan Bautista

Road map B4. 🏔 1,650. 🚌 from Hollister. 🛈 650 San Benito St, Hollister, (831) 637-5315.
🅦 sanjuanbautistaca.com

For a quick insight into California's multifaceted history, there is no better place than San Juan Bautista. This small town has retained its rural character, despite being a mere 30 miles (48 km) from the heart of the high-tech Silicon Valley (see p432).

The main attraction of the town is Mission San Juan Bautista, which stands to the west of the central plaza. The largest of the missions built during Spanish colonial rule, it is also the only one to have aisles along the nave. Alfred Hitchcock used the mission's facade for the final scenes of his film *Vertigo*. The adjacent monastery has been converted into a museum, displaying mission artifacts and photographs of the town at various stages of development.

El Camino Real sign

On the north side of the church there is a cemetery, next to which a faint trail marks the historic route of El Camino Real. This 650-mile (1,050-km) path linked the 21 California missions, all within a day's journey of their nearest mission (see pp50–51). By coincidence, this trail also follows the San Andreas Fault, the underlying source of all California's earthquakes (see pp28–9). A seismograph on the edge of the town's plaza monitors tectonic activity.

The east and south sides of the plaza are lined by three historic buildings, all of which have been preserved as part of San Juan Bautista State Historic Park. The Plaza Hotel incorporates part of the original barracks built in 1813. The town's stables now house antique carriages and stagecoaches, and Castro House was owned by Patrick Breen, a survivor of the tragic Donner Party (see p490).

The Loma Prieta Earthquake

The powerful tremor that rocked San Francisco on October 17, 1989, had its epicenter beneath Loma Prieta, a hill between Santa Cruz and San Juan Bautista. Although the international media concentrated on the extensive damage caused in and around San Francisco, the worst damage occurred in Santa Cruz and the surrounding communities, where a number of homes and commercial buildings were destroyed. Approximately 40 businesses were forced to relocate to tentlike temporary buildings occupying three full blocks. The downtown district of Santa Cruz was a vast building site until the end of 1994. The majority of the damaged structures have now been repaired or replaced, but empty lots still remain where buildings once stood.

Destruction caused by the Loma Prieta earthquake in 1989

❹ Santa Cruz

Perched at the northern tip of Monterey Bay, Santa Cruz is a composite of small-town California, with an agricultural rather than suburban feel. Its surrounding farmland forms a broad shelf between the bay and the densely forested Santa Cruz Mountains that rise to the east. These mountains separate Santa Cruz from the more urban Silicon Valley *(see p432)* and, along with the scenic coastline, provide residents and visitors with an easy access to nature. The city's past is preserved in a replica 18th-century mission and in the excellent local history museum. The large University of California campus above town, attracting students and professors from all over the world, also gives Santa Cruz a cosmopolitan and erudite character.

Reconstructed facade of Santa Cruz Mission

Exploring Santa Cruz

The downtown, which centers on Pacific Avenue, is 875 yards (800 m) inland. Much of this area was badly damaged by the Loma Prieta earthquake *(see p509)*, but the city has recovered swiftly, with many good bookstores, art galleries, and cafés lining the streets. The historic core of the city, including the remains of the 1791 Mission Santa Cruz, is on a hill to the northeast of the town.

Detail of the Giant Dipper

The highlight of this place is the waterfront, including the Santa Cruz Beach Boardwalk Amusement Park and scenic West Cliff Drive that runs along the coast.

🎡 Santa Cruz Beach Boardwalk Amusement Park

400 Beach St. **Tel** (831) 423-5590. **Open** call ahead for opening times. 🌐 **beachboardwalk.com**

The last surviving old-style amusement park on the West Coast, the Santa Cruz Beach Boardwalk offers a variety of attractions and games lined up along the beachfront. Visitors can wander freely, deciding which of the rides to try. The main attraction is the Giant Dipper roller coaster, built in 1924 by Arthur Looff and now a National Historic Landmark. The car travels along the 1-mile (1.6-km) wooden track at 55 mph (88 km/h). The carousel nearby features horses and chariots hand-carved by Looff's father, craftsman Charles Looff, in 1911. The ride is accompanied by a 100-year-old pipe organ. The park also has 27 more modern rides and an Art Deco dance hall.

🏛 Mission Santa Cruz

Emmet & High Sts. **Tel** (831) 426-5686. **Open** 10am–4pm Mon, Thu–Sat, 10am–2pm Sun. Donation.

On top of a hill overlooking the town, Mission Santa Cruz was founded on September 25, 1791 by Father Lasuén, as the 12th Franciscan mission in California. The buildings were completed three years later. The mission was never a great success, however, due to earthquakes, poor weather, and its isolated location, all of which have eliminated any remains of the original structure. A park outlines the site, and a 1931 replica of the mission has been constructed. This houses a small museum.

🏛 Museum of Art and History at the McPherson Center

705 Front St. **Tel** (831) 429-1964. **Open** 11am–5pm Tue–Sun (to 9pm Fri). **Closed** Jan 1, Thanksgiving, Dec 25. 📷 🌐 **santacruzmah.org**

One positive development to arise out of the rubble of the 1989 Loma Prieta earthquake was this 20,000 sq ft (1,858 sq m) cultural center, which opened in 1993 to house the local art and history galleries. The Art Gallery shows works primarily by north central artists depicting the local landscape. The History Gallery includes a series of displays tracing the development of Santa Cruz County, from the pre-colonial and mission eras through to the present day.

Also in the History Gallery are exhibits detailing the region's agricultural and industrial heritage, with photographs of late 19th-century and early 20th-century farms and logging operations. The museum also incorporates the adjacent Octagon Gallery that was completed in 1882 as the County Hall of Records.

Giant Dipper roller coaster in the Boardwalk Amusement Park

Eroded archway at the Natural Bridges State Beach

Natural Bridges State Beach

2531 W Cliff Dr. **Tel** (831) 423-4609.
Open daily. Visitors' Center end
of W Cliff Drive. **Open** 8am–sunset
daily. **W** parks.ca.gov

Natural Bridges State Beach takes
its name from the picturesque
archways that were carved into
the cliffs by the ocean waves.
Two of the three original arches
collapsed but one still remains,
through which waves roll into a
small sandy cove. The park also
preserves a eucalyptus grove
and a nature trail, showing all
the stages in the life cycle of the
monarch butterfly *(see p223)*.

Santa Cruz Surfing Museum

Lighthouse Point, 701 W Cliff Drive
Tel (831) 420-6289. **Open** winter:
noon–4pm Thu–Mon; summer:
10am–5pm Wed–Mon.
Closed public hols. Donation.
W santacruzsurfingmuseum.org

In a lighthouse overlooking the
region's main surfing area, this
museum has artifacts from
every era of Santa Cruz surfing.
The sport was brought here
from Hawaii, making Santa Cruz
the birthplace of surfing on the
US mainland. It evolved into a
truly Californian pursuit with the
music of the Beach Boys in the
1960s *(see pp202–3)*. The surfboards range from the redwood
planks of the 1930s to today's
high-tech laminates.

Mystery Spot

465 Mystery Spot Rd.
Tel (831) 423 8897. **Open** daily.
W mysteryspot.com

Two miles (3 km) east of Santa
Cruz, a redwood grove has been
drawing visitors for decades
due to various strange events.
Balls roll uphill, parallel lines
converge, and the laws of
physics seem to be suspended.
Part tourist trap, part genuine
oddity, the Mystery Spot has
to be seen.

Santa Cruz City Center

① Natural Bridges State Beach
② Santa Cruz Surfing Museum
③ Santa Cruz Beach Boardwalk
   Amusement Park
④ Museum of Art and History at the
   McPherson Center
⑤ Mission Santa Cruz

0 meters 250
0 yards 250

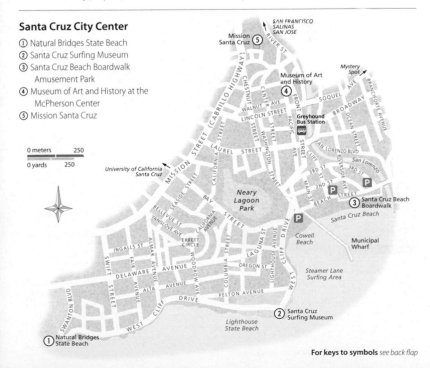

Street-by-Street: Monterey

The Spanish explorer, Sebastián Vizcaíno, landed here in 1602 and named the bay after his patron, the Count of Monterrey. But it was not until the Spanish captain Gaspar de Portolá (1717–1784) and Father Serra *(see pp50–51)* landed here in 1770 and established a church and presidio that the garrison grew into a pueblo. Monterey served as the capital of California until 1848. After the Gold Rush *(see pp52–3)* the city lost its status to San Francisco and settled into the role of a hardworking fishing port, market town, and military base.

Today, visitors come to tour the historic sites, dine on seafood at Fisherman's Wharf, and visit the globally renowned Monterey Bay Aquarium.

California's First Theater
Built in 1847 as a boarding house, it became a theater in 1848.

★ **Colton Hall**
The California State Constitution was first signed here in 1849. The hall now houses a museum commemorating the event.

Key

— Suggested route

0 meters   100
0 yards   100

Larkin House
Thomas Larkin, an East Coast merchant, built this house in 1832. The architecture has become representative of Monterey style *(see pp34–5)*.

The Sherman Quarters were General Sherman's military base from 1847–1849.

The Cooper-Molera Complex combines a garden, a carriage display and personal mementos of three generations of the Cooper family, who occupied the house between 1832 and 1900.

FRANKLIN STREET
PIERCE STREET
PACIFIC STREET
CALLE PRINCIPAL
JEFFERSON STREET
MUNRAS AVENUE

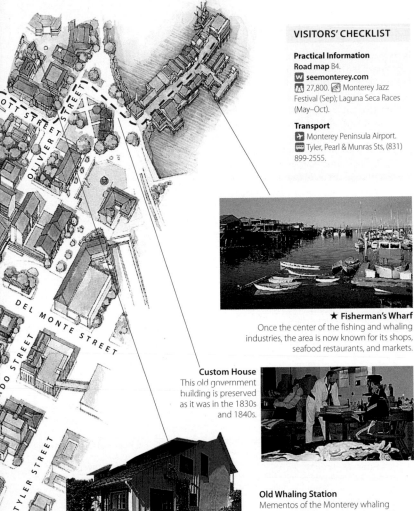

★ **Fisherman's Wharf**
Once the center of the fishing and whaling
industries, the area is now known for its shops,
seafood restaurants, and markets.

Custom House
This old government
building is preserved
as it was in the 1830s
and 1840s.

Old Whaling Station
Mementos of the Monterey whaling
industry are displayed in the house. The
paving outside the building was made
using whale bones.

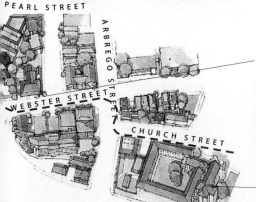

**Robert Louis Stevenson Silverado
Museum**
Robert Louis Stevenson *(see p30)* lived here in
1879. The house is now a museum.

The Royal Presidio Chapel,
built 1791–4, is the town's
oldest surviving building.

Exploring the Monterey Peninsula

Writers and artists have long extolled the spectacular coastline of the Monterey Peninsula. Its granite rocks have been cut into rugged coves and jutting points by the ocean. Forests of Monterey cypress and pine trees, wintering grounds of the monarch butterfly, cover the inland area. Otters and sea lions swim in the kelp forests beyond the shore. The peninsula is home to three main towns: Monterey, the capital of Spanish California *(see pp512–13)*; the former religious retreat, Pacific Grove; and the picturesque village of Carmel-by-the-Sea.

Marine bird at the Monterey Bay Aquarium

🐟 Monterey Bay Aquarium
886 Cannery Row, Monterey. **Tel** (831) 648-8888. **Open** daily. **Closed** Dec 25.
🖼 **W** montereybayaquarium.org
Monterey Bay Aquarium is one of the largest aquariums in the US, with more than 500 species and tens of thousands of specimens from the Monterey Bay area. Among the exhibits are an enclosed kelp forest, a rock pool, and a live jellyfish display. Visitors are allowed to touch the specimens, including sea stars and bat rays.

A pool connected to the open bay attracts sea otters. The Outer Bay Wing has a huge tank in which the conditions of the ocean are re-created. It contains yellowfin tuna, ocean sunfish, green sea turtles, and barracuda. The Research Institute offers a chance for visitors to watch the marine scientists at work, and the Splash Zone is a hands-on aquarium/museum for kids.

🏛 Cannery Row
800 Cannery Row, Monterey.
Tel (831) 649-6690. **Open** daily.
W cannery row.com
This six-block harbor-front street, celebrated by John Steinbeck in his ribald novels *Cannery Row*

and *Sweet Thursday (see p521)*, was once the site of more than 20 fish-packing plants that processed sardines from Monterey Bay. The canneries thrived from the early 20th century, reaching their greatest volume of production in the early 1940s. In 1945 the sardines suddenly disappeared, perhaps as a result of overfishing, and most of the canneries were abandoned, later to be demolished or burned down. The buildings that remain today house an eclectic collection of shops and restaurants. One notable historic building that remains, at No. 800, is the old laboratory of "Doc" Ricketts, noted marine biologist, beer drinker, and best friend of Steinbeck. The building is now a private club.

Street sign in Cannery Row

🏛 Pacific Grove
Road Map B4. ℹ️ Forest & Central Aves, (831) 373-3304, (800) 656-6650. **Open** daily. **Closed** Jan 1, Thanksgiving, Dec 25. **W** pacificgrove.org
This sedate town was founded in 1889 as a religious retreat, where alcohol, dancing, and even the Sunday newspaper

were banned. Today it is best known for its wooden houses, many now converted into inns, its beautiful coastal parks, and the monarch butterflies that arrive between October and April *(see p223)*. The annual return of the insects, which are protected by city ordinance, occasions a lively parade.

The Point Pinos Lighthouse was built in 1852 and is now the oldest operating lighthouse in California.

🏛 Carmel-by-the-Sea
Road Map B4. ℹ️ San Carlos, 5th & 6th Sts, (831) 624-2522, (800) 550-4333. **Open** Mon–Sat. **Closed** Jan 1, Thanksgiving, Dec 25.
W carmelcalifornia.org
The varied array of homes in this picturesque village border the steep hillsides down to the ocean. City ordinances restricting streetlights, mail deliveries, and sidewalks gives the town its quaint atmosphere. Art galleries and shops abound along Ocean Ave. The town sponsors an annual playwriting contest, a Bach Festival, and art exhibitions.

🏖 Carmel River State Beach
Carmelo & Scenic Rds. **Road Map** B4.
W parks.ca.gov
This 109-acre (270-ha) state park straddles the mouth of the Carmel River, containing a lagoon and wetland nature preserve for a bountiful population of native and migratory birds. Fishing is permitted on the beach, but swimming is discouraged because of dangerous currents and cold temperatures. The beach is a favorite picnic spot of Carmel residents.

Point Pinos Lighthouse at Pacific Grove

For hotels and restaurants in this area see p543 and pp576–7

The 17-Mile Drive

Sightseers may tour the Monterey Peninsula via a toll road, the 17-Mile Drive. The road offers spectacular views of what the area has to offer, including crashing surf, coastal flora, and the Del Monte Forest. The extraordinary beauty of the region has also attracted many wealthy people to build imposing estates and mansions in the area. Most celebrated of all its attractions are the country clubs and championship golf courses.

① Spanish Bay
The shore within this cove at the southern edge of Pacific Grove is a popular picnicking area.

⑥ Spyglass Hill
This golf course was named after a location in Robert Louis Stevenson's *Treasure Island*. Stevenson often described the local scenery in his novels.

② Huckleberry Hill
This hill in the Del Monte Forest is popular in the summer with hikers.

Tips for Drivers

Duration of journey: 3 hours. Entrance: There is a toll charge for each car. Cycling is free.
Getting there: There are four toll gates: 17-Mile Drive, San Antonio Ave, Hwy 1, and SFB Morse Drive. The tour is marked by red and yellow lines.
When to go: Summer can be crowded and foggy. In any season, traffic is lighter during the week.
Where to stay and eat: Carmel, Monterey, and Pacific Grove have a wide range of hotels and restaurants *(see p543 and p577)*.
Visitor Information: Monterey County Convention & Visitors' Bureau, 150 Olivier St, (877) 666-8373. **W** seemonterey.com

⑤ Lone Cypress
On a rock overlooking the ocean, this is perhaps one of the most photographed trees in the world.

④ Tor House
This striking rock house was built by the poet Robinson Jeffers between 1918 and 1919.

③ Carmel Mission
At one time this beautiful mission was the administrative center for northern California *(see pp516–17)*.

Key

⬜ Tour route
= = Other roads
⬜ Golf courses

0 meters   500
0 yards   500

❼ Carmel Mission

Founded in 1770 by Father Junípero Serra (1713–84) and built of adobe brick by Native American laborers, Carmel Mission served as the administrative center for all the Northern California missions *(see pp50–51)*. Father Serra resided here until his death and is now buried at the foot of the altar. The mission was secularized and abandoned in 1834, quickly falling into disrepair. Restoration work began in 1924, carefully following the plans of the original mission, and replanting the gardens. The reconstructed living quarters detail 18th-century mission life. The mission still functions as a Catholic church.

The sarcophagus depicts Father Serra recumbent in death, surrounded by three mourning padres. It is among the finest of its type in the United States.

Kitchen
This restored room shows the kitchen as it was in missionary days, including the oven brought from Mexico. A section of the original adobe wall can be seen.

Statue of Junípero Serra
Set within the beautiful front courtyard, a statue of Serra faces the mission church he founded.

★ Serra's Cell
Father Serra's simple way of life is evident in this sparse, restored cell. The wooden bed, chair, desk, and candlestick were the only pieces of furniture he possessed. He died here in 1784.

Facade and front courtyard of Carmel Mission

KEY

① **Dining room**

② **Bell tower**

③ **The chapel window** is the only place where the original paintwork can still be seen.

④ **Father Serra's burial place** under the altar is marked with a plaque.

⑤ **The cemetery** contains the graves of 18th-century missionaries.

⑥ **The museum**, in the old living quarters, contains several relics belonging to Father Serra.

★ **Main Altar**
The Gothic arch of Carmel's altar, with its ornate decoration, is the only one of its kind among all the 21 Franciscan missions in California.

❽ Big Sur

In the late 18th century, Spanish colonists at Carmel named this stretch of land *El Pais Grande del Sur*, the "big country to the south," and the coastline of Big Sur has been attracting hyperbole ever since. The novelist Robert Louis Stevenson called it "the greatest meeting of land and sea in the world," and the 100 miles (160 km) of breathtaking mountains, cliffs, and rocky coves still leave visitors grasping for adjectives.

The scenic Hwy 1 was constructed across this rugged landscape during the 1930s, but otherwise Big Sur has been preserved in its natural state. There are no large towns and very few signs of civilization in the area. Most of the shoreline is protected in a series of state parks that offer dense forests, broad rivers, and crashing surf, all easily accessible within a short walk of the road.

Crashing surf and rocky cliffs, typical of the Big Sur coastline

Point Lobos State Reserve
This is the habitat of the Monterey cypress, the only tree to survive the region's mixture of fog and salt spray. Its branches are shaped by the sea winds.

Bixby Creek Bridge
This photogenic arched bridge was built in 1932. For many years it was the world's largest single-arch span, at 260 ft (79 m) tall and 700 ft (213 m) long. Hwy 1 was named the state's first scenic highway here in 1966.

KEY

① **Point Sur Lighthouse** sits atop a volcanic cone. It was manned until 1974 but is now automated.

② **Nepenthe** *(see p576)* is a lovely restaurant hidden from the road by oak trees. It has long been frequented by Hollywood movie stars.

③ **The Esalen Institute** was set up in the 1960s to hold New Age seminars. Its hot springs were first frequented by Native Americans and still attract visitors *(see p445)*.

④ **San Simeon Point** is a natural harbor that was used by William Randolph Hearst to ship in materials for his estate, Hearst Castle®, on the inland hilltop *(see pp216–17)*.

Andrew Molera State Park
Opened in 1972, this park includes 10 miles (16 km) of hiking trails and 2.5 miles (4 km) of quiet, sandy beach.

Julia Pfeiffer Burns State Park
A tunnel under Hwy 1, accessible only on foot, leads to the 100-ft (30-m) high bluff from which the McWay Creek waterfall spills into the Pacific Ocean.

Ventana Wilderness
Part of the Los Padres National Forest, many of the steep ridges of this beautiful wilderness are accessible only to experienced hikers. Camp sites cover the lower reaches.

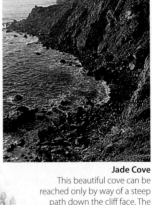

Jade Cove
This beautiful cove can be reached only by way of a steep path down the cliff face. The removal of jade is prohibited above the high tide level.

0 kilometers 10

0 miles 10

Ventana Wilderness

Tassajara Creek

Los Padres National Forest

Big Creek

Lucia

Nacimiento Fergusson Rd

Antonio River

Lake San Antonio

Los Burros Rd

Plaskett Creek

Nacimiento River

Lake Nacimiento

Alder Creek

San Simeon

Key

══ Minor road

━━ Scenic route

- - ∙ Hiking trails

── National park boundaries

〰 Rivers and lakes

For additional map symbols *see back flap*

Nobel prize-winning author John Steinbeck (1902–68)

❾ Salinas

Road map B4. 🗺 151,000. 🚆 🚌
ℹ 119 E Alisal St, (831) 424-7611.
🔤 seemonterey.com

Situated at the north end of the predominantly agricultural Salinas Valley, which stretches for more than 50 miles (80 km) between San Francisco and San Luis Obispo, Salinas is the region's primary agricultural center. Vegetable-packing plants and canneries line the major highways and railroad tracks. The region is often referred to as the "salad bowl of the nation," its prime produce being lettuce, as well as tomatoes and garlic.

The town is perhaps best known, however, as the birthplace of the Nobel prize- winning author John Steinbeck, who set many of his naturalistic stories here and in the surrounding area. A selection of books, manu-scripts, photographs, and personal memorabilia relating to the author is on permanent display in a special room of the **National Steinbeck Center Museum**. The library also

supplies information on Steinbeck-related places to visit in the area, and on the Steinbeck Festival, held in Salinas every August.

Hat in Three Stages of Landing, a large-scale, bright yellow steel sculpture of three cowboy hats by the acclaimed Pop artist Claes Oldenberg, was erected in the town in the 1970s. It stands, appropriately, in front of the entrance to the California State Rodeo. Each Fourth of July one of the largest rodeos in the world is held here.

🏛 **National Steinbeck Center Museum**
1 Main St. **Tel** (831) 775-4721.
Open 10am–5pm daily. **Closed** public hols. 🔤 steinbeck.org

❿ Pinnacles National Monument

500 Hwy 146, Paicines. **Road map** B4.
Tel (831) 389-4485. 🚆 King City & Soledad. **Open** daily. 🎫 🚹 some trails. 🚹 🔤 nps.gov/pinn

High in the hills above the Salinas Valley, 12 miles (20 km) east of the town of Soledad on US101, the Pinnacles National Monument preserves 16,000 acres (6,500 ha) of a unique volcanic landscape. A solid ridge of lava flows, eroded over millions of years into oddly contorted crags and spires, runs through the center of the park, in places forming cliffs more than 500 ft (150 m) tall. There are no roads across the park, but there are many carefully maintained hiking trails.

One of the most popular and accessible spots in the park is the Balconies formation, reached by a 1.5-mile (2.5 km) leisurely trail. Here beautiful red and gold cliffs rise high above the ground, attracting rock-climbers, photo-graphers, and bird-watchers. At the base of the cliffs, huge boulders caught between the narrow canyons have formed a series of dark talus caves. These were reputedly used in the past as outlaws' hideouts.

The park is best visited in spring, when the temperature is cool and the wildflowers are in bloom. Mountain lions, coyotes, and eagles can occasionally also be sighted.

Volcanic crags of the Pinnacles National Monument

⓫ Fresno

Road map C4. 🗺 509,000. ✈ Fresno Air Terminal. 🚆 🚌 ℹ 1550 E Shaw Ave, (559) 981-5200, (800) 788-0836.
🔤 playfresno.org

The city of Fresno is located at approximately the geographical center of the state, and is its eighth largest city. It is often referred to as the "Raisin Capital of the World" because of its abundant production of the

Vegetable pickers and packers in the Salinas Valley

dried fruit. The small **Fresno Art Museum** is worth a visit. The city's location makes it a good base for excursions to the High Sierras, Kings Canyon, Sequoia, and Yosemite National Parks *(see pp486–501)*.

Homegrown
Fresno raisins

🏛 Fresno Art Museum
2233 N First St.
Tel (559) 441-4221.
Open 11am–5pm Thu–Sun.
W fresnoartmuseum.org

Environs
In Kearney Park, 7 miles (11 km) west of Fresno, is **Kearney Mansion**, an elaborate French Renaissance-style house built in 1903 by Theodore Kearney, an agriculturalist who helped found California's raisin industry. The house is now a period museum.

🏛 Kearney Mansion
7160 W. Kearney Blvd, Hwy 99.
Tel (559) 441-0862. **Open** 1–3pm Fri–Sun. 🅿 📷 **W** historicfresno.org

Colonel Allen Allensworth, resident of Hanford

⑫ Hanford
Road map C4. 🏬 53,000. 🚌 🚃 ℹ
200 Santa Fe Ave, Suite D, (559) 582-5024). **W** hanfordchamber.com

One of many medium-sized farming communities in the area, Hanford is significant because of its multiethnic heritage. The China Alley neighborhood was once inhabited by one of the largest Chinese communities in California, many of whom worked on the construction of the transcontinental railroad *(see pp54–5)*. Located east of the town center, China Alley surrounds the historic **Taoist Temple**, built in 1893. The temple operated as a hostel for Chinese immigrants and a Chinese school as well as a religious shrine. Downtown Hanford, around Courthouse Square, has a beautiful antique carousel and a number of elegant buildings dating from the late 19th century, now converted into shops and restaurants.

🎭 Taoist Temple Museum
12 China Alley. **Tel** (559) 582-4508.
Open by appointment only. 🅿 📷
W chinaalley.com

Environs
The **Colonel Allensworth State Historic Park** is 30 miles (50 km) south of Hanford. Colonel Allen Allensworth believed his fellow African-Americans could combat racism by building their own future. He established a unique farming community in 1908 with a group of African-American families. Memorabilia of this independent community are now on display in the old farmhouses.

🏛 Colonel Allensworth State Historic Park
Off Hwy 99 on County Rd J22, Earlimart. **Tel** (661) 849-3433.
Open daily. 🅿 **W** parks.ca.gov

John Steinbeck

One of California's most successful 20th-century writers, John Steinbeck (1902–68) was born in Salinas to an established family of farmers and ranchers. When he dropped out of Stanford University *(see p431)*, Steinbeck moved to the Monterey Peninsula in the late 1920s to write fiction. After several attempts he eventually gained a measure of success with the publication of the novella *Tortilla Flat* in 1935. Steinbeck then began a series of short stories and novels, the majority of them focusing on the people and places he knew well in the Salinas Valley and Monterey area. These included some of his greatest work: *Of Mice and Men* (1937), *Cannery Row* (1945), and *East of Eden* (1952).

His best-known work is *The Grapes of Wrath* (1939). The novel fictionalizes the mass westward migration that took place during the Depression of the 1930s, by documenting the struggles of the Joad family as they fled the dust bowl of Oklahoma for the greener pastures of California. It was an immediate bestseller and earned Steinbeck a Pulitzer Prize, although many Californians took its unhappy ending as an insult to their state, and even as Communist propaganda. Steinbeck reacted to this antipathy in 1943 by going to North Africa and becoming a war correspondent. On his return to the United States in 1945 he settled on Long Island, New York. In 1962, he was awarded the Nobel Prize for Literature. Steinbeck was the first American author to receive both the Pulitzer Prize and the Nobel Prize.

He died in New York City on December 20, 1968, but is buried in his hometown, in the Garden of Memories at No. 768 Abbott Street.

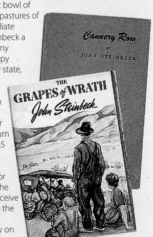

First editions of Steinbeck's famous works, *Cannery Row* and *The Grapes of Wrath*

The Inn at Furnace Creek set amongst desert oasis *(see p535)* ▶

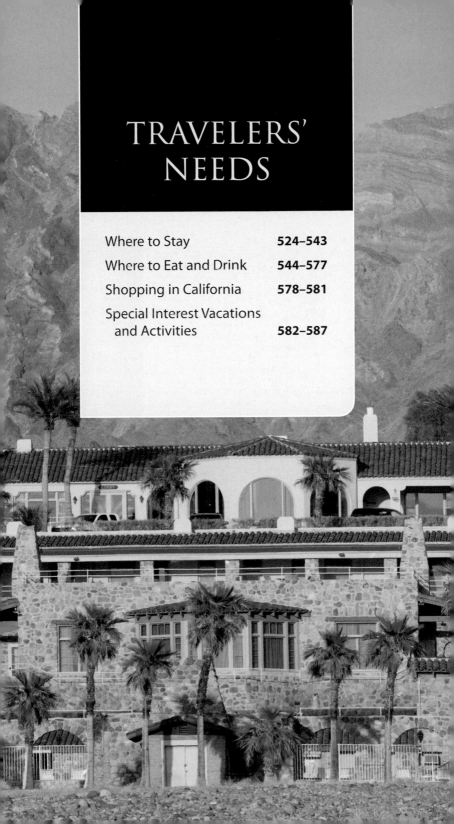

TRAVELERS' NEEDS

WHERE TO STAY

Home to the soaring Sierra Nevada mountain range, lush wooded hills, sophisticated urban centers, and a long, fabled stretch of coastline, California is a premier vacation destination. There is a wealth of accommodation options to suit every budget – from rustic lodges and family vacation resorts to five-star hotels. Top hotels can range from film-star luxury to high-tech business centers.

The widespread budget options vary from roadside motels to historic inns and high-rise hotels, and most come with double beds, en-suite bathrooms, and comfortable surroundings. Camping and RV facilities are also available for those who prefer the great outdoors. The listings on pages 528–43 give full descriptions of quality accommodations throughout the state to suit all budgets.

Hotel Classifications

California is recognized for its wide variety of accommodations that cater to visitors from around the world. The diamond rating system of the California State Automobile Association is an excellent guideline of value for travelers. Every lodging, from the most expensive four-diamond hotel to a budget one-diamond motel, is rated for service, cleanliness, and the range of facilities offered.

Hotels

In California, hotels come in every shape and size. There are numerous historic showplaces, some originally built to lure East Coast visitors to the West, including the Palace Hotel in San Francisco (see p536), the Millennium Biltmore in Los Angeles (see p528), and the Ahwahnee in Yosemite National Park (see p543). California is also famous for trendy, urban hostelries with stunning architecture such as the Hotel Vitale in San Francisco (see p537) and the Mondrian in West Hollywood (see p531). Some of the major hotels boast acclaimed restaurants, state-of-the-art conference centers, and lavish swimming pool terraces, while others might have well-tended gardens, a souvenir shop or boutique, or even a chandeliered ballroom. Boutique hotels and bed-and-breakfast inns tend to focus more on charm and intimacy, and have far fewer guest rooms. Several hotels built on Native American land have Las Vegas-style casinos attached.

Most California hotels have fitness facilities, spas, laundry services, and high-tech amenities such as in-room Wi-Fi, movies, and video games, plus work desks with ergonomic chairs and computer consoles. Pets are usually welcome, even in many five-star hotels. Non-smoking rooms are always available – many hotels have entire floors reserved for nonsmokers and

Lounge bar in the exclusive Beverly Wilshire Hotel, Los Angeles (see p528)

smoke-free hotels are becoming more common. Hotel restaurants throughout the state are smoke-free, as are most public spaces, including lobbies.

Prices

Room rates range from about $150 per night to a moderate $250, while upscale hotels may range from $250 upwards. Luxury destinations in Beverly Hills, Big Sur, San Francisco, and Napa Valley may charge $300 to $900 a night in high season. Note that additional city and state taxes may apply – 14 percent in San Francisco and 15.5 percent in Los Angeles. Other charges may include parking, resort fees, and outgoing telephone calls. Wi-Fi is available in-room at many hotels, but some upscale hotels may charge a daily fee for Wi-Fi.

Millennium Biltmore Hotel in Los Angeles (see p528)

When to Book

California is a world-renowned tourist destination and room rates soar during high seasons, which runs through the summer months throughout the state, and the winter months in the ski areas and along the southern beaches. It is worth looking into discounts and packages well in advance. California sunshine throughout the year makes the prospect of off-season travel attractive, too.

Corporate Hotels

These properties cater to business travelers by offering weekly and monthly rates. There are a number of all-suite hotels with living rooms and large work areas featuring Wi-Fi and fax connections. Many business hotels have in-house, 24-hour business centers with computers and printing facilities.

Chain Hotels

Guests can count on good service, moderate prices, and comfortable surroundings at a chain hotel. Popular chains include **Westin**, **Hilton**, **Sheraton**, **Marriott**, **Ramada**, **Hyatt**, and **Holiday Inn**. Some operate more than

Chateau Marmont on Sunset Boulevard, Los Angeles *(see p531)*

Sign over small boutique hotel

one hotel in each city. All chain hotels listed on page 527 have websites, or you can call the hotel's toll-free number to ask about rates and availability.

Tipping

A tip of $2 per bag is fair for bellhops who carry the luggage to and from your room. If the hotel has valet parking, 15–20 percent of the parking charge should be given to the driver upon departure. Room service requires a 15–20 percent tip, and a $10 tip for the maid is appreciated.

Resorts

California's legendary vacation resorts are spread out on landscaped grounds or in pristine natural surroundings, often with a diverse range of accommodations from rooms and suites to cottages, condos, and villas.

Resorts are concentrated in the Wine Country, in the mountains, along the coast, and in prime vacation destinations such as San Diego and Monterey. They usually offer a wide variety of activities from horseback riding to tennis and golf. They also often have a large swimming pool, yoga sessions, surfing or skiing lessons, a full-service spa, a decent restaurant, and children's programs.

San Diego Marriott Marquis and Marina Hotel, on San Diego Bay *(see p534)*

The historic Carter House Inns in Eureka, North California *(see p541)*

Motels

Inexpensive roadside motels sprang up in California in the 1950s, as a product of an increasingly car-oriented lifestyle. Affordable and basic, motels usually offer minimal amenities – beds, TVs, telephones, tea and coffee-making facilities, and en-suite bathrooms; parking is always included. Most have outdoor pools – a necessity for travelers in summer heat – and some have kitchen facilities and non-smoking rooms. Pets are usually welcome, with advance notice.

Motels belonging to the big chains can be found peppered along the highways of the state, and rates begin at around $50 a night. **Best Western** motels, in particular, have a reputation for clean rooms and good service at reasonable prices.

Historic Inns

Rich in regional history, these inns are often housed in the few remaining late 19th-century buildings in many of California's small towns. As well as reflecting local history, some inns also have their own story to tell having been, perhaps, a hunting and fishing lodge, a stern-wheeler riverboat, a Victorian mansion, or a hideaway for Hollywood movie stars in earlier times. Whatever their heritage, they all share a unique architecture and ambience. Many such inns, built during the era of railroad

expansion in the West, have achieved protected status and cannot be demolished or architecturally altered.

Similar to B&B hotels in atmosphere, historic inns are larger, with 20–100 rooms. Most serve complimentary Continental breakfasts, afternoon snacks, and wine in the evening. For more information, contact **California Inns**.

Grand historic lodges and rustic cabins can be found in some of the National Parks, and are maintained by the **National Park Service**. A few architecturally significant motels have been spruced up as well.

Smaller lodgings also have rustic charm. Some individual cabins have kitchen facilities for self-catering. Rarely do these inns have on-site restaurants, cafés, or room service. Most of them allow pets, many have outdoor pools, and larger ones may also have tennis courts. Check in advance whether smoking is allowed in the cabins – some inns in the state now pride themselves on providing guests with a completely smoke-free environment.

B&B Accommodations

Most B&Bs in California are restored homes that retain the charm of bygone eras. In addition to breakfast, afternoon snacks and evening drinks are usually offered. Rates start at about $80 upwards a night,

often with a two-night minimum stay required. Bathrooms may be en suite or shared, and libraries, parlors, and lush gardens are sometimes open to guests. For more information, contact the **California Association of Boutique and Breakfast Inns**.

Rooms in Private Homes

Booked through local vacation rental agencies or online with sites such as **Airbnb**, private homes are available to rent for nightly rates of $300 to $3,000, depending on the size, location, and standard of amenities. Contact any town's Chamber of Commerce or visitors' center for agency referrals.

Another option, especially for families and for travelers planning longer stays, is to arrange a house exchange with residents of California. **INTERVAC**

Inn At The Presidio, San Francisco *(see p538)*

US is part of a worldwide home exchange network and publishes quarterly directories of people willing to exchange their homes for yours during vacations. Annual fees to obtain or be listed in this directory range from $65 to $85.

Youth Hostels

The least expensive accommodation option, hostels offer clean, modern amenities, including communal kitchen facilities. Hostels are often set in enviable locations offering convenience in city centers or access to nature in National Parks. Dormitory-style, single sex rooms are most common, although many hostels nowadays do have private rooms available for couples or families. There is no age limit. **Hostelling International USA** can provide a list of lodgings.

Camping, Trailers, and RVs

Campers are always welcome in California's vast National and State Park systems (see p582), and there is also a large network of privately run campsites throughout the state. Those camping in tents will have the best choice of pitches, but there are plenty of beautiful sites for trailers and RVs, with electricity hook-ups

Deetjen's Big Sur Inn on the edge of a redwood forest, North Central California (see p543)

and disposal stations, too. Safe drinking water, picnic areas, and a general store are standard at most camp grounds. Information on camping can be obtained from **Reserve America** and **California State Park Campgrounds**.

Recommended Hotels

A variety of accommodation choices – from high-rise hotels to quaint B&Bs, from affordable motels and hostels to luxurious inns – have been listed in this guide (see pp528–43). Each hotel has been categorized as Boutique, Luxury, Resort, Historic,

B&B, or Budget and represents the very best that California has to offer. These establishments have been selected on two main criteria – location and service – and feature a wide selection to suit all requirements.

For the best of the best, look out for hotels highlighted as DK Choice. They have been selected for their exceptional quality and charm, and may be set in a beautiful location or in a historic landmark building, boast splendid views, or offer excellent facilities and service. These hotels are among California's most popular places to stay, so be sure to book in advance.

Where to Stay

Los Angeles
Airport

The Concourse Hotel $$
Budget   **Road map** inset A
6225 W Century Blvd, 90045
Tel *(424) 702-1234*
W concoursehotellax.hyatt.com
Ideal for business travelers, this place offers a pool, gym, and business center. Shuttle service to the airport.

Westin Los Angeles Airport $$
Luxury   **Road map** inset A
5400 W Century Blvd, 90045
Tel *310-216-5858*
W westinlosangelesairport.com
Extensive business amenities, top-notch fitness facility, and a good restaurant in the lobby.

Bel Air

Luxe Sunset Boulevard $$$
Luxury   **Road map** inset A
11461 Sunset Blvd, 90049
Tel *310-476-6571*
W luxehotels.com/sunset
Sophisticated place with sizable rooms and amenities such as plush bathrobes and luxury soaps.

Beverly Hills

Avalon Hotel $$$
Boutique   **Map** 5 F4
9400 W Olympic Blvd, 90212
Tel *310-277-5221*
W avalonbeverlyhills.com
This splendid boutique option has an award-winning restaurant and friendly service.

The Beverly Hills Hotel $$$
Luxury   **Map** 5 D2
9641 Sunset Blvd, 90210
Tel *310-276-2251*
W beverlyhillshotel.com
Centrally located famed property *(see p99)* set amid lush gardens. Tennis courts, and full-service spa.

The Beverly Hilton $$$
Luxury   **Map** 5 D4
9876 Wilshire Blvd, 90210
Tel *310-274-7777*
W beverlyhilton.com
Chic LA icon, home to the Golden Globe Awards. Rooms feature state-of-the-art amenities.

Beverly Wilshire $$$
Luxury   **Map** 5 F4
9500 Wilshire Blvd, 90212
Tel *310-275-5200*
W fourseasons.com
European charm and style in a central location. Spacious, well-appointed rooms.

Hotel Bel-Air $$$
Luxury   **Map** 4 A1
701 Stone Canyon Rd, 90077
Tel *310-472-1211*
W hotelbelair.com
Established in 1922, Hotel Bel-Air is set in beautiful, landscaped gardens *(see p99)* and has supremely comfortable rooms. Many Hollywood stars have stayed here.

Maison 140 $$$
Luxury   **Map** 5 E4
140 Lasky Dr, 90212
Tel *310-281-4000*
W maison140.com
Small, stylish place offering upscale luxury at good prices. Chic rooms.

The Peninsula Beverly Hills $$$
Luxury   **Map** 5 E4
9882 S Santa Monica Blvd, 90212
Tel *310-551-2888*
W beverlyhills.peninsula.com
Refined, elegant destination with well-equipped rooms, and a top-rated spa and restaurant.

Century City

Hyatt Regency Century Plaza $$$
Luxury   **Map** 5 D5
2025 Ave of the Stars, 90067
Tel *310-228-1234*
W centuryplaza.hyatt.com
A local icon, popular with heads of state and Hollywood stars. First-rate spa and dining facilities.

InterContinental Los Angeles Hotel $$$
Luxury   **Map** 5 D5
2151 Ave of the Stars, 90067
Tel *310-284-6500*
W intercontinentallosangeles.com
Modern option renowned for its business facilities. All rooms have a balcony or a patio.

Rooftop pool and bar area of Luxe Sunset Boulevard, Bel Air

Downtown

Best Western Dragon Gate Inn $
Budget   **Map** 11 F2
818 N Hill St, 90012
Tel *(213) 617-3077*
W dragongateinn.com
Clean, friendly place with large rooms. Conveniently location close to Downtown attractions.

Ramada Wilshire Center $
Budget   **Map** 9 D4
3900 Wilshire Blvd, 90010
Tel *(213) 736-5222*
W ramada.com
Tidy, reliable, great-value option within easy reach of attractions.

Miyako Hotel $$
Budget   **Map** 11 E4
328 E 1st St, 90012
Tel *(213) 617-2000*
W miyakoinn.com
Japanese hospitality, with simple, tasteful rooms, and a long list of health treatments in the spa.

Sheraton Los Angeles Downtown Hotel $$
Budget   **Map** 11 C4
711 S Hope St, 90017
Tel *(213) 488-3500*
W sheratonlosangelesdowntown.com
Large, airy rooms with business amenities. Linked to Macy's Plaza shopping complex.

Hilton Checkers $$$
Luxury   **Map** 11 D4
535 S Grand Ave, 90071
Tel *(213) 624-0000*
W hiltoncheckers.com
This place from the 1920s offers large rooms with grand bathrooms.

Luxe City Center $$$
Luxury   **Map** 10 C5
1020 S Figueroa St, 90015
Tel *(213) 748-1291*
W luxecitycenter.com
All rooms have comfortable beds with lounge areas. Across the street from the shopping district.

Millennium Biltmore $$$
Luxury   **Map** 11 D4
506 S Grand Ave, 90071
Tel *(213) 624-1011*
W thebiltmore.com
This LA icon with an ornate, Spanish-style lobby, dates to 1923. Small, nicely furnished rooms.

Omni Los Angeles Hotel **$$$**
Luxury **Map** 11 D5
51 S Olive St, 90012
Tel *(213) 617-3300*
W omnihotels.com
Mid-sized hotel ideally situated
for the main shopping and
entertainment areas.

The Ritz-Carlton **$$$**
Luxury **Map** 10 C5
900 W Olympic Blvd, 90015
Tel *213-743-8800*
W ritzcarlton.com
Plush hotel with fine city views
from all rooms. Lounge, bar, and
rooftop pool on the 26th floor.

Glendale

Hilton Los Angeles North/
Glendale **$$**
Budget **Road map** inset A
100 W Glenoaks Blvd, 91202
Tel *(818) 956-5466*
W hiltonlosangelesglendale.com
A well located, comfortable hotel,
with a pool, spa, and full-service
fitness center.

Hermosa Beach

The Beach House **$$$**
Boutique **Road map** inset A
1300 The Strand, 90254
Tel *310-374-3001*
W beach-house.com
In a fun neighborhood, this
oceanfront hideaway features
luxurious studio suites.

Hollywood

Hollywood Hotel **$$**
Budget **Map** 9 F1
1160 N Vermont Ave, 90029
Tel *(323) 315-1800*
W hollywoodhotel.net
Perfect for family, leisure, and
business travelers, this option has
complete conference facilities
and a pool set in gardens.

Hollywood Orchid Suites **$$**
Budget **Map** 2 B4
1753 Orchid Ave, 90028
Tel *(323) 874-9678*
W orchidsuites.com
Directly behind the famed TCL
Chinese Theatre, this converted
apartment-hotel has tidy rooms.

The Hollywood Roosevelt
Hotel **$$$**
Historic **Map** 2 B4
7000 Hollywood Blvd, 90028
Tel *(323) 856-1970*
W thehollywoodroosevelt.com
A refurbished classic, The Hollywood
Roosevelt features cabana-style
suites surrounding a courtyard pool.
It has played host to countless
Hollywood icons.

The extensive and popular Hyatt Regency Longbeach

Loews Hollywood Hotel **$$$**
Luxury **Map** 2 B4
1755 N Highland Ave, 90028
Tel *(323) 856-1200*
W loewshotels.com
Spacious, well-appointed rooms
with an array of amenities feature
here, as well as rooftop pool.

Magic Castle Hotel **$$$**
Historic **Map** 2 B4
7025 Franklin Ave, 90028
Tel *(323) 851-0800*
W magiccastlehotel.com
Renowned for its whimsical,
castle-like design. Offers suites
and studios with full kitchens.

The Standard Hotel **$$$**
Boutique **Map** 2 B4
8300 Sunset Blvd, 90069
Tel *(323) 650-9090*
W standardhotels.com/hollywood
A hip Sunset Strip hotel with
cutting-edge style.

W Hollywood **$$$**
Luxury **Map** 2 B4
6250 Hollywood Blvd, 90028
Tel *(323) 798-1300*
W whotels.com
Sleek, ultra-modern rooms.
Rooftop pool and bar, luxury spa.

Long Beach

Hotel Queen Mary **$**
Historic **Road map** inset A
1126 Queen's Hwy, 90802
Tel *(877) 342-0738*
W queenmary.com
Restored historic cruise liner
with all modern comforts. Enjoy
the fascinating ship tours.

Inn of Long Beach **$**
Budget **Road map** inset A
185 Atlantic Ave, 90802
Tel *(562) 435-3791*
W innoflongbeach.com
Pleasant motel at a convenient
downtown location, close to the
beach and family-friendly sights.

Hyatt Regency **$$**
Budget **Road map** inset A
200 S Pine Ave, 90802
Tel *(562) 491-1234*
W longbeach.hyatt.com
Chain option popular with
business travelers at a fantastic
harborside location. Recreational
facilities include a heated outdoor pool and full-service gym.

Renaissance **$$**
Budget **Road map** inset A
111 E Ocean Blvd, 90802
Tel *(562) 437-5900*
W renaissancelongbeach.com
Large property close to harbor
attractions. Well-appointed rooms.

Malibu

Malibu Beach Inn **$$$**
Luxury **Road map** inset A
22878 Pacific Coast Hwy, 90265
Tel *310-651-7777*
W malibubeachinn.com
Intimate hotel overlooking the
Pacific boasting its very own
beach. Every room has sea views.

Villa Graziadio
Exectuive Center **$$$**
Luxury **Road map** inset A
*Pepperdine University, 24255 Pacific
Coast Hwy, 90265*
Tel *310-506-1100*
W villagraziadio.com
This small hotel on the Pepper-
dine University campus offers
exquisite ocean views, attentive
staff, and a convenient location.

Marina del Rey

Foghorn Harbor Inn **$$**
Budget **Road map** inset A
4140 Via Marina, 90292
Tel *310-823-4626*
W foghornhotel.com
This modest hotel near the beach
provides good value for its
location. Comfortably appointed
rooms with patios or balconies.

For more information on types of hotels *see pages 524–7*

Monrovia

Doubletree Hilton $$
Budget   **Road map** inset A
924 W Huntington Dr, 91016
Tel *(626) 357-1900*
ⓦ doubletree.com
Chain option with spacious,
nicely appointed rooms.

Palos Verdes

Terranea Resort $$$
Luxury   **Road map** inset A
100 Terranea Way Dr, 90275
Tel *310-265-2800*
ⓦ terranea.com
Plush resort with a golf course,
pools, and hiking trails. Choose
from a bungalow, *casita*, or suite.

Pasadena

Comfort Inn $
Budget   **Road map** inset A
2300 W Colorado Blvd, 90041
Tel *(323) 256-1199*
ⓦ choicehotels.com
No-frills rooms set in scenic
surroundings. Good option for
families on a budget.

Bissell House $$
B&B   **Road map** inset A
201 Orange Grove Ave, 91030
Tel *(626) 441-3535*
ⓦ bissellhouse.com
Individually decorated rooms
with period furnishings.

Hilton Pasadena $$
Budget   **Road map** inset A
168 South Los Robles Ave, 91101
Tel *(626) 577-1000*
ⓦ hilton.com
Business-friendly option with
comfortably furnished rooms.

Sheraton Pasadena $$
Budget   **Road map** inset A
303 E Cordova St, 91101
Tel *(626) 449-4000*
ⓦ sheratonpasadena.com
Central spot connected to the
Convention Center and offering
executive-friendly features, such
as a 24-hour business center.

The Westin Pasadena $$
Budget   **Road map** inset A
191 N Los Robles Ave, 91101
Tel *626-792-2727*
ⓦ starwoodhotels.com
Rooftop pool, restaurant, and bar
at this upscale destination.

The Langham Hotel $$$
Luxury   **Road map** inset A
1401 S Oak Knoll Ave, 91106
Tel *(626) 568-3900*
ⓦ pasadena.langhamhotels.com
In a historic building at a secluded
location away from the city center,
this hotel offers exemplary service.

Redondo Beach

Portofino Hotel & Marina $$$
Luxury   **Road map** inset A
260 Portofino Way, 92077
Tel *(800) 468-4292*
ⓦ hotelportofino.com
Oceanfront property with floor-
to-ceiling windows offering
views of sailboats and sunsets.

Santa Monica

Best Western Gateway Hotel $$
Budget   **Road map** inset A
1920 Santa Monica Blvd, 90404
Tel *310-829-9100*
ⓦ gatewayhotel.com
Basic yet comfortable rooms at
this budget option. Multilingual
staff and beach shuttle service.

Doubletree Suites $$$
Luxury   **Road map** inset A
1707 4th St, 90401
Tel *310-395-3332*
ⓦ doubletree.com
Large property near the beach,
with spacious two-room suites.

Fairmont Miramar
Hotel & Bungalows $$$
Luxury   **Road map** inset A
101 Wilshire Blvd, 90401
Tel *310-576-7777*
ⓦ fairmont.com/santamonica
This cliffside property is frequented
by the rich and famous. Sweeping ocean views.

Georgian Hotel $$$
Historic   **Road map** inset A
1415 Ocean Ave, 90401
Tel *310-395-9945*
ⓦ georgianhotel.com
High-end comfort at this well-
preserved historic property.

Hotel California $$$
Luxury   **Road map** inset A
1670 Ocean Ave, 90401
Tel *310-393-2363*
ⓦ hotelca.com
Charming find with plenty of
beach activities and ocean views.

Loews Santa Monica
Beach Hotel $$$
Luxury   **Road map** inset A
1700 Ocean Ave, 90401
Tel *310-458-6700*
ⓦ santamonicaloewshotel.com
Resort-style property offering
sumptuously appointed rooms.

Palihouse $$$
Boutique   **Road map** inset A
1001 3rd St, 90403
Tel *310-394-1279*
ⓦ palihousesantamonica.com
Unwind in style at this hip, trendy
destination. Welcoming staff.

Shutters on the Beach $$$
Boutique   **Road map** inset A
1 Pico Blvd, 90405
Tel *310-458-0030*
ⓦ shuttersonthebeach.com
This deluxe hotel on the beach,
popular with celebrities, has
spacious rooms with spectacular
ocean views. There is a poolside
lounge area and beachside spa.

Torrance

Courtyard by Marriott $$
Budget   **Road map** inset A
2633 Sepulveda Blvd, 90505
Tel *310-533-8000*
At this stylish hotel rooms have
luxury bedding and basic
amenities, including a pool.

Universal City

The Beverly Garland $$
Boutique   **Road map** inset A
4222 Vineland Ave, 91602
Tel *(818) 980-8000*
Quiet, family-friendly option
situated near Universal Studios.

Hilton $$$
Luxury   **Road map** inset A
555 Universal Hollywood Dr, 91608
Tel *(818) 506-2500*
ⓦ hilton.com
A huge family-friendly option
offering a range of rooms with
attractive decor and modern
amenities. The hotel is located
opposite Universal City Walk.

The grand historic exterior of The Langham, Pasadena

For key to prices *see page 528*

The elegant yet minamilist design at Andaz, West Hollywood

Sheraton Universal $$$
Historic   Road map inset A
333 Universal Hollywood Dr, 91608
Tel *(866) 716-8130*
🆆 sheratonuniversal.com
A Universal City landmark
since 1969, residing on the
backlot of Universal Studios.
Shuttle service to CityWalk.

Van Nuys

Holiday Inn Express $
Budget   Road map inset A
8244 Orion Ave, 91406
Tel *(818) 989-5010*
🆆 hiexpress.com
Convenient choice, and a short
drive from Universal Studios.
Spacious rooms with work areas.

Venice

The Cadillac Hotel $$
Boutique   Road map inset A
8 Dudley Ave, 90291
Tel *310-399-8876*
🆆 thecadillachotel.com
Hip, historic property located
directly on the famed Venice
Beach boardwalk. Rooms have
lovely ocean views.

DK Choice

Hotel Erwin $$$
Boutique   Road map inset A
1697 Pacific Ave, 90291
Tel *310-452-1111*
🆆 hotelerwin.com
A charming destination in
colorful Venice, Hotel Erwin
attracts a wide variety of
travelers. The trendy rooms are
filled with eclectic art and
modern features such as luxury
beds, HD TVs, and desks with
ergonomic chairs. Enjoy views
of the ocean and boardwalk
from private balconies and the
open-air rooftop bar.

The Inn at Venice Beach $$$
B&B   Road map inset A
327 Washington Blvd, 90291
Tel *310-821-2557*
🆆 innatvenicebeach.com
Pleasant Inn with bright, cheerful
rooms. Next to the yacht club.

Su Casa $$$
B&B   Road map inset A
431 Ocean Front Walk, 90291
Tel *310-452-9700*
🆆 sucasavenice.com
Casual B&B with a superb beach
location on the boardwalk. Rooms
have HD TVs and kitchenettes.

The Venice Beach House $$$
B&B   Road map inset A
15 30th Ave, 90291
Tel *310-823-1966*
🆆 venicebeachhouse.com
Secluded, intimate spot set
on well-manicured grounds.
Close to the beach.

West Hollywood

Best Western Sunset Plaza $$
Budget   Map 1 A5
8400 Sunset Blvd, 90069
Tel *(323) 654-0750*
🆆 sunsetplazahotel.com
Well-appointed chain option
with attractive rooms, plenty of
amenities, and a central location.

DK Choice

Andaz West Hollywood $$$
Boutique   Map 1 A5
8401 Sunset Blvd, 90069
Tel *(323) 656-1234*
🆆 andaz.hyatt.com
Infused with an ambience of
simple luxury, the Andaz offers
high-spec rooms that are stylish
and comfortable. Impeccable
service, and an ideal location with
easy access to some of LA's finest
shops, restaurants, and clubs.

Chateau Marmont $$$
Luxury   Map 1 B5
8221 Sunset Blvd, 90046
Tel *(323) 656-1010*
🆆 chateaumarmont.com
Celebrity hideaway with an
attractive collection of rooms,
suites, and private cottages.
Top-notch service.

Mondrian Hotel $$$
Luxury   Map 1 A5
8440 Sunset Blvd, 90069
Tel *(323) 650-8999*
🆆 mondrianhotel.com
Offering spacious rooms with full
kitchens and work spaces, this is
one of the Strip's hottest spots.

Sunset Tower Hotel $$$
Historic   Map 1 A5
8358 Sunset Blvd, 90069
Tel *(323) 654-7100*
🆆 sunsettowerhotel.com
Art Deco property with a rich
history. Elegant, well-equipped
rooms and gorgeous suites.

Westwood

Royal Palace Westwood Hotel $
Budget   Map 4 A4
1052 Tiverton Ave, 90024
Tel *310-208 6677*
🆆 royalpalacewestwood.com
Inexpensive, no-frills option in
the heart of Westwood Village.

Hilgard House Hotel $$
Boutique   Map 4 A4
927 Hilgard Ave, 90024
Tel *(910) 208-3945*
🆆 hilgardhouse.com
A cozy budget option near the
UCLA campus and the Hammer
Museum *(see p102)*.

Palomar $$$
Boutique   Map 4 B4
10740 Wilshire Blvd, 90024
Tel *310-475-8711*
🆆 hotelpalomar-lawestwood.com
Sizable rooms furnished with
upscale amenities. Conveniently
located near local attractions.

Le Parc Suites $$$
Boutique   Map 4 A4
733 N West Knoll Ave, 90069
Tel *310-855-8888*
🆆 leparcsuites.com
Stylish property in a residential
part of town. Lovely pool, full-
service spa, and fitness center.

W Los Angeles Westwood $$$
Boutique   Map 4 A4
930 Hilgard Ave, 90024
Tel *310-208-8765*
🆆 wlosangeles.com
Sleek, stylish rooms, state-of-the-
art spa, two outdoor pools, and
high-profile lounge and bar areas.

For more information on types of hotels *see pages 524–7*

The breakfast area at the Courtyard by Marriott business hotel, Bakersfield

South Central California

BAKERSFIELD: Courtyard by Marriott $
Budget **Road map** C5
3601 Marriott Dr, 93308
Tel *(661) 324-6660*
W marriott.com
Clean, modern hotel situated near the local airport. Good option for business travelers.

CAMBRIA: Cambria Pines Lodge $$
B&B **Road map** B5
2905 Burton Dr, 93428
Tel *(800) 966-6490*
W cambriapineslodge.com
Quaint lodge and cottages surrounded by expansive gardens. Simple, tasteful rooms with brightly painted walls.

CAMBRIA: Pelican Inn & Suites $$
B&B **Road map** B5
6316 Moonstone Beach Dr, 93428
Tel *(888) 454-4222*
W pelicansuites.com
Bright, cheerful inn with rooms featuring oceanfront balconies.

MONTECITO: Montecito Inn $$$
Historic **Road map** C5
1295 Coast Village Rd, 93108
Tel *(805) 969-7854*
W montecitoinn.com
Comfortable Mediterranean-style option with luxurious features. Built in 1928 by Charlie Chaplin.

MONTECITO: San Ysidro Ranch $$$
Luxury **Road map** C5
900 San Ysidro Ln, 93108
Tel *(805) 565-1700*
W sanysidroranch.com
Stunning spot in the mountains, perfect for a peaceful getaway.

MORRO BAY: Embarcadero Inn $$
B&B **Road map** B5
456 Embarcadero Blvd, 93442
Tel *(888) 223-5777*
W embarcaderoinn.com
Friendly inn on the harbor; rooms have balconies and fireplaces.

MORRO BAY: Inn at Morro Bay $$
B&B **Road map** B5
60 State Park Rd, 93442
Tel *(800) 321-9566*
W innatmorrobay.com
Charming French country-style inn offering contemporary rooms. The patio also has a hot tub.

OJAI: Ojai Valley Inn & Spa $$$
Luxury **Road map** C5
905 Country Club Rd, 93023
Tel *(800) 422-6524*
W ojairesort.com
Rambling white adobe buildings with red-tile roofs, a lavish spa, and an award-winning golf course.

PASO ROBLES: Paso Robles Inn $
Budget **Road map** B5
1103 Spring St, 93446
Tel *(805) 238-2660*
W pasoroblesinn.com
A popular Mission destination set in lush grounds that feature a creek and natural hot springs.

PASO ROBLES: Hotel Cheval $$$
Luxury **Road map** B5
1021 Pine St, 93446
Tel *(866) 522-6999*
W hotelcheval.com
Modern rooms with fireplaces. Convenient location close to many acclaimed wineries.

SAN LUIS OBISPO: Garden Street Inn $$
B&B **Road map** B5
1212 Garden St, 93401
Tel *(800) 488-2045*
W gardenstreetinn.com
Housed in a restored 1860 Victorian building. Rooms are furnished with antiques; some have fireplaces and Jacuzzis.

SAN LUIS OBISPO: Madonna Inn $$$
B&B **Road map** B5
100 Madonna Rd, 93405
Tel *(805) 543-3000*
W madonnainn.com
Amusement park-like facade, and individually themed rooms.

SANTA BARBARA: Hotel Santa Barbara $$
Historic **Road map** C5
533 State St, 93101
Tel *(805) 957-9300*
W hotelsantabarbara.com
Charming 1926 property with tidy, well-equipped rooms.

SANTA BARBARA: Inn by the Harbor $$
B&B **Road map** C5
433 W Montecito St, 93101
Tel *(800) 626-1986*
W innbytheharbor.com
Ideal for families, located close to the beach. Rooms feature French country decor and pine furniture.

DK Choice

SANTA BARBARA: The Biltmore $$$
Luxury **Road map** C5
1260 Channel Dr, 93108
Tel *(805) 969-2261*
W fourseasons.com
This elegant Spanish Colonial-style property is set on sprawling grounds, across a beach and away from town. The sumptuous rooms and secluded cottages are equipped with all modern amenities. Exquisite seaside luxury and great attention to detail.

SANTA BARBARA: Simpson House Inn $$$
B&B **Road map** C5
121 E Arrellaga St, 93101
Tel *(800) 676-1280*
W simpsonhouseinn.com
Delightful, award-winning inn in a gorgeous garden setting.

SANTA PAULA: Santa Paula Inn $
B&B **Road map** C5
111 N 8th St, 93060
Tel *(805) 933-0011*
W santapaulainn.com
Quaint property in a pastoral setting amid lemon and avocado groves. Snug rooms with Jacuzzis.

SIMI VALLEY: Best Western Plus Posada Royale $
Budget **Road map** C5
1775 Madera Rd, 93065
Tel *(805) 584-6300*
W posadaroyale.com
Comfortable option near the Ronald Reagan Presidential Library.

SOLVANG: Hadsten House $$
B&B **Road map** C5
1450 Mission Dr, 93463
Tel *(800) 457-5373*
W hadstenhouse.com
Pleasant hotel for exploring the area's wineries and restaurants.

SOLVANG: Alisal Guest Ranch $$$
Luxury **Road map** C5
1054 Alisal Rd, 93463
Tel *(805) 688-6411*
W alisal.com
Plush ranch offering rooms with wood-burning fireplaces and floor-to-ceiling windows.

Orange County

ANAHEIM: Anaheim Desert Inn & Suites $
Budget   Road map D6
1600 S Harbor Blvd, 92802
Tel *714-772-5050*
🆆 anaheimdesertinn.com
Family- and business-friendly option located across Disneyland's main entrance.

ANAHEIM: Candy Cane Inn $$
Budget   Road map D6
1747 S. Harbor Blvd, 92802
Tel *(800) 345-7057*
🆆 candycaneinn.net
A convenient base for the park with free shuttle service.

ANAHEIM: Disney's Grand Californian Hotel® and Spa $$$
Luxury   Road map D6
1600 S Disneyland Dr, 92802
Tel *714-635-2300*
🆆 disneyland.disney.go.com
Magnificent spot inside Disney's California Adventure Park. Features pools, a spa, and a kids' club.

ANAHEIM: Disney's Paradise Pier® Hotel $$$
Boutique   Road map D6
1717 S Disneyland Dr, 92802
Tel *714-999-0990*
🆆 disneyland.disney.go.com
A bright, California beach-themed hotel in the Disneyland Park.

AVALON: Hotel Vista del Mar $$
Boutique   Road map C6
417 Crescent Ave, 90704
Tel *(800) 601-3836*
🆆 hotel-vistadelmar.com
Many rooms have ocean views at this cozy spot in a garden courtyard.

COSTA MESA: Ayres Hotel & Suites $$
Boutique   Road map D6
325 Bristol St, 92626
Tel *(800) 322-9992*
🆆 ayreshotels.com
The charming rooms are decorated in French country-style.

COSTA MESA: Residence Inn $$
Budget   Road map D6
881 W Baker St, 92626
Tel *714-241-8800*
🆆 marriott.com
Rooms have kitchenettes and separate living areas.

DANA POINT: Blue Lantern Inn $$
B&B   Road map D6
34343 St of the Blue Lantern, 92629
Tel *(949) 661-1304*
🆆 bluelanterninn.com
Romantic spot overlooking the harbor. Luxurious rooms have

fireplaces. Suites have private decks and spectacular views.

HUNTINGTON BEACH: Shorebreak Hotel $$$
Boutique   Road map D6
500 Pacific Coast Hwy, 92648
Tel *(877) 212-8597*
🆆 shorebreakhotel.com
This hotel offers comfortable rooms plus many extras, including a complimentary wine hour in the evening.

DK Choice

LAGUNA BEACH: Surf & Sand Resort $$$
Resort   Road map D6
1555 S Coast Hwy, 92651
Tel *(949) 494-2897*
🆆 surfandsandresort.com
A top-rated California resort located on prime beachfront property. Each welcoming guest room and suite features contemporary design, luxury fittings, and views of the ocean. Excellent facilities including a spa, pools, and restaurant make this a popular getaway destination.

NEWPORT BEACH: Fairmont $$$
Luxury   Road map D6
4500 MacArthur Blvd, 92660
Tel *(949) 476-2001*
🆆 fairmont.com
Large, well-appointed rooms and friendly service. European elegance with Californian flair.

San Diego County

CARLSBAD: Pelican Cove Inn $
B&B   Road map D6
320 Walnut Ave, 92008
Tel *(760) 434-5995*
🆆 pelican-cove.com
Snug rooms with fireplaces. Excellent breakfast spread.

CARLSBAD: Beach Terrace Inn $$$
B&B   Road map D6
2775 Ocean St, 92008
Tel *(800) 433-5415*
🆆 beachterraceinn.com
Comfortable beach resort. Suites feature kitchenettes and fireplaces; some have ocean views.

CORONADO: Hotel Del Coronado $$$
Historic   Road map D6
1500 Orange Ave, 92118
Tel *(619) 435-6611*
🆆 hoteldel.com
Iconic Victorian resort located on the beach. Modern rooms and cottages with lots of amenities.

DEL MAR: Clarion Del Mar Inn $$
Budget   Road map D6
720 Camino Del Mar, 92014
Tel *(858) 755-9765*
🆆 delmarinn.com
Quaint property set amid English-style gardens. Courteous staff.

DEL MAR: L'Auberge Del Mar $$$
Luxury   Road map D6
1540 Camino Del Mar, 92014
Tel *(858) 259-1515*
🆆 laubergedelmar.com
Elegant resort with spacious, well-furnished rooms, and a plush spa.

LA JOLLA: The Bed and Breakfast Inn at La Jolla $$
B&B   Road map D6
7753 Draper Ave, 92037
Tel *(858) 456-2066*
🆆 innlajolla.com
Modern comfort with old-world charm. Individually decorated rooms with ocean views.

LA JOLLA: Estancia La Jolla $$$
Luxury   Road map D6
9700 N Torrey Pines Rd, 92037
Tel *(858) 454-0771*
🆆 lavalencia.com
Ranch-style architecture set within lush gardens. Saltwater pool and an award-winning spa.

Fairmont, Newport Beach luxury hotel

For more information on types of hotels *see pages 524–7*

Outdoor pool overlooking the golf course at Lodge at Torrey Pines, La Jolla

LA JOLLA: The Lodge at Torrey Pines $$$
Resort Road map D6
11480 N Torrey Pines Rd, 92037
Tel (858) 453-4420
w lodgetorreypines.com
Handsome property overlooking the famous Torrey Pines golf course. Award-winning restaurant.

JULIAN: Orchard Hill Country Inn $$
B&B Road map D6
2502 Washington St, 92036
Tel (760) 765-1700
w orchardhill.com
This craftsman-style lodge, set in peaceful grounds, features 22 beautiful and cozy rooms.

RANCHO SANTA FE: Rancho Valencia $$$
Resort Road map D6
5921 Valencia Circle, 92067
Tel (858) 756-1123
w ranchovalencia.com
Peaceful and secluded resort with spacious hacienda-style rooms.

SAN DIEGO: Keating House $
Historic Road map D6
2331 2nd Ave, 92101
Tel (619) 239-8585
w keatinghouse.com
Elegant Victorian house with a lovely parlor, surrounded by lush grounds. Spacious rooms.

SAN DIEGO: Old Town Inn $
Budget Road map D6
4444 Pacific Hwy, 92110
Tel (619) 260-8024
w oldtown-inn.com
Modest, family-owned inn with a variety of rooms, including large apartments with kitchenettes.

SAN DIEGO: Sheraton Mission Valley Hotel $
Budget Road map D6
1433 Camino Del Rio S, 92108
Tel (619) 260-0111
w sheratonmissionvalley.com
A comfortable and convenient establishment near the beaches.

SAN DIEGO: Bahia Hotel $$
Resort Road map D6
998 W Mission Bay Dr, 92109
Tel (858) 488-0551
w bahiahotel.com
Family-friendly resort on a beach peninsula in the heart of Mission Bay. Modern amenities.

SAN DIEGO: Catamaran $$
Resort Road map D6
3999 Mission Blvd, 92109
Tel (858) 488-1081
w catamaranresort.com
Casual, elegant resort adjacent to Mission Bay and Pacific shoreline. Relax in the tropical outdoor pool.

SAN DIEGO: Doubletree by Hilton Golf Resort $$
Budget Road map D6
14455 Penasquitos Dr, 92129
Tel (858) 672-9100
w doubletree.com
Contemporary rooms some with either a patio or balcony. Golf course, tennis courts, and pool.

SAN DIEGO: Paradise Point $$
Luxury Road map D6
1404 Vacation Rd, 92109
Tel (858) 274-4630
w paradisepoint.com
Bungalow-style rooms are scattered across a 44-acre (18-ha) private island. Award-winning spa.

SAN DIEGO: The Beach Cottages $$$
Historic Road map D6
4255 Ocean Blvd, 92109
Tel (858) 483-7440
w beachcottages.com
Family-run place with a range of lodgings, from basic rooms to cottages with full kitchens.

SAN DIEGO: Hotel Solamar $$$
Boutique Road map D6
435 6th Ave, 92101
Tel (619) 819-9500
w hotelsolamar.com
Stylish hotel with chic furnishings and sumptuous amenities. Rooftop pool and bar.

SAN DIEGO: San Diego Marriott Marquis & Marina $$$
Luxury Road map D6
333 West Harbor Dr, 92101
Tel (619) 234-1500
w marriott.com
Large, business-friendly property with a nautical theme. Rooms offer lovely views of downtown.

DK Choice

SAN DIEGO: The US Grant $$$
Historic Road map D6
326 Broadway, 92101
Tel (619) 232-3121
w usgrant.net
A landmark since 1910, this historic property located in the heart of downtown is a prime spot for visiting the city's major attractions. Rooms have a period feel, yet are equipped with modern, luxurious amenities. The lobby and public areas are regal and opulent. Opt for in-room dining or enjoy a delicious meal in the excellent restaurant.

The Inland Empire and Low Desert

BIG BEAR LAKE: Northwoods Resort $$$
Luxury Road map D5
40650 Village Dr, 92315
Tel (909) 866-3121
w northwoodsresort.com
The only full-service hotel at Big Bear Lake. Ideal for families.

BORREGO SPRINGS: Borrego Springs Resort $$
Luxury Road map D6
1112 Tilting T Dr, 92004
Tel (760) 767-5700
w borregospringsresort.com
Spacious rooms and outstanding service. A prime destination with three nine-hole golf courses, a spa, and tennis courts.

DESERT HOT SPRINGS: Two Bunch Palms $$
Boutique Road map D6
67425 Two Bunch Palms Trail, 92240
Tel (760) 329-8791
w twobunchpalms.com
This adults-only oasis is renowned for its rejuvenating mineral pools and spa treatments.

IDYLLWILD: Quiet Creek Inn $
B&B Road map D6
26345 Delano Dr, 92549
Tel (951) 468-4208
w quietcreekinn.com
Comfortable cabins with fireplaces in a secluded forest setting. Hiking trails nearby.

For key to prices see page 528

INDIAN WELLS: Indian Wells Resort Hotel $
Historic   Road map D6
76–661 Hwy 111, 92210
Tel *(800) 248-3220*
w indianwellsresort.com
Luxurious desert resort on a golf course. Opulent rooms.

INDIO: Best Western Date Tree Hotel $
Budget   Road map D6
81909 Indio Blvd, 92201
Tel *(760) 347-3421*
w datetree.com
Quiet, well-run hotel with tastefully decorated rooms.

PALM DESERT: JW Marriott Desert Springs Resort & Spa $$
Luxury   Road map D6
74855 Country Club Dr, 92260
Tel *(760) 341-2211*
w desertspringsresort.com
Spectacular hotel with a lake in its lobby. Lavishly appointed rooms with gorgeous views.

DK Choice

PALM SPRINGS: Ace Hotel & Swim Club $
Boutique   Road map D6
701 E Palm Canyon Dr, 92264
Tel *(760) 325-9900*
w acehotel.com/palmsprings
The chic vibe of this trendy boutique hotel makes it a popular hipster hangout. Rooms are decorated with contemporary Americana and furnished with comfortable beds and amenities. Take a dip in the outdoor pool or enjoy a massage in a Mongolian yurt.

PALM SPRINGS: Colt's Lodge $
Budget   Road map D6
1586 E Palm Canyon Dr, 92264
Tel *(760) 323-2231*
w coltslodgeps.com
Peaceful hideaway with lovely gardens and an elegant pool.

PALM SPRINGS: Desert Riviera $
Budget   Road map D6
610 E Palm Canyon Dr, 92264
Tel *(760) 327-5314*
w desertrivierahotel.com
Vintage building with manicured gardens and splendid mountain views. Friendly staff.

PALM SPRINGS: Orbit In $$
Boutique   Road map D6
562 West Arenas Rd, 92262
Tel *(760) 323-3585*
w orbitin.com
Restored mid-century property with in-room massage facilities. Spectacular views.

PALM SPRINGS: The Saguaro Palm Springs $$
Boutique   Road map D6
1800 E Palm Canyon Dr, 92264
Tel *(760) 323-1711*
w thesaguaro.com
Charming desert oasis with stylish, colorful rooms, a garden courtyard, and mountain views.

PALM SPRINGS: Colony Palms Hotel $$$
Luxury   Road map D6
572 North Indian Canyon Dr, 92262
Tel *(800) 557-2187*
w colonypalmshotel.com
Sophisticated destination in the heart of downtown. Features luxurious in-room amenities, a croquet lawn, and cabanas.

PALM SPRINGS: Hilton Palm Springs $$$
Luxury   Road map D6
400 E Tahquitz Canyon Dr, 92262
Tel *(760) 320-6868*
w hiltonpalmsprings.com
Spacious rooms situated around a large pool. Popular poolside lounge and restaurant.

RIVERSIDE: Mission Inn $$
Historic   Road map D6
3649 Mission Inn Ave, 92501
Tel *(951) 784-0300*
w missioninn.com
Iconic property dating back to 1888. Exquisite rooms with Spanish Colonial charm.

The Mojave Desert

BARSTOW: Ramada Inn $
Budget   Road map D5
1511 E Main St, 92311
Tel *(760) 256-5673*
w ramada.com
Mission-style motor inn. Clean and comfortable rooms.

The wood beamed lounge at Inn at Furnace Creek, Death Valley

DEATH VALLEY: Amargosa Opera House and Hotel $
Historic   Road map D4
Death Valley Junction, 92328
Tel *(760) 852-4441*
w amargosa-opera-house.com
Quirky place with a cabaret theater. Snug but eccentric rooms without TV or phone.

DEATH VALLEY: Stovepipe Wells Village $
Budget   Road map D4
Hwy 190, 92328
Tel *(760) 786-2387*
w escapetodeathvalley.com
Rustic retreat in a stunning desert landscape. Contemporary guest rooms available in various sizes. Perfect for hiking the dunes.

DK Choice

DEATH VALLEY: The Inn at Furnace Creek $$$
Resort   Road map D4
Hwy 190, 92328
Tel *(760) 786-2345*
w furnacecreekresort.com
A historic landmark, this gorgeous desert oasis offers elegant rooms, services and amenities on par with top luxury resorts. Recreation activities on site include a spring-fed pool, horseback riding, yoga classes, golf, and tennis. Enjoy lovely sunset views from quaint patios and stroll through the gardens.

LAKE HAVASU: Hidden Palms Resort Condominiums $
Budget   Road map E5
2100 Swanson Ave, 86403
Tel *(928) 855-7144*
w hiddenpalms.com
Spacious, one-bedroom suites near the lake featuring separate dining areas and kitchenettes.

LAKE HAVASU: The Nautical Beachfront Resort $
Budget   Road map E5
1000 McCulloch Blvd, 86403
Tel *(928) 855-2141*
w nauticalinn.com
Lakefront property with a private beach, water activities, and large rooms with patios. Suites have full kitchens and boat docks.

MOJAVE: Best Western Plus Desert Winds $
Budget   Road map D5
16200 Sierra Hwy Mojave, 93501
Tel *(661) 824-3601*
w bestwestern.com
Clean and comfortable rooms at this popular chain hotel. Friendly staff. Outdoor pool on site and hiking trails nearby.

For more information on types of hotels *see pages 524–7*

San Francisco

Downtown

Cornell Hotel de France $
B&B   **Map** 5 B4
715 Bush St, 94108
Tel *(415) 421-3154*
W cornellhotel.com
A family-run, French country-style
hotel with snug rooms.

The Donatello $
Budget   **Map** 5 B5
501 Post St, 94102
Tel *(415) 441-7100*
W shellhospitality.com
Spacious rooms with modern
amenities and a fitness center.

The Donatello, located in Downtown, San Francisco

Golden Gate Hotel $
Budget   **Map** 5 B4
775 Bush St, 94108
Tel *(415) 392-3702*
W goldengatehotel.com
Quaint Edwardian-style inn.
Rooms have claw-foot tubs
and antiques. Dog friendly.

**Hostelling International San
Francisco Downtown** $
Budget   **Map** 5 B5
312 Mason St, 94102
Tel *(800) 909-4776*
W sfhostels.org
A variety of private and shared
rooms with kitchen facilities, daily
maid service, and free Wi-Fi.

Hotel Bijou $
Budget   **Map** 5 B5
111 Mason St, 94102
Tel *(415) 771-1200*
W hotelbijou.com
A quirky gem with decor
themed around San Francisco's
cinematic history.

Hotel Carlton $
Budget   **Map** 5 B4
1075 Sutter St, 94109
Tel *(415) 673-0242*
W jdvhotels.com
Classic European-style hotel with
colorful, well-furnished rooms.

Hotel des Arts $
Budget   **Map** 5 B4
447 Bush St, 94108
Tel *(415) 956-3232*
W sfhoteldesarts.com
The hip rooms are individually
decorated by different artists.
Includes breakfast.

San Remo Hotel $
Budget   **Map** 5 B5
2237 Mason St, 94133
Tel *(415) 776-8688*
W sanremohotel.com
Small, intimate and neatly kept
rooms with shared bathrooms.
Excellent rooftop penthouse.

Chancellor Hotel $$
Budget   **Map** 5 B4
433 Powell St, 94102
Tel *(415) 362-2004*
W chancellorhotel.com
This classic hotel has well-
maintained rooms with small
bathrooms. Café-bar on site.

Courtyard by Marriott $$
Budget   **Map** 6 D5
299 2nd St, 94105
Tel *(800) 321-2211*
W marriott.com
Rooms with work stations and
several meeting venues on site.
Popular with business travelers.

Galleria Park Hotel $$
Luxury   **Map** 5 C4
191 Sutter St, 94104
Tel *(415) 781-3060*
W jdvhotels.com
Upscale modern rooms with
latest high-tech amenities.

Handlery Union Square Hotel $$
Budget   **Map** 5 B5
351 Geary St, 94102
Tel *(415) 781-7800*
W sf.handlery.com
Family-owned hotel with well-
furbished rooms and suites. Pool,
sauna, and restaurant-bar on site.

Hotel Adagio $$
Luxury   **Map** 5 B5
550 Geary St, 94102
Tel *(415) 775-5000*
W hoteladagiosf.com
Sizable, well-equipped rooms
with a warm, Mediterranean look.

Hotel Diva $$
Luxury   **Map** 5 B5
440 Geary St, 94102
Tel *(415) 885-0200*
W hoteldiva.com
Ultra-modern rooms with deluxe
furnishings. On-site café and a
24-hour fitness center. Games
for kids in the Little Divas suite.

Hotel Metropolis $$
Boutique   **Map** 5 B5
25 Mason St, 94102
Tel *(415) 775-4600*
W haiyi-hotels.com
Sleek, contemporary rooms
and family suites. Library and a
Southern-style restaurant on site.

Hotel Rex $$
Boutique   **Map** 5 B4
562 Sutter St, 94102
Tel *(415) 433-4434*
W jdvhotels.com
A welcoming place reminiscent
of the literary salons of the 1920s
and 30s. Enjoy live jazz on Friday
evenings in the Library Bar.

Mystic Hotel $$
Boutique   **Map** 5 C4
417 Stockton St, 94108
Tel *(415) 400-0500*
W mystichotel.com
Smart, sleek luxury in a renovated
hotel near Union Square.

Palace Hotel $$
Historic   **Map** 5 C5
2 New Montgomery St, 94105
Tel *(415) 512-1111*
W sfpalace.com
A Downtown landmark since 1909
(see p321). Famous stained-glass-
domed Garden Court restaurant.

Sir Francis Drake Hotel $$
Historic   **Map** 5 B4
450 Powell St, 94102
Tel *(415) 392-7755*
W sirfrancisdrake.com
This hotel has small rooms but
with a 1930s flair. Excellent dining
options on site. Pets allowed.

Villa Florence $$
Budget   **Map** 5 B5
225 Powell St, 94102
Tel *(415) 397-7700*
W villaflorence.com
Pretty European-style rooms
equipped with modern comforts.

For San Francisco map references *see San Francisco Street Finder maps pages 404–13*

Clift Hotel $$$
Historic　　　　　Map 5 B5
495 Geary St, 94102
Tel *(415) 775-4700*
W morganshotelgroup.com
A century-old Theater District
hostelry updated with flamboyant
Philippe Starck-designed decor.
Romantic bar-lounge.

**Four Seasons Hotel San
Francisco** $$$
Luxury　　　　　Map 5 C5
757 Market St, 94103
Tel *(415) 633-3000*
W fourseasons.com/sanfrancisco
Large rooms with sophisticated
decor and floor-to-ceiling windows.
Renowned for its service.

Grand Hyatt San Francisco $$$
Luxury　　　　　Map 5 C4
345 Stockton St, 94108
Tel *(415) 398-1234*
W grandsanfrancisco.hyatt.com
Hyatt's flagship property offers
luxurious rooms, suites, and
meeting venues. The restaurant
has legendary panoramic views.

Hotel Monaco $$$
Boutique　　　　Map 5 B5
501 Geary St, 94102
Tel *(415) 292-0100*
W monaco-sf.com
Excellent facilities including a spa
with sauna, and a 24-hour gym.

Hotel Vitale $$$
Luxury　　　　　Map 5 C5
8 Mission St, 94105
Tel *(888) 890-8688*
W jdvhotels.com
Large deluxe rooms are the
norm at this waterfront hotel.
Spa and hot tubs on the roof.

Hotel Zelos $$$
Boutique　　　　Map 5 C5
12 4th St, 94103
Tel *(415) 348-1111*
W hotelzelos.com
Brightly colored, comfortable
rooms in a historic 1905 building.
High-tech amenities.

**Loews Regency
San Francisco** $$$
Luxury　　　　　Map 5 C3
222 Sansome St, 94104
Tel *(415) 276-9888*
W loewshotels.com
Elegant rooms on the top 11 floors
of a 48-story building provide
breathtaking views of the city.

The Orchard Garden Hotel $$$
Boutique　　　　Map 5 C4
466 Bush St, 94108
Tel *(415) 399-9807*
W theorchardgardenhotel.com
Eco-chic in a modern residential-
style hostelry. Enjoy sustainable
seafood at the restaurant-bar.

St. Regis San Francisco $$$
Luxury　　　　　Map 6 D5
125 3rd St, 94105
Tel *(415) 284-4000*
W stregissanfrancisco.com
Minimalist, Asian-influenced decor
at this high-rise. Remède spa, infinity
pool, and acclaimed cuisine.

**San Francisco
Marriott Marquis** $$$
Luxury　　　　　Map 5 C5
55 4th St, 94103
Tel *(415) 896-1600*
W marriott.com
Caters to business travelers, but
great for tourists as well. Rooms
have excellent amenities.

Taj Campton Place $$$
Boutique　　　　Map 5 C4
340 Stockton St, 94108
Tel *(415) 781-5555*
W tajhotels.com
Indulge in ultimate luxury at this
hotel with sumptuous rooms and
a Michelin-starred restaurant.

W San Francisco $$$
Luxury　　　　　Map 6 D5
181 3rd St, 94103
Tel *(415) 777-5300*
W wsanfrancisco.com
Über-stylish, contemporary decor
with a trendy café-bar in the
lobby and a fantastic spa.

Chinatown and Nob Hill

Baldwin Hotel $
Budget　　　　　Map 5 C4
321 Grant Ave, 94108
Tel *(415) 781-2220*
W baldwinhotel.com
Vintage European-style hotel with
small but clean rooms, antique
tubs, and attentive service.

Hotel Triton $
Boutique　　　　Map 5 C4
342 Grant Ave, 94108
Tel *(415) 394-0500*
W hoteltriton.com
Hip, eclectic, Chagall-like decor
throughout this affordable inn.
A 24-hour fitness center.

The Mosser $
Budget　　　　　Map 5 C5
54 4th St, 94103
Tel *(415) 986-4400*
W themosser.com
Modern rooms with Victorian charm.
Some have shared bathrooms.

Executive Hotel Vintage Court $$
Boutique　　　　Map 5 C4
650 Bush St, 94108
Tel *(415) 781-5555*
W executivehotels.net
An elegant, European-style inn
with Wine Country-inspired decor.
Upscale, high-tech amenities.

Petite Auberge $$
Boutique　　　　Map 5 B4
863 Bush St, 94108
Tel *(415) 928-6000*
W jdvhotels.com
French Provincial-styled hotel
mixing luxurious and rustic
designs. Exceptional service.

The Fairmont San Francisco $$$
Luxury　　　　　Map 5 B4
950 Mason St, 94108
Tel *(415) 772-5000*
W fairmont.com
A century-old Nob Hill classic,
The Fairmont is opulent, service-
focused, and luxurious.

**Intercontinental
Mark Hopkins** $$$
Luxury　　　　　Map 5 B4
1 Nob Hill, 94108
Tel *(415) 392-3434*
W intercontinentalmarkhopkins.com
Business-class clientele as well as
tourists love this iconic hostelry.
Stunning views from every room.

Omni San Francisco $$$
Luxury　　　　　Map 5 C4
500 California St, 94104
Tel *(415) 677-9494*
W omnihotels.com
Understated elegance in a 1926
Florentine Renaissance building
adorned with Italian marble and
crystal chandeliers.

Palatial exterior of The Fairmont, Nob Hill, San Francisco

For more information on types of hotels *see page 524*

Elegant dining area, Hyatt at Fisherman's Wharf, San Francisco

The Ritz-Carlton, San Francisco $$$
Historic   Map 5 C4
600 Stockton St, 94108
Tel *(415) 296-7465*
Ⓦ ritzcarlton.com
A 1909 Neo-Classical landmark with marble floors and Oriental carpets. Superb service.

The Scarlet Huntington $$$
Historic   Map 5 B4
1075 California St, 94108
Tel *(415) 474-5400*
Ⓦ thescarlethotels.com
A landmark hotel since 1924, with small, lavishly furnished rooms and an excellent spa.

Stanford Court $$$
Luxury   Map 5 B4
905 California St, 94108
Tel *(415) 989-3500*
Ⓦ stanfordcourt.com
Plush, spacious rooms with city views. Fitness center and highly acclaimed restaurant on site.

Fisherman's Wharf and North Beach

Hostelling International San Francisco Fisherman's Wharf $
Budget   Map 4 E1
240 Fort Mason, 94109
Tel *(800) 909-4776*
Ⓦ sfhostels.org
This lovely hostel has an incredible waterfront park setting. Private and shared rooms with kitchen facilities, and daily maid service.

Hotel Bohème $
Budget   Map 5 C3
444 Columbus Ave, 94133
Tel *(415) 433-9111*
Ⓦ hotelboheme.com
Small, eclectic rooms at this 1950s relic located amid cafés, bars, and shops. Great for city explorers.

For key to prices *see page 528*

Best Western Tuscan Inn $$
Budget   Map 5 B1
425 North Point St, 94133
Tel *(415) 561-1100*
Ⓦ tuscaninn.com
Steps from the waterfront, this inn has colorful rooms and an Italian restaurant.

Hyatt at Fisherman's Wharf $$
Luxury   Map 5 B1
555 North Point St, 94133
Tel *(415) 563-1234*
Ⓦ fishermanswharf.hyatt.com
Contemporary place offering rooms with armchairs and oversized high-tech desks.

Sheraton Fisherman's Wharf Hotel $$
Luxury   Map 5 B1
2500 Mason St, 94133
Tel *(415) 362-5500*
Ⓦ sheratonatthewharf.com
Sleek and contemporary decor in spacious rooms with sofas and ergonomic desk chairs.

Suites at Fisherman's Wharf $$
Budget   Map 5 A2
2655 Hyde St, 94109
Tel *(415) 771-0200*
Ⓦ shellhospitality.com
One- and two-bedroom bay-view suites with kitchenettes.

Argonaut Hotel $$$
Boutique   Map 5 A1
495 Jefferson St, 94109
Tel *(415) 563-0800*
Ⓦ argonauthotel.com
This place boasts authentic sea-side character, from the decor to the on-site restaurant. Pet friendly.

Fairmont Heritage Place, Ghirardelli Square $$$
Luxury   Map 4 F1
900 North Point St, 94109
Tel *(415) 268-9900*
Ⓦ fairmont.com
A residential-style hotel with two- and three-bedroom apartment units with kitchens, living rooms, and dining areas.

Pacific Heights

Buena Vista Motor Inn $
Budget   Map 4 E2
1599 Lombard St, 94123
Tel *(415) 923-9600*
Ⓦ buenavistamotorinn.com
A basic motel at a good location. Rooftop patio and free parking.

Hotel Kabuki $
Boutique   Map 4 E4
1625 Post St, 94115
Tel *(415) 922-3200*
Ⓦ jdvhotels.com
Japanese-style hotel; deep soaking tubs and a Zen-like ambience.

The Kimpton Buchanan $
Budget   Map 4 E4
1800 Sutter St, 94115
Tel *(415) 921-4000*
Ⓦ thebuchananhotel.com
Colorful, stylish property with spacious rooms. Popular with families.

Hotel del Sol $$
Boutique   Map 4 D2
3100 Webster St, 94123
Tel *(415) 921-5520*
Ⓦ jdvhotels.com
Hip, colorful 1950s motor lodge, turned hotel, with a pool and sauna.

Hotel Drisco $$
Boutique   Map 3 C3
2901 Pacific Ave, 94115
Tel *(415) 346-2880*
Ⓦ hoteldrisco.com
Spacious and elegant. 1940s glamour with modern amenities.

DK Choice

Inn at the Presidio $$
Boutique   Map 3 A2
42 Moraga Ave, 94129
Tel *(415) 689-4287*
Ⓦ innatthepresidio.com
Housed in a 1903 officers' quarters, this inn has sumptuous rooms with views of the Golden Gate Bridge. Relax and enjoy breakfast on the front porch or on the patio, which has a fire pit.

The relaxing rooftop area of Fairmont Heritage Place, San Francisco

The foyer area at the historic Inn at the Presidio, Golden Gate

Jackson Court Hotel $$
B&B   Map 4 E3
2198 Jackson St, 94115
Tel *(415) 929-7670*
W jacksoncourt.com
A brownstone mansion dating back to 1900 with rooms furnished with antiques. Some rooms have fireplaces.

Laurel Inn $$
Budget   Map 3 C4
444 Presidio Ave, 94115
Tel *(415) 567-8467*
W jdvhotels.com
A stylish, modern hotel offering bright studio-apartment-style rooms, some with kitchenettes.

Queen Anne Hotel $$
Boutique   Map 4 F4
1590 Sutter St, 94109
Tel *(415) 441-2828*
W queenanne.com
Authentic period character and charming decor at this stately Victorian hotel. Great service.

The Civic Center

Hayes Valley Inn $
Budget   Map 4 E4
417 Gough St, 94102
Tel *(415) 431-9131*
W hayesvalleyinn.com
B&B charm within budget. Pretty rooms with shared bathrooms. Complimentary breakfast.

Hostelling International San Francisco City Center $
Budget   Map 4 F4
685 Ellis St, 94109
Tel *(800) 909-4776*
W sfhostels.org
A range of comfortable rooms, all with en-suite baths.

Hotel Vertigo $
Budget   Map 4 E4
940 Sutter St, 94109
Tel *(415) 885-6800*
W haiyi-hotels.com
Hitchcock fans rejoice – this place is a fun take on the classic film. Excellent amenities.

Sleep Over Sauce $
Budget   Map 4 E4
135 Gough St, 94102
Tel *(415) 621-0896*
W sleepsf.com
Charming place with small, comfortable rooms in a trendy area.

Inn at the Opera $$
B&B   Map 4 F5
333 Fulton St, 94102
Tel *(415) 863-8400*
W shellhospitality.com
A long-established favorite in a 1920s building. Elegant French-style rooms with free Wi-Fi.

Phoenix Hotel $$
Boutique   Map 4 F5
601 Eddy St, 94109
Tel *(415) 776-1380*
W jdvhotels.com
Retro tropical-themed motel, popular with rock bands (and fans).

Haight Ashbury and The Mission

Americania Hotel $
Budget
121 7th St, 94103
Tel *(415) 626-0200*
W americaniahotel.com
Bright, colorful rooms with pop-culture decor. Heated pool.

Carriage Inn $
Budget
140 7th St, 94103
Tel *(415) 552-8600*
W carriageinnsf.com
Individually themed rooms have decor inspired by famous San Franciscans. Outdoor hot tub.

Good Hotel $
Budget
112 7th St, 94103
Tel *(415) 621-7001*
W thegoodhotel.com
Eco-friendly hotel with minimalist decor using recycled material such as water-bottle lights.

The Inn San Francisco $
B&B   Map 10 F3
943 South Van Ness Ave, 94110
Tel *(415) 641-0188*
W innsf.com
Elaborate Victorian mansion with comfortable beds, gorgeous fireplaces, and antiques. Enjoy a hearty breakfast in the parlor.

The Red Victorian $
B&B   Map 9 B1
1665 Haight St, 94117
Tel *(415) 864-1978*
W embassynetwork.com
Bright red building leftover from the Summer of Love. Each room here is a different hippie haven. Some share bathrooms. No TV.

The Bay Area

DK Choice

BERKELEY:
Berkeley City Club $$
Historic   Road map inset B
2315 Durant Ave, 94704
Tel *(510) 848-7800*
W berkeleycityclubhotel.com
Built in 1929, this hotel is a stunning example of a Julia Morgan masterpiece *(see p219)*. It boasts charming, if small, guest rooms and elegant public spaces. Take a dip in the gorgeous indoor pool or make use of the superb fitness center. The on-site club hosts performances and lectures.

BERKELEY:
Hotel Shattuck Plaza $$
Historic   Road map inset B
2086 Allston Way, 94704
Tel *(510) 845-7300*
W hotelshattuckplaza.com
Classic 1920s decor with 21st-century amenities. Bay views from many rooms.

CORTE MADERA: Best Western Corte Madera Inn $
Budget   Road map inset B
56 Madera Blvd, 94925
Tel *(415) 924-1502*
W cortemaderainn.com
An attractive, family-friendly motel arranged around gardens and lawns. Excellent restaurant.

HALF MOON BAY: Half Moon Bay Inn $$
Boutique   Road map inset B
401 Main St, 94019
Tel *(650) 726-1177*
W halfmoonbayinn.com
Pet-friendly hotel in a landmark 1932 Spanish Revival building. Rooms have luxurious amenities.

HALF MOON BAY: Half Moon Bay Lodge $$
Resort   Road map inset B
42400 S Cabrillo Highway, 94019
Tel *(650) 726-9000*
W pacificahotels.com
Rooms have either patios or balconies overlooking gardens. Nearby coastal hiking trails.

For more information on types of hotels *see pages 524–7*

HALF MOON BAY: Oceano Hotel & Spa $$
Luxury   Road map inset B
280 Capistrano Rd, 94019
Tel *(650) 726-5400*
W oceanohalfmoonbay.com
Upscale accommodations in a shopping and restaurant complex at the harbor. On-site spa.

HALF MOON BAY: Ritz-Carlton Half Moon Bay $$$
Luxury   Road map Inset B
1 Miramontes Point Rd, 94019
Tel *(650) 712-7000*
W ritzcarlton.com
Magnificent setting on a high oceanside cliff. Boasts two golf courses and a full-service spa.

LAFAYETTE: Lafayette Park Hotel & Spa $$$
Luxury   Road map inset B
3287 Mount Diablo Blvd, 94549
Tel *(925) 283-3700*
W lafayetteparkhotel.com
Grand French chateau-style ambience and first-class service.

MARSHALL: Nick's Cove & Cottages $$
Boutique   Road map A3
23240 Hwy 1, 94940
Tel *(415) 663-1033*
W nickscove.com
Comfortable cottages with rustic interiors, right on Tomales Bay.

MILLBRAE: El Rancho Inn $
Budget   Road map inset B
1100 El Camino Real, 94030
Tel *(650) 588-8500*
W elranchoinn.com
Well-decorated rooms and apartment-style suites. Impeccable service.

OAKLAND: Waterfront Hotel $$
Budget   Road map inset B
10 Washington St, 94607
Tel *(510) 836-3800*
W jdvhotels.com
Nautical-themed rooms, some with balconies and bay views.

OLEMA: Point Reyes Seashore Lodge $$
B&B   Road map A3
10021 Coastal Hwy 1, 94956
Tel *(415) 663-9000*
W pointreyesseashore.com
A luxurious country estate in an idyllic garden setting. Comfortable rooms and two cottages.

PALO ALTO: Garden Court Hotel $$$
Luxury   Road map inset B
520 Cowper St, 94301
Tel *(650) 322-9000*
W gardencourt.com
A boutique hotel within walking distance of restaurants and shops.

A country estate setting at Point Reyes Seashore Lodge, Olema

PESCADERO: Pescadero Creek Inn $$
B&B   Road map B4
393 Stage Rd, 94060
Tel *(650) 879-1898*
W pescaderocreekinn.com
Peaceful getaway amid organic gardens. Snuggle under a down comforter or relax in an antique claw-foot tub.

SAN JOSE: Hotel Valencia $$
Luxury   Road map inset B
355 Santana Row, 95128
Tel *(408) 551-0010*
W hotelvalencia-santanarow.com
Sophisticated Spanish-style architecture and elegant accommodations. Lively bar.

SAUSALITO: Hotel Sausalito $$
Boutique   Road map inset B
16 El Portal, 94965
Tel *(415) 332-0700*
W hotelsausalito.com
A 1915 Mission Revival-style landmark near the San Francisco ferry. Rooftop garden.

SAUSALITO: Casa Madrona $$$
Boutique   Road map inset B
801 Bridgeway Ave, 94965
Tel *(415) 332-0502*
W casamadrona.com
Victorian-era gem with rooms and cottages on a bayview hillside. Spa services on site.

SAUSALITO: Cavallo Point $$$
Historic   Road map inset B
601 Murray Circle, 94965
Tel *(415) 339-4700*
W cavallopoint.com
Spa resort at the base of the Golden Gate Bridge with a Michelin-starred restaurant.

SUNNYVALE: Wild Palms Hotel $$
Budget   Road map inset B
910 E Fremont Ave, 94087
Tel *(408) 738-0500*
W jdvhotels.com
A Mediterranean atmosphere with courtyards, murals, and

mosaics. Bungalow-style rooms with living rooms and sofabeds.

TIBURON: Lodge at Tiburon $$
Resort   Road map inset B
1651 Tiburon Blvd, 94920
Tel *(415) 435-3133*
W thelodgeattiburon.com
Modern Craftsman-style hostelry near the waterfront. Suites have living rooms and kitchenettes.

TIBURON: Waters Edge Hotel $$
Boutique   Road map inset B
25 Main St, 94920
Tel *(415) 789-5999*
W marinhotels.com
Minimalist chic hotel at the ferry dock. Water view rooms with private balconies or decks.

TIBURON: Inn Above Tide $$$
Boutique   Road map inset B
30 El Portal, 94965
Tel *(415) 332-9535*
W innabovetide.com
Romantic destination with rooms perched over the bay. Hot tubs, ferry access, and free breakfasts. Many rooms have private fireplaces and decks.

The North

DUNSMUIR: Railroad Park Resort $
Budget   Road map B2
100 Railroad Park Rd, 96025
Tel *(530) 235-4440*
W rrpark.com
Simple rooms and cabins in restored freight cars and cabooses arranged around a swimming pool. On-site restaurant.

EUREKA: Abigail's Elegant Victorian Mansion $$
Historic   Road map A2
1406 C St, 95501
Tel *(707) 444-3144*
W eureka-california.com
A charming, antique-filled inn located in a Victorian building.

DK Choice

EUREKA: Carter House Inns
Historic $$$
301 L St, 95501
Tel *(707) 444-8062*
W carterhouse.com
Carter House Inns are set in a complex of five historic buildings, including a replica of a Victorian house. Each has plush rooms and suites with spa tubs, four-poster beds, marble fireplaces, and dressing parlors. There is also a Michelin-starred restaurant. Impeccable service.

LASSEN VOLCANIC NATIONAL PARK: Drakesbad Guest Ranch $$
Resort   Road map B2
Warner Valley Rd, 96020
Tel *(530) 529-1512*
W drakesbad.com
A century-old hot springs resort in scenic surroundings. Choice of rooms, cabins, and bungalows.

MOUNT SHASTA CITY: Mount Shasta Resort $
Resort   Road map B1
1000 Siskiyou Lake Blvd, 96067
Tel *(530) 926-3030*
W mountshastaresort.com
One- and two-bedroom chalets in a pretty, wooded setting. Well equipped with all basic amenities. Golf course, restaurant, and bar.

TRINITY CENTER: Coffee Creek Guest Ranch $
Resort   Road map A2
4310 Coffee Creek Rd, 96091
Tel *(530) 266-3343*
W coffeecreekranch.com
Rustic cabins with summer camp atmosphere. Hearty, family-style meals, heated pool, and more.

Wine Country

BODEGA BAY: Bodega Bay Lodge $$
Boutique   Road map A3
103 Hwy 1, 94923
Tel *(707) 875-3525*
W bodegabaylodge.com
Deluxe rooms amid pines and landscaped dunes. Seaview pool and a fine-dining restaurant.

BODEGA BAY: Inn at the Tides $$
Resort   Road map A3
800 Hwy 1, 94923
Tel *(800) 541-7788*
W innatthetides.com
Two-story buildings with fireplaces, sitting areas, sea views, and excellent dining options.

CALISTOGA: Indian Springs $$
Resort   Road map A3
1712 Lincoln Ave, 94515
Tel *(707) 942-4913*
W indianspringscalistoga.com
A spa resort since 1865, with huge heated pools filled with natural geyser mineral water.

DK Choice

CALISTOGA: Solage Calistoga $$$
Luxury   Road map A3
755 Silverado Trail, 94515
Tel *(866) 942-7442*
W solagecalistoga.com
Solage is a sprawling, chic, eco-focused resort with a Michelin-starred restaurant, trendy bar, and an exotic geothermal spa. Offers cottage-style studios with fireplaces, patios, and vineyard views. Daily fitness classes and free bikes.

FORT BRAGG: The Beach House Inn $$
Budget   Road map A2
100 Pudding Creek Rd, 95437
Tel *(888) 559-9992*
W beachinn.com
Waterfront inn surrounded by lovely wetlands. Simple rooms with spa tubs and fireplaces.

GLEN ELLEN: Olea Hotel $$
B&B   Road map A3
5131 Warm Springs Rd, 95442
Tel *(707) 996-5131*
W oleahotel.com
Hillside rooms and cottages with plush duvets and robes, high-tech amenities, and lovely gardens.

GUALALA: Mar Vista Cottages $
Boutique   Road map A3
35101 S Hwy 1, 95445
Tel *(707) 884-3522*
W marvistamendocino.com
Choice of 12 comfortable vintage cottages with fireplaces and

Relaxing bathroom suite at Carter House Inns, Eureka

kitchens but no TV, radio, or phone. Perfect for a getaway.

HEALDSBURG: Camellia Inn $$
B&B   Road map A3
211 North St, 95448
Tel *(707) 433-8182*
W camelliainn.com
Romantic rooms in an 1869 Italianate Victorian house in lush gardens. Sumptuous breakfasts.

HEALDSBURG: Honor Mansion $$$
B&B   Road map A3
14891 Grove St, 95448
Tel *(800) 554-4667*
W honormansion.com
A spectacular inn set in beautiful gardens. Lavish rooms with a wealth of amenities.

LITTLE RIVER: Little River Inn $$$
Boutique   Road map A3
7751 Hwy 1, 95456
Tel *(888) 466-5683*
W littleriverinn.com
A country resort in a 19th-century mansion overlooking the sea. Top-notch restaurant and a nine-hole golf course.

MENDOCINO: The Stanford Inn by the Sea $$
Resort   Road map A3
Hwy 1 & Comptche-Ukiah Rd, 95460
Tel *(800) 331-8884*
W stanfordinn.com
Rooms and suites with private, oceanview decks. Surrounded by gardens. Spa services on site.

NAPA: Andaz Napa $$$
Luxury   Road map B3
1450 First St, 94559
Tel *(707) 224-3900*
W napa.andaz.hyatt.com
A chic, urban hotel featuring spacious rooms with excellent facilities. Wine bar and restaurant.

NAPA: Senza Hotel $$$
Boutique   Road map B3
4066 Howard Ln, 94558
Tel *(707) 253-0337*
W senzahotel.com
Romantic French barn and 19th-century mansion set amid pretty gardens. This property is owned by the Hall winemaking family.

NAPA: Silverado Resort and Spa $$$
Resort   Road map B3
1600 Atlas Peak Rd, 94558
Tel *(707) 257-0200*
W silveradoresort.com
A huge, pillared 19th-century mansion with condo-style units and cottages, a full-service spa, restaurants, and sports facilities.

For more information on types of hotels *see pages 524–7*

The relaxing spa at Fairmont Sonoma Mission Inn and Spa, Sonoma

ST. HELENA: El Bonita $
Boutique   Road map A3
195 Main St, 94574
Tel (707) 963-3216
W elbonita.com
An updated 1930s Art Deco motel with nicely appointed rooms, plus larger units with private balconies.

ST. HELENA: Harvest Inn $$
Resort   Road map A3
1 Main St, 94574
Tel (707) 963-9463
W harvestinn.com
Rooms, suites, and cottages with antiques, four-poster beds, fireplaces, and eclectic furnishings.

ST. HELENA: Meadowood $$$
Resort   Road map A3
900 Meadowood Ln, 94574
Tel (800) 458-8080
W meadowood.com
Luxurious accommodations and a Michelin-starred restaurant, set in a magical redwood forest.

SANTA ROSA: Flamingo $
Resort   Road map A3
2777 4th St, 95405
Tel 800) 848-8300
W flamingoresort.com
Modern hotel with a giant pool terrace, lawns, tennis court, and full-service health club.

SEA RANCH: Sea Ranch Lodge $
Boutique   Road map A3
60 Sea Walk Dr, 95497
Tel (707) 785-2371
W searanchlodge.com
A small lodge on oceanfront headlands offering clean rooms. Restaurant and bar with views.

SONOMA: Ramekins Inn $$
Boutique   Road map A3
450 W Spain St, 95476
Tel (415) 933-0452
W ramekins.com
Situated in an iconic rammed-earth building housing a cooking school. Spacious rooms with views of the countryside.

SONOMA: The Fairmont Sonoma Mission Inn and Spa $$$
Resort   Road map A3
18140 Hwy 12, 95476
Tel (888) 270-1118
W fairmont.com
A 1920s-style pink palace with an award-winning spa. Elegant café.

SONOMA: Inn at Sonoma $$$
B&B   Road map A3
630 Broadway, 95476
Tel (707) 939-1340
W innatsonoma.com
Plush rooms with fireplaces, sitting areas, and either private balconies or patios. Rooftop hot tub.

YOUNTVILLE: Bardessono $$$
Luxury   Road map B3
6526 Yount St, 94599
Tel (707) 363-7295
W bardessono.com
An upscale lodge famous for its sustainable design. Villa-style suites in a Mediterranean setting.

Gold Country and The Central Valley

AMADOR CITY: Imperial Hotel $
B&B   Road map B3
14202 Hwy 49, 95601
Tel (209) 267-9172
W imperialamador.com
Charming little hotel. Rooms with Victorian-era decor.

AUBURN: Power's Mansion Inn $
B&B   Road map B3
164 Cleveland Ave, 95603
Tel (530) 885-1166
W powersmansioninn.com
Elegant property with parlors and antiques. Wine tours available.

DK Choice
GRASS VALLEY: The Holbrooke Hotel $
Historic   Road map B3
212 W Main St, 95945
Tel (530) 273-1353
W holbrooke.com
Established in 1851 to cater to Gold Rush pioneers, this historic property is a local landmark and a bastion of Gold Country hospitality. Rooms are furnished with antiques and have exposed brick walls and claw-foot tubs.

MURPHYS: Murphys Historic Hotel $
Historic   Road map B3
457 Main St, 95247
Tel (209) 728-3444
W murphyshotel.com
Longest-operating hotel in California. Lively saloon.

NEVADA CITY: The Madison House Bed & Breakfast $$
B&B   Road map B3
427 Broad St, 95959
Tel (530) 265-9478
W themadisonhouse.net
Comfortable Victorian-era establishment. Quiet and romantic.

SACRAMENTO: Sterling Hotel $
Historic   Road map B3
1300 H St, 95814
Tel (800) 365-7660
W sterlinghotelsacramento.com
Elegant, beautifully restored Victorian mansion combining charm and luxury.

SOMERSET: Gold Mountain Winery and Lodge $$
Boutique   Road map B3
7750 Fair Play Rd, 95684
Tel (800) 245-9166
W goldmountainwineryandlodge.com
Idyllic location complements the modern and elegant rooms with great views. Relax on the garden patio or explore the wineyards.

SONORA: Barretta Gardens Inn $$
B&B   Road map B3
700 Barretta St, 95370
Tel (209) 532-6039
W barrettagardens.com
Individually decorated, wine-themed rooms. Good breakfasts.

SUTTER CREEK: Sutter Creek Inn $$
B&B   Road map B3
75 Main St, 95685
Tel (209) 267-5606
W suttercreekinn.com
This country-style 1859 inn has private cottages with fireplaces. Many rooms have private patios.

The High Sierras

FISH CAMP: The Narrow Gauge Inn $$
Budget   Road map C4
48571 Hwy 41, 93623
Tel (559) 683-7720
W narrowgaugeinn.com
A romantic gem with quaint rooms and a fabulous restaurant. Some rooms have balconies.

JUNE LAKE: Gull Lake Lodge $
Budget   Road map C3
132 Bruce St, 93529
Tel (760) 648-7516
W gulllakelodge.com
Intimate lodge in a residential area within walking distance of the lakes. One-bedroom apartments with kitchenettes and en-suite baths.

For key to prices see page 528

KINGS CANYON NATIONAL PARK: Montecito Sequoia Lodge $
Budget   Road map C3
63410 Generals Hwy, 93633
Tel *(559) 565-3388*
w montecitosequoia.com
Lodge-style rooms and cabins, popular with families. Many activities are offered including guided hikes, rock-climbing and campfires. Meals included.

MAMMOTH LAKES: Austria Hof Lodge $$
Budget   Road map C4
924 Canyon Blvd, 93546
Tel *(760) 934-2764*
w austriahof.com
This charming mountain lodge near the ski lift has snug rooms, some with fireplaces and kitchenettes. Friendly staff.

SOUTH LAKE TAHOE: Beach Retreat and Lodge $
Budget   Road map C3
3411 Lake Tahoe Blvd, 96150
Tel *(530) 541-6722*
w tahoebeachretreat.com
Full-service establishment with a lakeside location. Great for both summer and winter activities, including kayaking, paddle boarding, and lakeside dining.

SQUAW VALLEY: Resort at Squaw Creek $$$
Luxury   Road map B3
400 Squaw Creek Rd, 96146
Tel *(530) 583-6300*
w squawcreek.com
Luxuriously appointed resort with many recreational activities including golf and skiing. Free transport to Squaw Valley.

TAHOE CITY: Chaney House $
B&B   Road map B3
4725 W Lake Blvd, 96145
Tel *(530) 525-7333*
w chaneyhouse.com
This traditional stone and timber lodge exudes charm. Large fireplace. Private beach access.

TRUCKEE: The Richardson House $$$
Historic   Road map B3
10154 High St, 96160
Tel *(530) 563-6874*
w therichardsonhouse.com
Restored Victorian house in historic downtown. Comfortable rooms with lavish amenities.

YOSEMITE NATIONAL PARK: Cedar Lodge $
Budget   Road map C3
9966 Hwy 140, 95318
Tel *(209) 379-2612*
w stayyosemitecedarlodge.com
Family-friendly place with a wide range of rooms, from standard size to 14-person suites.

DK Choice

YOSEMITE NATIONAL PARK: The Ahwahnee $$$
Historic   Road map C3
Yosemite Valley, 95389
Tel *(559) 253-5636*
w yosemitepark.com
Opened in 1927, this famed rustic lodge *(see p495)* is built of stone and timber and is designed to highlight its natural surroundings. The elegant Ahwahnee features a soaring lobby, well-appointed rooms, a beautiful solarium, and an excellent restaurant *(see p576)*. A variety of lodging options and warm hospitality make this the top choice for a stay in the valley.

North Central California

BIG SUR: Deetjens Big Sur Inn $$
Historic   Road map B4
48865 Hwy 1, 93920
Tel *(831) 667-2377*
w deetjens.com
A tranquil forest retreat with cozy, eclectic rooms. Pretty gardens and an excellent restaurant.

CARMEL: Los Laureles Lodge $
Boutique   Road map B4
313 W Carmel Valley Rd, 93924
Tel *(831) 659-2233*
w loslaureles.com
Eclectic rooms built into former horse stables. Lovely grounds and generous amenities.

DK Choice

CARMEL: Pine Inn $$
B&B   Road map B4
Ocean Ave & Monte Verde, 93921
Tel *(831) 624-3851*
w pineinn.com
This iconic inn, the oldest in town, offers elegant rooms and suites equipped with all modern comforts. The on-site restaurant is popular with the locals. Conveniently located near boutiques and galleries, and just blocks from the beach.

MONTEREY: Lone Oak Lodge $
Budget   Road map B4
2221 North Fremont St, 93940
Tel *(831) 372-4924*
w loneoaklodge.com
Popular with scuba divers but also great for families. Rooms are basic; suites have kitchenettes.

MONTEREY: InterContinental The Clement Monterey $$$
Luxury   Road map B4
750 Cannery Row, 93940
Tel *(831) 375-4500*
w ictheclementmonterey.com
Luxury establishment with upscale contemporary decor. Rooms and suites with ocean views.

MONTEREY: Monterey Bay Inn $$$
B&B   Road map B4
242 Cannery Row, 93940
Tel *(831) 373-6242*
w montereybayinn.com
Comfortable rooms, many with spectacular bay views. Excellent amenities. Central location.

SANTA CRUZ: Sea and Sand Inn $$
Budget   Road map B4
201 West Cliff Dr, 95060
Tel *(831) 427-3400*
w santacruzmotels.com
Oceanview rooms, suites, and studios on the clifftop near the beach. Breakfast included.

SANTA CRUZ: Beach Street Inn and Suites $$$
Boutique   Road map B4
125 Beach St, 95060
Tel *(831) 423-3031*
w beachstreetinn.com
Bright rooms with a retro feel and ocean views. Beachside location.

Stone and timber exterior of The Ahwahnee, Yosemite National Park

For more information on types of hotels *see pages 524–7*

WHERE TO EAT AND DRINK

Of all the states in the US, California is known for a wide variety of places to eat and some of the healthiest, most beautifully presented restaurant food. Pioneered in the 1970s by chefs such as Jeremiah Towers, Wolfgang Puck, and Alice Waters, "California Cuisine" has evolved into an internationally recognized style that incorporates ethnic fusion with seasonal, locally sourced ingredients. A plethora of Italian, Mexican, and Asian eateries – serving a wide selection of dishes including Japanese sushi, Thai noodles, Chinese dim sum, Middle Eastern falafel, and Indian tandoori – reflect the cultural diversity of the state's population. Beside the multicultural choices, there is no shortage of classic, all-American diners and fast-food joints serving hamburgers, French fries, and soda. The restaurants listed on pages 550–77 have been selected for their variety, service, and good value. Some typical meals served in California are featured on pages *546–7*.

California Eating Patterns

American breakfasts, none the least those in California, are known for their generous portions. The huge breakfast menus typically offer omelets with fries and toast; pancakes or waffles topped with fruit and syrup; frittatas; and eggs and bacon or sausage served with toast or a muffin. Less filling choices include international-style Continental breakfasts: brewed or specialty coffee with a bagel or pastry, or cereal and yogurt topped with raisins or bananas. Breakfast is usually served from 6 to 11am, and all day in some diners. Weekend brunches, served into mid-afternoon, are often buffets with all the breakfast items plus salads, quiches, seafood, fruit, and elaborate desserts.

California lunch can be light – soup and salad or a sandwich. Dinner, served any time between 5 and 10pm, is often the main meal of the day for Americans, and many fine-dining restaurants are dinner destinations.

Prices and Tipping

A snack in a café usually costs around $12 per person, while a main meal in a diner can be around $20. A three-course meal in an average restaurant, excluding wine, may cost $40–$70, and gourmet meals and fixed price menus usually start at about $70.

Based on satisfactory service, a 15 percent tip is expected; when service is superlative, leave 20 percent. Make sure the tip is calculated on the net cost of the meal, not including the tax, which is up to 8.25 percent.

Healthy Eating

A number of restaurants in California follow the American Heart Association's (AHA) guidelines for reducing cholesterol and dietary fat.

A red heart beside a dish denotes an AHA-approved "Healthy Heart" meal, and calories are sometimes noted. If a restaurant does not offer healthy choices, diners can request a waiter to adjust ingredients, where possible. Salads are usually on offer, and there are many restaurants, in particular Asian eateries, that focus on vegetarian dishes.

Restaurants serving Californian cuisine strive to use fresh, locally sourced ingredients low in saturated fats and high in fresh vegetables and fruits. Another cuisine that uses fresh local products is Modern American – these restaurants serve traditional American food imaginatively fused with foreign cuisines, with a stress on high quality and sophisticated cooking techniques.

Fast Food

An ubiquitous feature of the California landscape, fast-food outlets are widespread. These offer filling, inexpensive food, and are a great way to save money. Chain-owned diners and drive-ins include Denny's, Sizzler, Applebee's, and Red Lobster. While the seating areas are large and menu selections are extensive, the food is prepared in bulk and may therefore be rather ordinary.

Coffee Houses, Tea Houses, and Cafés

Coffee houses can be found all over California. Many

BOA Steakhouse, West Hollywood *(see p555)*

The Restaurant at Meadowood, St.Helena, The Wine Country *(see p573)*

specialize in Italian favorites such as latte and cappuccino, and offer an assortment of pastries and cakes to go with them. Many offer free Wi-Fi. Some of the larger bookstores also have small cafés for their customers.

California's sunny climate lends itself to outdoor living, so many eateries have sidewalk or patio tables.Many of the upscale hotels in major cities serve elegant, formal afternoon tea services.

Picnics and Takeouts

Delicatessens and super-markets with deli counters stock cold meats, cheeses, pickles, and salads. They may also make fresh sandwiches to order which can be enjoyed in one of California's many parks or open areas. Guests can also order takeout from many casual restaurants – at the same price as eating in the restaurant.

Sidewalk patio of the rustic Los Olivos Café & Wine Merchant *(see p556)*

Craft Beer Bars

Craft beer bars have become very popular in most cities. These bars and pubs serve a range of national and international beers, as well as unique local specialties, such as Anchor Steam in San Francisco and Karl Straus Amber Lager in San Diego. Some pubs even brew and offer their hand-crafted specialty beers *(see p549)*. A variety of snack foods and tapas-style items are typically served at these bars to soak up the beer.

Smoking

California is an anti-smoking state and has banned smoking in all restaurants and in most public places, including some beaches and parks. Some restaurants with outdoor tables may turn a blind eye, however, and allow guests to smoke outside. Cigars are rarely allowed except in "cigar bars."

Wheelchair Access

All new restaurants in California and established restaurants undergoing renovation must make their sites accessible to wheelchair users. This usually means that there should be ramps or no steps into the restaurant or to the tables, and wide bathroom doors.

Children's Facilities

Most restaurants are child-friendly and offer a kids' menu and high chairs or booster

seats. However, in the quieter, upscale restaurants, parents are expected to keep children seated at the table, so as not to disturb other customers. It is best to check with the restaurant.

Booking Ahead

It is always best to make a reservation in advance to avoid disappointment. Popular city restaurants and fashionable places are often very busy and sometimes booked up more than a month in advance.

Recommended Restaurants

The restaurants listed in this guide have been selected for their exceptional food and memorable location, and showcase the state's plethora of ethnic, international, and unique California cuisines. They cover a range of prices from budget and moderately priced to upscale. Many of the venues have patios, terraces, or water-front views to take advantage of the mild weather.

A selection of restaurants have been highlighted as "DK Choice." Some of these serve excellent regional specialties, others may be set in particularly atmospheric environs, while some may offer cuisine created by world-class chefs. The DK Choices cover an eclectic range of cuisines from Asian and Mexican to Italian and local American food. They can be very popular so remember to book in advance.

The Flavors of California

One heady whiff of a California farmer's market and you will understand how California cuisine – rooted in the simple concept that ingredients should be fresh, healthful, and homegrown – developed in the sun-kissed Golden State. Ethnic cuisine, too, especially sizzling Mexican but also Mediterranean and spicy Chinese and Thai, makes a bold appearance across the state. And, of course, traditionalists can indulge in the all-American burger and fries at a classic diner. Better yet, for a quintessential California car culture moment, pull into a drive-through for a burger-on-the-dash meal.

Coriander and bay leaves

Stalls at a Californian market, laden with local produce

Locally Grown Vegetables and Herbs

The seasons reign supreme in California cuisine and chefs develop their menus around what is fresh at the market. The summer warmth brings forth heavy vine tomatoes, zucchini, and a rainbow of peppers, while the autumnal cool reaps lush broccoli, artichokes, cauliflower, and acorn squash. A birds-eye view of the state reveals verdant herb gardens unfolding from one end to the other; wild mustard fields giving way to scented swathes of cilantro (coriander), bay, and basil, to be used in everything from sauces to salads.

Fresh Fruits and Nuts

Fruits and nuts flourish in California's year-round sunny climate. The healthy soil, fed by an abundance of fresh water, yields downy-skinned peaches, caramel-sweet dates, and the state's famed avocados. The world's most popular avocado

White peaches
Dates
Persimmons
Papaya
Mango
Kumquats
Fresh figs

Mouthwatering selection of ripe Calfornian fruits

Californian Dishes and Specialties

Jalapeño chilis

Due to similarities in climate, Californian cooking is strongly influenced by Mediterranean cuisine. However, traditional Italian or Provençal recipes are often given a twist with the addition of New World ingredients, resulting in innovative pizzas and pasta dishes and exotic, colorful salads. Sauces and salad dressings tend to be light and fresh, designed to enhance and complement the key ingredients of the dish. A popular dish is the Cobb salad, consisting of chopped salad green vegatables, tomato, crisp bacon, chicken breast, hard-boiled egg, chives, avocado, blue cheese, and red-wine vinaigrette. Locally produced goat cheese is used liberally in dishes, its tangy flavor pairing beautifully with vegetables and meat. Desserts make the most of local fruits, and will often be as simple as a mixed-fruit platter with a passion-fruit sauce or home-made ice cream.

Mesclun salad with dates and goat cheese Mixed baby greens mingle with sweet dates and crumbled cheese.

A bustling Mexican snack bar in San Francisco's lively Haight neighborhood

Mexican Cuisine

There is no need to head south of the border for *comida mexicana*. Nearly every town has its share of casual, colorful *taquerias* where you can dig into Mexican fare at a price that is easy on the wallet. At less than $10 for a blimp-sized burrito or platter overflowing with seasoned rice, beans and chicken, a Mexican meal remains one of the best bargains in the state.

The Mexican Menu

Tortilla A Mexican staple, this is a round, flat unleavened corn- or wheat-flour bread.

Burrito Warmed tortilla, filled with *arroz* (rice), *frijoles* (beans), and *pollo* (chicken), *carne* (meat) or veggies.

Quesadilla Tortilla stuffed with *queso* (cheese) and other fillings, then grilled or pan-fried to melt the cheese.

Taco A crisp or soft tortilla folded, and stuffed with a savory filling.

Chile Relleno Stuffed green chili pepper fried in batter.

Salsas Spicy fresh sauces, from traditional chunky tomato to trendy slivers of papaya, mango, or peach to vegetable salsas with corn and black beans.

Mole This rich, dark sauce is an aromatic blend of bitter chocolate, spices, and chilis, often drizzled over chicken.

is the rough-skinned Haas variety, a California native, prized for its silky texture and mild, nutty flavor and used extensively in salads and sandwiches and to concoct velvety dips. The thin-skinned, green Fuerte avocado is another creamy favorite, as are California black walnuts, whose rock-hard shells hide an intensely flavorful meat used by chefs as a nutty seasoning.

Fish and Seafood

California's seas and rivers abound with fish and shellfish, from delicate Dungeness crab to meaty swordfish and albacore tuna, and many waterfront restaurants serve up fish so fresh it is practically flopping on your plate. Petrale sole, found everywhere from Fort Bragg to Monterey, is the premium flatfish at the market, with a fine-textured,

low-fat flesh that grills to perfection. Named after their rock-hard shell, Ridgeback Santa Barbara shrimp can be tough little guys to peel but boast the sweetest tasting meat in the Pacific. The best freshwater fish is the state's king salmon, which spawns in the Sacramento and San Joaquin rivers and is prized for its delicate, velvety meat that melts on the tongue.

Succulent crabs plucked straight from the Pacific ocean

Salmon on watercress with citrus vinaigrette Local fish and peppery leaves are offset by a piquant vinaigrette.

Grilled chicken breasts with tomato salsa Whole black beans and guacamole complement this healthy dish.

Poached fresh persimmons A luscious concoction of silky persimmons are draped over vanilla ice cream.

What to Drink in California

Californians are devoted to the consumption of beverages, partly because they tend to do so much outdoor exercise in the heat and partly as a social activity. Sodas, water, and other non-alcoholic cold drinks play the largest role in the state's beverage culture, although hard liquor is still popular. Many restaurants tempt weekend customers with champagne brunches. Beer can be enjoyed at craft beer bars and pubs (see p545), beach bars, or while watching a game of baseball. Wine, particularly local California wine (see pp442–3), is popular with dinner.

Sign in the Napa Valley wine-producing region in Northern California

A popular brand of Tequila

Colorful Sunset Strip

Strawberry Daiquiri

Margarita with slice of lime

Cocktails

Sipping cocktails beside the ocean at sunset is part of the popular image of the "California dream." The margarita cocktail still ranks as the firm favorite throughout the state. Served in wide glasses, margaritas are a blend of tequila, lime juice, and an orange-flavored liqueur, with the rim of the glass dipped in salt. The Sunset Strip, named after the once infamous section of Sunset Boulevard (see pp106–108), consists of equal parts of gin, rum, triple sec, vodka, pineapple juice, and lemonade. Another cocktail that is popular in the state is the piña colada. This is a blend of fresh pineapple juice, cream of coconut, and sometimes papaya juice, lime, and orange juice. A shot of rum is added, and the finished drink is served over ice in tall, elegant glasses.

Non-Alcoholic Cold Beverages

Californians are generally very health-conscious, and fresh fruit and vegetable juices and smoothies are popular. Juice bars are almost as ubiquitous as fast-food restaurants. Here, patrons can get fresh fruits and vegetables – from strawberries to kale – pressed or squeezed to order. Nutritious seeds or spirulina are often added to smoothies.

Most fast-food outlets offer a range of non-alcoholic cold drinks in three sizes, although the same products can usually be purchased much less expensively from shops or supermarkets.

The most popular non-alcoholic drink in the state remains the all-American cola, including diet and caffeine-free versions. However, there is a health awareness campaign to reduce the consumption of sugary drinks, including colas and other carbonated beverages.

Sports-loving Californians often carry bottled water or flexible thermos flasks filled with drinks chilled overnight in the refrigerator.

Freshly squeezed strawberry juice

Tea and Coffee

"Designer" coffee is very popular in California. Caffè latte, café au lait, cappuccino, and other coffee concoctions, both hot and iced, and flavored brews, such as almond and mocha, are typically on hand at coffee houses. Tea, especially green tea, is also becoming increasingly popular, and imported teas come in every imaginable flavor.

Cappuccino

Caffè latte

Iced coffee

Tea with lemon

Wine

Grape vines thrive in the mild climate of Northern California, where cooling fogs help the fruit to reach perfection. There are over 100 types of grape across the state. The main red wine varieties grown in the region are Cabernet Sauvignon, Pinot Noir, Merlot, and Zinfandel *(see pp442–3)*. White wines are also classified by grape variety, with Chardonnay by far the most popular of recent years. Grown throughout the West Coast region, this prestige grape produces wines varying in character from dry, light, lemon, and vanilla-scented to the more headstrong and oaky.

California has acquired an international reputation for excellent champagne-style wines at the right price, reflected in the fact that the finest French producers have huge investments in the state. Moët & Chandon and Mumm, among others, have set up wineries in the Napa Valley *(see pp466–7)* and elsewhere.

Wine is of course much cheaper in supermarkets or liquor stores than in restaurants. Many restaurants allow customers to bring their own bottles (call ahead to check); the corkage fee generally starts at $10.

Sparkling Cuvée Napa by Mumm

Rosé or blush wine

Napa Chardonnay

Cabernet Sauvignon

Water

A variety of mineral waters is produced in the state, the best of which comes from the spa town of Calistoga in the Napa Valley *(see p465)*. Many mineral waters are flavored with fresh fruit and most are carbonated. Most public places, including office buildings, have water dispensers. California tap water is fresh, clean, and safe to drink.

Calistoga mineral water

Alcohol Regulations

Alcohol cannot be purchased or consumed in California by anyone under the age of 21. It is not uncommon for shops and bars to refuse service or admittance to anyone not carrying documents proving that they are at least 21 years old. Licensing hours, however, are relaxed; those old enough to drink legally can buy or consume alcohol from 6am until 2am, seven days a week.

Busy bar in Santa Barbara

Beer

Beers of every variety – foreign, American, even homemade – have become highly desirable. The recent resurgence in small breweries across the United States can be credited to the success of San Francisco's Anchor Brewery, whose Steam Beer, Liberty Ale, and other products show that American beer need not be bland and tasteless. Other excellent local brews to look out for include Mendocino County's rich Boont Amber and Red Tail Ale.

Copying the self-brewing concept that began in Canada, a few Californians are now opening do-it-yourself breweries. Experts are on hand to assist with malting, boiling, carbonating, hopping, fermenting, and bottling. A personal-label brew takes two to six weeks to ferment. Craft beers, brewed on the premises of a bar *(see p545)*, are also extremely popular.

Anchor Steam Beer

Red Tail Ale

Liberty Ale

Where to Eat and Drink

Los Angeles
Airport

Truxton's American Bistro $$
American   **Road map** inset A
8611 Truxton Ave, 90045
Tel *310-417-8789*
Varied menu of finely prepared dishes – house favorites include Cobb salad (*see p546*), buttermilk-fried chicken, and spaghetti with meatballs. Efficient service and close proximity to LAX.

Bel Air

Vibrato Grill Jazz $$$
Modern
American   **Road map** inset A
2930 Beverly Glen Circle, 90077
Tel *310-474-9400*   **Closed** Mon
Conceived by renowned jazz trumpeter Herb Alpert. Jazz artists perform while patrons dine on upscale dishes. The bar area is perfect for a date.

Beverly Hills

Nate 'n Al $
Delicatessen   **Map** 5 F3
414 N Beverly Dr, 90210
Tel *310-274-0101*
Traditional deli in one of the fanciest neighborhoods in town, serving classic potato knishes (pasty), frothy egg creams, and savory pastrami sandwiches. on rye bread.

Da Pasquale Restaurant $$
Italian   **Map** 5 E3
9749 Santa Monica Blvd, 90210
Tel *310-859-3884*
This friendly family-run restaurant celebrates the cuisine of Naples. Popular with the entertainment industry crowd, Da Pasquale is known for its thin-crust pizzas and home-made pastas.

The Farm of Beverly Hills $$
American   **Map** 5 F3
439 N Beverly Dr, 90210
Tel *310-273-5578*
Brings a refreshing bit of the American heartland with an array of classic food, such as meat-loaf and fried chicken. Airy, unpretentious setting with a sunny sidewalk patio.

Fred's $$
Delicatessen   **Map** 5 F4
9570 Wilshire Blvd, 90212
Tel *310-777-5877*
Set in Barneys department store, this chic deli serves fine fare for lunch, dinner, and cocktails

as well as a weekend brunch. Terrace provides great views.

The Bazaar $$$
Spanish   **Map** 6 C3
465 S La Cienega Blvd, 90048
Tel *310-246-5567*
Celebrity chef Jose Andrés' comprehensive gourmet playground lures foodies from all over the world. Guests have a number of areas to choose from – striking dining rooms, a breezy Mediterranean-style terrace, and a welcoming patisserie.

Crustacean $$$
Vietnamese/French   **Map** 6 A2
9646 Santa Monica Blvd, 90210
Tel *310-205-8990*
Roasted crab, grilled rack of lamb, and garlic noodles are the top picks at this elegant, intimate spot. Dinner in the wine cellar is a favorite for special occasions.

The Grill on the Alley $$$
American   **Map** 5 F3
9560 Dayton Way, 90210
Tel *310-276-0615*
Premier power-lunch setup where studio heads discuss their next mega-deal over Cobb salads, perfectly grilled steaks, and pastas. Classic chophouse atmosphere with high-backed leather booths.

Lawry's Prime Rib $$$
Steakhouse   **Map** 6 C4
100 N La Cienega Blvd, 90211
Tel *310-652-2827*
Beloved LA dining tradition since 1938, Lawry's Prime Rib is still the place for an expertly carved steaks with all the trimmings – served in a grand dining room.

> **Price Guide**
> For a three-course meal for one, a glass of house wine, and all unavoidable extra charges, including tax.
>
> $ up to $40
> $$ $40 to $70
> $$$ over $70

Matsuhisa $$$
Japanese   **Map** 6 B4
129 N La Cienega Blvd, 90211
Tel *310-659-9639*
This flagship restaurant of sushi chef Nobu Matsuhisa attracts hordes of celebrities. Specializes in modern sushi with diverse influences from the world over.

Spago $$$
Modern American   **Map** 5 F3
176 N Cañon Dr, 90210
Tel *310-385-0880*
Celebrity chef Wolfgang Puck's flagship restaurant is one of LA's most entertaining dining spots. Stylish dining room, often filled with recognizable faces. Upscale regional and Austrian cuisine.

Wolfgang's Steakhouse $$$
Steakhouse   **Map** 5 F3
445 N Cañon Dr, 90210
Tel *310-385-0640*
Part of an elegant steakhouse chain run by Wolfgang Zwiener, this restaurant features excellent steaks, seafood, and wine. The cordial ambience and upscale setting includes a piano and bar.

Century City

Clementine $
American   **Map** 5 D4
1751 Ensley Ave, 90024
Tel *310-552-1080*   **Closed** Sun
This welcoming Parisian-style café has colorfully draped tables

Dining room at the renowned The Grill on the Alley, Beverly Hills

For Los Angeles map references *see Los Angeles Street Finder maps pages 186–97*

spilling onto the sidewalk. It is a perfect morning spot for freshly baked treats and gourmet coffee. The afternoon brings tasty soups, salads, and hearty sandwiches.

Culver City

Tender Greens $
American   **Road map** inset A
9523 Culver Blvd, 90232
Tel *310-842-8300*
This popular chain has a seasonal menu that utilizes fresh produce sourced from local farms: organic meat, fresh bread, and local wine and beer. Outstanding versions of Cobb salad and tuna nicoise.

Downtown

Hae Jang Chon Korean BBQ Restaurant $
Korean   **Map** 11 D4
3821 W 6th St, 90020
Tel *(213) 389-8777*
Head to this eatery in bustling Koreatown for authentic fare. Servers explain the menu's traditional intricacies. Exceptionally popular with celebratory groups.

Langer's Deli $
Delicatessen   **Map** 10 A4
704 S Alvarado St, 90057
Tel *(213) 483-8050*   **Closed** *Sun*
Serving award winning pastrami and diner fare since 1947, this is one of the nation's most acclaimed delis. Sit in a vintage booth to eat old-time favorites.

Philippe The Original $
Delicatessen   **Map** 11 F3
1001 N Alameda St, 90012
Tel *(213) 628-3781*
Founded in 1908, this is one of the city's oldest restaurants and the self-proclaimed originator of the French dip sandwich, including beef, lamb, pork, and turkey versions. The interior is casual with communal dining tables.

Bäco Mercat $$
Spanish   **Map** 11 E4
408 S Main St, 90013
Tel *(213) 687-8808*
Foodies from all over come to the historic Old Bank district to sample the young chef's signature flatbread sandwiches. Try the original version that combines crispy pork belly and beef *carnitas* with caraway pepper.

Bottega Louie $$
Italian   **Map** 11 D4
700 S Grand Ave, 90017
Tel *(213) 802-1470*
Vibrant spot for appetizing pizzas, pastas, and small plates. The

Elegant interiors of Water Grill, Downtown LA

bustling gourmet market and patisserie offers a range of delicious Italian specialties, including beautiful macaroons.

Guelaguetza $$
Mexican   **Map** 9 D5
3014 W Olympic Blvd, 90006
Tel *(213) 427-0608*
Award-winning Oaxaca cuisine, made using authentic recipes and ingredients. Sauces can be ordered to take away. Vibrant bar area serves an exceptional variety of *mezcal*. Live Mexican music.

Traxx $$
Modern American   **Map** 11 F3
800 N Alameda St, 90012
Tel *(213) 625-1999*
Upscale American fare prepared in a bustling open kitchen, located just off the concourse in historic Union Station. The hidden outdoor courtyard provides a quieter dining option.

Cicada $$$
Italian   **Map** 11 D4
617 S Olive St, 90014
Tel *(213) 488-9488*   **Closed** *Mon & Tue*
One of the city's grandest dining rooms, housed in the historic Oviatt Hotel with dramatic Art Deco design. Blends modern Italian and American fare.

Faith & Flower $$$
Modern American   **Map** 10 C5
705 W 9th St, 90015
Tel *(213) 239-0642*
Sample rustic fare and an inventive craft cocktail list created by skilled mixologists at this hip spot with vintage decor.

Patina $$$
Modern American   **Map** 11 D3
141 S Grand Ave, 90012
Tel *(213) 972-3331*   **Closed** *Mon*
Housed in the stunning Walt Disney Concert Hall, this temple of gastronomy has an indulgent caviar cart and acclaimed wine list.

Water Grill $$$
American   **Map** 11 D4
544 S Grand Ave, 90071
Tel *(213) 891-0900*
A premier seafood restaurant that combines an oyster bar with a classy dining room. Inviting raw bar items and complex preparations of fresh seafood. Friendly, efficient service.

Glendale

La Cabañita $
Mexican   **Road map** inset A
3447 N Verdugo Rd, 91208
Tel *(818) 957-2711*
This small, festive eatery enjoys a strong following. The bustling kitchen churns out classics such as *chiles en nogada* finished with a pecan sauce, mole enchiladas, and *pozole* (maize soup with meat and chili peppers).

Hollywood

Canter's Deli and Restaurant $
Delicatessen   **Map** 7 D2
419 N Fairfax Ave, 90036
Tel *(323) 651-2030*
This iconic deli has been an LA institution since 1931. Serves big portions of classic kosher fare 24 hours a day. Casual atmosphere.

Fred 62 $
American   **Road map** inset A
1850 N Vermont Ave, 90027
Tel *(323) 667-0062*
Open round the clock, this diner has a lengthy menu catering to a diverse crowd – from young rockers to businessmen.

Jitlada $
Thai   **Map** 10 C1
5233 W Sunset Blvd, 90027
Tel *(323) 667-9809*   **Closed** *Mon*
This friendly, casual spot tucked into a strip mall has won national acclaim for its assortment of over 100 authentic offerings from Southern Thailand.

For more information on types of restaurants *see pages 544–5*

Pink's Famous Hot Dogs $
Hot Dogs   Map 7 F1
709 N La Brea Ave, 90038
Tel *(323) 931-4223*
Legendary hot dog stand where
Orson Welles once ate 18
frankfurters. The classic chili dog
is a crowd favorite. Also has hot
dogs named after celebrities.

**Roscoe's House of
Chicken & Waffles** $
American   Map 3 D5
1514 N Gower St, 90028
Tel *(323) 466-7453*
Iconic chain specializing in
Southern-style fried chicken
accompanied by fresh hot
waffles, covered in hot sauce or
sweet syrup. Always crowded.

Umami Burger $
American   Map 2 C4
1520 N Cahuenga Blvd, 90028
Tel *(323) 469-3100*
Popular chain serving gourmet
burgers with inventive, flavorful
toppings. The limited menu also
includes salads, sandwiches, and
craft beers. Hip, minimalist decor.

AOC $$
Mediterranean   Map 7 D3
8022 W 3rd St, 90048
Tel *(323) 653-6359*
Offers over 50 wines by the
glass and a number of tapas-
like small bites. Home-made
charcuterie includes pâtés and
sausages. Sophisticated
and romantic ambience.

Animal $$
Modern American   Map 7 D2
435 N Fairfax Ave, 90048
Tel *(323) 782-9225*
The two young chef/owners
have won national acclaim for
their eclectic menu. Try the *foie
gras* with home-made biscuits
and maple-sausage gravy. Huge
selection of wines by the glass.

Ca' Brea $$
Italian   Map 7 F4
346 S La Brea Ave, 90036
Tel *(323) 938-2863*
Multi-tiered, art-filled space near
some of the city's top restaurants
and art galleries. Enjoy inventive
antipasti, pastas, and hearty
entrées. Extensive wine list.

Cheebo $$
American   Map 11 D1
7533 Sunset Blvd, 90046
Tel *(323) 850-7070*
Keeps crowds happy with terrific
rectangular pizza "slabs." Also
on offer are entrées, salads, and
sandwiches such as the signature
mesquite-grilled burger with
applewood-smoked bacon.

For key to prices *see page 550*

Angelini Osteria $$$
Italian   Map 7 F2
7313 Beverly Blvd, 90036
Tel *(323) 297-0070*   **Closed** *Mon*
One of LA's most popular Italian
chefs churns out rustic dishes
such as flavorsome lasagne with
herb sauce, made using his
grandmother's recipe.

Carlitos Gardel $$$
Steakhouse   Map 7 D1
7963 Melrose Ave, 90046
Tel *(323) 655-0891*
Beef- and wine-lover's paradise,
also serving pastas, chicken
dishes, and signature garlic fries.
The undisputed draw is all-
natural, grass-fed, USDA certified
prime cuts of Black Angus beef.

DK Choice

Musso and Frank Grill $$$
Steakhouse   Map 1 B4
6667 Hollywood Blvd, 90028
Tel *(323) 467-7788*   **Closed** *Sun &
Mon*
Hollywood's oldest restaurant,
Musso and Frank never seems
to go out of style. Classic
mahogany and red leather
decor and a crowd of both
tourists and locals who belly
up to the bar for expertly made
martinis. Old-school menu
favorites include chicken pot
pie, liver and onions, and
huge, juicy steaks.

Providence $$$
Seafood   Map 7 D1
5955 Melrose Ave, 90038
Tel *(323) 460-4170*
Sophisticated restaurant with
French and Japanese influences.
The kitchen sources fresh fish
daily and the award-winning
wine list features more than
400 labels by the glass.

Long Beach

Parkers' Lighthouse $$
Seafood   **Road map** inset A
435 Shoreline Village Dr, 90802
Tel *(562) 432-6500*
With a working lighthouse,
this Long Beach landmark has
great views of the harbor and
the *Queen Mary* ocean liner. The
menu showcases mesquite-
grilled seafood, most of it flown
in daily from Alaska and Hawaii.

Sir Winston's $$$
Modern
American   **Road map** inset A
1126 Queen's Hwy, 90801
Tel *(562) 435-3511*
The *Queen Mary*'s most romantic
dining option. Serves Continental
favorites such as caviar, *foie gras*,
lobster bisque, rack of lamb, and
chocolate soufflé. Perfect for a
special occasion.

Malibu

**Malibu Seafood Fresh Fish
Market & Patio Café** $
Seafood   **Road map** inset A
25653 Pacific Coast Hwy, 90265
Tel *(310) 456-3430*
This no-frills seafood market and
eatery dating back to 1972 is
owned and operated by
commercial fishermen. Get the
hand-battered cod and home-
made clam chowder to go, or
enjoy a meal on the casual patio.

Duke's Malibu $$$
American   **Road map** inset A
21150 Pacific Coast Hwy, 90265
Tel *310-317-0777*
Duke's Malibu attracts hordes
of locals and travelers owing to
its inviting menu and huge,
ocean-front picture windows.
House favorites include panko-
crusted calamari and Hawaiian
huli-huli chicken.

Classic dining at Musso and Frank Grill, Downtown Los Angeles

Geoffrey's $$$
Modern
American   **Road map** inset A
27400 Pacific Coast Hwy, 90265
Tel *310-457-1519*
In a stunning location perched on a cliff above the Pacific Coast, Geoffey's has a casual atmosphere with umbrella-laden tables and fire pits to keep diners cozy. Menu highlights include Maine lobster and Kobe beef.

Saddle Peak Lodge $$$
Modern
American   **Road map** inset A
419 Cold Canyon Rd, 91302
Tel *(818) 222-3888*
Rustic restaurant in an old hunting lodge, tucked away in the Santa Monica Mountains. The kitchen serves game – elk, buffalo, venison – with aplomb. Romantic, candlelit atmosphere.

Manhattan Beach
Manhattan Beach Post $$
Modern
American   **Road map** inset A
1142 Manhattan Ave, 90266
Tel *310-545-5405*
Stylish space just two blocks from the beach, with an inviting and eclectic menu of small plates that are paired with hand-crafted cocktails and boutique wines. Friendly servers make sure diners are satisfied with their meal.

Marina del Rey
Café del Rey $$
International   **Road map** inset A
4451 Admiralty Way, 90292
Tel *310-823-6395*
This sophisticated dining venue enjoys a dockside location and expansive windows with panoramic views. The eclectic menu features many Pacific Rim-inspired dishes. Weekend brunch on the patio is an LA tradition.

The Cheesecake Factory $$
American   **Road map** inset A
4142 Via Marina, 90292
Tel *310-306-3344*
Massive portions of well-prepared savory and sweet dishes, the stars being the huge variety of cheesecakes. Perched on the marina overlooking the bay.

Cast & Plow $$$
American   **Road map** inset A
4375 Admiralty Way, 90292
Tel *310-574-4333*
Housed in the Ritz-Carlton hotel, this restaurant offers farm-to-table sustainable cuisine. Enjoy a variety of small plates made

Clean and contemporary dining at The Royce Wood-Fired Steakhouse, Pasadena

with the fresh seasonal local ingredients and complemented with beautiful waterfront views.

Midtown
Chan Dara $$
Asian   **Map** 8 B2
310 N Larchmont Blvd, 90004
Tel *(323) 467-1052*
Flavorful noodles, soups, satays, and curries offered at reasonable prices at this restaurant, housed in a charming little bungalow just north of Larchmont Village.

Pizzeria Mozza $$
Pizza   **Map** 8 A4
641 N Highland Ave, 90036
Tel *(323) 297-0101*
Head here for the creative pies served straight from the stone oven, within sight of the diners. The Italian wines on offer are modestly priced. Sister restaurant Osteria Mozza right next door.

Monrovia
LeRoy's The Original Restaurant $
American   **Road map** inset A
523 W Huntington Dr, 91016
Tel *626-357-5076*
A good choice for hearty breakfasts and lunches, where generous portion sizes and service make up for the no-frills atmosphere. Crowd favorites include giant omelets, hot turkey sandwiches, and juicy pork chops.

Pasadena
Dog Haus $
German   **Road map** inset A
93 E Green St, 91105
Tel *(626) 683-0808*
Fun, casual eatery specializing in gourmet hot dogs and sausages. Choose from the long list of inventive toppings. Signature

"Sooo Cali" dog is topped with arugula, tomato, fried onions, spicy basil aioli, and avocado.

Mi Piace $$
Italian   **Road map** inset A
25 E Colorado Blvd, 91105
Tel *(626) 795-3131*
This trattoria offers traditional pastas and pizzas, plus a few more innovative dishes. Trendy setting popular with a youthful crowd. Stylish martini lounge with stainless steel bar and red leather couches.

Parkway Grill $$$
Modern
American   **Road map** inset A
510 S Arroyo Pkwy, 91105
Tel *(626) 795-1001*
Parkway Grill has been a favorite since 1985 for its wood-fired pizzas and creative cuisine with Southwestern influences. Adjacent organic garden ensures great salads, and wild game is a specialty. Casually elegant, garden-like setting.

The Royce Wood-Fired Steakhouse $$$
Steakhouse   **Road map** inset A
1401 S Oak Knoll Ave, 91106
Tel *(626) 568-3900*
Luxury hotel restaurant offering a fine selection of cuts and chops. Australian wagyu and Kobe Japanese beef are perfectly prepared over an oak-fired grill.

Shiro $$$
Asian   **Road map** inset A
1505 Mission St, S Pasadena, 91030
Tel *(626) 799-4774* **Closed** *Mon & Tue*
Shiro's signature dish is a whole, deep-fried catfish with *ponzu* (a citrus-based sauce) and fresh cilantro. The varied wine list features several Californian award-winners. Highly rated servers and an attractive dining area.

For more information on types of restaurants *see pages 544–5*

Entrance to the classy Mélisse, Santa Monica

Playa del Rey

Cantalini's Salerno Beach Restaurant $$
Italian **Road map** inset A
193 Culver Blvd, 90293
Tel *310-821-0018*
Freshly made pastas, New York-style pizzas, fresh seafood, and a good children's menu make this an affordable family-friendly option, just a block from the beach. Friendly staff.

The Tripel $$
American **Road map** inset A
333 Culver Blvd, 90293
Tel *(310) 821-0333*
An eclectic gastropub a short stroll away from the Pacific, The Tripel offers excellent pub fare and has an extensive craft beer selection.

Redondo Beach

Chez Mélange $$
International **Road map** inset A
1611 S Catalina Ave, 90277
Tel *310-540-1222*
Crowd-pleasing and upscale comfort cuisine served in an airy dining room. The eclectic menu's inspirations range from Louisiana to Italy. Located in Palos Verdes Inn.

San Pedro

Raffaello's Italian Ristorante $$
Italian **Road map** inset A
400 S Pacific Ave, 90731
Tel *310-514-0900*
Rustic dishes made with fresh ingredients. Crowd favorites include *osso buco*, fettucine alfredo, and seafood risotto. Welcoming staff.

For key to prices *see page 550*

Santa Monica

Border Grill $$
Mexican **Road map** inset A
1445 4th St, 90401
Tel *310-451-1655*
Local institution founded by celebrity chefs. The menu contains authentic recipes from across Mexico and the well-informed servers deliver delicious margaritas from an attractive bar.

Father's Office $$
Modern American **Road map** inset A
1018 Montana Ave, 90403
Tel *310-736-2224*
Enjoy the convivial atmosphere inside or sit outdoors on the large patio. The menu features gastropub fare, craft beers and inventive cocktails. Do not miss the famed Office Burger.

Tar & Roses $$
International **Road map** inset A
602 Santa Monica Blvd, 90401
Tel *310-587-0700*
Trendy destination that lures foodies with its inventive preparations of farm-fresh cuisine. Crispy pig tails, braised lamb belly, and oxtail dumplings are typical fare here.

Chinois on Main $$$
Asian/French **Road map** inset A
2709 Main St, 90405
Tel *310-392-9025*
Wolfgang Puck's pioneering restaurant is one of the first to perfect Asian-French fusion cuisine. Constantly evolving menu and impressive service.

The Lobster $$$
Seafood **Road map** inset A
1602 Ocean Ave, 90401
Tel *310-458-9294*
Lively fish house at the foot of the Santa Monica pier. The namesake crustacean is served in a variety of crowd-pleasing forms. Terrace provides lovely sunset views.

DK Choice

Mélisse $$$
French **Road map** inset A
1104 Wilshire Blvd, 90401
Tel *310-395-0881* **Closed** *Sun & Mon*
One of the city's most glamorous restaurants, Mélisse specializes in modern French cuisine and is perfect for dining on special occasions. The tasting menus change seasonally and feature the finest Californian ingredients. An impressive wine list complements the excellent food.

Valentino $$$
Italian **Road map** inset A
3115 Pico Blvd, 90405
Tel *310-829-4313* **Closed** *Sun & Mon*
One of the area's best Italian restaurants, specializing in creative and contemporary fine dining dishes. The wine list is backed by a cellar of around 200,000 bottles.

Sherman Oaks

Café Bizou $$
Californian **Road map** inset A
14016 Ventura Blvd, 91423
Tel *(818) 788-3536*
Popular spot housed in an inviting old bungalow. Lengthy menu of Californian crowd favorites, with most entrées priced under $20. A favorite with wine buffs for its $2 corkage fee.

Studio City

Art's Deli $
Delicatessen **Road map** inset A
12224 Ventura Blvd, 91604
Tel *(818) 762-1221*
A bit more expensive than most delis, but the diners do not seem to mind as the huge sandwiches are billed as "works of art." Savory pastrami, smoked fish, and big breakfasts are the favorites here.

Universal City

Ca' del Sole $$
Italian **Road map** inset A
4100 Cahuenga Blvd, 91602
Tel *(818) 985-4669*
Attractive dining room that feels homey with its fireplace, hanging copper pots, and cozy booths. Fresh salads, first-rate pastas, and attractively priced mains.

The inviting and colorful interior of Border Grill, Santa Monica

Venice

Jody Maroni's
Sausage Kingdom $
Hot Dogs **Road map** inset A
2011 Ocean Front Walk, 90291
Tel *310-822-5639*
Although there are franchised
locations around town, the
original is a boardwalk landmark.
Sausages such as tequila-chicken
and Bombay curried lamb are
served in freshly baked rolls.

The Rose $
Café **Road map** inset A
220 Rose Ave, 90291
Tel *310-399-0711*
Representative of the city's old
bohemian vibe, with roomy
interiors and a pleasant patio.
Choose from an assortment of
pastries, quiches, salads, and well-
made specialty coffees.

Superba Snack Bar $$
Italian **Road map** inset A
533 Rose Ave, 90291
Tel *310-399-6400*
Hip foodie hangout serving
pastas and inventive small
plates made with fresh, local
ingredients. Try dishes such
as spaghetti with sea urchin,
served with miso butter, and
pickled jalapeños.

Joe's Restaurant $$$
Californian/
Mediterranean **Road map** inset A
1023 Abbot Kinney Blvd, 90291
Tel *310-399-5811* **Closed** *Mon*
The cuisine at Joe's Restaurant
has French and Mediterranean
themes, reflected on the menu,
such as potato-scaled red
snapper with red wine sauce.
Friendly staff and laid-back yet
sophisticated dining area.

West Hollywood

La Bohème $$
International **Map** 6 C1
8400 Santa Monica Blvd, 90069
Tel *310) 848-2360* **Closed** *Mon*
With a fireplace and chandeliers,
La Bohème's gothic-like space
provides a romantic setting. The
eclectic cuisine is made with fresh
ingredients from the farmers'
market. Outdoor patio.

Bossa Nova Brazilian Cuisine $$
Brazilian **Map** 6 B2
685 N Robertson Blvd, 90069
Tel *310-657-5070* **Closed** *Sun*
Caipirinha drinks prove to be a
popular accompaniment to the
large portions of grilled chicken,
black beans, and plantains.
There is usually a long wait for
outside tables, which are perfect
for people-watching.

The über cool interior of BOA Steakhouse, West Hollywood

Jinpachi $$
Japanese **Map** 6 C1
8711 Santa Monica Blvd, 90069
Tel *310-358-9134* **Closed** *Sun*
Amazingly fresh sushi and
sashimi is served in a dining
room with just a handful of
tables. Other specialties include
halibut *carpaccio*, Scottish
salmon with jalapeño, and blue-
fin tuna.

Mandarette Café $$
Chinese **Map** 6 C2
8386 Beverly Blvd, 90048
Tel *(323) 655-6115*
A casual spin-off of a fancy
Beverly Hills restaurant. Choose
from a value-oriented menu or
the house favorites: noodle
dishes, fresh salads, and curried
chicken dumplings.

Ago $$$
Italian **Map** 6 C1
8478 Melrose Ave, 90069
Tel *(323) 655-6333*
Considered by many the
best Italian fare in the city,
Ago is often packed with
loyal customers, including
celebrities. Boasts an extensive
wine list.

BOA Steakhouse $$$
Steakhouse **Map** 6 A1
9200 Sunset Blvd, 90069
Tel *310-278-2050*
Diners enjoy top-quality
steaks complemented by an
assortment of unusual rubs,
sauces, and condiments at this
trendy venue popular with
celebrities. It also serves
excellent fresh seafood.

Dan Tana's $$$
Italian **Map** 6 A2
9071 Santa Monica Blvd, 90069
Tel *310-275-9444*
This landmark restaurant serves
classic Italian fare. The red-and-
white tablecloths complement
the old-school setting.

Jar $$$
Steakhouse **Map** 6 C2
8225 Beverly Blvd, 90048
Tel *(323) 655-6566* **Closed** *Mon*
A modern chophouse with a
stylish retro feel provided by a zinc
bar, deep wood tones, club chairs,
and cork floor. Head here for
inventive spins on familiar dishes.

Lucques $$$
French **Map** 6 C2
8474 Melrose Ave, 90069
Tel *(323) 655-6277*
A superbly skilled chef prepares
a mix of modern and traditional
French fare. The dining room
is carved out of the former
carriage house of silent film
star Harold Lloyd.

Petrossian $$$
French **Map** 6 B2
321 N Robertson Blvd, 90048
Tel *310-271-6300*
Petrossian's caviar-focused
menu includes dishes such as
poached eggs, smoked salmon,
duck confit salad, and even
desserts with caviar. Modern
interior with lively paintings
by local artists.

RH Restaurant $$$
Californian **Map** 1 A5
8401 W Sunset Blvd, 90069
Tel *(323) 785-6090*
Romantic spot with a bustling
open kitchen. Traditional
cuisine is prepared using local
ingredients. Seasonal dishes are
made using the freshest
vegetables and organic meat.
Impressive wine list.

Wa Sushi & Bistro $$$
Sushi/French **Map** 1 A5
1106 N La Cienega Blvd, 90069
Tel *310-854-7285* **Closed** *Mon*
A trio of chefs from the renowned
Matsuhisa *(see p550)* run this
restaurant with a hillside view of
the city. Superb sushi and sashimi,
plus classic French-inspired dishes.

For more information on types of restaurants *see pages 544–5*

Westwood

Apple Pan $
American   Road map inset A
10801 W Pico Blvd, 90064
Tel *310-475-3585*   **Closed** *Mon*
This old-school diner, with a single horseshoe-shaped counter, is an LA icon. Delicious burgers are topped with Tillamook cheddar and BBQ sauce. Fresh apple and banana cream pies provide a sweet finish to the meal.

John O'Groats $
Café   Road map inset A
10516 Pico Blvd, 90064
Tel *310-204-0692*
Coffee shop serving some of the best breakfasts in LA, complete with perfect home-made biscuits. Popular items include pumpkin or blueberry pancakes and *huevos rancheros* (eggs baked in spicy tomato sauce).

Versailles $
Cuban   Road map inset A
10319 Venice Blvd, 90034
Tel *310-558-3168*
No-frills eatery with a big menu of Cuban specialties. Among the favorites are *ropa vieja* (shredded pork on tortillas), paella, and garlic chicken. Many dishes are accompanied by flavorful black beans, rice, and plantains.

La Serenata de Garibaldi $$
Mexican   Road map inset A
10924 W Pico Blvd, 90064
Tel *310-441-9667*
Casual spin-off of a venerable East LA restaurant, packed with diners getting their fix of Mexican seafood. Dishes include *ceviche*, mahi mahi tacos, and *gorditas* stuffed with shrimp.

Mori Sushi $$$
Japanese   Road map inset A
11500 W Pico Blvd, 90064
Tel *310-479-3939*   **Closed** *Sun*
Unassuming establishment where the chef is a master at aesthetic creations presented on unique plates fired in his own kiln. Rare species of fish are crafted into edible works of art.

South Central California

BAKERSFIELD: Wool Growers $
Spanish   Road map C5
620 E 19th St, 93305
Tel *(661) 327-9584*   **Closed** *Sun*
Family-style meals in a region with Basque heritage. The hearty mains include lamb chops, oxtail stew, and fried chicken; sides include soups, beans, and veggies.

Casual dining room at John O'Groats, Westwood

BUELLTON: The Hitching Post II $$
Steakhouse   Road map B5
406 E Hwy 246, 93427
Tel *(805) 688-0676*
This Wine Country favorite was featured in the road trip movie *Sideways* (2004). It is famous for its oak-grilled steaks and chops, complemented by a good selection of local wines, including their own. Low-key, rustic charm.

CAMBRIA: Wild Ginger $
Asian   Road map B5
2380 Main St, 93428
Tel *(805) 927-1001*   **Closed** *Thu*
Locals flock to Wild Ginger for what some call the best Asian food on the Central Coast. The varied menu features dishes such as Singapore chicken satay, Thai chicken wings, and Vietnamese caramelized prawns.

CAYUCOS: Schooners Wharf $$
Seafood   Road map C5
171 N Ocean Ave, 93430
Tel *(805) 995-3883*
This restaurant and bar serving fresh fish has been a local favorite since 1993. The dining room has a retro nautical theme and the patio offers splendid views of the ocean.

LOS OLIVOS: Los Olivos Café & Wine Merchant $$
International   Road map C5
2879 Grand Ave, 93441
Tel *(805) 688-7265*
Ideal spot for recharging after a day of wine tasting. Rustic little dining room with a charming, wisteria-covered sidewalk patio. Light bites include pizzas, olives, and artisanal cheeses, while heartier dishes such as pasta, lamb, and pot roast are also served.

MONTECITO: Lucky's $$$
Steakhouse   Road map C5
1279 Coast Village Rd, 93108
Tel *(805) 565-7540*
Top-notch steaks and seafood. Relaxed ambience for enjoying a well-made martini. Sunday brunch is a especially popular.

MORRO BAY: Windows on the Water $$$
Modern American   Road map B5
699 Embarcadero, 93442
Tel *(805) 772-0677*
Spacious restaurant with large windows that provide striking views of the water and Morro Rock. Favorites include crab cakes with jalapeño aioli, cedar-planked salmon, and Pacific *bouillabaisse*.

OJAI: Suzanne's Cuisine $$
Californian   Road map C5
502 W Ojai Ave, 93023
Tel *(805) 640-1961*   **Closed** *Tue*
American dishes prepared with a French twist, using local, organic ingredients. Considered the best eatery in town by many, including celebrities.

PASO ROBLES: Bistro Laurent $$$
French   Road map B5
1202 Pine St, 93446
Tel *(805) 226-8191*   **Closed** *Sun & Mon*
Wine Country bistro serving familiar favorites in an attractive dining room housed in an old brick structure. Sit on the breezy patio and sip on local wines.

PISMO BEACH: Splash Café $
American   Road map B5
197 Pomeroy Ave, 93449
Tel *(805) 773-4653*
Funky beachside spot popular with surfers. Outstanding clam

chowder is served in a sourdough bread bowl. Baskets of fish 'n' chips are also popular.

SAN LUIS OBISPO: Buona Tavola $$
Italian   Road map B5
1037 Monterey St, 93401
Tel *(805) 545-8000*
Cosmopolitan, art-filled trattoria with a lovely garden patio next to the historic Fremont Theatre. The moderately priced menu offers a wide choice of antipasti, pastas, steaks, and seafood. Great wine list.

SAN LUIS OBISPO: Novo Restaurant and Lounge $$
International   Road map B5
726 Higuera St, 93401
Tel *(805) 543-3986*
Modern eatery serving tapas with a twist. Fusing South American and Southeast Asian flavors with Spanish classics, the kitchen turns out small bites like prawns *muqueca* – a Brazilian stew – and *piquillo*-cheese empanadas with chutney.

SAN LUIS OBISPO: Ciopinot $$$
Italian   Road map B5
1051 Nipomo St, 93401
Tel *(805) 547-1111*
Family-owned seafood grill and oyster bar. The extensive wine list focuses on white and red Pinots from around the globe and the no corkage fee appeals to local wine lovers. Warm, friendly service.

SANTA BARBARA: La Super-Rica $
Mexican   Road map C5
622 N Milpas St, 93103
Tel *(805) 963-4940* **Closed** *Tue & Wed*
Little roadside shack with a devoted clientele that patiently stands in line for simple Mexican fare. Try the tacos, made from

Local favorite bistro, Bouchon, Santa Barbara

Ocean views from the dining area at Bella Vista, Santa Barbara

freshly grilled tortillas, and filled with marinated pork, beef, chicken, chorizo, and more.

SANTA BARBARA: Arigato Sushi $$
Sushi   Road map C5
1225 State St, 93101
Tel *(805) 965-6074*
This award-winning sushi spot serves all the standards as well as inventive rolls, plus dozens of cooked options. Efficient servers maintain a relaxed atmosphere. Offers wines and sakes.

SANTA BARBARA: Brophy Bros. Restaurant & Clam Bar $$
Seafood   Road map C5
119 Harbor Way, 93109
Tel *(805) 966-4418*
Head to this dockside eatery with harbor views and sample fresh seafood, expertly prepared. Excellent clam bar with raw shellfish and bowls of legendary chowder.

SANTA BARBARA: The Hungry Cat $$
Seafood   Road map C5
1134 Chapala St, 93101
Tel *(805) 884-4701*
Small and always busy, this is one of the city's top spots for seafood. Locals devour generous portions of oysters, fried shrimp, and fish 'n' chips. The casual atmosphere is great for people-watching.

SANTA BARBARA: Louie's California Bistro $$
Californian   Road map C5
1404 de la Vina St, 93101
Tel *(805) 963-7003*
Charming, no-frills eatery tucked into a 19th-century boutique hotel. Gourmet pizzas and pastas share the menu with regional American

classics. Quiet and romantic atmosphere. Lovely patio seating.

SANTA BARBARA: Olio e Limone $$
Italian   Road map C5
17 W Victoria St, 93101
Tel *(805) 899-2699*
One of the city's favorite trattorias, with authentic Sicilian specialties and familiar favorites served in an intimate dining room. Gracious staff helpfully suggest wines from an extensive list.

SANTA BARBARA: The Palace Grill $$
Cajun   Road map C5
8 E Cota St, 93101
Tel *(805) 963-5000*
This crowd-pleaser delivers traditional New Orleans-style fare in friendly, colorful, and fun environs. From savory gumbo and *étouffée* (shellfish served with rice) to blackened redfish flown in from the "Big Easy," it has all the tastes of New Orleans.

SANTA BARBARA: Trattoria Vittoria $$
Italian   Road map C5
30 E Victoria St, 93103
Tel *(805) 962-5014*
Traditional trattoria run by an Italian family. The pasta is hand-made, soups are made daily, and sauces have deep flavors that come from cooking for days.

SANTA BARBARA: Bella Vista $$$
Italian   Road map C5
The Biltmore, 1260 Channel Dr, 93108
Tel *(805) 969-2261*
This local favorite has large windows overlooking the ocean. Bella Vista's menu focuses heavily on local produce and seafood prepared with an Italian twist. Sunset dinners and Sunday brunch service are popular.

DK Choice

SANTA BARBARA: Bouchon $$$
French   Road map C5
9 W Victoria St, 93101
Tel *(805) 730-1160*
A classy, inviting bistro that exudes a comfortable, warm aura. The kitchen churns out an array of well-prepared French classics. Favorites include bourbon- and maple-glazed duck, buffalo tartare, and warm chocolate molten lava cake for dessert. Servers detail the menu's intricacies while offering expert wine-pairing advice. Couples will enjoy the romantic atmosphere and attentive service.

For more information on types of restaurants *see pages 544–5*

Cozy interior of Julienne in downtown Santa Barbara

SANTA BARBARA: Downey's $$$
Modern American   Road map C5
1305 State St, 93101
Tel *(805) 966-5006*   **Closed** *Mon*
A classic regional cuisine experience in an elegant dining room. Crab, lobster, and mussels from local waters often feature on the daily changing menu, and top-quality meats are finished with perfect sauces.

SANTA BARBARA: Julienne $$$
Modern American   Road map C5
138 E Canon Perdido, 93101
Tel *(805) 845-6488*   **Closed** *Mon*
The award-winning Julienne has a daily changing menu focusing on sustainably sourced, local ingredients. It offers top-notch seafood, housemade charcuterie, and fixed-price wine menus.

SANTA YNEZ: Trattoria Grappolo $$
Italian   Road map C5
3687 Sagunto St, 93460
Tel *(805) 688-6899*
Bustling trattoria filled with colorful murals. Gourmet pizzas, generously plated pastas, and hearty main courses are on the menu. Moderately priced wine list that honors local wineries. Efficient servers and welcoming environs.

SOLVANG: Solvang Restaurant $
Danish   Road map C5
1672 Copenhagen St, 93463
Tel *(800) 654-0541*
One of the country's most comprehensive Scandinavian-themed eateries. The house favorite is *aebleskiver*, a sort of Danish pastry that is topped with raspberry jam and powdered sugar.

For key to prices *see page 550*

SOLVANG: Root 246 $$
Modern American   Road map C5
420 Alisal Rd, 93463
Tel *(805) 686-8681*   **Closed** *Mon*
This celebrity-chef-driven eatery is an oasis of contemporary design and food in an otherwise kitschy tourist town. Hand-cut fries, braised meats, and fresh local salads provide a perfect end to a day of wine tasting.

VENTURA: Andria's Seafood Restaurant & Market $
Seafood   Road map C5
1449 Spinnaker Dr, 93001
Tel *(805) 654-0546*
A no-frills favorite on the harbor. Menu includes fresh seafood – lobster, fish 'n' chips, and more – at affordable prices. Casual counter service, with seating both indoors and outside.

Orange County

ANAHEIM: Mimi's Café $
American   Road map D6
1400 S Harbor Blvd, 92802
Tel *(714) 956-2223*
Close to the Disneyland resort, Mimi's Café is part of a family-friendly chain serving filling and budget-friendly fare such as quiche, steak, and pot pie.

ANAHEIM: Goofy's Kitchen $$
American   Road map D6
1150 Magic Way, 92803
Tel *(714) 781-3463*
A taste of Disneyland even before entering the park. Kids love the buffet featuring Mickey Mouse-shaped waffles, peanut-butter-and-jelly pizza, and chocolate cake. Disney characters interact with patrons.

ANAHEIM: Anaheim White House Restaurant $$$
International   Road map D6
887 S Anaheim Blvd, 92805
Tel *(714) 722-1381*
The grand facade of this old home fronts an elegant interior and a sprawling veranda. Refined cuisine combines Northern Italian, French, and Asian influences. Artfully presented dishes.

ANAHEIM: Napa Rose $$$
Modern American   Road map D6
1313 Disneyland Dr, 92802
Tel *(714) 635-2300*
Fine-dining restaurant in Disney's Grand Californian Hotel. Gourmet dishes feature farm-fresh ingredients that encapsulate the flavors of California Wine Country. World-renowned vintage wines complement the cuisine.

BUENA PARK: Mrs. Knott's Chicken Dinner Restaurant $
American   Road map D6
8039 Beach Blvd, 90620
Tel *(714) 220-5055*
A local institution since 1934. Chicken dinners are served with biscuits, mashed potatoes, gravy, and veggies. Try the diner's signature boysenberry pie for a sweet finish.

CATALINA ISLAND: Avalon Grille $
American   Road map C6
423 Crescent Ave, Avalon, 90704
Tel *(310) 510-7494*
The menu features a range of dishes varying from burgers to seafood. There is a well-stocked bar with live music on Saturday nights during summer. Large windows offer beautiful views of the Pacific.

CORONA DEL MAR: Five Crowns $$
Steakhouse/British   Road map D6
3801 East Coast Hwy, 92965
Tel *(949) 760-0331*
Old-fashioned Tudor-style house featuring a crackling fireplace and wooden beams. Prime rib is the specialty but lamb, duck, and seafood also impress. Sunday brunch in the garden is appealing in good weather.

COSTA MESA: Memphis Café $
Southern   Road map D6
2920 S Bristol St, 92626
Tel *(714) 432-7685*
Favored by a young crowd, Memphis Café serves updated versions of soul food favorites. Pulled-pork sandwiches, gumbo, jambalaya, and catfish omelets (for breakfast) are the menu's highlights. Kitsch 1960s decor.

Elegant wooden furnishing at Studio, Laguna Beach

COSTA MESA: Scott's Restaurant & Bar $$
Seafood Road map D6
3300 Bristol St, 92626
Tel *(714) 979-2400*
This San Francisco import's old–school kitchen turns out classics such as oysters Rockefeller, lobster bisque, and *cioppino* (fish stew), along with steaks. Try the bread pudding or a slice of cheesecake for dessert.

COSTA MESA: Mastro's Steakhouse $$$
Steakhouse Road map D6
633 Anton Blvd, 92626
Tel *(714) 546-7405*
Enjoy contemporary fine dining at this sophisticated restaurant. Prime steak, prime rib, and fresh seafood top the menu and the wine list is extensive. There is live music every evening.

HUNTINGTON BEACH: Sandy's $$
American Road map D6
315 Pacific Coast Hwy, 92648
Tel *(714) 374-7273*
Located on the pier, Sandy's offers scenic views of the ocean. Locally sourced ingredients are used wherever possible. Surf and turf is a specialty, with the pecan-crusted sea bass being a favorite. Good range of wines and cocktails.

IRVINE: Javier's Cantina $
Mexican Road map D6
45 Fortune Dr, 92618
Tel *(949) 872-2101*
Regional homestyle cuisine in a sophisticated setting. Popular dishes include Dungeness crab enchiladas in tomatillo sauce, *tamales* (fried corn snack), and *carnitas* (braised meat). The bar boasts a huge selection of tequilas.

IRVINE: Bistango $$$
Modern American Road map D6
19100 Von Karman Ave, 92612
Tel *(949) 752-5222* **Closed** *Sun*
Modern art, a lively bar scene, and live jazz sets the tone at Bistango. The menu offers Californian cuisine featuring creative pizzas, seafood, pastas, and paellas. Award-winning wine list.

LAGUNA BEACH: Alessa Laguna $
Italian Road map D6
234 Forest Ave, 92651
Tel *(949) 497-8222*
Alessa Laguna's kitchen serves high-quality Italian cuisine. Dishes on offer include ravioli, calamari, chicken marsala, and lasagna. Regular patrons attest to this restaurant's popularity.

Modern interiors of Three Seventy Common, Laguna Beach

LAGUNA BEACH: Las Brisas $
Mexican Road map D6
360 Cliff Dr, 92652
Tel *(949) 497-5434*
The menu at Las Brisas features specialties such as *ceviche*, red snapper stuffed with shrimp, and a seafood stew. Wide selection of tequilas on offer. Sprawling coastal restaurant offering spectacular ocean views.

LAGUNA BEACH: Zinc Café & Market $
International Road map D6
350 Ocean Ave, 92651
Tel *(949) 494-6302*
Combination café and market open for breakfast and lunch. Market is great for picnickers. Specialties include Tuscan white-bean soup, vegetarian chili, and personal-sized pizzas. Lovely garden patio.

LAGUNA BEACH: 230 Forest Avenue Restaurant & Bar $$
Seafood Road map D6
230 Forest Ave, 92651
Tel *(949) 494-2545*
Chic, intimate spot across from the beach specializing in fresh seafood. Chopped seafood salad and grilled freshly caught fish are favorites and the chocolate croissant bread pudding is a delight. Extensive wine list and martini selection.

LAGUNA BEACH: Three Seventy Common $$
Modern American Road map D6
370 Glenneyre, 92651
Tel *(949) 494-8686*
This trendy spot features rustic decor with industrial accents. The menu offers locally sourced dishes: local greens, pork belly, and *poutine* (french fries topped with gravy and cheese) are the highlights. Cobblers and cakes make for excellent sweet treats.

LAGUNA BEACH: Studio $$$
French Road map D6
30801 S Coast Hwy, 92651
Tel *(949) 715-6420* **Closed** *Mon*
Beachfront structure on the grounds of the exclusive Montage Resort. Modern French preparations feature innovative use of artisanal local ingredients. Fabulous tasting menu.

NEWPORT BEACH: Mama D's Italian Kitchen $
Italian Road map D6
3012 Newport Blvd, 92663
Tel *(949) 675-6262*
Expansive menu featuring large portions of all the classic Italian favorites. Complimentary fresh-baked cookies at the end of the meal. Friendly service.

NEWPORT BEACH: Roy's Restaurant $$
Hawaiian Road map D6
453 Newport Center Dr, 92660
Tel *(949) 640-7697*
Unique fine-dining experience with a menu of sushi and fish dishes. Try the *misoyaki* butterfish. Martinis and other innovative cocktails.

DK Choice

ORANGE: The Hobbit $$$
French Road map D6
2932 E Chapman Ave, 92669
Tel *(714) 997-1972* **Closed** *Mon & Tue*
The Hobbit offers one of Southern California's most exciting dining experiences. The seven-course, *prix fixe* "feasts" begin in the wine cellar and include an "intermission" when guests may tour the kitchen. The menu is influenced by a range of European cuisines and the main entrée changes weekly. Book ahead.

For more information on types of restaurants *see pages 544–5*

SAN CLEMENTE: Iva Lee's $
Creole **Road map** D6
555 N El Camino Real, 92672
Tel *(949) 361-2855*
Standout dishes at Iva Lee's
include fried green tomatoes
with goat cheese, grilled pork
chops, and jambalaya. End
with Bananas Foster. Warm
atmosphere enhanced by
live blues and jazz.

SAN JUAN CAPISTRANO:
Cedar Creek Inn $$
Modern American **Road map** D6
26860 Ortega Hwy, 92675
Tel *(949) 240-2229*
Spanish Mission-inspired design
provides a casually elegant
atmosphere. Choose from an
extensive menu that features
pasta, seafood, and prime rib.
Patio with a view of Mission
San Juan Capistrano.

**SANTA ANA: Antonello
Ristorante** $$
Italian **Road map** D6
3800 S Plaza Dr, 92704
Tel *(714) 751-7153* **Closed** *Sun*
Highly revered spot with an
old-world ambience. The classic
menu features *spaghetti alla
puttanesca, cioppino,* scampi,
and risotto. Impressive wine list.

**SUNSET BEACH: Harbor
House Café** $
Diner **Road map** D6
16341 Pacific Coast Hwy, 90742
Tel *(562) 592-5404*
Inviting roadside spot decorated
with surfing gear, movie posters,
and collectables. Head here
for American dishes including
tasty burgers, over 20 kinds of
omelets, and malts. Open round
the clock.

TUSTIN: Zov's Bistro $
International **Road map** D6
17440 E 17th St, 92780
Tel *(714) 838-8855*
The food at this local favorite
shows influences from Greece,
Italy, Lebanon, Morocco, and
beyond. Versatile wine list
and a bakery that produces
delectable cakes, tarts, cookies,
and breads.

San Diego County

CORONADO: Candelas $$
Mexican **Road map** D6
1201 1st St, 92118
Tel *(619) 435-4900*
Innovative dishes of modern
Mexican fare with French accents
focus on meats, seafood, and
surprising vegetarian options.

For key to prices *see page 550*

The sophisticated dining area at 1500 Ocean, Coronado

CORONADO: Mistral $$
Mediterranean **Road map** D6
*Loews Coronado Bay Resort,
4000 Coronado Bay Rd, 92118*
Tel *(619) 424-4000* **Closed** *Mon & Tue*
Dazzling dining room with views
of the Coronado Bay bridge and
San Diego skyline. Offers globally
inspired cuisine with a focus on
small plates. Diverse wine list
and winning desserts.

CORONADO: 1500 Ocean $$$
Mediterranean **Road map** D6
1500 Orange Ave, 92118
Tel *(619) 522-8490* **Closed** *Sun & Mon*
Hotel Del Coronado's signature
beachfront restaurant. Farm-to-
table cuisine makes use of
California's coastal ingredients.
Seasonal cocktails incorporate
fresh herbs. Extensive wine list.

DEL MAR: Kitchen 1540 $$
Modern American **Road map** D6
1540 Camino Del Mar, 92014
Tel *(858) 793-6460*
Relaxed and modern, with an
open kitchen, wine bar, and an
outdoor dining terrace. The diverse
menu offers organic traditional
classics with innovative creations.

**DEL MAR: Market
Restaurant & Bar** $$
Modern American **Road map** D6
3702 Via de la Valle, 92014
Tel *(858) 523-0007*
This sleek establishment offers
hearty dishes prepared using the
freshest local ingredients. Steaks
draw rave reviews and the sushi
bar is a popular spot. Views of Del
Mar Racetrack.

LA JOLLA: Alfonso's of La Jolla $
Mexican **Road map** D6
1251 Prospect Ave, 92037
Tel *(858) 454-2232*
Fresh seafood and Mexican flavors
in a festive setting. Lobster fajitas
and burritos, and shrimp *ceviche*
join chicken and beef dishes.
Patio seating and great margaritas.

LA JOLLA: Brockton Villa $
American **Road map** D6
1235 Coast Blvd, 92037
Tel *(858) 454-7393*
Seaside cottage-turned-eatery
offering views of the cove. Fresh
local fare is served all day, with
a great wine list and creative
"Brocktails." Friendly service.

LA JOLLA: The Cottage $
Café **Road map** D6
7702 Fay Ave, 92037
Tel *(858) 454-8409*
A local favorite for breakfast.
Excellent stuffed French
toast, crab cakes Benedict,
specialty omelets, breakfast
burritos, and fresh scones.
Sample burgers, flat-iron steak,
or meatloaf for lunch.

LA JOLLA: Living Room $
Café **Road map** D6
1010 Prospect Ave, 92037
Tel *(858) 459-1187*
Serving all day until late night,
with a menu that has waffles,
bagels, soups, sandwiches, pasta
dishes, and more. Huge selection
of fresh fruit tarts, cheesecakes,
cookies, and coffees.

Brockton Villa, offering beautiful views
of La Jolla Cove

LA JOLLA: Regents Pizzeria $
Pizza **Road map** D6
4150 Regents Park, Row 170, 92037
Tel *(858) 550-0406*
Serves both New York- and
Chicago-style pizzas. Standout
dishes include the meat-lover's
pizza with sausage, meatballs,
and pepperoni, as well as
chicken alfredo with a garlic
cream sauce.

LA JOLLA: Roppongi $
Asian–European **Road map** D6
875 Prospect St, 92037
Tel *(858) 551-5252*
Intriguing menu featuring tapas-
style dishes, sushi, and sashimi
plus other innovative specialties.
The stylish dining room is filled
with Asian antiques. Sleek lounge
and charming patio.

LA JOLLA: Whisknladle $$
Modern American **Road map** D6
1044 Wall St, 92037
Tel *(858) 551-7575*
Serves dishes with an imaginative
flair. Eclectic array of seafood and
a glistening raw bar. An ideal
happy hour spot, with tapas-
sized plates and seasonal cocktails.

DK Choice

**LA JOLLA: George's
California Modern** $$$
Modern American **Road map** D6
1250 Prospect St, 92037
Tel *(858) 454 4244*
This hip restaurant has a
menu that boasts cleverly
conceived seafood dishes
made using local ingredients.
An extensive wine list and
craft cocktails complement
the inventive cuisine. Gorgeous
views of the ocean and
modern design make this
an indulgent dining choice.
Refined service.

LA JOLLA: The Marine Room $$$
International **Road map** D6
2000 Spindrift Dr, 92037
Tel *(858) 459-7222*
An oceanfront icon serving
innovative dishes that harmonize
Asian and French influences, with
seafood as the star. Pricey, but a
wonderful dining experience.

LA JOLLA: Tapenade $$$
French **Road map** D6
7612 Fay Ave, 92037
Tel *(858) 551-7500*
Tapenade serves cuisine from the
south of France. *Escargots*, duck,
and *steak au poivre* are highlights
as well as Maine lobster in salad,
soup, and risotto. Decadent
desserts and fine cheeses.

**PACIFIC BEACH: Nick's at
the Beach** $
American **Road map** D6
809 Thomas Ave, 92109
Tel *(858) 232-2436*
Order from a diverse menu that
includes hearty omelets and
pancakes for breakfast, a wide
choice of seafood, sandwiches,
and more for lunch and dinner.
Happy hour draws a lively crowd.

**RANCHO SANTA FE:
Mille Fleurs** $$$
French **Road map** D6
6009 Paseo Delicias, 92067
Tel *(858) 756-3085*
Hidden away in an exclusive San
Diego suburb, this romantic
venue has great service. Superb
ingredients – local and flown in
from top sources – enhance the
modern French cuisine.

SAN DIEGO: Big Kitchen Café $
Diner **Road map** D6
3003 Grape St, 92102
Tel *(619) 234-5789*
Endearing gem of a diner behind
Balboa Park, popular for huge
breakfasts featuring omelets,
pancakes, and *huevos rancheros*.
Enjoy coffee on the patio.

SAN DIEGO: Hodad's $
American **Road map** D6
5010 Newport Ave, 92107
Tel *(619) 224-4623*
This beachside joint has served
up huge burgers to hungry
surfers and locals for decades.
Hefty patties stacked high with
fresh toppings, accompanied by
a basket of "frings" – fries and rings.

**SAN DIEGO: Karl Strauss
Brewing Company** $
American **Road map** D6
1157 Columbia St, 92101
Tel *(619) 234-2739*
Downtown microbrewery
offering pub fare and a wide
assortment of handcrafted
beers on tap. Menu favorites
include meatloaf, burgers, salads,
and wings.

**SAN DIEGO: South Beach
Bar & Grille** $
Seafood/Mexican **Road map** D6
5059 Newport Ave, 92107
Tel *(619) 226-4577*
Beachfront hangout renowned
for its mahi mahi fish tacos. Daily
specials, extensive bar menu,
and TVs draw lively crowds. A
variety of seafood, burgers, and
vegetarian dishes also available.

SAN DIEGO: Sushi Ota $
Japanese **Road map** D6
4529 Mission Bay Dr, 92109
Tel *(858) 270-5670*
Modest eatery serving some of
the city's best sushi and other
authentic offerings. Skilled chefs
focus on traditional dishes crafted
from the freshest ingredients.

SAN DIEGO: El Zarape $
Mexican **Road map** D6
4642 Park Blvd, 92116
Tel *(619) 692-1652* **Closed** *Mon*
This lively spot rustles up
adventurous but economical
tacos and burritos. Try the fresh
and flavorful lobster burritos,
potato-rolled tacos, and other
traditional offerings.

SAN DIEGO: El Agave $$
Mexican **Road map** D6
2304 San Diego Ave, 92110
Tel *(619) 220-0692*
Lively hacienda-style dining
room and sunny patio. The varied
menu features ancient Mexican
recipes with European influences.
Savory, chocolate-flavor mole
dishes are especially popular.
Impressive tequila selection.

SAN DIEGO: Dobson's $$
Modern American **Road map** D6
956 Broadway Circle, 92101
Tel *(619) 231-6771* **Closed** *Sun*
Old-fashioned dining room and
antique bar. Californian cuisine is
laced with European and Asian
influences and the dishes are
beautifully presented. Choice of
mussel *bisque en croûte*, sautéed
salmon, rack of lamb, and pastas.

Karl Strauss Brewing Company, San Diego

For more information on types of restaurants *see pages 544–5*

Fine dining with impressive views at Bertrand at Mister A's, San Diego

SAN DIEGO: Garage Kitchen & Bar $$
American Road map D6
655 4th Ave, 92101
Tel *(619) 231-6700*
One of the best pubs in the Gaslamp district, Garage Kitchen gives an interesting twist to regular favorites. Stop by for light bites such as ahi (tuna) tartare nachos.

SAN DIEGO: Indigo Grill $$
Modern American Road map D6
1536 India St, 92101
Tel *(619) 234-6802*
Popular spot for innovative fare. Totem poles and artifacts from indigenous American cultures adorn the dining room, while the menu puts a twist on regional cooking, from Mexico to Alaska.

SAN DIEGO: The Prado at Balboa Park $$
Modern American Road map D6
1549 El Prado, Balboa Park, 92101
Tel *(619) 557-9441*
Grand dining spot in the House of Hospitality. Fusion menu with Italian, Latin, and Asian influences. Try the *hamachi* fish tacos and paella with lobster saffron broth.

SAN DIEGO: AVANT $$$
Californian Road map D6
17550 Bernardo Oaks Dr, 92128
Tel *(858) 675-8500*
Inviting setting with a menu offering contemporary cuisine. Vibrant, creative dishes made with fresh, seasonal ingredients. Inspired artisanal cocktails.

SAN DIEGO: Bertrand at Mister A's $$$
Modern American Road map D6
2550 5th Ave, 92103
Tel *(619) 239-1377*
Upscale restaurant with attentive staff, exquisite food, and views of the skyline. The menu has classic as well as innovative meat, seafood, and vegetarian options.

SAN DIEGO: The Westgate Room $$$
Californian Road map D6
1055 2nd Ave, 92101
Tel *(619) 238-1818*
Ideal for special occasions with its European elegance and a striking dining area that has a hint of Versailles. Continental-Californian menu features perfectly executed and formally presented game and seafood.

SAN DIEGO: WineSellar & Brasserie $$$
French Road map D6
9550 Waples St, 92121
Tel *(858) 450-9557* **Closed** *Sun, Mon*
Acclaimed addition to a renowned wine shop. Tuck into the classic but elevated cuisine with creative touches. Award-winning wine list and knowledgeable staff.

The Inland Empire and Low Desert

BIG BEAR CITY: Peppercorn Grille $
American Road map D6
553 Pine Knot Ave, 92315
Tel *(909) 866-5405*
Welcoming spot in the heart of the village. There is something for everyone – high-quality meats, seafood, pizza, and pastas. Good wine list. Friendly service. Perfect for relaxing after outdoor activities.

CHINO: Centro Basco $
Basque Road map D6
13432 S Central Ave, 91710
Tel *(909) 628-9014* **Closed** *Mon*
Formerly part of an old lodging house for Basque sheep herders. Generous portions served in a sprawling dining room. Soup terrines, meatloaf, burgers, beef tongue, trout, prime rib, and more. Communal tables offer a unique experience.

IDYLLWILD: Restaurant Gastrognome $$
Modern American Road map D6
54381 Ridgeview Dr, 92549
Tel *(951) 659-5055*
The "Gnome" boasts a delightfully rustic dining room in a forest. Hearty fare includes crab cakes, orange-glazed roast duck, salmon with hollandaise sauce, and lobster tacos. Deck seating with forest and mountain views.

LA QUINTA: Louise's Pantry $
American Road map D6
47150 Washington St, 92253
Tel *(760) 771-3330*
A popular old-style coffee shop offering big breakfasts, chicken dumplings, grilled sandwiches, and fresh apple pie. The Reuben sandwich (beef, Swiss cheese and Sauerkraut) is a favorite.

PALM DESERT: Cuistot $$$
French Road map D6
72595 El Paseo, 95562
Tel *(760) 340-1000*
One of Palm Desert's premier culinary attractions, Cuistot is located in a French country farmhouse-inspired building. Serves expertly cooked food.

PALM DESERT: Jillian's $$$
European Road map D6
74155 El Paseo, 92260
Tel *(760) 776-8242* **Closed** *Sun*
A romantic spot for dining and music under the stars. The menu features roasted meats and grilled fish with innovative twists. Award-winning wine list.

PALM SPRINGS: Europa $$
European Road map D6
1620 S Indian Trail, 92264
Tel *(760) 327-2314* **Closed** *Mon*
One of Coachella Valley's most romantic spots, Europa features an intimate dining room with a fireplace and patio. Highlights include rack of lamb, *saumon en papillote*, and duck confit.

DK Choice

PALM SPRINGS: Melvyn's Restaurant $$
American Road map D6
200 W Ramon Rd, 92260
Tel *(760) 325-2323*
This establishment has been a special occasion restaurant for over three decades. Antiques, waiters in linen jackets, and old photographs transport diners to a bygone era. The menu of classics is well regarded and many dishes are prepared table-side. Enjoy an after-dinner drink in the piano lounge.

Entrance to Melvyn's Restaurant, Palm Springs

PALM SPRINGS: Palm Springs Chop House $$
Steakhouse   Road map D6
262 S Palm Canyon Dr, 92262
Tel *(760) 320-4500*
A locals favorite in the heart of Downtown. Great people-watching from the patio. Prime beef and encyclopedic wine list are the highlights, along with lamb, pork chops, rib chops, and Brussels sprout hash.

PALM SPRINGS: Le Vallauris $$$
French   Road map D6
385 W Tahquitz Canyon Way, 92262
Tel *(760) 325-5059*
Grand dame of Palm Springs. Refined, elegant dining room features tapestries and antique furniture. French specialties share a menu with creative seafood dishes. Impressive list of Bordeaux. First-class service.

RANCHO MIRAGE: Las Casuelas Nuevas $
Mexican   Road map D6
70-050 Hwy 111, 92270
Tel *(760) 328-8844*
Hacienda-style restaurant that specializes in enchiladas, fajitas, and *carnitas*. Live entertainment, potent margaritas, and a long list of premium tequilas keep things lively. A favored destination for Sunday brunch.

RANCHO MIRAGE: Fleming's Steakhouse & Wine Bar $$
Steakhouse   Road map D6
71800 Hwy 111, 92270
Tel *(760) 776-6685*
Bustling spot in the River entertainment area. Traditional favorites include USDA prime beef and fresh seafood, plus rich sides such as potatoes with jalapeño, cream, and cheddar. More than 100 wines by the glass.

RANCHO MIRAGE: Shame on the Moon $$
American   Road map D6
69550 Frank Sinatra Dr, 92270
Tel *(760) 324-5515*
A camp local institution much favored by locals. The menu features traditional fare such as steaks, pastas, fish, veal, and meatloaf. Warm and friendly service. Reservations recommended.

RANCHO MIRAGE: Wally's Desert Turtle $$$
American   Road map D6
71775 Hwy 111, 92270
Tel *(760) 568-9321*   Closed *Mon*
Grand desert dining room with mirrored ceilings, Peruvian artifacts, and elegant murals. Try rack of lamb and filet of beef with Béarnaise sauce, all made with top ingredients.

REDLANDS: Carolyn's Café $
American   Road map D6
1711 W Lugonia Ave, 92374
Tel *(909) 335-8181*   Closed *Sun*
Coffee cake is the star at this welcoming spot. Big breakfasts include eggs, waffles, and more. Lunch features home-made soups, salads, and sandwiches. Friendly service and a welcoming atmosphere.

REDLANDS: Joe Greensleeves $$
Italian   Road map D6
220 N Orange St, 92373
Tel *(909) 792-6969*   Closed *Sun*
Endearing local favorite housed in an old building. Subtly romantic decor with cozy booths and a fireplace. The glass-enclosed kitchen serves up wild game, lobster ravioli, pastas, and steaks cooked over a wood grill.

RIVERSIDE: Las Campanas $
Mexican   Road map D6
3649 Mission Inn Ave, 92501
Tel *(951) 784-0300*
Charming courtyard and garden shaded by towering palm trees. At dinner, outdoor candle-light creates a romantic setting. The upscale menu features *filet mignon flautas*, and rotisserie chicken with apricot chipotle sauce. The signature fresh fruit margaritas are popular.

RIVERSIDE: Mario's Place $$
Italian   Road map D6
3646 Mission Inn Ave, 92501
Tel *(951) 684-7755*   Closed *Sun*
Sleek, cosmopolitan establishment with Art Deco touches. The kitchen skillfully prepares Northern Italian specialties in a wood-burning oven. Asian and French influences are apparent. Live jazz on weekends.

RIVERSIDE: Duane's Prime Steak & Seafood $$$
Steakhouse   Road map D6
3649 Mission Inn Ave, 92501
Tel *(888) 326-4448*   Closed *Sun*
Located in one of California's most historic hotels. Dark wood and elegant table settings create a refined atmosphere. Superb steaks accompanied by all the traditional sides. Good wine list.

TEMECULA: Meritage Restaurant at Callaway Vineyards $$
Mediterranean   Road map D6
32720 Rancho California Rd, 92593
Tel *(951) 587-8889*
This wine country destination offers beautiful views of Callaway Vineyards. The exceptional menu focuses on small plates with local ingredients and Mediterranean flavors. Unique wine pairings and friendly service.

The Mojave Desert

BAKER: The Mad Greek $
Mediterranean   Road map D5
72112 Baker Blvd, 92309
Tel *(760) 733-4354*
Pit stop on the way to Las Vegas or Death Valley. Tasty gyros (roasted meat in a tortilla), hummus, kebabs, and other dishes, alongside burgers and fries. Popular strawberry shakes.

BARSTOW: Idle Spurs $
Steakhouse   Road map D5
690 Hwy 58, 92311
Tel *(760) 256-8888*   Closed *Mon*
Traditional steakhouse with a popular bar. Try the jalapeño poppers, fiery chicken wings, and tender-aged steaks all smothered in home-made BBQ sauce. The tree-shaded patio is a relaxing seating option.

Formal dining room at popular Italian Mario's place, Riverside

For more information on types of restaurants *see pages 544–5*

The dining area at the historic Inn at Furnace Creek, Death Valley

BARSTOW: Lola's Kitchen $
Mexican   **Road map** D5
1244 E Main St, 92311
Tel *(760) 255-1007*   **Closed** *Sun*
Everything is freshly made at this lively restaurant, from tortilla chips to tacos. The green chili enchiladas are recommended.

DK Choice

DEATH VALLEY: Inn at Furnace Creek Dining Room $$$
Modern
American   **Road map** D4
Hwy 190, 92328
Tel *(760) 786-2345*
Housed in a historic adobe-and-stone resort, this upscale dining room offers gorgeous views. The sophisticated menu features Southwestern and Pacific Rim influences. While dishes such as cactus salad and rattlesnake empanadas reflect the desert environment, simpler fare and vegetarian options are also available. Afternoon tea in the lobby has been going since 1927.

LAKE HAVASU: Barley Brothers Restaurant & Brewery $
American   **Road map** E5
1425 McCulloch Blvd, 86403
Tel *(928) 505-7837*
A romantic spot with views of London Bridge. Delicious wood-fired pizzas and entrées such as seafood, burgers, and pastas, complemented by a large choice of handcrafted beers.

LAKE HAVASU: Shugrue's Restaurant $$
American   **Road map** E5
1425 McCulloch Blvd, 86403
Tel *(928) 505-7837*
Quiet family restaurant with tasteful interiors and a view of London Bridge. Steaks, seafood, burgers, and pastas are the highlights. Excellent desserts.

San Francisco

Downtown

David's Deli $
American   **Map** 5 A5
474 Geary St, 94102
Tel *(415) 276-5950*
Head to David's Deli and sit at the counter for gigantic hot pastrami sandwiches, New York-style cheesecake, matzo ball soup, huge slices of pie, and many more deli favorites.

Out the Door $
Vietnamese   **Map** 6 E3
No. 5, 1 Ferry Building, 94111
Tel *(415) 321-3740*
Fresh, healthy snacks and meals to eat in or takeout. Choose from imperial rolls, green papaya salad, noodle dishes, stir-fries, grills, steam buns, five-spice chicken soup, and clay-pot chicken. Located in the Ferry Building *(see p320)*.

San Francisco Soup Company $
American   **Map** 6 D4
50 Fremont St, 94105
Tel *(415) 904-7660*
Spotless, casual café, one of many branches across the city. Offers a range of soups, from favorites like vegetable, potato leek, and chicken noodle to gumbo, mushroom barley, and ethnic varieties. Other offerings include salads, sandwiches, and cookies. Pastries for breakfast.

Sears Fine Food $
American   **Map** 5 B4
439 Powell St, 94108
Tel *(415) 986-1160*
Sears has been serving generous portions of comfort food since 1938. Breakfast includes sourdough French toast and Swedish pancakes, strawberry waffles, shrimp and crab omelets.

Show Dogs $
American   **Map** 5 C5
1020 Market St, 94102
Tel *(415) 558-9560*
Head here for killer classic all-beef frankfurters and corn dogs, veggie dogs, and wild boar sausages. Also serves Philly cheese steak, fish sandwiches, and fried chicken. Good place for BBQ, beer, and people-watching.

Tin Vietnamese Cuisine $
Vietnamese   **Map** 5 C5
937 Howard St, 94103
Tel *(415) 882-7188*
A busy place for perfect *pho* and traditional dishes like green papaya salad, savory clay-pot fish, and other seafood. Also serves noodle dishes, rice plates, grilled veggies, and chili-lemongrass chicken, plus wine and beer.

Amber India $$
Indian   **Map** 5 C5
25 Yerba Buena Ln, 94103
Tel *(415) 777-0500*
Located in the Yerba Buena Gardens museum and hotel district, Amber India attracts a crowd for its take on Indian food. Excellent butter chicken, yogurt-marinated lamb, and duck tikka.

Bar Agricole $$
American   **Map** 10 F1
355 11th St, 94103
Tel *(415) 355-9400*
Always memorable daily menu of locally sourced produce, seafood, and meats. Choose from roasted pork, oxtail terrine, buckwheat *beignets*, pear *galette*, and pulled duck leg sandwich. Try the unique and exotic cocktails.

Popular All-American diner Show Dogs, Downtown San Francisco

For San Francisco map references *see San Francisco Street Finder maps pages 404–13*

Bocadillos $$
Spanish **Map** 5 C4
710 Montgomery St, 94111
Tel *(415) 982-2622*
Head for appetizers or dinner
to this cozy, brick-walled café
serving sandwiches, small-plate
tapas, and Basque dishes. Items
on the menu include halibut
ceviche, cod fritters, octopus
carpaccio, braised tripe, grilled
chorizo, and lamb burgers.

Delancey Street Restaurant $$
American **Map** 6 E5
600 Embarcadero, 94107
Tel *(415) 512-5179*
Great reliable cooking is to be
enjoyed at this restaurant with a
lovely dining room and bay view
patio. The huge menu includes
BBQ ribs, crab cakes, antipasti,
and pizza, as well as many
rotisserie and grill meats, poultry,
fish, and hearty, healthy specials.

Epic Roasthouse $$
American **Map** 6 E4
369 Embarcadero, 94105
Tel *(415) 369-9955*
In an unbeatable waterfront
location with a bay view dining
room and patio beneath the Bay
Bridge, Epic Roasthouse offers
dry-aged Kobe beefsteaks, pork
and lamb, and steakhouse
burgers as well as oven-roasted
dishes. There is a also a charming,
intimate bar with a bar menu.

M.Y. China $$
Chinese **Map** 5 C5
845 Market St, 94103
Tel *(415) 580-3001*
This restaurant in the Westfield
Centre is owned by celebrity chef
Martin Yan. Noodle-pulling demos
and a busy open kitchen will
entice diners to try noodle dishes,
dim sum, stir-fries, BBQ pork, and
Chairman Mao's chicken.

Tadich Grill $$
American **Map** 6 D4
240 California St, 94111
Tel *(415) 391-1849*
The oldest restaurant in San
Francisco (first opened in 1849 as
a coffee stand) has cozy booths. It
serves a wide range of seafood
dishes, *cioppino*, crab cocktails, pot
roast, and legendary martinis.

Yank Sing $$
Chinese **Map** 6 E4
101 Spear St, 94105
Tel *(415) 957-9300*
Over 80 choices of dim sum and
great service in a 250-seat
setting. Peking duck, signature
cabbage, walnut and honey
salad, shrimp *har gau*, honey-
glazed sea bass, and custard tarts.

BIX $$$
Modern American **Map** 5 C3
56 Gold St, 94133
Tel *(415) 433-6300*
Glamorous supper club with live
jazz, superb cocktails and an old
Hollywood feel. Favorites include
chicken hash, table-side steak
tartare, and crab rolls.

Boulevard $$$
American **Map** 6 E4
1 Mission St, 94105
Tel *(415) 543-6084*
A culinary landmark, with a chic
interior, from one of the top chefs
in the city. The daily changing
menu features wood oven-
roasted local lamb, pork and
beef, and tasty local seafood.

Coi $$$
French **Map** 5 A3
373 Broadway, 94133
Tel *(415) 543-2222*
This Michelin-starred restaurant
has a spectacular multi-course,
regularly changing menu
sourced from the farmers' market.

Hakkasan San Francisco $$$
Chinese **Map** 5 C1
1 Kearny St, 94108
Tel *(415) 829-8148*
A stand-out in a city famous
for Chinese restaurants, Hakkasan
serves Cantonese dishes with a
modern twist. It is housed in a
classic "flatiron" building, with
stylish white leather banquettes,
and flamboyant iron grillwork.

House of Prime Rib $$$
American **Map** 5 A5
1906 Van Ness Ave, 94109
Tel *(415) 885-4605*
A landmark since 1949, with a
paneled interior and a fireplace in
each dining room. Enjoy prime
rib roasted in a rock salt crust and
carved table-side, along with
salad and classic sides.

Kokkari Estiatorio $$$
Greek **Map** 6 D3
200 Jackson St, 94111
Tel *(415) 981-0983*
The rustic ambience at this
attractive eatery is highlighted
by the dishes. Savory meats and
poultry are cooked on an open
fire. A traditional menu offers
avgolemono soup, grilled
meatballs, lamb riblets, grilled
octopus, and moussaka.

Michael Mina $$$
American/Japanese **Map** 5 B4
252 California St, 94111
Tel *(415) 397-9222*
This restaurant is Michelin-starred
for its specialties such as *ahi* tuna
tartare, *wagyu shabu shabu*, and

Exterior of Delancey Street Restaurant,
Downtown San Francisco

duck-leg tacos, as well as its
signature dessert tasting. The
counter menu is popular with
the busy bar crowd.

Prospect $$$
Californian **Map** 6 E4
300 Spear St, 94105
Tel *(415) 247-7770*
The organic, changing menu
features dishes such as black cod
with shiso fritters, and quail with
sweetbreads, served in a
sophisticated, lively interior.

Saison $$$
Californian
178 Townsend St, 94107
Tel *(415) 828-7990*
Housed in a historic building,
this Michellin-starred, acclaimed
restaurant offers a multi-course,
daily-changing tasting menu.
All dishes use seasonal
ingredients sourced from
local farms and fisheries,
paired with the best wines.

DK Choice

The Slanted Door $$$
Vietnamese **Map** 6 E3
1 Ferry Building, 94111
Tel *(415) 861-8032*
Situated on the bayfront, this
nationally acclaimed restaurant
serves everything from
traditional street food to plates
with a French twist. Sip on
signature cocktails while trying
dishes such as caramelized
shrimp, cellophane crab
noodles, chicken clay-pot,
lemongrass tofu, and many
vegetarian options. Advance
booking is essential.

For more information on types of restaurants *see pages 544–5*

Sons & Daughters $$$
Californian   Map 5 B4
708 Bush St, 94108
Tel *(415) 391-8311*
A 28-seat dining room awaits at
this tiny gem of a restaurant
tucked away off Union Square.
Locally grown ingredients make
the food sing. Menu changes daily.

Chinatown and Nob Hill

Great Eastern $
Chinese   Map 5 C3
649 Jackson St, 94133
Tel *(415) 986-2500*
One of the top Cantonese-style
seafood restaurants in town, with
tanks of live cod, crab, prawns, and
more. Also serves Peking duck,
dim sum, and savory clay-pots.

Hunan Home's $
Chinese   Map 5 C3
622 Jackson St, 94133
Tel *(415) 982-2844*
Popular with local Chinese
residents, Hunan Home's serves
delicious, authentic food at
reasonable prices. The potstickers
(fried dumplings) win rave reviews.

R and G Lounge $
Chinese   Map 5 C4
631 Kearny St, 94108
Tel *(415) 982-7877*
Sit in a huge, brightly lit dining
room, and choose from a huge
menu of Cantonese-style
seafood. Whole steamed fish,
fried catfish, roasted crab, and
savory clay-pots.

Acquerello $$
Californian   Map 5 A4
1722 Sacramento St, 94109
Tel *(415) 567-5432*
Elegant and formal restaurant
serving consistently top-notch,
seasonal *prix fixe* and tasting
menus for over two decades.
Kobe beef and house-made
exotic pastas are on offer. The
presentation is worth a photo.

Cocotte $$
French
1521 Hyde St, 94109
Tel *(415) 292-4415*
Watch cable cars pass by while
enjoying French rotisserie chicken
at this Nob Hill spot. Also on the
menu: *coq au vin*, steak, veggie
gratins, duck breast, profiteroles,
and more. Takeout available.

House of Nanking $$
Chinese   Map 5 C4
919 Kearny St, 94133
Tel *(415) 421-1429*
One of the most renowned
Chinese restaurants in town has
an elaborate menu featuring
Shanghai-style specialties such as
sautéed pea shoots with scallops,
and black bean-glazed eggplant.

Aurea $$$
Californian   Map 5 A4
905 California St, 94108
Tel *(866) 942-5019*
Casual restaurant in the upscale
Stanford Court Hotel. On offer are
dishes such as rack of lamb, Harris
Ranch steaks, BBQ pork sliders,
and Kurobuta pork. Open till late.

Big 4 $$$
American   Map 5 B4
1075 California St, 94108
Tel *(415) 474-5400*
Romantic restaurant and bar in
the Huntington Hotel. Wild
game, Arctic char, Dungeness
crab, as well as legendary cheese
and dessert presentations. Live
piano music and a fireplace.

Fisherman's Wharf and North Beach

Boudin at the Wharf $
Seafood   Map 5 A1
160 Jefferson St, 94133
Tel *(415) 928-1849*
Popular with tourists, this venue
has a casual café downstairs and a
bistro and bar upstairs. Choose

from chowder in bread bowls,
fresh seafood, sourdough pizza
and more San-Francisco
specialties. Watch bread-baking
through an observation window.

Molinari Delicatessen $
Italian   Map 5 A2
373 Columbus Ave, 94133
Tel *(415) 421-2337*
Order takeout or sit at a sidewalk
table and enjoy the dizzying
aroma of cheeses, salamis, and
sausages. The North Beach special
sandwich with prosciutto, sun-
dried tomatoes, provolone, and
sweet peppers is recommended.

My Canh $
Vietnamese   Map 5 A3
626 Broadway St, 94133
Tel *(415) 397-8888*
A family-owned hole-in-the-wall,
My Canh is famous for some of
the best Vietnamese noodle
soup – *pho*. Cheap, fast, and
fabulous fare. Open until 2am.

Pier 23 Café $
American   Map 6 D2
Pier 23 The Embarcadero, 94111
Tel *(415) 362-5125*
Watch boats on the bay from the
deck while sipping a cocktail and
munching on clam chowder,
roasted Dungeness crab, and
more seafood dishes. Burgers
and bar bites too. Live music.

Alioto's $$
Seafood
8 Fisherman's Wharf, 94133
Tel *(415) 673-0183*
A 1920s landmark with a three-
story dining room and bay views.
Fresh Pacific seafood and Italian
dishes include Dungeness crab,
lobster, *cioppino*, clam chowder,
and seasonal fish. There is also a
casual waterside café.

**The Franciscan Crab
Restaurant** $$
Seafood   Map 5 B1
Pier 43 1/2 Fisherman's Wharf, 94133
Tel *(415) 362-7733*
There are panoramic views of
Alcatraz and the bay from this Art
Deco restaurant. Dungeness crab
and local seafood dominate the
extensive menu. Try the home-
made cheeses and cured meats.

L'Osteria del Forno $$
Italian   Map 5 A2
519 Columbus Ave, 94133
Tel *(415) 982-1124*
This long-established place serves
Northern Italian specialties fresh
from the oven. Try the focaccia
sandwiches, roast pork, thin-crust
pizzas, roast of the day, and
roasted vegetables on polenta.

Impressive pier location of Scoma's, Fisherman's Wharf

For key to prices *see page 550*

Neptune's Waterfront Grill & Bar
Seafood $$
Map 5 B1
PIER 39, 94133
Tel *(415) 434-2260*
With dazzling views of the bridge, the bay, and Alcatraz, this popular place serves impressive seafood, pizza, steaks, calamari, and clam chowder.

Ristobar
Italian $$
Map 5 A2
2300 Chestnut St, 94123
Tel *(415) 923-6464*
Rustic Italian fare of artisanal pizza, home-made pasta, luscious pastry, and *charcuterie*. Enjoy wine and cocktails on a heated patio.

Rose Pistola
Italian $$
Map 5 A2
532 Columbus Ave, 94133
Tel *(415) 399-0499*
Rose Pistola serves up excellent Italian fare such as pastas and wood-fired pizzas, hearty *cioppino*, signature whole roasted crab and fish, and generous antipasti. Order gelato for dessert.

Scoma's
Seafood $$
Map 5 A1
Pier 47 Fisherman's Wharf , 94133
Tel *(800) 644-5852*
This historic spot does not disappoint with its fresh seafood, friendly service, and a classic white-linen experience – all with minimum fuss.

The Square Bar & Kitchen
American $$
Map 5 B1
1707 Powell St, 94133
Tel *(415) 525-3579*   **Closed** *Mon & Tue*
This neighborhood restaurant on Washington Square serves sophisticated comfort food. Weekend brunches and daily happy hours provide good value.

The Waterfront Restaurant
Seafood $$
Map 6 D2
Pier 7 The Embarcadero, 94111
Tel *(415) 391-2696*
Spread over three levels on the bayfront. Dine on perfectly prepared seafood, *cioppino*, whole fish and crab roasted in the wood-fired oven, as well as smoked salmon, and calamari.

Wipeout Bar and Grill
American $$
Map 5 B1
PIER 39 Embarcadero, 94133
Tel *(415) 986-5966*
At this surf-themed eatery, sit by the outdoor fire pit and snack on burgers, burritos, sandwiches, pastas, and pizza. Sports on big TVs. Wipeout-To-Go takeout menu at the VW van window.

Italian favorite L'Osteria del Forno, North Beach

Pacific Heights

Mel's Drive-In
American $
Map 3 C2
2165 Lombard St, 94123
Tel *(415) 921-3039*
Historic diner with jukeboxes, thick shakes, burgers, and BLTs, as well as turkey dinner, home-made pie, meatloaf, and banana splits. Open early till late; this is one of several in the city.

Mifune
Japanese $
Map 5 A5
1737 Post St, 94117
Tel *(415) 922-0337*
One of the best noodle houses in the city, famous for traditional *udon* and *soba*. Huge menu of pork *katsu*, *karaage*, *nabeyaki udon*, vegetable *ramen*, *unagi* rolls and much more. Fast service.

Pizzeria Delfina
Italian $
Map 5 A4
2406 California St, 94115
Tel *(415) 440-1189*
Enjoy exceptional Neapolitan-style thin-crust pizzas with traditional and exotic toppings such as *salsiccia* (Italian sausage) or cherrystone clams. Antipasti, pasta, and gelato are served too.

Betelnut
Asian $$
Map 4 E2
2030 Union St, 94123
Tel *(415) 929-8855*
In the style of a Shanghai speakeasy with open kitchen, the menu features serves curried chicken, firecracker shrimp, glazed short ribs, and dumplings. Lively bar.

Dobbs Ferry Restaurant
American $$
Map 4 E2
409 Gough St, 94102
Tel *(415) 551-7700*
Serving west coast food with east coast style, comfort food includes *scarpariello* (chicken with pickled peppers), steak, and pizzas.

Elite Café
American $$
Map 4 D4
2049 Fillmore St, 94115
Tel *(415) 673-5483*
A favorite for New Orleans-style cuisine, specializing in jambalaya, *étouffée*, *andouille* sausage, and *beignets*. There is a raw bar and a cocktail bar too.

Gamine French Bistrot
French $$
Map 4 E2
2223 Union St, 94123
Tel *(415) 771-7771*
Classic French bistro fare from *moules marinière* to lamb stew, steak frites, *charcuterie*, crêpe suzettes, *tarte tatin*, steak tartare plus burgers and paninis.

Greens
Vegetarian $$
Map 4 E1
Building A, Fort Mason, 94123
Tel *(415) 771-6222*
This is the city's top veggie restaurant. Daily menu with hearty, organic, sustainable produce from family farms and Greens' own garden.

Mamacita
Mexican $$
Map 4 D2
2317 Chestnut St, 94123
Tel *(415) 346-8494*
Dine here for updated specialties such as pulled pork tamales, lamb enchiladas, and seafood *posole*. Dishes are made with ingredients fresh from the chef's family farm.

Original Joe's
Italian $$
Map 5 B2
601 Union St, 94133
Tel *(415) 775-4877*
Classic comfort food served in a charming 250-seat interior with a bar and fireplace. Choose from pot roast, sweetbreads, veal Milanese, linguine alfredo, signature broiled chicken, and clam chowder. Popular with local politicians.

For more information on types of restaurants *see pages 544–5*

Ristorante Capannina $$
Italian   Map 4 E2
1809 Union St, 94123
Tel *(415) 409-8001*
Diners have a choice of several
home-made pastas, gnocchi,
risotto, brick-pressed chicken,
seafood dishes, rack of lamb,
and braised short ribs. Early
bird specials and a cozy bar, plus
sidewalk tables.

Rose's Café $$
Italian   Map 4 D3
2298 Union St, 94123
Tel *(415) 775-2200*
A pretty bistro-café known
for food made from all-organic,
local ingredients. The menu
features pizzas, roasted fish,
poultry and meats, gnocchi, and
freshly-made pasta.

Swan Oyster Depot $$
Seafood   Map 5 A3
1517 Polk St, 94109
Tel *(415) 673-1101*   **Closed** *Dinner*
Since 1912, Swan Oyster Depot
has been serving some of the
city's best clam chowder, oyster
on the half-shell, cracked crab,
lobster, and fresh seafood
from its 18-stool counter.
Beer and wine are available.
No credit cards.

Gary Danko $$$
French   Map 5 A2
800 North Point St, 94109
Tel *(415) 749-2060*
Gary Danko is one of the top
eateries on the West Coast.
Formal setting, superb service,
and classic French and inventive
local cuisine. Daily *prix fixe*
menu, a great wine list, and
fantastic cheese cart.

The Civic Center

Arlequin Café $
Café   Map 4 F5
384 Hayes St, 94102
Tel *(415) 626-1211*
Tasty gourmet sandwiches,
salads and desserts all at
reasonable prices. This cozy café
has a lovely atmosphere and
great breakfasts, too. Popular
with locals.

Hayes Street Grill $$
Seafood   Map 4 F5
320 Hayes St, 94102
Tel *(415) 863-5545*
Located near the opera and
symphony halls and popular
for pre-concert meals, Hayes
Street Grill is known for quick
service grilled seafood, calamari
fritto misto, and fish soup.
Guests get to choose the fish,
its preparation, and the sauce.

For key to prices *see page 550*

Indigo $$
American   Map 4 F5
687 McAllister St, 94102
Tel *(415) 673-9353*
Indigo's multi-ethnic menu
ranges from dishes such as
ahi tuna tartare to pan-roasted
pork tenderloin, salmon with
mango salsa, veggie specials,
and lavender *crème brûlée*.
Prix fixe specials.

Absinthe $$$
French   Map 4 F5
398 Hayes St, 94102
Tel *(415) 551-1590*
This classic brasserie bar serves
French onion soup and *coq au
vin*, roasted duck breast, steak
frites, spectacular cheeses, and
memorable burgers.

AQ $$$
Mediterranean   Map 5 C5
1085 Mission St, 94103
Tel *(415) 341-9000*
Serves creative and exotically
presented Mediterranean small
plates. Smoked chowder, short
ribs, suckling pig, and striped
bass feature on the menu as well
as artisanal cheeses. Full bar.

Jardinière $$$
French   Map 4 E5
300 Grove St, 94102
Tel *(415) 861-5555*
Celebrity chef Traci Des Jardins
creates spectacular dishes using
sustainable seasonal produce –
from Faro lasagna with boar *sugo*
to duck confit and schnitzel.

Haight Ashbury and the Mission

American Grilled Cheese Kitchen $
American
2400 Harrison St, 94110
Tel *(415) 243-0107*   **Closed** *dinner*
Super-popular sandwich café
offering many specialties made
with regionally sourced cheeses,

accompanied by specialty
coffees, craft beers on tap, and
wine by the glass.

Kasa Indian Eatery $
Indian   Map 9 C3
4001 18th St, 94114
Tel *(415) 621-6940*
Unassuming neighborhood
place serving large portions of
delicious chicken tikka, turkey
kebabs, cauliflower and potato
curry, and daily veggie specials.

Kate's Kitchen $
American   Map 9 B1
471 Haight St, 94117
Tel *(415) 626-3984*
Friendly spot famous for French
toast, biscuits and gravy, bacon-
cheddar cornmeal pancakes,
home-made chicken soup,
and other comfort food.

Lovejoy's Tea Room $
British   Map 10 E1
1351 Church St, 94114
Tel *(415) 648-5895*
Anglophiles flock to this cozy,
quirky English tea room for its
pots of imported teas, fresh warm
scones, delicate finger sand-
wiches, and amiable service.

Namu Gaji $
Korean   Map 10 E2
499 Dolores St, 94110
Tel *(415) 431-6268*
A casual restaurant serving
Korean tacos, local seafood,
noodles, dumplings, stone-pot
vegetables, and produce from
their own farm. Sake and rice ale
specials at happy hour.

La Oaxaquena $
Mexican   Map 10 F1
2128 Mission St, 94110
Tel *(415) 621-5446*
This is a favorite venue for
burritos, tamales, *enmoladas*, BBQ
goat, and ostrich and salmon
tacos. There are also veggie *sopes*
and guacamole plus Mexican hot
chocolate, and wines.

The busy bar area at Swan Oyster Depot, Pacific Heights

Contemporary dining area at Foreign Cinema, the Mission

St. Francis Fountain $
American   Map 10 D4
2801 24th St, 94110
Tel *(415) 826-4210*
Since 1918, St. Francis has been drawing crowds with its neon signs and soda-fountain decor. Excellent sodas, shakes, root beer floats, egg creams (milkshakes), and grilled cheese sandwiches.

La Taqueria $
Mexican   Map 10 F4
2889 Mission St, 94110
Tel *(415) 285-7117*
At this popular place, murals are the backdrop for fresh-fruit sodas, *carne asada, carnitas,* grilled chicken, steak tacos, and burritos. Takeout available.

Bernal Star $$
American
410 Cortland Ave, 94110
Tel *(415) 695-8777*
Head here for upscale burgers and brunch favorites, made with organic meats and eggs. A daily beer-and-burger happy hour draws in the regulars. Movies are shown on the heated patio.

Café Jacqueline $$
French   Map 5 C2
1454 Grant Ave, 94133
Tel *(415) 981-5565*
This popular restaurant has a limited bistro menu. It is famous for French onion soup and dessert soufflés that take some time to prepare but are worth the wait.

Cha Cha Cha $$
Latin American   Map 10 F3
2327 Mission St, 94110
Tel *(415) 824-1502*
As much a lively bar as a restaurant, Cha Cha Cha serves small tapas plates and excellent sangria against a background of foot-tapping Latin music. Gets crowded on Friday and Saturday nights.

Foreign Cinema $$
Californian/
Mediterranean   Map 10 F1
2534 Mission St, 94110
Tel *(415) 648-7600*
Sit in the industrial chic dining room or on the tented patio to watch foreign films, and munch on rustic Mediterranean fare and local seafood at the raw bar.

ICHI Sushi $$
Japanese   Map 10 F1
3369 Mission St, 94110
Tel *(415) 525-4750*
Sustainable seafood on a sushi menu with a twist – salmon *nigiri* with bonito shavings, *somen* noodle salad in *shiso* pesto, oysters, hot plates, and specialty rolls.

Izakaya Yuzuki $$
Japanese   Map 10 E2
598 Guerrero St, 94110
Tel *(415) 556-9898*
Perfectly prepared, beautifully presented dishes that are focused on rice and fermented ingredients such as *miso, yakitori,* plus tofu, and grilled items.

Piqueo's $$
Peruvian
830 Cortland Ave, 94110
Tel *(415) 282-8812*
Charming restaurant and tapas bar serving Peruvian fusion cuisine – BBQ pulled pork, curry, *ceviche,* seafood paella and pan-seared scallops. Also serves small plates such as yucca balls, and *dulce de leche* parfait.

Wine Kitchen $$
Californian   Map 10 D1
507 Divisadero St, 94115
Tel *(415) 525-3485*
A casual wine bar and café serving bistro-style dishes such as *maitake* tempura with spiced chickpea puree, seafood in Romesco broth, and short ribs.

Atelier Crenn $$$
French   Map 10 E1
3127 Fillmore St, 94123
Tel *(415) 440-0460*
The first female chef in the US to earn two Michelin stars, Dominique Crenn creates "poetic culinaria" of edibile molecular gastronomy in her tiny restaurant.

SPQR $$$
Italian   Map 10 E1
1911 Fillmore St, 94115
Tel *(415) 771-7779*
This Michelin-starred restaurant has a seasonal menu of Italian dishes – from *wagyu* beef tartare to quail with burnt orange sauce or roasted rabbit with dried fruit – and a great wine list.

Golden Gate Park and The Presidio

de Young Café $
American/European   Map 9 A1
JFK and Tea Garden Dr, 94118
Tel *(415) 863-3330*
Enjoy lunch or snacks in this delightful museum café serving classic dishes, either indoors or on the covered patio adjacent to the sculpture garden. There is a selection of wines. Takeout is also available.

Park Chow $
American   Map 9 A4
1240 9th Ave, 94122
Tel *(415) 665-9912*
Park Chow offers comfort food such as pastas, grilled meats, sandwiches, and soups. It also has a great kids' menu with burgers, chicken fingers, and grilled cheese. It is located a block from Golden Gate Park.

Transit Café at the Presidio $
American   Map 3 B2
215 Lincoln Blvd, 94129
Tel *(415) 561-4435*
Pick up a picnic to enjoy in the park or relax at a bay view terrace table. There is a range of morning pastries, wood oven-baked pizzas, grilled hamburgers, sandwiches, and salads to choose from, as well as wine and beer. Wi-Fi available.

Warming Hut $
American   Map 3 A2
Crissy Field, 94123
Tel *(415) 561-3040*
A casual spot by the beach at Crissy Field, Warming Hut is great for drinks, light meals, and snacks. Hot dogs, hot chocolate, soups, sandwiches, and espresso drinks all feature on the menu. It also sells guidebooks and souvenirs.

For more information on types of restaurants *see pages 544–5*

Aziza $$
Moroccan Map 8 E1
5800 Geary Blvd, 94121
Tel *(415) 752-2222*
A Richmond District standout, Aziza has been awarded a Michelin star for its tasting menu. Chicken with preserved lemon, duck confit, savory lamb shank, and other North African-inspired dishes in a romantic setting.

Beach Chalet $$
American Map 7 A2
1000 Great Hwy, 94121
Tel *(415) 386-8439*
A 1920s masterpiece of architecture at Ocean Beach. The brewpub upstairs has an upscale bistro menu. Downstairs, the Park Chalet Garden Restaurant is a café with indoor and outdoor seating and Golden Gate Park views.

Cliff House $$
Historic Map 7 A1
1090 Point Lobos Ave, 94121
Tel *(415) 386-3330*
An Art Deco-style restaurant and tourist destination at Ocean Beach. Overlooking the waves of the Pacific there is an affordable bistro, a takeout counter, and the upscale restaurant Sutro's.

Outerlands $$$
Californian Map 7 B3
4001 Judah St, 94122
Tel *(415) 661-6140*
The menu at this popular rustic dining room comprises exotic preparations for black cod, locally sourced poultry, meats, and seafood, as well as vegetarian options, home-made bread and artisinal cheeses.

The Bay Area

BERKELEY: Bette's Oceanview Diner
American Road map inset B $
1807 Fourth St, 94710
Tel *(510) 644-3230*
An all-American, 1940s café with booths and counter seating. Opens at 6:30am and goes full blast all day long. The epitome of comfort food to take out or eat in.

BERKELEY: Belli Osteria $$
Italian Road map inset B
2016 Shattuck Ave, 94704
Tel *(510) 704-1902*
Exotic and seasonal pastas such as braised lamb pappardelle served in a rustic environment. Frequently changing entrées include whole grilled sea bass, and hanger steak sandwiches.

BERKELEY: Skates on the Bay $$
American Road map inset B
100 Seawall Dr, 94710
Tel *(510) 549-1900*
Fresh Pacific seafood from oysters to *ahi*, salmon to sushi, plus steaks, pasta, burgers and chicken. Gorgeous Zowie bay and harbor views. Raw bar and a lively cocktail bar scene.

BERKELEY: Chez Panisse $$$
Californian Road map inset B
1517 Shattuck Ave, 94709
Tel *(510) 548-5525*
Chef Alice Waters' flagship venue comprises a restaurant on the first floor and a second-floor café. The seasonal menu is made from local, organic ingredients.

BOLINAS: Coast Café $
American Map A3
46 Wharf Rd, 94924
Tel *(415) 868-2298*
Sit amid vintage surfboards and enjoy local seafood and organic produce, poultry, and meats. Famous for its sourdough bread, big burgers, and gardener's pie.

HALF MOON BAY: Barbara's Fish Trap $
Seafood Road map inset B
281 Capistrano St, 94019
Tel *(650) 728-7049*
A little red building on stilts complete with a heated covered patio and water views. Offers daily fresh fish specials, chowder, Dungeness crab, burgers, and thick-cut fries.

HALF MOON BAY: Cameron's Pub & Inn $
Gastropub Road map inset B
1410 South Cabrillo Hwy, 94019
Tel *(650) 726-5705*
Look for the London double-decker buses – one is a kids' game room – at this British outpost. Hearty fare including delicious fish 'n' chips, chili, steak, and pizza.

HALF MOON BAY: Miramar Beach Restaurant $$
American Road map inset B
131 Mirada Rd, 94019
Tel *(650) 726-9053*
A former prohibition roadhouse that now serves seafood and steaks, pastas, salads, and soups. Patio with lovely oceanfront views. Live music on weekends.

LARKSPUR: Left Bank Brasserie $$
French Road map inset B
507 Magnolia Ave, 94939
Tel *(415) 927-3331*
Left Bank serves bistro favorites such as *cassoulet, coq au vin, charcuterie, escargots*, and onion soup. Sit at a shady sidewalk table or in the lovely dining room.

LOS GATOS: Manresa $$$
Californian Road map inset B
320 Village Ln, 95030
Tel *(408) 354-4330*
Los Gatos has earned Michelin stars for its *prix fixe* and tasting menus, and great service. Dishes include suckling pig on huckleberry sauce with walnut foam.

MARSHALL: Nick's Cove Restaurant & Oyster Bar $$
Seafood Road map A3
23240 Hwy 1, 94940
Tel *(415) 663-1033*
A restaurant with hunting lodge ambience. Serves farm-to-table cuisine, plus crab macaroni and cheese, and other seafood. Small plates at the bar.

MILL VALLEY: Buckeye Roadhouse $$
American Road map inset B
15 Shoreline Hwy, 94941
Tel *(415) 331-2600*
Located conspicuously along the freeway, this warm and inviting Bavarian-style lodge with cushy booths and Big Band-era music, serves American comfort food and ethnic specialties.

Art Deco-style Cliff House, offering stunning ocean views

MONTARA: La Costanera **$$$**
Peruvian **Road map** inset B
8150 Cabrillo Hwy, 94037
Tel *(650) 728-1600* **Closed** *Mon*
Awarded a Michelin star for its
Peruvian specialties and top
service. Slow-cooked pork
shoulder, paella, seafood, steak,
and lots of small plates make up
the menu. Floor to ceiling
windows make the most of the
beach-front location. Bar with
evening happy hour weeknights.

**MOSS BEACH: Moss Beach
Distillery** **$**
Seafood **Road map** inset B
140 Beach Way, 94038
Tel *(650) 728-5595*
The best place to enjoy a cocktail,
whether seated in a double
rocker or covered with blankets
with the waves crashing below.
Moss Beach Distillery serves fresh
local seafood for lunch and
dinner, and for the elaborate
weekend brunch.

OAKLAND: Bakesale Betty **$**
American **Map** inset B
5098 Telegraph Ave, 94609
Tel *(510) 985-1213*
There are plenty of gourmet
baked treats at this popular cafe.
The famous fried chicken
sandwiches are not to be
missed. Take away available.

PALO ALTO: Baumé **$$$**
French **Map** inset B
201 S California Ave, 94306
Tel *(650) 328-8899*
Michelin-starred restaurant in a
Japanese-inspired dining room.
Spectacular 12-course modern
and traditional French offerings.
Famous for molecular gastronomy,
breathtaking presentations, and a
daily-changing seasonal menu.

PESCADERO: Duarte's Tavern **$**
Seafood
202 Stage Rd, 94060
Tel *(650) 879-0464*
Belly up to the bar with local
ranchers in this tiny fishing village.
In an Old West-style building
dating back to 1894, Duarte's
Tavern serves hearty local dishes
and classics such as artichoke
soup, steaks, and the famous
olallieberry pie (a cross between
a logan berry and a youngberry).

**POINT REYES STATION: Bovine
Bakery** **$**
American **Map** A3
11315 Hwy 1, 94956
Tel *(415) 663-9420*
Expect long lines at this eatery,
popular for its organic morning
buns, pastries, pizza, sandwiches,
and croissants. Also serves tarts,

Relaxed dining room with sea views at Moss Beach Distillery, Moss Beach

pies, and quiche by the slice, plus
organic fair-trade coffees.

**POINT REYES STATION: The
Station House Café** **$$**
American **Map** A3
11180 Hwy 1, 94956
Tel *(415) 663-1515*
A high-ceilinged dining room
and patio. Dine on warm pop-
overs, fried calamari and other
local seafood, free-range poultry
and meats, and pecan pie.

**SAN RAFAEL: Sol Food Puerto
Rican Cuisine** **$**
Puerto Rican **Road map** inset B
901 Lincoln Ave, 94901
Tel *(415) 451-4765*
A friendly, casual resaurant serving
authentic comfort food. Highlights
include *pollo al horno* (oven-
roasted chicken), garlic-fried
plantains, and mango iced tea.

DK Choice

**SAN RAFAEL: Terrapin
Crossroads** **$$**
American **Map** inset B
100 Yacht Club Dr, 94901
Tel *(415) 524-2773*
A popular place in an upscale
yet rustic setting. Owned by
Grateful Dead legend Phil Lesh,
who often plays with bands in
the bar and concert hall. Eat in
the lounge, the bar, or in one
of the sprawling dining rooms.
Diners have a choice of wood-
oven pizzas, meats, and veggies,
plus lots of small plates.

SAUSALITO: Fish **$**
Seafood **Road map** inset B
350 Harbor Dr, 94965
Tel *(415) 331-3474*
Sit at picnic tables on the harbor-
front and enjoy fish 'n' chips,

pasta, fish tacos, chocolate
bread pudding, and root beer
floats. Fun, casual atmosphere.

**SAUSALITO: Salito's
Crab House & Prime Rib** **$$**
Seafood **Road map** inset B
1200 Bridgeway, 94965
Tel *(415) 331-3226*
Casual dining room and
waterfront deck where the
bay views complement a surf 'n'
turf menu. Signature dishes
include roasted Dungeness
crab, shellfish skillets, and
prime rib. Excellent *beignets*
and kettle bread.

SAUSALITO: Murray Circle **$$$**
Californian **Road map** inset B
602 Murray Circle, 94965
Tel *(415) 339-4750*
Urban-chic hideaway with
a locally sourced, seasonal
menu by a Michelin-starred
chef. Boasts a 2,000-bottle
wine list. Small plates in the
intimate bar.

**STINSON BEACH: Sand
Dollar Restaurant** **$**
Seafood **Map** A3
3458 Shoreline Hwy, 94970
Tel *(415) 868-0434*
In a charming 1920s building
near the beach. Hearty fare of
steak frites, burgers, fish 'n' chips,
and ribs. Big wine list. Live music
on weekends.

TIBURON: Sam's Anchor Café **$$**
Seafood **Road map** inset B
27 Main St, 94920
Tel *(415) 435-4527*
A lively crowd can be found
here enjoying clam chowder,
cracked crab, steaks, lots of
appetizers, and Ramos Fizz
brunches. Dock with good
skyline views.

For more information on types of restaurants *see pages 544–5*

The North

ARCATA: Abruzzi's $$
Italian   **Road map** A2
780 Seventh St, 95521
Tel *(707) 826-234*
A mid-19th-century building with stained glass and antiques. Famous for pasta, pizzas, steak, seafood, sweet potato crab cakes, and eggplant parmesan.

EUREKA: Samoa Cookhouse $
American   **Road map** A2
79 Cookhouse Ln, Samoa, 95564
Tel *(707) 442-1659*
Hearty meals are served in an Old West cookhouse by the bay that once served loggers. There is also a museum with logging artifacts and photos *(see also p450)*.

DK Choice

EUREKA: Restaurant 301 $$$
Californian   **Road map** A2
301 L St, 95501
Tel *(707) 444-8062*
This is an award-winning foodie Mecca in an elegant Victorian building in Old Town. The daily-changing menu includes home grown organic vegetables from the kitchen gardens, local seafood, poultry, and meats. Oenophiles make pilgrimages here for the winemaker dinners and for rare vintages from the 3,400-bottle wine list.

FERNDALE: VI Restaurant & Tavern $$
Californian   **Road map** A2
400 Ocean Ave, 95536
Tel *(707) 786-4950*
Dine in a spectacular Victorian building. The menu features delicious house-smoked salmon, goat cheese ravioli, cherry-glazed chicken, steaks, and local seafood. There is a top-notch regional wine list.

LITTLE RIVER: Little River Inn $$
American   **Road map** A3
7751 Hwy 1, 95456
Tel *(707) 937-5942*
This has been one of the top eateries on the coast for decades. Dine on local seafood, grass-fed lamb and beef, and end the meal with olallieberry cobbler. Cozy bar.

MOUNT SHASTA CITY: Highland House Restaurant $
American   **Road map** B1
1000 Siskiyou Lake Blvd, 96067
Tel *(530) 926-3030*   **Closed** *Mon–Thu in off-peak season*
Clubhouse-style eatery with mountain views. Serves steaks, pasta, and grilled chicken. Appetizers at the bar.

MOUNT SHASTA CITY: Lilys $
American   **Road map** B1
1013 S Mount Shasta Blvd, 96067
Tel *(530) 926-3372*
Hearty food served on the deck in the garden. Mexican dishes plus steaks, eggs, and veggies.

Wine Country

BODEGA BAY: Spud Point Crab Company $
Seafood   **Road map** A3
1860 Westshore Rd, 94923
Tel *(707) 875-9472*
Fresh catch is turned into delicious meals served at picnic tables. Try the crab and shrimp sandwiches.. Tri-tip cuts of beef with chili, and hot dogs are also served.

CALISTOGA: Buster's Southern Barbecue $
American   **Road map** A3
1207 Foothill Blvd, 94515
Tel *(707) 942-5605*
Famous for oak-fire-roasted meats served at picnic tables, with slaw and baked beans. Also on offer are pork loin, ribs, sandwiches, or platters; shakes and beer, too.

CALISTOGA: Calistoga Inn Restaurant & Brewery $$
American   **Road map** A3
1250 Lincoln Ave, 94515
Tel *(707) 942-4101*
An 1880s inn with a dining terrace on the Napa River and a microbrewery. Choose from hearty sandwiches, meal-sized salads, pot roast, seafood, ribs, appetizers, and grilled local meats.

CALISTOGA: Solbar $$$
Californian   **Road map** A3
755 Silverado Trail , 94515
Tel *(707) 226-0800*
A Michelin-starred eatery focused on organic local ingredients, free-range poultry and meats, seafood, Niman Ranch pork, and spectacular veggies and desserts.

ELK: Greenwood Pier Café $
American   **Road map** A3
5928 Hwy 1, 95432
Tel *(707) 877-3400*
Located in a flower garden on cliffs above the ocean. Serves seafood, grilled lamb and steak as well as pastas, sandwiches, and salads. Lovely cliffside wine bar.

FORESTVILLE: Farmhouse Inn and Restaurant $$$
Californian   **Road map** A3
7871 River Rd, 95436
Tel *(800) 464-6642*   **Closed** *Tue, Wed*
A Michelin-starred restaurant with a creative menu and top service. Savor dishes such as pear and parmesan ravioli and venison loin, alongside a stellar wine list.

FORT BRAGG: North Coast Brewing Company $
Gastropub   **Road map** A2
444 N Main St, 95437
Tel *(707) 964-2739* **Closed** *Mon, Tue*
Casual atmosphere and a hearty menu of fish, Cajun black beans and rice, jerk chicken, and Route 66 chili. Cheese and beer pairings.

DK Choice

GEYSERVILLE: Rustic Francis's Favorites $$$
Italian   **Road map** A3
300 Via Archimedes, 95441
Tel *(707) 857-1485*
On the Francis Ford Coppola Winery, this Italian spot offers favorite family recipes, Mrs. Scorsese's lemon chicken, habit-forming ribs, and florentine steak. Diners can also eat at the movie memorabilia-surrounded bar or around the swimming pool. Sit indoors by the Argentine-style *parrilla* or on the terrace with views of the vineyard.

Elegant dining room at Restaurant 301, Eureka

For key to prices *see page 550*

Grand exterior of the Madrona Manor, Healdsburg

HEALDSBURG: Oakville Grocery
Californian $ **Road map** A3
124 Matheson St, 95448
Tel (707) 433-3200
A table on the plaza-side terrace is the spot to enjoy gourmet sandwiches, rotisserie chicken, and snacks. The grocery sells local produce, artisanal cheeses, charcuterie, and wines.

HEALDSBURG: Bistro Ralph $$
Bistro **Road map** A3
109 Plaza St, 95448
Tel (707) 433-1380
Local produce is used to create tasty dishes such as lamb with roasted garlic and polenta, osso buco, and peach shortcake. Ask for the Local Stash wine list.

HEALDSBURG: Madrona Manor $$$
Californian **Road map** A3
1001 Westside Rd, 95448
Tel (707) 433-4231
Five elaborate dining rooms in a 1881 historic mansion. Awarded a Michelin star for its dishes featuring local meats, poultry and seafood, and artisanal cheeses.

MENDOCINO: Café Beaujolais $$
Californian **Road map** A3
961 Ukiah St, 95460
Tel (707) 937-5614
Located in a 1910 sunny yellow house, Café Beaujolais serves organic beef, seafood, pizza, and artisanal breads, plus chocolate and cherry cake.

MENDOCINO: Ravens' Restaurant $$
Vegetarian **Road map** A3
44850 Comptche Ukiah Rd, 95460
Tel (707) 937-5615
This eatery on the coast serves only vegetarian fare: soups, pizzas, pastas, and grilled veggies. Come early and visit the organic gardens.

NAPA: Bistro Don Giovanni $$$
Italian **Road map** B3
4110 Howard Ln, 94558
Tel (707) 224-3300
Head here for pastas, fritto misto, wood-oven pizzas, local seafood, roasted half-chicken, and Bostini trifle. Bar and patio seating.

RUTHERFORD: Rutherford Grill $$
American **Road map** A3
1880 Rutherford Rd, 94558
Tel (707) 962-1782
Choose from smoky baby back ribs, feathery onion rings, and grilled and spit-roasted meats. Big booths inside and umbrella tables and a wine bar outside.

ST. HELENA: Gott's Roadside Tray Gourmet $
American **Road map** A3
933 Main St, 94574
Tel (707) 963-3486
Upscale version of a 1950s stand with outdoor tables. Burgers, fish tacos, beer, and a big wine list. Plenty of shakes – try the espresso bean, mint chip, or pistachio.

ST. HELENA: Wine Spectator Greystone Restaurant $$
Californian **Road map** A3
2555 Main St, 94574
Tel (707) 967-1010
At the grand Culinary Institute of America, this is an elegantly casual restaurant with a terrace. Graduate chefs prepare "world flavor" cuisine from local produce.

ST. HELENA: The Restaurant at Meadowood $$$
Californian **Road map** A3
900 Meadowood Ln, 94574
Tel (877) 963-3646 **Closed** Sun
This formal restaurant has achieved three Michelin-stars for its cuisine. The daily changing menu may include dishes such as coal-roasted sturgeon or pine-cured venison.

SONOMA: The Red Grape $
Italian **Road map** A3
529 1st St W, 95476
Tel (707) 996-4103
This family-friendly eatery's pizza is considered the best in town. Also serves New Haven-style pies with classic and exotic toppings. Leafy patio and a small bar.

SONOMA: The Girl and the Fig $$$
French **Road map** A3
110 W Spain St, 95476
Tel (707) 938-3634
Enjoy French cuisine in art-filled dining rooms or on the patio. Choice of artisanal cheeses and charcuterie, tartares, steak frites, and creative veggie dishes. Sip on local wine at the antique bar.

YOUNTVILLE: Bottega Napa Valley $$$
Italian **Road map** B3
6525 Washington St, 94599
Tel (707) 945-1050
This is Food Network star Michael Chiarello's trendy place, housed in an old brick winery. Contemporary Italian cuisine made with local ingredients, wood-roasted meats, poultry, and whole fish. Exceptional pastas and risottos.

YOUNTVILLE: Bouchon $$$
French **Road map** B3
6534 Washington St, 94599
Tel (707) 944-8037
Sample the skill of critically acclaimed chef Thomas Keller at this bistro. Exquisite steak frites and extensive raw bar.

Wine Spectator Greystone Restaurant, St. Helena

For more information on types of restaurants see pages 544–5

Sierra Nevada Tap Room & Restaurant, Chico

YOUNTVILLE: French Laundry $$$
Californian **Road map** B3
6640 Washington St, 94599
Tel *(707) 944-2380*
Three Michelin stars make this one of the country's top restaurants. It is set in a century-old stone building that conjures a French countryside feel. The spectacular nine-course menu changes nightly.

YOUNTVILLE: Mustards Grill $$$
Californian **Road map** A3
7399 St Helena Hwy, 94558
Tel *(707) 944-2424*
Iconic West Coast chef Cindy Pawlcyn prepares home-made pastas, grilled and spit-roasted poultry, baby back ribs, and rabbit roulade. Enjoy a glass from the extensive wine list.

Gold Country and the Central Valley

CHICO: Sierra Nevada Tap Room & Restaurant $
American **Road map** B2
1075 E 20th St, 95928
Tel *(530) 345-2739*
This working brewery is popular for its craft beers and serves memorable pale ale-steamed clams, beer-cheese burgers, and wood-fired pizzas. Frequented by a young crowd, it is upbeat and lively, especially on weekends.

GRASS VALLEY: South Pine Café $
American **Road map** B3
102 N Richardson St, 95945
Tel *(530) 274-0261*
A local favorite, this family-run downtown eatery offers good-value meals and friendly service. Brunch options include eggs with jalapeno hollandaise and fresh home-made juices.

JAMESTOWN: National Hotel Restaurant $$
American/ Mediterranean **Road map** B3
18183 Main St, 95370
Tel *(209) 984-3446*
Set in a historic Gold Rush-era structure this is a cheery place with an impressive menu that includes steaks and an extensive list of appetizers. Home-made desserts and an excellent wine.

NEVADA CITY: Matteo's Public $
American **Road map** B3
300 Commercial St, 95959
Tel *(530) 265-6248* **Closed** *Mon*
Inventive gastropub fare focusing on local and sustainable ingredients used in skillfully prepared and artistically presented dishes. Live music and a large patio draw crowds.

NEVADA CITY: New Moon Café $$
Modern American **Road map** B3
203 York St, 95959
Tel *(530) 265-6399* **Closed** *Mon*
This small but inviting spot treats customers like family. Local ingredients steer the fresh, inventive, always-changing menu. Fresh ravioli of the day is a favorite.

DK Choice

SACRAMENTO: Chando's Tacos $
Mexican **Road map** B3
863 Arden Way, 95815
Tel *(916) 641-8226*
This brightly colored roadside stand is consistently named as one of Sacramento's best restaurants. The tacos in particular are exceptional. All of the meats – such as *adobado* and *carnitas* – are perfectly spiced, grilled, and tucked into fresh-made tortillas. The *tortas* are also a hit as are the home-made sauces.

SACRAMENTO: Morant's Old-Fashioned Sausage Kitchen $
European **Road map** B3
5001 Franklin Blvd, 95820
Tel *(916) 731-4377* **Closed** *Sun & Mon*
Part butcher shop, part deli, specializing in German sausages, though other types are available. Very casual, but the commitment to quality ingredients attracts chefs, foodies, and loyal fans.

SACRAMENTO: Tower Café $
International **Road map** B3
1518 Broadway, 95818
Tel *(916) 441-0222*
Immensely popular, especially for the palm-shrouded courtyard seating. The menu is casual and is influenced by continents from Asia to Africa. Extensive beer and wine list that spans the globe. Friendly service.

SACRAMENTO: Esquire Grill $$
American **Road map** B3
1213 K St, 95814
Tel *(916) 448-8900* **Closed** *Sun*
This New York-style bistro draws a well-dressed downtown crowd. The menu and extensive beer and wine list at this casual eatery feature both local and international options. Their banana cream pie is a delight.

SACRAMENTO: The Press Bistro $$
Mediterranean **Road map** B3
1809 Capitol Ave, 95811
Tel *(916) 444-2566* **Closed** *Mon*
Exudes a warm, friendly vibe, especially at the communal table. Italian-influenced tapas encourage sharing. While a farm-to-table approach ensures fresh cuisine made with local ingredients. Local house wines available.

Sleek interior and banquet seating at Esquire Grill, Sacramento

**SACRAMENTO: The Red
Rabbit** $$
American   **Road map** B3
2718 J St, 95816
Tel *(916) 706-2275*
This trendy neighborhood eatery
focuses on the local in all its ele-
ments, from ingredients to design.
The cuisine and the cocktail menu
impress with creativity, and the
brunch is a popular, sociable affair.

**SACRAMENTO:
The Firehouse** $$$
Modern American **Road map** B3
1112 2nd St, 95814
Tel *(916) 442-4772*
Set in a historic landmark building
in the heart of Old Sacramento.
Known for top-service and an
extensive wine list. Creative menus
include meat and seafood dishes
such as white corn lobster bisque
and *frutti di mare*.

SACRAMENTO: The Kitchen $$$
Modern American **Road map** B3
2225 Hurley Way, 95825
Tel *(916) 568-7171*   **Closed** *Mon,
Tue*
Special-occasion destination
with a monthly fixed, five-course
menu that is always innovative
and exceptional. Elegant dining
room, professional service, and
an open kitchen make for a
memorable experience.

SONORA: Banny's Café $
Mediterranean   **Road map** B3
17566 Lime Kiln Rd, 95370
Tel *(209) 533-4709*
Banny's menu features a mix of
regional styles, with an emphasis
on Mediterranean fare. Pastas are
home-made, salads are fresh, and
meats are flavorful. The wine bar
has an extensive list of local
vintages. Friendly service.

**SONORA: The Diamondback
Grill** $
Modern American **Road map** B3
93 S Washington St, 95370
Tel *(209) 532-6661*
Big, juicy burgers are the draw
at this family-run restaurant in
the historic downtown. Daily
specials are equally delicious
and the separate wine bar is a
popular gathering spot.

SONORA: Talulah's $
Modern American **Road map** B3
13 S Washington St, 95370
Tel *(209) 532-7278*   **Closed** *Sun
& Mon*
Seasonal, organic ingredients
make up the Italian-influenced
cuisine. Fresh ravioli, gorgonzola-
stuffed chicken, and meatloaf
are favorites, and all dishes are
served with fresh local veggies.

The High Sierras

BIG PINE: Copper Top BBQ $
American   **Road map** C4
310 N Main St, 93514
Tel *(760) 970-5577*
Customers sit at picnic tables at
this restaurant popular for its use
of certified Angus beef and
quality ingredients. Homey
atmosphere and friendly service.

BISHOP: Erick Schat's Bakkery $
Deli   **Road map** C4
763 N Main St, 93514
Tel *(760) 873-7156* **Closed** *Sat & Sun*
This Dutch bakery has been a
classic stop for hikers, skiers, and
holidaymakers for decades. It
produces made-from-scratch
items daily. The Sheepherder
Bread is famous; other sweet
and savory baked goods are
just as tasty.

BISHOP: The Village Café $
Breakfast   **Road map** C4
965 N See Vee Ln, 93515
Tel *(760) 872-3101* **Closed** *Mon & Tue*
Popular breakfast and lunch spot.
Known for its large portions, and
wide menu. Try the perfectly
cooked eggs, butter pecan French
toast, and strong coffee. Home-
cooking and friendly service.

DK Choice

**MAMMOTH LAKES: The
Restaurant at Convict Lake** $$
French   **Road map** C4
2000 Convict Lake Rd, 93546
Tel *(760) 934-3803*
This beautiful restaurant
warrants its high prices for the
atmosphere and alpine setting.
A perfect spot for special
occasions – the dining area has
a fireplace and windows that
look out onto the lake and forest.
Perfectly cooked local meats
and fish are paired with excellent
wines. It offers a lovely brunch.

MAMMOTH LAKES: Toomey's $$
Modern American **Road map** C4
6085 Minaret Rd, 93546
Tel *(760) 924-4408*
Popular local chef Matt Toomey
creates an all-day menu of
comfort dishes such as coconut
mascarpone pancakes, lobster
taquitos and wild buffalo meatloaf.

**NORTH LAKE TAHOE:
Bridgetender Tavern and Grill** $
American   **Road map** C3
65 W Lake Blvd, 96145
Tel *(530) 583-3342*
Casual tavern with outdoor
seating overlooking the lake.
The menu features juicy burgers
and fries as well as grilled seafood
options. Popular gathering spot.

**SOUTH LAKE TAHOE: Lake
Tahoe Pizza Company** $
Pizza   **Road map** C3
1168 Lake Tahoe Blvd, 96150
Tel *(530) 544-1919*
A great spot for brick-oven pies.
Traditional Italian favorites are on
the family-style menu along with
pastas, sandwiches, and lighter
selections. Good beer list.

**SOUTH LAKE TAHOE: The
Fresh Ketch** $$
Seafood   **Road map** C3
2435 Venice Dr, 96150
Tel *(530) 541-5683*   **Closed** *Sun*
Waterfront eatery with lovely
views and friendly service. The
seafood-centric menu has all the
usual offerings.

**STATELINE: Sage Room
Steakhouse** $$$
Steakhouse   **Road map** C3
Hwy 50 at Stateline Ave, NV 89449
Tel *(775) 588-2411*   **Closed** *Tue
& Wed*
This fine-dining spot has had a
loyal following since 1947. Steaks,
chops, and game dishes are
served in a Western-themed
setting. Bananas Foster (bananas
with vanilla ice cream in a liqueur
sauce) is the dessert specialty.

Rustic bar and dining area in The Red Rabbit, Sacramento

For more information on types of restaurants *see pages 544–5*

TAHOE CITY: Tahoe House Bakery & Gourmet $
European/Bakery   Road map B3
625 West Lake Blvd, 96145
Tel *(530) 583-1377*
A popular breakfast option, this Swiss-themed spot is also a take-away deli, and great for picnickers, offering cheeses, breads, and cakes. A menu of traditional Swiss dishes is available.

TAHOE CITY: Christy Hill Restaurant $$
Modern American   Road map C3
115 Grove St, 96145
Tel *(530) 583-8551*
Lakefront spot with outdoor seating on a lovely wooden deck, popular in the summer. Window seats inside also offer great views. The eclectic cuisine is well prepared. Superb wine list.

TRUCKEE: Moody's Bistro & Lounge $$
Modern American   Road map B3
10007 Bridge St, 96161
Tel *(530) 587-8688*
Moody's has a swanky, pioneer-style atmosphere, with a large bar. The modern menu features inventive sandwiches and salads, fresh pastas, and grilled meats. Excellent wine list pairs perfectly with the cuisine.

TRUCKEE: Pianeta $$
Italian   Road map B3
10096 Donner Pass Rd, 96161
Tel *(530) 587-4694*
This downtown spot has a mountain ambience and comfy booth seating. The reliable menu features well-prepared rustic Italian fare. Friendly service.

YOSEMITE NATIONAL PARK: Wawona Dining Room $$
American   Road map C3
8308 Wawona Rd, 95389
Tel *(209) 375-1425*   **Closed** *Nov, Jan (Dec reduced hours)*
Housed in the historic Wawona Hotel, this place is popular for its seasonal specialties and traditional favorites. Flavorful steak and trout are the highlight. The dining room has rustic flair, and there is a lovely outdoor veranda as well.

YOSEMITE NATIONAL PARK: Ahwahnee Dining Room $$$
Modern American   Road map C3
9013 Village Dr, 95389
Tel *(209) 372-1489*
Beautiful setting in a renowned hotel *(see p543)*. The menu features American standards, with the top choices being steaks and chops. Delectable desserts also served.

North Central California

APTOS: Bittersweet Bistro $$$
Seafood   Road map B4
787 Rio Del Mar Blvd, 95003
Tel *(831) 662-9799*
Excellent bistro fare, some of the best in the area. The menu features artfully presented Mediter-ranean dishes. Impressive wine list.

DK Choice

BIG SUR: Deetjen's Restaurant $$
American   Road map B4
48865 Hwy 1, 93920
Tel *(831) 667-2378*
This eatery is the highlight of the historic Deetjen's Big Sur Inn on the Pacific Coast Highway. Four uniquely decorated dining spaces in a secluded forest setting, plus friendly service, make for a lovely experience. The menu features Californian cuisine and the colorful breakfast menu is very popular. Reservations are recommended.

BIG SUR: Nepenthe Restaurant $$
Modern American   Road map B4
48510 Hwy 1, 93920
Tel *(831) 667-2345*
Stunning coastal spot that offers simple preparations of traditional fare alongside freshly made breads and desserts. Try the ambrosia burger.

BIG SUR: Sierra Mar $$$
Modern American   Road map B4
Hwy 1, 93920
Tel *(831) 667-2800*
This award-winning restaurant at the Post Ranch Inn offers magnificent views from its dining room. An innovative and daily-changing menu features seasonally inspired fare. Boasts one of North America's most extensive wine cellars.

CARMEL: Hog's Breath Inn $
American   Road map B4
Corner of San Carlos Ave & 5th St, 93921
Tel *(831) 625-1044*
Previously owned by Clint Eastwood, this bar and restaurant has a great patio and a fireplace. Hearty American fare is on the menu. Ribs and an extensive list of appetizers are specialties.

CARMEL: Katy's Place $
American   Road map B4
Mission St b/w 5th and 6th, 93921
Tel *(831) 624-0199*
A local favorite serving homey breakfasts and lunches. Katy's Place is famous for its French toast with strawberries, pecan waffles, variations of eggs Benedict, and several kinds of omelets. Catch all the action from a counter seat.

CARMEL: Restaurant at Mission Ranch $$
American   Road map B4
26270 Dolores St, 93923
Tel *(831) 624-6436*
Casual country setting with a fireplace and a patio with grand views. The traditional diner house menu includes steak and fresh local seafood. Features a piano bar and Sunday jazz brunch.

CARMEL: Anton & Michel $$$
French   Road map B4
Corner of Mission Ave & 7th St, 93921
Tel *(831) 624-2406*
Popular for its contemporary French-inspired cuisine and sophisticated ambience. Pan-

Ahwahnee Dining Room, Yosemite National Park

roasted duck breast is a favorite. Ask for a table on the quiet patio.

CARMEL: Casanova $$$
Italian   Road map B4
5th Ave b/w Mission & San Carlos St, 93921
Tel *(831) 625-0501*
This quaint, romantic spot is a Carmel favorite. Delicious fare is served in intimate dining rooms. The outdoor patio offers prime seating. Charming staff.

CARMEL: Pacific's Edge $$$
Californian   Road map B4
120 Highlands Dr, 93923
Tel *(831) 622-5445*
Elegant dining with stunning ocean views. The cuisine on offer includes beef, lamb, and an array of seafood choices. A chef's tasting menu, bar menu, and cigar menu are also available, along with award-winning wines.

CARMEL VALLEY: Running Iron Restaurant & Saloon $
American   Road map B4
24 E Carmel Valley Rd, 93924
Tel *(831) 659-4633*
A valley watering hole since the 1940s, this has a Western museum vibe, complete with boots and spurs. Steaks and south-of-the-border specialties are favorites, alongside fresh local seafood, fried chicken, and burgers.

MONTEREY: Compagno's Market & Deli $
Deli   Road map B4
2000 Prescott Ave, 93940
Tel *(831) 375-5987*
This traditional deli gets rave reviews for its fresh food and serving staff who treat customers like family. House-roasted meats and an assortment of fresh breads are on the menu. Their full-size sandwiches are a challenge worth tackling.

MONTEREY: Monterey's Fish House $
Seafood   Road map B4
2114 Del Monte Ave, 93940
Tel *(831) 373-4647*
This casual but classy joint is frequently packed with locals. Incredibly fresh seafood is served grilled, blackened, or poached. Substantial wine list. Enjoy drinks and fresh oysters at the bar.

MONTEREY: Old Fisherman's Grotto $$
Seafood   Road map B4
39 Fishermans Wharf, 93940
Tel *(831) 375-4604*
A touristy but beloved family-run spot on the wharf with stunning views of the harbor. Menu

Chic interior of Restaurant 1833, Monterey

includes fresh seafood as well as steaks, Italian pastas, and delicious homemade desserts.

MONTEREY: Tarpy's Roadhouse $$
American   Road map B4
2999 Monterey-Salinas Hwy, 93940
Tel *(831) 647-1444*
Rustic eatery with a loyal following in an old ranch house. The wide-ranging menu includes wood-fired wild game, steaks, fresh seafood, salads, and burgers. Cozy outdoor patio. Service is friendly and professional.

MONTEREY: Restaurant 1833 $$$
Modern American   Road map B4
500 Hartnell St, 93940
Tel *(831) 643-1833*
Historic building with elements of its past evident in the decor. Intimate outdoor dining features fire pits. Regional, seasonal ingredients are the highlights of the contemporary cuisine on offer. The craft cocktails are notable.

PACIFIC GROVE: Fandango $$$
French/Seafood   Road map B4
223 17th St, 93950
Tel *(831) 372-3456*
Cheery neighborhood spot serving reliable preparations of seafood and steak. The colorful upstairs room, alcove, cellar, and main dining room all have individual character. The scampi, rack of lamb, and *bouillabaisse* all come recommended.

SANTA CRUZ: The Crêpe Place $
French   Road map B4
1134 Soquel Ave, 95062
Tel *(831) 429-6994*
This quirky crêperie is a local favorite. The menu features a wide selection of crêpes and a

wealth of choices for creating your own. Soups and salads are also on the menu.

SANTA CRUZ: The Crow's Nest $
Seafood   Road map B4
2218 E Cliff Dr, 95062
Tel *(831) 476-4560*
A harbor icon since 1969, this entertaining eatery serves seafood specialties as well as pasta, steaks, and chops. The upstairs bar has a more casual atmosphere. Great views of the harbor.

SEASIDE: El Migueleno $
Salvadoran   Road map B4
1066 Broadway Ave, 93955
Tel *(831) 899-2199*
One of the few Salvadoran establishments in the region, El Migueleno blends both Mexican and Salvadoran culinary traditions. Go for the seafood stew made fresh with local fish. Friendly service.

Elegant place setting at Fandango, Pacific Grove

For more information on types of restaurants *see pages 544–5*

SHOPPING IN CALIFORNIA

California is a manufacturing giant and a major player in the global economy. It is the largest producer of children's clothing in the US, and is equally famous for its sportswear and swimwear. Produce from the San Joaquin Valley, including fruit, nuts, and vegetables, feeds the nation. Aside from the shopping districts of LA *(see pp170–73)* and San Francisco *(see pp386–91)*, the state's smaller towns and countryside offer a wide range of merchandise and local produce. Roadside food stands, wineries, antique shops, and crafts by local artisans are some of the attractions of California's backroads. Prices tend to be lower than in the cities, and in some places, such as flea markets, you will be expected to barter and negotiate.

Art galleries and shops in the picturesque village of Carmel *(see p514)*

Shopping Hours

Since the local population tends to view shopping as a recreational activity, most major stores are open for business seven days a week. Typical business hours are 10am–6pm (some till 9pm), Monday to Saturday, and 10am–5pm on Sundays. In smaller communities, stores may be closed on Sunday or Monday. Opening hours for stores in such smaller towns and villages tend to be 11am–7pm.

How To Pay

Most stores accept credit cards, including MasterCard, American Express, and Visa, and traveler's checks. Paying by traveler's checks requires some form of identification, such as a passport or driver's license. Few stores will accept checks drawn on foreign banks. Cash is the best way to pay for any small purchases *(see pp596–7)*.

Sales Tax

Sales tax (VAT) in California ranges from 7.25 to 8.5 percent. All items except groceries and prescription drugs are taxed. In general, tax is not included in the advertised price but is added separately at the cash register.

Rights and Refunds

Merchants are not required by law to give a cash refund or credit for returned goods, although most do so. All stores will refund the cost of a defective item, if it is not marked "flawed" or "sold as is." Inspect the item before you buy it and keep all receipts. If an item is faulty, go back to the store with the receipt and original pack-aging. Many stores will refund your money up to 30 days after purchase.

Shipping Packages

For a charge, most stores ship goods worldwide, or you can send your items home by Federal Express or US Express Mail Service *(see p599)* You will be asked to fill out a form giving a short description of the goods and stating their monetary value. Keep receipts of the transaction in case the items should get lost in transit.

Where to Shop

A number of coastal towns noted for their locally owned shops can be found along Hwy 1 or US 101. These include Santa Barbara *(see pp224–5)*, Big Sur *(see pp518–19)*, Carmel *(see p514)*, Santa Cruz *(see pp510–11)*, and Sausalito *(see p418)*.

On Hwy 99 and other roads that cross the San Joaquin Valley, many farms sell locally grown fruit and vegetables. Palm Springs *(see pp278–9)* is known for its fashion and second-hand stores. Antique dealers are plentiful in towns in the Sierra foothills, such as Sutter Creek *(see p480)*.

Fashion

California is known for its casual clothing – the dress-down Friday business look was invented here. However, the East Coast also looks to California for the very best of cutting-edge fashion. Seventy percent of all US swimwear is designed here, by big names in their field and can be found at chainstores like **Diane's Beach-wear**. Sixty-five percent

San Franciscan original, Gap

of the country's younger female fashion is also produced here. Try **The Children's Place**, **Gymboree**, and **Carter's** for kids' fashions.

Other local heroes include designer Max Azria, renowned for contemporary fashion label, **BCBGMAXAZRIA**, as well as the teen chainstore **Forever 21**, and **Chico's** for women. California is the birth place of denim, with Levi Strauss starting his San Francisco business in 1860 *(see p347)*; the flagship **Original Levi's Store** is downtown on Market Street. **The Gap**, now an international retail giant, also originated in San Francisco and was the first store to mass-market denim jeans.

Flea Markets

Flea markets (also called swap meets) are held on weekends, usually on Sundays. Vendors set up booths within a vast parking lot, football stadium, or even in the grounds of one of the famous missions. Just about everything imaginable is for sale. It is often possible to find a one-of-a-kind treasure at a good price, but do not accept the quoted price – bargaining is *de rigueur*. Be sure to bring cash with you because most vendors will not accept credit cards or traveler's checks.

Notable flea markets include the **Berkeley Flea Market**, the **San Jose Flea Market**, and the **Rose Bowl Flea Market** and **PCC Flea Market**, both in Pasadena. Flea markets may charge a nominal entrance fee of 75 cents or $1.

Cover of a vintage Hollywood magazine from the 1950s

Pop Culture Antiques

Memorabilia stores are a California specialty. San Fernando's **The Game Doc** sells a variety of old games for all ages. **Ekkehart Wilms Period Antiques** in Belmont specializes in late-19th-century and early-20th-century tech pieces, like antique telephones and radios. **Sarah Stocking Fine Antique Posters** specializes in old movie posters. A range of Hollywood

memorabilia is easily found in LA *(see pp170–71)* Other stores, such as **Sutter Creek Antiques** in Sutter Creek, also sell such items.

Outlet Centers

One of the state's most popular retail trends is factory outlet malls. These sell off-season or surplus goods, such as clothing and household items, directly to consumers at prices lower than those in department stores.

Outlet centers usually have at least 20 shops, but the **Vacaville Premium Outlets** has more than 100 stores. Other popular centers include the **American Tin Cannery Factory Outlets** in Pacific Grove, **Napa Premium Outlets**, **Cabazon Outlets**, **Citadel Outlets**, **Prime Outlets Pismo Beach**, and the **Camarillo Premium Outlets**. For special outlet center tours in San Francisco, contact **Shopper Stopper Tours**.

Size Chart

For Australian sizes follow the British and American conversions.

Children's clothing

American	2–3	4–5	6–6x	7–8	10	12	14	16 (size)	
British	2–3	4–5	6–7	8–9	10–11	12	14	14+ (years)	
Continental	2–3	4–5	6–7	8–9	10–11	12	14	14+ (years)	

Children's shoes

American	7½	8½	9½	10½	11½	12½	13½	1½	2½
British	7	8	9	10	11	12	13	1	2
Continental	24	25½	27	28	29	30	32	33	34

Women's dresses, coats and skirts

American	4	6	8	10	12	14	16	18
British	6	8	10	12	14	16	18	20
Continental	38	40	42	44	46	48	50	52

Women's blouses and sweaters

American	6	8	10	12	14	16	18
British	30	32	34	36	38	40	42
Continental	40	42	44	46	48	50	52

Women's shoes

American	5	6	7	8	9	10	11
British	3	4	5	6	7	8	9
Continental	36	37	38	39	40	41	44

Men's suits

American	34	36	38	40	42	44	46	48
British	34	36	38	40	42	44	46	48
Continental	44	46	48	50	52	54	56	58

Men's shirts

American	14	15	15½	16	16½	17	17½	18
British	14	15	15½	16	16½	17	17½	18
Continental	36	38	39	41	42	43	44	45

Men's shoes

American	7	7½	8	8½	9½	10½	11	11½
British	6	7	7½	8	9	10	11	12
Continental	39	40	41	42	43	44	45	46

Browsers at an open-air flea market in Sausalito

Antique shops in Temecula, near Carlsbad

Books, Music, and Crafts

Bookstores, whether part of a large chain or independent, are a feature of even the smallest California town.

The best selection of music and books is generally available only in big cities, in chains such as **Barnes & Noble**. If a town has a university, head toward the student district for new and used record stores.

Native American arts and crafts are available in a number of places; contact the **California Indian Museum and Cultural Center** for more information. Mexican arts and crafts can be found at **Fiesta de Reyes** in San Diego.

Antiques

California's small towns are awash with traditional antiques such as fine gold and silver jewelry, Native American artifacts, textiles, antique clothing, Bakelite jewelry, and period furniture dating back to the 18th and 19th centuries.

The West Coast is the port of entry to the US for many Pacific Rim countries and, as a result, many antique porcelain sculptures from Japan and China, and antique Asian furniture are available. Twentieth-century collectables include Arts and Crafts and Art Deco furniture, clothing, posters, prewar tin toys, blown glass, and pottery.

Antique dealers often rent space together in one large mall, barn, or warehouse building that is open to the public. Located north of Balboa Park in San Diego, is **Antique Row**, featuring antiques and collectible stores, vintage-clothing boutiques, and used bookstores.

Food

Many of California's farms, particularly in Sonoma or Fresno counties, sell their produce to visitors on self-guided farm trails. In Sonoma, contact the **Sonoma County Farm Trails** or the **Sonoma Valley Chamber of Commerce.** The Fresno County Blossom Trail is a 62-mile (100-km) trail passing through groves, orchards, and vineyards. It begins at **Simonian Farms,** which sells local fruits, honey, and mustards. Contact the **Fresno County Farm Bureau** for information.

California has a number of unique food shops scattered around the state. In Napa's Anderson Valley, the **Apple Farm** is a year-round fruit stand

Fresh local produce at a farmers' market

selling locally grown apples and pears. Also in Napa, the **Jimtown Store** sells local jams, honey, olives, mustards, vinegars, and salad dressings. On Hwy 152, east of Gilroy, **Casa de Fruta**, which began as a simple cherry stand in the 1940s, has grown into a vast complex with a fruit stand, coffee shop (Casa de Coffee), restaurant (Casa de Burger), and gift shop (Casa de Gift).

Harris Ranch, almost midway between LA and San Francisco on I-5, is a vast complex set amid a working cattle ranch. The Spanish-style hacienda has a gift shop featuring Harris Ranch produce and fresh meat, as well as a restaurant, coffee shop, and overnight lodging.

Italian Marketplace at the Viansa Winery

Wineries

As well as those in Napa and Sonoma counties, wineries throughout the state are known for the shops located inside their tasting rooms. A range of merchandise related to wine is for sale. For a list of California's wineries, contact the **Wine Institute of San Francisco**.

The Italian Marketplace at the **Viansa Winery** sells Italian cheeses and breads, cookbooks, and kitchenware. The **Sebastiani Vineyards** sell a variety of wine-related souvenirs. The gift shop in the **Sterling Vineyards** offers silk scarves, silver jewelry, and regional history books.

Family-owned **V Sattui Winery** has a gourmet deli, as well as a shaded picnic area to eat your purchases.

DIRECTORY

Fashion

BCBGMAXAZRIA
8634 W Sunset Blvd,
Los Angeles, CA 90069.
Tel 310-360-0946.

Carter's
Midtown Crossing, 4550
Pico Blvd, Los Angeles,
CA 90015.
Tel (323) 932-1630.

Chico's
1314 Montana Ave, Santa
Monica, CA 90403.
Tel 310-394-2481.

The Children's Place
Stonestown Galleria, 3251
20 Ave, San Francisco,
CA 94132.
Tel (415) 682-9404.

Diane's Beachwear
116 Main St, Huntington
Beach, CA 92648.
Tel 714-536-7803.

Forever 21
Beverly Center, 8522
Beverly Blvd #849 & #852,
Los Angeles, CA 90048.
Tel 310-854-1320.

The Gap
1355 3rd St, Promenade,
Santa Monica, CA 90401.
Tel 310-393-0719.

Gymboree
Santa Monica Place, 395
Santa Monica Pier, CA
90410. **Tel** 310-451-2751.

Original Levi's Store
815 Market St, San
Francisco, CA 94102.
Tel (415) 501-0100.

Flea Markets

Berkeley Flea Market
1937 Ashby Ave, Berkeley,
CA 94703.**Tel** (510) 644-
0744. **W** berkeleyflea
market.com

PCC Flea Market
1570 E Colorado Blvd,
Pasadena, CA 91106.
Tel (626) 585-7906.
W pasadena.edu/
fleamarket

Rose Bowl Flea Market
1001 Rose Bowl Drive,
Pasadena, CA 91103.
Tel (323) 560-7469.
W rgcshows.com

San Jose Flea Market
1590 Berryessa Road,
San Jose, CA 95133.
Tel (408) 453-1110.
W sjfm.com

Pop Culture Antiques

Ekkehart Wilms Period Antiques
248 Harbor Blvd,
Belmont, CA 94002.
Tel (650) 571-9070.
W vintagephone.com

The Game Doc
8927 Lankershim Blvd,
Sun Valley, CA 91352.
Tel (818) 504-0440.

Sarah Stocking Fine Antique Posters
368 Jackson St,
San Francisco,
CA 94111.
Tel (415) 984-0700.

Sutter Creek Antiques
28 Main St, Sutter Creek,
CA 95685.
Tel (209) 267-5574.

Outlet Centers

American Tin Cannery Factory Outlets
125 Ocean View Blvd,
Pacific Grove,
CA 93950.
Tel (831) 372-1442.
W americantin
cannery.com

Cabazon Outlets
48750 Seminole Rd,
Cabazon, CA 92230.
Tel (951) 922-3000.
W cabazonoutlets.com

Camarillo Premium Outlets
740 E Ventura Blvd,
Camarillo, CA 93010.
Tel (805) 445-8520.

Citadel Outlets
100 Citadel Dr,
Los Angeles, CA 90040.
Tel (323) 888-1724.
W citadeloutlets.com

Napa Premium Outlets
629 Factory Stores Dr,
Napa, CA 94558.
Tel (707) 226-9876.

Prime Outlets Pismo Beach
333 Five Cities Drive,
Pismo Beach, CA 93449.
Tel (805) 773-4620.
W premiumoutlets.
com/pismo

Shopper Stopper Tours
2489 Schaeffer Rd,
Sebastopol, CA 95473.
Tel (707) 829-1597.

Vacaville Premium Outlets
321–2 Nut Tree Rd,
Vacaville, CA 95687.
Tel (707) 447-5755.
W premiumoutlets.
com/vacaville

Books, Music, and Crafts

Barnes & Noble
791 S Main St, Orange, CA
92868. **Tel** (714) 558-0028.

California Indian Museum and Cultural Center
5250 Aero Dr, San Rosa,
CA 95403. **Tel** (707) 579-
3004. **W** cimcc.org

Fiesta de Reyes
Old Town, San Diego,
CA 92110.
Tel (619) 296-3161.
W fiestadereyes.com

Antiques

Antique Row
308 Adams Ave, San
Diego, CA 92103.
Tel (619) 282-7329.

Food

Apple Farm
18501 Greenwood Rd,
Philo, CA 95466.
Tel (707) 895-2333.
W philoapplefarm.com

Casa de Fruta
10021 Pacheco Pass Hwy,
Hollister, CA 95023.
Tel (408) 842-7282.
W casadefruta.com

Fresno County Farm Bureau
1274 West Hedges,
Fresno, CA 93728.
Tel (559) 237-0263.
W fcfb.org

Harris Ranch
24505 West Dorris Ave,
Coalinga, CA 93210.
Tel (800) 942-2333.
W harrisranch.com

Jimtown Store
6706 Hwy 128,
Healdsburg, CA 95448.
Tel (707) 433-1212.
W jimtown.com

Simonian Farms
2629 S Clovis Ave, Fresno,
CA 93725.
Tel (559) 237-2294.
W simonianfarms.com

Sonoma County Farm Trails
PO Box 6032, Santa Rosa,
CA 95606.
Tel (800) 207-9464.
W farmtrails.org

Sonoma Valley Chamber of Commerce
651-A Broadway,
Sonoma, CA 95476.
Tel (707) 996-1033.
W sonomachamber.
org

Wineries

Sebastiani Vineyards
389 Fourth St East,
Sonoma, CA 95476.
Tel (800) 888-5532.
W sebastiani.com

Sterling Vineyards
1111 Dunaweal Loane,
Calistoga, CA 94515.
Tel (707) 942-3300.
W sterlingvineyards.
com

V Sattui Winery
1111 White Lane, St
Helena, CA 94574.
Tel (707) 963-7774.
W vsattuiwinery.com

Viansa Winery
25200 Arnold Drive,
Sonoma, CA 95476.
Tel (707) 935-4700.
W viansa.com

Wine Institute of San Francisco
425 Market St, Suite 1000,
San Francisco, CA 94105.
Tel (415) 512-0151.
W wineinstitute.org

SPECIAL INTEREST VACATIONS AND ACTIVITIES

California is practically synonymous with the great outdoors. The state has protected its landscape so that future generations can visit places of beauty. The deserts, redwood forests, alpine meadows, granite mountains, lakes, and sandy beaches all attract visitors. California has a culture rich with physical activity, and wilderness is never far from any city. Golfers are well provided for around the Monterey Peninsula *(see p515)* and winter skiers flock to the resorts at Lake Tahoe *(see p491)*. Whether visitors are keen on hiking, surfing, horseback riding, or biking, California provides ample opportunities. For details of the main events in the sports calendar, see pages 40–43.

Tahquitz Golf Course, Palm Springs

Special Interest Vacations

Details of special interest vacations are available from the **California Office of Tourism**. One of the most popular of these are tours of California's missions along El Camino Real *(see pp50–51)*.

Writers who make California their home often give readings at local writers' workshops. The best of these are the **Santa Barbara Writers' Conference** and the **Squaw Valley Community of Writers.**

Artists can take advantage of the state's various craft centers. Nationally renowned artists hold painting courses at the **Mendocino Arts Center.**

Institutes such as **Gourmet Retreats** at Casa Lana in the Napa Valley and **Tante Marie's Cooking School** in San Francisco provide accommodations, cooking classes, shopping tours, visits to the Wine Country, and fine meals during week-long intensive courses in the summer months.

Camping

California has always valued its wilderness: Yosemite Valley *(see pp492–3)* and the Mariposa Grove of giant redwoods were protected parkland as early as 1864. Today there are more than 250 places classified as either state parks, wilderness areas, historic sites, or recreation areas.

At every site, there are hiking trails and parking lots. Many also provide bathrooms and camp sites. All state and federal parks allow day-use visitors, charging a small parking fee. For camping, reserve a site with **State Park Reservations**, **Reserve America**, or **Yosemite Reservations**. It is advisable to book in advance. Camping trips into the state's desert are organized by **Desert Survivors.** They include environmental information.

Hiking

Day hikes and longer trips in the country are popular with both residents and visitors. There are more than 1 million miles (1.6 million km) of trails in California, the longest being the Pacific Crest Trail. The 2,654-mile (4,270-km) route stretches from Canada to Mexico. One of its highlights is the 211-mile (340-km) John Muir Trail, from Yosemite's high country to Mount Whitney *(see pp492–9)*. The **Sierra Club** organizes guided outings and provides detailed maps.

Hiking along the John Muir Trail at Mount Whitney

Horseback Riding

Equestrians will find a wide variety of riding trails in California, across all types of landscape – pine-covered mountains, lush meadows, chaparral hills, and dry valleys. Many state and national parks allow horses and pack mules on their trails.

Traditional cowboy life can still be found at privately owned ranches. These are working ranches, and guests can ride with the ranch hands and herd animals, or simply ride for pleasure on their extensive network of trails. **Alisal Guest Ranch and Resort** holds annual roundups and cattle drives or just let **Hidden Trails** organize a ranch holiday for you.

Horseback riding in Ventura County

Mountain Biking

Many state parks allow cyclists on their hiking trails. One spectacular trail for cyclists begins at High Camp in Squaw Valley, Lake Tahoe *(see p491)*. A 2,000-ft (610-m) ascent via an aerial tram is followed by a downhill ride to Shirley Lake. Contact the **Northern California Nevada Cycling Association** to find out where mountain bikes are welcome in Northern California.

Outfitters such as **Backroads** also lead groups of cyclists on tours of the state's countryside, often with stops for leisurely gourmet lunches. Transport vans accompany the cyclists, carrying heavy equipment and camping gear for week-long trips. Popular destinations

Mountain biking in Marin County

include the Napa Valley *(see pp466–7)* and the country lanes of Sonoma, Monterey, and Santa Barbara Counties.

Beaches

Beaches along California's 1,100- mile (1,770-km) coastline vary considerably. Some have rough waves and rocky shores, ideal for rock pool exploration and quiet reflection. Others have the white sand, arching waves, and warm water that attract the surfers of California legend.

Whether you want to surf or simply watch the golden boys of summer, the best beaches include the Leo Carrillo State Beach north of Malibu *(see p71)*, Windansea Beach in La Jolla *(see pp252–3)*, and Corona del Mar in Newport Beach *(see pp234–5)*. The **Club Ed Surf School** offers a 7-day surfing camp for beginners to the sport, which is held between April and October.

Many spots along the coast are good diving areas, including Scripps Shoreline Underwater Preserve in La Jolla *(see p253)*, the coves of Laguna Beach *(see p235)*, and Monterey Bay *(see p515)*. Equipment can be rented from **Glen's Aquarius II Dive Shop**. The **Oceanside Scuba & Swim Center** in Oceanside also offers beginners' diving lessons.

Natural Bridges State Park in Santa Cruz *(see pp510–11)* and Pfeiffer State Beach in Big Sur *(see pp418–19)* are good sites for rock pool exploration, where the ocean has eroded the rock in unusual formations. Torrey Pines State Beach *(see p252)* offers forests and dramatic white-capped swells. Pismo Beach is famous for its sand dunes, surfing, and clam digging *(see p212)*.

Southern California's water is warm enough for swimming from April to November. In the sea north of San Francisco a wet suit should be worn at all times of the year.

Golden beaches of La Jolla cove

Whitewater Rafting and Kayaking

Whitewater rafting is like a thrilling roller-coaster ride combined with stunning scenic views. Specialty outfitters such as **UCFS Outdoors Program** and **Whitewater Voyages** provide rafts, paddles, and life jackets. They take groups ranging from six to eight people, accompanied by a guide, down a tributary of one of California's major rivers. Trips may last one day only or include an overnight stay.

The rafting season lasts from April to September. Trips are graded by their level of difficulty: Classes I and II are relatively safe, with a few exciting twists and turns. Beginners wanting a safe but more exciting ride should book a trip on a Class III river. Only experienced rafters should go on a Class IV, or higher, trip.

Most organizations that offer river rafting also provide kayak and canoe trips. For more information on this, contact the **American River Touring Association**.

Waterskiing in San Diego

Water Sports

The lakes and beaches in California offer a variety of activities. Houseboats are available to rent for a slow cruise through the maze of inlets in the Sacramento Delta. Speedboats are available at Lake Tahoe *(see p491)*, Lake Shasta *(see p456)*, and the man-made lakes that are part of the state recreation system.

One of the popular sports is parasailing. With waterskis and a parachute, participants are harnessed to a speedboat and launched into the air for an exhilarating ride. It is a safe sport, but life jackets should be worn. Contact **Parasailing Catalina** for details.

Bird-Watching

In autumn, ducks, geese, and other shorebirds leave Canada to winter in South America, stopping in California along the way. The Point Reyes National Seashore *(see pp416–18)* supports at least 45 percent of US bird species. More than 425 species have been sighted here. **Shearwater Journeys** offers bird-watching cruises from Monterey. In southern San Diego, the **Tijuana River National Estuarine Research Reserve** hosts some 400 species, best seen in spring and autumn.

Bird-watching in La Jolla *(see p265)*

Fishing

California is an angler's paradise. From the end of April through to the middle of November, anglers head to the rivers and streams of the Sierra Nevada Mountains for trout fishing. Bass fishing in California's multitude of lakes and reservoirs is plentiful throughout the year. During the autumn and winter months, schools of salmon and steelhead make their way upriver, with especially good fishing in the Klamath, American, Eel, and Sacramento rivers. Sturgeon and striped bass can also readily be caught in the Sacramento River Delta.

Almost every coastal city in the state offers charter boats for deep-sea ocean fishing. In Northern California, the summer months are particularly good for halibut and ocean salmon, but throughout the Pacific, from autumn to early spring, 40–50-lb (18–23-kg) hauls of cod and rock fish are not unusual. In the warmer waters off Southern California, blue fin, yellow fin, and skipjack tuna, as well as

Rafting at Yosemite National Park *(see pp492–5)*

Fishing on Lake Molena in San Diego

barracuda are particularly plentiful during the summer. To rent a charter boat for fishing, contact **Anchor Charter Boats** or **Stagnaro's Sport Fishing**.

To find out which fish are in season, contact the **State Department of Fish and Game**. Information on fly fishing, another popular California sport, is available from the **Troutfitter Guide Service** at Mammoth Lakes.

Rock Climbing and Caving

Rock climbing combines the dexterity of gymnastics with the grace of dance, as individuals scale vertical rock walls using only their hands and high-friction shoes. The sport can be practiced throughout the year in

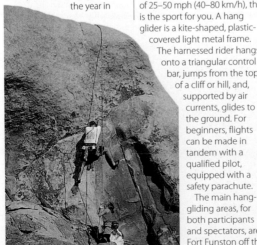

Rock climbing at Joshua Tree National Park

rock-climbing gyms In major cities. Other places to learn how to rock climb or simply to watch others in action are the Joshua Tree National Park *(see pp282–3)*, Idyllwild, near Palm Springs *(see p280)*, and Squaw Valley in Lake Tahoe *(see p491)*. Contact the **American Mountain Guides Association** or **Touchstone Climbing & Fitness** for information.

Spelunkers (cave explorers) should head for the Pinnacles National Monument *(see p521)* or Lassen Volcanic National Park *(see p457)*, where volcanoes have created unusual caves and rock formations.

Hang Gliding

If you have ever wanted to ride the thermal air currents at speeds of 25–50 mph (40–80 km/h), this is the sport for you. A hang glider is a kite-shaped, plastic-covered light metal frame. The harnessed rider hangs onto a triangular control bar, jumps from the top of a cliff or hill, and, supported by air currents, glides to the ground. For beginners, flights can be made in tandem with a qualified pilot, equipped with a safety parachute.

The main hang-gliding areas, for both participants and spectators, are Fort Funston off the Bay Area coastline

(see pp416–17), **Torrey Pines Gliderport** in San Diego, or Vista Point in Palm Desert *(see p278)*. If you want to learn the sport, they will recommend instructors. They also sell and rent gliding equipment.

Gardens

The warm, sunny climate of California has inspired numerous skilled and amateur gardeners to experiment with horticulture. The result is a rich variety of arboretums, botanical gardens, city parks, and private estates all over the state that are now open to the public.

Huntington Library Art Collections and Botanical Gardens are Henry Huntington's idealistic monument to art and culture. Work began on the gardens in 1904. They cover three-quarters of the 200-acre (80-ha) estate and are among the finest of their kind in California *(see pp162–5)*.

The **Descanso Gardens** in La Cañada offer 4 acres (1.6 ha) of roses, an impressive 30-acre (12-ha) grove of live oaks, and a protected forest of camellia trees. William Bourn's landscaped grounds and elegant estate of Filoli in the Bay Area town of Woodside *(see p431)* and **Villa Montalvo Arboretum** in Saratoga are both carefully tended so that their flowers are in bloom all year long. Weekend jazz concerts are held at Saratoga during the summer months, adding to the cultured environment.

Hot air ballooning over California's landscape

Hot Air Ballooning

Hot air ballooning is a popular excursion in the Napa Valley (see pp466–7), Monterey (see pp514–15), Palm Springs (see pp278–80), and Temecula. The rides are taken at sunrise or sunset when there is the least wind and are quiet and gentle, offering incomparable panoramic views of the countryside. Outfitters such as **Panorama Balloon Tours** and **Napa Valley Balloons** provide private and group outings, which are then followed by a picnic.

Whale Watching

From December through to April, gray whales journey 7,000 miles (11,260 km), passing the California coast having left Alaska's Bering Strait for the warmer climate of Mexico's Baja Peninsula. Ocean cruises offer views of these impressive mammals. Humpback, killer whales, pilot, and blue whales also frequent the coast between San Francisco and Monterey in late summer. Charter operators provide a glimpse of the gray whales, as well as the dolphins and porpoises that accompany them on their trips. For more information, contact **Oceanic Society Expeditions**.

Hot Springs

A long soak in a hot spring (a bubbling tributary of an underground river, heated by the earth) is said to be very good for one's health. Calistoga in Northern California (see p465) has numerous spas, offering everything from heated pools with mineral water to mud baths, steam baths, and massages. Contact the **Calistoga Chamber of Commerce** for a full list of area resorts.

Island Hopping

Five volcanic islands off the coast of Southern California make up the Channel Islands National Park (see p228). This stark nature preserve is ideal for hiking, viewing wildlife, and exploring rock pools. It is also an excellent spot to see whales and dolphins, as well as many species of shore birds. Ferries depart from Ventura and Santa Barbara harbors. Reserve your trip with **Island Packers**.

Catalina Island (see pp246–7) is accessible by ferry from San Pedro, Long Beach, and Dana Point. It is more developed than the Channel Islands National Park, with shops, restaurants, and accommodations. Developed as a summer resort in the 1920s by chewing-gum magnate William Wrigley, Jr, the island offers trails for cycling, hiking, and opportunities for diving and snorkeling (see pp246–7). You can also take a trip into the mountains to see the bison.

Farther north, **Angel Island**, in San Francisco Bay, is a 740-acre (300-ha) marine sanctuary, reached by ferry from Fisherman's Wharf. Extensive hiking trails, picnic areas, and camp sites are available to visitors. Gray whales and a wide range of shore birds can be observed.

Two Harbors on Catalina Island

DIRECTORY

Special Interest Vacations

California Office of Tourism
PO Box 1499, Sacramento, CA 95812.
Tel (916) 444-4429.
W visitcalifornia.com

Gourmet Retreats
Casa Lana, 1316 S Oak St, Calistoga, CA 94515.
Tel (877) 968-2665.
W gourmetretreats.com

Mendocino Arts Center
45200 Little Lake St, Mendocino, CA 95460.
Tel (707) 937-5818.
W mendocinoarts.org

Santa Barbara Writers' Conference
27 W Anapamu St, Suite 305 Santa Barbara, CA 93101. Tel (805) 964-0367. W sbwriters.com

Squaw Valley Community of Writers
PO Box 1416, Nevada City, CA 95959.
Tel (530) 470-8440.
W squawvalleywriters.org

Tante Marie's Cooking School
Broderick St, San Francisco, CA 94115.
Tel (415) 788-6699.
W tantemarie.com

Camping

Desert Survivors
PO Box 20991, Oakland, CA 94620-0991.
Tel (510) 357-6585.
W desert-survivors.org

Reserve America
Tel (877) 444-6777.
Tel (518) 885-3639.
W reserveamerica.com

State Park Reservations
Tel (800) 444-7275.
W parks.ca.gov

Yosemite Reservations
Tel (877) 444-6777.
W reserveamerica.com

Hiking

Sierra Club
85 Second St, San Francisco, CA 94105.
Tel (415) 977-5500.
W sierraclub.org

Horseback Riding

Alisal Guest Ranch and Resort
1054 Alisal Rd, Solvang, CA 93463. Tel (805) 688-6411. W alisal.com

Hidden Trails
202–380 West 1st Ave Vancouver, BC V5Y 3T7.
Tel (888) 9-TRAILS.
W hiddentrails.com

Mountain Biking

Backroads
801 Cedar St, Berkeley, CA 94710. Tel (800) 462-2848.
W backroads.com

Northern California Nevada Cycling Assoc.
W ncnca.org

Beaches

Club Ed Surf School
2350 Paul Minnie Ave, Santa Cruz, CA 95062.
Tel (800) 287 SURF.
W club-ed.com

Glen's Aquarius II Dive Shop
32 Cannery Row, Monterey, CA 93940.
Tel (866) 375 6605.
W aquarius2.com

Oceanside Scuba & Swim Center
225 Brooks St, Oceanside, CA 92054. Tel (760) 722-7826. W oceansidescubaswim.com

Whitewater Rafting and Kayaking

American River Touring Association
24000 Casa Loma Rd, Groveland, CA 95321.
Tel (800) 323-2782.
W arta.org

Whitewater Voyages
5225 San Pablo Dam Rd, El Sobrante, CA 94820.
Tel (800) 400-7238.
W whitewatervoyages.com

UCSF Outdoors Program
500 Parnassus Ave, San Francisco, CA 94143.
Tel (415) 476-2078.
W campuslifeservices.ucsf.edu

Water Sports

Parasailing Catalina
105 Pebbly Beach Rd, Avalon, CA 90704.
Tel 310-510-1777.
W parasailcatalina.com

Bird-Watching

Shearwater Journeys
PO Box 190, Hollister, CA 95024.
Tel (831) 637-8527.
W shearwaterjourneys.org

Tijuana River Reserve
301 Caspian Way, Imperial Beach, CA 91932. Tel (619) 575-2704. W trnerr.org

Fishing

Anchor Charter Boats
32260 N Harbor Dr, Fort Bragg, CA 95437. Tel (707) 964-4550. W anchorcharterboats.com

Stagnaro's Sport Fishing
1718 Brommer St, Santa Cruz, CA 95062.
Tel (831) 427-2334.
W stagnaros.com

State Department of Fish and Game
1416 9th St, 12th Fl, Sacramento, CA 95814.
Tel (916) 445-0411.
W dfg.ca.gov

Troutfitter Guide Service
PO Box 1734, Mammoth Lakes, CA 93546.
Tel (800) 637-6912.
W thetroutfly.com

Rock Climbing and Caving

American Mountain Guides Association
1209 Pearl St, Boulder, CO 80302.
Tel (303) 271-0984.
W amga.com

Touchstone Climbing & Fitness
2295 Harrison St, San Francisco, CA 94110.
Tel (415) 550-0515.
W touchstoneclimbing.com

Hang Gliding

Torrey Pines Gliderport
2800 Torrey Pines Scenic Drive, La Jolla, CA 92037.
Tel (858) 452-9858.
W flytorrey.com

Gardens

Descanso Gardens
1418 Descanso Dr, La Canada, CA 91011.
Tel (818) 949-4200.
W descansogardens.org

Villa Montalvo Arboretum
15400 Montalvo Rd, Saratoga, CA 95071.
Tel (408) 961-5800.
W montalvoarts.org

Hot Air Ballooning

Napa Valley Balloons
4086 Byway E Napa, CA 94558. Tel (800) 253-2224.
W napavalleyballoons.com

Panorama Balloon Tours
PO Box 218, Del Mar, CA 90214. Tel (800) 455-3592.
W gohotair.com

Whale Watching

Oceanic Society Expeditions
30 Sir Francis Drake Blvd, Ross, CA 94957.
Tel (800) 326-7491.
W oceanicsociety.org

Hot Springs

Calistoga Chamber of Commerce
1506 Lincoln Ave, Calistoga, CA 94515.
Tel (707) 942-6333.
W visitcalistoga.com

Island Hopping

Angel Island Ferry
Tel (415) 435-2131.
W angelislandferry.com

Island Packers
Tel (805) 642-1393.
W islandpackers.com

SURVIVAL GUIDE

PRACTICAL INFORMATION

California is a vibrant state with something to appeal to every taste: from the clubs, restaurants, and bustling downtowns of San Francisco and Los Angeles to the charming plazas and peaceful vistas of rural towns; from the snow-capped mountains and redwood forests of the north to the surfer haunts of San Diego. And no matter where you go in the "Golden State," you will be welcomed and looked after. Even so, it is advisable to plan ahead to ensure that you experience the best the state has to offer. Most places will have knowledgable visitors' centers offering travel advice and information on sights and visits and this Survival Guide contains valuable information to help you plan your trip. Personal Security and Health *(pp594–5)* outlines some recommended precautions.

Downhill skiers overlooking the slopes above Lake Tahoe

When to Go

The season from mid-April to September sees a rush of visitors to the state's major tourist destinations, but be advised that summer often brings San Francisco's foggiest weeks. The winter months are also popular with visitors, either for the warm climate of the south or for the ski slopes of Lake Tahoe. During the quieter off-season in early April or November it is possible to visit many of the attractions at lower admission prices and without the usual crowds.

Visas and Passports

Citizens of countries that qualify for the Visa Waiver Program (many EU countries, Australia, New Zealand, plus others), who plan to stay less than 90 days, need to apply for entry to the US in advance via the **Electronic System for Authorization**, which will charge all applicants a $14 processing fee. Canadians are generally allowed to stay for up to six months. Canadians arriving by air must present a valid passport; if arriving by land or sea an enhanced driver's license or ID card will be sufficient. Visitors from other parts of the world need a valid passport and a non-immigrant visitor's visa, which can be obtained from a US Embassy or Consulate. Check the **US Customs and Border Protection** website for the latest information on entry requirements.

Customs Information

Visitors arriving in the US by air and sea are issued with customs declaration forms before arrival; these need to be filled in and handed to passport control. If you are an adult non-resident, you are permitted to bring in a limited amount of duty-free items. These include 0.2 gal (1 liter) of alcoholic beverages (beer, wine, or spirits), 200 cigarettes, 50 cigars (but not Cuban), or 4.4 lb (2 kg) of smoking tobacco, and $100 worth of gifts for other people. Non-residents will be subjected to a retina scan and be fingerprinted and asked a handful of questions about the purpose of their visit.

Tourist Information

Advance information can be obtained from the **California Division of Tourism** or the nearest **California Welcome Center**. Maps, guides, event listings, and discount passes for public travel and tourist attractions are available from both state and local Visitors' and Convention Bureaus. Welcome Center offices are open from 9am–5:30pm, Monday to Friday.

The Directory below right provides the addresses and telephone numbers of the primary tourist information offices throughout the state.

Consulates

Most countries have consulates in both San Francisco and Los Angeles. Consulates are generally open from 9am to 5pm, Monday to Friday. Although they are not in existence expressly to deal with visitors' problems, staff can help with lost passports and give advice on legal matters in emergencies. Consulate contact details can usually be found on the relevant embassy's website.

California Welcome Center, Santa Rosa

◀ Road bridge on Highway One near Big Sur, North Central California

Admission Charges

Major museums, theme parks, art galleries, and other attractions generally charge an admission fee. Entry fees range from $10 to $20 (up to $80 per person for amusement parks), and there are often discounts for the disabled, students, senior citizens, and children *(see p592)*. Smaller sights are either free or request a small donation. At many larger institutions entrance is free on one day a month (call or check their website for details). Visitors can get discounted admission to a number of venues by purchasing "Fun Spots" coupons from the Visit California website (www. visitcalifornia.com). These provide money off entry to many sights. Discounts to San Francisco attractions are available with a CityPass (www. citypass.com; $84 adults, $59 children), which also covers a week's public travel, including cable car rides.

Opening Hours

Most businesses are open from 9am–5pm, Monday to Saturday and do not close for lunch. Many are also open 11am–5pm Sundays. Some groceries, drugstores, and gas stations

Entrance of the San Diego Museum of Art

in the larger towns and cities are open 24 hours a day. In large cities, most shops will often stay open until 7pm or 8pm.

Many museums close on Mondays and/or Tuesdays and on major public holidays, but on some days they stay open until early evening.

Californians tend to eat early in the evenings, and some restaurants often have their last sitting at about 10pm. You may find that some restaurants will be closed on Monday or Tuesday evenings, so be sure to check this before heading out for dinner.

Most bars are open until 2am, particularly on Fridays and Saturdays.

Smoking

It is illegal to smoke in any public building throughout the entire state of California. Ask about smoking policies when reserving a hotel room if you are concerned about it. Remember that in California smoking is banned in restaurants, bars, and in all public places. However, In Los Angeles and San Francisco, several bars are employee-owned and can decide whether or not to allow smoking, and, in an effort to attract more patrons, many of them do. Visitors can ask around to find these spots, or search a local website for details, such as www.yelp.com.

DIRECTORY

Visas and Passports

Electronic System for Authorization
Ⓦ esta.cbp.dhs.gov

US Customs and Border Protection
Ⓦ cbp.gov

Tourist Information

California Division of Tourism
PO Box 1499,
Sacramento,
CA 95814.
Tel (800) 862-2543.
Ⓦ visitcalifornia.com

Welcome Centers
Ⓦ visitcwc.com

Central Coast
Pismo Beach, 333 5 Cities
Dr. **Tel** (805) 773-7924.

High Sierras
Truckee, 10065 Donner
Pass Rd. **Tel** (530) 587-2757.

Los Angeles
685 S Figueroa St. **Tel** (213)
689-8822. Ⓦ discover
losangeles.com

Orange County
Anaheim, 800 W Katella
Ave. **Tel** 714-765-8888.
Ⓦ anaheimoc.org

San Diego
1140 N Harbor Dr.
Tel (619) 236-1212.
Ⓦ sandiego.org

San Francisco
San Francisco, PIER 39, 2nd
Level. **Tel** (415) 981-1280.
Ⓦ sanfrancisco.travel

South Central
Santa Barbara, 1601 Anacapa St. **Tel** (805) 966-9222.
Ⓦ santabarbaraca.com

Southern California
Oxnard, 1000 Town
Center Dr, Ste 135.
Tel (805) 988-0717

Wine Country
Santa Rosa, 9 4th St.
Tel (800) 404-7673.

Consulates

Australian Consulate
575 Market St, Suite 1800,
San Francisco. **Map** 6 D4.
Tel (415) 644-3620.

British Consulate General
1 Sansome St, San
Francisco. **Map** 5 C4.
Tel (415) 617-1300.

Canadian Consulate
550 S Hope St, 9th floor,
Los Angeles. **Map** 11 D4.
Tel (213) 346 -2700.

French Consulate
88 Kearney St, No. 600,
San Francisco. **Map** 5 C4.
Tel (415) 397- 4330.

German Consulate
1960 Jackson St, San
Francisco. **Map** 4 C3.
Tel (415) 775-1061.

Japanese Consulate
275 Battery St #2100, San
Francisco. **Map** 6 D4.
Tel (415) 780-6000.

Taxes and Tipping

The California State Government levies an 8.25 percent general sales and use tax. In major cities, an additional 1–1.5 percent tax is added to all bought items except those for out-of-state delivery, to-go food, and food for preparation. There are no sales tax charges on hotel rooms, but a 12–14 percent transient occupancy tax is generally incurred.

In restaurants, it is normal to tip 15–20 percent of the total bill. Allow for a tip of 15 percent for taxi drivers, bar staff, and hairdressers. Porters at hotels and airports expect $2 per bag. It is also common to leave hotel cleaning staff $1–2 for each day of your stay.

Travelers with Special Needs

California law requires that every public building is accessible to people with disabilities, which includes not only ramps and accessible bathrooms, but also clearly marked disabled parking. Direction signs and entrances are also specially adapted for blind and disabled visitors. Disabled people also receive privileges such as reserved seating at event venues and on public transport, free parking, and admission reductions to many national and state parks.

It is advisable to notify sights and hotels in advance of your arrival, so that they can prepare

Parking bays for the disabled are clearly marked

for any special needs that you may have.

The Society for the Advancement of Travel for the Handicapped (SATH) uses a blue H sign to symbolize special facilities in restaurants, hotels, and at tourist sights. For further information on disability rights in California, contact the **Disability Rights, Education, and Defense Fund**.

Traveling with Children

California has some of the country's best child-friendly attractions, such as Disneyland® and Universal Studios℠ in Los Angeles, the San Diego Zoo, and the Exploratorium and California Academy of Sciences in San Francisco. And then, of course, there are the state's many beaches and parks, all of which are free. Along Highway 1 from Cambria up to Point Reyes, there are numerous wildlife viewing points where kids will love to watch elephant seals, elk, or the area's many birds.

There are discounts for children at many theme parks and museums and there are kid's menus with discounted meal prices at restaurants all over California. Many hotels offer "kids stay free" or "kids eat free" deals and children aged five and under ride public transport for free.

Senior Travelers

Seniors aged 65 and older get discounts at many restaurants, movies, and at most attractions. Discount travel and reserved seating for seniors is available on all public transport. The **American Association of Retired People** offers a website which includes recommendations for sights and information on available discounts.

Gay and Lesbian Travelers

California has a long history of celebrating gay rights. The largest Gay Pride Parade in the world is held in San Francisco

each year, and there is a general focus on equality throughout much of the state. California's large gay community is mainly focused in the major cities, particularly in the Castro District of San Francisco *(see p364)*, Hillcrest in San Diego, the West Hollywood area of LA *(see p105)*, and Palm Springs. Free newspapers and magazines that contain gay listings include the *LA Weekly* in Los Angeles and the several magazines in San Francisco, such as *Out in San Francisco* and *The Advocate*.

ISIC student card gives discount entry to many attractions

Traveling on a Budget

There are many ways to take advantage of the best of California on a budget. Students receive discounted entry to several attractions and movie theaters, as well as discounted ski lift tickets in Tahoe and Mammoth resorts. Most museums have a discount night, often Tuesday or Thursday, when entry is reduced or free.

There are a number of websites offering discounts on hotel rooms, restaurants, and other activities. Try **Jetsetter** for hotel and spa deals and **Groupon** and **Living Social** for restaurant discounts. To save money on lodging, consider renting a house or apartment. **Vacation Rentals by Owner** or **AirBnB** offer rooms from $75 a night for a studio/1 bed and up to $300 a night for a house that sleeps 10. **Hostelling International – American Youth Hostels** provides safe and inexpensive accommodation in both rural and urban areas.

The **Student Travel Association** is one of the biggest travel organizations that specializes in holidays for students and young people.

Self-Realization Fellowship in LA, an alternative place of worship

Religious Organizations

California, and particularly Northern California, has the reputation of attracting unconventional forms of worship *(see pp444–5)*. Sects, cults, and alternative religions seem to thrive in the state as much as the more conventional churches and temples. The Catholic Church has the largest following, with nearly a quarter of its members of Hispanic origin. Los Angeles has the second largest Jewish community in the US, and there are many beautiful synagogues. Hindu temples, Islamic mosques, and a range of shrines, such as the Self-Realization Temple in LA, abound throughout the state.

California Time

California is in the Pacific Time Zone. Daylight Saving Time begins on the second Sunday in March (at 2am) when clocks are set ahead one hour. It ends on the first Sunday in November (at 2am) when clocks are set back one hour.

Electricity

In the United States all electrical current flows at a standard 110–120 volts AC (alternating current). To operate 220-volt appliances requires a voltage converter and an adapter plug with two flat parallel prongs to fit US outlets. The same applies to battery pack rechargers. Many hotels have hairdryers mounted on the bathroom wall and special plugs for electric shavers that carry 110- or 220-volt current.

Conversion Chart

Remember to bear in mind that 1 US pint (0.5 liter) is a smaller measure than 1 UK pint (0.6 liter).

US Standard to Metric
1 inch = 2.54 centimeters
1 foot = 30 centimeters
1 mile = 1.6 kilometers
1 ounce = 28 grams
1 pound = 454 grams
1 US quart = 0.947 liter
1 US gallon = 3.8 liters

Metric to US Standard
1 centimeter = 0.4 inch
1 meter = 3 feet 3 inches
1 kilometer = 0.6 miles
1 gram = 0.04 ounce
1 kilogram = 2.2 pounds
1 liter = 1.1 US quarts

green spa network™
Vital People. Vital Planet.

Green Spa Network logo

Responsible Tourism

California leads the way on all things "green" in the United States, from the sustainable food movement to the green building boom. Recycling bins are available everywhere, and plastic reduction is also becoming a focus, with cities throughout the state passing bans on plastic bags and bottles. A number of incentive programs have spurred more renewable energy development, so it is not uncommon to see solar or wind farms along rural roads or solar panels atop high-rises. Green business associations, such as the **Green Hotels Association**, the **Green Spa Network**, and the **Green Chamber of Commerce** make it easy for visitors to find and support green businesses.

DIRECTORY

Travelers with Special Needs

Disability Rights, Education, and Defense Fund
2212 6th St, Berkeley, CA 94710.
Tel (510) 644-2555.
w dredf.org

Senior Travelers

American Association of Retired People
Tel (202) 434-3525.
w aarp.org

Traveling on a Budget

AirBnB
w airbnb.com

Groupon
w groupon.com

Hosteling International – American Youth Hostels
733 15th St NW, Suite 840,
Washington, DC 20005.
Tel (800) 909-4776.
w hiusa.org

Jetsetter
w jetsetter.com

Living Social
w livingsocial.com

Student Travel Association
Tel (800) 781-4040.
w statravel.com

Vacation Rentals by Owner (VRBO)
w vrbo.com

Responsible Tourism

Green Chamber of Commerce
821 Irving St, #225278,
San Francisco.
Tel (415) 839-9280.
w greenchamberofcommerce.net

Green Hotels Association
Tel (713) 789-8889.
w greenhotels.com

Green Spa Network
Tel (800) 275-3045.
w greenspanetwork.org

Personal Security and Health

Like most major cities, the cities of California have some dangerous neighborhoods. Check with the tourist office or hotel staff about which parts of town are considered unwise to visit, either alone or at night. San Francisco is believed to be one of the safest large cities in the US; unfortunately, problems are more visible in some areas of LA. When traveling in the countryside, always carry a good local map, particularly in the deserts and the mountains. It is important to take the advice of the local authorities seriously and in cases of all outdoor pursuits, normal safety procedures should be observed.

Motorcycle police patrolling the streets, San Francisco

Police

Uniformed and plain-clothes police regularly patrol the streets on foot, as well as in cars and motorcycles. The Highway Patrol monitor speeding on the highways and are first-responders in case of accidents. All non-emergency crimes should be reported to the local police station, the number for which can be found easily online or in the Blue Pages of the telephone book (phone books are placed in most hotel rooms; otherwise call the concierge or hotel operator for important phone numbers).

What to Be Aware Of

The notorious gangs of California, particularly in Los Angeles, are rarely seen outside their own areas and are not interested in approaching visitors. Visitors are more likely to be the target of theft or car crime.

Lock any valuables away in the hotel safe – do not carry them around with you. If you rent a car, do not leave valuables in view when you park, even if it seems like a safe neighborhood. Make sure you know where you are going so you don't enter a bad neighborhood, especially on your own and at night.

Pedestrians should observe road safety laws: jaywalking, or crossing the road anywhere except at an intersection, can result in a fine.

Outside of the cities, in wilderness areas pay attention to posted warnings and heed the advice of local rangers.

In an Emergency

For emergencies that require medical, police, or fire services, call 911 in the first instance. US hospital emergency rooms can often be crowded and it may take time to be seen. City-owned hospitals are listed in the Blue Pages of the telephone book, private hospitals in the Yellow Pages, or check online. When requested, hotels will usually call a doctor or dentist to visit you in your room. The national organization **Travelers' Aid Society** can also provide some assistance in many kinds of emergency.

Lost and Stolen Property

Although the chances of retrieving property lost in the street are very slim, telephone the **Police Non-Emergency Line** to report lost or stolen items. If you want to make an insurance claim on your return home, you will need to obtain a copy of the police report to send to the insurance company. In most cities, you can now file the report online at www.sco.ca.gov and print a copy for your records. In case of loss, it is always useful to have a photocopy of all documents kept separately as proof of possession.

If your passport is lost or stolen, get in contact with your consulate immediately (see p591). For lost or stolen traveler's checks or credit cards, you should call the issuing company's relevant hotline (see p597).

Hospitals and Pharmacies

There are both public and private hospitals in the US, with private hospitals generally offering nicer facilities and shorter wait times. Low-cost clinics are walk-in clinics that charge a small fee and can be

Fire engine, Santa Rosa

Police car, Los Angeles

Ambulance, San Bernardino County

a good option for travelers in need of care for minor illnesses. The main pharmacies in California are **Walgreens** and **CVS**. Some pharmacies offer clinics, and these will be listed in the phone book and can be easily found online. If you take medication, bring a back-up prescription with you. Pharmacies are open from 9am–6pm; many 24-hour pharmacies exist in the cities.

Travel and Health Insurance

Travel insurance is strongly recommended for the US. You should take out adequate coverage for emergency medical and dental care while also insuring your personal property. If you visit a doctor's office, hospital, or low-cost clinic in the US without insurance, be prepared to pay exorbitant fees. Even with medical coverage, you may still have to pay for some services, then claim reimbursement from your insurance company.

It is also advisable to make sure your travel insurance covers for lost or stolen baggage and travel documents, accidental death or injury, trip cancellation, and legal advice.

A park fire warning sign indicating the level of risk

Safety Outdoors

Outside of the cities, pay attention to posted warnings and heed the advice of rangers and locals. The Pacific Ocean is rarely warm, even in summer. The ocean can also be rough, more suited to surfers than swimmers, with a strong undertow.

It is important to have the proper equipment before hiking in the wilderness. Notify

Ranger with a cross-country skiing group at Yosemite National Park

someone of your plans before setting off. Leave the area as you found it, and be wary of the occasionally dangerous wildlife in many of the parks. As forest fires can start fast, check with the park ranger whether camp fires are allowed.

There are services for climbers in many parks *(see p585)*. Contact local ranger services via the **California State Parks** for advice on instructors, equipment required, and current weather conditions.

Be careful in the desert. At lower levels, it is usually hot and dry; at high elevations, temperatures often drop below freezing at night. Always carry extra gas and water in your car. If your car overheats, do not leave it to go for help.

It is also worth checking the **California Department of Transportation** websites for updates on road conditions and precautions to take.

Earthquakes

The expectation and fear of earthquakes should not get in the way of everyday activities. You may experience a tremor, but the most important thing is not to panic. Precautions are important, such as keeping shoes and a flashlight by the bed when asleep, in case of broken glass or power cuts. Most injuries occur from falling material so, if indoors, stand in a doorway or crouch under a

table. If you are in a car, slow down, pull to the side of the road, and stop. When outside, avoid standing under or being near trees, power lines, or bridges. For further information on earthquake precautions, contact **The United States Geological Survey**.

DIRECTORY

Police

Police Non-Emergency Lines

Los Angeles
Tel (877) 275-5273.

San Francisco
Tel (415) 553-0123.

In an Emergency

All Emergencies
Tel 911.

Travelers' Aid Society
Inland Empire
Tel (909) 544-5378.

San Diego
Tel (619) 295-8393.

Pharmacies

CVS
Tel (888) 607-4287.
W cvs.com

Walgreens
Tel (800) 925-4733.
W walgreens.com

Safety Outdoors

California Department of Transportation To check highway and road conditions.
W dot.ca.gov

California State Parks
Tel 800-777-0369.
W parks.ca.gov

Earthquake Information

The United States Geological Survey
Earth Science Information Centers, 345 Middlefield Rd, Menlo Park, CA 94025.
Tel (650) 329-4390. W usgs.gov

Banking and Currency

San Francisco and LA are major West Coast financial centers. California has a wealth of local, regional, and major national banks, plus some retail branches of the leading foreign banks. For the convenience of residents and visitors alike, there are numerous ATMs that operate 24 hours a day. In smaller towns, some banks may not exchange foreign currency or traveler's checks, so it is best to call the bank in advance. Credit cards are very useful, and are typically required as a form of security for checking in at hotels or for renting a car.

Banks and Exchange Bureaus

Bank opening times vary throughout the state, but they usually open between 10am and 5pm Monday to Friday. Banking hours within major cities may be longer: some open as early as 7:30am and close at 6pm, and are often open on Saturday mornings too. Credit Unions serve only their own members and deal with local business, so look for banks that offer services to the general public. **Chase**, **Bank of America**, and **Wells Fargo** all have hundreds of branches throughout the whole of California.

Major banks will exchange currency, but larger exchange bureaus are also available at major airports and in the financial districts of California. Exchange bureaus are open 9am–5pm on weekdays, and note that commissions will be charged. The best-known companies are **Travelex Currency Service** and **Currency Exchange International** and both have offices throughout California.

ATMs

Most ATMs accept debit cards from the main international banks and many credit cards, and can be found in most bank foyers or on the outside wall near the bank's entrance. The ATM machines that are located in bank foyers can be accessed outside normal banking hours via a card-reader at the door, which accepts all major cards. ATM machines usually issue American bank notes in $20 denominations. Ask your card provider which ATM system your card can access in California and how much each transaction will cost. The more popular systems used throughout California are Cirrus and Plus.

Bars and convenience stores often offer ATMs but these machines will usually charge a fee to every cardholder. Withdrawals from bank ATMs may provide a better foreign currency exchange rate than cash transactions, but you will be charged.

On a cautionary note, be aware of your surroundings when using any ATM. Make sure you shield your PIN, and if available, use a machine located within a bank. Be careful when removing your card at the machine.

If you are traveling from Europe, and use a chip & pin card, you may need to sign for some transactions, as the technology is still being introduced in the US.

Travelex exchange bureau logo

Credit Cards and Prepaid Debit Cards

Credit cards are extremely common in the US and can even be used for purchases costing $1, as well as for public transport fares and parking. Most hotels will ask for a credit card number on check-in, and almost all car rental companies require a credit card. Some will accept the use of a debit card. Hospitals will accept most credit cards in payment. **American Express**, **MasterCard**, and **Visa** are widely accepted throughout California.

If your credit or debit card is lost or stolen, contact your card company immediately. In order to ensure your card works overseas, it is worth contacting your bank or credit card provider to let them know of your travel plans. Precautions against fraud may cause your card to be blocked if unexpected transactions are made from a foreign country.

Traveler's checks issued by American Express in US dollars are less widely accepted than they used to be, and places that do take them, will ask for ident-ification such as a passport or driver's license. If you lose your checks, contact the **American Express Helpline** immediately.

Prepaid debit cards are more commonly used than traveler's cheques – they are also protected against loss but do not require ID as they operate on a PIN system for identification. The card is preloaded with the currency of your choice and used like a debit card to pay for things and withdraw money from an ATM.

ATMs at the Bank of America, San Francisco

Coins

*American coins come in 1-, 5-, 10-, 25-
and 50-cent pieces. The gold-tone
$1 coin is also in circulation, as are
the State quarters, which feature a
historical scene on one side. Each coin
has a popular name: 25-cent pieces
are called quarters, 10-cent pieces are
dimes, 5-cent pieces are nickels, and
1-cent pieces are pennies.*

25-cent coin
(a quarter)

10-cent coin
(a dime)

5-cent coin
(a nickel)

1-cent coin
(a penny)

Bank Notes

*Units of currency in the United States are dollars and cents.
There are 100 cents to a dollar. Notes come in the following
denominations: $1, $5, $10, $20, $50 and $100. Security features
include subtle color hues and color-shifting ink in the lower right
hand corner of the face of each note. Each bank note features a
different US president.*

DIRECTORY

Banks

Bank of America
Tel (800) 432-1000.
W bankofamerica.com

Chase
Tel (800) 432-3117.
W chase.com

Wells Fargo
Tel (800) 869-3557.
W wellsfargo.com

Exchange Bureaus

**Currency Exchange
International**
865 Market St, San Francisco.
Map 6 D4. **Tel** (415) 974-6600.

Travelex Currency Service
443 Castro St, San Francisco.
Map 10 D3. **Tel** (415) 552-3108.
W travelex.com

Credit Cards and
Traveler's Checks

American Express Helpline
Tel (800) 221-7282.

MasterCard
Tel (800) 307-7309.

Visa
Tel (800) 847-2911.

1-dollar bill ($1)

10-dollar bill ($50)

50-dollar bill ($50)

5-dollar bill ($5)

20-dollar bill ($20)

100-dollar bill ($100)

Communications and Media

As the home of Silicon Valley, California is always ahead when it comes to communication technologies. High-speed Wi-Fi is freely available throughout much of the state, and visitors can pick up pay-as-you-go cell (mobile) phones for use while in California. Public pay phones can still be found in hotels, airports, and some street corners. Los Angeles is a communications and media hub, and the base of several listings magazines, a variety of national and international newspapers and world news TV channels. No matter where you are in the state, it is generally easy to keep up with what is happening back home.

International and Local Telephone Calls

Local calls are free from most hotels, whereas long-distance and international calls are billed at very high rates. Visitors are better off purchasing prepaid phone cards (available at pharmacies and convenience stores, or online) to make calls from pay phones and cell phones, especially if calling international numbers. To use most phone cards you call the toll-free number printed on the card, enter the pin, and then dial the required number. All phone cards have instructions both printed on the card and spoken clearly to the caller when they phone the toll-free number.

To make a call from a public telephone or cell phone, you will need to dial 0 before the number. To call US numbers outside the city you are staying in, you will need to dial 1 and then the number. To call outside the US, dial 011, the country code and the number.

SIM cards for use. Both can be ordered online, however buying in-store ensures that you get a phone or SIM card that is compatible. Calls to phones outside the US are billed at premium rates, while calls to land lines are cheaper.

at&t

AT&T cell phone logo

Cell Phones

Visitors to the US who wish to use their own cell phone will need a tri-band phone and a SIM card that has been activated for "roaming." Ask your cell provider if your phone has been set up to be used abroad.

The primary cell phone providers in the United States are **T-Mobile**, **AT&T**, **Verizon** and **Sprint**. All offer prepaid and pay-as-you-go phones and

Public Telephones

Modern pay phones have a hand receiver and a 12-button key pad. Pacific Bell (PacBell) operates the majority of public pay phones. Although public phones are becoming increasingly rare, they are still typically available in airports, public transit terminals, and on main streets in large cities. Calls cost a minimum of 50 cents and most phones accept both coins and credit cards. If you need help or information, call the operator by dialing 0; for directory assistance, dial 411.

Cell phones, more widely used than public telephones

Reaching the Right Number

- Direct-dial call outside the local area code, but within the US and Canada: dial 1, then the area code and then the local number.
- International direct-dial call: dial 011 followed by country code (UK: 44; Australia: 61; New Zealand: 64), then the city or area code (omit the first 0) and then the local number.
- International call via the operator: dial 01, then the country code, then the area code (without the first 0), and then the local number.
- International directory inquiries: dial 00.
- International operator assistance: dial 01.
- A 1-800, 866, 888, 844 or 877 prefix indicates a free call.
- Local directory inquiries: dial 411.
- For calls within the local area code do not use an area code first. Exceptions: 310, 657, and 714 area codes must be keyed in for all calls, even local.
- For emergency police, fire, or ambulance services, dial 911.

Internet

Visitors can find free wireless Internet access throughout much of California, including on all major public transport systems.

Some hotels provide Internet access for free, while others charge a daily fee. In a few cases, hotels provide hardwired Ethernet access rather than wireless; such establishments have Ethernet cables available at the front desk. Public Wi-Fi is now so common in California that Internet cafés are becoming rare, but most coffee shops offer Wi-Fi (either free or for an hourly rate), and hotel business centers have Internet-ready computers and printers available to use. **FedEx** offers computers for hire with Internet and printing

A busy café with Wi-Fi facility, San Francisco

capabilities, as well as services in store. Libraries also have public computers with free Internet access available.

Postal Services

Apart from post offices, letters can be sent from hotel reception desks or mailed in letter slots in office buildings, in mailboxes on the street, and at rail, air, and bus terminals. Stamps can be purchased at post offices, hotel reception desks, or in some cases from bank ATMs. Different stamps are required for postcards; check postage rules and rates on the **United States Postal Service** website or at the post office. Flat rate envelopes are a great way to reduce postage costs; you can send as much as you can fit into the envelope for a flat $13 rate (available for domestic and international mail).

US Postal Service logo

All domestic mail usually arrives within 1 to 5 days. International airmail to New Zealand, Australia, Canada, Ireland, and the United Kingdom takes 5–10 working days. The federal post office offers Priority Mail, which promises delivery faster than first class mail, and the more expensive Express Mail, which delivers next day within the US, and within 72 hours to many international destinations. Private express and international mail can be arranged through **FedEx**, **DHL** or **UPS**, the numbers for which are listed in the Yellow Pages.

If you wish to receive mail during your visit it can be sent care of **General Delivery** to a local address. This service is available in the larger city post offices. Undelivered mail sent c/o General Delivery will be held for 30 days before being returned to the sender.

Newspapers and Magazines

The *New York Times*, the *Wall Street Journal*, and *USA Today* are available throughout much of California. There are also several local daily papers, many of which can be bought from street distribution bins or newsstands. Local magazines such as *LA Weekly*, *Angeleno*, and *Los Angeles* magazine in LA and the *SF Weekly*, *Bay Guardian*, and *San Francisco Magazine* in San Francisco provide information on local restaurants and events.

Television and Radio

The choice of TV stations in California is vast. Much of it is supplied by cable or satellite systems. Most hotel rooms have a TV, with a full range of cable channels, including BBC America and HBO. Bars frequently have screens showing sports. There is a wide selection of national and local channels, most of them showing sitcoms, magazine programs, children's cartoons, movies, and talk shows. There are also Spanish

and Asian foreign-language channels such as KRCA, as well as news and music channels. Most cable or satellite TV set-ups include a menu channel with listings.

There are several radio stations in California; public radio stations run news and talk programs. Wilderness areas typically have a dedicated frequency for news of road closures and weather issues. Hotels may provide a list of radio frequencies, or there are useful websites such as www.radio-locator.com.

DIRECTORY

Cell Phones

AT&T
Tel (800) 331-0500.
w att.com

Sprint
Tel (888) 211-4727.
w sprint.com

T-Mobile
Tel (800) 866-2453.
w tmobile.com

Verizon
Tel (800) 922-0204.
w verizon.com

Postal Services

DHL
Tel (800) 225-5345.
w dhl.com

FedEx
Tel (800) 463-3339.
w fedex.com

General Delivery
Los Angeles
c/o General Delivery, LA Main Post Office, 900 N Alameda, Los Angeles, CA 90086.
San Diego
c/o General Delivery, San Diego Main Post Office, San Diego, CA 92110.
San Francisco
c/o General Delivery, Civic Center, 101 Hyde St, San Francisco, CA 94142.

UPS
Tel (800) 742-5877.
w ups.com

United States Postal Service
Tel (800) 275-8777.
w usps.gov

TRAVEL INFORMATION

San Francisco and Los Angeles are the two main gateways for visitors traveling to California by air. You can also reach California by car, Amtrak train, long-distance bus, or by ocean liner. Despite continuing problems with traffic congestion and the rapid increase in gas prices, large comfortable cars and a comprehensive network of roads make driving an efficient and pleasurable way to tour the state. Public transportation is also a viable and inexpensive option. In some major cities, historic cable cars and ferries work alongside modern buses and mass transit systems as an efficient way to get around.

The modern concourse at San Jose airport, California

Arriving by Air

Air travel is an essential part of exploring America, and California is no exception. All the major airports are efficiently designed, with computerized ticketing systems for faster check-in.

Los Angeles (LAX) and San Francisco (SFO) are the two main airports used by visitors. International flights also land at San Diego (SAN), Oakland (OAK), Ontario (ONT), and San Jose (SJC). With vast numbers of passengers passing through, airports such as LA and San Francisco can be busy and at peak times, lines at customs and immigration are inevitable. It will help to take this into consideration when planning your transport from the airport.

All airports have disabled facilities, although it is advisable to check with the airline if you require help.

Air Fares and Tickets

Fare prices vary according to the season, with the most expensive fares being during the summer and holiday periods, such as Christmas and Thanksgiving *(see p43)*. It is always cheaper to travel on weekdays rather than on weekends. Tickets can be purchased from a reputable travel agent or they can often be booked for less online with easy to use websites such as **Travelocity** and **Kayak**, which provide airline price comparisons on all flights.

Domestic Air Travel

With over 30 airports for domestic flights including Sacramento and Ontario (also international), Santa Barbara, John Wayne/Orange County, and Fresno – air travel within California is easy and fairly cheap with prices starting from around $100 each way. **Southwest**, **Jet Blue**, and **Virgin America** all offer low prices and high quality amenities during the flight. Jet Blue flies out of smaller airports, but offers extra leg room and in-flight satellite TV on personal screens. Southwest will get you anywhere in the US, with a stop over. Virgin America flies to many major airports and boast planes with personal entertainment systems and in-flight Wi-Fi.

Getting into the Cities from the Airport

Car hire desks *(see p604)*, currency exchange facilities *(see pp596–7)*, and shuttle bus

Airport	Information	Distance from City
Los Angeles (LAX)	**Tel** (855) 463-5252 W **lawa.org**	15 miles (24 km) from Downtown
San Francisco (SFO)	**Tel** (650) 821-8211 W **flysfo.com**	14 miles (22 km) from city center
Oakland (OAK)	**Tel** (510) 563-3300 W **flyoakland.com**	8 miles (12 km) from city center
San Diego (SAN)	**Tel** (619) 400-2404 W **san.org**	3 miles (5 km) from city center
San Jose (SJC)	**Tel** (408) 392-3600 W **flysanjose.com**	8 miles (12 km) from city center
Sacramento (SMF)	**Tel** (916) 929-5411 W **sacairports.org**	12 miles (19 km) from city center
Palm Springs (PSP)	**Tel** (760) 318-3800 W **palmspringsca.gov**	2 miles (3 km) from city center

services can be found at all airports. Most car hire companies supply a shuttle bus to the car pick-up points, usually located on the outskirts of the airport.

In San Francisco, the subway Shuttle buses and shared-ride vans or private sedans *(see p401)* can also be called for a door-to-door service to and from the airport and a specific city address. Cheaper than using a taxi, one-way fares vary in price, depending on the distance covered. Bay Area Rapid Transit (or BART) is another option, and has a desk located in the arrivals terminal. It is a 35-minute ride into the city and costs $8 to $10.

Taxi ranks can be found outside most main terminals and will take you into the city. Prices will vary.

Arriving by Land and Sea

The primary interstate freeways into California are the I-80 in the Bay Area and the North, and I-15, I-10, and I-40 in the South. Patrols at state borders will sometimes stop cars to check for illegal substances, but there are no tolls at these crossings and often no one patrolling them.

If driving into California from Las Vegas on the I-15, from Phoenix on the I-10, or from Flagstaff on the I-40, make sure you are well prepared as these roads are quite desolate. Cars can become extremely hot during the summer; drivers are advised to travel in the cooler morning and evening. In winter, cars on I-80 are advised to be equipped with four-wheel drive and snow tires or they will be stopped and made to put on snow chains.

Train travel in the US provides regular and easy connections between all major cities. **Amtrak** runs direct, long-distance routes from LA to Chicago, Seattle, Orlando, San Antonio and Albuquerque.

Bus rides from neighboring states cost $80–$100 on average for a round-trip. From Las Vegas it is possible to hop on to a four-to five-hour bus ride with **LuxBus** to LA with minimal stops.

Northern routes and buses originating farther away than Nevada are longer journeys; the ride from Portland to San Francisco is about 20 hours (90 minutes by air). **Greyhound Lines** is the primary bus line with a depot in every major city. **Green Tortoise** offers slower green buses with chances to break the journey at hostels *(see p602)*.

American as well as international cruise ships ply Californian waters. The primary ports for the arrival, departure and stopping of cruise ships are Long Beach and San Pedro, in Southern California, and San Francisco in Northern California.

Greyhound Lines logo

DIRECTORY

Arriving by Air

American Airlines
Tel (800) 433-7300.
W aa.com

British Airways
Tel (800) 247-9297.
W britishairways.com

Delta
Tel (800) 221-1212.
W delta–air.com

United
Tel (800) 241-6522.
W united.com

US Airways
Tel (800) 428-4322.
W usairways.com

Virgin Atlantic
Tel (800) 862-8621.
W virgin-atlantic.com

Air Fares and Tickets

Kayak
W kayak.com

Travelocity
W travelocity.com

Domestic Air Travel

Jet Blue
Tel (800) 538-2583.
W jetblue.com

Southwest
Tel (800) 435-9792.
W southwest.com

Virgin America
Tel (877) 359-8474.
W virginamerica.com

Arriving by Land and Sea

Amtrak
Tel (800) 872-7245.
W amtrak.com

Green Tortoise
494 Broadway, San Francisco,
CA 94133. Tel (800) 867-8647.
W greentortoise.com

Greyhound Lines
Tel (800) 231-2222.
W greyhound.com

LuxBus America
W luxbusamerica.com

The Port of Los Angeles
425 S. Palos Verdes Street
P.O. Box 151, San Pedro, CA
90733-0151. Tel 310-732-7678.
W portoflosangeles.org

An ocean liner arriving at Long Beach

Getting Around California

Although often more time-consuming, traveling by train, bus, and ferry can be an inexpensive and rewarding way of getting around California. Within the major cities of San Francisco (see pp400–403), Los Angeles (see pp182–5), and San Diego (see pp270–71), there are public transportation networks of buses, trams, Metro trains, ferries, and cable cars although they are very busy during the rush-hour periods. Taxis and shuttle buses are also useful in the cities. The network of Amtrak railroad lines and connecting bus services serves the state's most populous areas and offers some scenic journeys.

Cycling past Crissy Fields and the Golden Gate Bridge, San Francisco

Green Travel

Although California may lack the sophisticated rail infrastructure of Europe, the state does have some green travel options. In San Francisco, Los Angeles, and San Diego, public transport systems are modern and convenient, easily connecting visitors to the most popular sights and attractions. Many California cities use electric or hybrid buses and there are several "green taxi" fleets with electric and hybrid cars including **Green Taxi Santa Monica**, **Organic Taxi**, and **SF GreenCab**. Most hire car companies also offer a variety of hybrid car options.

While some cities have better public transportation systems than others (San Francisco is leagues ahead of Los Angeles), sustainable transport options are available throughout the state. Cycling is heavily encouraged in most places with designated lanes along scenic routes and in towns, and incentives are offered for lower-emission

vehicles, including carpool lanes for cars with two passengers and lower toll fees.

For those concerned about the carbon emissions from air travel, carbon offsets can be bought through companies such as TerraPass, www.terrapass.com.

Traveling by Rail

In California, the rail network, operated by **Amtrak**, is divided into three sections: the Pacific Surfliner Route (Paso Robles to San Diego), the Capitol Corridor (San Jose to Sacramento), and the San Joaquin Route (connecting Emeryville and Bakersfield). The Amtrak Thruway line services all main stations. A bus service also stops along these lines. Local commuter lines include **Caltrain** (linking San Jose and San Francisco); the Coast Starlight Connection (between San Luis Obispo and Santa Barbara); LA Metrolink; and the Coaster (connecting San Diego and Oceanside).

Long-Distance Buses

In California, Greyhound Lines bus services (see p601) include scenic coastal connections as well as frequent express routes linking major cities.

Guided tours provide a leisurely way of sightseeing. Several companies offer short package trips in deluxe buses visiting sights such as Hearst Castle® (see pp216–19), Yosemite National Park (see pp492–5), and Monterey (see pp512–15). Information about these can be found online.

For travelers with more time to spare, the Green Tortoise company (see p601) offers budget travel between the major cities of the Pacific Coast. Passengers can break their trip to camp, make meals, and explore the area. This company also operates hostels along its routes, which is a great deal for those wanting to book bus and lodging together and is very popular with younger travelers wanting to explore the state.

Taxis

Taxis or cabs can usually be found outside all airport terminals, main transportation terminals, and outside most major hotels. Taxis can also be hailed on the street in the downtown areas of all cities. They are expensive and fares are metered according to the distance traveled. Credit cards are often accepted, but it is best to inquire in advance. A tip of 15 percent is expected.

Pacific-Surfliner Amtrak train, a scenic line at Del Mar, San Diego County

Boats and Ferries

Express boat services provide a fast link from Los Angeles to Santa Catalina Island (see pp246–7). In San Francisco you can take a leisurely cruise across the bay (see pp402–3) to Sausalito, Alameda, and Larkspur. Most ferries carry foot passengers and bicycles, but not motor vehicles.

Commuter ferries provide a breezy alternative to the smog of rush-hour traffic and congestion. Some routes, such as the San Diego–Coronado ferry, provide a pleasant and reasonably priced way to enjoy traveling to different cities. For ferry timetables, prices, and locations in San Francisco and the Bay Area (see p403); in San Diego (see p271).

Tickets and Fares

The average ticket price on public transport in major cities such as San Francisco and Los Angeles is $2 each way. Although San Diego, San Jose, Los Angeles, and San Francisco transit systems all offer day and weekly passes, only San Francisco's CityPass (see p401) is priced to save visitors money. A 7-day unlimited Muni and cable car ticket, plus entry to local attractions costs $94 for adults and $69 for children (aged 5–12).

Ferry fares vary drastically. The ferry from Oakland to San Francisco is only 3 miles (5 km) and is $6.25 each way, while from Long Beach to Santa Catalina island, 22 miles (35 km), it costs $68.25.

DIRECTORY

Green Travel

Green Taxi Santa Monica
Tel 310-430-1882.
W mygreentaxi.com

Organic Taxi
Tel 310-877-6350.
W organictaxi.com

SF GreenCab
Tel (415) 626-4733.
W 626green.com

Traveling by Rail

Amtrak
Tel (800) 872-7245.
W amtrak.com

Caltrain
Tel (800) 660-4287.
W caltrain.com

Amtrak Routes

This map shows the main Amtrak routes within California, as well as the Amtrak Thruway feeder services to the main stations. Amtrak also has several interstate services to other major cities in the US.

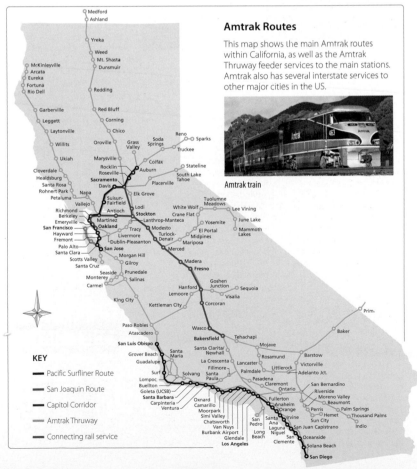

Amtrak train

KEY

— Pacific Surfliner Route
— San Joaquin Route
— Capitol Corridor
— Amtrak Thruway
— Connecting rail service

Traveling by Car

Driving is an essential part of the California way of life, and for both residents and visitors it is the most convenient way to travel around the state. Roads are well maintained so that they are able to cope with the great volume of rush-hour traffic that pours in and out of the main cities every weekday. The state has an efficient network of major roads linking the cities and towns. In remote areas, such as in the deserts and mountains, it is sometimes necessary to use a four-wheel-drive vehicle.

The Bixby Creek Bridge at Big Sur, part of the scenic Highway 1

Car Hire

It is best to arrange a fly-drive package before arriving in California. Take note of exactly what is included in the deal, and find out whether any extra payments may arise when the car is picked up. These additions – which can include optional fuel purchase, extended insurance cover, collision damage waiver, delivery or drop-off charges, and vehicle rental tax (a daily city vehicle rental tax) – can double the original prepaid fee. It is particularly important to find out exactly what is included in the insurance policy offered by the rental company. Drivers should remember that in California, where litigation is an everyday occurrence, it is sensible to be fully insured.

To rent a car, the driver must be over 25 and have a US or internationally valid driver's license. A major credit card is vital as a guarantee. Some companies may rent to younger drivers or accept a debit card in lieu of a credit

card number, but expect higher charges as a result. Taking a rented car across the border into Mexico is not permitted without prior arrangement.

The gas tank should be full when you return the vehicle, and you must allow sufficient time to process and check your final bill. If you plan on driving around enough to use a full tank of gas, the prepaid fuel option is a good idea to avoid having to stop at the gas station before returning the vehicle, and also paying the local price per gallon rate. Car rental is generally least expensive at airports *(see p601)*, but call the

free numbers advertised by rental companies to find out about discounts and deals. Rental cars usually have automatic transmission. If requested, some companies supply cars with manual transmission ("stick-shift"). Alternative hire vehicles such as Harley-Davidson motorcycles and RVs (motor homes) can be rented from **USA RV Rentals** and **Dubbelju Motorcycle**.

Roads and Tolls

The most common routes within the state are Highway 101 and I-5 from southern California to the north; Highway 1, which provides a scenic, coastal drive from the central coast to Mendocino in the north; and I-80, which runs northeast from San Francisco to Sacramento and Lake Tahoe. Tolls are uncommon on roads, but typical on bridges, mostly around the Bay Area, where it costs between $4 and $7 to cross the region's various bridges.

Rules of the Road

Americans drive on the right. Seat belts are compulsory for both driver and passengers. In the US, speed limits are individually set by each state. In California, the maximum speed limit is generally 65 mph (104 kmh), though selected freeways have a speed limit of 70 mph (110 kmh). In cities, the speed limits are restricted – check road signs as they vary. These limits are rigorously enforced. In Los Angeles, the

Traffic Signs

Drivers should take note of the different signs that give warnings and instructions. Speed limits may vary every few miles, depending on the road conditions and the amount of traffic, and should be adhered to. In more remote areas, drivers must look out for wildlife that occasionally strays onto roads. Disregarding traffic signs may result in a Highway Patrol fine.

Traffic flows in a single direction

Wildlife warning

Maximum speed

speed limit is 55 mph (88 kmh), including freeways. Drunk driving is a serious offense and carries heavy penalties. Highways without traffic lights or intersections are called freeways. Bicycles are not allowed on freeways or Interstates. Some freeways have less congested diamond (or carpool) lanes, which only cars with more than one passenger (and in some areas more than two) are permitted to use during rush hour (7–10am and 3–7pm).

Violating carpool lanes carries fines of $250 or more. It is permissible to turn right on red at traffic lights if there is nothing coming the other way, and unless otherwise indicated. The first vehicle to reach a stop sign junction has the right of way.

The **Automobile Association of America** (AAA) supplies maps, has an emergency road service, and offers discounts at hotels and restaurants. It is linked with many automobile clubs abroad, so inquire ahead whether they will honor your membership.

Parking

Parking in Californian cities is strictly controlled and can be expensive. Valet parking is obligatory if you pull up outside many hotels and restaurants. Hand the keys to the attendant and pay on departure. Most parking meters accept nickels, dimes, and quarters, but some

systems require dollar bills to be "posted" into the slot for the parking space. Parking lots have their own set prices. Parking is generally free at shopping malls or you can have your ticket validated at any store where you have made a purchase in order to reduce or eliminate the fee.

Parking restrictions are indicated by curb colors. If the curb is painted red, parking is prohibited; yellow indicates a loading zone; green allows limited parking and white is for drop off and pick up only. Blue curbs are for disabled parking. If parking on a hill in San Francisco, apply the handbrake and turn your wheels into the road if facing uphill and toward the curb if facing downhill. If your vehicle is towed, contact the local **Department of Transportation**.

PARK AT 90 DEGREES

PREVENT RUNAWAYS CURB WHEELS PARK IN GEAR SET BRAKE

Signs to prevent cars rolling downhill

Gasoline

Gas, or gasoline, is either unleaded or diesel quality. It is sold in gallons rather than liters. Inexpensive by European standards, the price includes a hefty gasoline tax. Gas stations are not as widespread as many visitors expect, so be sure to fill up the tank before driving into the mountains, desert, or through other remote areas. Few gas stations have pump attendants. Most pumps take credit cards, and it is common to pay for the gas before putting it into the car.

Driving through the historic district of San Diego's Gaslamp Quarter

General Index

Acknowledgments

Dorling Kindersley would like to thank the following people whose contributions and assistance have made the preparation of this book possible.

Main Contributor
Jamie Jensen grew up in LA and now lives in Northern California. He contributed to San Francisco in the DK Guides series, and his most recent book is *Road Trip USA: Cross-Country Adventures on America's Two-Lane Highways.*
Ellen Payne is Managing Editor of *Los Angeles Magazine* and has worked on numerous travel publications.
J Kingston Pierce is a Seattle writer specializing in West Coast history. He is a contributing editor of *San Francisco Focus* and *Seattle* magazines and his book credits include *San Francisco, You're History!*
Rebecca Poole Forée is Editor-in-Chief at Foghorn Press, San Francisco. She has written many travel books, including *Northern California Best Places.*
Nigel Tisdall is the author of several travel guides. He has contributed to *France, Seville and Andalusia* and *Portugal* in the DK series.
Stanley Young lives in LA. He has written several books including *The Missions of California* and *Paradise Found: The Beautiful Retreats and Sanctuaries of California and the Southwest.*

Contributors and Consultants
Virginia Butterfield, Dawn Douglas, Rebecca Renner, Tessa Souter, Shirley Streshinsky, Barbara Tannenbaum, Michael Webb, John Wilcock.

Additional Photography
Brenna Alexander, Max Alexander, Christopher P Baker, Demetrio Carassco, Lee Foster, Steve Gorton, Gary Grimaud, Bonita Halm, Nelson Hancock, Trevor Hill, Robert Holmes, Kirk Irwin, Neil Lukas, Neil Mersh, Ian O'Leary, Angus Osborn, David Peevers, Peter Peevers, Erhard Pfeiffer, Martin Richardson 12bl, Chris Stowers, Robert Vente, Paul Whitfield, Francesca Yorke.

Additional Illustrators
James A Allington, Arcana Studios, Hugh Dixon, Richard Draper, Dean Entwhistle, Eugene Fleury, Chris Forsey, Andrew Green, Steve Gyapay, Toni Hargreaves, Philip Hockey, John Lawrence, Nick Lipscombe, Mel Pickering, Sallie Alane Reason, Peter Ross, Simon Roulston, John See, Tristan Spaargaren, Ed Stuart, Paul Williams.

Cartography
Lovell Johns Ltd, Oxford, UK; ERA-Maptec Ltd, Dublin, Ireland; Alok Pathak, Kunal Singh. Street Finder Maps based upon digital data, adapted with permission from original survey by ETAK INC 1984–1994.
Map Co-ordinators Emily Green, David Pugh

Revisions Team
Publishing Director Georgina Dee
Publisher Vivien Antwi
Managing Editor Rachel Fox
Emma Anacootee, Lydia Baillie, Shahnaaz Bakshi, Peter Bennett, Marta Bescos Sánchez, Vandana Bhagra, Hilary Bird, Julie Bond, Sophie Boyak, Sherry Collins, Lisa Cope, Joanna Craig, Cullen Curtiss, Donna Dailey, Dipika Dasgupta, Stephanie Driver, Caroline Elliker, Michael Ellis, Nicola Erdpresser, Rob Farmer, Emer FitzGerald, Niki Foreman, Anna Freiberger, Rhiannon Furbear, Jo Gardner, Camilla Gersh, William Gordon, Emily Green, Roger Grody, Eric Grossman, Swati Gupta, Bonita Halm, Vinod Harish,

Mohammed Hassan, Paul Hines, Jacqueline Jackson, Stuart James, Claire Jones, Thomas A Knight, Rahul Kumar, Esther Labi, Kathryn Lane, Maite Lantaron, Gerrish Lopez, Nicola Malone, Bhavika Mathur, Megan McCrea, Kathy McDonald, Alison McGill, Ciaran McIntyre, Annie McQuitty, Sam Merrell, Nancy Mikula, Ella Milroy, Karen Misuraca, Sonal Modha, Mary Ormandy, Catherine Palmi, Carolyn Patten, Helen Peters, Rada Radojicic, Mani Ramaswamy, Natalie Rios, Ellen Root, Shailesh Sharma, Marlene Scribner, Jonathan Schultz, Azeem Siddiqui, Asavari Singh, Rituraj Singh, Tarini Singh, Meredith Smith, AnneLise Sorensen, Anna Streiffert Limerick, Alka Thakur, Nikhil Verma, Richa Verma, Lauren Viera, Ingrid Vienings, Marek Walisiewicz, Amy Westervelt, Hugo Wilkinson.

Special Assistance
Marianne Babel, Wells Fargo History Museum, San Francisco; Liz Badras, LA Convention and Visitors' Bureau; Craig Bates, Yosemite Museum; Joyce Bimbo, Hearst Castle, San Simeon; Elizabeth A Borsting and Ron Smith, the *Queen Mary*, Long Beach; Jean Bruce-Poole, El Pueblo de Los Angeles National Monument; Carolyn Cassady; Covent Garden Stamp Shop; Marcia Eymann and Joy Tahan, Oakland Museum of California; Donna Galassi; Mary Jean S Gamble, Salinas Public Library; Mary Haas, California Palace of the Legion of Honor; Nancy Masten, Photophile; Miguel Millar, US National Weather Service, Monterey; Warren Morse, LA County Metropolitan Transportation Authority; Anne North, San Diego Visitors' and Convention Bureau; Donald Schmidt, San Diego Zoo; Vito Sgromo, Sacramento State Capitol Museum; Dawn Stranne and Helen Chang, San Francisco Visitors' and Convention Bureau; Cherise Sun and Richard Ogar, Bancroft Library; Gaynell V Wald, Mission San Juan Capistrano; Chris Wirth, Wine Institute, San Francisco; Cynthia J Wornham and Lori Star, the J Paul Getty Trust.

Photography Permissions
Dorling Kindersley would like to thank the following for their assistance and kind permission to photograph at their establishments: Balboa Park, San Diego; Columbia State Historic Park; Disney Enterprises, Inc.; J Paul Getty Museum, LA; Hearst Castle, San Simeon; Huntington Library, San Marino; Knotts Berry Farm, Buena Park; Los Angeles Children's Museum; Los Angeles County Museum of Art; Museum of Contemporary Art, LA; Museum of Miniatures, LA; Museum of Television and Radio, LA; Museum of Tolerance, LA; Norton Simon Museum, Pasadena; Petersen Automotive Museum, LA; *Queen Mary*, Long Beach; Sacramento State Capitol; San Diego Aerospace Museum; San Diego Automotive Museum; San Diego Museum of Art; San Diego Wild Animal Park; San Diego Zoological Society; Santa Barbara Mission; Southwest Museum, LA; John Steinbeck Library, Salinas; Tao House, Danville; Timken Museum of Art, San Diego; Universal Studios, LA; University of California, Berkeley; University of California, LA; University of Southern California, LA; Wells Fargo History Room, San Francisco; Winchester Mystery House, San Jose; and all other churches, missions, museums, parks, wineries, hotels, restaurants, and sights too numerous to thank individually. References to various Disney copyrighted characters, trademarks, marks, and registered marks are owned by The Walt Disney Company and Disney Enterprises, Inc.

Picture Credits
a = above; b = below/bottom; c = center; f = far; l = left; r = right; t = top.

oil on canvas, 87crb; Rembrandt, *The Abduction of Europa* (1632), oil on a single oak panel, 87b; Jean-François Millet, *Man with a Hoe* (1860–2), oil on canvas, 80 x 99cm, 88cla; Carleton E Watkins, *Cape Horn, Columbia River, Oregon* (negative 1867, print 1881–3), albumen, 40.5 x 52.3 cm, 88br; Sèvres Porcelain Manufactory, Basket (1756), soft paste porcelain, gilding, 22 x 20.1 x 18 cm, 89tc; Footed Bowl (Venice, c.1500–50), free-blown calcedonio glass, 12.5 x 19.5 cm, 89cl; Gos-pels (Helmarshausen, c.1120–40), tempera colours, gold and silver on vellum bound between paper boards covered with brown calf, 22.8 x 16.4 cm, 89br; **Golden Gate Bridge Highway and Transportation District:** 59t, 384clb, 384br, 385tl, 385cra, 385br; Charles M Hiller 59tl; © **J. Paul Gettytrust:** (c) 2005 Richard Ross with the courtesy of the J. Paul Getty Trust 90b; **Golden Gate National Re-creation Area, National Park Service:** 343cb, 343bl; **Ronald Grant Archive:** 106cr, 109cl, 111crb, 611t; Capitol 202tr; *LA Story*, Warner Bros 24tc; *Rebel Without A Cause*, Warner Bros 72cra; *The Last Action Hero* Columbia Pictures 72crb; *Gidget*, Columbia Pictures 202cl. **Green Spa Network:** 593c; **Greyhound Lines, Inc.:** 601c; **The Grill on the Alley:** 550br; **Guerilla Atelier:** Hero B. Stevenson 167bl; **Hearst Castle/Hearst San Simeon State Historical Monument:** Z Baron 216br; John Blades 216tr, 216clb, 21/bl, 218cla, 219c; V Garagliano 216bc; Ken Raveill 216ca, 217tl, 217cra, 218br; Amber Wisdom 217crb; **Phoebe Hearst Museum of Anthropology:** 49crb; **Robert Holmes Photography:** Markham Johnson 309bl; **Hotel Casa del Mar:** 178bl; **Hulton Getty:** 61crb, 109tr; **Huntingdon Library, Art Collections, and Botanic Gardens:** 33b, 162clb, 162br, 163ca, 164br; Gutenberg Bible 163tl; *Blue Boy*, Thomas Gains-borough 163cr; *Diana the Huntress*, Houdon 164tr; The Wife of Bath from *The Canterbury Tales*, Chaucer (Ellesmere MS), 164c; **Hutchison Library:** B Regent 170cla; **Hyatt hotels:** 529tr, 531tl, 538tl. **Image Bank:** David Hamilton 27tl; **Image Works:** Lisa Law 444–5c; **Ingleside Inn:** 563tl; **Inn at the Presidio:** 526br, 539tl; **International Surf Festival:** 41br; **Kirk Irwin:** 24b, 201tr, 222cl, 222bl, 295br, 449tr, 620–21. **John O'Groats:** 556tr; **Jose Cuervo:** 548cla; **Julienne:** 558tl; **Karl Strauss Brewing Company:** 561br; **Catherine Karnow:** 204br; **Katz Pictures:** Lamoine 170cr; Saba /Steve Starr 29tl, Lara Jo Regan 73bl; **Robert E Kennedy Library:** Special Collections, California Polytechnic State University 219tr; **Knott's Berry Farm:** 240-1c, 240br, 241br, 278br; **Howard Koby:** www. photographersdirect.com 111crb; **www.kodaktheater.com:** 112cr; **Kobal Collection:** *LA Story*, Guild Film Distribution 73cla, *The Big Sleep*, Warner Bros 83br; *The Wild One*, Columbia Pictures 204bl. **LA County Museum of art:** *La Trahison des Images (Ceci n'est pas une pipe)*, René Magritte, purchased with funds provided by the Mr & Mrs William Preston Harrison Collection, 74tc; *In the Woods at Giverny: Blanche Hoschedé at Her Easel with Suzanne Hoschedé Reading*, Claude Monet, Mr & Mrs George Gard De Sylva Collection 118tr; *Soap Bubbles* (after 1739) Jean-Baptiste-Simón Chardin Gift of The Ahmanson Foundation 118cla; *The Hope Athena* (2nd century AD) William Randolph Hearst Collection 118bl; *Mulholland Drive: The Road to the Studio*, David Hockney, purchased with funds provided by the F Patrick Burnes Bequest 119tl; Plate, purchased with funds provided by the Art Museum Council 119cr; *Magdalen with the Smoking Flame*, Georges de La Tour, gift of The Ahmanson Foundation 120tr; *Monument to Honoré de Balzac*, Auguste Rodin, gift of B Gerald Cantor; 120c; *The Cotton Pickers*, Winslow Homer, Acquisition made possible by museum trustees 120bl; Pair of Officials, China, 618–907, Gift of Leon Lidow 121tr; Dunes, *Oceano*, Edward Weston,

© 1981 Center for Creative Photography, Arizona Board of Regents 121bl; **LA Department of Water and Power:** 56clb, 206bc; **Ladodgers Inc:** 156br; **Langham Hotels International Limited:** 530bl, 553tr; **Las Vegas Convention & Visitors Authority:** 293cl; **The Lodge Torey Pines:** 534tl; **Los Angeles Food & Wine Festival:** Gina Sinotte 40cla; **Los Angeles Philharmonic:** Tom Bonner 129br; **Legoland® California Resort:** 266tr; **Jack London Collection:** California State Parks 30br; **Luxe Sunset Boulevard:** 528bc. **Madrona Manor:** 573tl; **Magnes Museum Permanent Collections:** 19th-century blue velvet embroidery brocade robe, 423tc; **Magnum Photos:** Michael Nichols 60br; **Marine World Africa USA:** Charlotte Fiorito 302tr; **Mario's Place:** 563br; **Marriot Hotels:** 532tl; **Barry McGee:** 428bl; **Andrew Mckinney Photography:** 51cl, 304tr, 305cr, 306tr, 307tr, 307br, 311cr, 311tc, 317crb, 335tr, 350c, 373bl, 385bl, 418tl; **The Restaurant at Meadowood:** 545t; **Mélisse:** 554tl; **Mendocino Brewing Company:** 549bc; **Metropolitan Transit Development Board, San Diego:** Stephen Simpson 270cla; **Metropolitan Water District of Southern California:** 206clb; **Mineta San José International Airport:** 600cla; **Robert Mondavi Winery:** 466br; **Moss Beach Distillery:** 571tr; **John Muir National Historic Site:** National Park Service 419br; **Muni** 401ca, 401bl; **Mumm Napa:** 549tc; **Museum of Television and Radio:** Grant Mudford 94tr. **The Names Project:** AIDS Memorial Quilt © 1988 Matt Herron 61clb; **The National Motor Museum, Beaulieu:** 205bl; **The Palace Hotel:** 321b; **Peter Newark's American Pictures:** 51br, 52br, 205tl, 307crb; **Peter Newark's Western Americana:** 52cla, 52bl, 52–3c, 257br, 645 (inset); **NHPA:** Joe Blossom 85tr; Rich Kirchner 43tl, 464c; Stephen Krasemann 507cra; P McDonald 246br; David Middleton 440ca, 452cla; Kevin Schafer 440bc; John Shaw 223bc, 234cl, 283ca, 440clb, 495cr; Roger Tidman 245bl; **New York Public Library:** I N Phelps Stokes Collection, Miriam and Ira D Wallach Division of Art, Prints and Photo-graphs, The New York Public Library, Astor, Lenox and Tilden Foundations 52clb; **The Norton Simon Foundation, Pasadena:** Still Life with Lem-ons, Oranges and a Rose, Francisco de Zurbaran (1633) 160br; Buddha Enthroned, Kashmir, India (8th century) 161br; *Woman with a Book*, Pablo Picasso (1832), Estate of Robert Ellis Simon, 1969, 160cla; *Saints Paul and Frediano*, Filippino Lippi (1483) 161tc; *Self-Portrait*, Rembrandt van Rijn (c.1636–38) 161cr; *The Little Fourteen-Year-Old Dancer*, Edgar Degas (1878–81) 160clb. **Courtesy of the Oakland Museum of California:** 429bl; Jeff Warrin 429cra; *Yosemite Valley*, Albert Bierstadt (1868) 8–9; *Figure on a Porch*, Richard Diebenkorn (1959) 32cl; *Ocean Park 107* Richard Diebenkorn (1958) 428clb; *Afternoon in Piedmont*, Xavier Tizoc Martinez (c.1911) 32br; *California Venus*, Rupert Schmid (c.1895) 33cr; The Oakland Museum History Department 28bl, 47b, 48cla, 48–9cb (2), 49cla, 51cr, 53ca, 53crb, 56tr, 57cb, 60bl, 383br, 428tr, 429tl, 445tl; The Oakland Museum Kahn Collection 479br; The Oakland Tribune Collection, Gift of Alameda Newspaper Group 58bc, 444cl, 444bc; **Los Olivos:** 545bl; **PalmSprings Aerial Tramway:** 279tl; **Palm Springs Art Museum:** 279cr; **Pasadena Convention And Visitors' Bureau:** 158bl; **Edward Pfeiffer:** 29tr, 34tr, 34b, 35br, 67bl, 77tl, 94bl, 95cra, 126cl, 136cla, 136b, 137tl, 137cr, 137br, 145b; **Photolibrary:** JTB Photo 127bl; **Photo Network:** Mary Messenger 580bc; Phyllis Picardi 205br; Woodard 40bc; **Photophile:** 38crb, 65tl, 200clb; Scott Crain 22c; Arthur Fox 584tc; Mark Gibson 579br; Jim Gray 201br; Michael Hall 72tr; Matt Lindsay 25br, 41cl, 270bl, 271bc, Sal Maimone 131bl, 171tr, 200bc, 256br, 438bl; **Photo Trek Inc:** M J Wickham 438clb;

Petersen Automotive Museum: Scott Williamson 122tr; **Pictor International–London:** 66tr, 66bl, 66br, 204tr, 240bl; 296bl, 517tl; **Pictures Colour Library:** 26t, 43bl, 127tl; Leo de Wys 583cl; **Point Reyes Seashore Lodge:** 540tr; **Popperfoto:** 520tl. **Precita Eyes Mural Arts and Visitors Center:** Balloon Journey ©2008 Precita Eyes Muralists, by Kristen Foskett 310crb; Hillcrest Elementary School © 2007 Precita Eyes Muralists 310c; Oakland, Stop the Violence © 2007 Precita Eyes Muralists. Directed by Joshua Stevenson. Designed and painted by AYPAL youth (Asian Pacific Islander Youth Promoting Advocacy and Leadership) including Recy, Marcus, and many Others. Acrylic paint on Tyvek 310b; **Presidio of San Francisco:** NPS staff photos 381tl, 381cra; **Presidio Trust:** 381br; **The Red Rabbit Kitchen and Bar:** 575br; **Red & White Fleet:** 403bl; **Restaurant 1833:** Patrick Tragenza 577tr; **Reuters:** Kimberley White 61ca **Rex Features:** 364bl; **Rex Shutterstock:** Brian Moody 363br; Most Wanted 101tl; **Riverside Municipal Museum:** Chris Moser 48cr; **Robert Harding Picture Library:** 200ca, 207cr 580tl; Walter Bibikow 458; Bildagentur/Schuster 202br; Russ Bishop 436-7; Neale Clarke 290-1; Richard Cummins 134t; Neil Emmerson 368; Eye Ubiquitous 92; FPG 28cl, 56cla, 57clb, 59cra; Jon Gardey 501tl; Tony Gervis 487b; Glow Images 76tr; James Hager 272; Gavin Hellier 298-9, 588-9; Michael J Howell 27tr; Dave Jacobs 441br, 500tr; Robert Landau 77crb; Rich Reid Photography.com 284; Westlight/Bill Ross 154tr, Steve Smith 27br 37tc; **Salinas Public Library:** Courtesy of the Steinbeck Archives, 31tl, 521br; **San Diego Air and Space Museum:** 260cl; **San Diego Metropolitan Transit System:** 270cla; **San Francisco Art Institute:** D Wakely 345cl; **San Francisco Cable Car Museum:** 307tl, 307bl; **San Francisco Convention and Visitors' Bureau:** 43br, Mark Gibson 306cl; Courtesy of Brown, Zukov & Associates 386t; **San Francisco Museum of Modern Art:** Country Dog Gentlemen, 1972, by Roy De Forest, polymer on canvas, gift of the Hamilton-Wells Collection, 323br; Orange Sweater, 1955, by Elmer Bischoff, oil on canvas, gift of Mr and Mrs Mark Schorer, 327cr; Back View, 1977, Philip Guston, oil on canvas, gift of the artist, 309cr; Henrik Kam 322tr; Gerhard Richter 323cr; No. 14, 1960 by Mark Rothko 322c; Richard Shaw 323clb; Steelblue 323cb; **San Francisco Public Library History Room:** 58cla, 343bla, 373crb; **San Mateo County Historical Association:** 416cla; **Santa Barbara Mission Archive Library:** 50cl, 51tl; **Santa Barbara Museum of Art:** The Ripened Wheat, Jules Bastien-Lepage (1884), Museum purchase with funds provided by Suzette and Eugene Davidson and the Davidson Endow-ment Fund 224cl; **Santa Rosa Convention & Visitors Bureau:** 590br, 594cr; **Science Photo Library:** NASA 288c; George Bernard 432bc; Simon Fraser 22tl; David Parker 28tr; Peter Menzel 28cr, 509br;

Shell Vacations Hospitality: 536tr; **Showdogs Resturant:** 564br; **Sierra Nevada Tap Room & Restaurant:** 574tl; **Sonoma Valley Visitors' Bureau:** Bob Nixon 469br; **Southwest Museum:** ID CT.126, Photo by Don Meyer (491.G.802) 75tr; **Spectrum Colour Library:** 476tr, 513cra, 582br; **STA Travel Group:** 592cra; **The Standard, Downtown LA:** Martin Kunz 178cla; **Stanford University Archives:** Department of Special Collections, 55b; **Stevenson House Collection, Monterey State Historic Park:** Sharon Fong 512tr, 513cr, 513br; **Tony Stone Images:** 42br, 417crb, 438cla, 488crb; Jerry Alexander 467tl; Ken Biggs 67tl, 182cla; David Carriere 584bl; Chad Ehlers 67tr; Johan Elzenga 287tr, 294c, 296cl; Roy Giles, 338cla; Lorentz Gullachsen 23t; Gavin Hellier 498tl; D C Lowe 491tr; David Madison 583tr; David Maisel 302bc; A&L Sinibaldi 23br, 439crb; Alan Smith 219b; Larry Ulrich 447bc; **Levi Strauss & Co:** 347cr, 347bc; **Tim Street-Porter:** 36bl, 37bl, 76bl; **Superstock:** Ambient images Inc 454-5; Design Pics 502. **Tate Gallery London:** It's a Psychological Fact that Pleasure helps your Disposition, 1948, Eduardo Paolozzi 58–9c; **Edward Thomas Photography:** 36tr. **Three Seventy Common:** 559tr; **Travelex Currency Services INC.:** 596cra; **Ulster Museum, Belfast:** By kind perm-ission of the Trustees 49cl; © 2000 **Universal Studios Inc** All Rights Reserved 151b, 152cl, 152br, 153tr, 152bl; **US National Park Services:** 381br; **By Courtesy of the US Postal Service:** 618t; Stamp Designs © 1995, 321c, 599c. **Water Grill:** 551tr; **Wells Fargo Bank:** 53bl, 316bl, 318b, 483br; **Westfield City Century:** 97cb; **Westfield Horton Plaza:** 254bl; **Williams-Sonoma, Inc.:** 388cr; **Wine Spectator Restaurant:** 573br; **World Pictures:** 151c, 610c. **Yosemite Museum:** National Park Service 48cra, Craig & Jennifer Bates 48cl; Michael Dixon 48clb; **Yosemite National Park Research Library:** 55ca. ©**Zefa:** 43c, 442cl; **Bill Zeldis Photography:** 46; **Zeum:** 326clb; **Zoological Society of San Diego:** 263br.

All other images © Dorling Kindersley. See www.DKimages.com for more information.

Front Endpaper
Alamy Images: Brenda Kean Lbr; Jim Lundgren Rtl; David Nixon Lcl; Photoshot Holdings Ltd Lbc; **Dreamstime.com:** Hotshotsworldwide Rc; Photoquest Lbl; **Getty Images:** Woodward Payne Rtc; **Robert Harding Picture Library:** Walter Bibikow Lcla; James Hager Rcrb; Gavin Hellier Lc; Rich Reid Photography.com Rcr; **Superstock:** Design Pics Rtr.

Jacket
Front - **Dreamstime.com:** Hasan Can Balcioglu bl;. **Getty Images:** Mint Images – Frans Lanting; **Spine:** Getty Images: Mint Images – Frans Lanting.

Special Editions of DK Travel Guides

DK Travel Guides can be purchased in bulk quantities at discounted prices for use in promotions or as premiums. We are also able to offer special editions and personalized jackets, corporate imprints, and excerpts from all of our books, tailored specifically to meet your own needs.

To find out more, please contact:
in the United States **specialsales@dk.com**
in the UK **travelguides@uk.dk.com**
in Canada DK Special Sales at **specialmarkets@dk.com**
in Australia **penguincorporatesales@penguinrandomhouse.com.au**